Garfield
FAT CAT 3-PACK
VOLUME 5

BY
JIM DAVIS

BALLANTINE BOOKS • NEW YORK

2010 Ballantine Books Trade Paperback Edition

Published in the United States by Ballantine Books, an imprint of The Random House Publishing Group, a division of Random House, Inc., New York.

Originally published as three separate volumes, in both black and white and color, as *Garfield Food for Thought*, *Garfield Swallows His Pride*, and *Garfield Worldwide*. This compilation was originally published in black and white in 1996.

ISBN 978-0-345-49180-0

Printed in the United States of America

www.ballantinebooks.com

First Colorized Edition

9 8 7 6 5 4 3

Garfield
food for thought

BY JIM DAVIS

Ballantine Books • New York

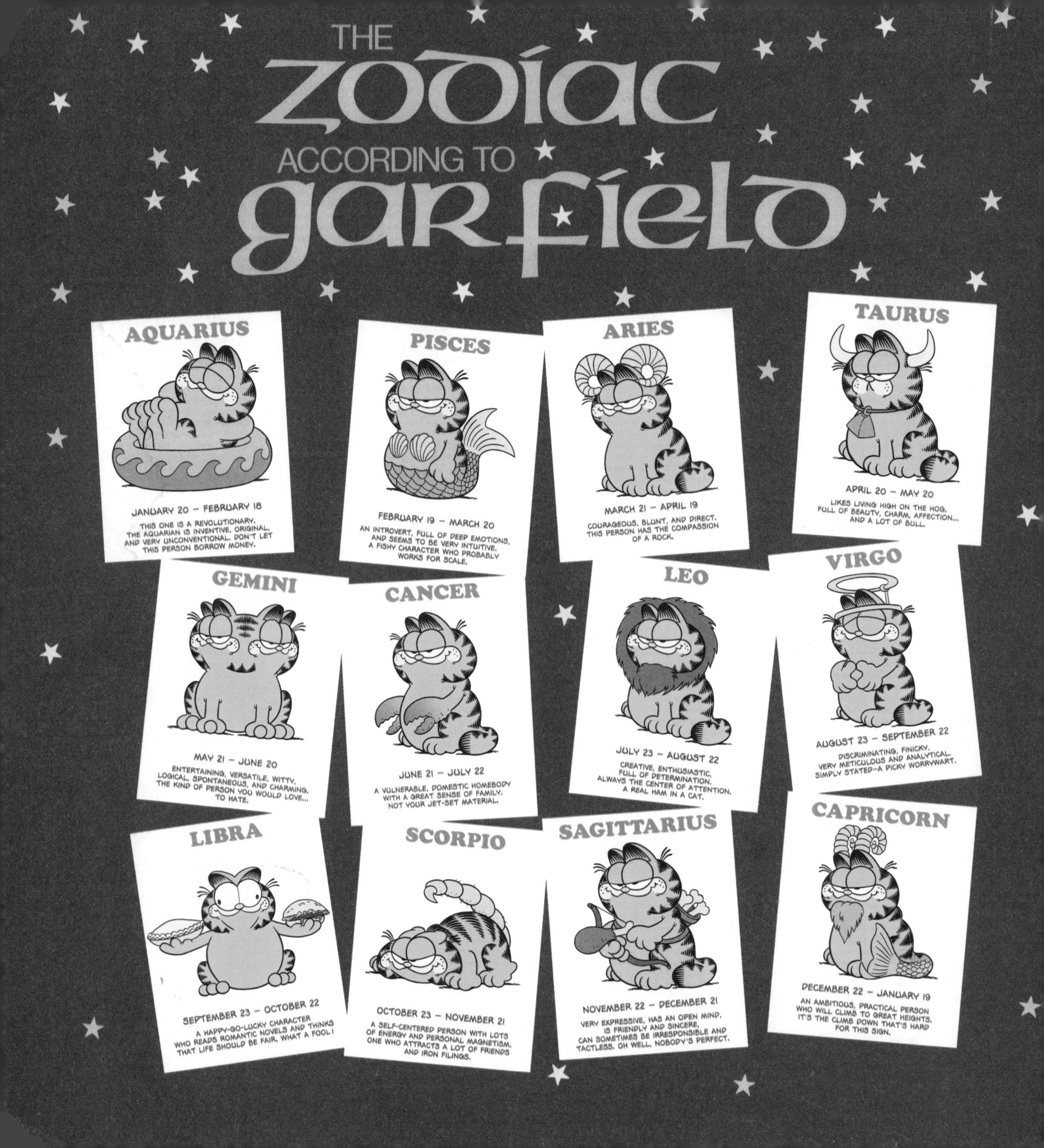
THE
ZODIAC
ACCORDING TO
garfield
AQUARIUS
JANUARY 20 – FEBRUARY 18
THIS ONE IS A REVOLUTIONARY. THE AQUARIAN IS INVENTIVE, ORIGINAL, AND VERY UNCONVENTIONAL. DON'T LET THIS PERSON BORROW MONEY.
PISCES
FEBRUARY 19 – MARCH 20
AN INTROVERT, FULL OF DEEP EMOTIONS, AND SEEMS TO BE VERY INTUITIVE. A FISHY CHARACTER WHO PROBABLY WORKS FOR SCALE.
ARIES
MARCH 21 – APRIL 19
COURAGEOUS, BLUNT, AND DIRECT. THIS PERSON HAS THE COMPASSION OF A ROCK.
TAURUS
APRIL 20 – MAY 20
LIKES LIVING HIGH ON THE HOG. FULL OF BEAUTY, CHARM, AFFECTION... AND A LOT OF BULL.
GEMINI
MAY 21 – JUNE 20
ENTERTAINING, VERSATILE, WITTY, LOGICAL, SPONTANEOUS, AND CHARMING. THE KIND OF PERSON YOU WOULD LOVE... TO HATE.
CANCER
JUNE 21 – JULY 22
A VULNERABLE, DOMESTIC HOMEBODY WITH A GREAT SENSE OF FAMILY. NOT YOUR JET-SET MATERIAL.
LEO
JULY 23 – AUGUST 22
CREATIVE, ENTHUSIASTIC, FULL OF DETERMINATION. ALWAYS THE CENTER OF ATTENTION. A REAL HAM IN A CAT.
VIRGO
AUGUST 23 – SEPTEMBER 22
DISCRIMINATING, FINICKY, VERY METICULOUS AND ANALYTICAL. SIMPLY STATED—A PICKY WORRYWART.
LIBRA
SEPTEMBER 23 – OCTOBER 22
A HAPPY-GO-LUCKY CHARACTER WHO READS ROMANTIC NOVELS AND THINKS THAT LIFE SHOULD BE FAIR. WHAT A FOOL!
SCORPIO
OCTOBER 23 – NOVEMBER 21
A SELF-CENTERED PERSON WITH LOTS OF ENERGY AND PERSONAL MAGNETISM. ONE WHO ATTRACTS A LOT OF FRIENDS AND IRON FILINGS.
SAGITTARIUS
NOVEMBER 22 – DECEMBER 21
VERY EXPRESSIVE, HAS AN OPEN MIND, IS FRIENDLY AND SINCERE. CAN SOMETIMES BE IRRESPONSIBLE AND TACTLESS. OH WELL, NOBODY'S PERFECT.
CAPRICORN
DECEMBER 22 – JANUARY 19
AN AMBITIOUS, PRACTICAL PERSON WHO WILL CLIMB TO GREAT HEIGHTS. IT'S THE CLIMB DOWN THAT'S HARD FOR THIS SIGN.

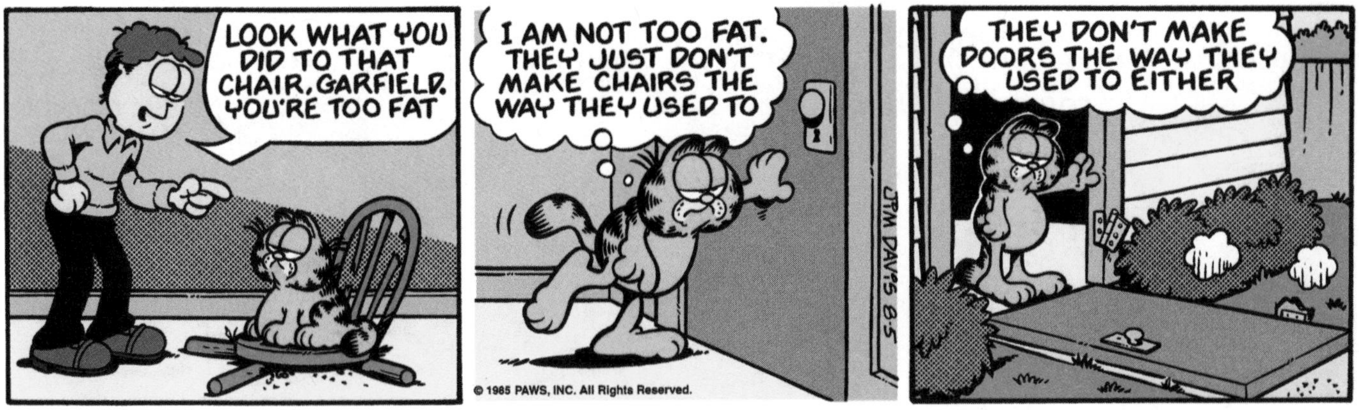
LOOK WHAT YOU DID TO THAT CHAIR, GARFIELD. YOU'RE TOO FAT
I AM NOT TOO FAT. THEY JUST DON'T MAKE CHAIRS THE WAY THEY USED TO
JIM DAVIS 8-5
© 1985 PAWS, INC. All Rights Reserved.
THEY DON'T MAKE DOORS THE WAY THEY USED TO EITHER

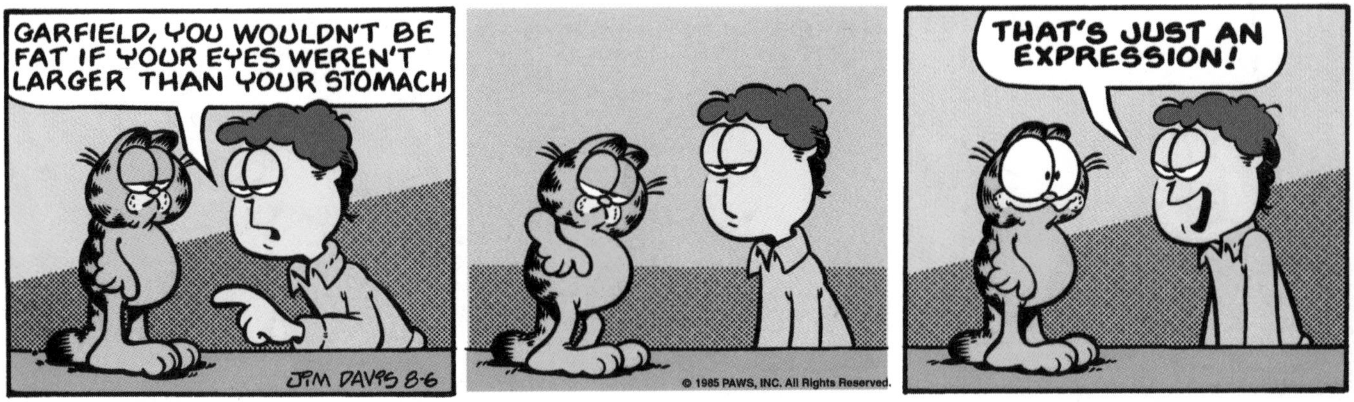
GARFIELD, YOU WOULDN'T BE FAT IF YOUR EYES WEREN'T LARGER THAN YOUR STOMACH
JIM DAVIS 8-6
© 1985 PAWS, INC. All Rights Reserved.
THAT'S JUST AN EXPRESSION!

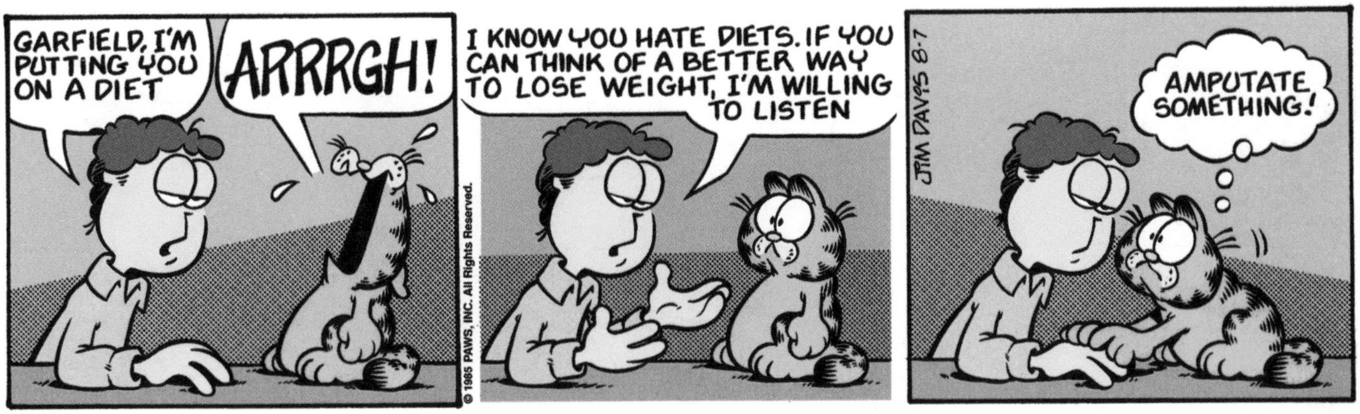
GARFIELD, I'M PUTTING YOU ON A DIET
ARRRGH!
© 1985 PAWS, INC. All Rights Reserved.
I KNOW YOU HATE DIETS. IF YOU CAN THINK OF A BETTER WAY TO LOSE WEIGHT, I'M WILLING TO LISTEN
JIM DAVIS 8-7
AMPUTATE SOMETHING!

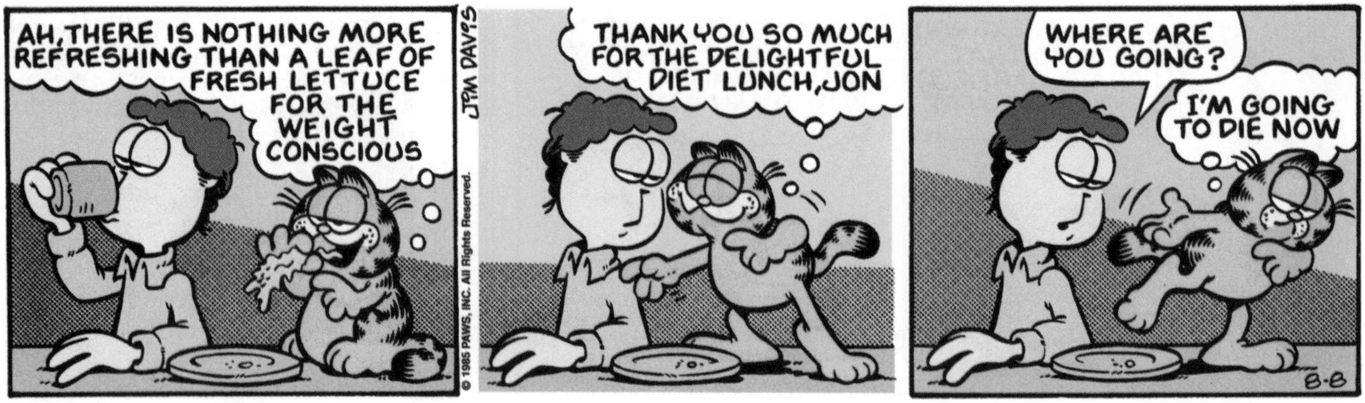
AH, THERE IS NOTHING MORE REFRESHING THAN A LEAF OF FRESH LETTUCE FOR THE WEIGHT CONSCIOUS
JIM DAVIS
© 1985 PAWS, INC. All Rights Reserved.
THANK YOU SO MUCH FOR THE DELIGHTFUL DIET LUNCH, JON
WHERE ARE YOU GOING?
I'M GOING TO DIE NOW
8-8

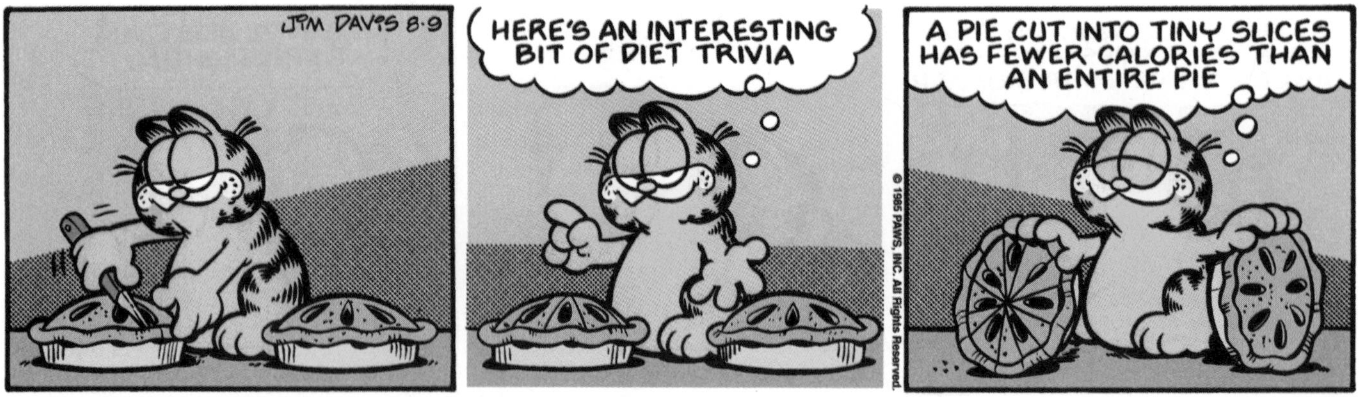
JIM DAVIS 8-9
HERE'S AN INTERESTING BIT OF DIET TRIVIA
© 1985 PAWS, INC. All Rights Reserved.
A PIE CUT INTO TINY SLICES HAS FEWER CALORIES THAN AN ENTIRE PIE

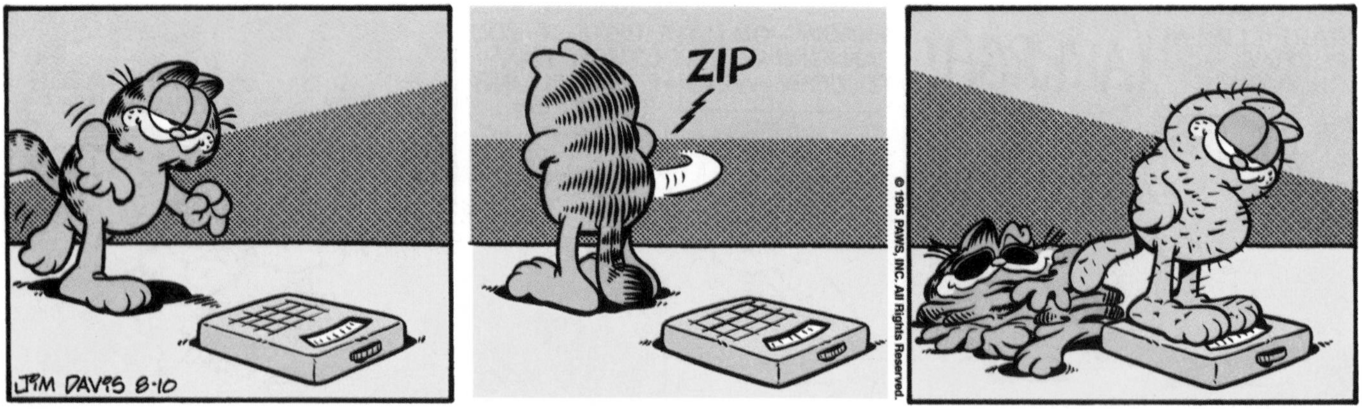
JIM DAVIS 8-10
ZIP
© 1985 PAWS, INC. All Rights Reserved.

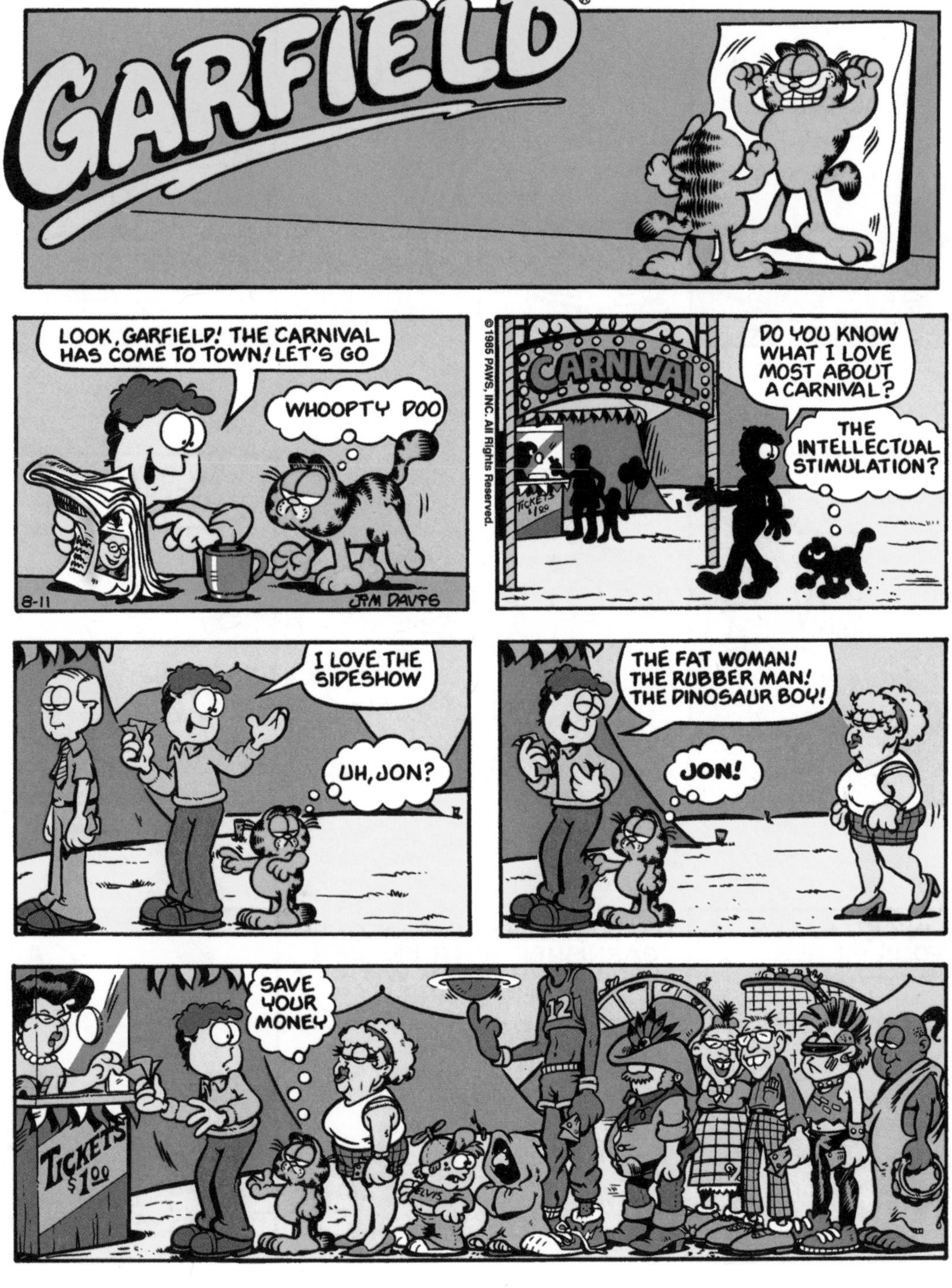
GARFIELD®
LOOK, GARFIELD! THE CARNIVAL HAS COME TO TOWN! LET'S GO
WHOOPTY DOO
8-11
JIM DAVIS
© 1985 PAWS, INC. All Rights Reserved.
CARNIVAL
TICKETS $1.00
DO YOU KNOW WHAT I LOVE MOST ABOUT A CARNIVAL?
THE INTELLECTUAL STIMULATION?
I LOVE THE SIDESHOW
UH, JON?
THE FAT WOMAN! THE RUBBER MAN! THE DINOSAUR BOY!
JON!
SAVE YOUR MONEY
TICKETS $1.00
12
ELVIS

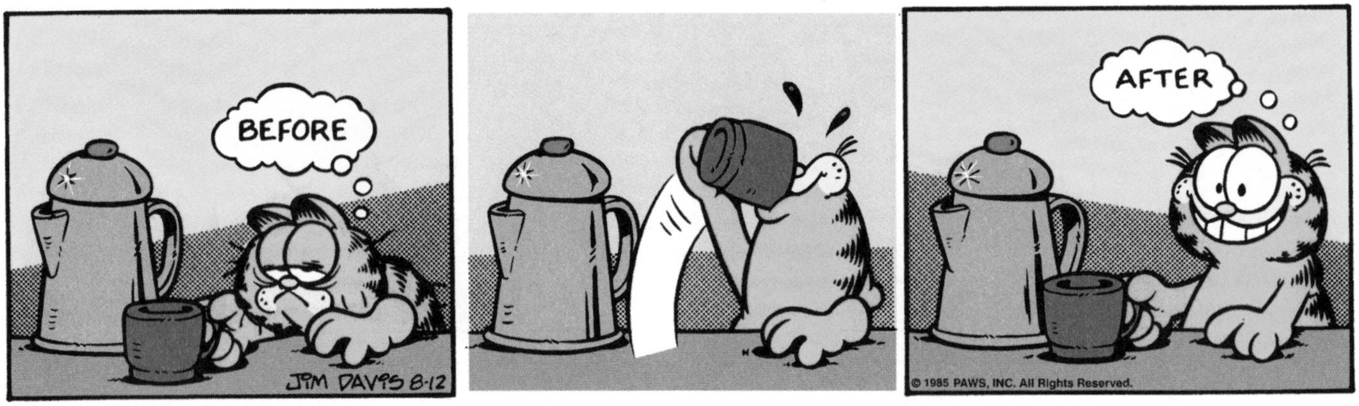
BEFORE
JIM DAVIS 8-12
AFTER
© 1985 PAWS, INC. All Rights Reserved.

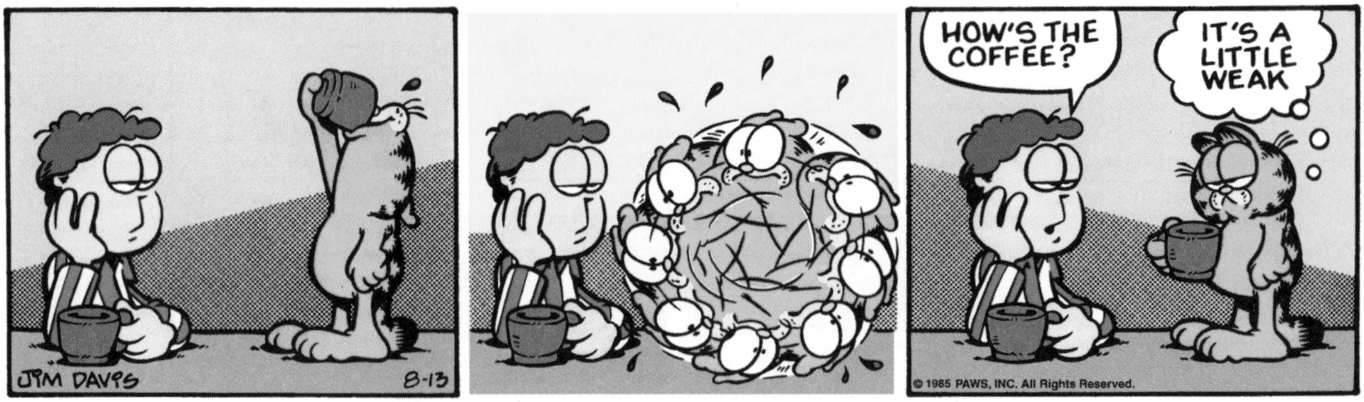
JIM DAVIS
8-13
HOW'S THE COFFEE?
IT'S A LITTLE WEAK
© 1985 PAWS, INC. All Rights Reserved.

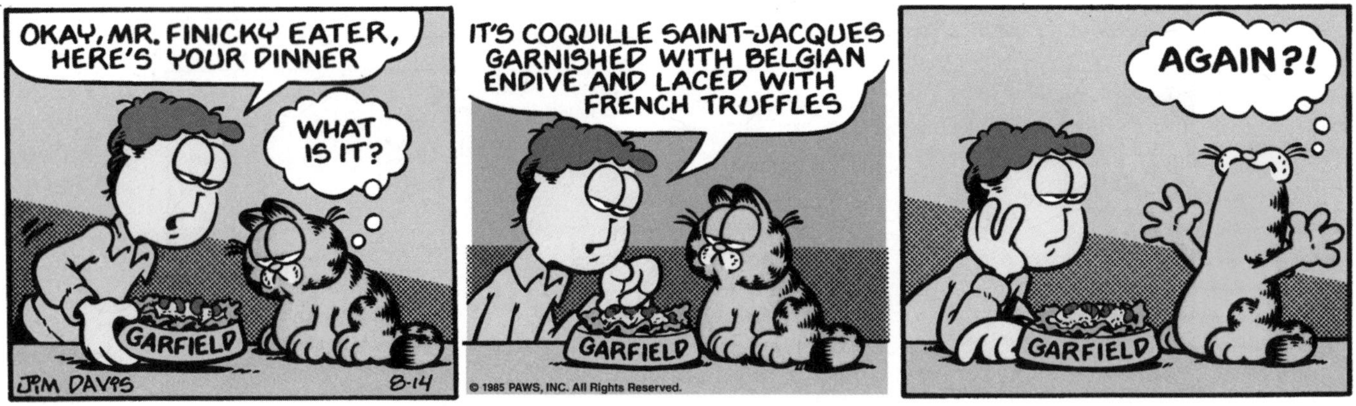
OKAY, MR. FINICKY EATER, HERE'S YOUR DINNER
WHAT IS IT?
GARFIELD
JIM DAVIS
8-14
IT'S COQUILLE SAINT-JACQUES GARNISHED WITH BELGIAN ENDIVE AND LACED WITH FRENCH TRUFFLES
GARFIELD
© 1985 PAWS, INC. All Rights Reserved.
AGAIN?!
GARFIELD

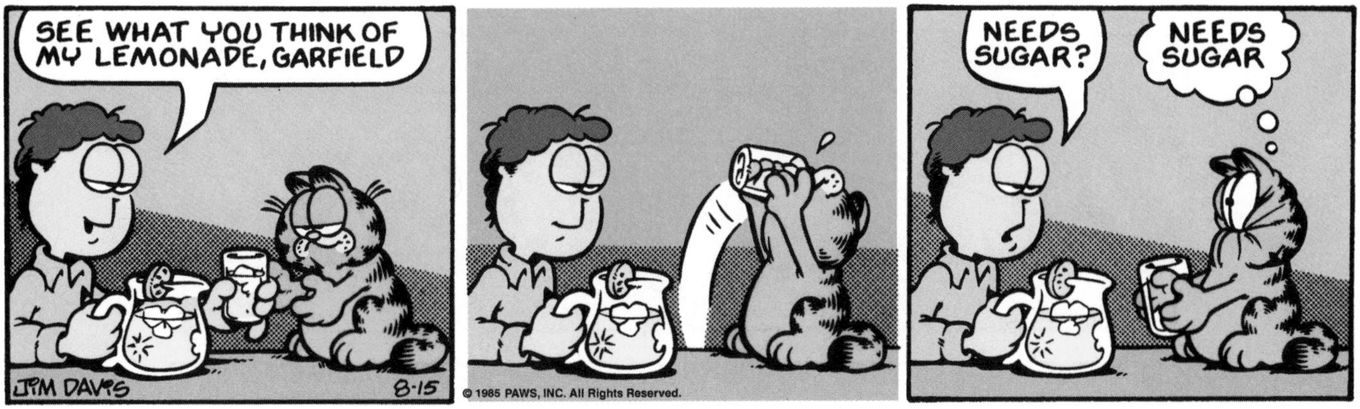
SEE WHAT YOU THINK OF MY LEMONADE, GARFIELD
JIM DAVIS
8-15
© 1985 PAWS, INC. All Rights Reserved.
NEEDS SUGAR?
NEEDS SUGAR

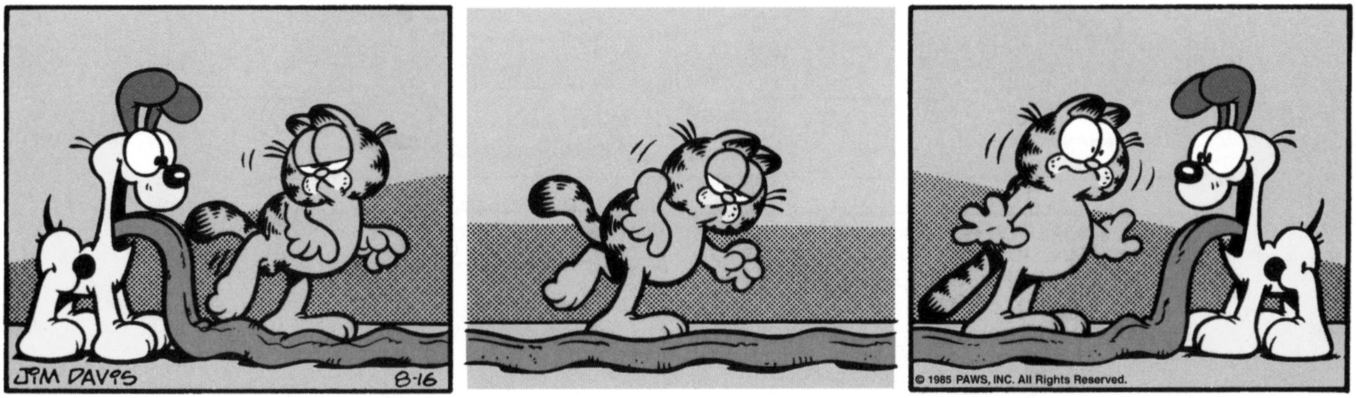
JIM DAVIS
8-16
© 1985 PAWS, INC. All Rights Reserved.

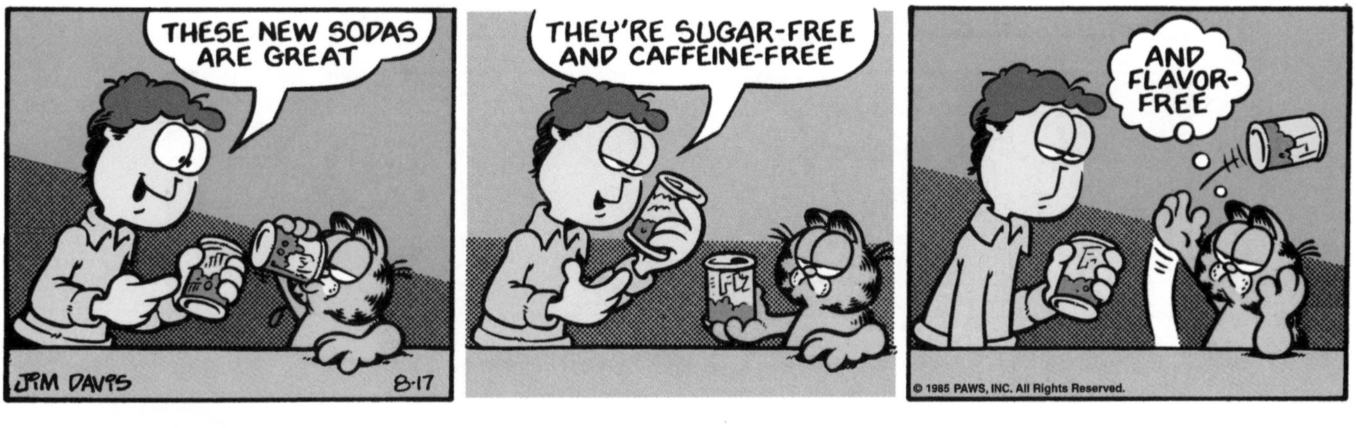
THESE NEW SODAS ARE GREAT
JIM DAVIS
8-17
THEY'RE SUGAR-FREE AND CAFFEINE-FREE
AND FLAVOR-FREE
© 1985 PAWS, INC. All Rights Reserved.

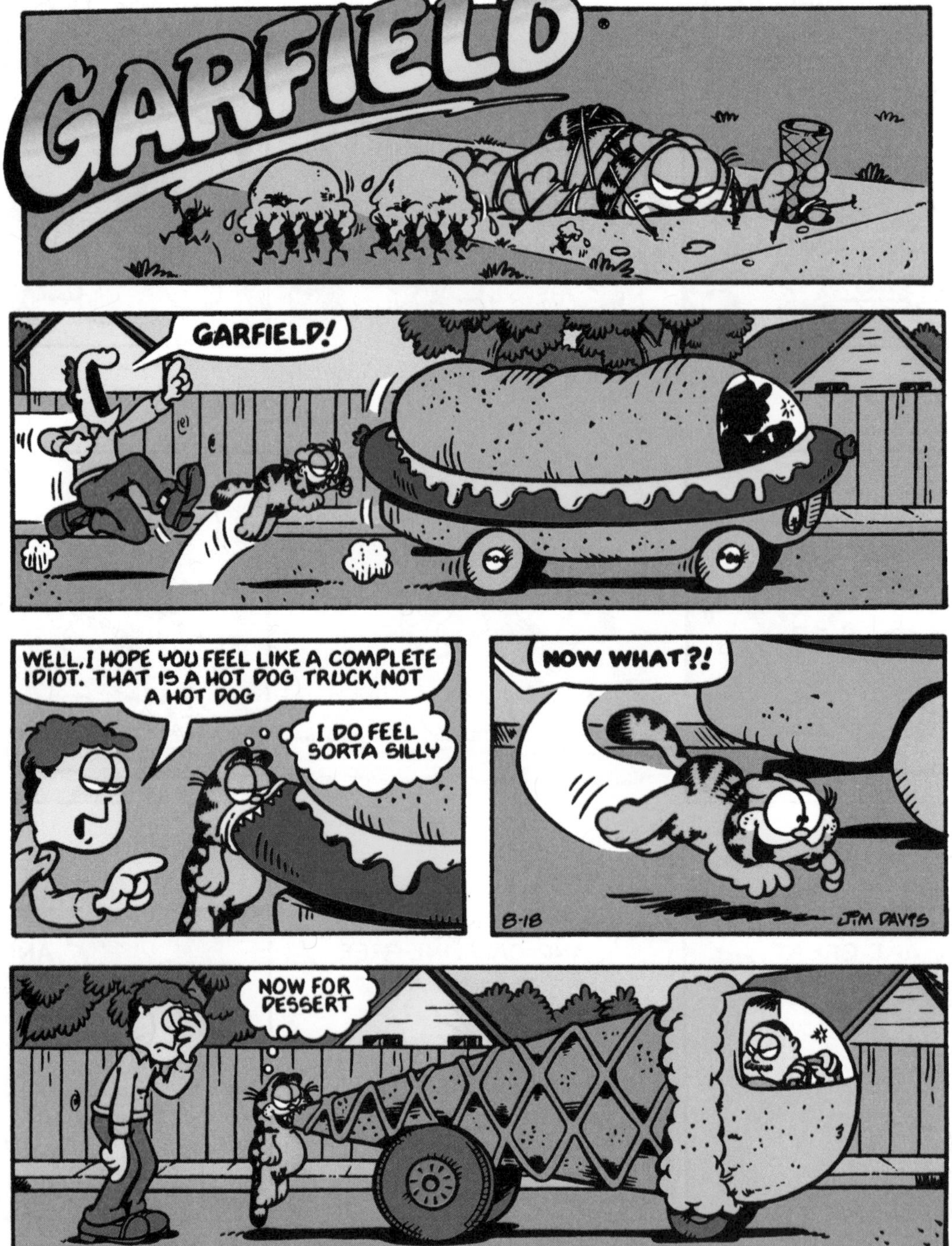
GARFIELD®
GARFIELD!
WELL, I HOPE YOU FEEL LIKE A COMPLETE IDIOT. THAT IS A HOT DOG TRUCK, NOT A HOT DOG
I DO FEEL SORTA SILLY
NOW WHAT?!
8-18
JIM DAVIS
NOW FOR DESSERT
© 1985 PAWS, INC. All Rights Reserved.

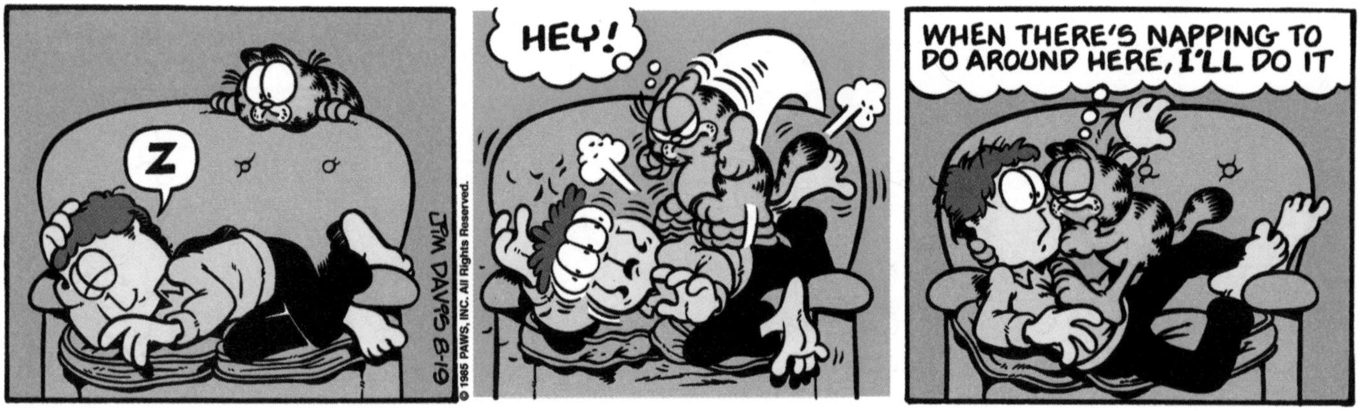
Z
JIM DAVIS 8-19
© 1985 PAWS, INC. All Rights Reserved.
HEY!
WHEN THERE'S NAPPING TO DO AROUND HERE, I'LL DO IT

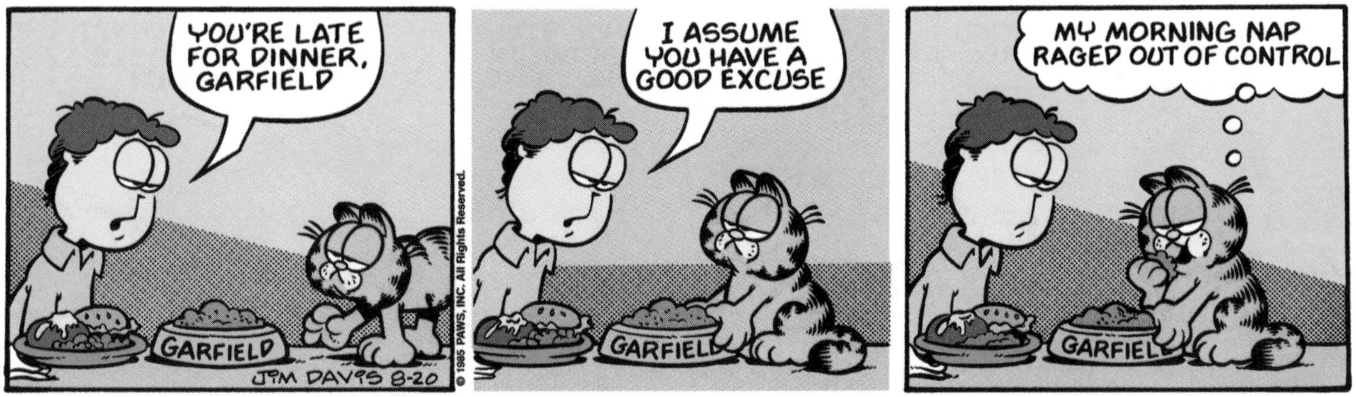
YOU'RE LATE FOR DINNER, GARFIELD
GARFIELD
JIM DAVIS 8-20
© 1985 PAWS, INC. All Rights Reserved.
I ASSUME YOU HAVE A GOOD EXCUSE
GARFIELD
MY MORNING NAP RAGED OUT OF CONTROL
GARFIEL

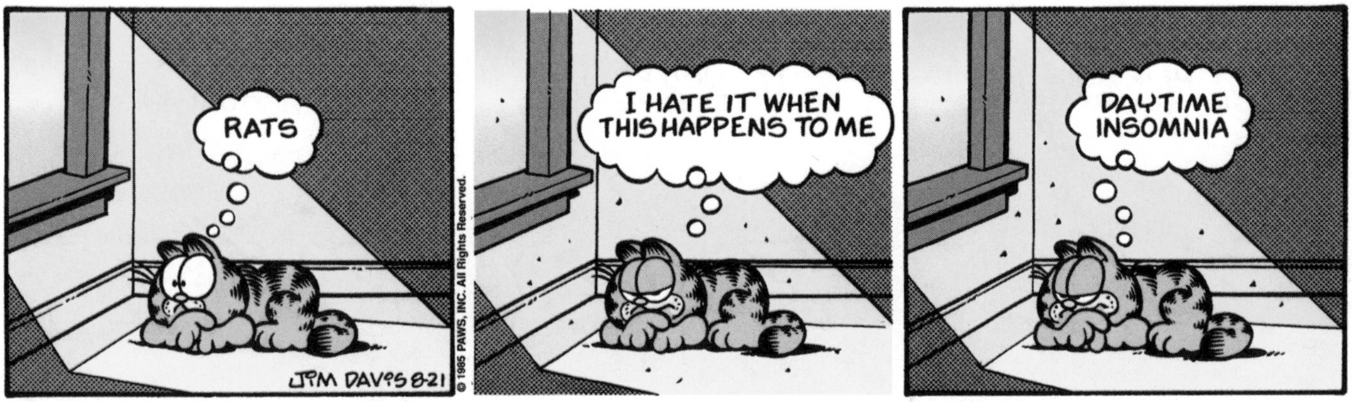
RATS
JIM DAVIS 8-21
© 1985 PAWS, INC. All Rights Reserved.
I HATE IT WHEN THIS HAPPENS TO ME
DAYTIME INSOMNIA

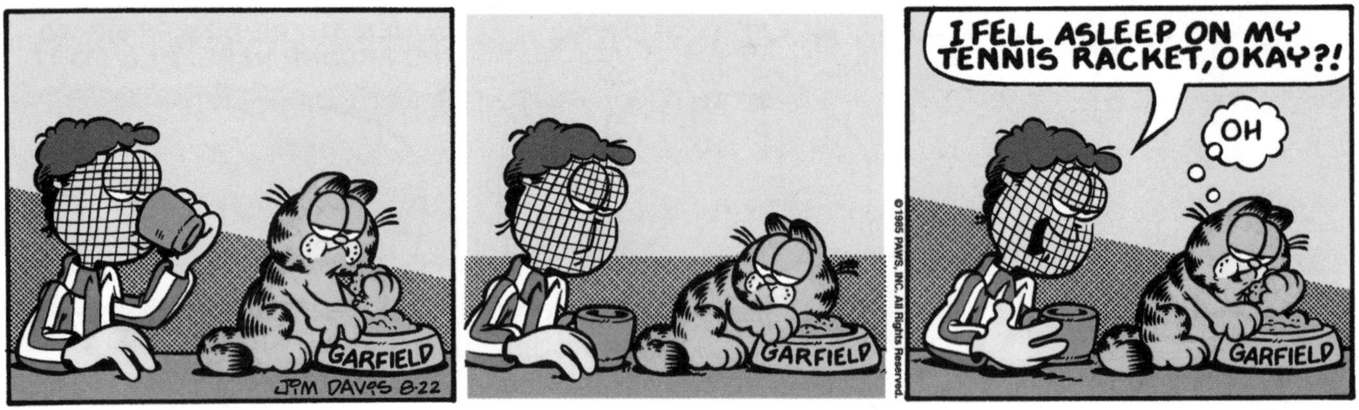
GARFIELD
GARFIELD
JIM DAVIS 8-22
© 1985 PAWS, INC. All Rights Reserved.
I FELL ASLEEP ON MY TENNIS RACKET, OKAY?!
OH
GARFIELD

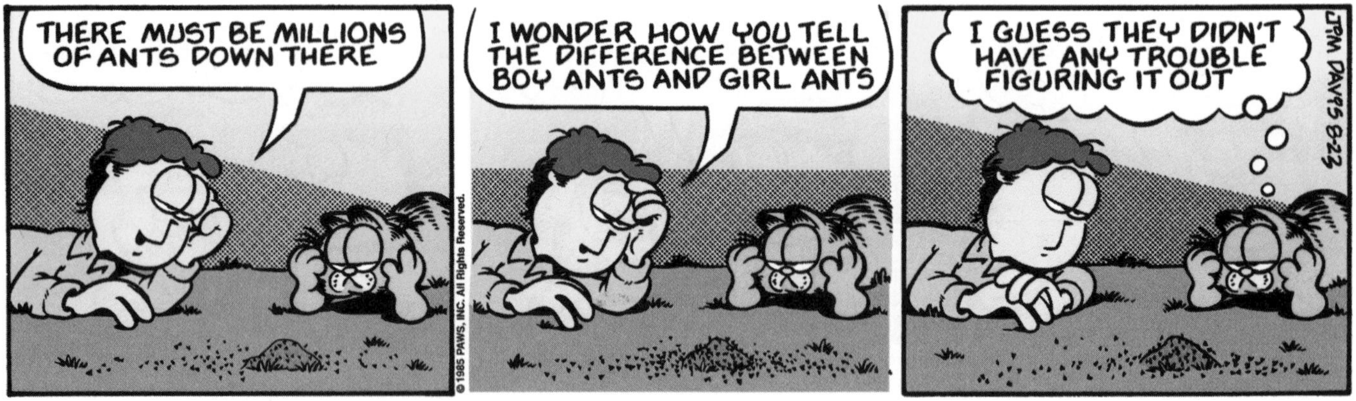
THERE MUST BE MILLIONS OF ANTS DOWN THERE
© 1985 PAWS, INC. All Rights Reserved.
I WONDER HOW YOU TELL THE DIFFERENCE BETWEEN BOY ANTS AND GIRL ANTS
I GUESS THEY DIDN'T HAVE ANY TROUBLE FIGURING IT OUT
JIM DAVIS 8-23

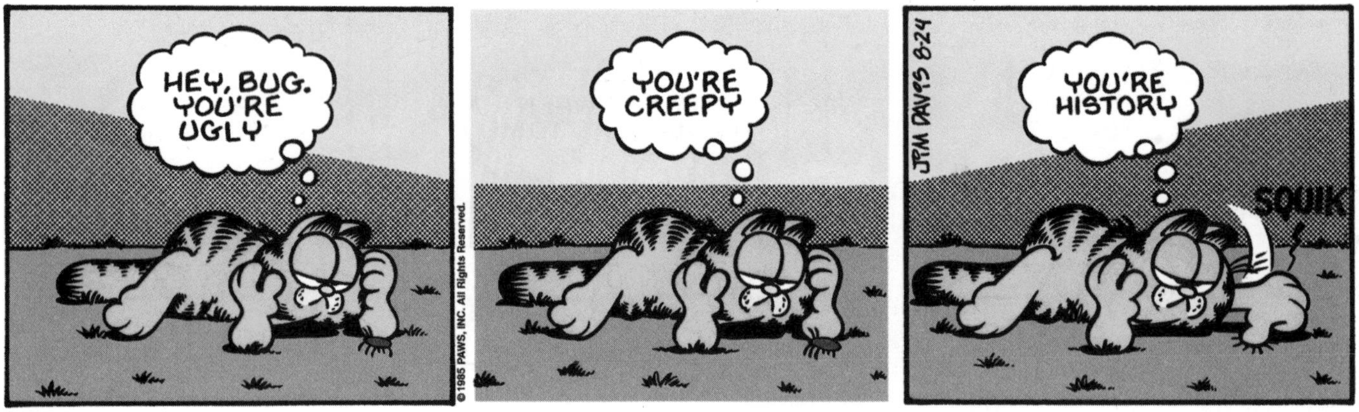
HEY, BUG. YOU'RE UGLY
© 1985 PAWS, INC. All Rights Reserved.
YOU'RE CREEPY
JIM DAVIS 8-24
YOU'RE HISTORY
SQUIK

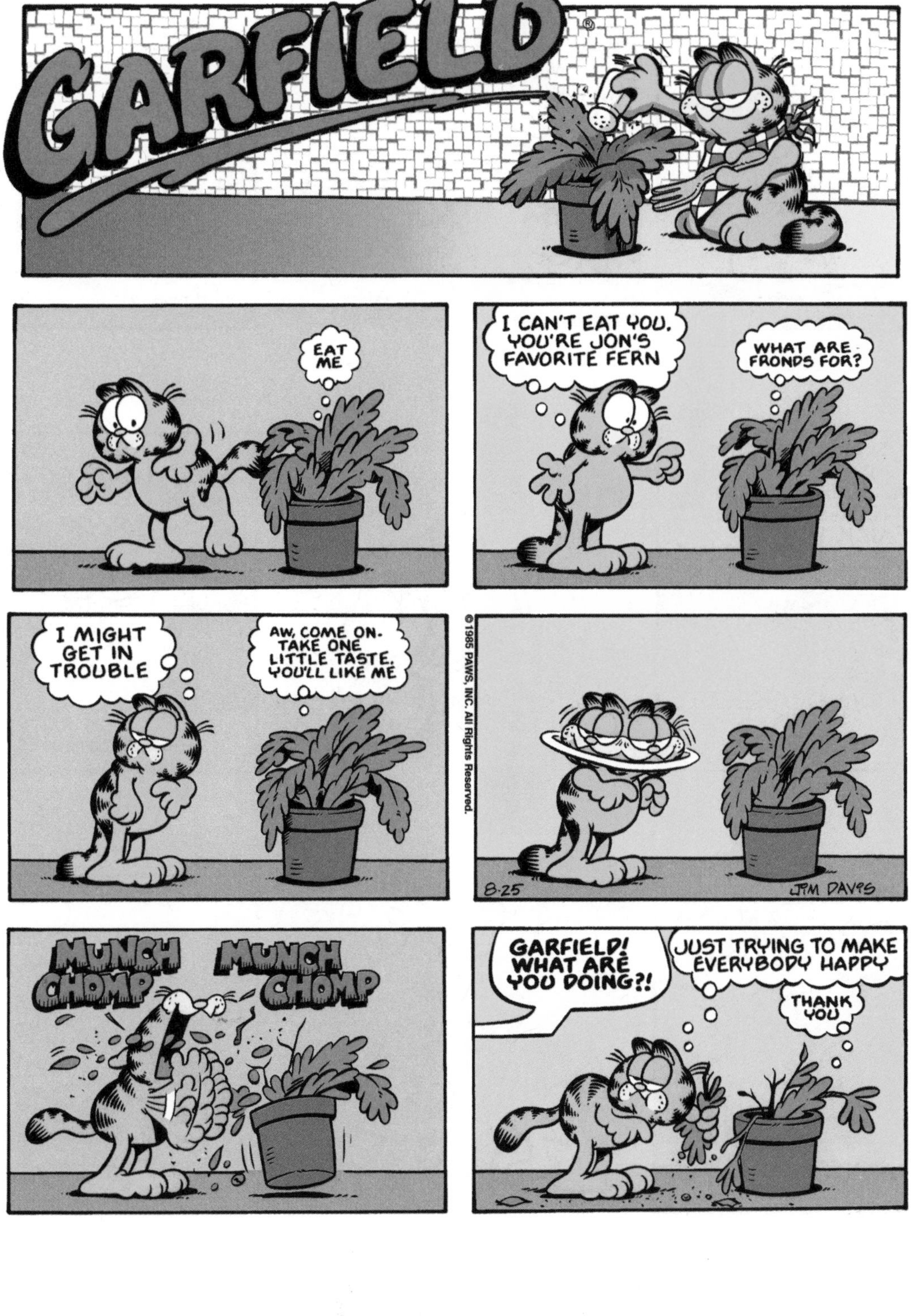
GARFIELD®
EAT ME
I CAN'T EAT YOU. YOU'RE JON'S FAVORITE FERN
WHAT ARE FRONDS FOR?
I MIGHT GET IN TROUBLE
AW, COME ON. TAKE ONE LITTLE TASTE. YOU'LL LIKE ME
8-25
JIM DAVIS
MUNCH CHOMP
MUNCH CHOMP
GARFIELD! WHAT ARE YOU DOING?!
JUST TRYING TO MAKE EVERYBODY HAPPY
THANK YOU

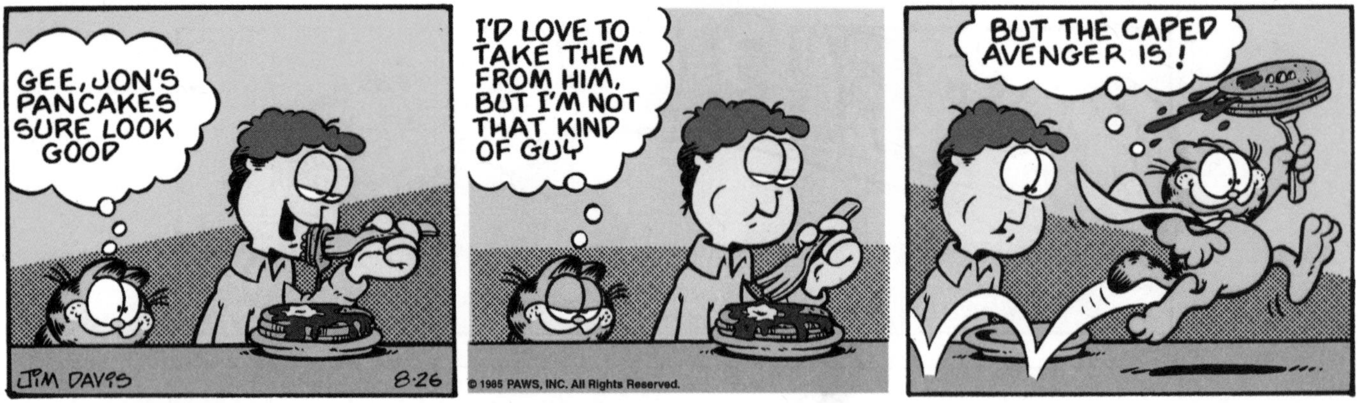
GEE, JON'S PANCAKES SURE LOOK GOOD
JIM DAVIS
8·26
I'D LOVE TO TAKE THEM FROM HIM, BUT I'M NOT THAT KIND OF GUY
© 1985 PAWS, INC. All Rights Reserved.
BUT THE CAPED AVENGER IS!

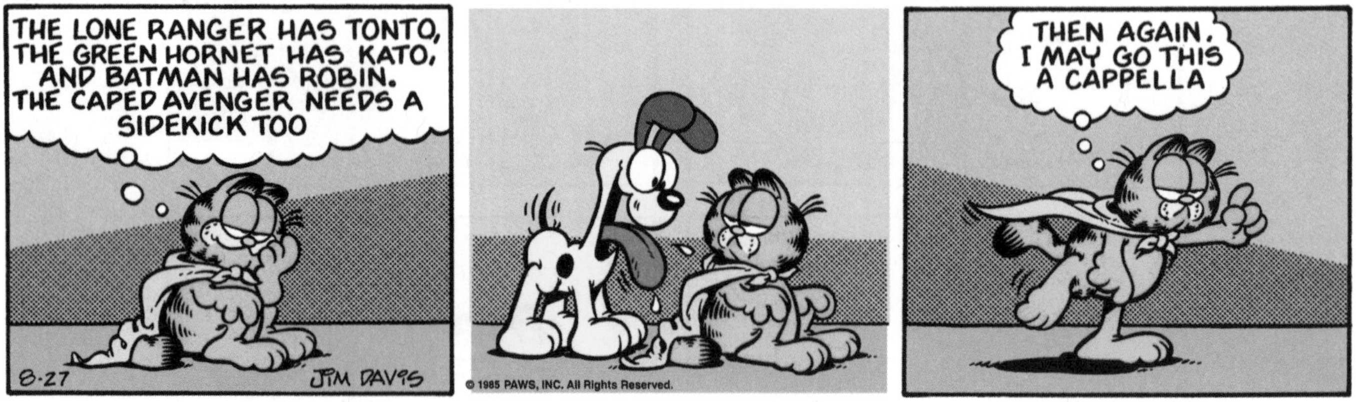
THE LONE RANGER HAS TONTO, THE GREEN HORNET HAS KATO, AND BATMAN HAS ROBIN. THE CAPED AVENGER NEEDS A SIDEKICK TOO
8·27
JIM DAVIS
© 1985 PAWS, INC. All Rights Reserved.
THEN AGAIN, I MAY GO THIS A CAPPELLA

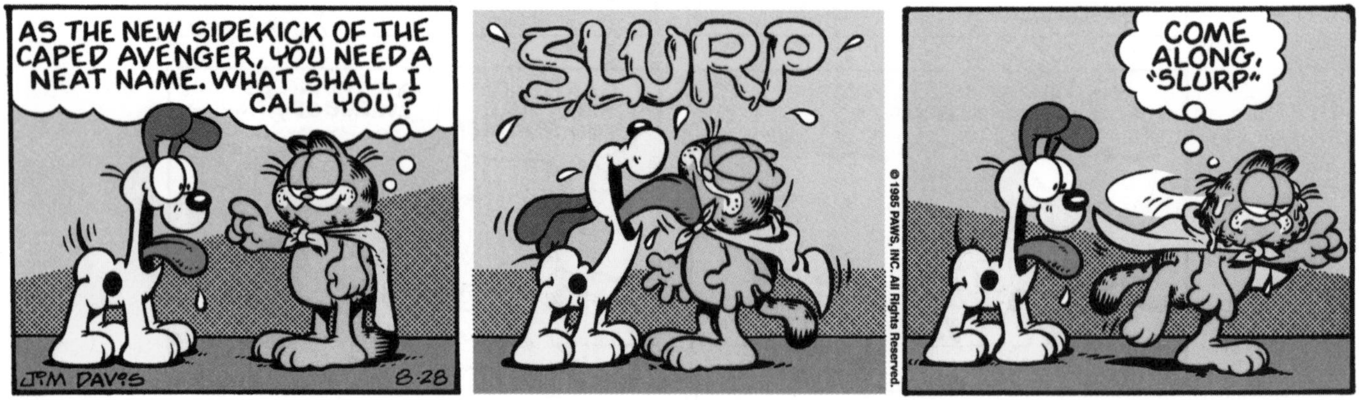
AS THE NEW SIDEKICK OF THE CAPED AVENGER, YOU NEED A NEAT NAME. WHAT SHALL I CALL YOU?
JIM DAVIS
8·28
SLURP
© 1985 PAWS, INC. All Rights Reserved.
COME ALONG, "SLURP"

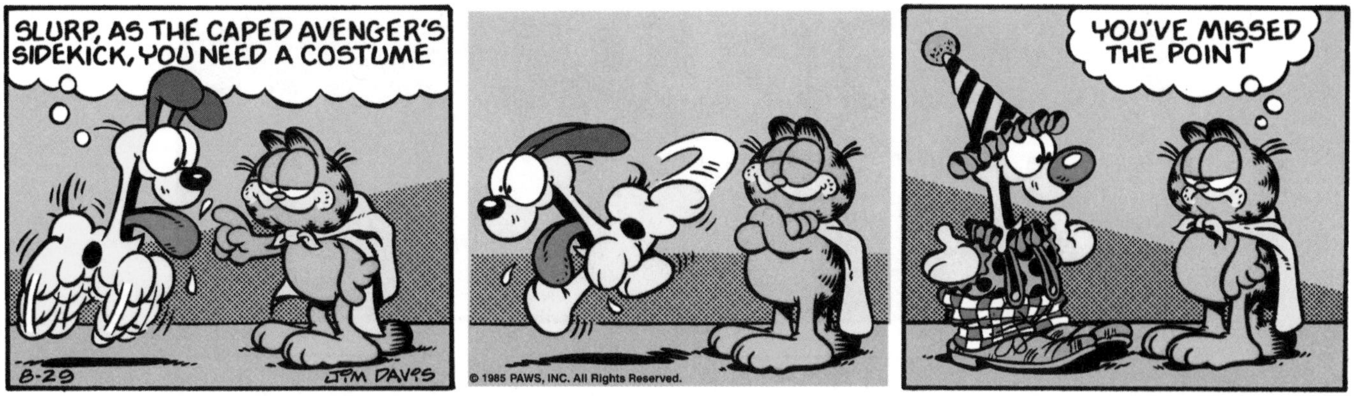
SLURP, AS THE CAPED AVENGER'S SIDEKICK, YOU NEED A COSTUME
8-29
JIM DAVIS
© 1985 PAWS, INC. All Rights Reserved.
YOU'VE MISSED THE POINT

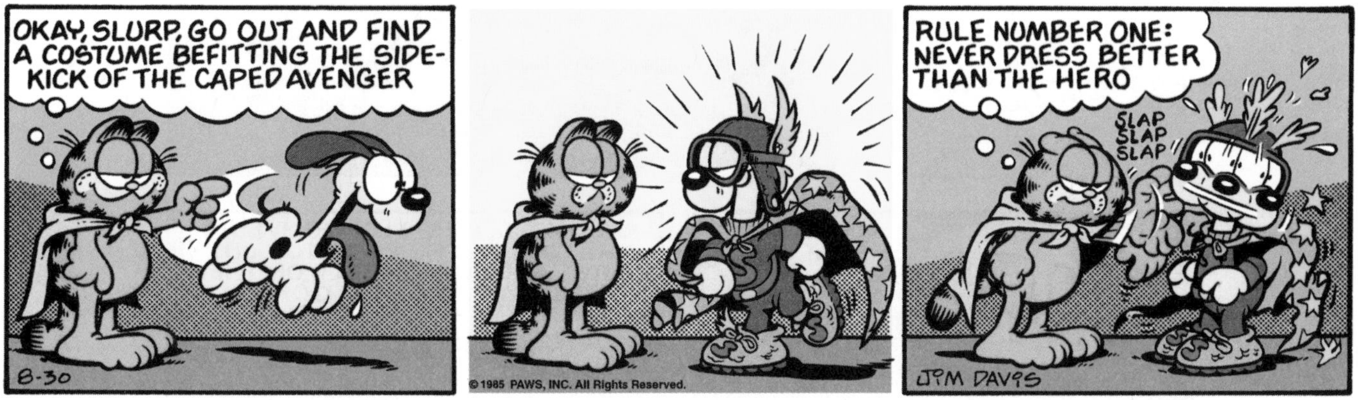
OKAY, SLURP, GO OUT AND FIND A COSTUME BEFITTING THE SIDE-KICK OF THE CAPED AVENGER
8-30
© 1985 PAWS, INC. All Rights Reserved.
RULE NUMBER ONE: NEVER DRESS BETTER THAN THE HERO
SLAP SLAP SLAP
JIM DAVIS

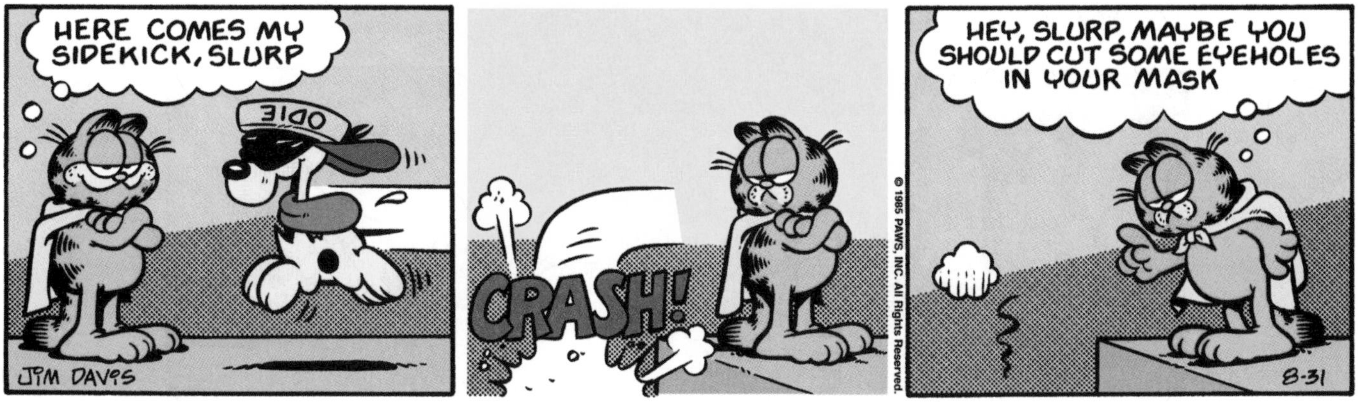
HERE COMES MY SIDEKICK, SLURP
ODIE
JIM DAVIS
CRASH!
© 1985 PAWS, INC. All Rights Reserved.
HEY, SLURP, MAYBE YOU SHOULD CUT SOME EYEHOLES IN YOUR MASK
8-31

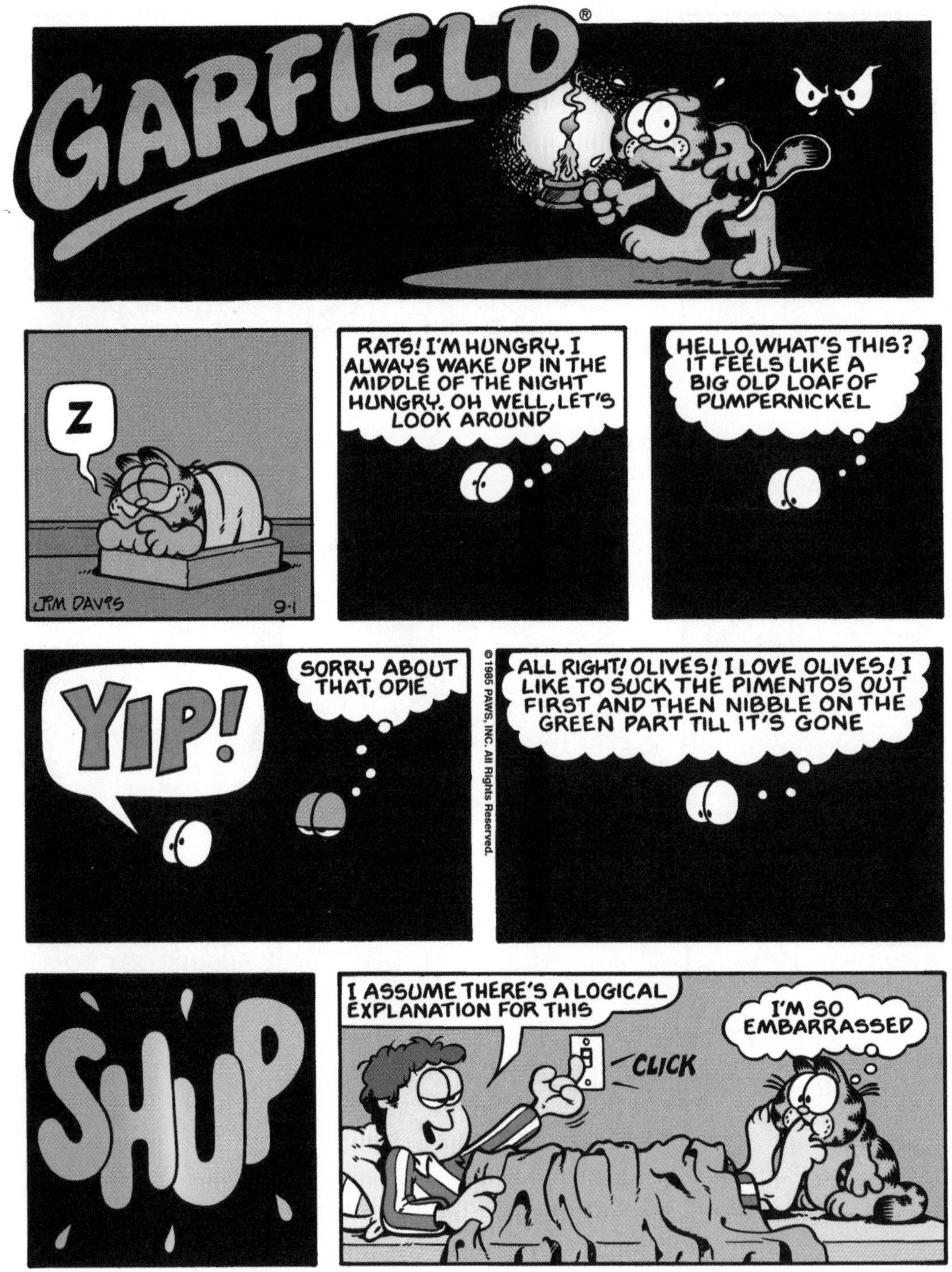
GARFIELD®
Z
JIM DAVIS
9-1
RATS! I'M HUNGRY. I ALWAYS WAKE UP IN THE MIDDLE OF THE NIGHT HUNGRY. OH WELL, LET'S LOOK AROUND
HELLO, WHAT'S THIS? IT FEELS LIKE A BIG OLD LOAF OF PUMPERNICKEL
YIP!
SORRY ABOUT THAT, ODIE
ALL RIGHT! OLIVES! I LOVE OLIVES! I LIKE TO SUCK THE PIMENTOS OUT FIRST AND THEN NIBBLE ON THE GREEN PART TILL IT'S GONE
SHUP
I ASSUME THERE'S A LOGICAL EXPLANATION FOR THIS
CLICK
I'M SO EMBARRASSED

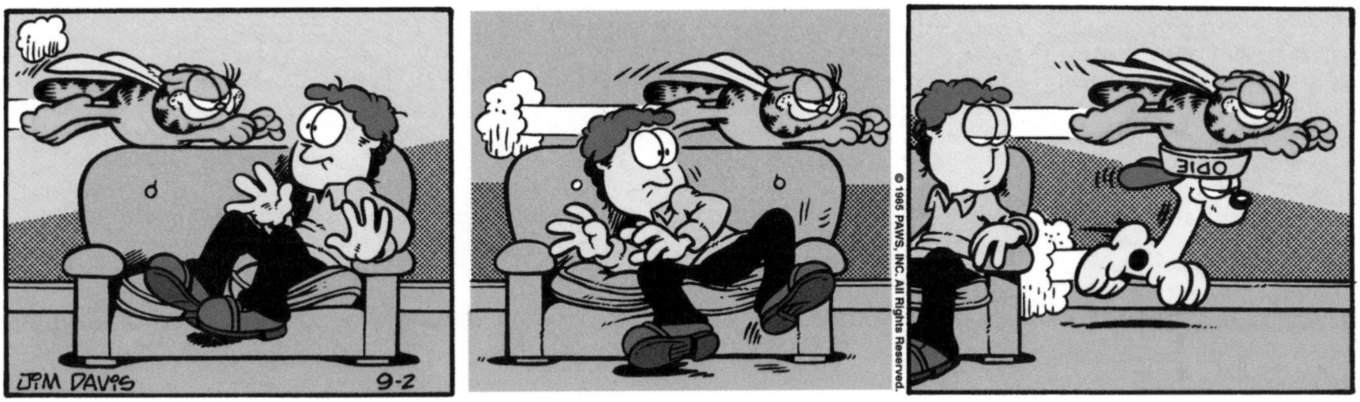
JIM DAVIS
9-2
© 1985 PAWS, INC. All Rights Reserved.

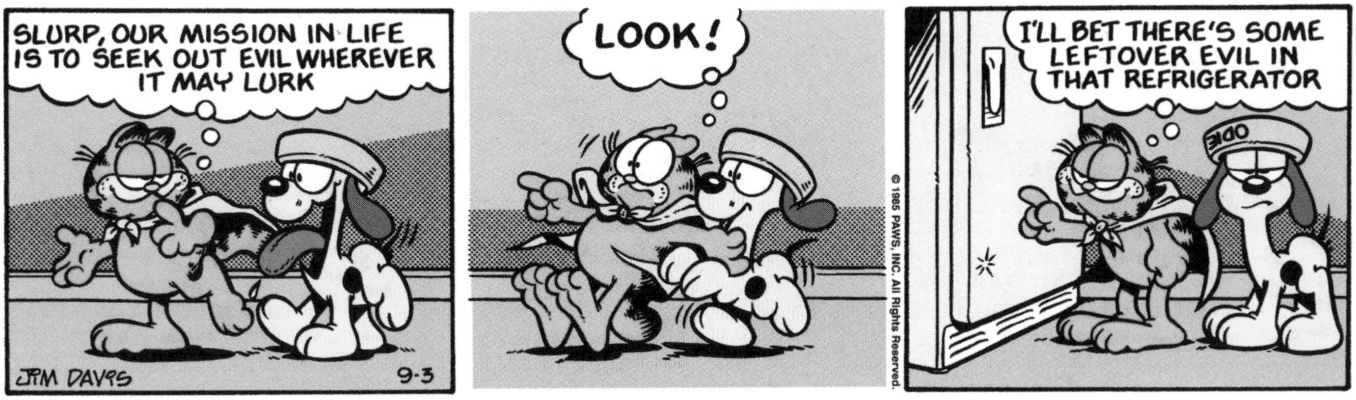
SLURP, OUR MISSION IN LIFE IS TO SEEK OUT EVIL WHEREVER IT MAY LURK
JIM DAVIS
9-3
LOOK!
I'LL BET THERE'S SOME LEFTOVER EVIL IN THAT REFRIGERATOR
© 1985 PAWS, INC. All Rights Reserved.

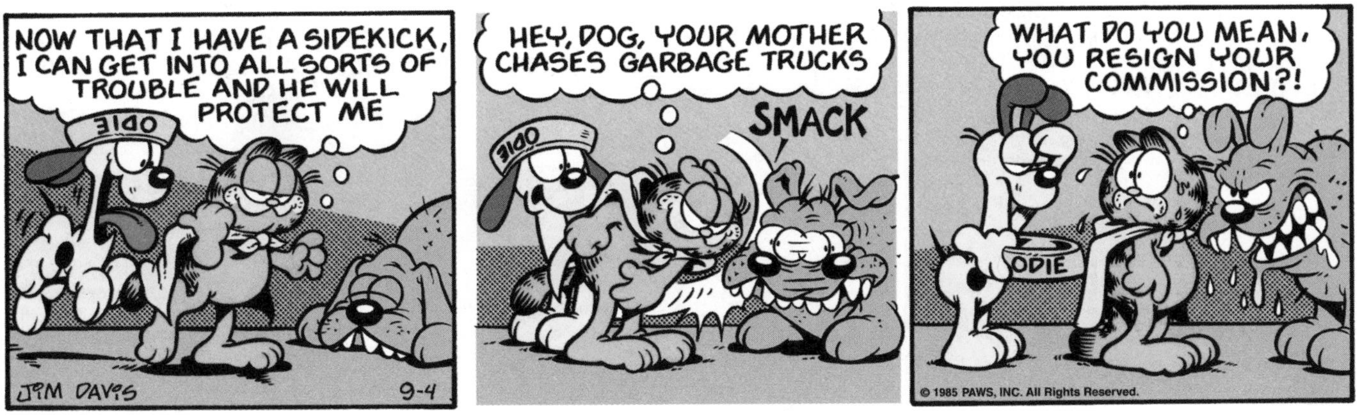
NOW THAT I HAVE A SIDEKICK, I CAN GET INTO ALL SORTS OF TROUBLE AND HE WILL PROTECT ME
ODIE
JIM DAVIS
9-4
HEY, DOG, YOUR MOTHER CHASES GARBAGE TRUCKS
ODIE
SMACK
WHAT DO YOU MEAN, YOU RESIGN YOUR COMMISSION?!
ODIE
© 1985 PAWS, INC. All Rights Reserved.

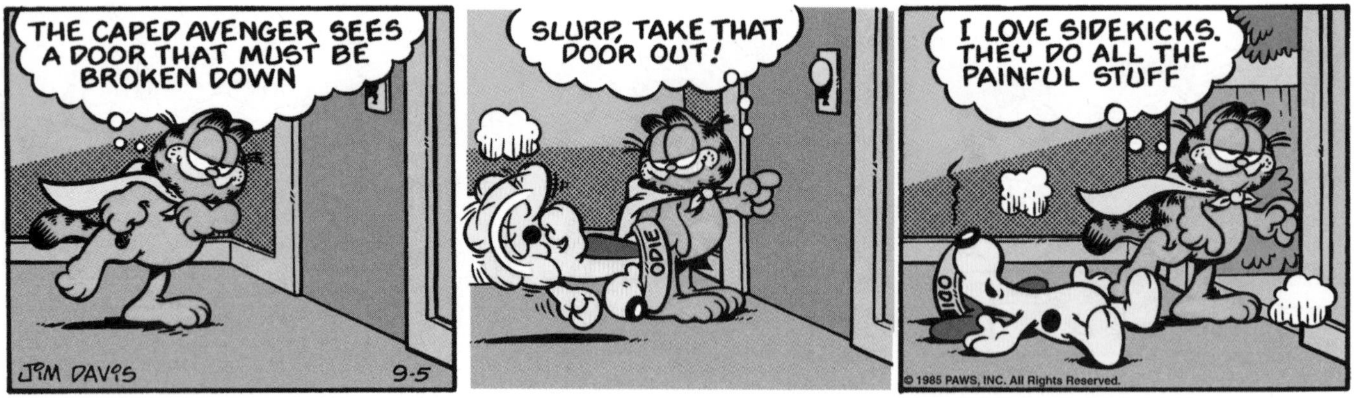
THE CAPED AVENGER SEES A DOOR THAT MUST BE BROKEN DOWN
JIM DAVIS 9-5
SLURP, TAKE THAT DOOR OUT!
ODIE
I LOVE SIDEKICKS. THEY DO ALL THE PAINFUL STUFF
ODIE
© 1985 PAWS, INC. All Rights Reserved.

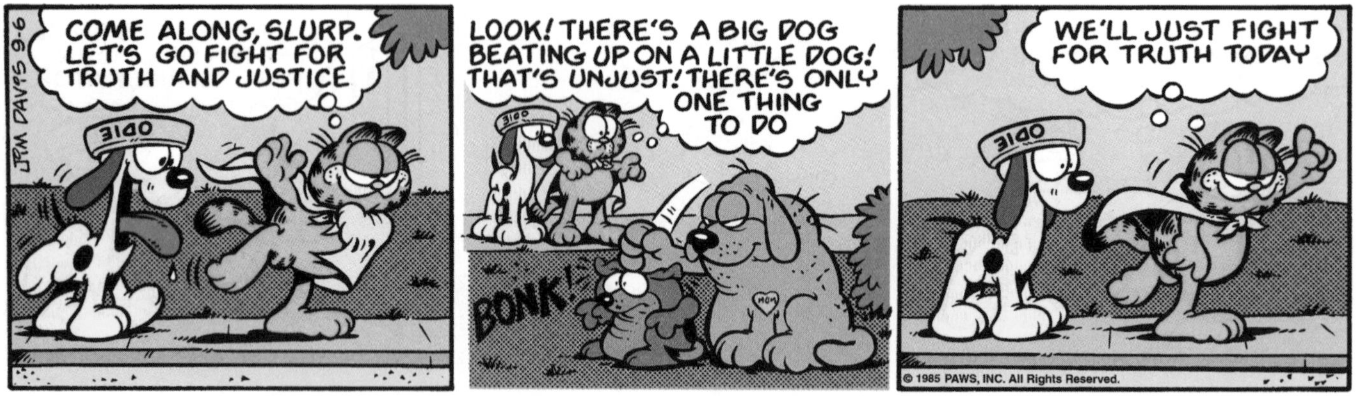
COME ALONG, SLURP. LET'S GO FIGHT FOR TRUTH AND JUSTICE
JIM DAVIS 9-6
ODIE
LOOK! THERE'S A BIG DOG BEATING UP ON A LITTLE DOG! THAT'S UNJUST! THERE'S ONLY ONE THING TO DO
BONK!
MOM
WE'LL JUST FIGHT FOR TRUTH TODAY
ODIE
© 1985 PAWS, INC. All Rights Reserved.

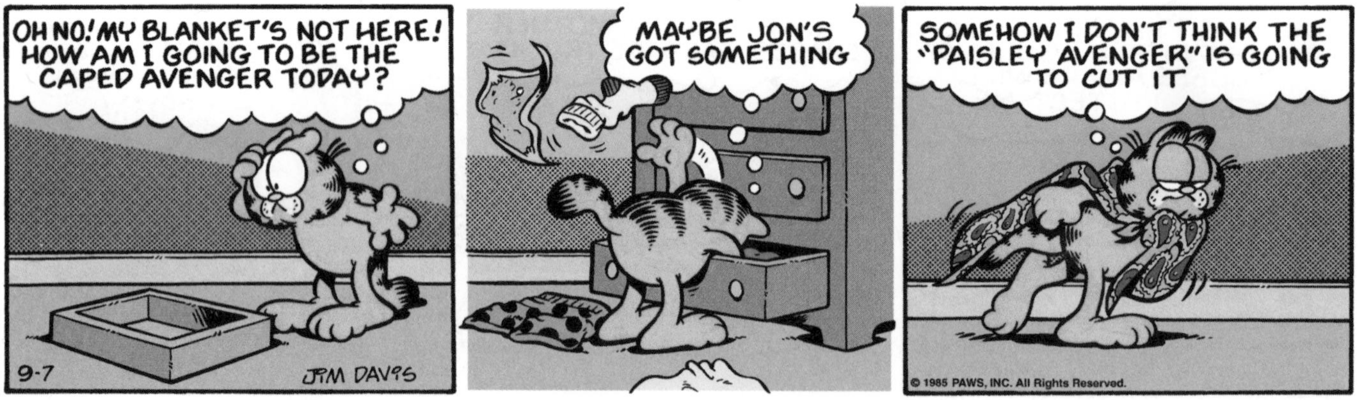
OH NO! MY BLANKET'S NOT HERE! HOW AM I GOING TO BE THE CAPED AVENGER TODAY?
9-7
JIM DAVIS
MAYBE JON'S GOT SOMETHING
SOMEHOW I DON'T THINK THE "PAISLEY AVENGER" IS GOING TO CUT IT
© 1985 PAWS, INC. All Rights Reserved.

GARFIELD®
LOOK AT ALL THOSE POOR ANIMALS IN THERE ALL CAGED UP. THIS LOOKS LIKE A JOB FOR...
FREEDOM FIGHTER!
YOU'RE FREE! YOU'RE FREE!
JIM DAVIS 9-8
GO FOR IT!
HMMM, FOLKS MUST NOT BE HEAVILY INTO FREEDOM THESE DAYS
YOU'RE SECURE! YOU'RE SECURE!
SLAM!

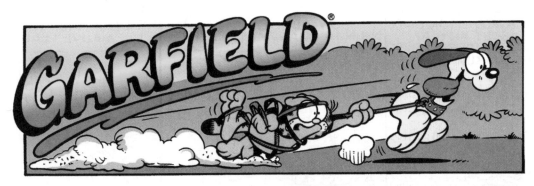

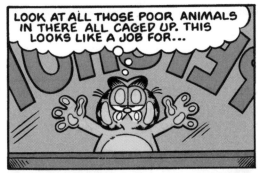

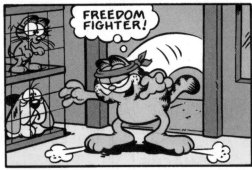

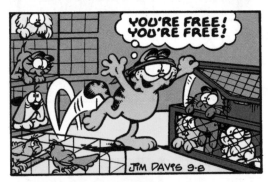

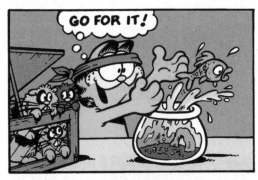

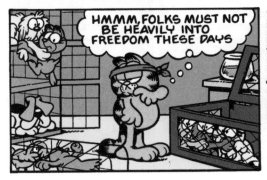

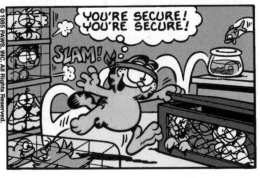

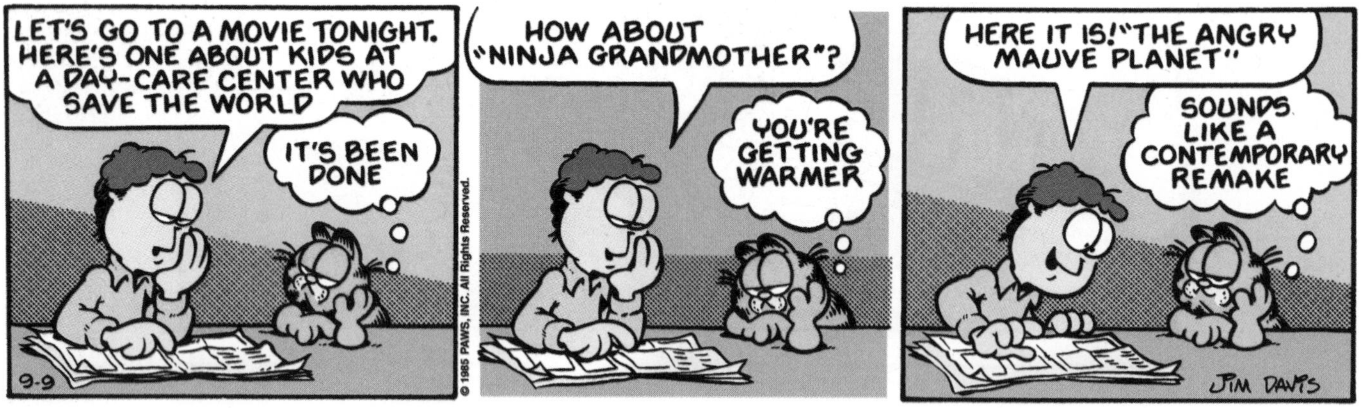
LET'S GO TO A MOVIE TONIGHT. HERE'S ONE ABOUT KIDS AT A DAY-CARE CENTER WHO SAVE THE WORLD
IT'S BEEN DONE
9-9
© 1985 PAWS, INC. All Rights Reserved.
HOW ABOUT "NINJA GRANDMOTHER"?
YOU'RE GETTING WARMER
HERE IT IS! "THE ANGRY MAUVE PLANET"
SOUNDS LIKE A CONTEMPORARY REMAKE
JIM DAVIS

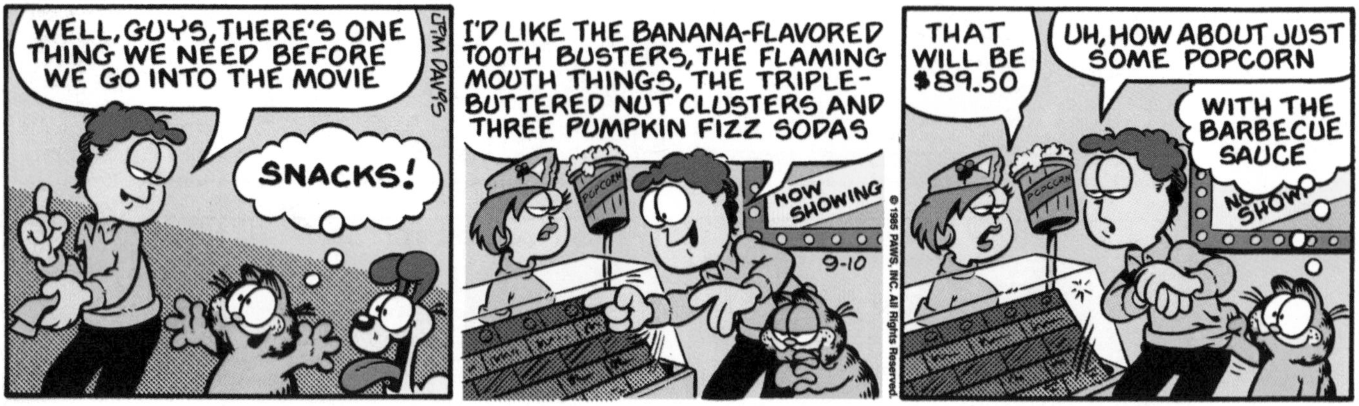
WELL, GUYS, THERE'S ONE THING WE NEED BEFORE WE GO INTO THE MOVIE
SNACKS!
JIM DAVIS
I'D LIKE THE BANANA-FLAVORED TOOTH BUSTERS, THE FLAMING MOUTH THINGS, THE TRIPLE-BUTTERED NUT CLUSTERS AND THREE PUMPKIN FIZZ SODAS
POPCORN
NOW SHOWING
9-10
© 1985 PAWS, INC. All Rights Reserved.
THAT WILL BE $89.50
UH, HOW ABOUT JUST SOME POPCORN
WITH THE BARBECUE SAUCE

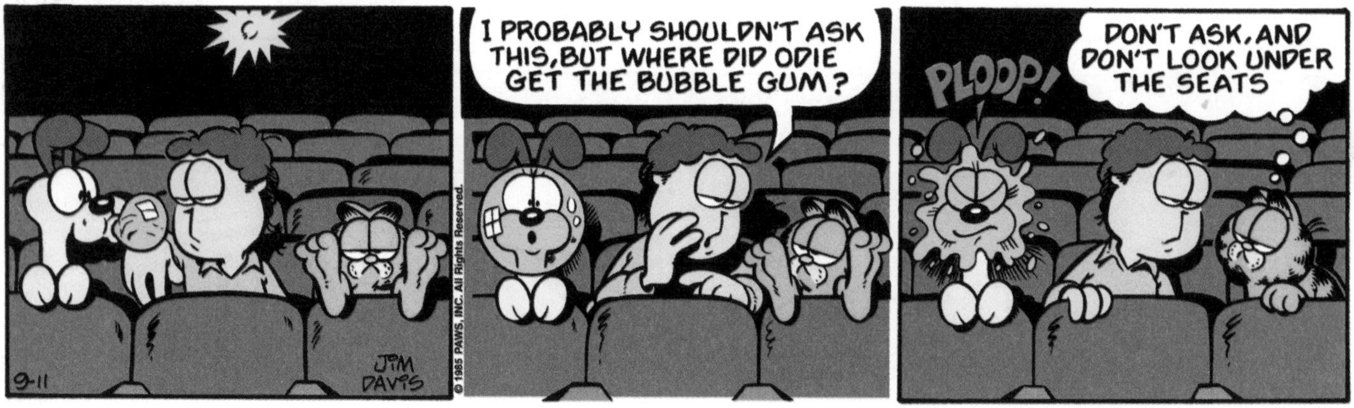
9-11
JIM DAVIS
© 1985 PAWS, INC. All Rights Reserved.
I PROBABLY SHOULDN'T ASK THIS, BUT WHERE DID ODIE GET THE BUBBLE GUM?
PLOOP!
DON'T ASK, AND DON'T LOOK UNDER THE SEATS

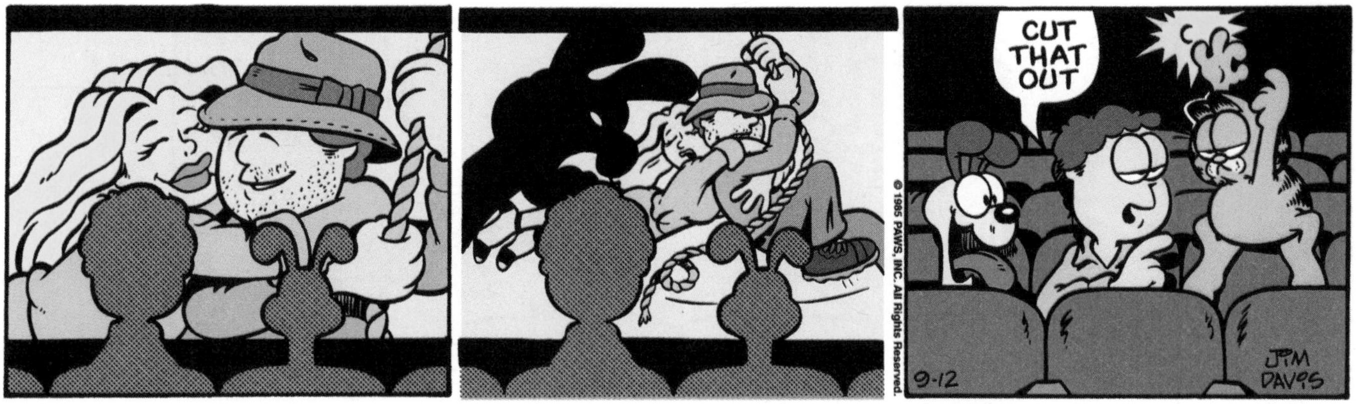
CUT THAT OUT
© 1985 PAWS, INC. All Rights Reserved.
9-12
JIM DAVIS

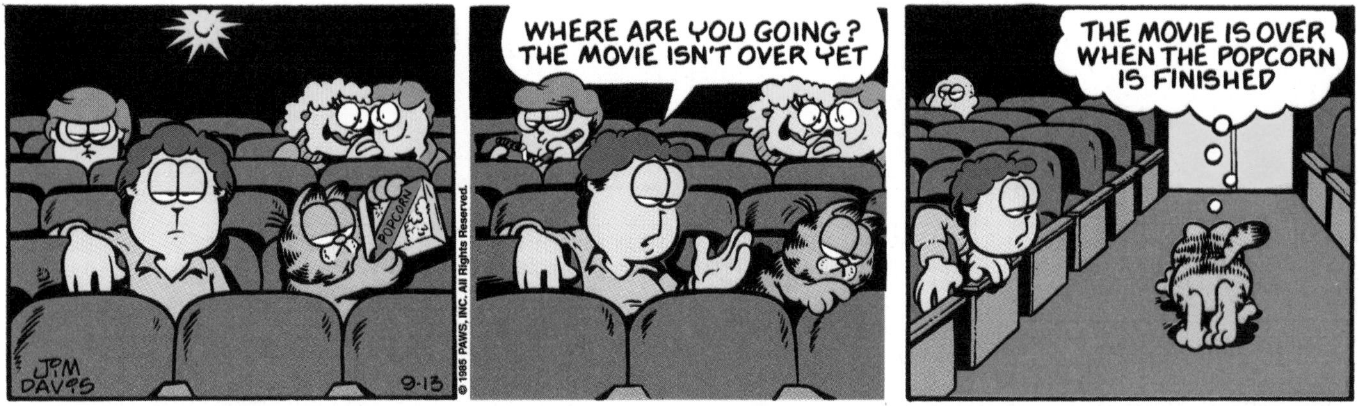
POPCORN
JIM DAVIS
9-13
© 1985 PAWS, INC. All Rights Reserved.
WHERE ARE YOU GOING? THE MOVIE ISN'T OVER YET
THE MOVIE IS OVER WHEN THE POPCORN IS FINISHED

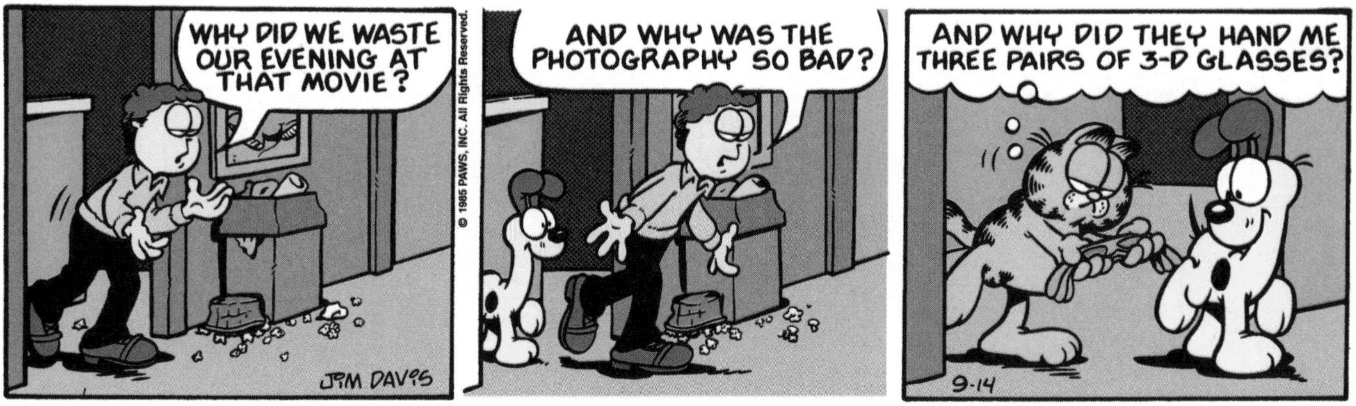
WHY DID WE WASTE OUR EVENING AT THAT MOVIE?
JIM DAVIS
© 1985 PAWS, INC. All Rights Reserved.
AND WHY WAS THE PHOTOGRAPHY SO BAD?
AND WHY DID THEY HAND ME THREE PAIRS OF 3-D GLASSES?
9-14

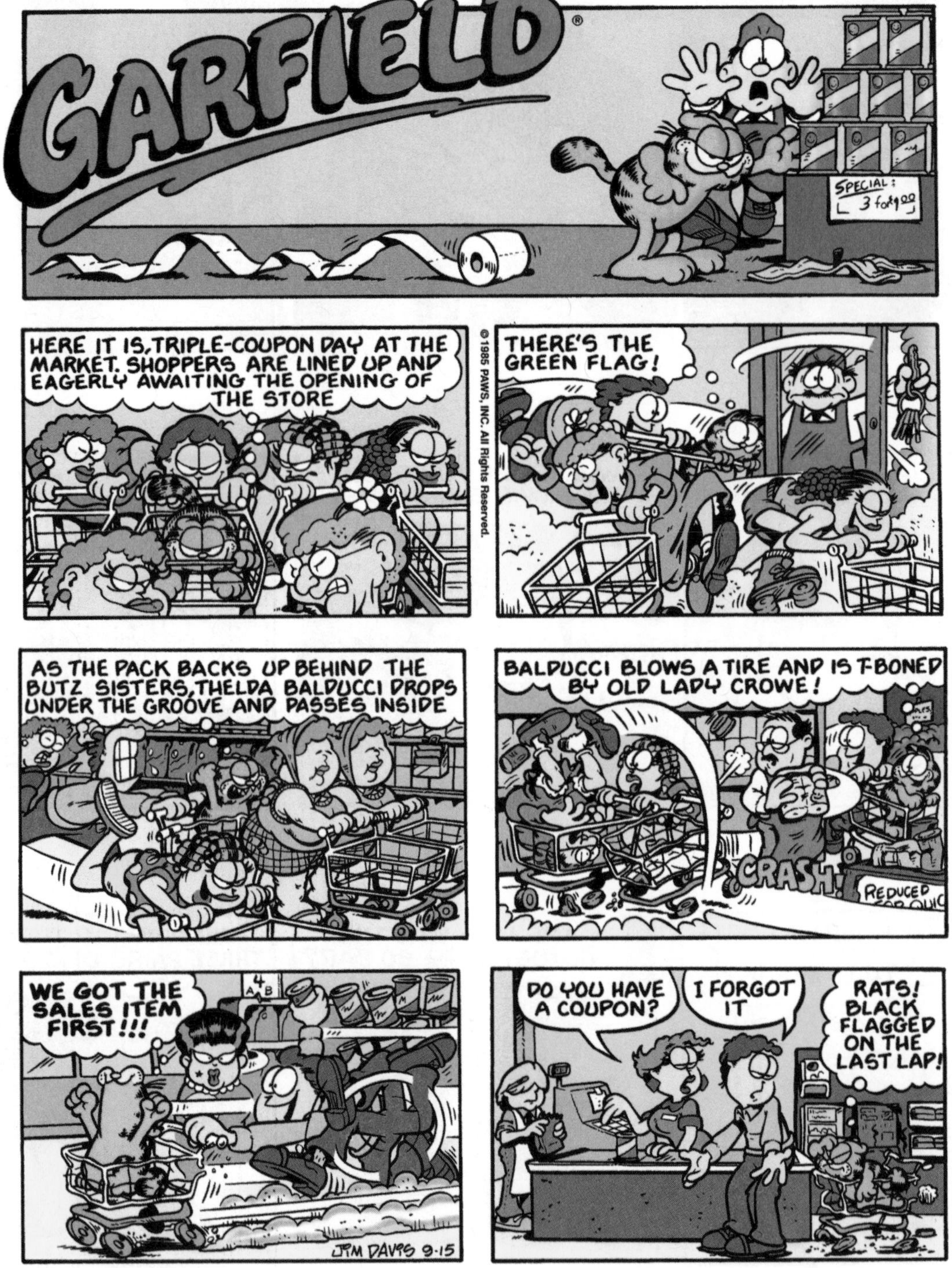
GARFIELD
SPECIAL:
HERE IT IS, TRIPLE-COUPON DAY AT THE MARKET. SHOPPERS ARE LINED UP AND EAGERLY AWAITING THE OPENING OF THE STORE
© 1985 PAWS, INC. All Rights Reserved.
THERE'S THE GREEN FLAG!
AS THE PACK BACKS UP BEHIND THE BUTZ SISTERS, THELDA BALDUCCI DROPS UNDER THE GROOVE AND PASSES INSIDE
BALDUCCI BLOWS A TIRE AND IS T-BONED BY OLD LADY CROWE!
CRASH!
REDUCED
WE GOT THE SALES ITEM FIRST!!!
JIM DAVIS 9-15
DO YOU HAVE A COUPON?
I FORGOT IT
RATS! BLACK FLAGGED ON THE LAST LAP!

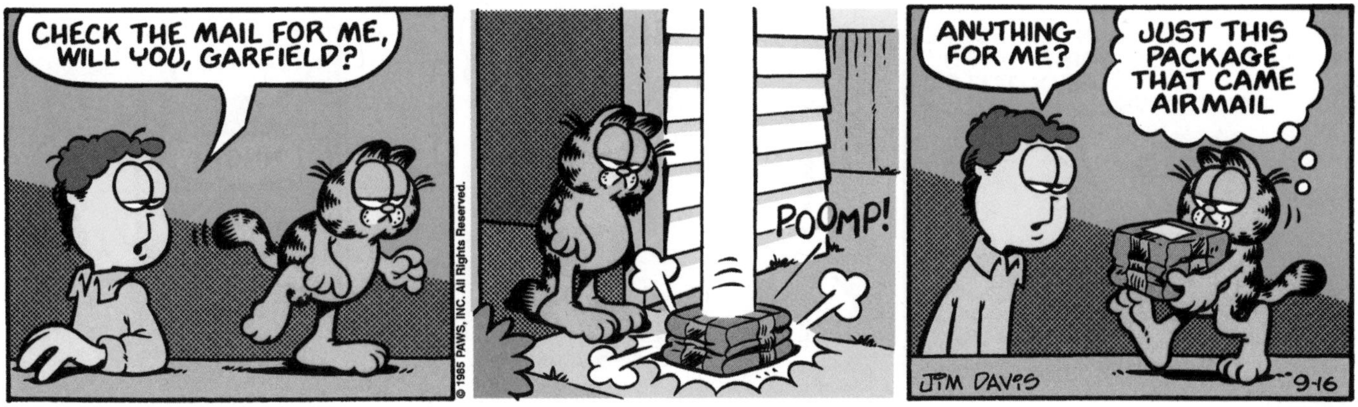
CHECK THE MAIL FOR ME, WILL YOU, GARFIELD?
© 1985 PAWS, INC. All Rights Reserved.
POOMP!
ANYTHING FOR ME?
JUST THIS PACKAGE THAT CAME AIRMAIL
JIM DAVIS
9-16

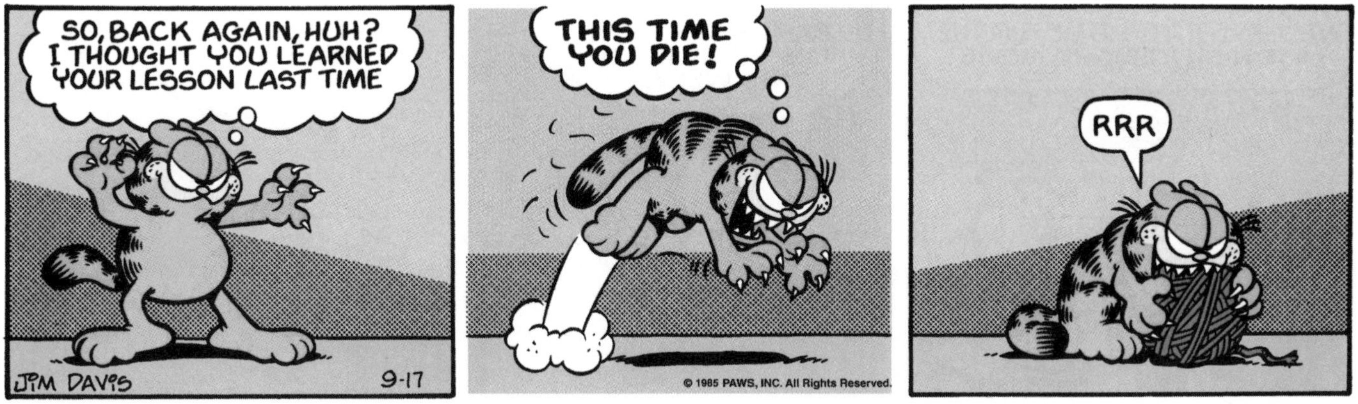
SO, BACK AGAIN, HUH? I THOUGHT YOU LEARNED YOUR LESSON LAST TIME
JIM DAVIS
9-17
THIS TIME YOU DIE!
© 1985 PAWS, INC. All Rights Reserved.
RRR

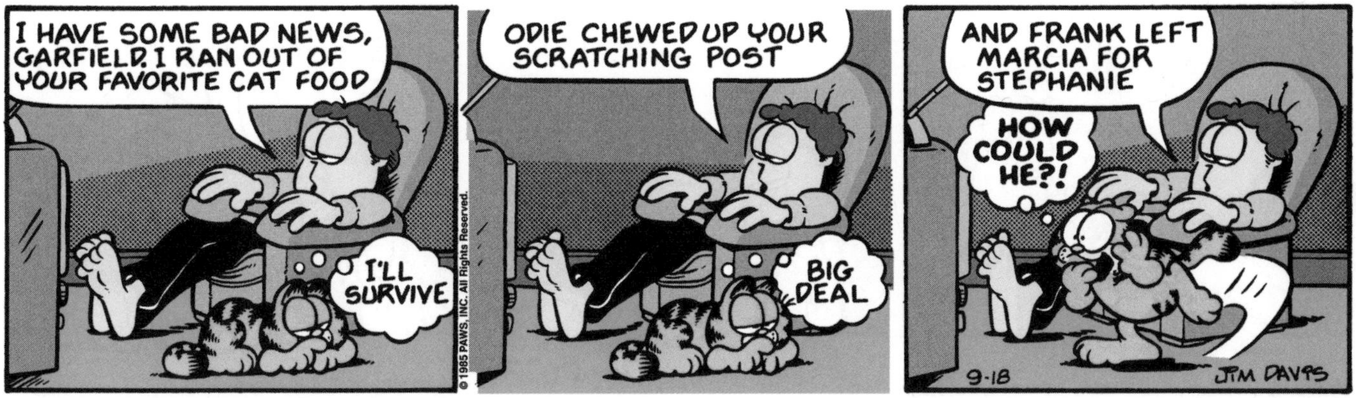
I HAVE SOME BAD NEWS, GARFIELD. I RAN OUT OF YOUR FAVORITE CAT FOOD
I'LL SURVIVE
© 1985 PAWS, INC. All Rights Reserved.
ODIE CHEWED UP YOUR SCRATCHING POST
BIG DEAL
AND FRANK LEFT MARCIA FOR STEPHANIE
HOW COULD HE?!
9-18
JIM DAVIS

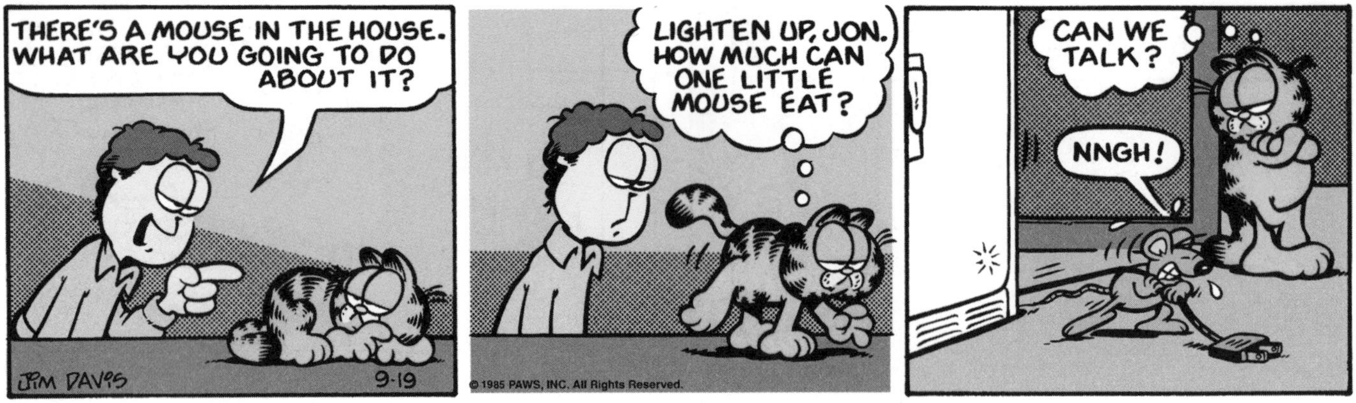
THERE'S A MOUSE IN THE HOUSE. WHAT ARE YOU GOING TO DO ABOUT IT?
JIM DAVIS
9-19
LIGHTEN UP, JON. HOW MUCH CAN ONE LITTLE MOUSE EAT?
© 1985 PAWS, INC. All Rights Reserved.
CAN WE TALK?
NNGH!

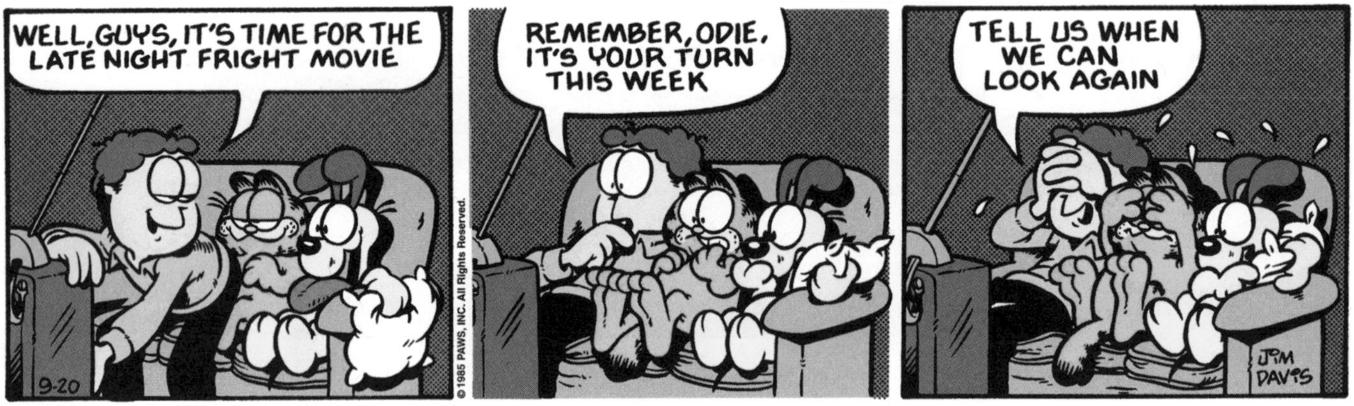
WELL, GUYS, IT'S TIME FOR THE LATE NIGHT FRIGHT MOVIE
9-20
© 1985 PAWS, INC. All Rights Reserved.
REMEMBER, ODIE. IT'S YOUR TURN THIS WEEK
TELL US WHEN WE CAN LOOK AGAIN
JIM DAVIS

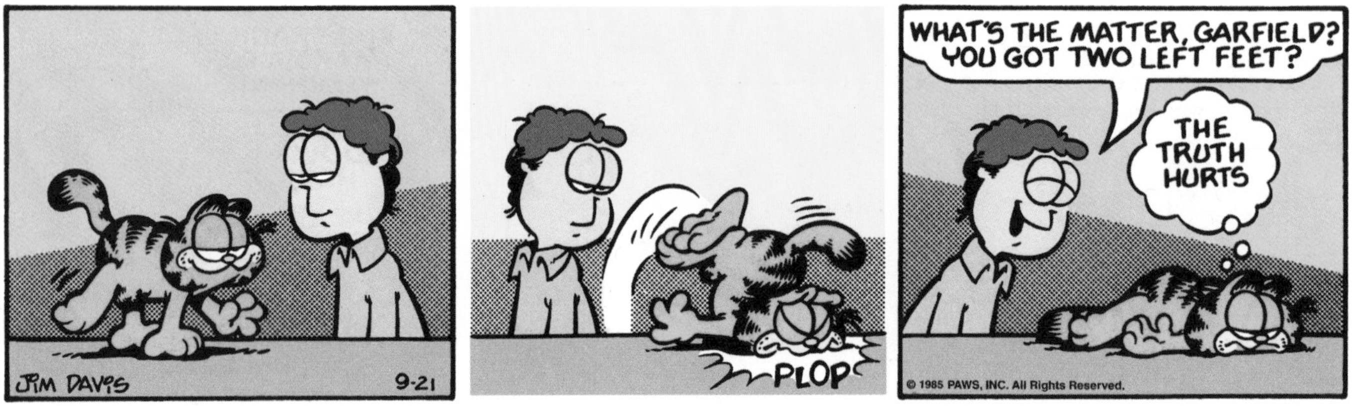
JIM DAVIS
9-21
PLOP
WHAT'S THE MATTER, GARFIELD? YOU GOT TWO LEFT FEET?
THE TRUTH HURTS
© 1985 PAWS, INC. All Rights Reserved.

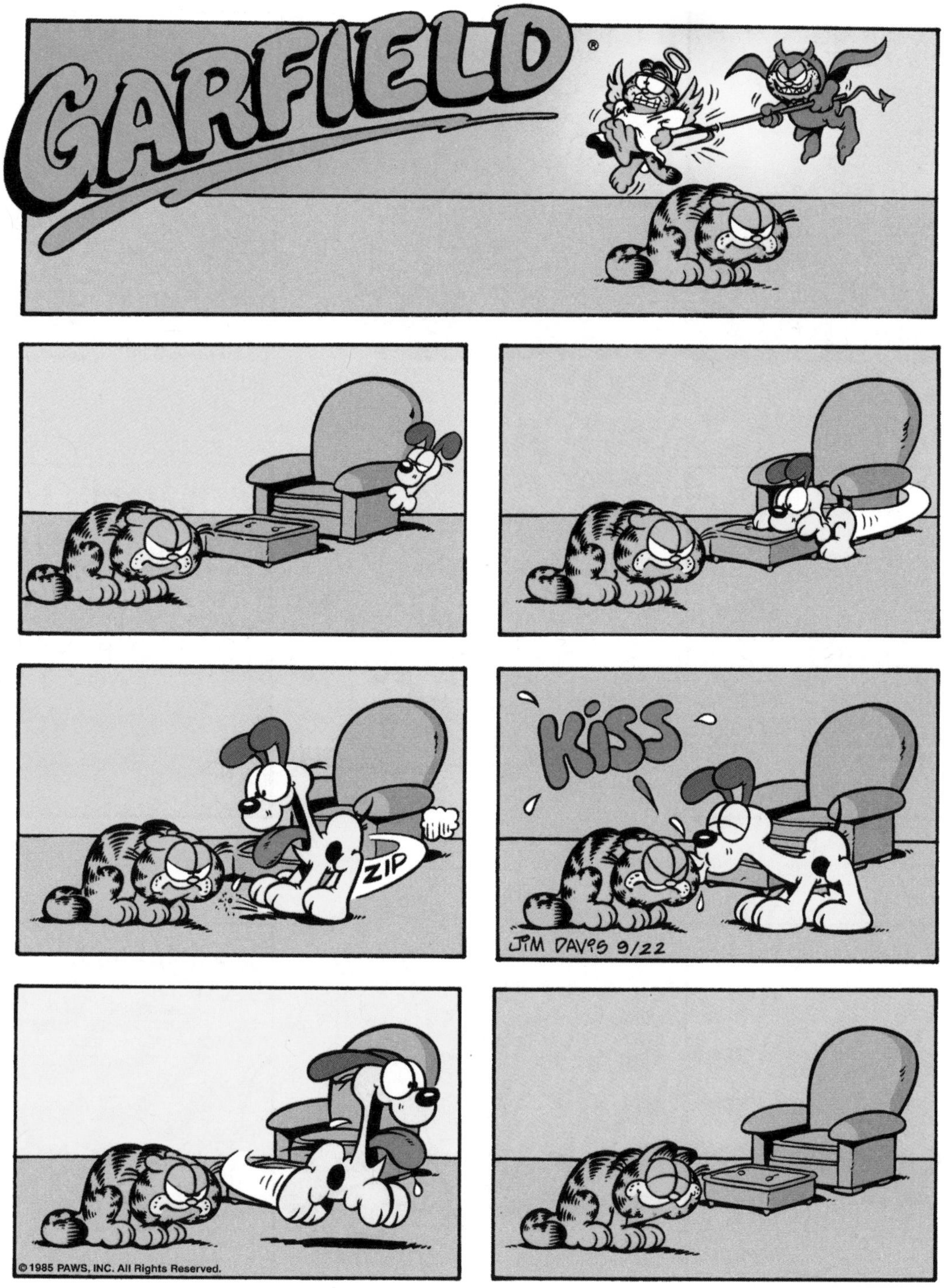
GARFIELD
ZIP
KISS
JIM DAVIS 9/22

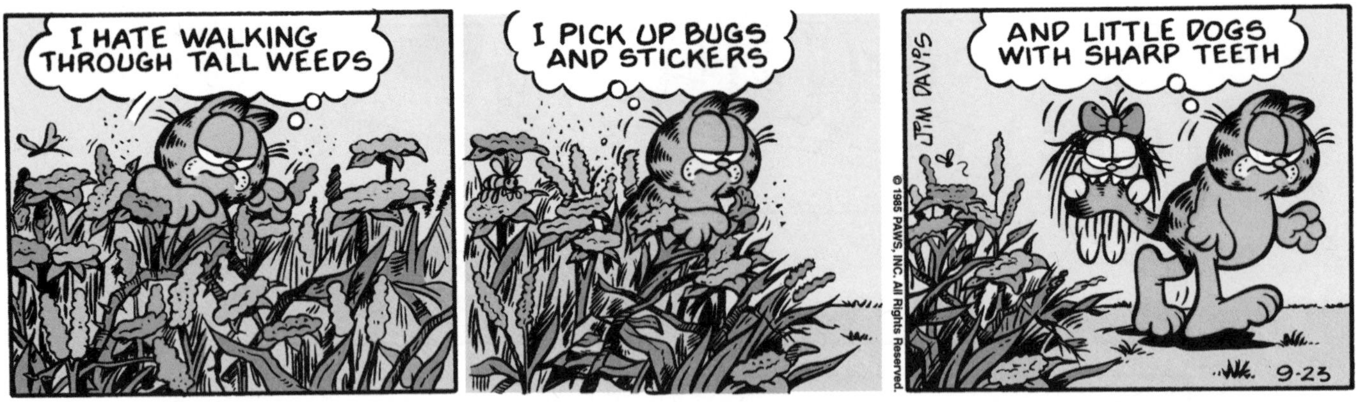
I HATE WALKING THROUGH TALL WEEDS
I PICK UP BUGS AND STICKERS
AND LITTLE DOGS WITH SHARP TEETH
JIM DAVIS
© 1985 PAWS, INC. All Rights Reserved.
9-23

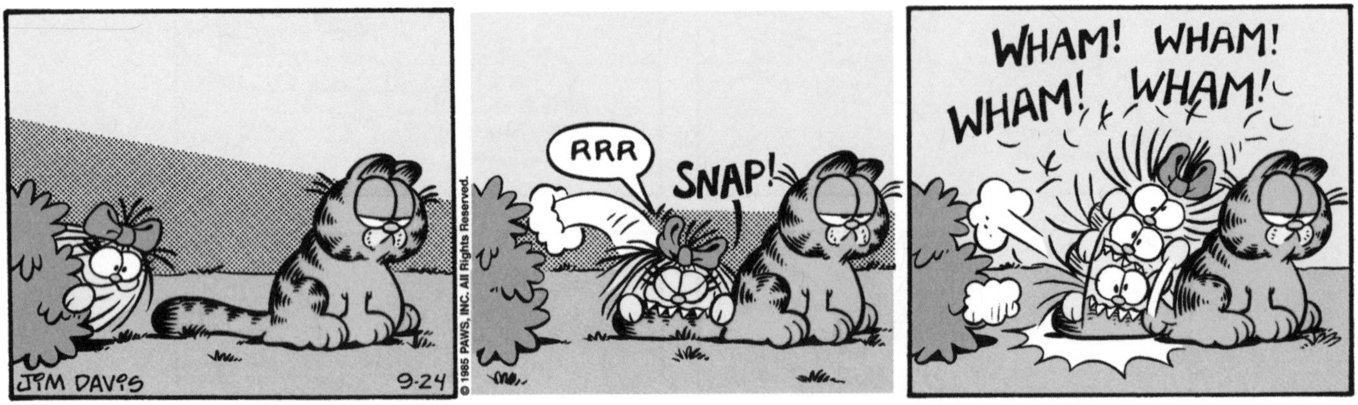
JIM DAVIS
9-24
© 1985 PAWS, INC. All Rights Reserved.
RRR
SNAP!
WHAM! WHAM!
WHAM! WHAM!

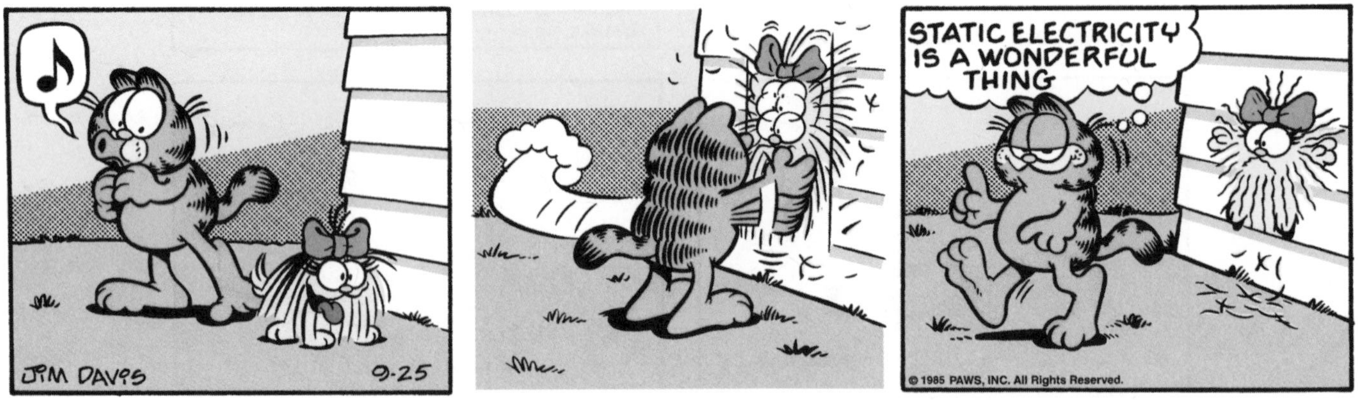
♪
JIM DAVIS
9-25
STATIC ELECTRICITY IS A WONDERFUL THING
© 1985 PAWS, INC. All Rights Reserved.

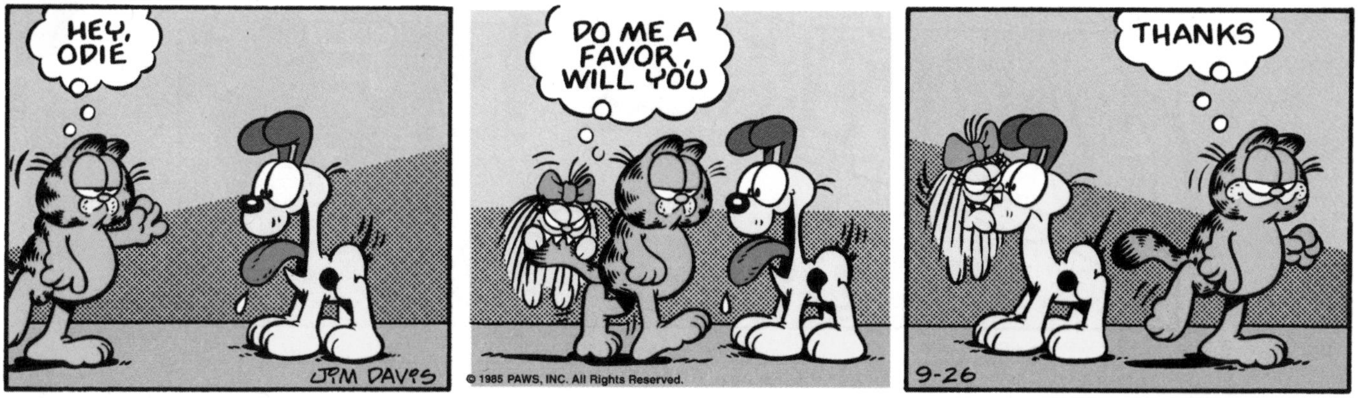
HEY, ODIE
JIM DAVIS
DO ME A FAVOR, WILL YOU
© 1985 PAWS, INC. All Rights Reserved.
THANKS
9-26

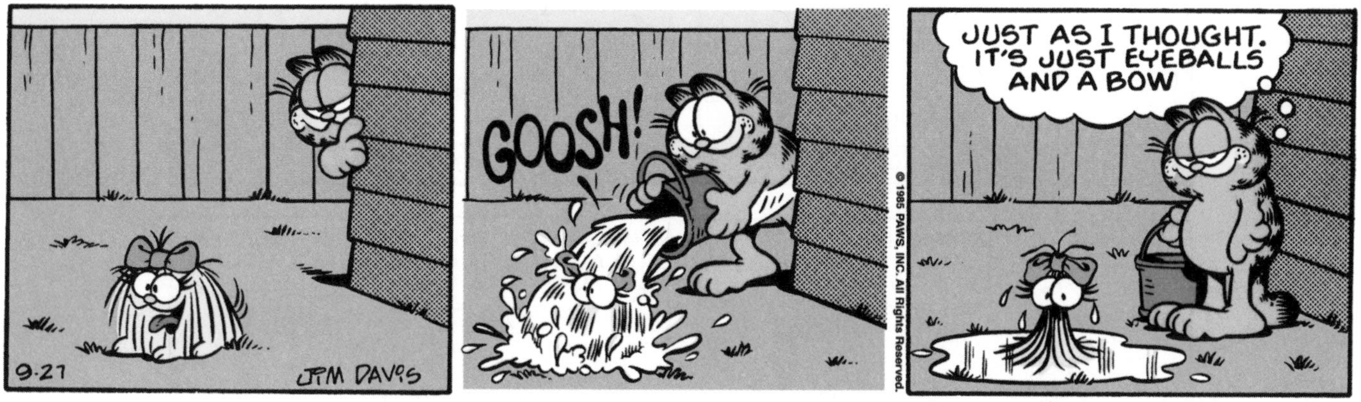
9-27
JIM DAVIS
GOOSH!
© 1985 PAWS, INC. All Rights Reserved.
JUST AS I THOUGHT. IT'S JUST EYEBALLS AND A BOW

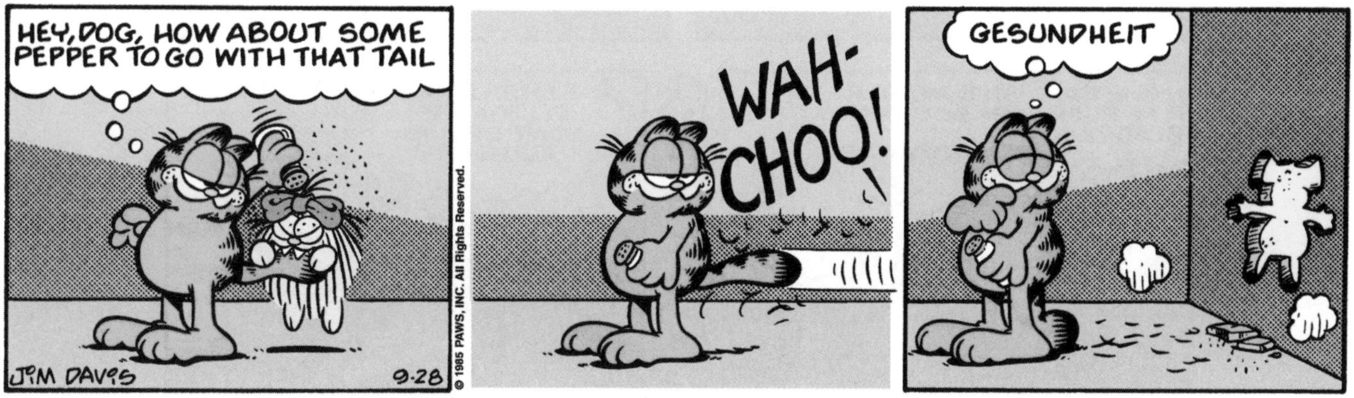
HEY, DOG, HOW ABOUT SOME PEPPER TO GO WITH THAT TAIL
JIM DAVIS
9-28
© 1985 PAWS, INC. All Rights Reserved.
WAH-CHOO!
GESUNDHEIT

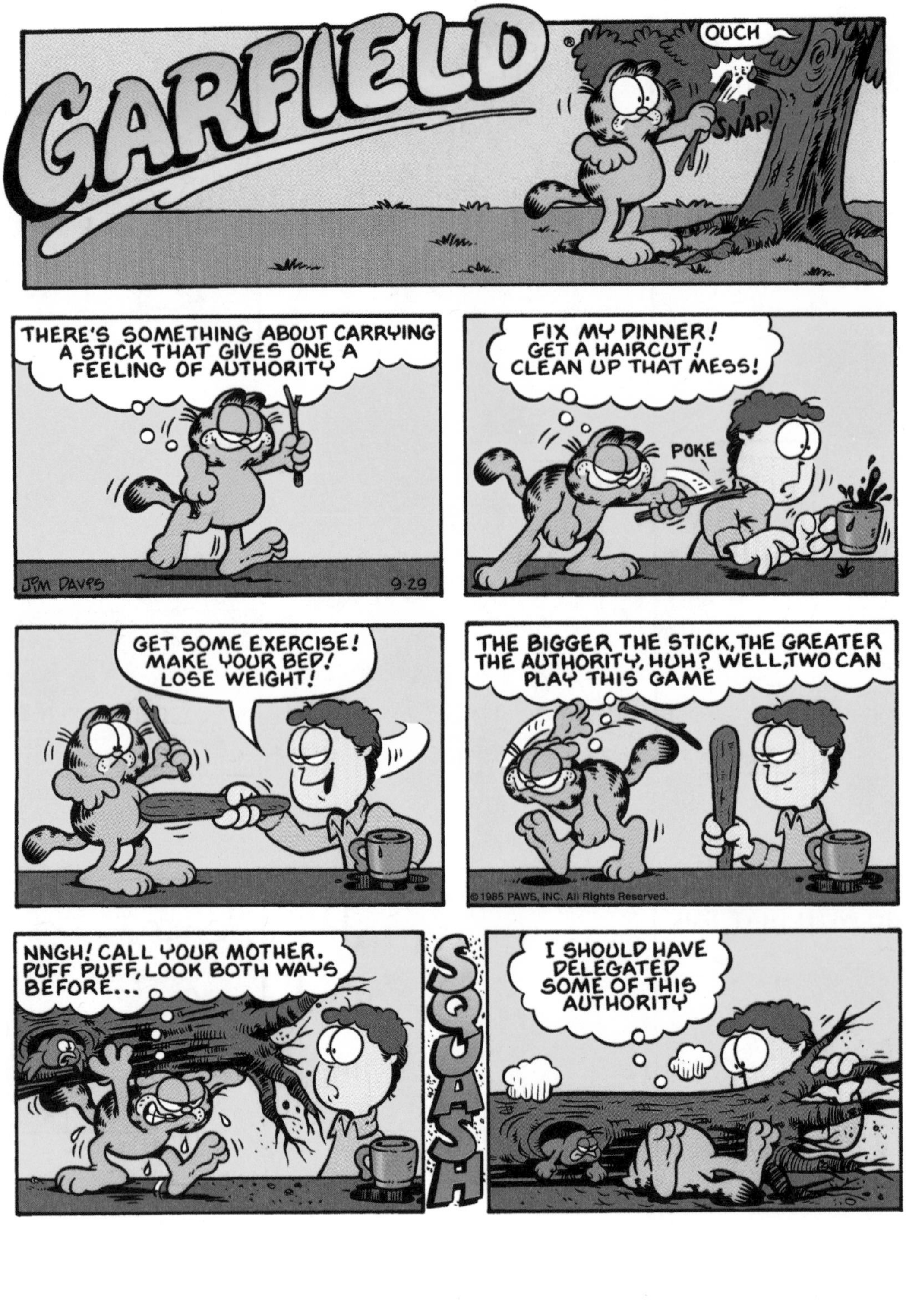
GARFIELD
OUCH
SNAP!
THERE'S SOMETHING ABOUT CARRYING A STICK THAT GIVES ONE A FEELING OF AUTHORITY
JIM DAVIS
9-29
FIX MY DINNER! GET A HAIRCUT! CLEAN UP THAT MESS!
POKE
GET SOME EXERCISE! MAKE YOUR BED! LOSE WEIGHT!
THE BIGGER THE STICK, THE GREATER THE AUTHORITY, HUH? WELL, TWO CAN PLAY THIS GAME
©1985 PAWS, INC. All Rights Reserved.
NNGH! CALL YOUR MOTHER. PUFF PUFF, LOOK BOTH WAYS BEFORE...
SQUASH
I SHOULD HAVE DELEGATED SOME OF THIS AUTHORITY

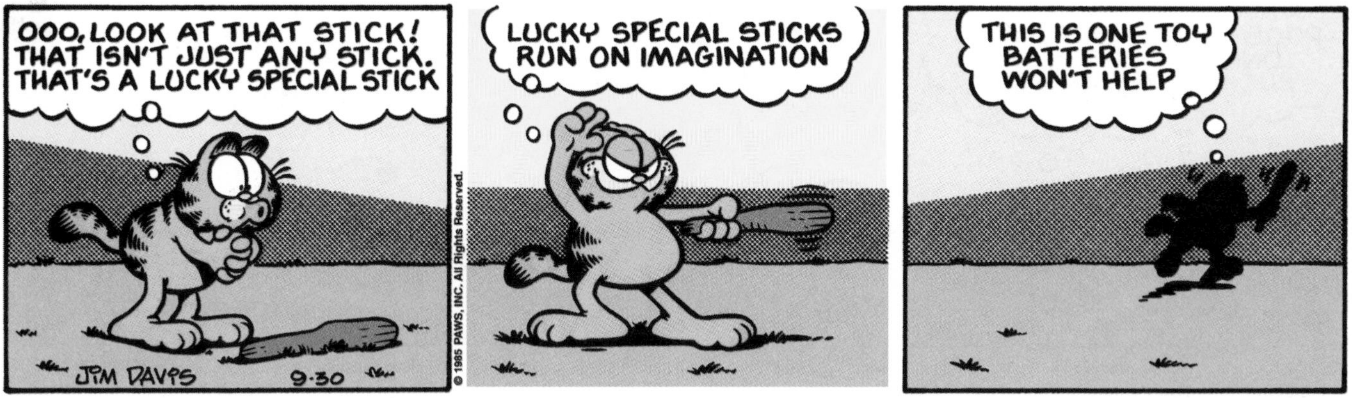
OOO, LOOK AT THAT STICK! THAT ISN'T JUST ANY STICK. THAT'S A LUCKY SPECIAL STICK
JIM DAVIS 9-30
© 1985 PAWS, INC. All Rights Reserved.
LUCKY SPECIAL STICKS RUN ON IMAGINATION
THIS IS ONE TOY BATTERIES WON'T HELP

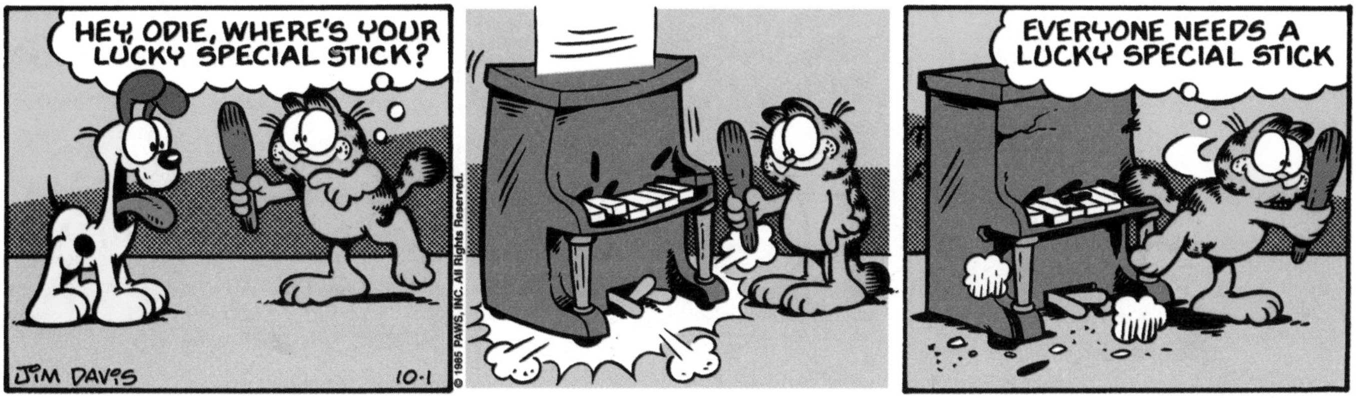
HEY, ODIE, WHERE'S YOUR LUCKY SPECIAL STICK?
JIM DAVIS 10-1
© 1985 PAWS, INC. All Rights Reserved.
EVERYONE NEEDS A LUCKY SPECIAL STICK

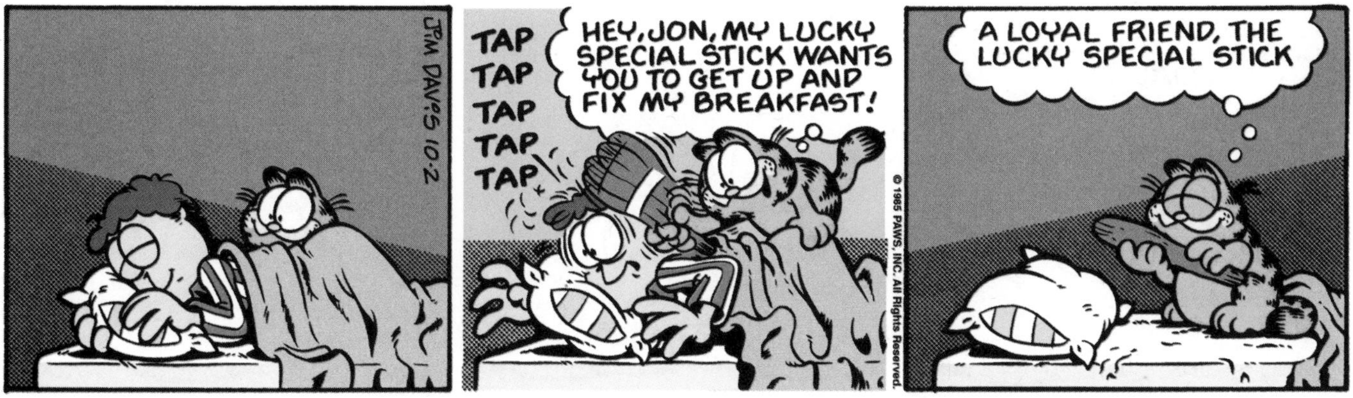
JIM DAVIS 10-2
TAP TAP TAP TAP TAP
HEY, JON, MY LUCKY SPECIAL STICK WANTS YOU TO GET UP AND FIX MY BREAKFAST!
© 1985 PAWS, INC. All Rights Reserved.
A LOYAL FRIEND, THE LUCKY SPECIAL STICK

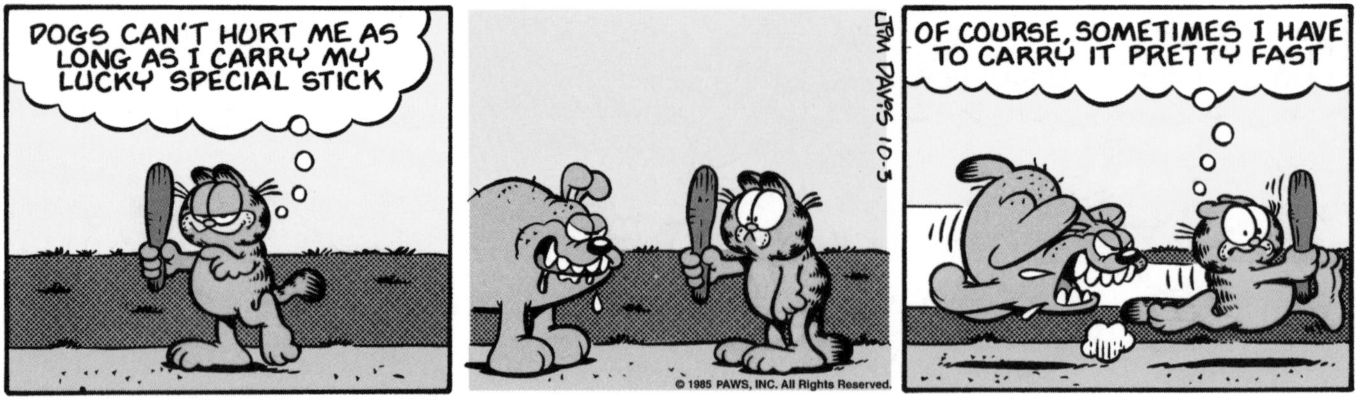
DOGS CAN'T HURT ME AS LONG AS I CARRY MY LUCKY SPECIAL STICK
JIM DAVIS 10-3
© 1985 PAWS, INC. All Rights Reserved.
OF COURSE, SOMETIMES I HAVE TO CARRY IT PRETTY FAST

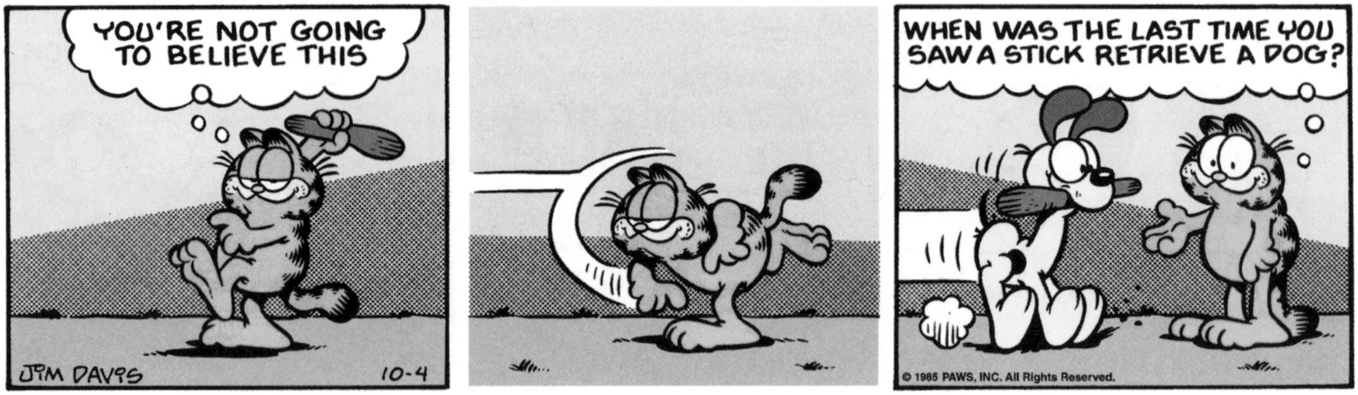
YOU'RE NOT GOING TO BELIEVE THIS
JIM DAVIS 10-4
WHEN WAS THE LAST TIME YOU SAW A STICK RETRIEVE A DOG?
© 1985 PAWS, INC. All Rights Reserved.

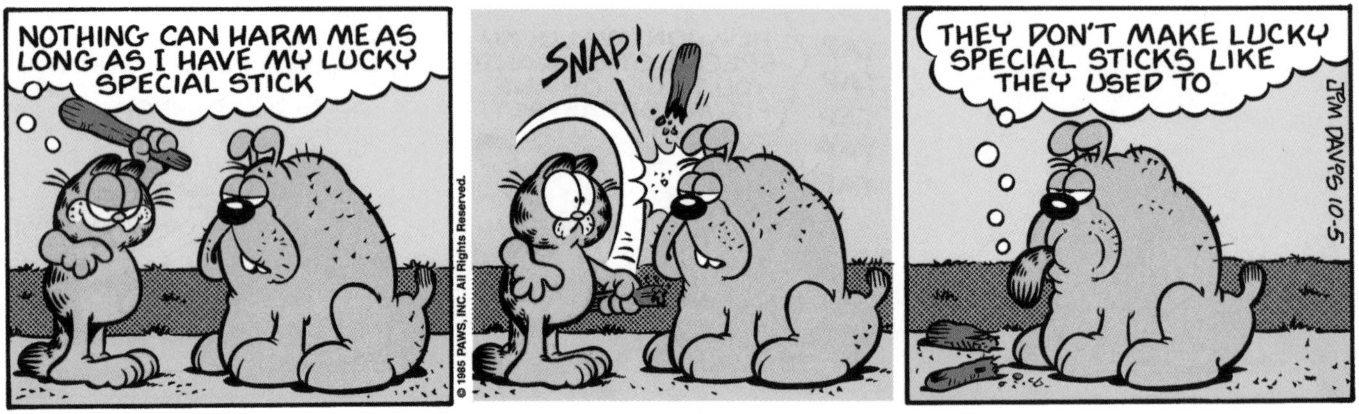
NOTHING CAN HARM ME AS LONG AS I HAVE MY LUCKY SPECIAL STICK
© 1985 PAWS, INC. All Rights Reserved.
SNAP!
THEY DON'T MAKE LUCKY SPECIAL STICKS LIKE THEY USED TO
JIM DAVIS 10-5

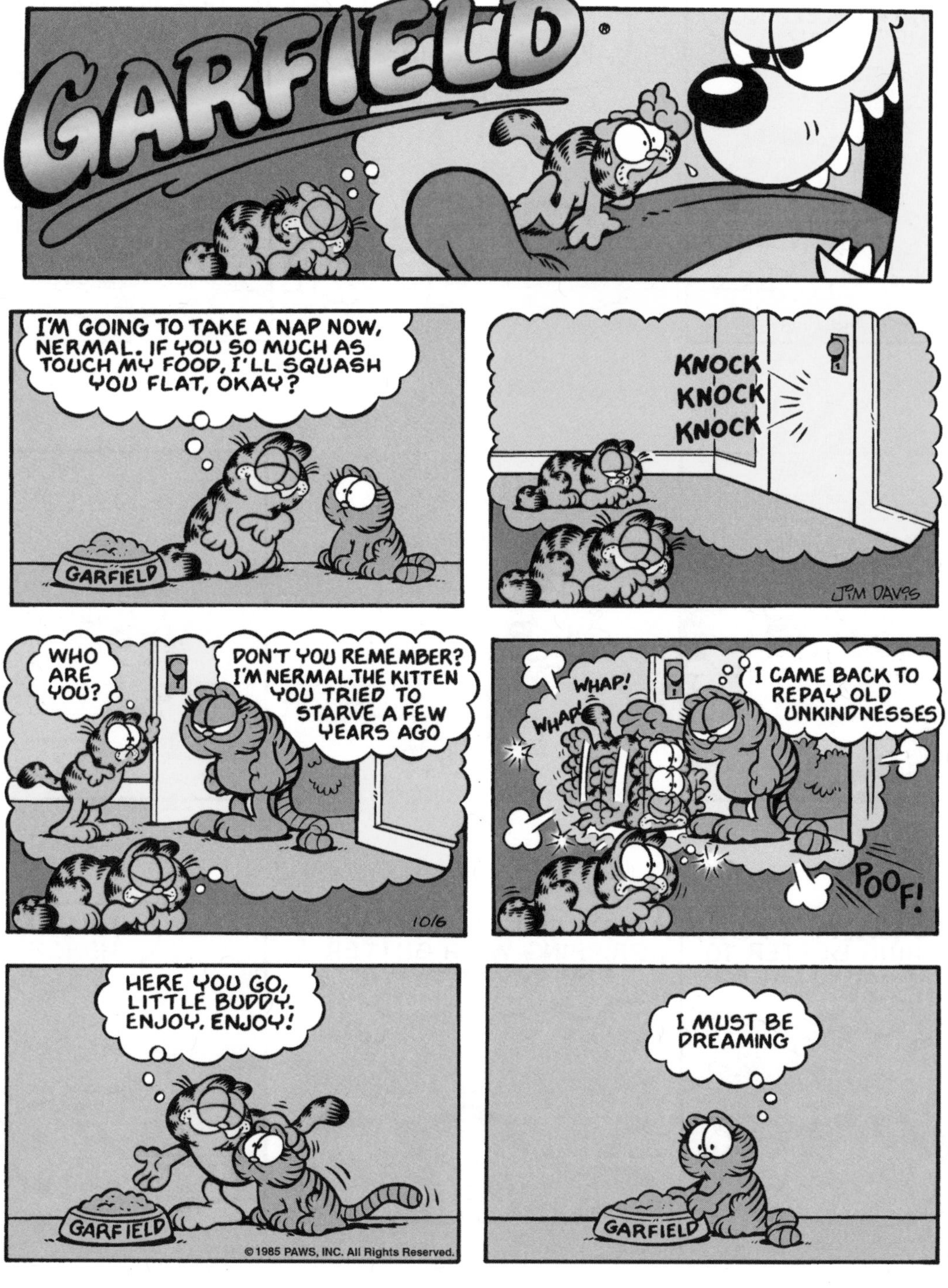
GARFIELD
I'M GOING TO TAKE A NAP NOW, NERMAL. IF YOU SO MUCH AS TOUCH MY FOOD, I'LL SQUASH YOU FLAT, OKAY?
GARFIELD
KNOCK
KNOCK
KNOCK
JIM DAVIS
WHO ARE YOU?
DON'T YOU REMEMBER? I'M NERMAL, THE KITTEN YOU TRIED TO STARVE A FEW YEARS AGO
10/6
WHAP!
WHAP!
I CAME BACK TO REPAY OLD UNKINDNESSES
POOF!
HERE YOU GO, LITTLE BUDDY. ENJOY, ENJOY!
GARFIELD
I MUST BE DREAMING
GARFIELD

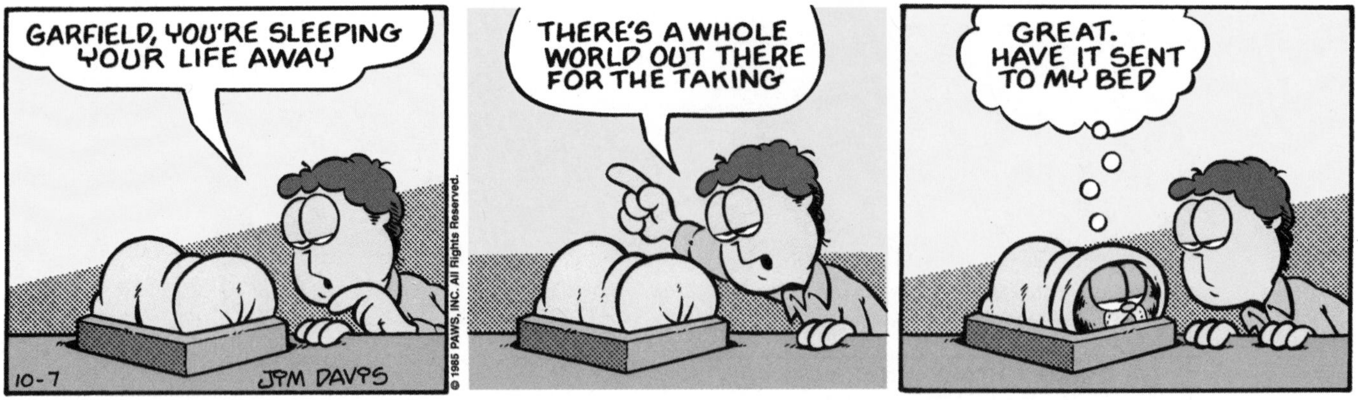
GARFIELD, YOU'RE SLEEPING YOUR LIFE AWAY
10-7
JIM DAVIS
© 1985 PAWS, INC. All Rights Reserved.
THERE'S A WHOLE WORLD OUT THERE FOR THE TAKING
GREAT. HAVE IT SENT TO MY BED

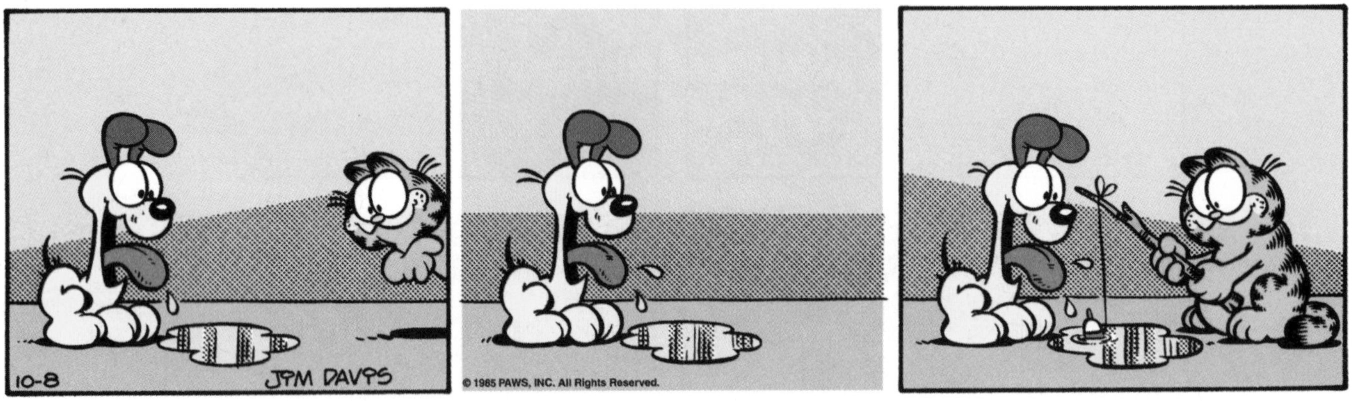
10-8
JIM DAVIS
© 1985 PAWS, INC. All Rights Reserved.

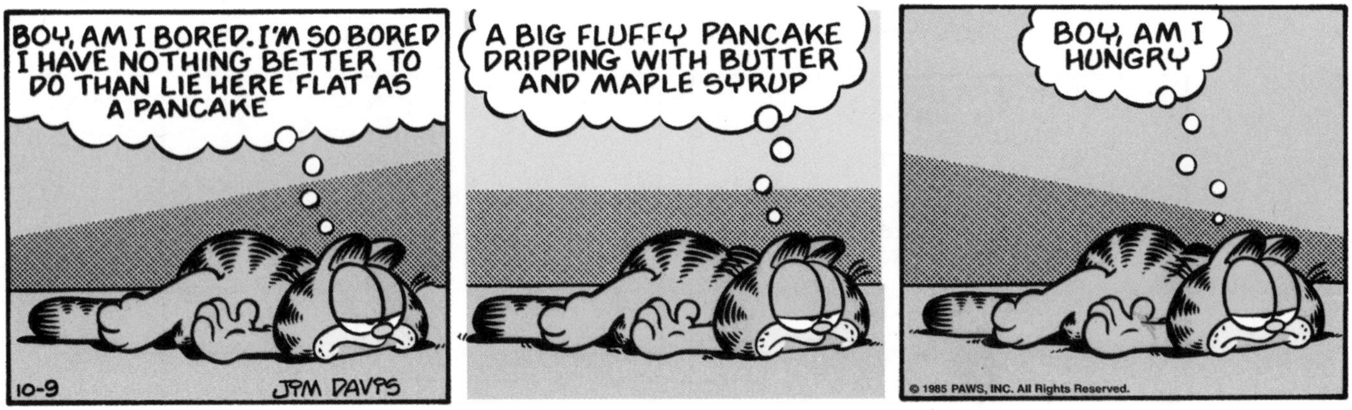
BOY, AM I BORED. I'M SO BORED I HAVE NOTHING BETTER TO DO THAN LIE HERE FLAT AS A PANCAKE
10-9
JIM DAVIS
A BIG FLUFFY PANCAKE DRIPPING WITH BUTTER AND MAPLE SYRUP
BOY, AM I HUNGRY
© 1985 PAWS, INC. All Rights Reserved.

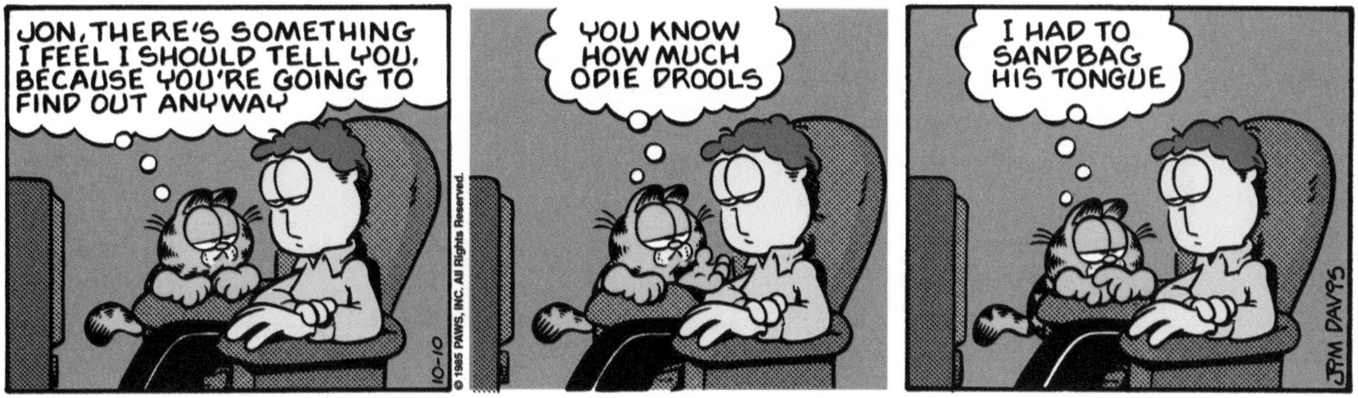
JON, THERE'S SOMETHING I FEEL I SHOULD TELL YOU, BECAUSE YOU'RE GOING TO FIND OUT ANYWAY
YOU KNOW HOW MUCH ODIE DROOLS
I HAD TO SANDBAG HIS TONGUE
© 1985 PAWS, INC. All Rights Reserved.

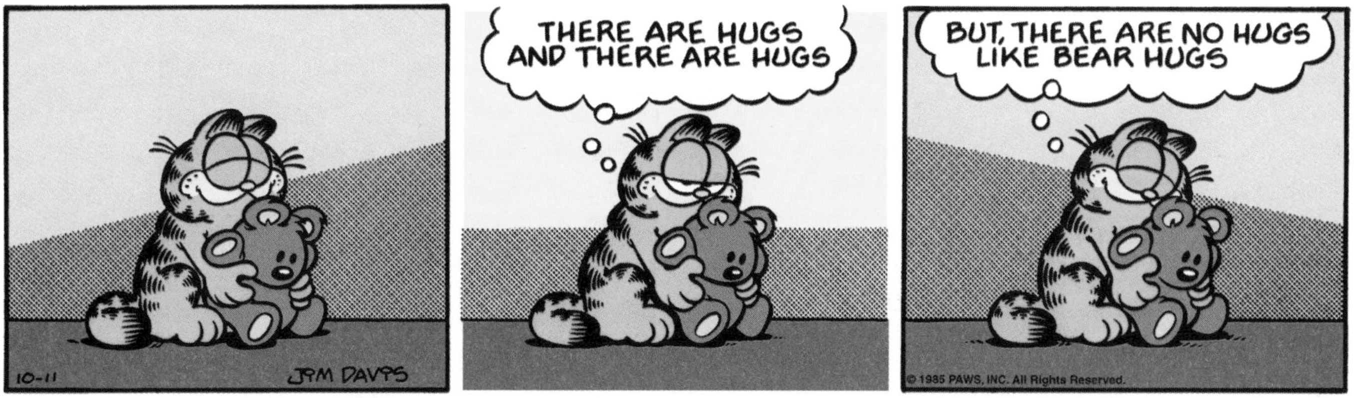
THERE ARE HUGS AND THERE ARE HUGS
BUT, THERE ARE NO HUGS LIKE BEAR HUGS
© 1985 PAWS, INC. All Rights Reserved.

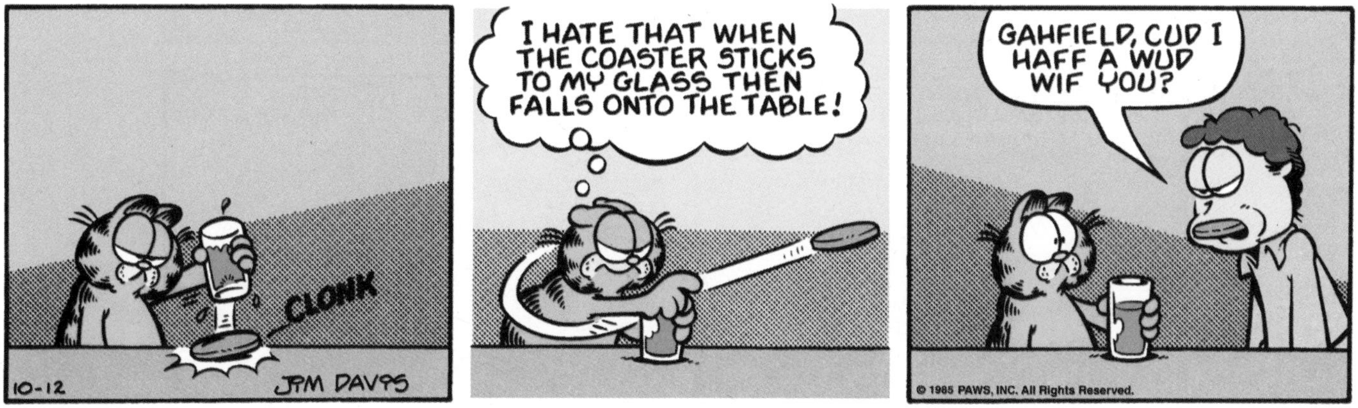
CLONK
I HATE THAT WHEN THE COASTER STICKS TO MY GLASS THEN FALLS ONTO THE TABLE!
GAHFIELD, CUD I HAFF A WUD WIF YOU?
© 1985 PAWS, INC. All Rights Reserved.

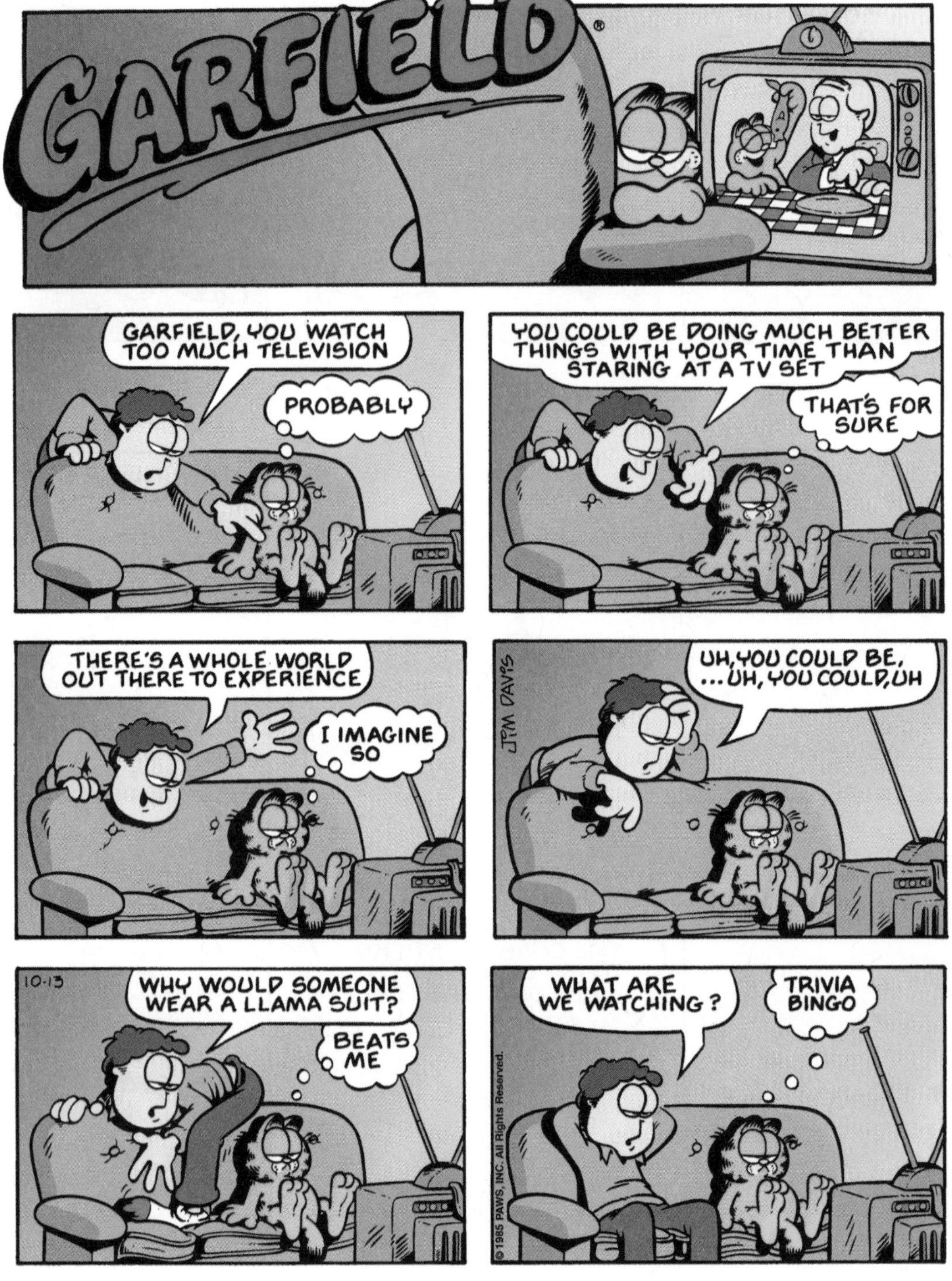
GARFIELD
GARFIELD, YOU WATCH TOO MUCH TELEVISION
PROBABLY
YOU COULD BE DOING MUCH BETTER THINGS WITH YOUR TIME THAN STARING AT A TV SET
THAT'S FOR SURE
THERE'S A WHOLE WORLD OUT THERE TO EXPERIENCE
I IMAGINE SO
JPM DAVIS
UH, YOU COULD BE, ...UH, YOU COULD, UH
10-13
WHY WOULD SOMEONE WEAR A LLAMA SUIT?
BEATS ME
©1985 PAWS, INC. All Rights Reserved.
WHAT ARE WE WATCHING?
TRIVIA BINGO

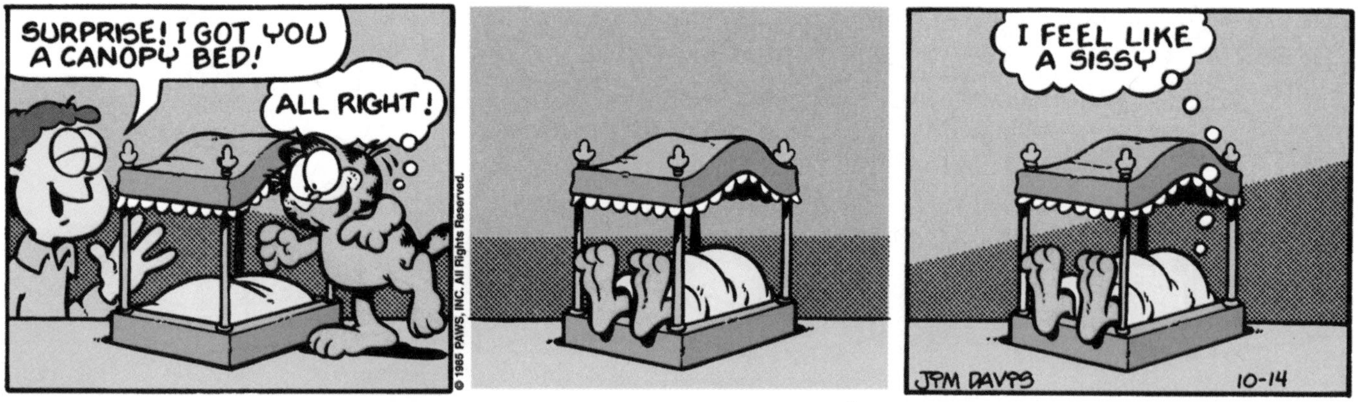
SURPRISE! I GOT YOU A CANOPY BED!
ALL RIGHT!
I FEEL LIKE A SISSY
© 1985 PAWS, INC. All Rights Reserved.
JIM DAVIS
10-14

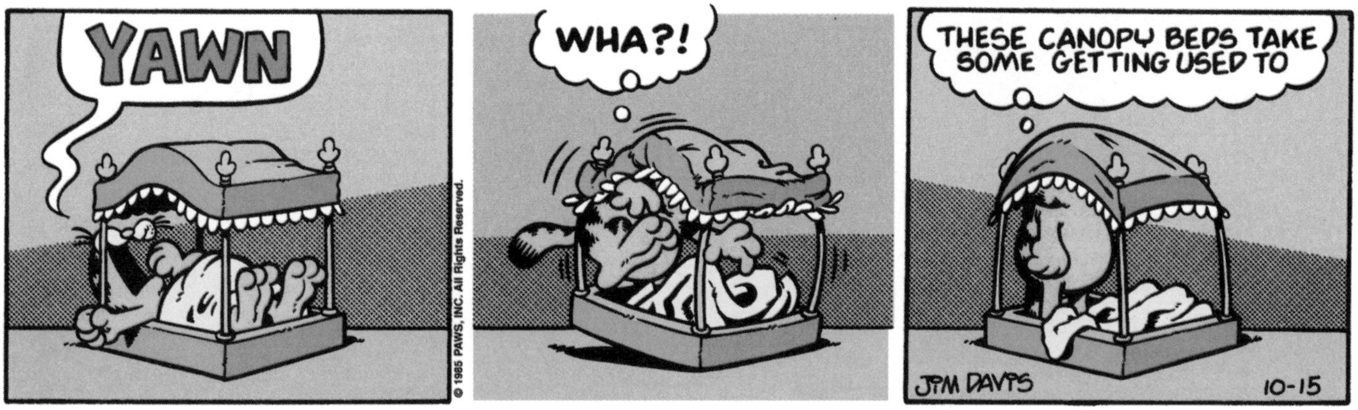
YAWN
WHA?!
THESE CANOPY BEDS TAKE SOME GETTING USED TO
© 1985 PAWS, INC. All Rights Reserved.
JIM DAVIS
10-15

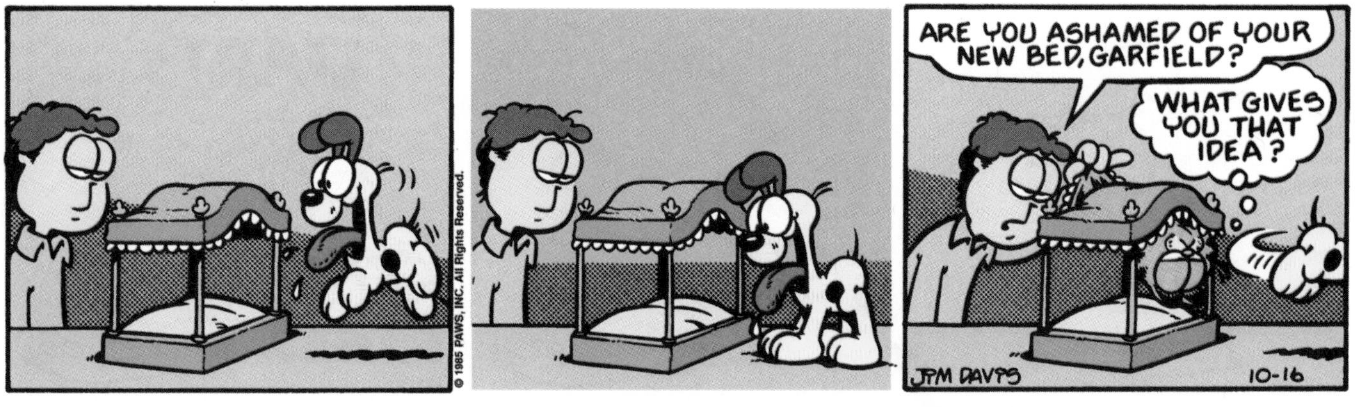
ARE YOU ASHAMED OF YOUR NEW BED, GARFIELD?
WHAT GIVES YOU THAT IDEA?
© 1985 PAWS, INC. All Rights Reserved.
JIM DAVIS
10-16

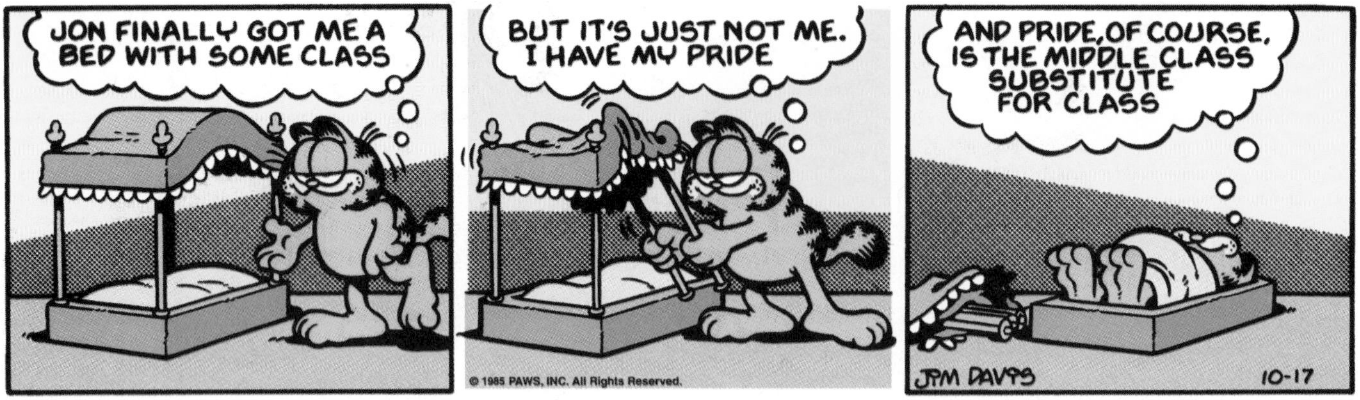
JON FINALLY GOT ME A BED WITH SOME CLASS
BUT IT'S JUST NOT ME. I HAVE MY PRIDE
AND PRIDE, OF COURSE, IS THE MIDDLE CLASS SUBSTITUTE FOR CLASS
© 1985 PAWS, INC. All Rights Reserved.
JIM DAVIS
10-17

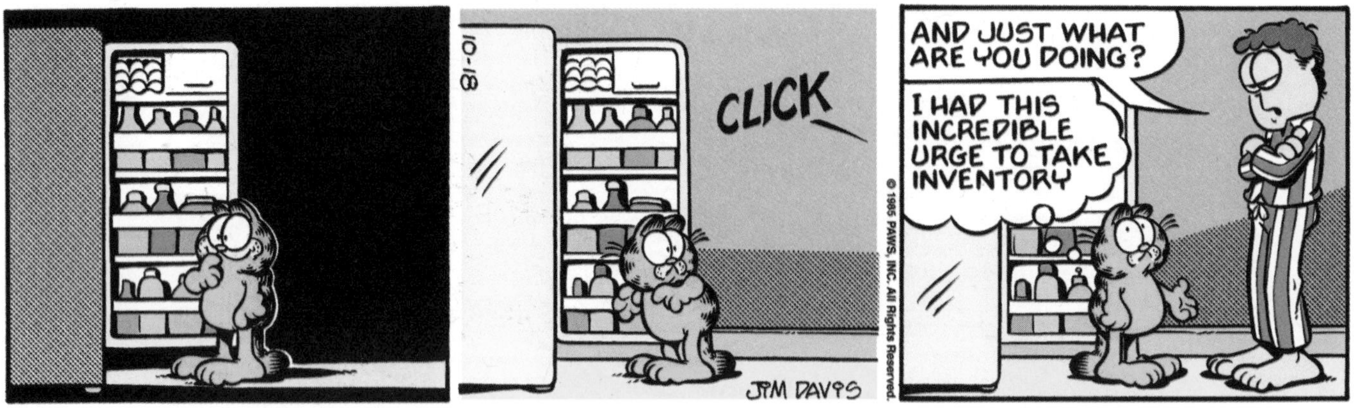
10-18
CLICK
JIM DAVIS
© 1985 PAWS, INC. All Rights Reserved.
AND JUST WHAT ARE YOU DOING?
I HAD THIS INCREDIBLE URGE TO TAKE INVENTORY

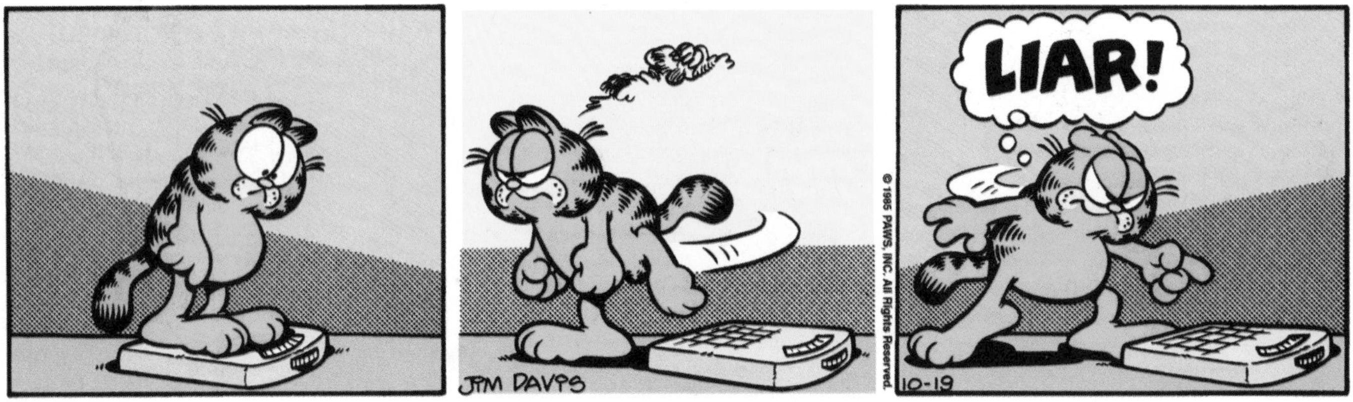
JIM DAVIS
© 1985 PAWS, INC. All Rights Reserved.
LIAR!
10-19

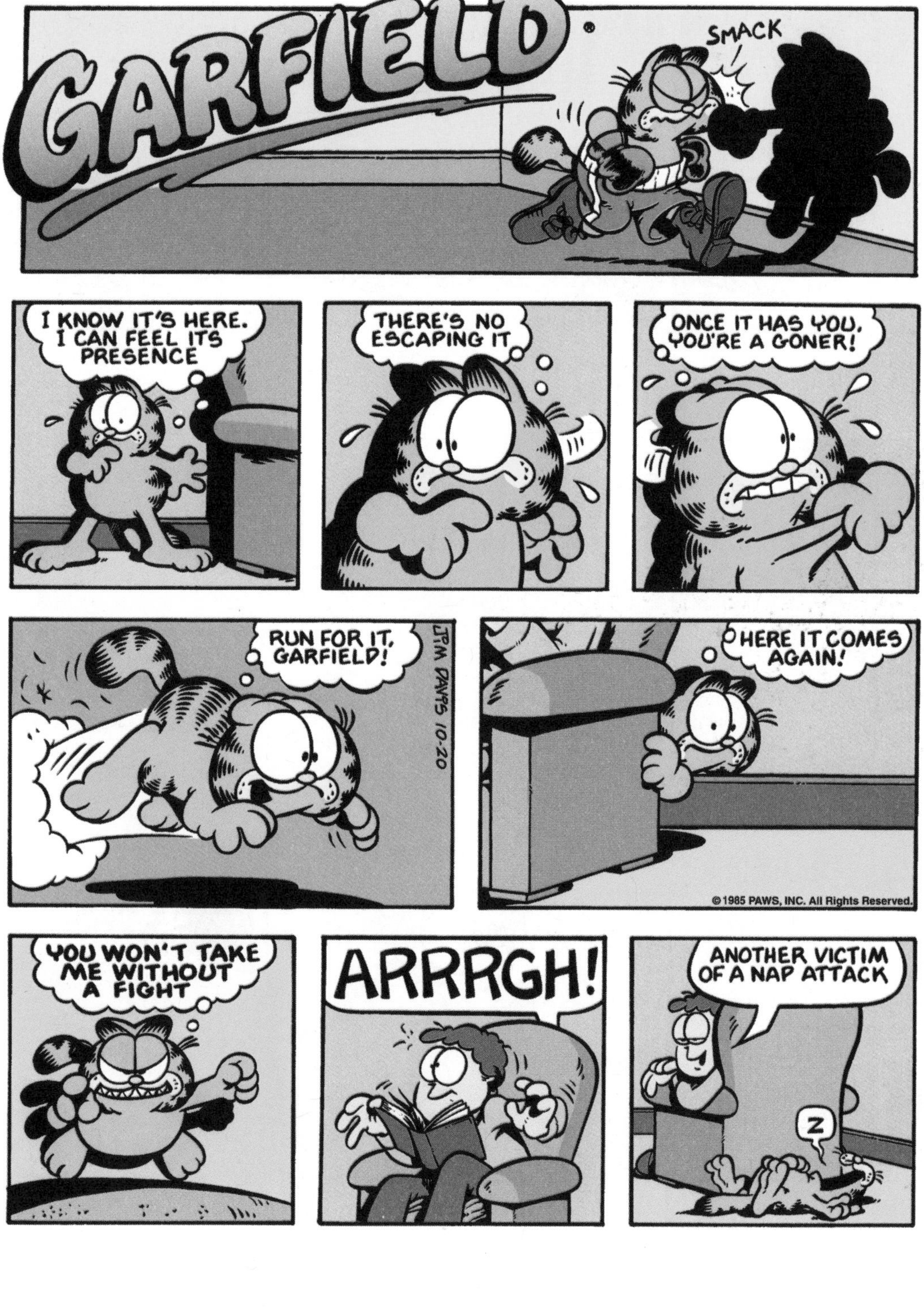
GARFIELD
SMACK
I KNOW IT'S HERE. I CAN FEEL ITS PRESENCE
THERE'S NO ESCAPING IT
ONCE IT HAS YOU, YOU'RE A GONER!
RUN FOR IT, GARFIELD!
JPM DAVIS 10-20
HERE IT COMES AGAIN!
© 1985 PAWS, INC. All Rights Reserved.
YOU WON'T TAKE ME WITHOUT A FIGHT
ARRRGH!
ANOTHER VICTIM OF A NAP ATTACK
Z

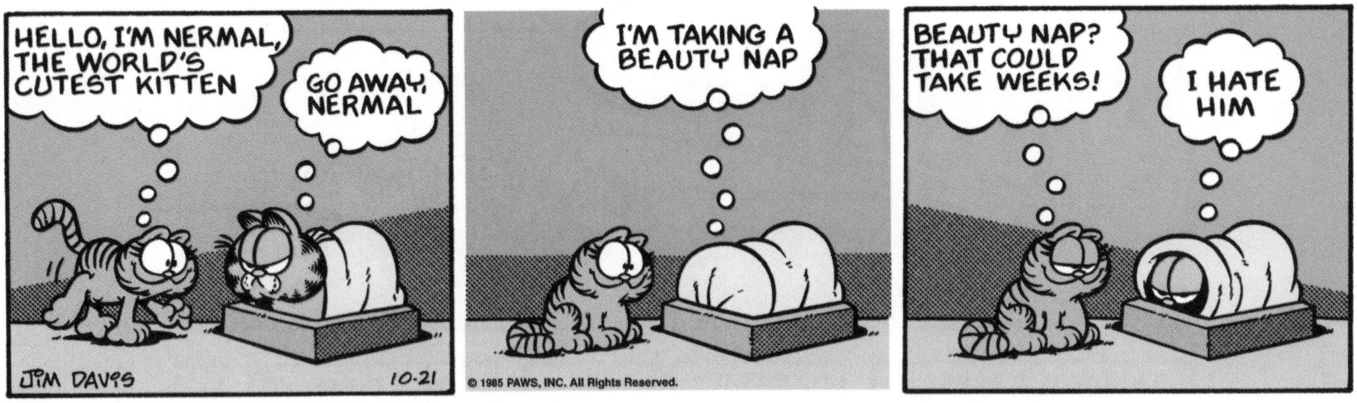
HELLO, I'M NERMAL, THE WORLD'S CUTEST KITTEN
GO AWAY, NERMAL
I'M TAKING A BEAUTY NAP
BEAUTY NAP? THAT COULD TAKE WEEKS!
I HATE HIM
JIM DAVIS
10-21
© 1985 PAWS, INC. All Rights Reserved.

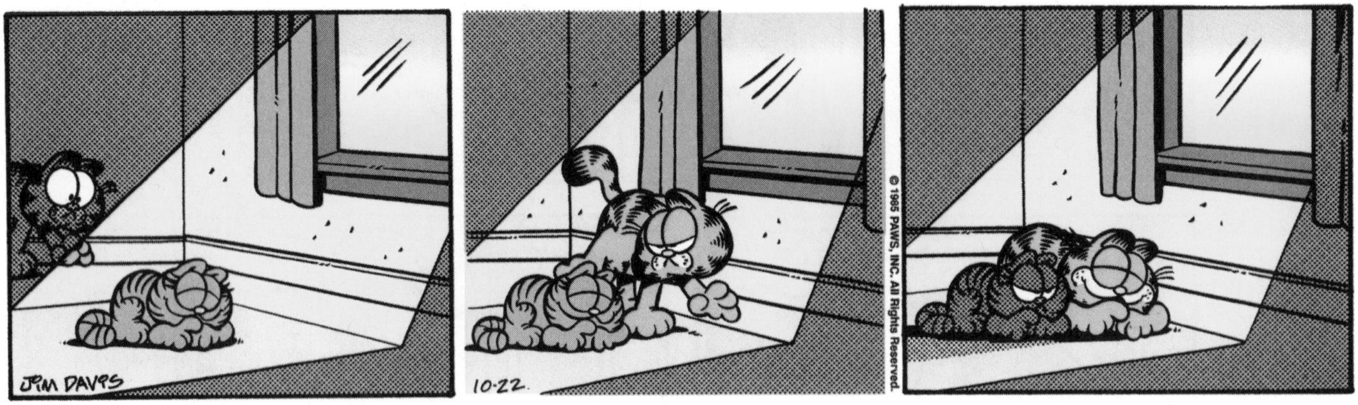
JIM DAVIS
10-22
© 1985 PAWS, INC. All Rights Reserved.

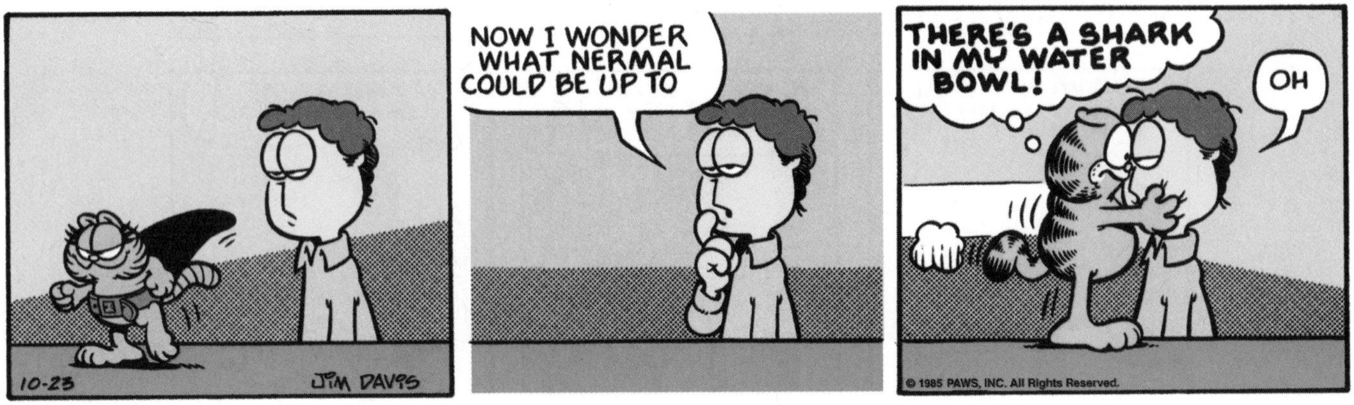
10-23
JIM DAVIS
NOW I WONDER WHAT NERMAL COULD BE UP TO
THERE'S A SHARK IN MY WATER BOWL!
OH
© 1985 PAWS, INC. All Rights Reserved.

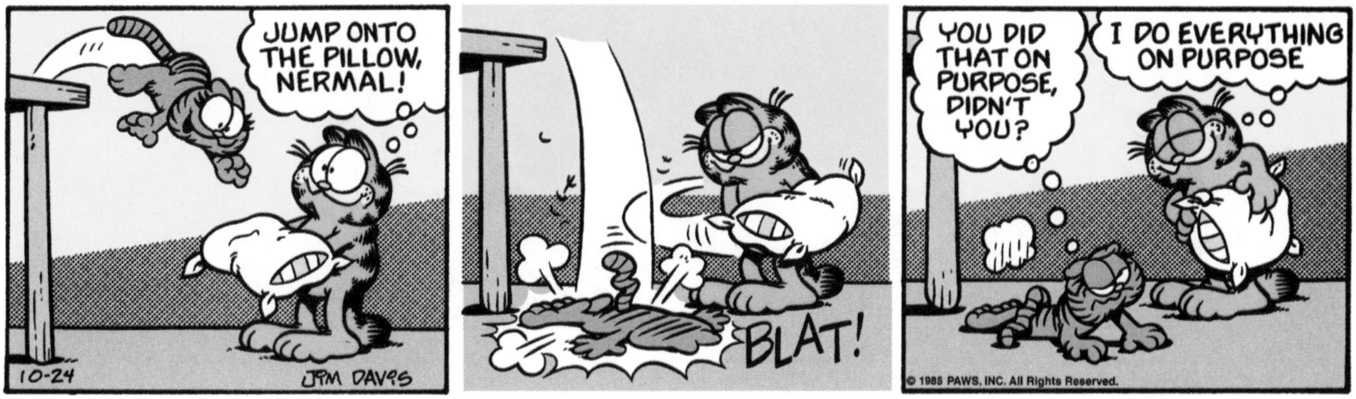
JUMP ONTO THE PILLOW, NERMAL!
10-24
JIM DAVIS
BLAT!
YOU DID THAT ON PURPOSE, DIDN'T YOU?
I DO EVERYTHING ON PURPOSE
© 1985 PAWS, INC. All Rights Reserved.

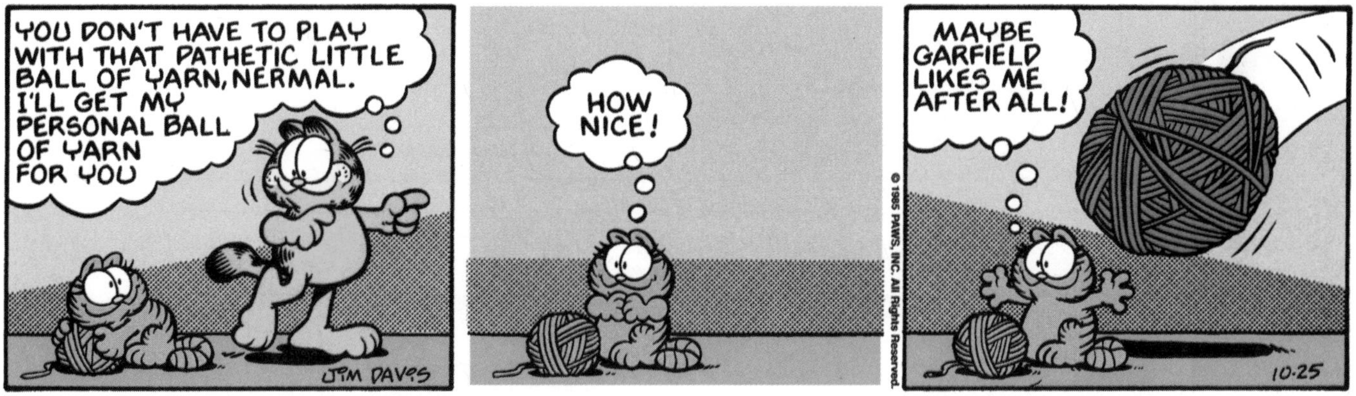
YOU DON'T HAVE TO PLAY WITH THAT PATHETIC LITTLE BALL OF YARN, NERMAL. I'LL GET MY PERSONAL BALL OF YARN FOR YOU
JIM DAVIS
HOW NICE!
© 1985 PAWS, INC. All Rights Reserved.
MAYBE GARFIELD LIKES ME AFTER ALL!
10-25

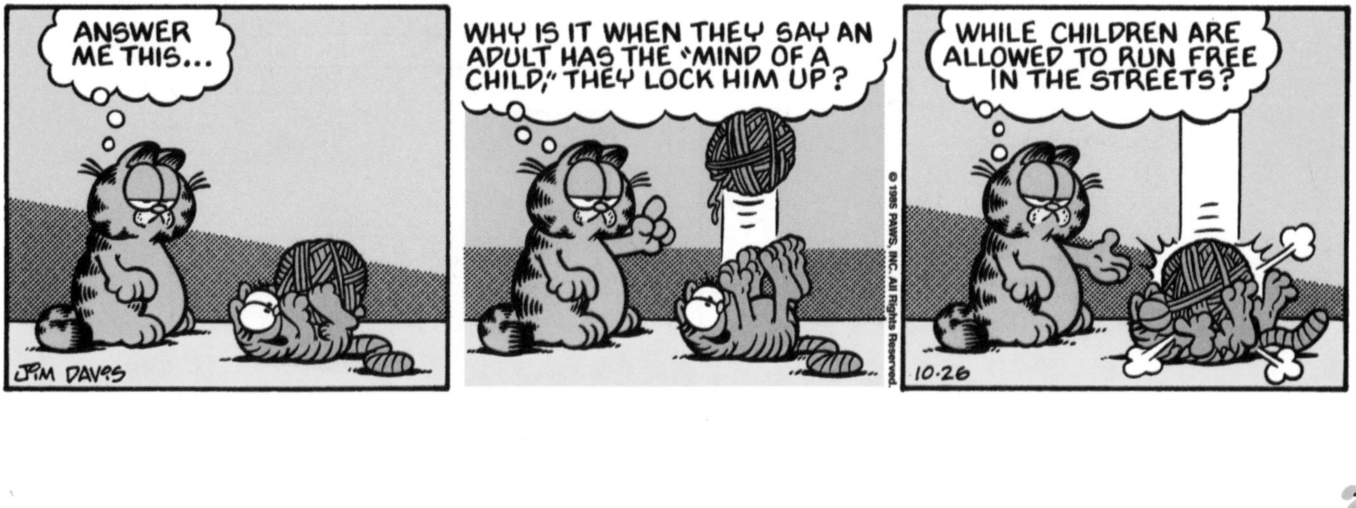
ANSWER ME THIS...
JIM DAVIS
WHY IS IT WHEN THEY SAY AN ADULT HAS THE "MIND OF A CHILD," THEY LOCK HIM UP?
© 1985 PAWS, INC. All Rights Reserved.
WHILE CHILDREN ARE ALLOWED TO RUN FREE IN THE STREETS?
10-26

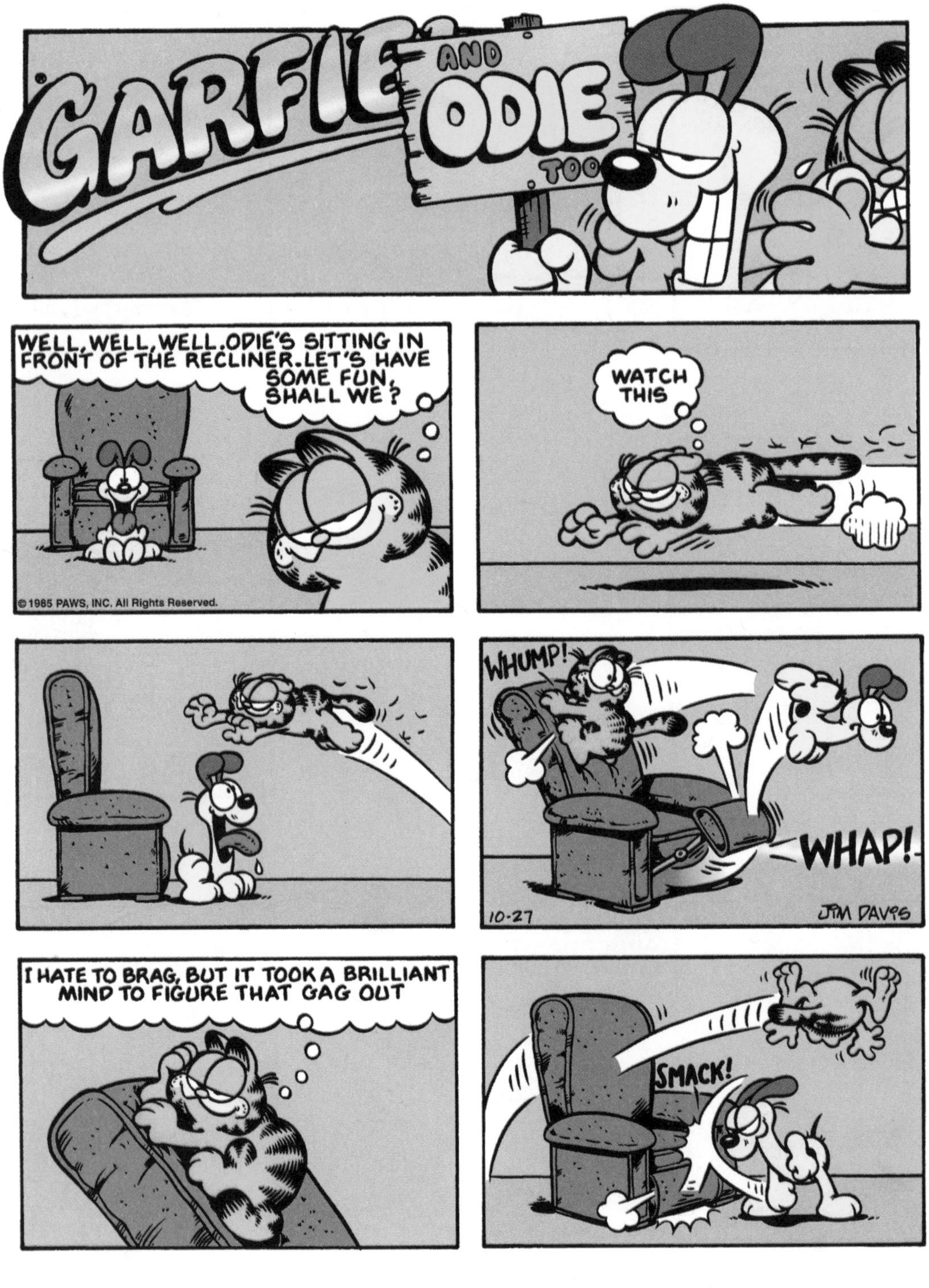
GARFIELD
AND ODIE TOO
WELL, WELL, WELL. ODIE'S SITTING IN FRONT OF THE RECLINER. LET'S HAVE SOME FUN, SHALL WE?
WATCH THIS
WHUMP!
WHAP!
10-27
JIM DAVIS
I HATE TO BRAG, BUT IT TOOK A BRILLIANT MIND TO FIGURE THAT GAG OUT
SMACK!

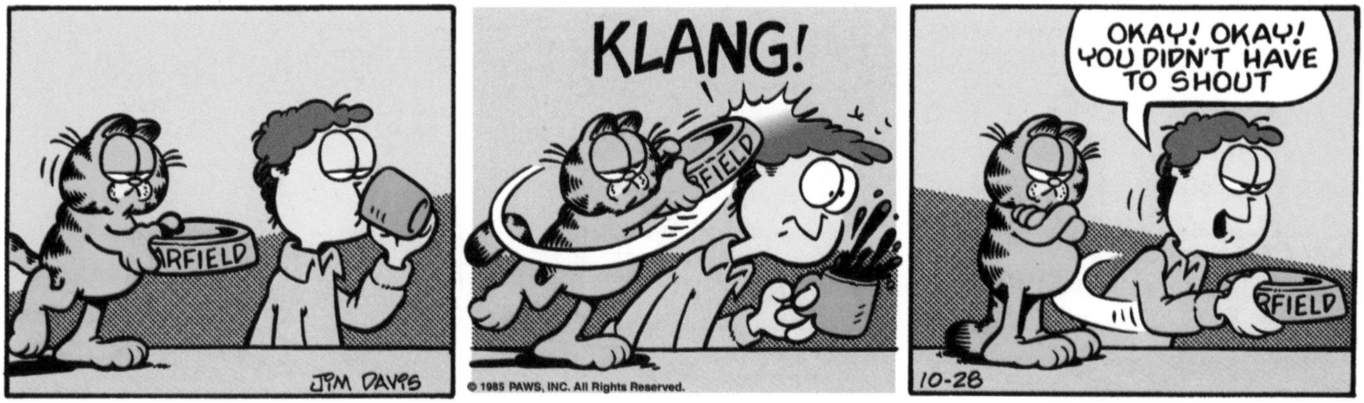
JIM DAVIS
KLANG!
© 1985 PAWS, INC. All Rights Reserved.
OKAY! OKAY! YOU DIDN'T HAVE TO SHOUT
10-28

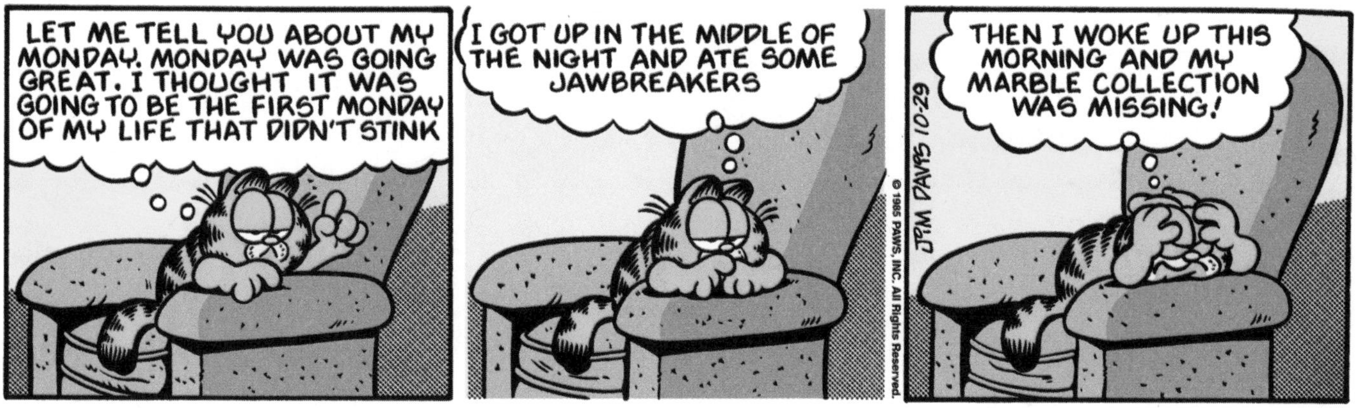
LET ME TELL YOU ABOUT MY MONDAY. MONDAY WAS GOING GREAT. I THOUGHT IT WAS GOING TO BE THE FIRST MONDAY OF MY LIFE THAT DIDN'T STINK
I GOT UP IN THE MIDDLE OF THE NIGHT AND ATE SOME JAWBREAKERS
JIM DAVIS 10-29
© 1985 PAWS, INC. All Rights Reserved.
THEN I WOKE UP THIS MORNING AND MY MARBLE COLLECTION WAS MISSING!

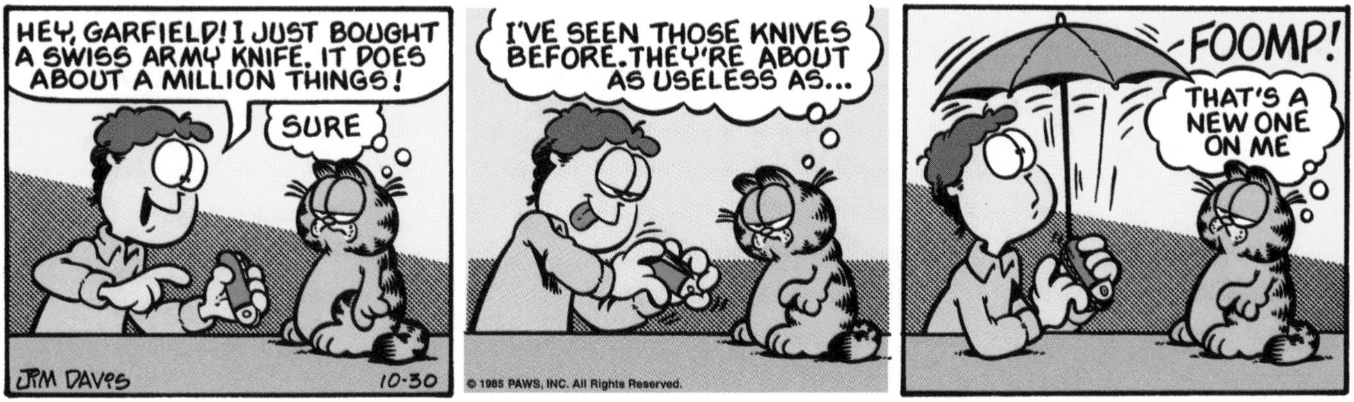
HEY, GARFIELD! I JUST BOUGHT A SWISS ARMY KNIFE. IT DOES ABOUT A MILLION THINGS!
SURE
JIM DAVIS
10-30
I'VE SEEN THOSE KNIVES BEFORE. THEY'RE ABOUT AS USELESS AS...
© 1985 PAWS, INC. All Rights Reserved.
FOOMP!
THAT'S A NEW ONE ON ME

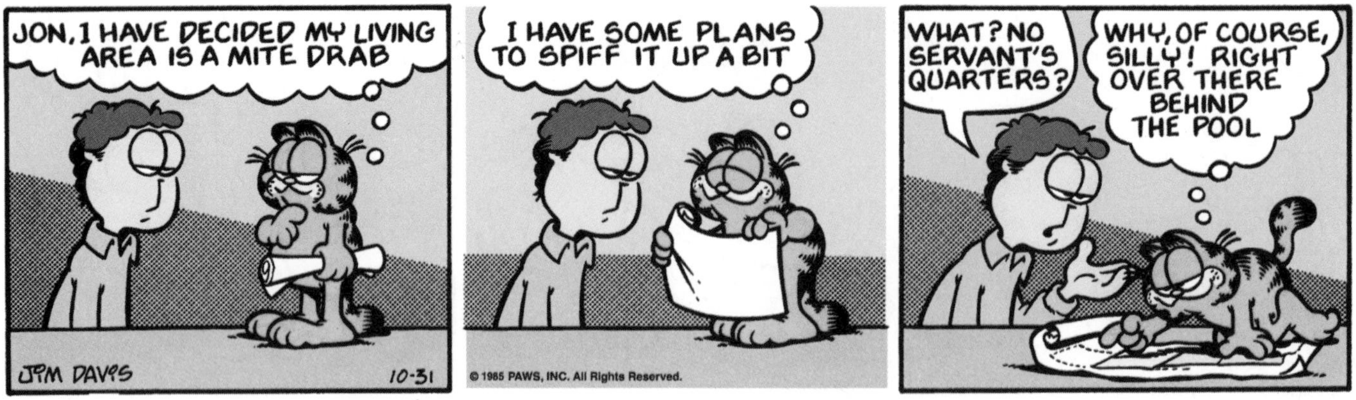
JON, I HAVE DECIDED MY LIVING AREA IS A MITE DRAB
JIM DAVIS
10-31
I HAVE SOME PLANS TO SPIFF IT UP A BIT
© 1985 PAWS, INC. All Rights Reserved.
WHAT? NO SERVANT'S QUARTERS?
WHY, OF COURSE, SILLY! RIGHT OVER THERE BEHIND THE POOL

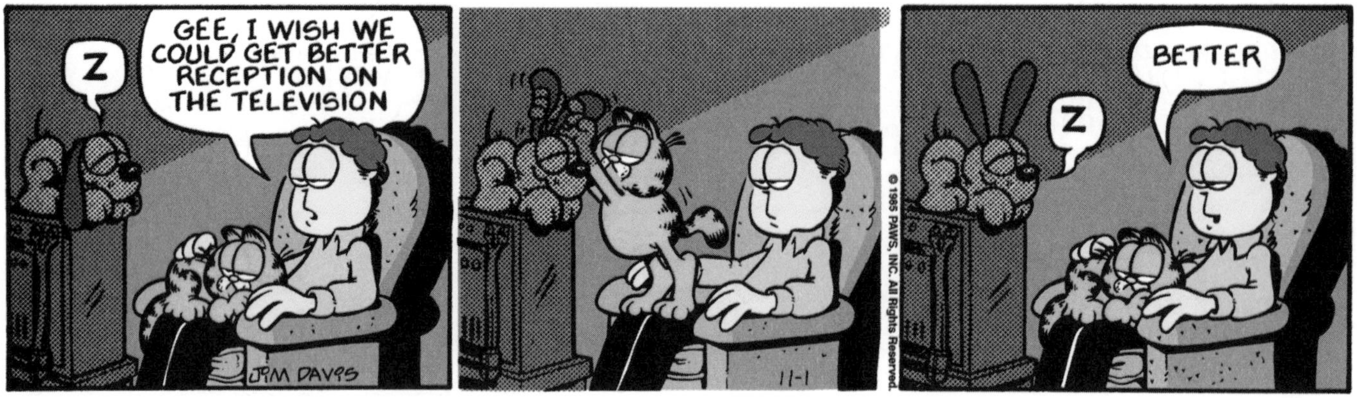
Z
GEE, I WISH WE COULD GET BETTER RECEPTION ON THE TELEVISION
JIM DAVIS
11-1
© 1985 PAWS, INC. All Rights Reserved.
Z
BETTER

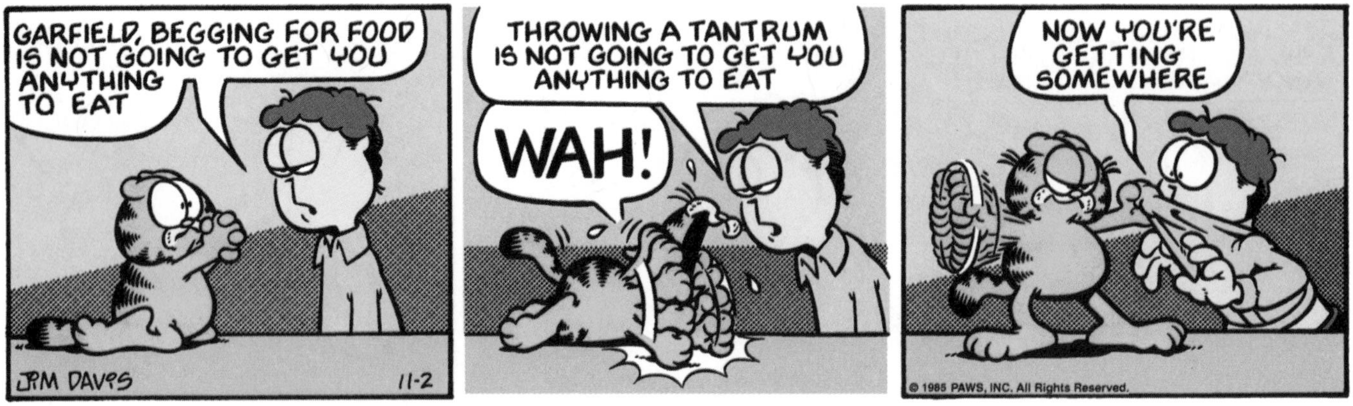
GARFIELD, BEGGING FOR FOOD IS NOT GOING TO GET YOU ANYTHING TO EAT
JIM DAVIS
11-2
THROWING A TANTRUM IS NOT GOING TO GET YOU ANYTHING TO EAT
WAH!
NOW YOU'RE GETTING SOMEWHERE
© 1985 PAWS, INC. All Rights Reserved.

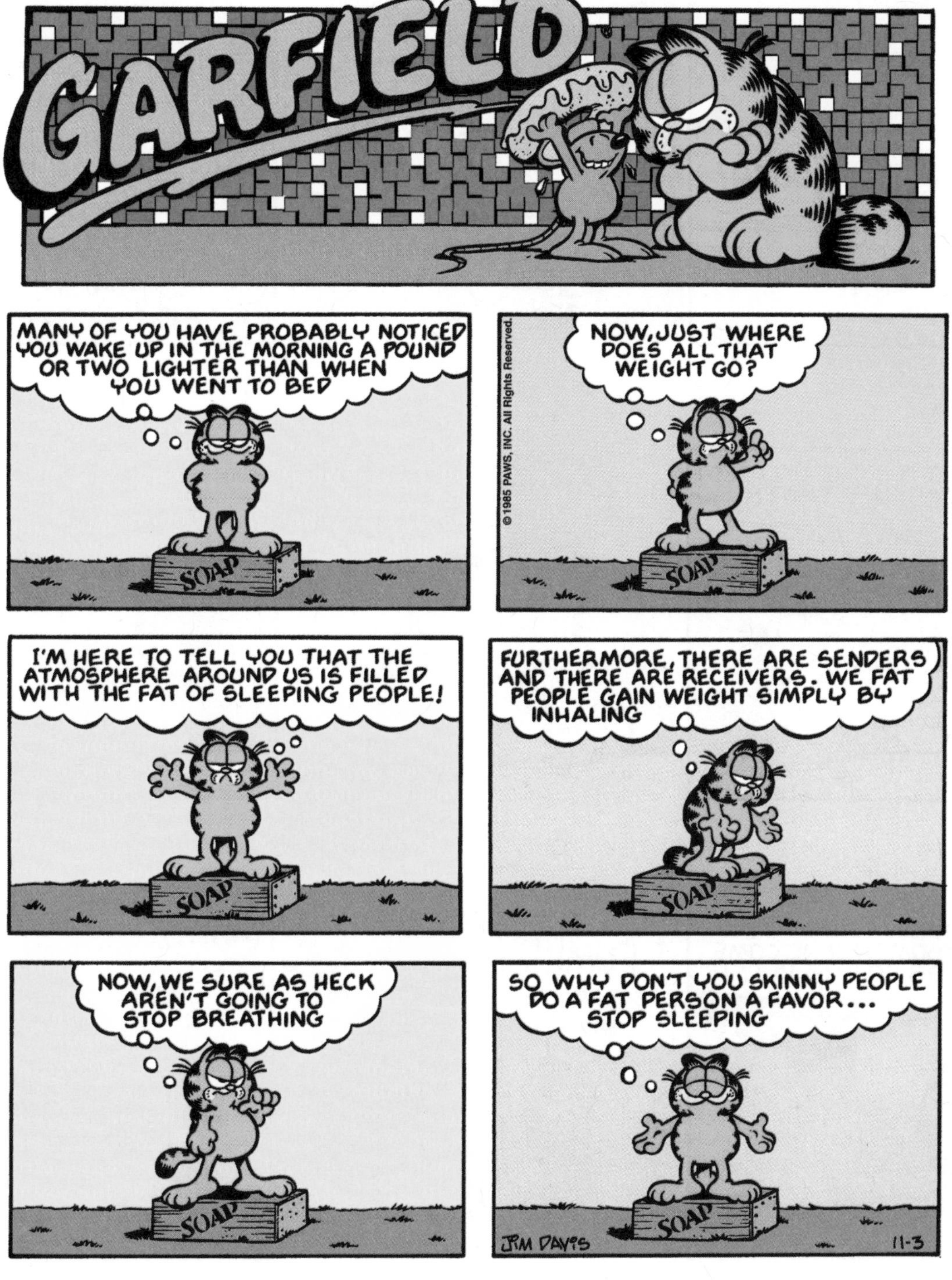
GARFIELD
MANY OF YOU HAVE PROBABLY NOTICED YOU WAKE UP IN THE MORNING A POUND OR TWO LIGHTER THAN WHEN YOU WENT TO BED
SOAP
© 1985 PAWS, INC. All Rights Reserved.
NOW, JUST WHERE DOES ALL THAT WEIGHT GO?
SOAP
I'M HERE TO TELL YOU THAT THE ATMOSPHERE AROUND US IS FILLED WITH THE FAT OF SLEEPING PEOPLE!
SOAP
FURTHERMORE, THERE ARE SENDERS AND THERE ARE RECEIVERS. WE FAT PEOPLE GAIN WEIGHT SIMPLY BY INHALING
SOAP
NOW, WE SURE AS HECK AREN'T GOING TO STOP BREATHING
SOAP
SO WHY DON'T YOU SKINNY PEOPLE DO A FAT PERSON A FAVOR... STOP SLEEPING
SOAP
JIM DAVIS
11-3

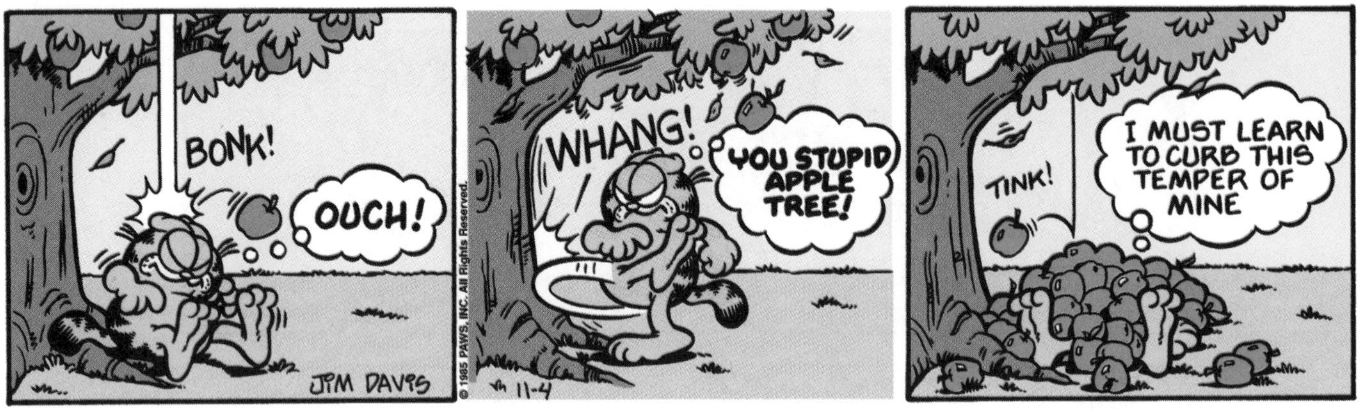
BONK!
OUCH!
JIM DAVIS
© 1985 PAWS, INC. All Rights Reserved.
11-4
WHANG!
YOU STUPID APPLE TREE!
TINK!
I MUST LEARN TO CURB THIS TEMPER OF MINE

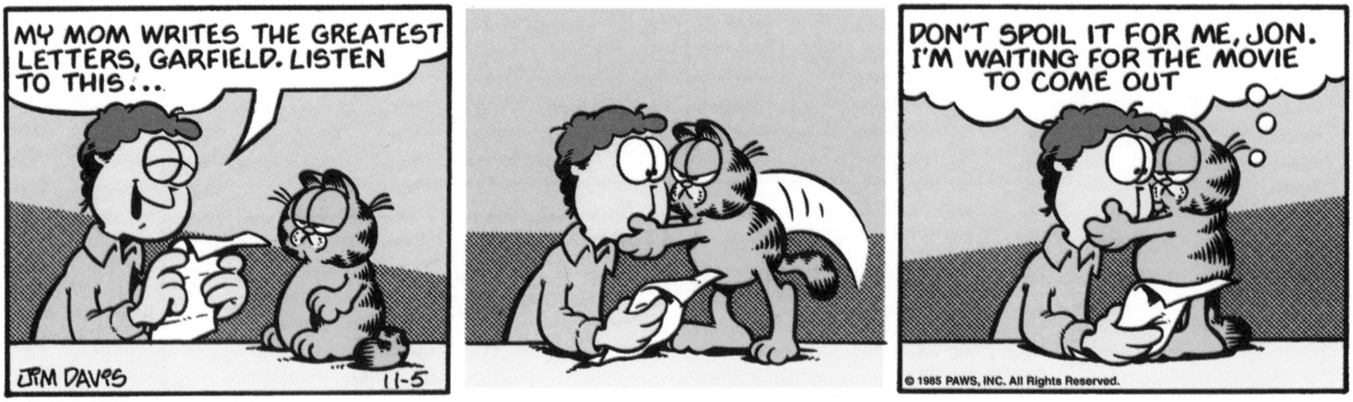
MY MOM WRITES THE GREATEST LETTERS, GARFIELD. LISTEN TO THIS...
JIM DAVIS
11-5
DON'T SPOIL IT FOR ME, JON. I'M WAITING FOR THE MOVIE TO COME OUT
© 1985 PAWS, INC. All Rights Reserved.

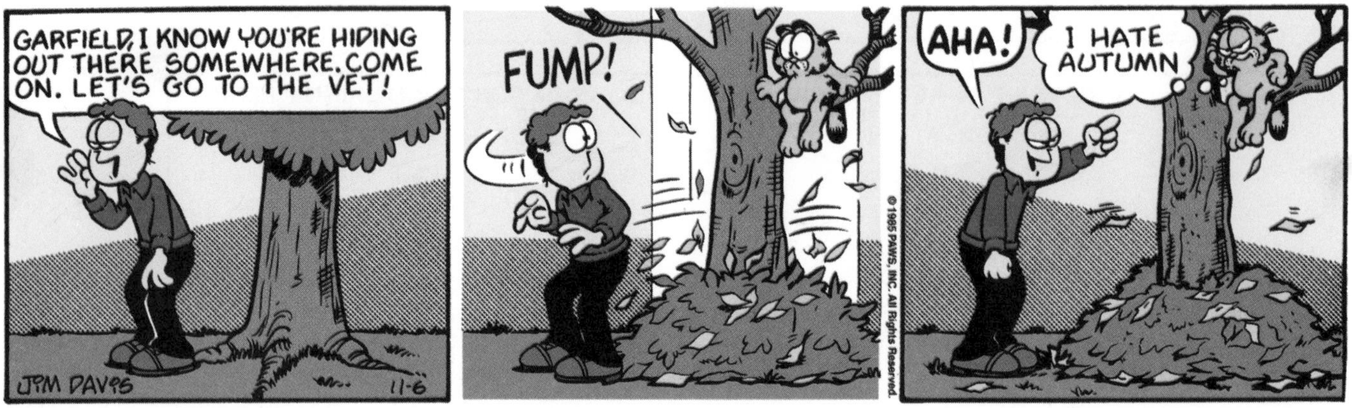
GARFIELD, I KNOW YOU'RE HIDING OUT THERE SOMEWHERE. COME ON. LET'S GO TO THE VET!
JIM DAVIS
11-6
FUMP!
© 1985 PAWS, INC. All Rights Reserved.
AHA!
I HATE AUTUMN

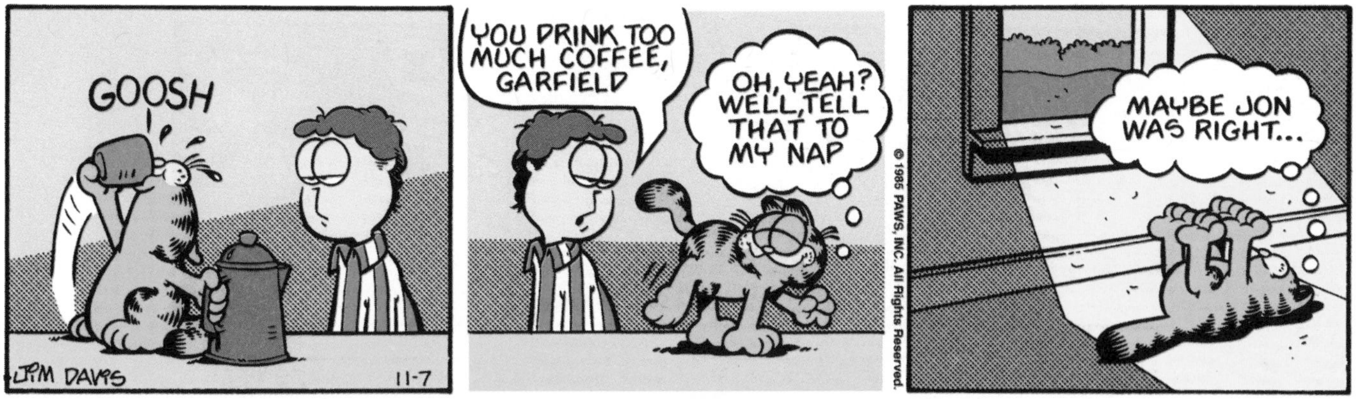
GOOSH
JIM DAVIS
11-7
YOU DRINK TOO MUCH COFFEE, GARFIELD
OH, YEAH? WELL, TELL THAT TO MY NAP
© 1985 PAWS, INC. All Rights Reserved.
MAYBE JON WAS RIGHT...

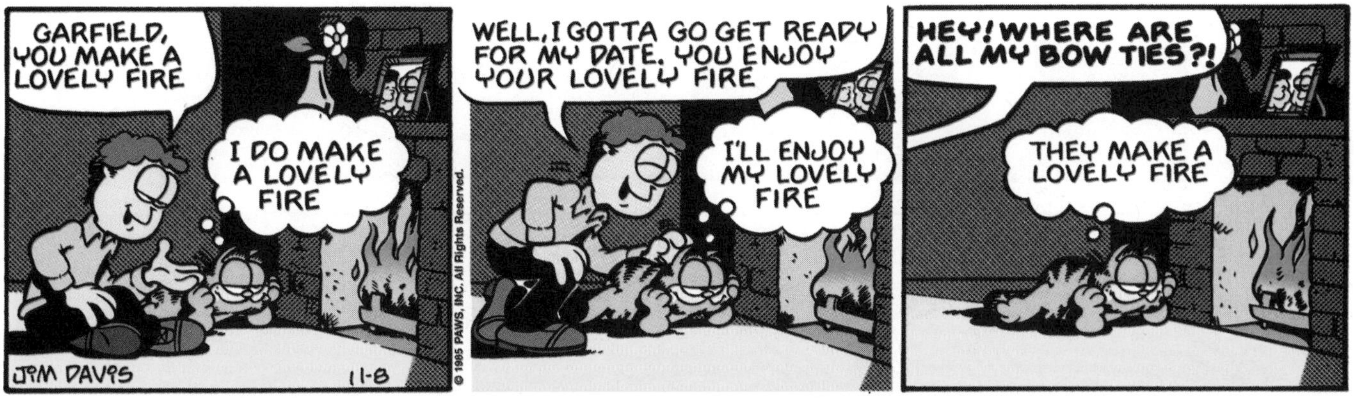
GARFIELD, YOU MAKE A LOVELY FIRE
I DO MAKE A LOVELY FIRE
JIM DAVIS
11-8
© 1985 PAWS, INC. All Rights Reserved.
WELL, I GOTTA GO GET READY FOR MY DATE. YOU ENJOY YOUR LOVELY FIRE
I'LL ENJOY MY LOVELY FIRE
HEY! WHERE ARE ALL MY BOW TIES?!
THEY MAKE A LOVELY FIRE

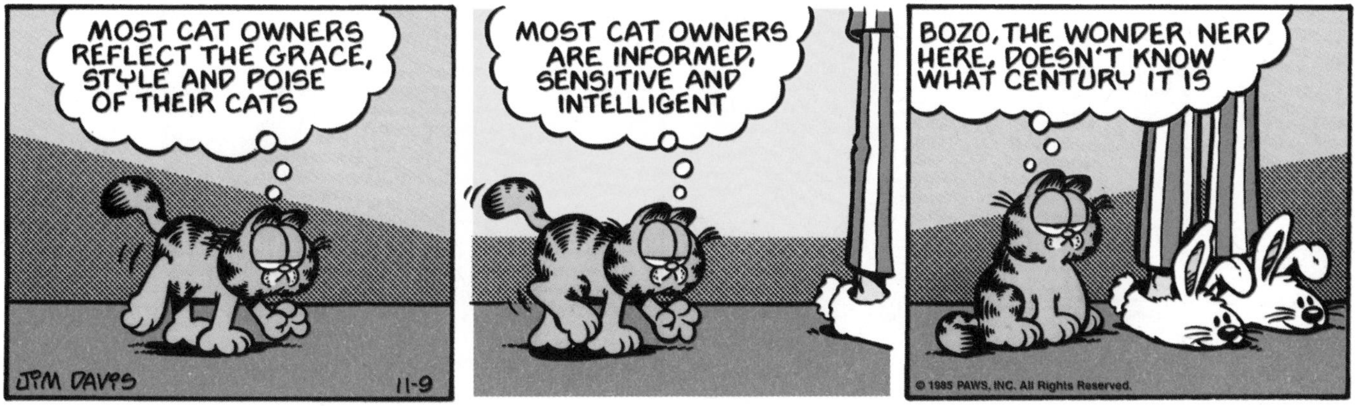
MOST CAT OWNERS REFLECT THE GRACE, STYLE AND POISE OF THEIR CATS
JIM DAVIS
11-9
MOST CAT OWNERS ARE INFORMED, SENSITIVE AND INTELLIGENT
BOZO, THE WONDER NERD HERE, DOESN'T KNOW WHAT CENTURY IT IS
© 1985 PAWS, INC. All Rights Reserved.

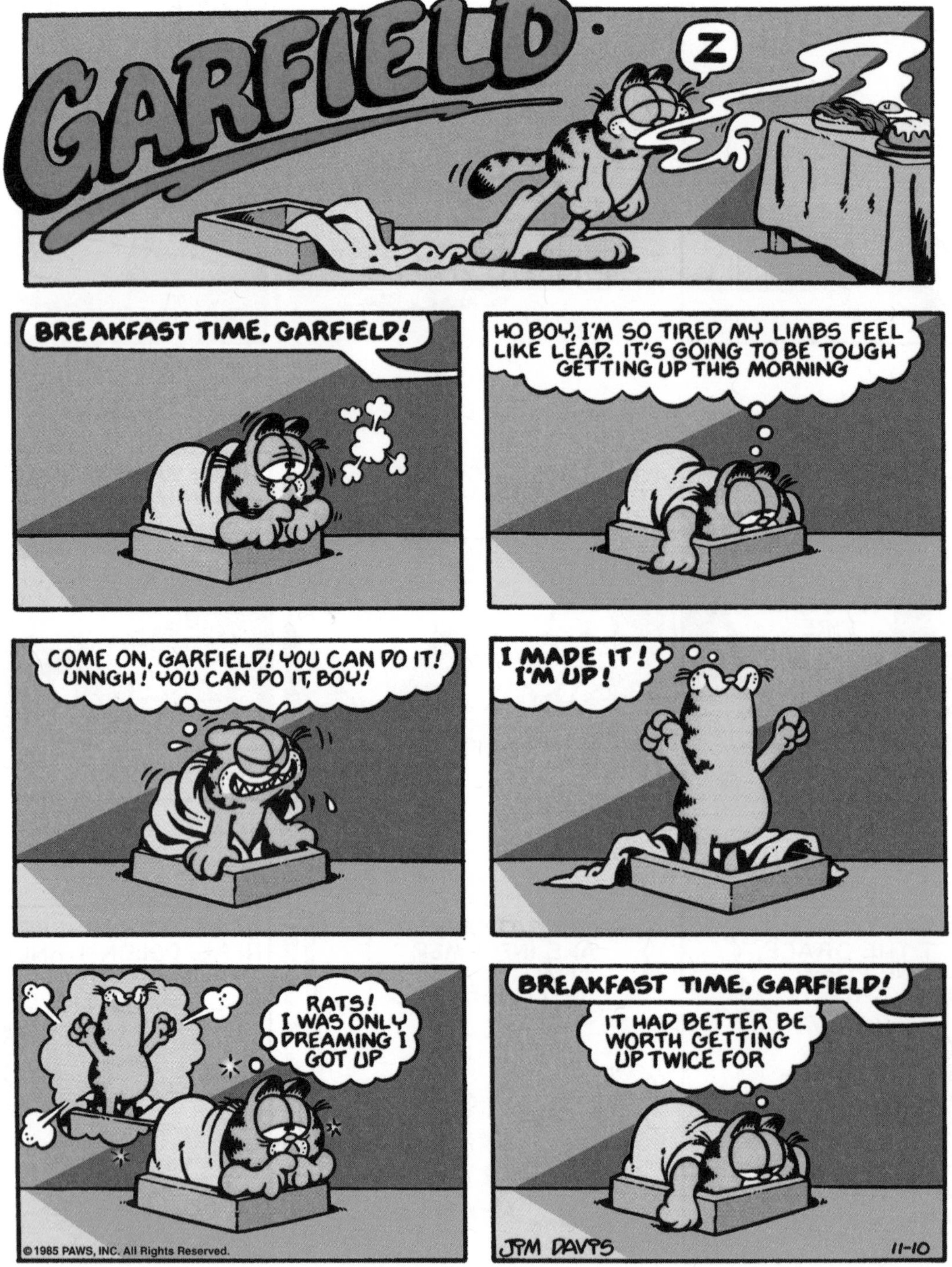
GARFIELD
Z
BREAKFAST TIME, GARFIELD!
HO BOY, I'M SO TIRED MY LIMBS FEEL LIKE LEAD. IT'S GOING TO BE TOUGH GETTING UP THIS MORNING
COME ON, GARFIELD! YOU CAN DO IT! UNNGH! YOU CAN DO IT, BOY!
I MADE IT! I'M UP!
RATS! I WAS ONLY DREAMING I GOT UP
BREAKFAST TIME, GARFIELD!
IT HAD BETTER BE WORTH GETTING UP TWICE FOR
© 1985 PAWS, INC. All Rights Reserved.
JIM DAVIS
11-10

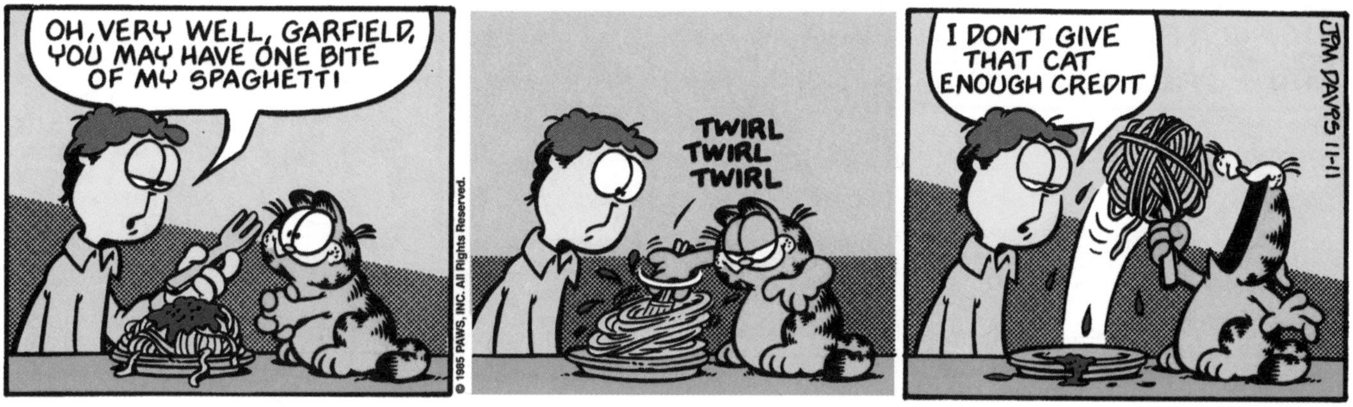
OH, VERY WELL, GARFIELD, YOU MAY HAVE ONE BITE OF MY SPAGHETTI
© 1985 PAWS, INC. All Rights Reserved.
TWIRL TWIRL TWIRL
I DON'T GIVE THAT CAT ENOUGH CREDIT
JIM DAVIS 11-11

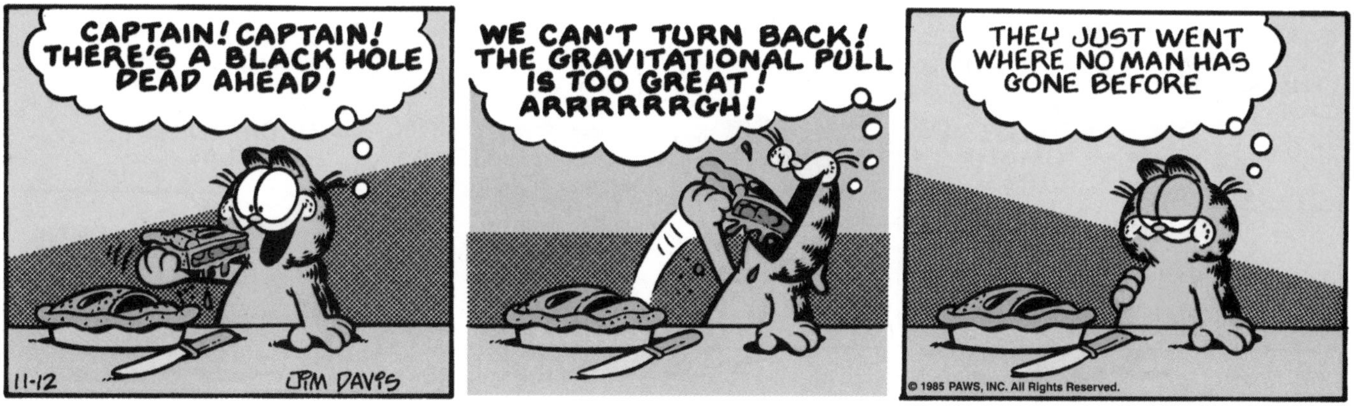
CAPTAIN! CAPTAIN! THERE'S A BLACK HOLE DEAD AHEAD!
11-12
JIM DAVIS
WE CAN'T TURN BACK! THE GRAVITATIONAL PULL IS TOO GREAT! ARRRRRRGH!
THEY JUST WENT WHERE NO MAN HAS GONE BEFORE
© 1985 PAWS, INC. All Rights Reserved.

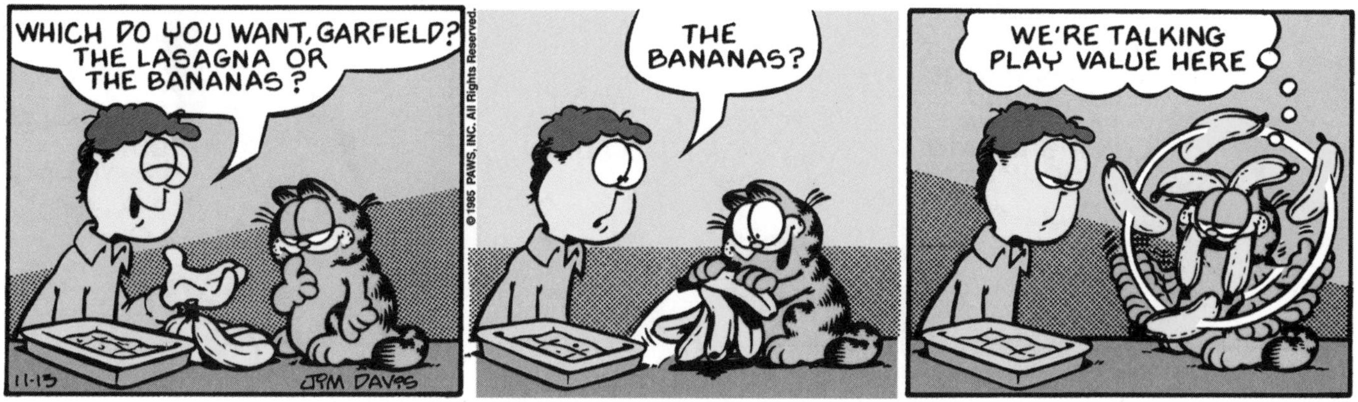
WHICH DO YOU WANT, GARFIELD? THE LASAGNA OR THE BANANAS?
11-13
JIM DAVIS
© 1985 PAWS, INC. All Rights Reserved.
THE BANANAS?
WE'RE TALKING PLAY VALUE HERE

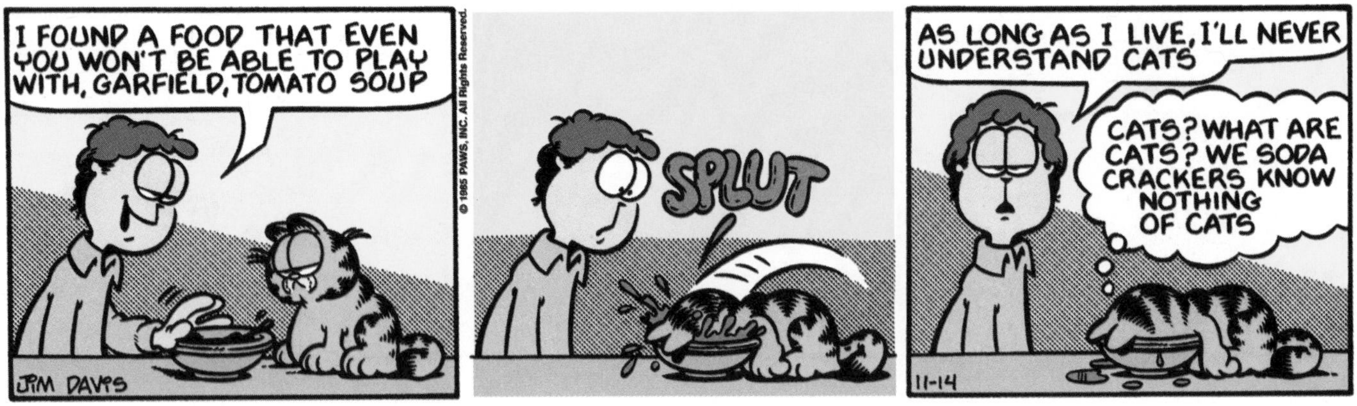
I FOUND A FOOD THAT EVEN YOU WON'T BE ABLE TO PLAY WITH, GARFIELD, TOMATO SOUP
JIM DAVIS
© 1985 PAWS, INC. All Rights Reserved.
SPLUT
AS LONG AS I LIVE, I'LL NEVER UNDERSTAND CATS
CATS? WHAT ARE CATS? WE SODA CRACKERS KNOW NOTHING OF CATS
11-14

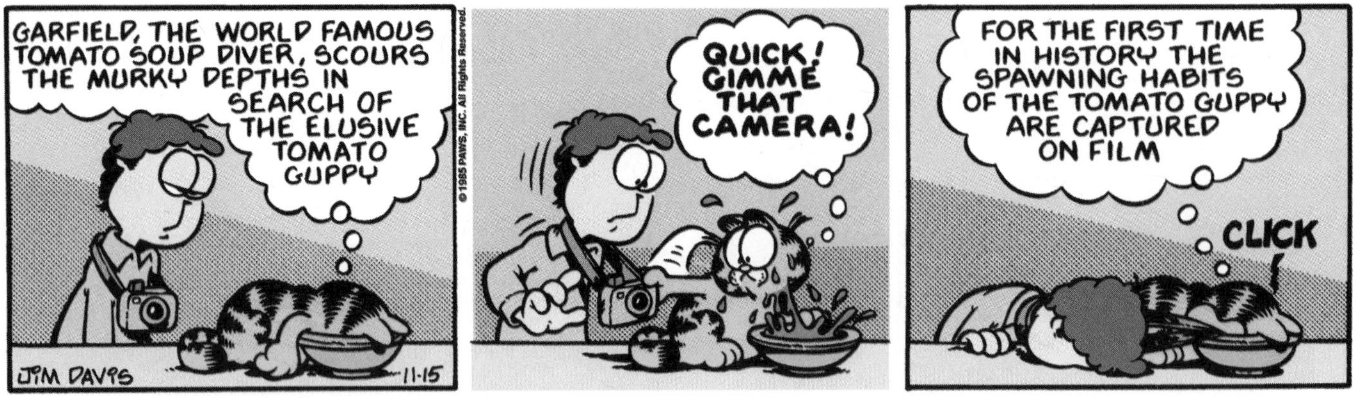
GARFIELD, THE WORLD FAMOUS TOMATO SOUP DIVER, SCOURS THE MURKY DEPTHS IN SEARCH OF THE ELUSIVE TOMATO GUPPY
JIM DAVIS
11-15
© 1985 PAWS, INC. All Rights Reserved.
QUICK! GIMME THAT CAMERA!
FOR THE FIRST TIME IN HISTORY THE SPAWNING HABITS OF THE TOMATO GUPPY ARE CAPTURED ON FILM
CLICK

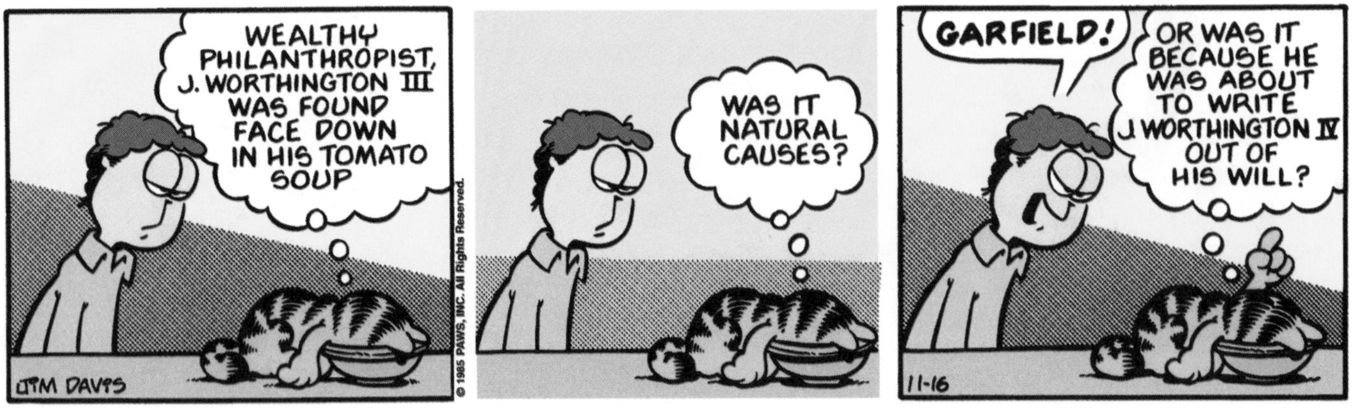
WEALTHY PHILANTHROPIST, J. WORTHINGTON III WAS FOUND FACE DOWN IN HIS TOMATO SOUP
JIM DAVIS
© 1985 PAWS, INC. All Rights Reserved.
WAS IT NATURAL CAUSES?
GARFIELD!
OR WAS IT BECAUSE HE WAS ABOUT TO WRITE J. WORTHINGTON IV OUT OF HIS WILL?
11-16

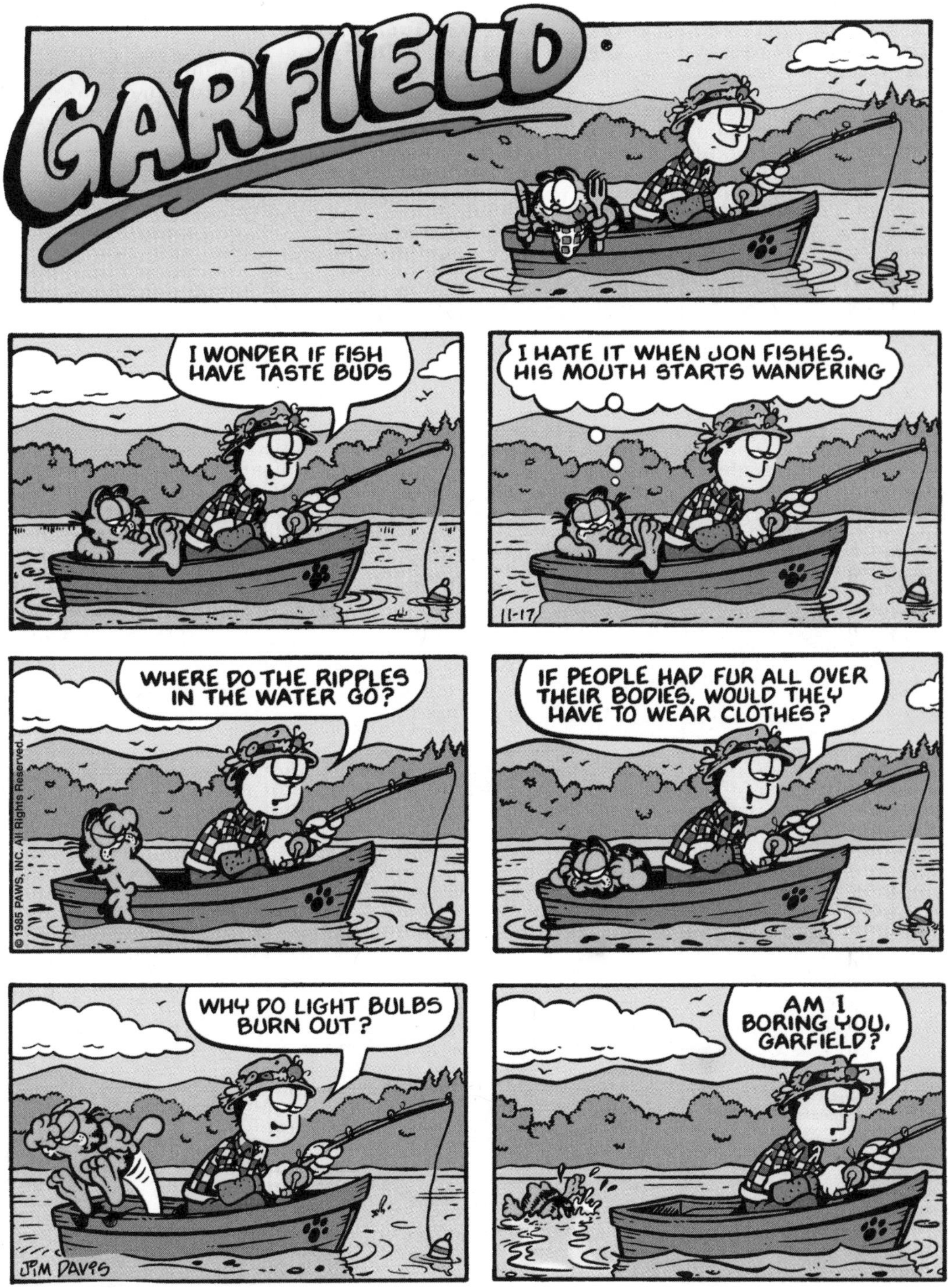
GARFIELD
I WONDER IF FISH HAVE TASTE BUDS
I HATE IT WHEN JON FISHES. HIS MOUTH STARTS WANDERING
11-17
WHERE DO THE RIPPLES IN THE WATER GO?
© 1985 PAWS, INC. All Rights Reserved.
IF PEOPLE HAD FUR ALL OVER THEIR BODIES, WOULD THEY HAVE TO WEAR CLOTHES?
WHY DO LIGHT BULBS BURN OUT?
JIM DAVIS
AM I BORING YOU, GARFIELD?

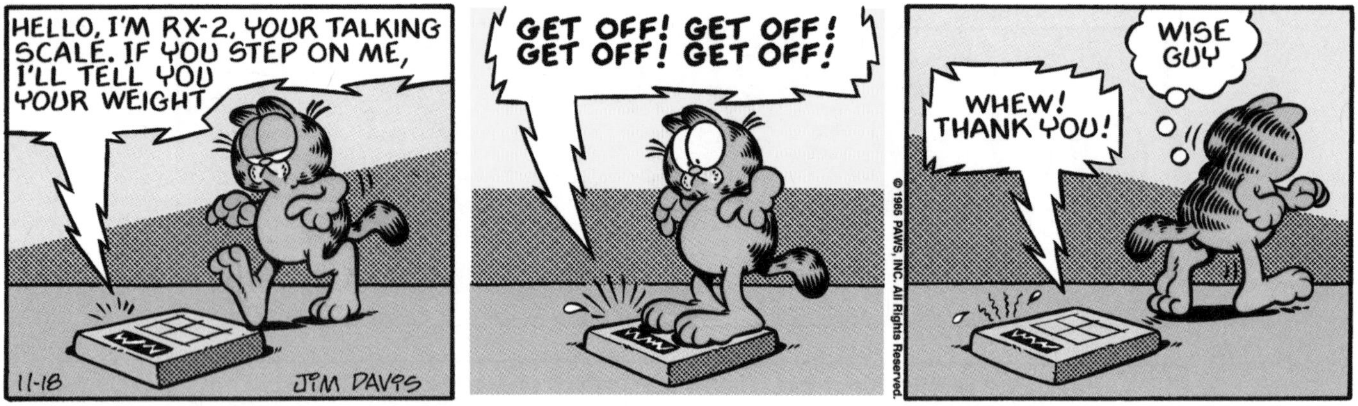
HELLO, I'M RX-2, YOUR TALKING SCALE. IF YOU STEP ON ME, I'LL TELL YOU YOUR WEIGHT
11-18
JIM DAVIS
GET OFF! GET OFF! GET OFF! GET OFF!
© 1985 PAWS, INC. All Rights Reserved.
WHEW! THANK YOU!
WISE GUY

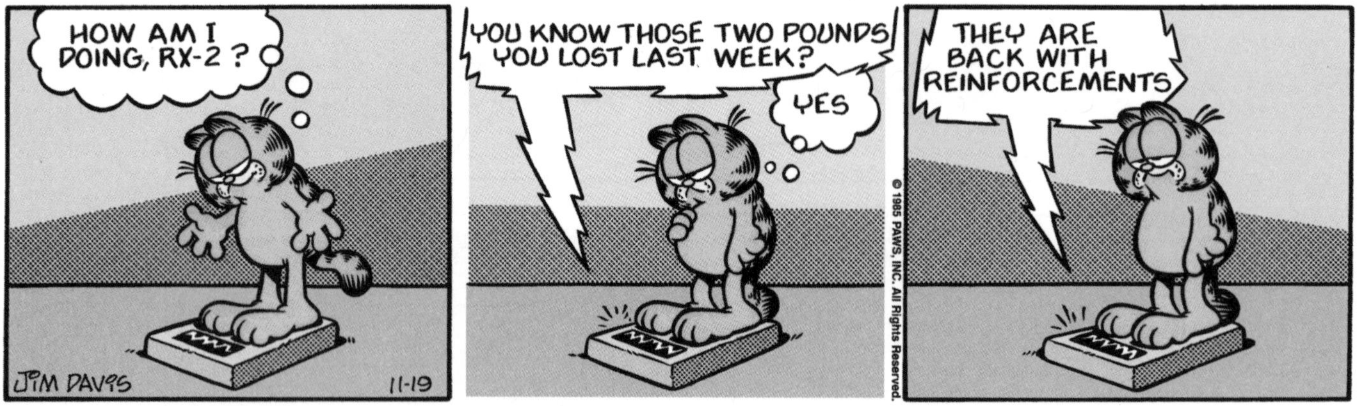
HOW AM I DOING, RX-2 ?
JIM DAVIS
11-19
YOU KNOW THOSE TWO POUNDS YOU LOST LAST WEEK?
YES
© 1985 PAWS, INC. All Rights Reserved.
THEY ARE BACK WITH REINFORCEMENTS

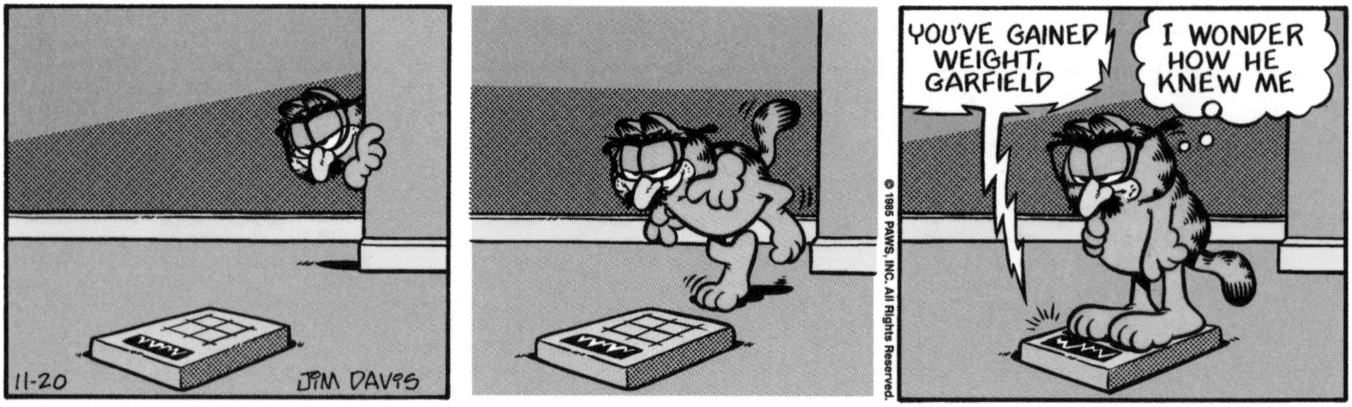
11-20
JIM DAVIS
© 1985 PAWS, INC. All Rights Reserved.
YOU'VE GAINED WEIGHT, GARFIELD
I WONDER HOW HE KNEW ME

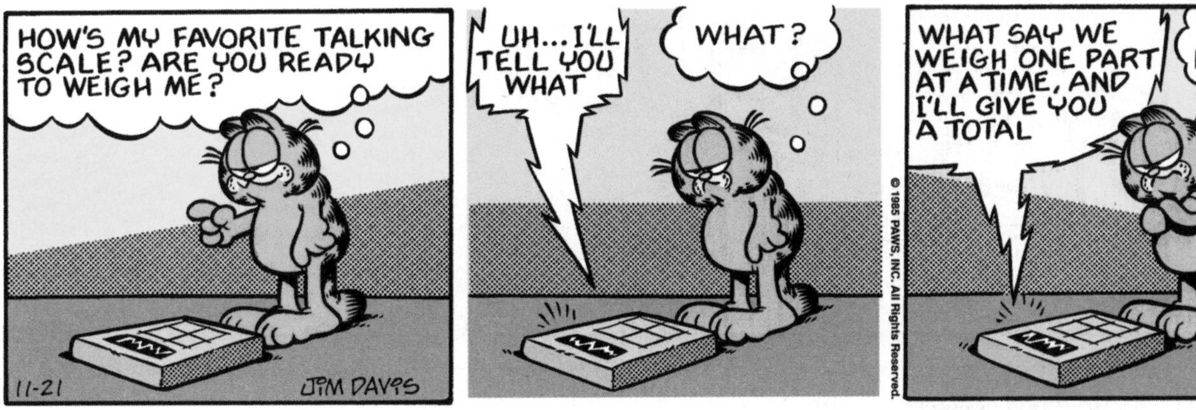
HOW'S MY FAVORITE TALKING SCALE? ARE YOU READY TO WEIGH ME?
11-21
JIM DAVIS
UH... I'LL TELL YOU WHAT
WHAT?
© 1985 PAWS, INC. All Rights Reserved.
WHAT SAY WE WEIGH ONE PART AT A TIME, AND I'LL GIVE YOU A TOTAL
VERY FUNNY

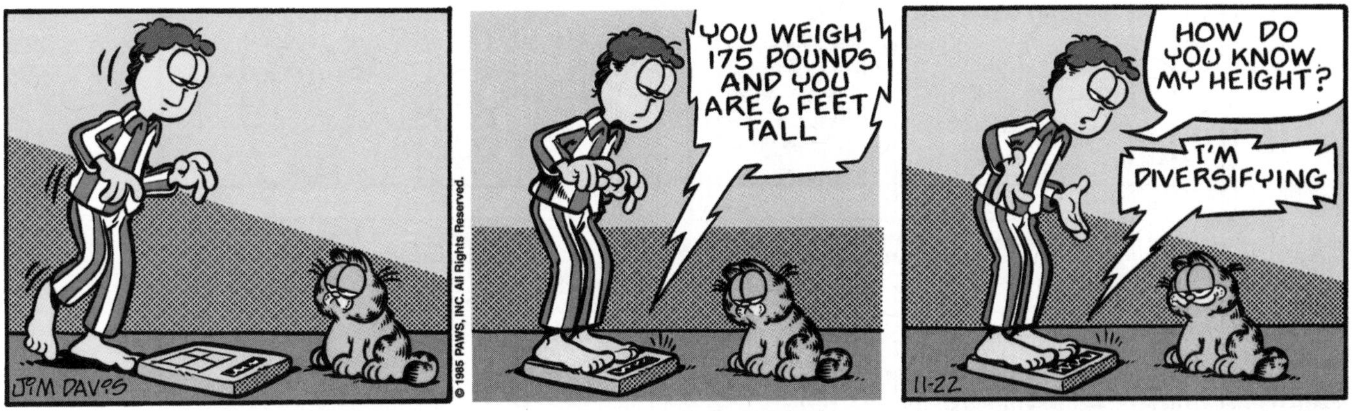
JIM DAVIS
© 1985 PAWS, INC. All Rights Reserved.
YOU WEIGH 175 POUNDS AND YOU ARE 6 FEET TALL
HOW DO YOU KNOW MY HEIGHT?
I'M DIVERSIFYING
11-22

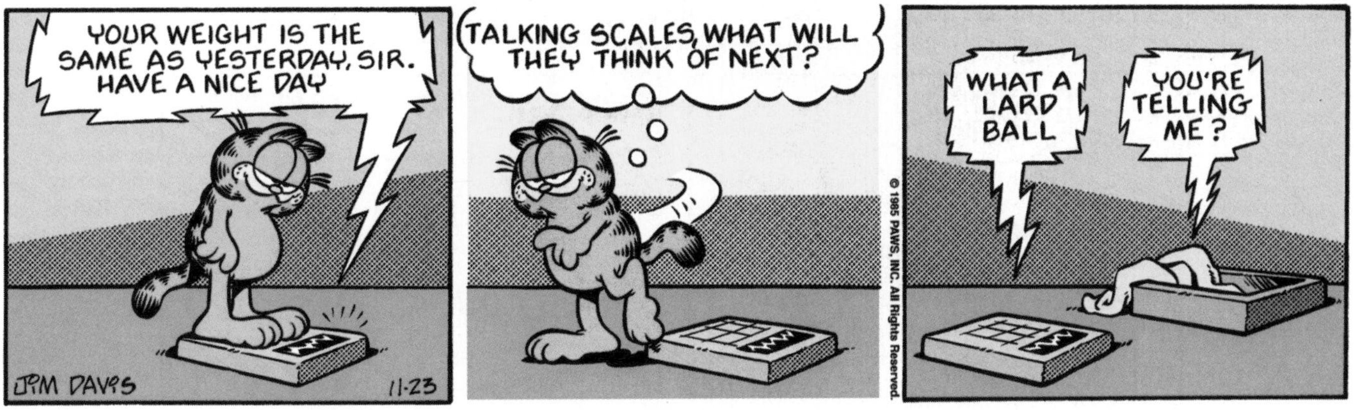
YOUR WEIGHT IS THE SAME AS YESTERDAY, SIR. HAVE A NICE DAY
JIM DAVIS
11-23
TALKING SCALES, WHAT WILL THEY THINK OF NEXT?
© 1985 PAWS, INC. All Rights Reserved.
WHAT A LARD BALL
YOU'RE TELLING ME?

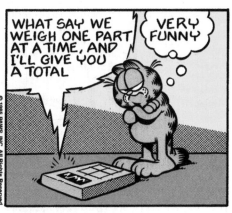

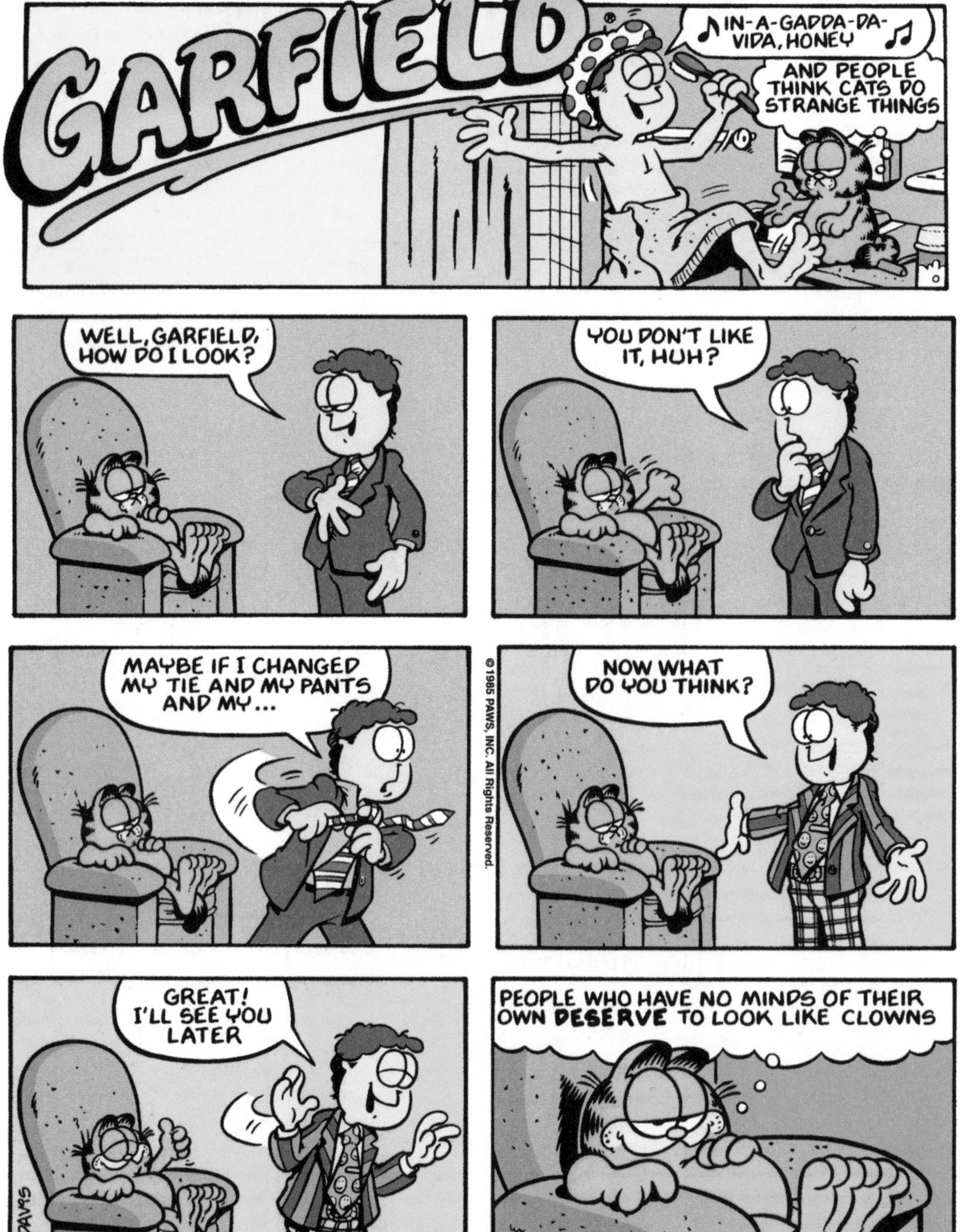
GARFIELD®
♪ IN-A-GADDA-DA-VIDA, HONEY ♫
AND PEOPLE THINK CATS DO STRANGE THINGS
WELL, GARFIELD, HOW DO I LOOK?
YOU DON'T LIKE IT, HUH?
MAYBE IF I CHANGED MY TIE AND MY PANTS AND MY...
© 1985 PAWS, INC. All Rights Reserved.
NOW WHAT DO YOU THINK?
GREAT! I'LL SEE YOU LATER
JIM DAVIS
11-24
PEOPLE WHO HAVE NO MINDS OF THEIR OWN **DESERVE** TO LOOK LIKE CLOWNS

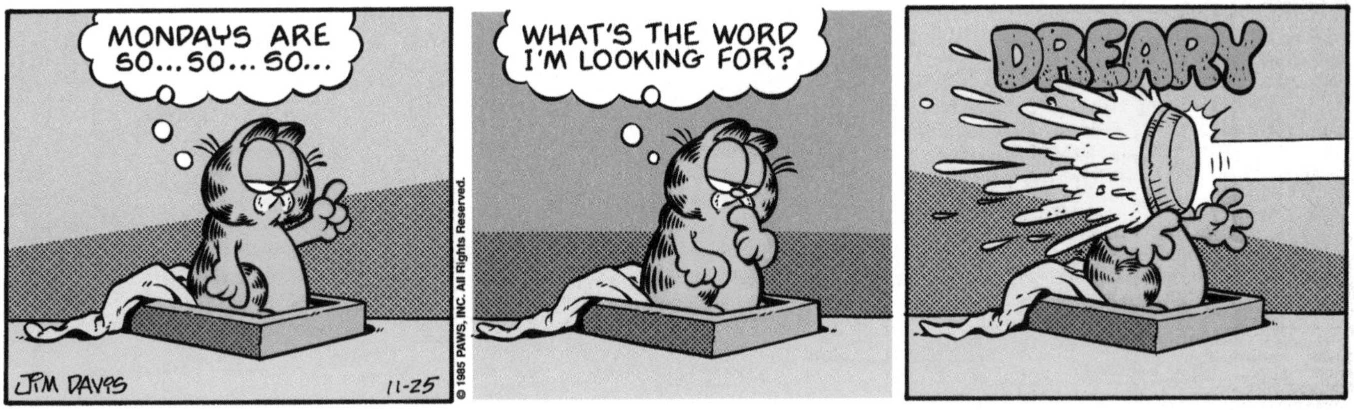
MONDAYS ARE SO... SO... SO...
JIM DAVIS
11-25
WHAT'S THE WORD I'M LOOKING FOR?
DREARY

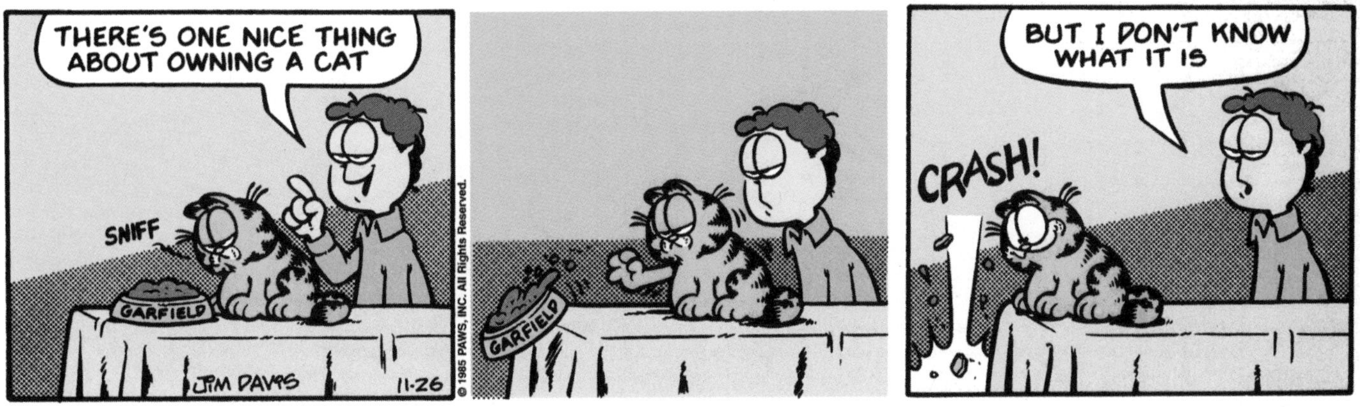
THERE'S ONE NICE THING ABOUT OWNING A CAT
SNIFF
GARFIELD
JIM DAVIS
11-26
GARFIELD
CRASH!
BUT I DON'T KNOW WHAT IT IS

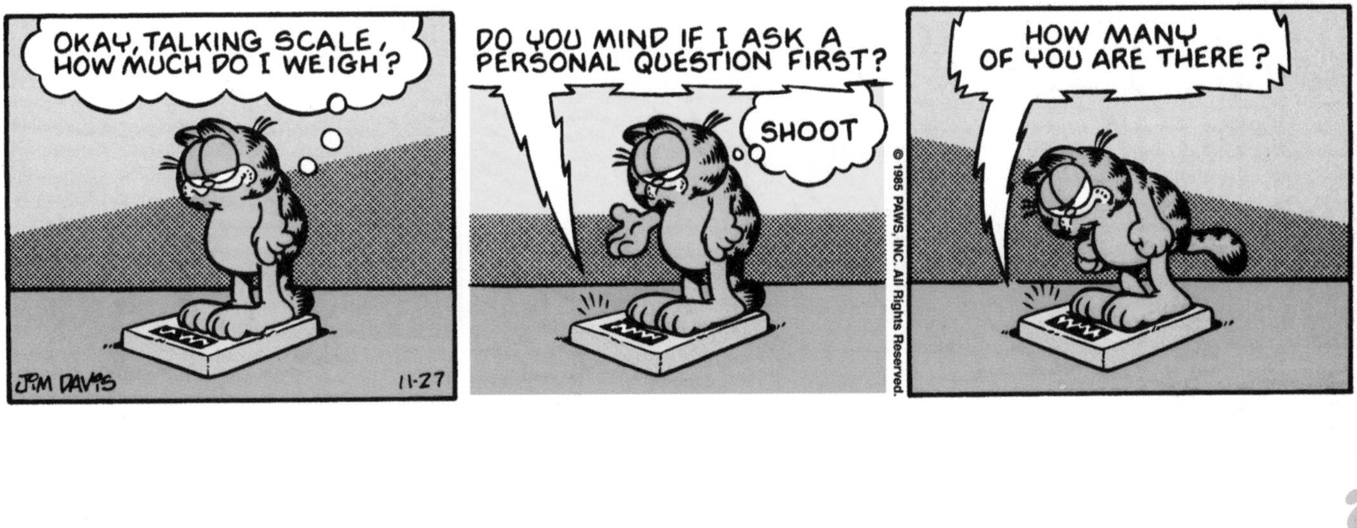
OKAY, TALKING SCALE, HOW MUCH DO I WEIGH?
JIM DAVIS
11-27
DO YOU MIND IF I ASK A PERSONAL QUESTION FIRST?
SHOOT
HOW MANY OF YOU ARE THERE?

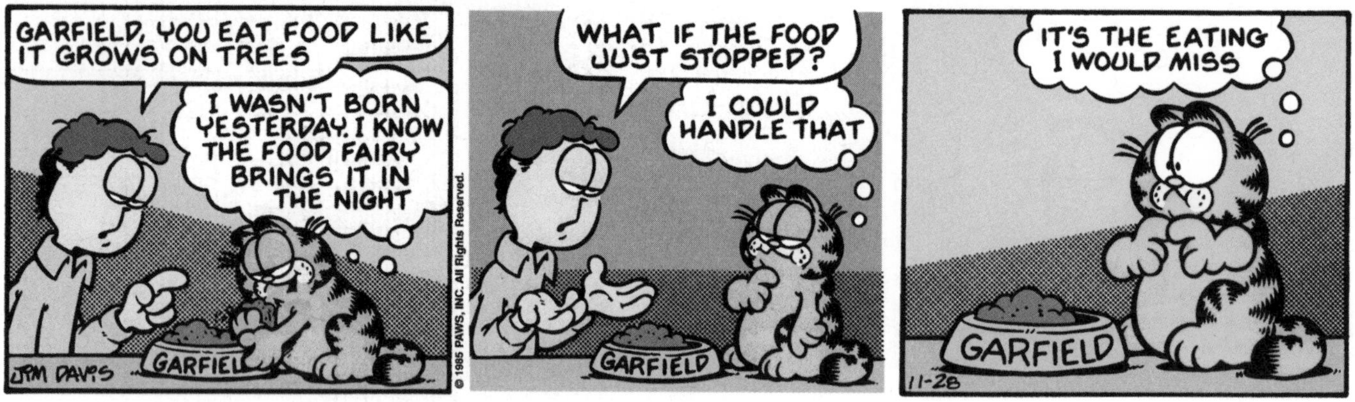
GARFIELD, YOU EAT FOOD LIKE IT GROWS ON TREES
I WASN'T BORN YESTERDAY. I KNOW THE FOOD FAIRY BRINGS IT IN THE NIGHT
GARFIEL
JIM DAVIS
© 1985 PAWS, INC. All Rights Reserved.
WHAT IF THE FOOD JUST STOPPED?
I COULD HANDLE THAT
GARFIELD
IT'S THE EATING I WOULD MISS
GARFIELD
11-28

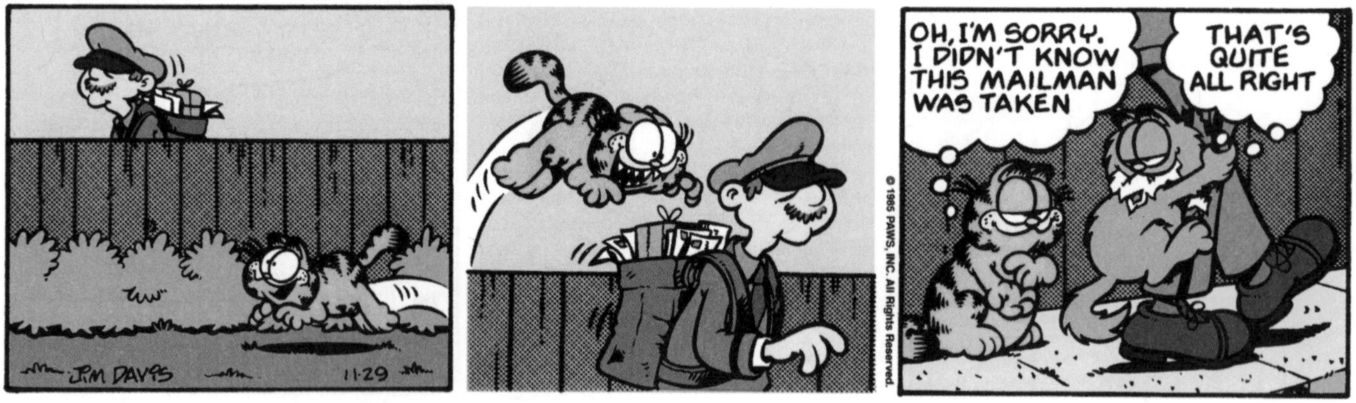
JIM DAVIS
11-29
© 1985 PAWS, INC. All Rights Reserved.
OH, I'M SORRY. I DIDN'T KNOW THIS MAILMAN WAS TAKEN
THAT'S QUITE ALL RIGHT

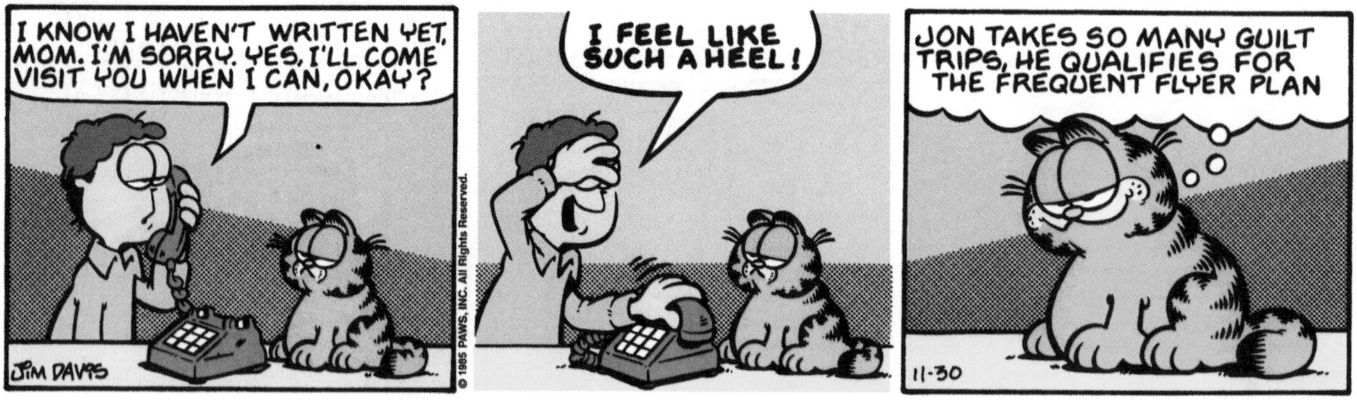
I KNOW I HAVEN'T WRITTEN YET, MOM. I'M SORRY. YES, I'LL COME VISIT YOU WHEN I CAN, OKAY?
JIM DAVIS
© 1985 PAWS, INC. All Rights Reserved.
I FEEL LIKE SUCH A HEEL!
JON TAKES SO MANY GUILT TRIPS, HE QUALIFIES FOR THE FREQUENT FLYER PLAN
11-30

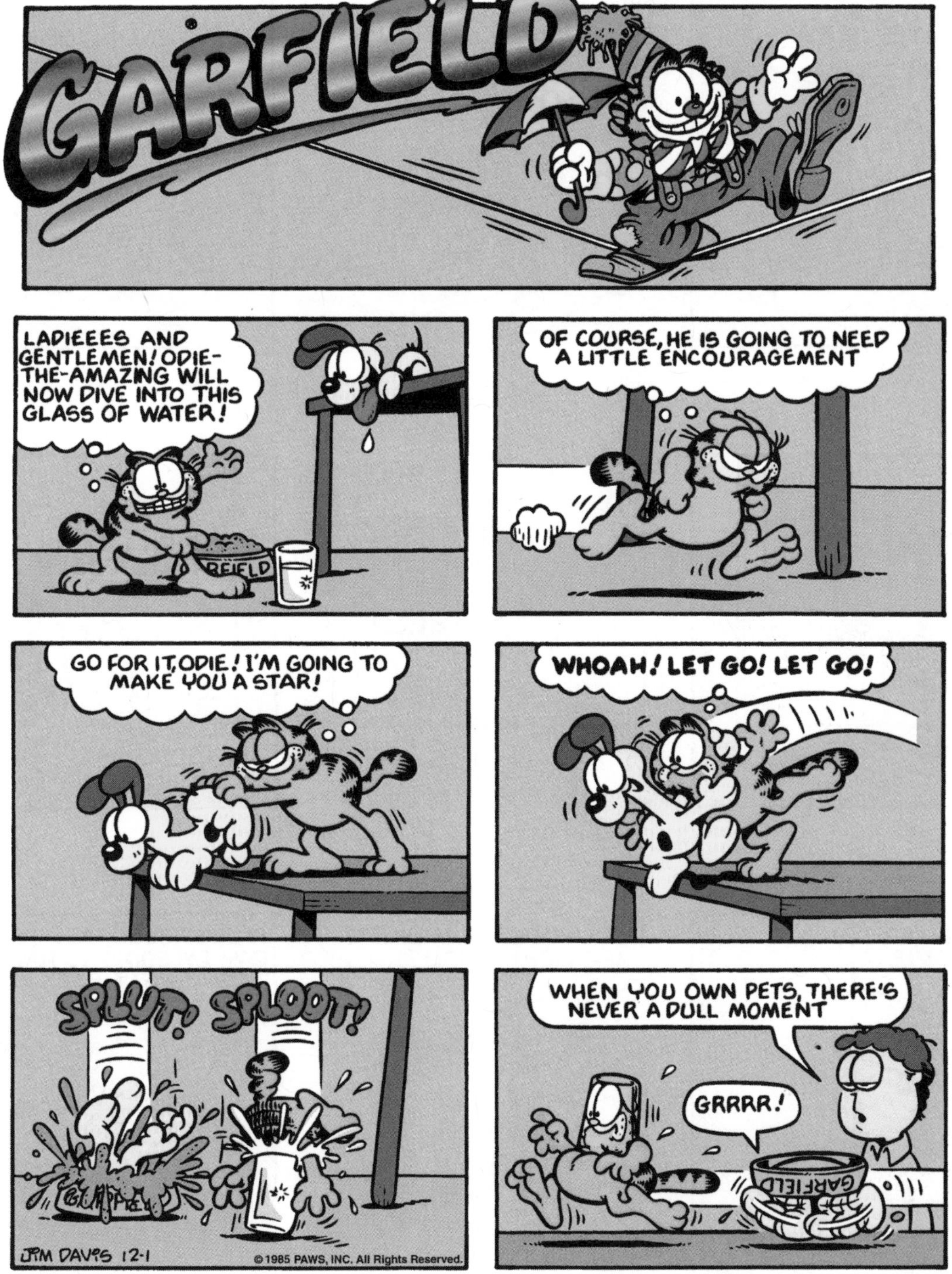
GARFIELD
LADIEEES AND GENTLEMEN! ODIE-THE-AMAZING WILL NOW DIVE INTO THIS GLASS OF WATER!
OF COURSE, HE IS GOING TO NEED A LITTLE ENCOURAGEMENT
GO FOR IT, ODIE! I'M GOING TO MAKE YOU A STAR!
WHOAH! LET GO! LET GO!
SPLUT! SPLOOT!
JIM DAVIS 12-1
© 1985 PAWS, INC. All Rights Reserved.
WHEN YOU OWN PETS, THERE'S NEVER A DULL MOMENT
GRRRR!
GARFIELD

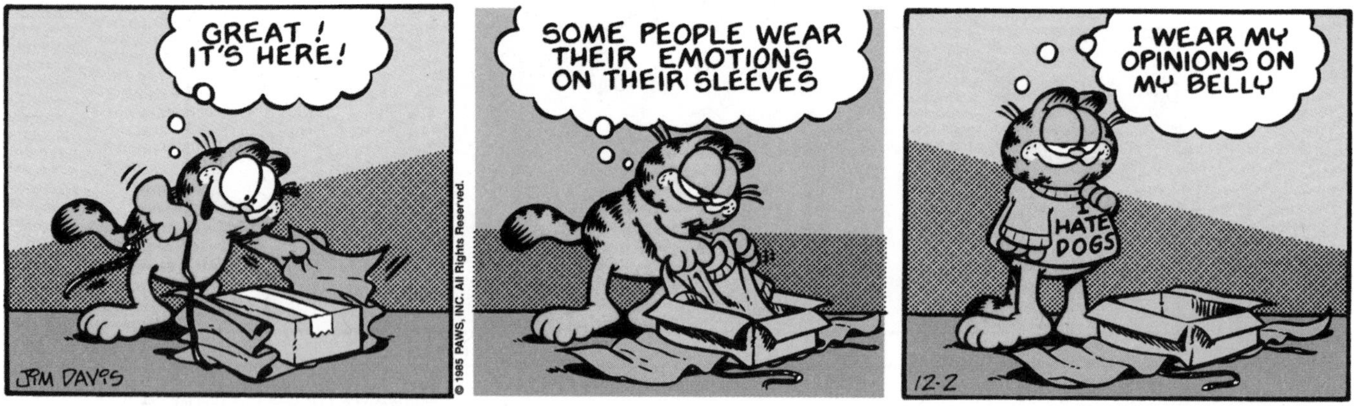
GREAT! IT'S HERE!
JIM DAVIS
© 1985 PAWS, INC. All Rights Reserved.
SOME PEOPLE WEAR THEIR EMOTIONS ON THEIR SLEEVES
I WEAR MY OPINIONS ON MY BELLY
I HATE DOGS
12-2

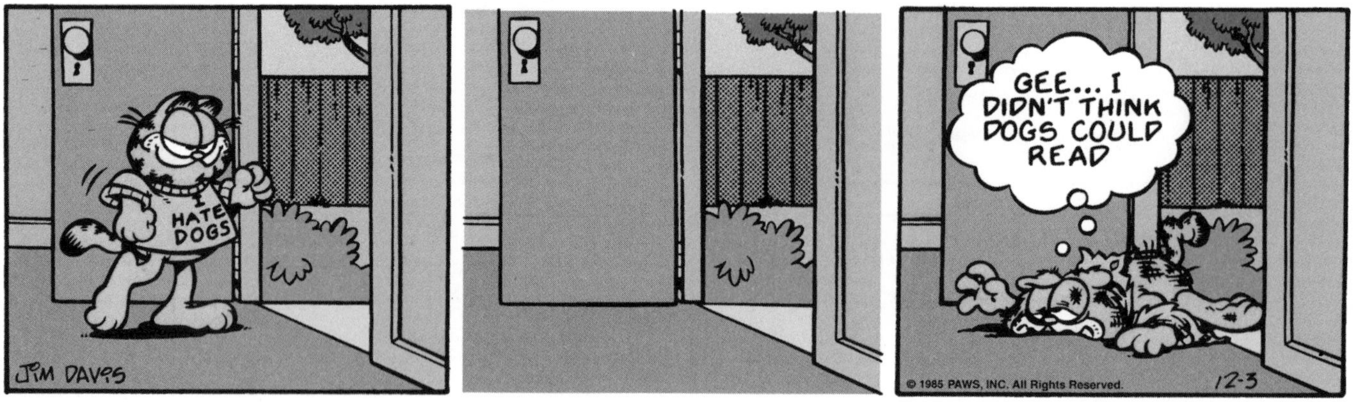
I HATE DOGS
JIM DAVIS
GEE... I DIDN'T THINK DOGS COULD READ
© 1985 PAWS, INC. All Rights Reserved.
12-3

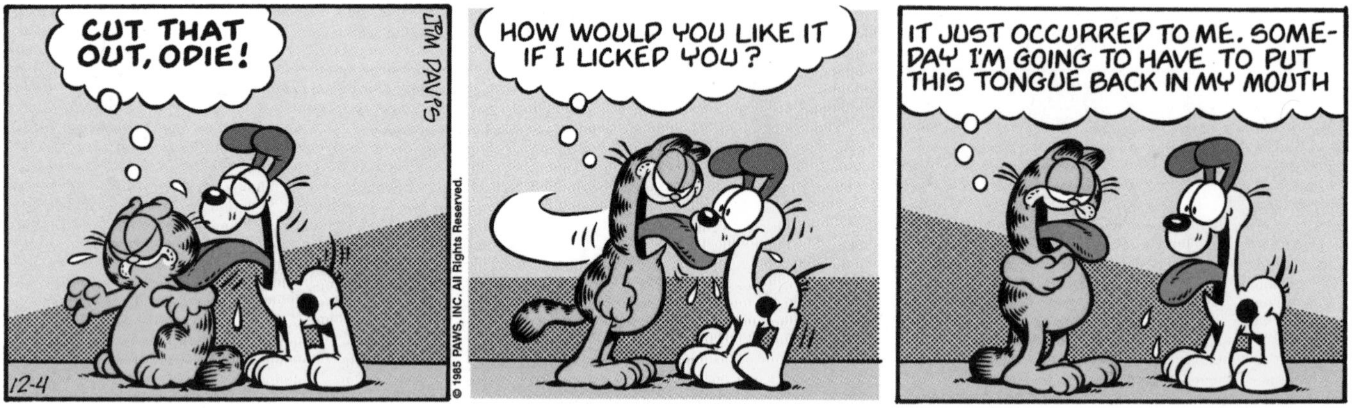
CUT THAT OUT, ODIE!
JIM DAVIS
12-4
© 1985 PAWS, INC. All Rights Reserved.
HOW WOULD YOU LIKE IT IF I LICKED YOU?
IT JUST OCCURRED TO ME. SOMEDAY I'M GOING TO HAVE TO PUT THIS TONGUE BACK IN MY MOUTH

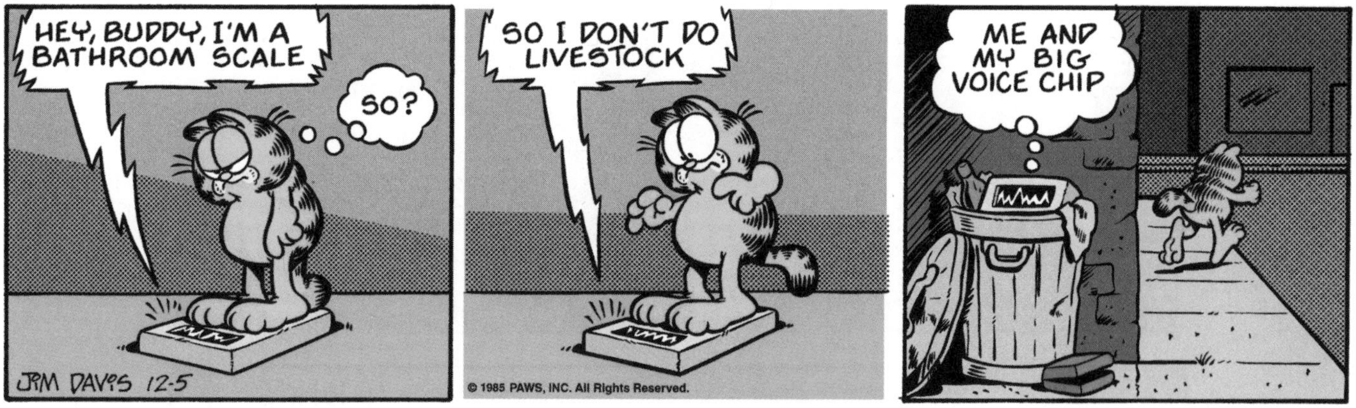
HEY, BUDDY, I'M A BATHROOM SCALE
SO?
JIM DAVIS 12-5
SO I DON'T DO LIVESTOCK
© 1985 PAWS, INC. All Rights Reserved.
ME AND MY BIG VOICE CHIP

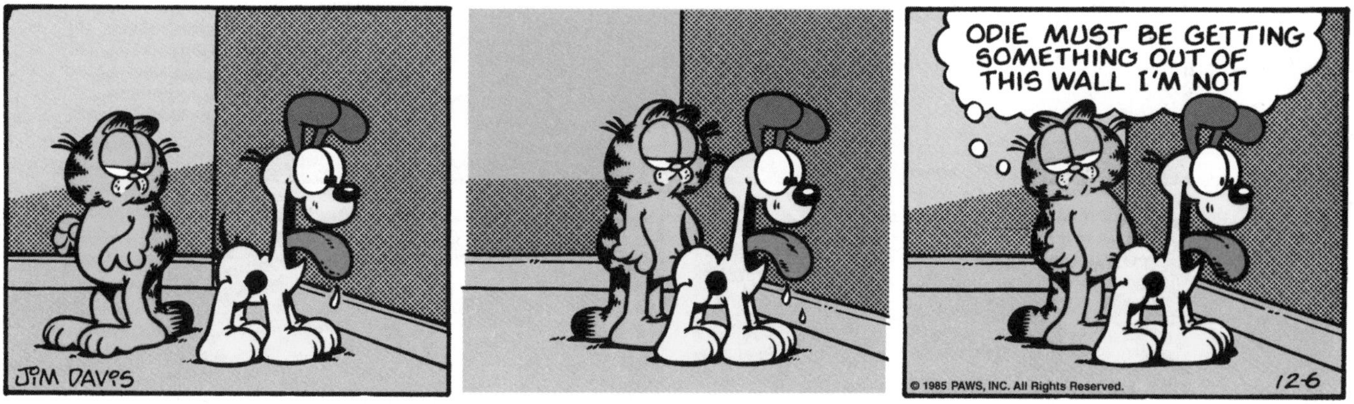
JIM DAVIS
ODIE MUST BE GETTING SOMETHING OUT OF THIS WALL I'M NOT
© 1985 PAWS, INC. All Rights Reserved.
12-6

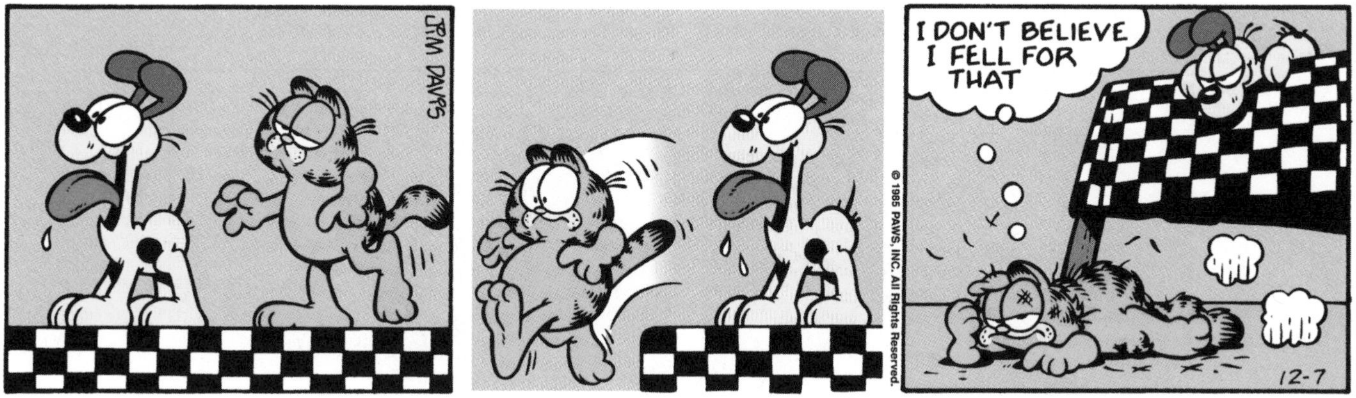
JIM DAVIS
© 1985 PAWS, INC. All Rights Reserved.
I DON'T BELIEVE I FELL FOR THAT
12-7

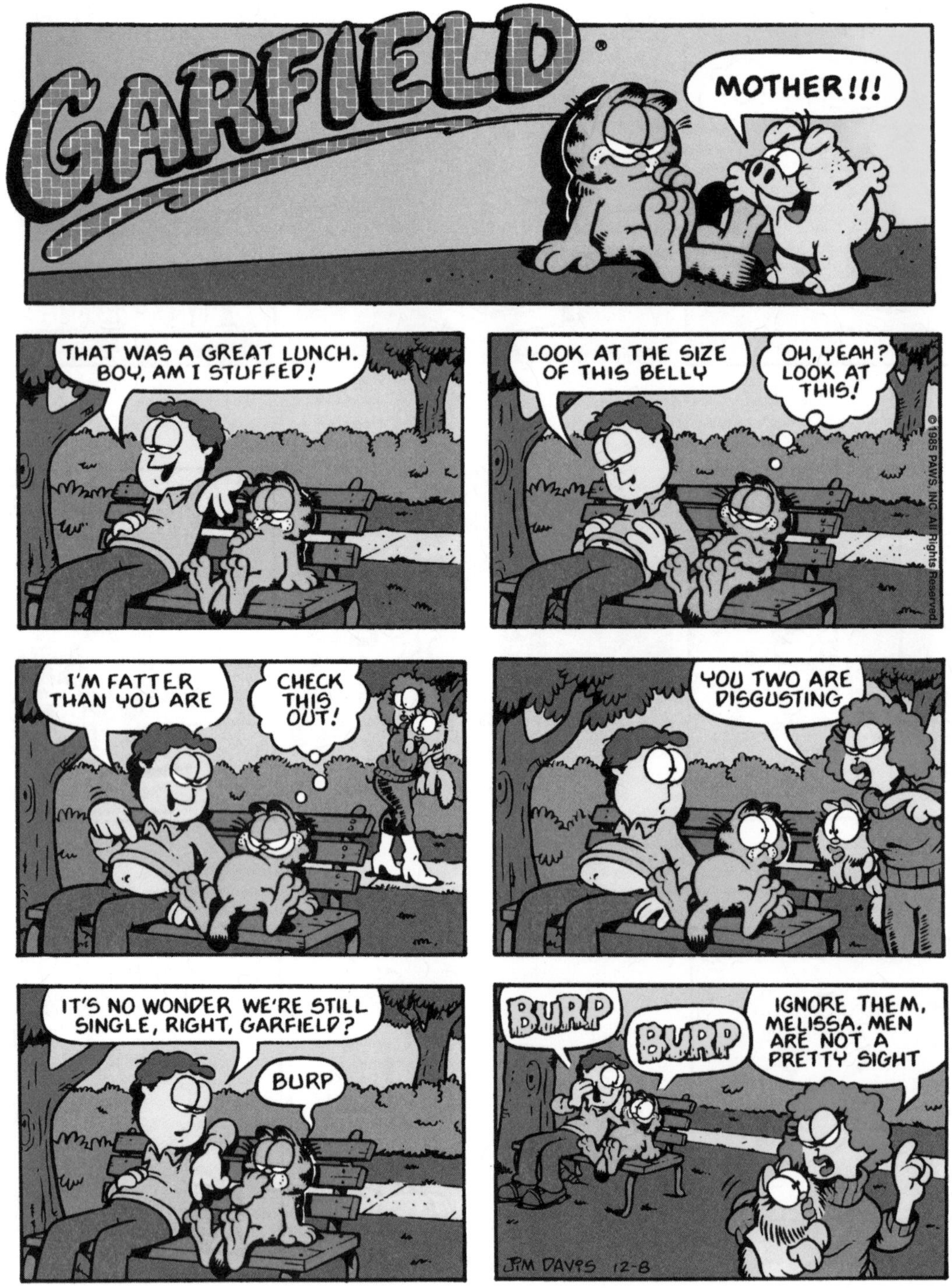
GARFIELD®
MOTHER!!!
THAT WAS A GREAT LUNCH. BOY, AM I STUFFED!
LOOK AT THE SIZE OF THIS BELLY
OH, YEAH? LOOK AT THIS!
© 1985 PAWS, INC. All Rights Reserved.
I'M FATTER THAN YOU ARE
CHECK THIS OUT!
YOU TWO ARE DISGUSTING
IT'S NO WONDER WE'RE STILL SINGLE, RIGHT, GARFIELD?
BURP
BURP
BURP
IGNORE THEM, MELISSA. MEN ARE NOT A PRETTY SIGHT
JIM DAVIS 12-8

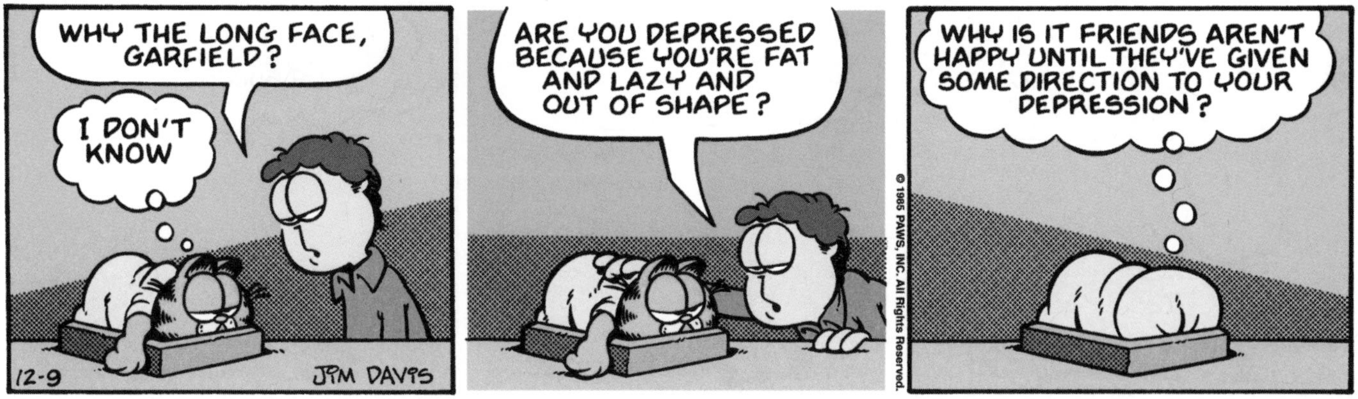
WHY THE LONG FACE, GARFIELD?
I DON'T KNOW
ARE YOU DEPRESSED BECAUSE YOU'RE FAT AND LAZY AND OUT OF SHAPE?
WHY IS IT FRIENDS AREN'T HAPPY UNTIL THEY'VE GIVEN SOME DIRECTION TO YOUR DEPRESSION?
12-9
JIM DAVIS
© 1985 PAWS, INC. All Rights Reserved.

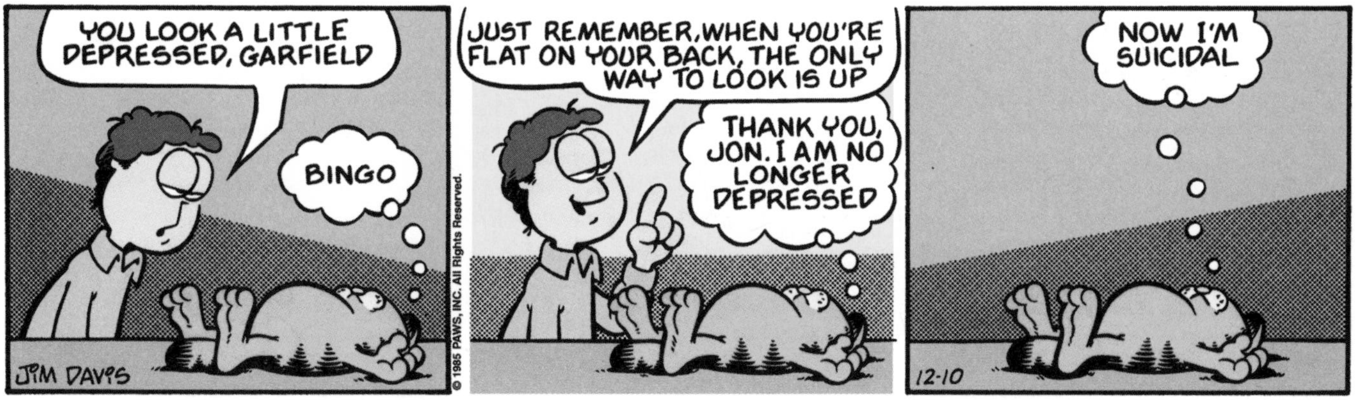
YOU LOOK A LITTLE DEPRESSED, GARFIELD
BINGO
JUST REMEMBER, WHEN YOU'RE FLAT ON YOUR BACK, THE ONLY WAY TO LOOK IS UP
THANK YOU, JON. I AM NO LONGER DEPRESSED
NOW I'M SUICIDAL
JIM DAVIS
12-10
© 1985 PAWS, INC. All Rights Reserved.

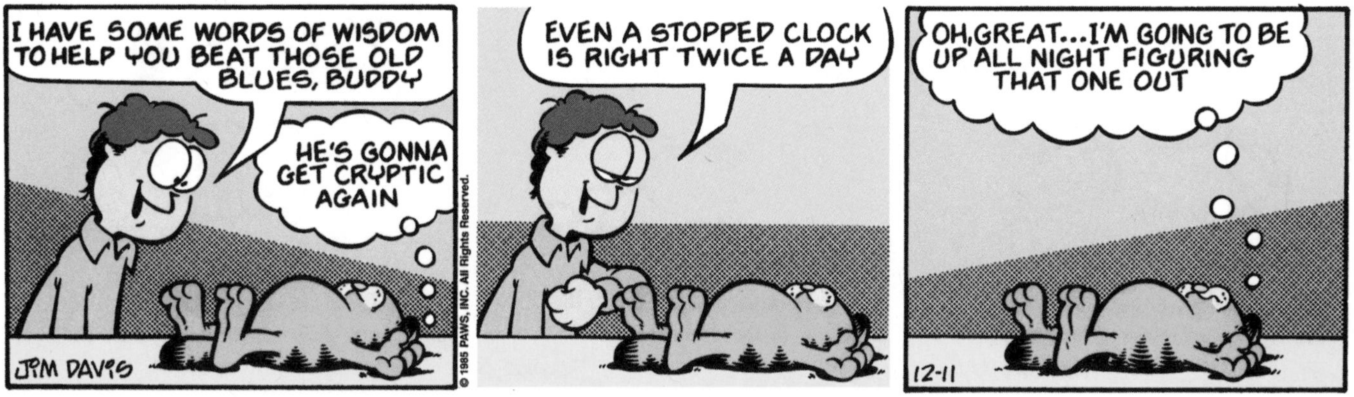
I HAVE SOME WORDS OF WISDOM TO HELP YOU BEAT THOSE OLD BLUES, BUDDY
HE'S GONNA GET CRYPTIC AGAIN
EVEN A STOPPED CLOCK IS RIGHT TWICE A DAY
OH, GREAT... I'M GOING TO BE UP ALL NIGHT FIGURING THAT ONE OUT
JIM DAVIS
12-11
© 1985 PAWS, INC. All Rights Reserved.

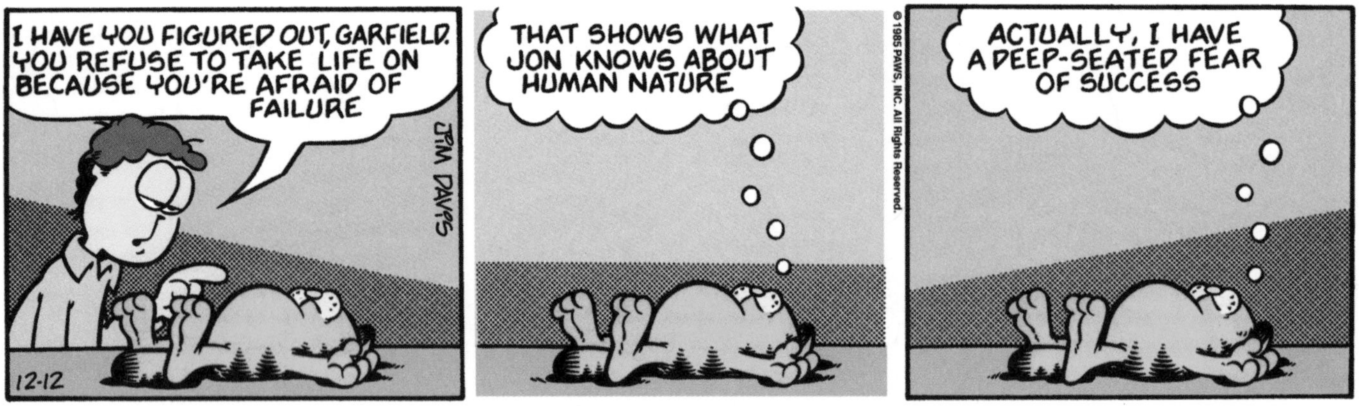
I HAVE YOU FIGURED OUT, GARFIELD. YOU REFUSE TO TAKE LIFE ON BECAUSE YOU'RE AFRAID OF FAILURE
JIM DAVIS
12-12
THAT SHOWS WHAT JON KNOWS ABOUT HUMAN NATURE
© 1985 PAWS, INC. All Rights Reserved.
ACTUALLY, I HAVE A DEEP-SEATED FEAR OF SUCCESS

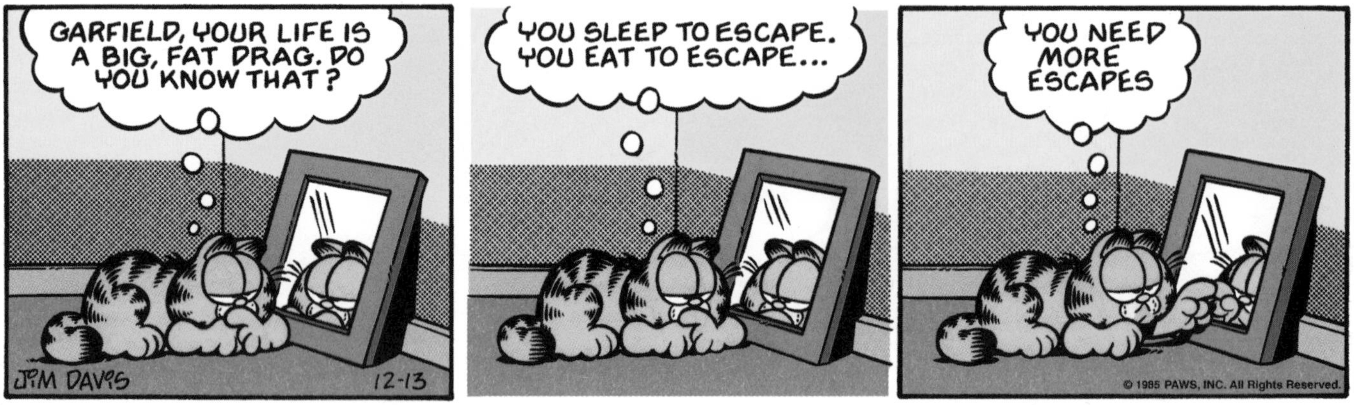
GARFIELD, YOUR LIFE IS A BIG, FAT DRAG. DO YOU KNOW THAT?
JIM DAVIS
12-13
YOU SLEEP TO ESCAPE. YOU EAT TO ESCAPE...
YOU NEED MORE ESCAPES
© 1985 PAWS, INC. All Rights Reserved.

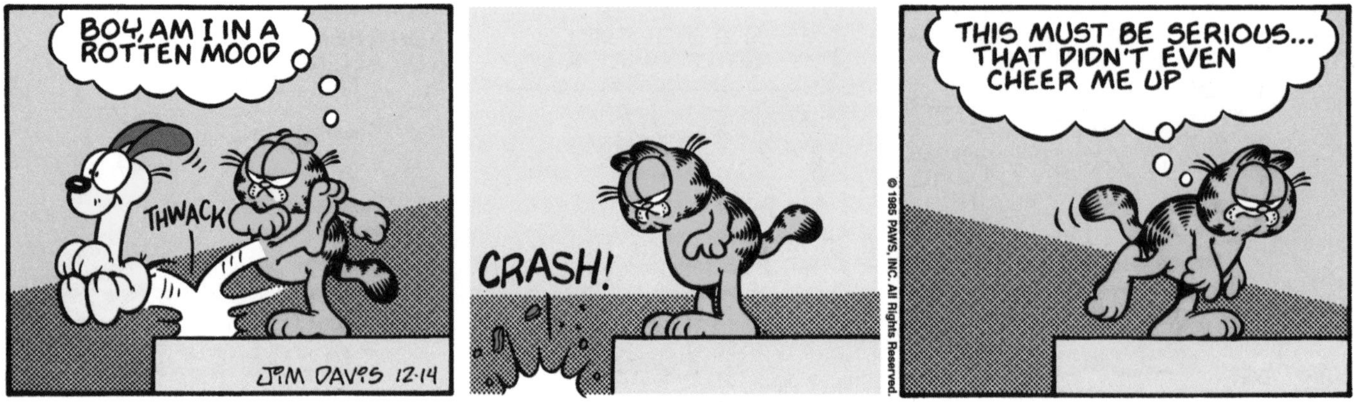
BOY, AM I IN A ROTTEN MOOD
THWACK
JIM DAVIS 12-14
CRASH!
© 1985 PAWS, INC. All Rights Reserved.
THIS MUST BE SERIOUS... THAT DIDN'T EVEN CHEER ME UP

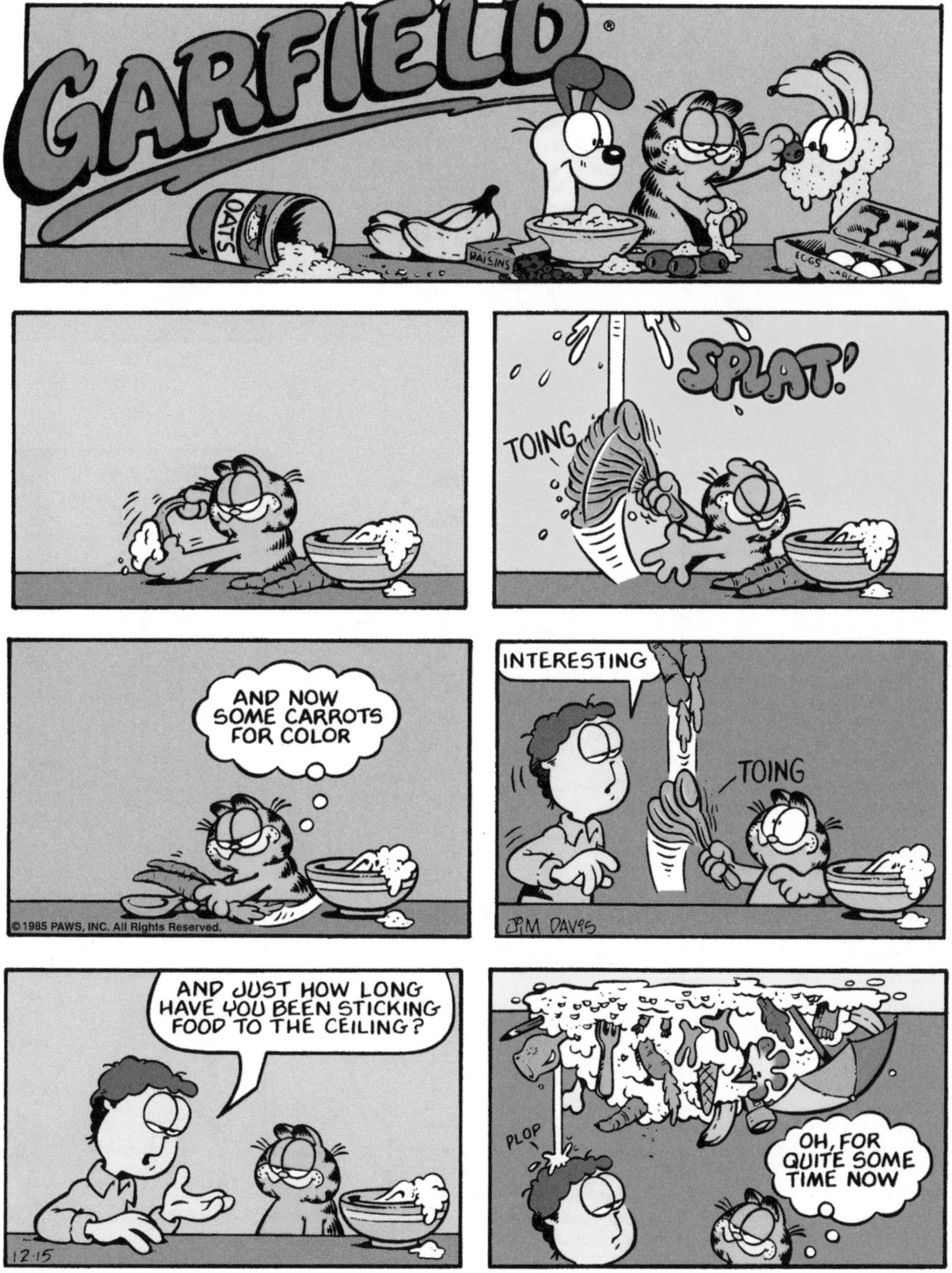

GARFIELD®
OATS
RAISINS
EGGS
SPLAT!
TOING
AND NOW SOME CARROTS FOR COLOR
© 1985 PAWS, INC. All Rights Reserved.
INTERESTING
TOING
JIM DAVIS
AND JUST HOW LONG HAVE YOU BEEN STICKING FOOD TO THE CEILING?
12·15
PLOP
OH, FOR QUITE SOME TIME NOW

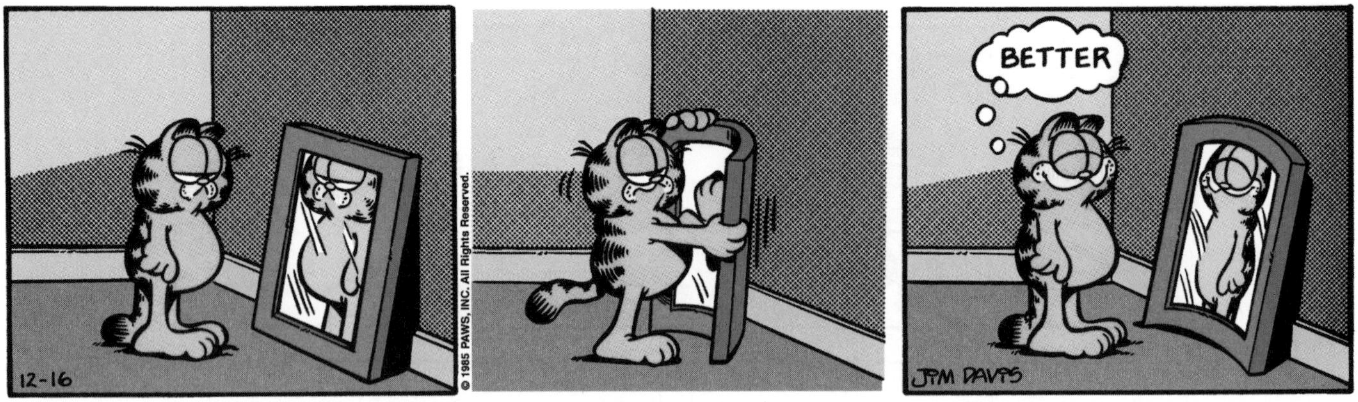
12-16
© 1985 PAWS, INC. All Rights Reserved.
BETTER
JIM DAVIS

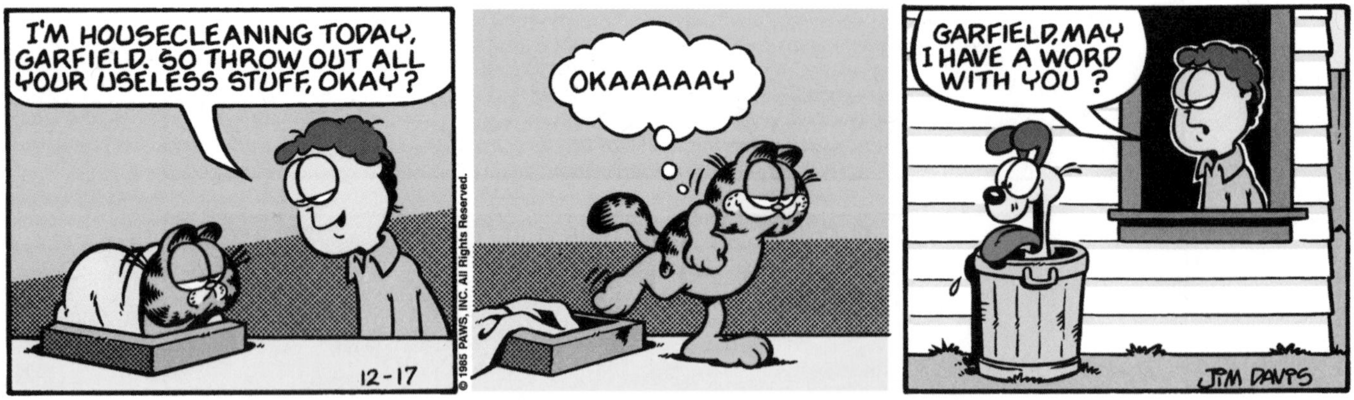
I'M HOUSECLEANING TODAY, GARFIELD. SO THROW OUT ALL YOUR USELESS STUFF, OKAY?
12-17
© 1985 PAWS, INC. All Rights Reserved.
OKAAAAAY
GARFIELD, MAY I HAVE A WORD WITH YOU?
JIM DAVIS

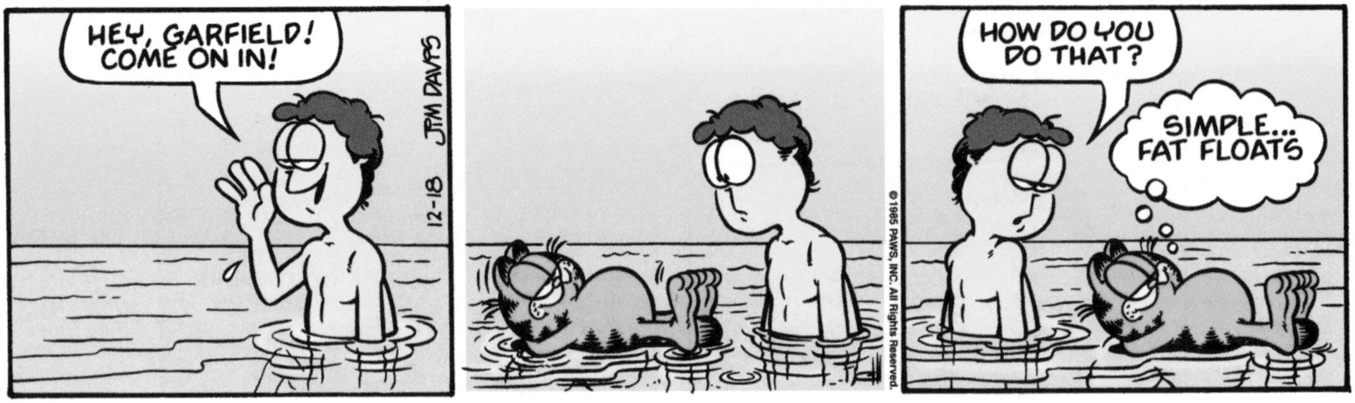
HEY, GARFIELD! COME ON IN!
JIM DAVIS
12-18
© 1985 PAWS, INC. All Rights Reserved.
HOW DO YOU DO THAT?
SIMPLE... FAT FLOATS

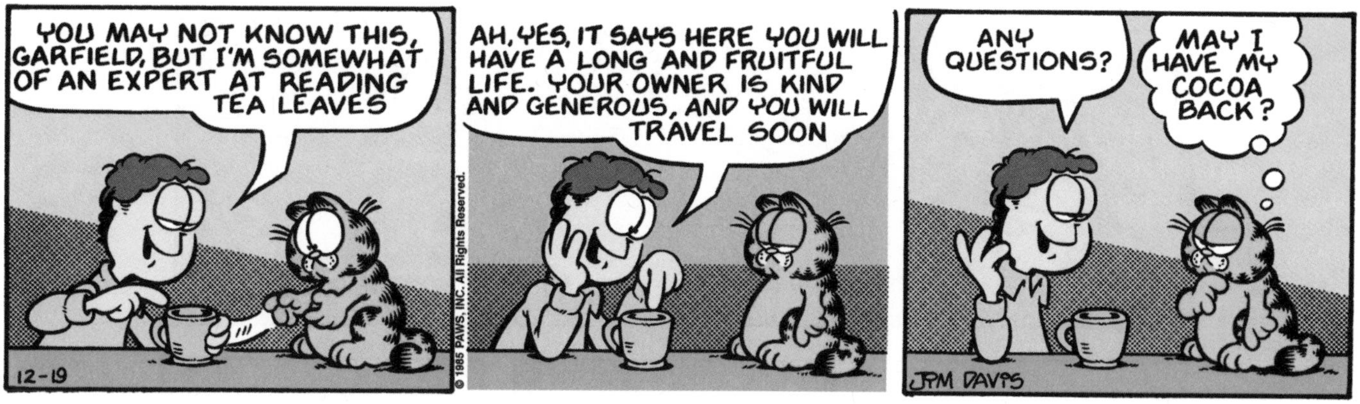
YOU MAY NOT KNOW THIS, GARFIELD, BUT I'M SOMEWHAT OF AN EXPERT AT READING TEA LEAVES
12-19
AH, YES, IT SAYS HERE YOU WILL HAVE A LONG AND FRUITFUL LIFE. YOUR OWNER IS KIND AND GENEROUS, AND YOU WILL TRAVEL SOON
© 1985 PAWS, INC. All Rights Reserved.
ANY QUESTIONS?
MAY I HAVE MY COCOA BACK?
JIM DAVIS

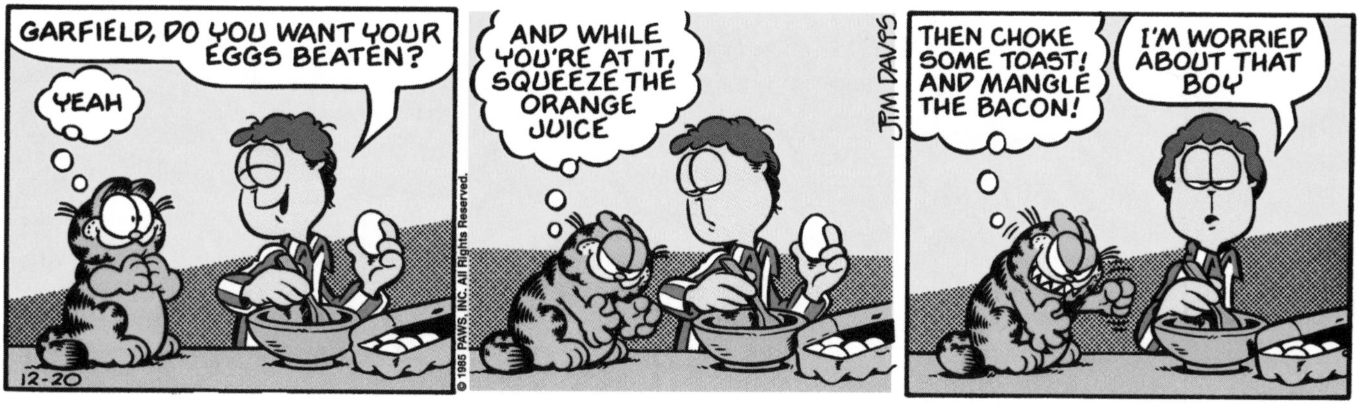
GARFIELD, DO YOU WANT YOUR EGGS BEATEN?
YEAH
12-20
© 1985 PAWS, INC. All Rights Reserved.
AND WHILE YOU'RE AT IT, SQUEEZE THE ORANGE JUICE
JIM DAVIS
THEN CHOKE SOME TOAST! AND MANGLE THE BACON!
I'M WORRIED ABOUT THAT BOY

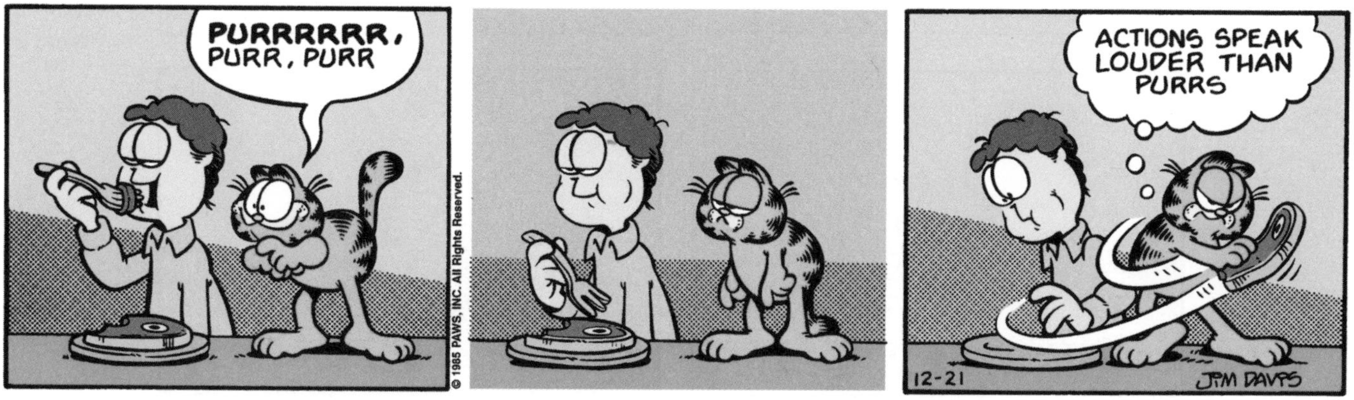
PURRRRRR, PURR, PURR
© 1985 PAWS, INC. All Rights Reserved.
ACTIONS SPEAK LOUDER THAN PURRS
12-21
JIM DAVIS

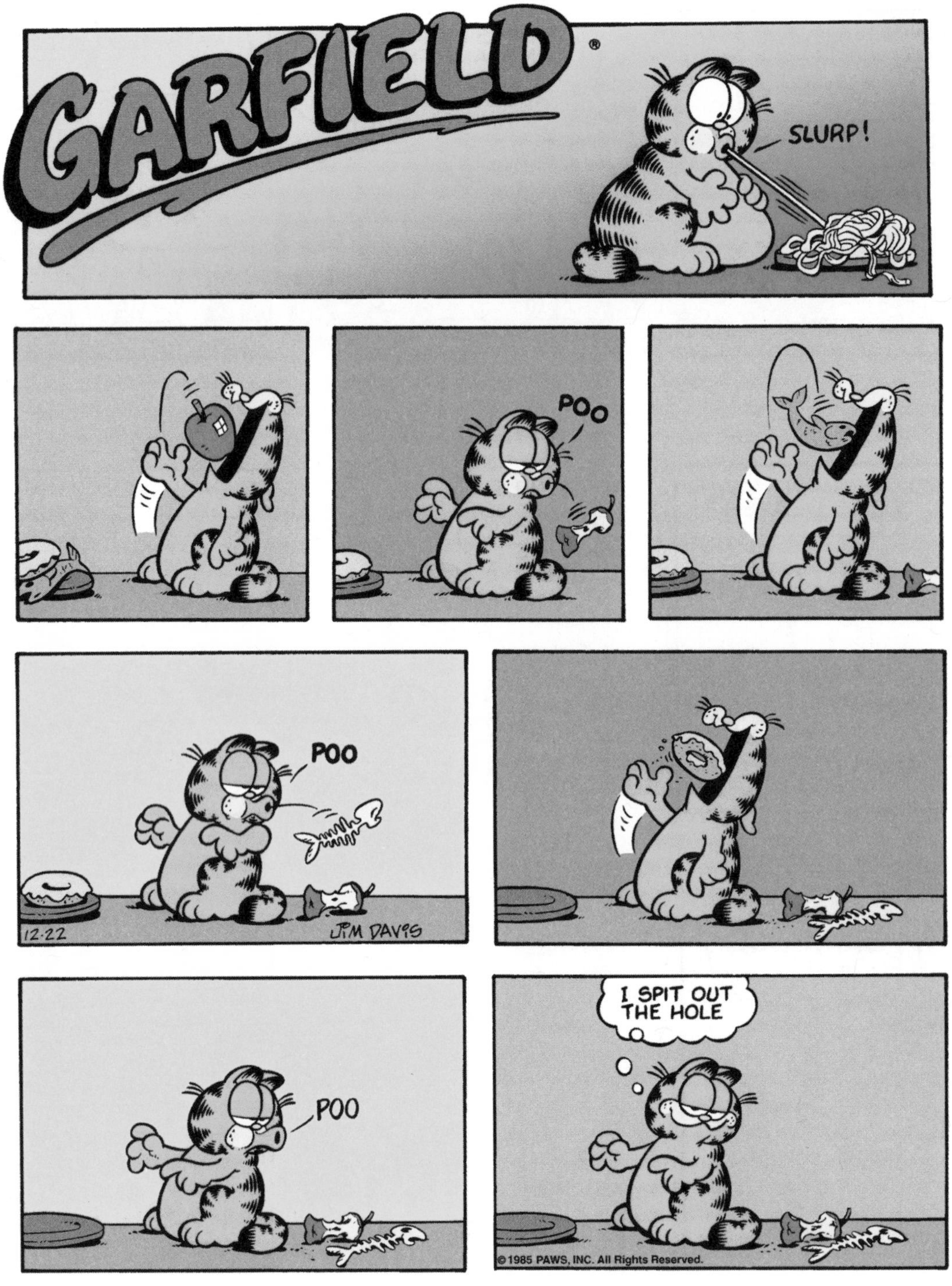
GARFIELD
SLURP!
POO
POO
12-22
JIM DAVIS
POO
I SPIT OUT THE HOLE
© 1985 PAWS, INC. All Rights Reserved.

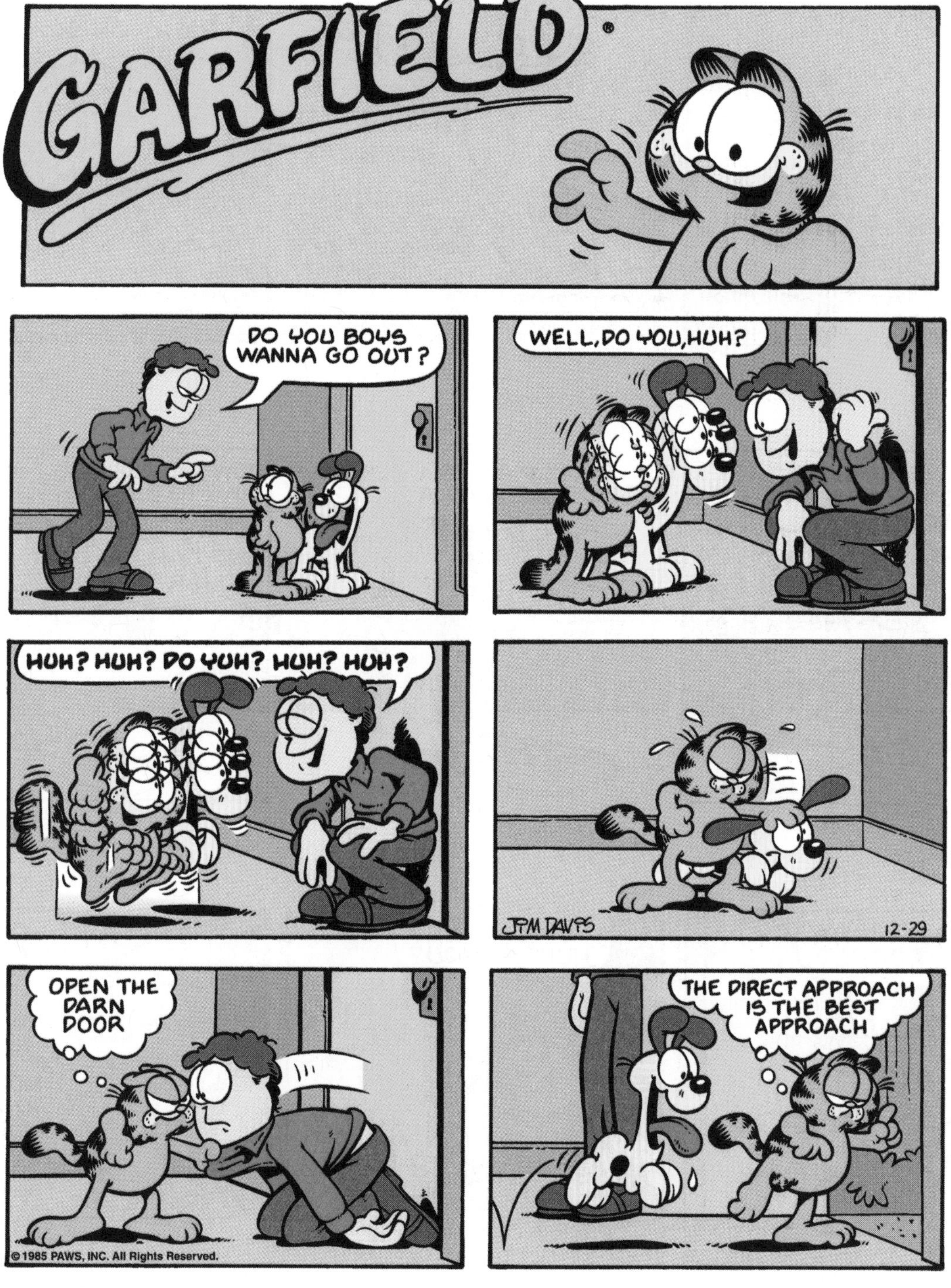
GARFIELD®
DO YOU BOYS WANNA GO OUT?
WELL, DO YOU, HUH?
HUH? HUH? DO YUH? HUH? HUH?
JIM DAVIS
12-29
OPEN THE DARN DOOR
THE DIRECT APPROACH IS THE BEST APPROACH
© 1985 PAWS, INC. All Rights Reserved.

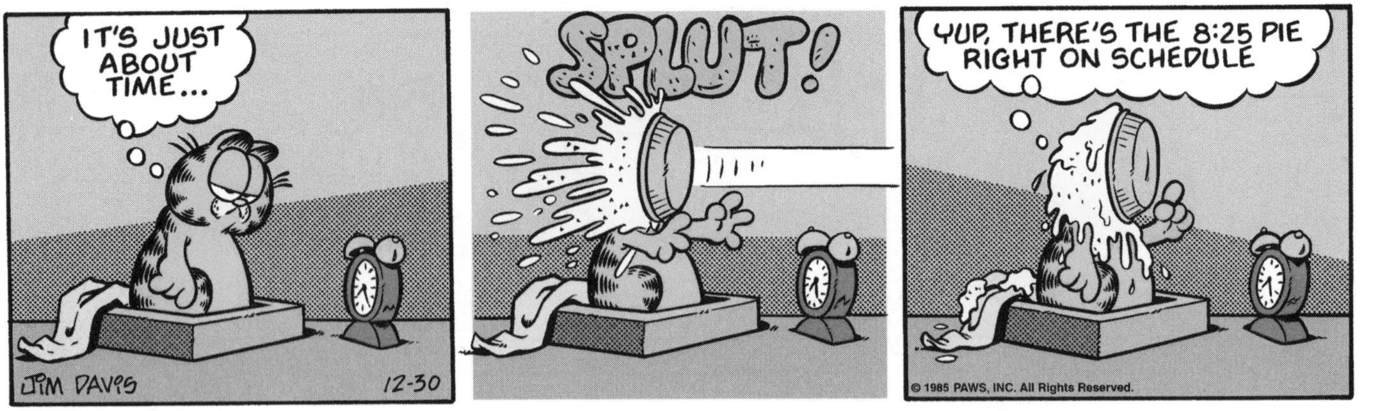
IT'S JUST ABOUT TIME...
JIM DAVIS
12-30
SPLUT!
YUP, THERE'S THE 8:25 PIE RIGHT ON SCHEDULE
© 1985 PAWS, INC. All Rights Reserved.

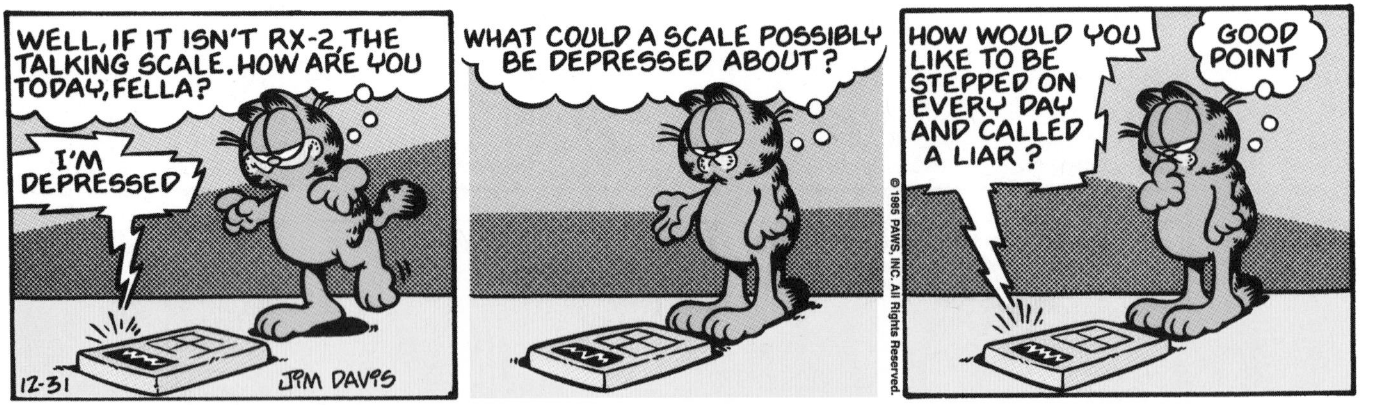
WELL, IF IT ISN'T RX-2, THE TALKING SCALE. HOW ARE YOU TODAY, FELLA?
I'M DEPRESSED
12-31
JIM DAVIS
WHAT COULD A SCALE POSSIBLY BE DEPRESSED ABOUT?
© 1985 PAWS, INC. All Rights Reserved.
HOW WOULD YOU LIKE TO BE STEPPED ON EVERY DAY AND CALLED A LIAR?
GOOD POINT

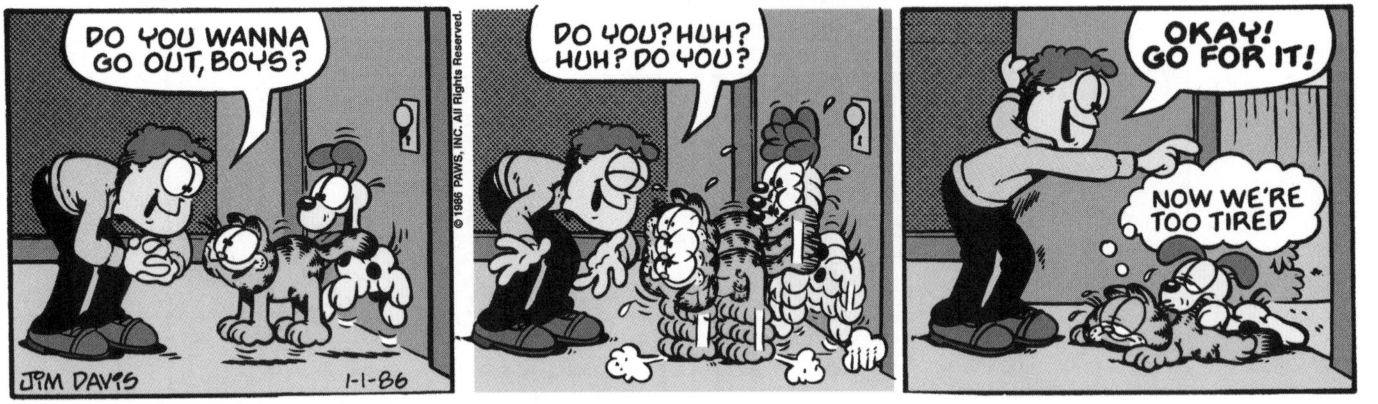
DO YOU WANNA GO OUT, BOYS?
JIM DAVIS
1-1-86
© 1986 PAWS, INC. All Rights Reserved.
DO YOU? HUH? HUH? DO YOU?
OKAY! GO FOR IT!
NOW WE'RE TOO TIRED

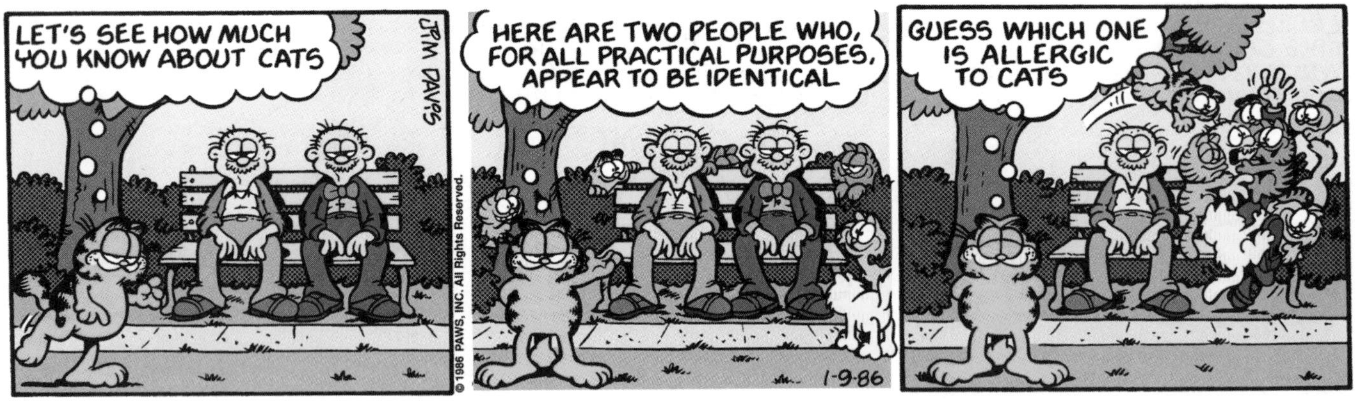
LET'S SEE HOW MUCH YOU KNOW ABOUT CATS
JIM DAVIS
© 1986 PAWS, INC. All Rights Reserved.
HERE ARE TWO PEOPLE WHO, FOR ALL PRACTICAL PURPOSES, APPEAR TO BE IDENTICAL
1-9-86
GUESS WHICH ONE IS ALLERGIC TO CATS

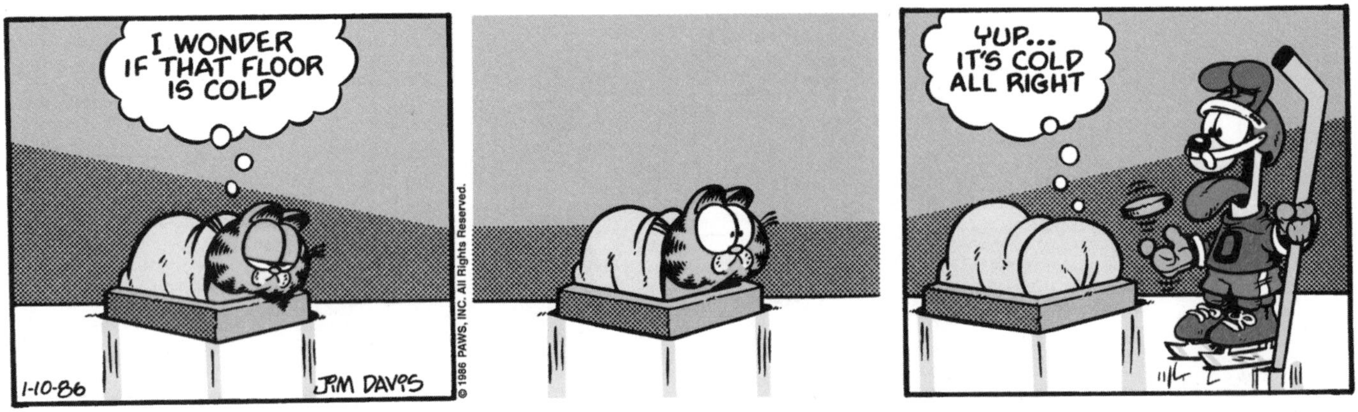
I WONDER IF THAT FLOOR IS COLD
1-10-86
JIM DAVIS
© 1986 PAWS, INC. All Rights Reserved.
YUP... IT'S COLD ALL RIGHT

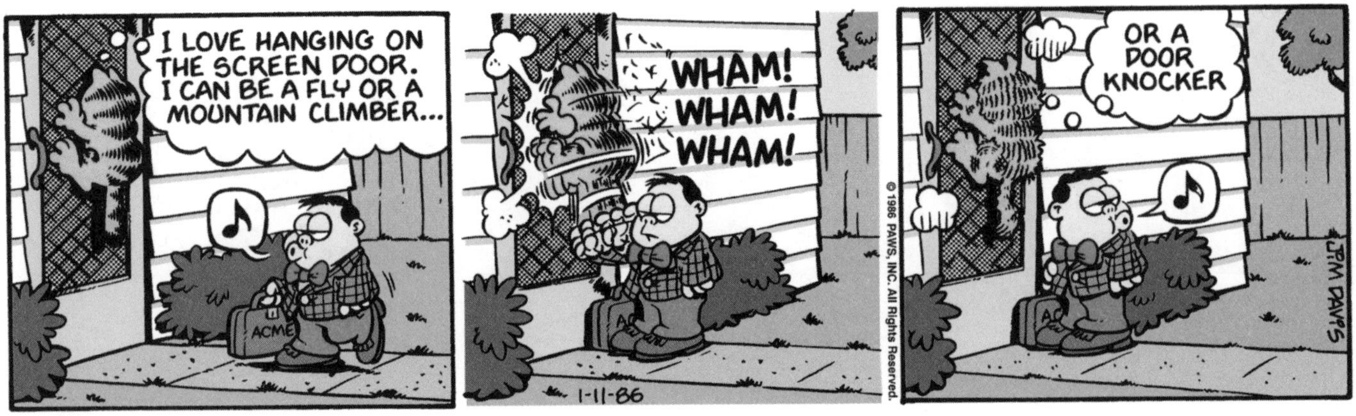
I LOVE HANGING ON THE SCREEN DOOR. I CAN BE A FLY OR A MOUNTAIN CLIMBER...
ACME
WHAM!
WHAM!
WHAM!
1-11-86
© 1986 PAWS, INC. All Rights Reserved.
OR A DOOR KNOCKER
JIM DAVIS

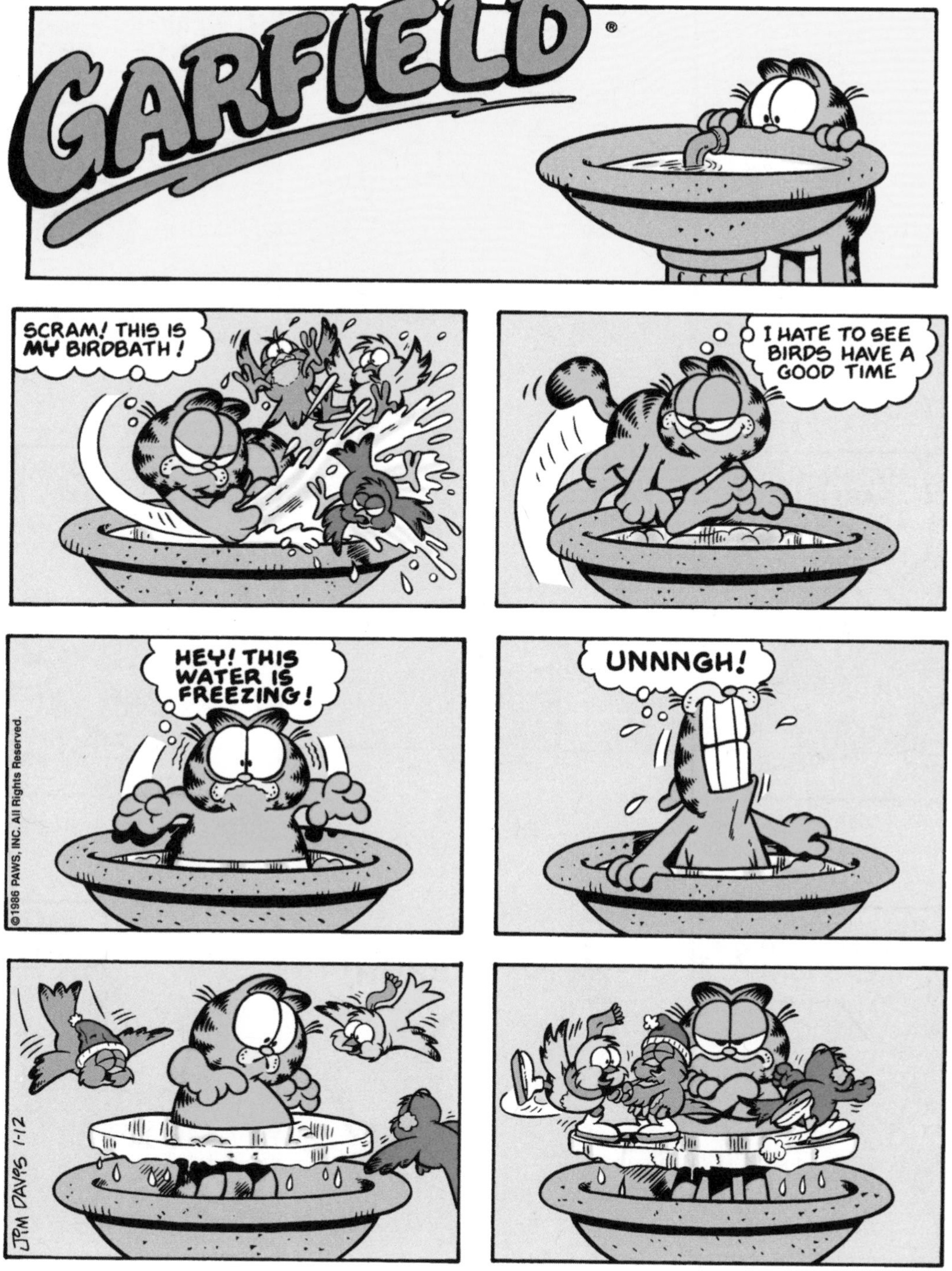
GARFIELD®
SCRAM! THIS IS MY BIRDBATH!
I HATE TO SEE BIRDS HAVE A GOOD TIME
HEY! THIS WATER IS FREEZING!
UNNNGH!
JPM DAVPS 1-12

74

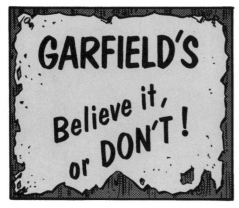

GARFIELD'S
Believe it,
or DON'T!

There is enough static electricity in 20 cats to start a car

But, it still won't start on a cold morning!

COME ON, GUYS. I'M LATE FOR WORK!

TAKE A HIKE, JACK

Z Z Z Z

Believe it, or DON'T!

GARFIELD'S
Believe it,
or DON'T!

A Jon Arbuckle claims to own a cat who can eat 10 times its body weight. To verify his claim we offered the cat 270 pounds of lasagna

The cat ate only 219 pounds of lasagna

THINGS WENT SO WELL IN REHEARSAL

Believe it, or DON'T!

GARFIELD'S
Believe it,
or DON'T!

Nick, a cat in Sweden, has eaten six mice a day for twelve years. That's over 26,000 mice!

In spite of his notoriety, poor Nick is still single

NICK, ABOUT YOUR BREATH...

Believe it, or DON'T!

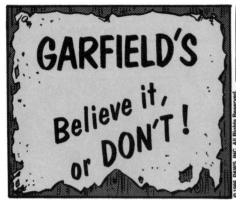

GARFIELD'S
Believe it,
or DON'T !

CATS AND DOGS EVOLVED FROM A SINGLE ANIMAL CALLED A "COG"...IT BECAME EXTINCT WHEN IT BARKED UP THE WRONG TREE...

BARK! BARK! BARK!

A TREE NAMED "BUBBA"

Believe it, or DON'T !

JIM DAVIS 1-23

GARFIELD'S
Believe it,
or DON'T !

IN 1957, A CAT IN OREGON SAVED A DROWNING CHILD

1-24

BUT, IT WAS UNDER THE LEGAL SIZE LIMIT, SO HE THREW THE KID BACK

Believe it, or DON'T !

JIM DAVIS

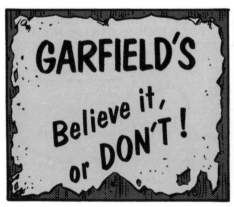

GARFIELD'S
Believe it,
or DON'T !

A CAT IN LUBBOCK, TEXAS GAVE BIRTH TO 57 KITTENS

WHEN ASKED HOW SHE FELT AFTER GIVING BIRTH TO QUINSEPTUPLETS, SHE SAID:

I'LL FEEL BETTER WHEN THEY START SLEEPING THROUGH THE NIGHT

JIM DAVIS 1-25

Believe it, or DON'T !

80

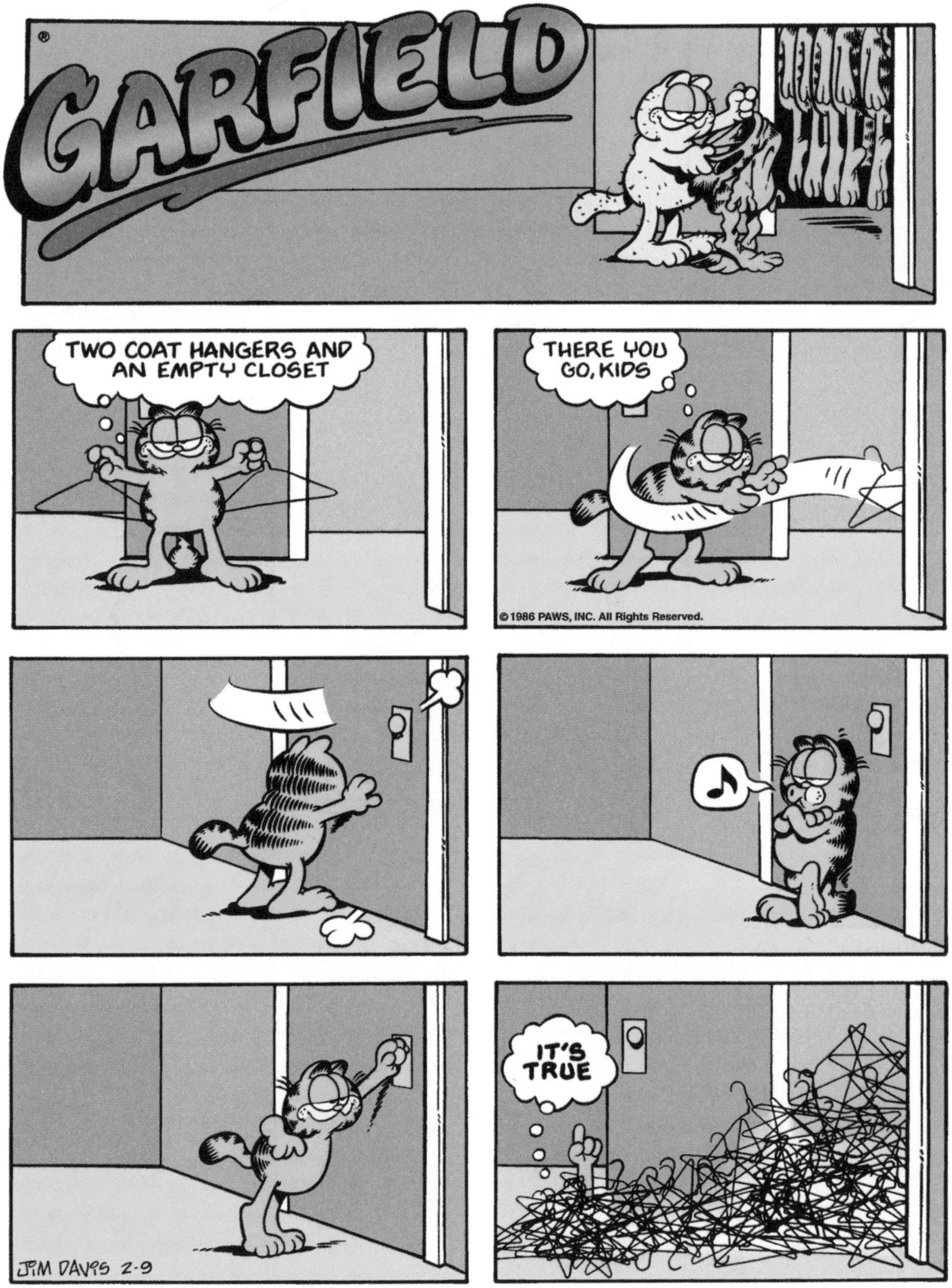
GARFIELD
TWO COAT HANGERS AND AN EMPTY CLOSET
THERE YOU GO, KIDS
© 1986 PAWS, INC. All Rights Reserved.
♪
JIM DAVIS 2-9
IT'S TRUE

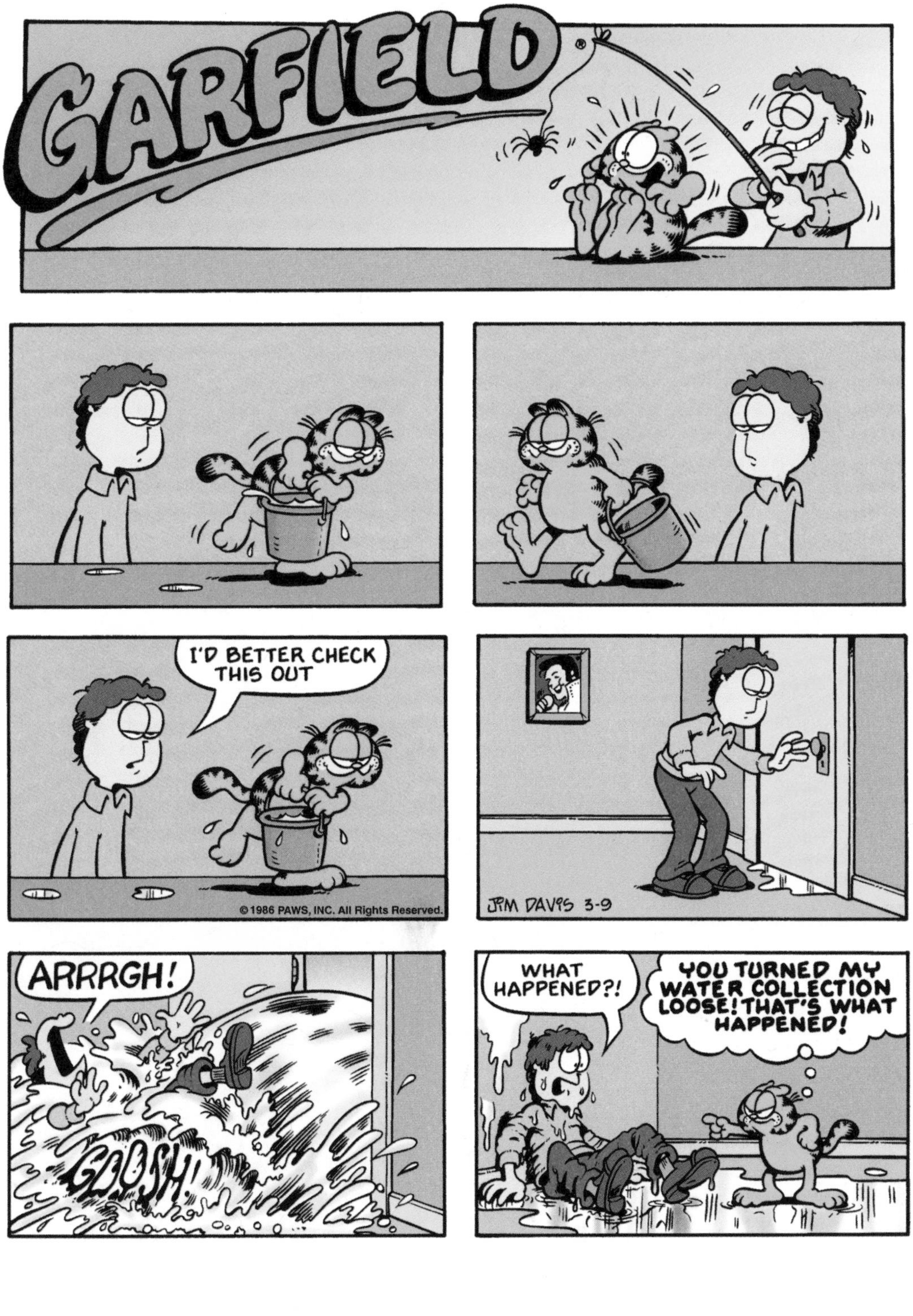
GARFIELD®
I'D BETTER CHECK THIS OUT
©1986 PAWS, INC. All Rights Reserved.
JIM DAVIS 3-9
ARRRGH!
GLOOSH!
WHAT HAPPENED?!
YOU TURNED MY WATER COLLECTION LOOSE! THAT'S WHAT HAPPENED!

GARFIELD'S 10 ALL-TIME FAVORITE BAD CAT JOKES

 1 What do you get when you cross a cat with a fish?
A carp that always lands on its feet.

 2 What does a cat take for a bad memory?
Milk of amnesia.

 3 Did you hear about the two cats who were inseparable?
They were Siamese twins.

 4 Why did the cat climb the drapes?
He had good claws to.

 5 Did you hear about the cat who was an overachiever?
He had ten lives.

 6 Why do cats eat fur balls?
They love a good gag.

 7 Did you hear about the cat who made a killing in sports?
He was in the tennis racket.

 8 I knew a cat who was so rich . . .
he had his mice monogrammed.

 9 What do you get when you cross a cat with a dog?
A badly injured dog.

 10 Can cats see in the dark?
Yes, but they have trouble holding the flashlight.

Garfield
swallows his pride

BY JIM DAVIS

Ballantine Books • **New York**

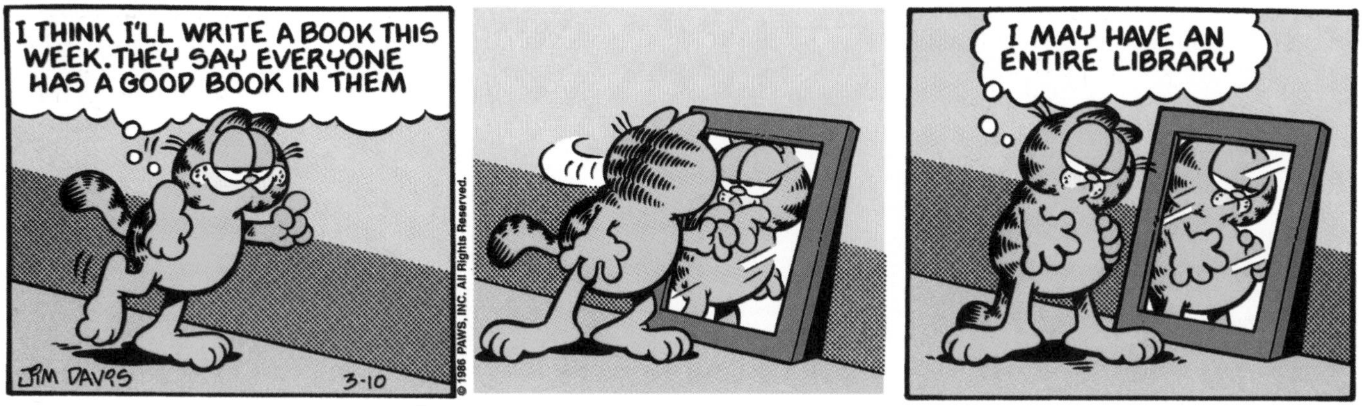
I THINK I'LL WRITE A BOOK THIS WEEK. THEY SAY EVERYONE HAS A GOOD BOOK IN THEM
I MAY HAVE AN ENTIRE LIBRARY
JIM DAVIS
3-10
© 1986 PAWS, INC. All Rights Reserved.

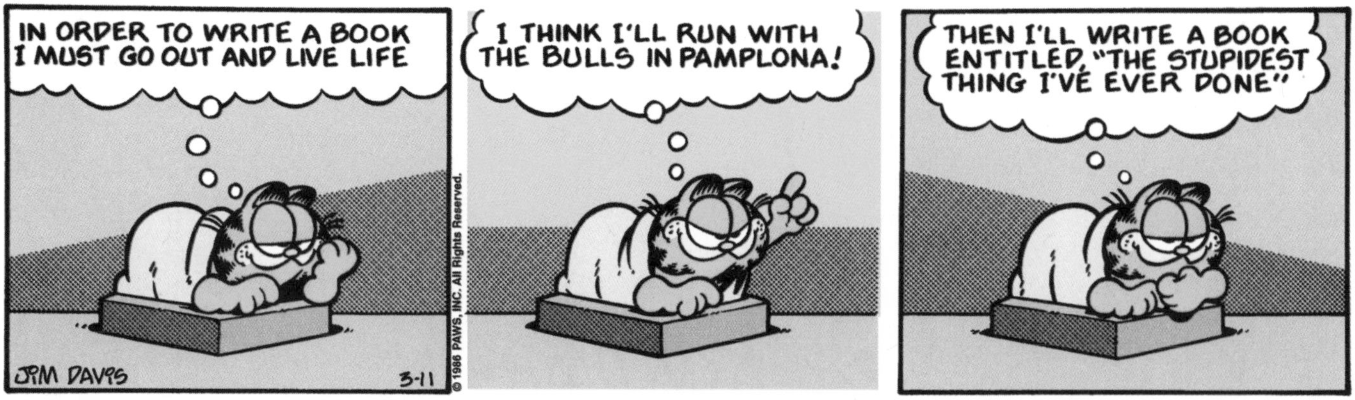
IN ORDER TO WRITE A BOOK I MUST GO OUT AND LIVE LIFE
I THINK I'LL RUN WITH THE BULLS IN PAMPLONA!
THEN I'LL WRITE A BOOK ENTITLED, "THE STUPIDEST THING I'VE EVER DONE"
JIM DAVIS
3-11
© 1986 PAWS, INC. All Rights Reserved.

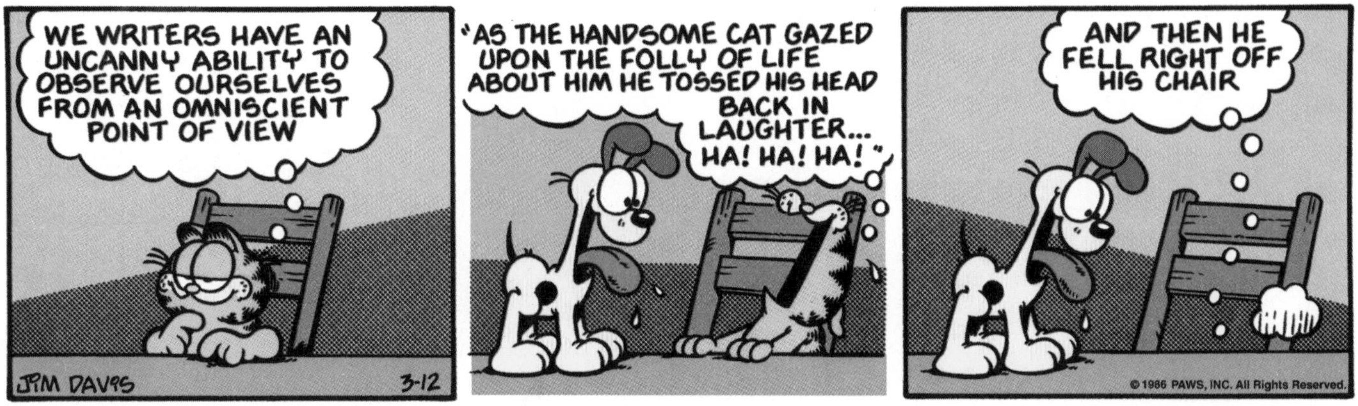
WE WRITERS HAVE AN UNCANNY ABILITY TO OBSERVE OURSELVES FROM AN OMNISCIENT POINT OF VIEW
"AS THE HANDSOME CAT GAZED UPON THE FOLLY OF LIFE ABOUT HIM HE TOSSED HIS HEAD BACK IN LAUGHTER... HA! HA! HA!"
AND THEN HE FELL RIGHT OFF HIS CHAIR
JIM DAVIS
3-12
© 1986 PAWS, INC. All Rights Reserved.

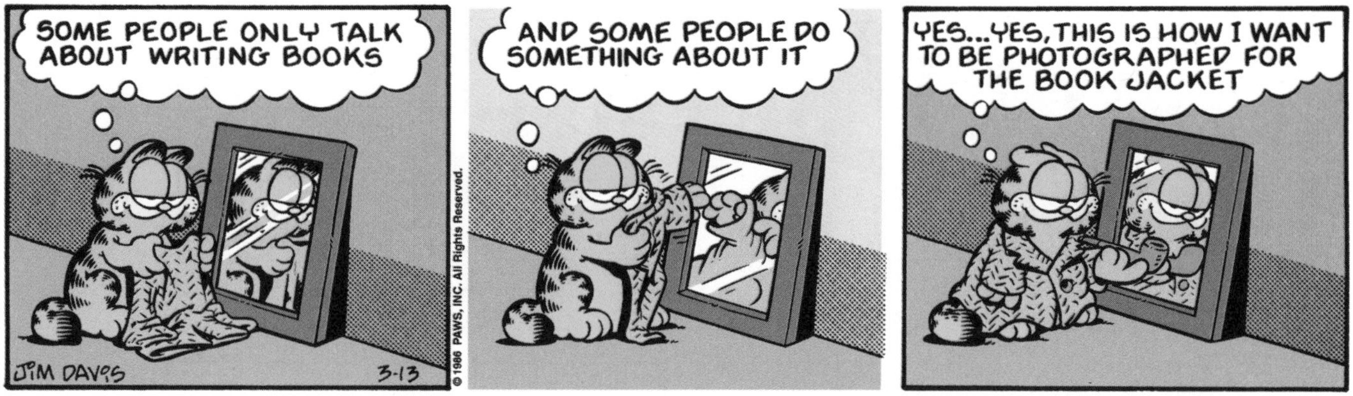
SOME PEOPLE ONLY TALK ABOUT WRITING BOOKS
JIM DAVIS 3-13
© 1986 PAWS, INC. All Rights Reserved.
AND SOME PEOPLE DO SOMETHING ABOUT IT
YES...YES, THIS IS HOW I WANT TO BE PHOTOGRAPHED FOR THE BOOK JACKET

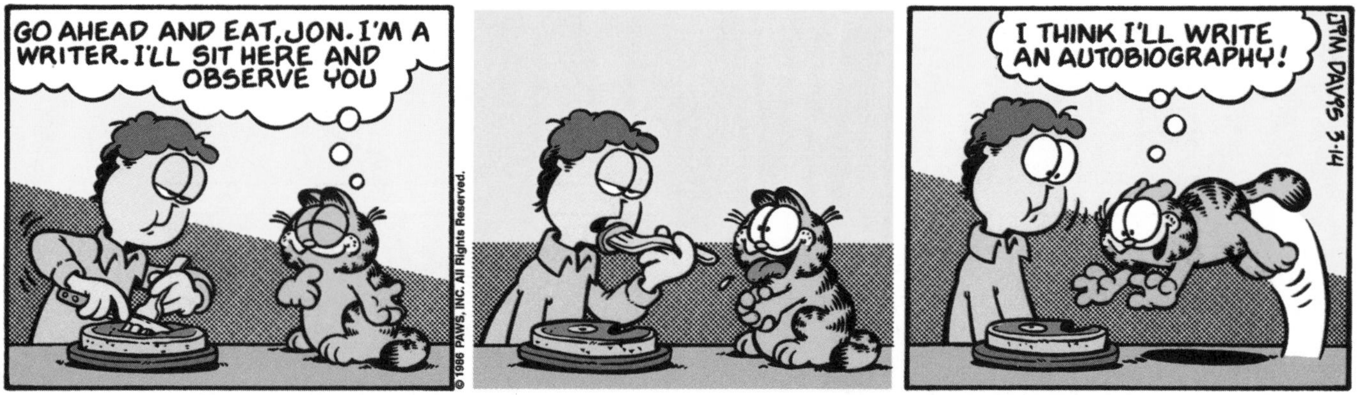
GO AHEAD AND EAT, JON. I'M A WRITER. I'LL SIT HERE AND OBSERVE YOU
© 1986 PAWS, INC. All Rights Reserved.
I THINK I'LL WRITE AN AUTOBIOGRAPHY!
JIM DAVIS 3-14

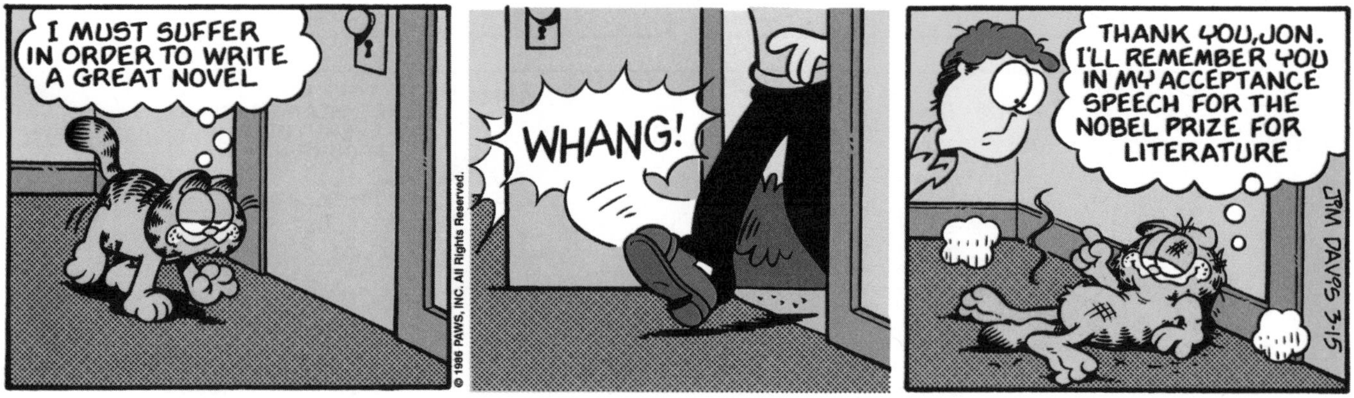
I MUST SUFFER IN ORDER TO WRITE A GREAT NOVEL
© 1986 PAWS, INC. All Rights Reserved.
WHANG!
THANK YOU, JON. I'LL REMEMBER YOU IN MY ACCEPTANCE SPEECH FOR THE NOBEL PRIZE FOR LITERATURE
JIM DAVIS 3-15

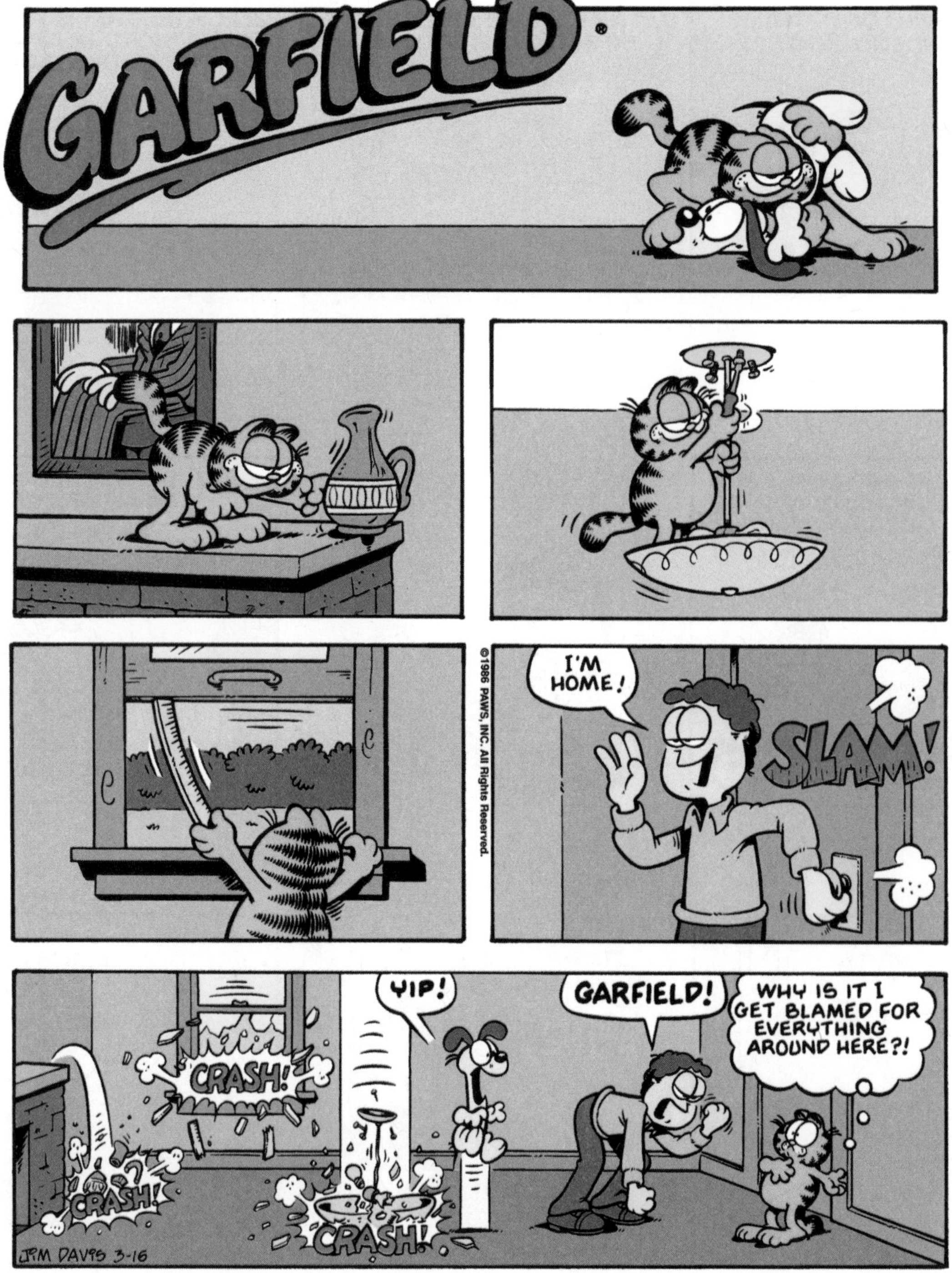

GARFIELD
©1986 PAWS, INC. All Rights Reserved.
I'M HOME!
SLAM!
CRASH!
CRASH!
YIP!
CRASH!
GARFIELD!
WHY IS IT I GET BLAMED FOR EVERYTHING AROUND HERE?!
JIM DAVIS 3-16

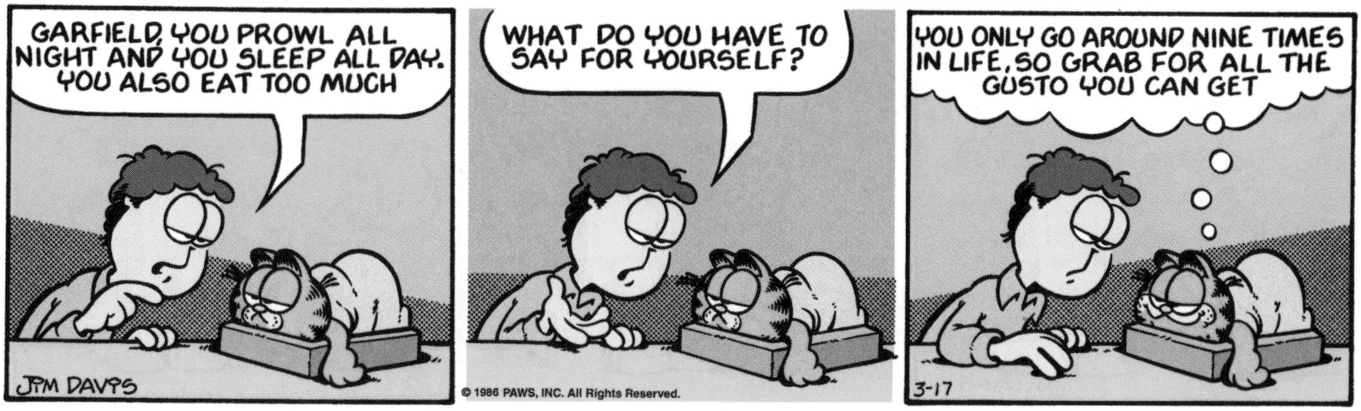
GARFIELD, YOU PROWL ALL NIGHT AND YOU SLEEP ALL DAY. YOU ALSO EAT TOO MUCH
JIM DAVIS
WHAT DO YOU HAVE TO SAY FOR YOURSELF?
© 1986 PAWS, INC. All Rights Reserved.
YOU ONLY GO AROUND NINE TIMES IN LIFE, SO GRAB FOR ALL THE GUSTO YOU CAN GET
3-17

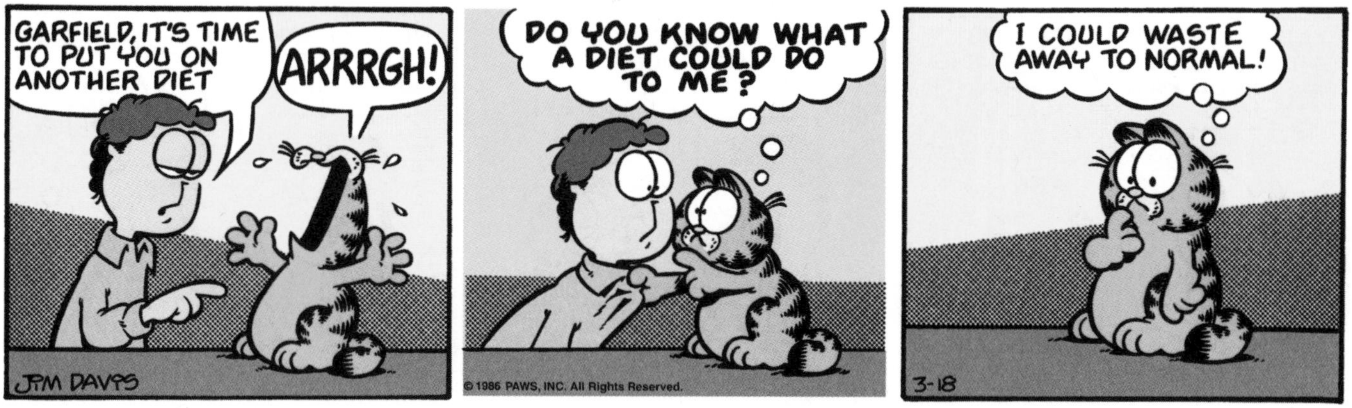
GARFIELD, IT'S TIME TO PUT YOU ON ANOTHER DIET
ARRRGH!
JIM DAVIS
DO YOU KNOW WHAT A DIET COULD DO TO ME?
© 1986 PAWS, INC. All Rights Reserved.
I COULD WASTE AWAY TO NORMAL!
3-18

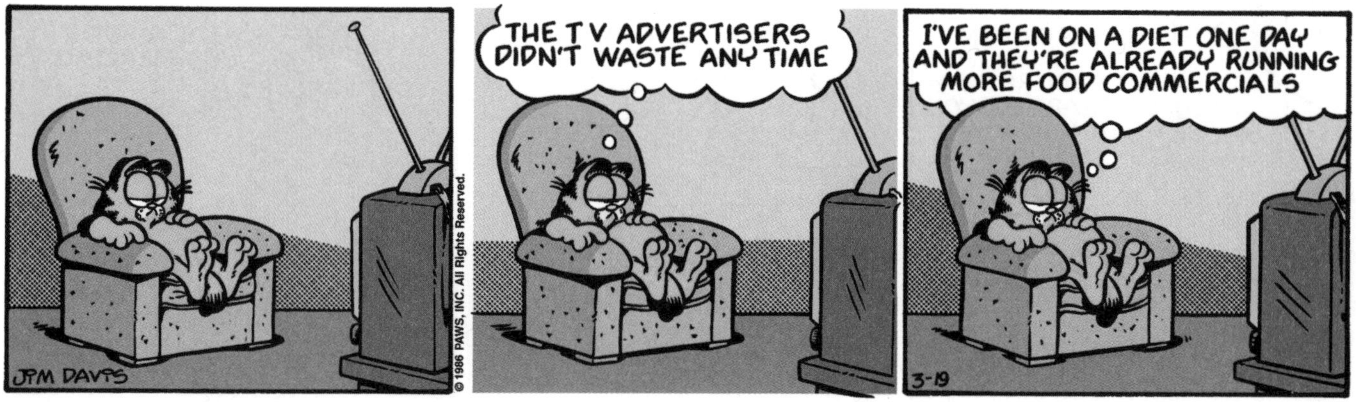
JIM DAVIS
© 1986 PAWS, INC. All Rights Reserved.
THE T V ADVERTISERS DIDN'T WASTE ANY TIME
I'VE BEEN ON A DIET ONE DAY AND THEY'RE ALREADY RUNNING MORE FOOD COMMERCIALS
3-19

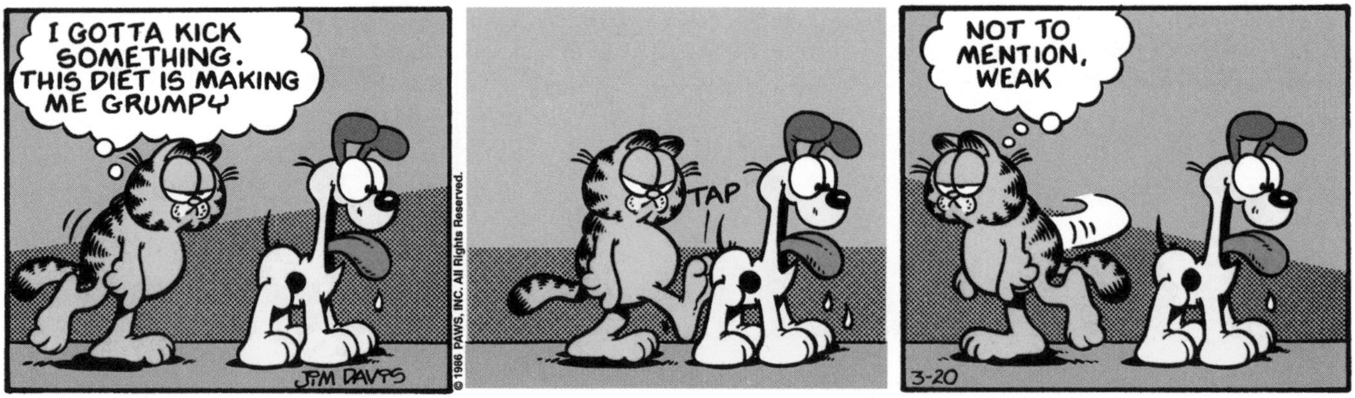
I GOTTA KICK SOMETHING. THIS DIET IS MAKING ME GRUMPY
JIM DAVIS
© 1986 PAWS, INC. All Rights Reserved.
TAP
NOT TO MENTION, WEAK
3-20

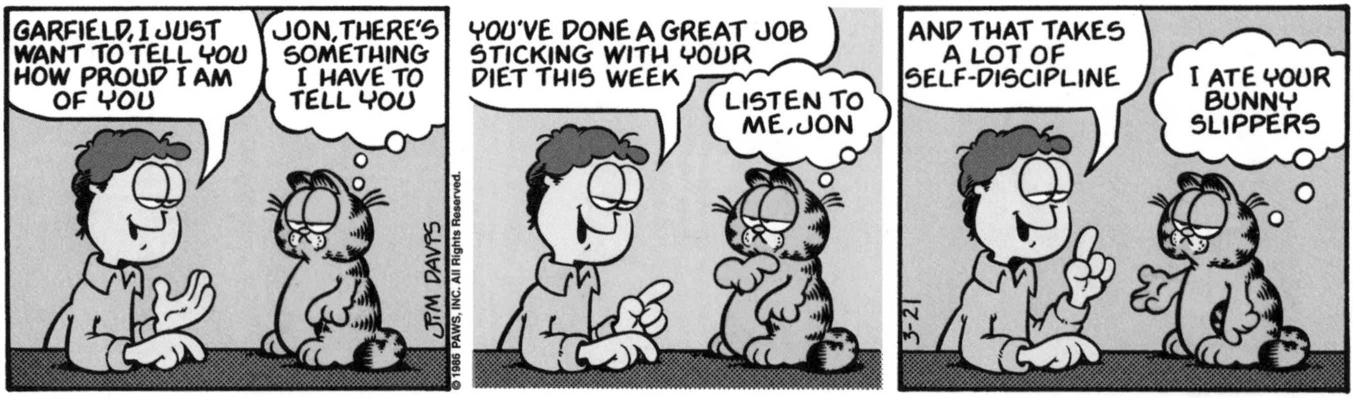
GARFIELD, I JUST WANT TO TELL YOU HOW PROUD I AM OF YOU
JON, THERE'S SOMETHING I HAVE TO TELL YOU
JIM DAVIS
© 1986 PAWS, INC. All Rights Reserved.
YOU'VE DONE A GREAT JOB STICKING WITH YOUR DIET THIS WEEK
LISTEN TO ME, JON
AND THAT TAKES A LOT OF SELF-DISCIPLINE
I ATE YOUR BUNNY SLIPPERS
3-21

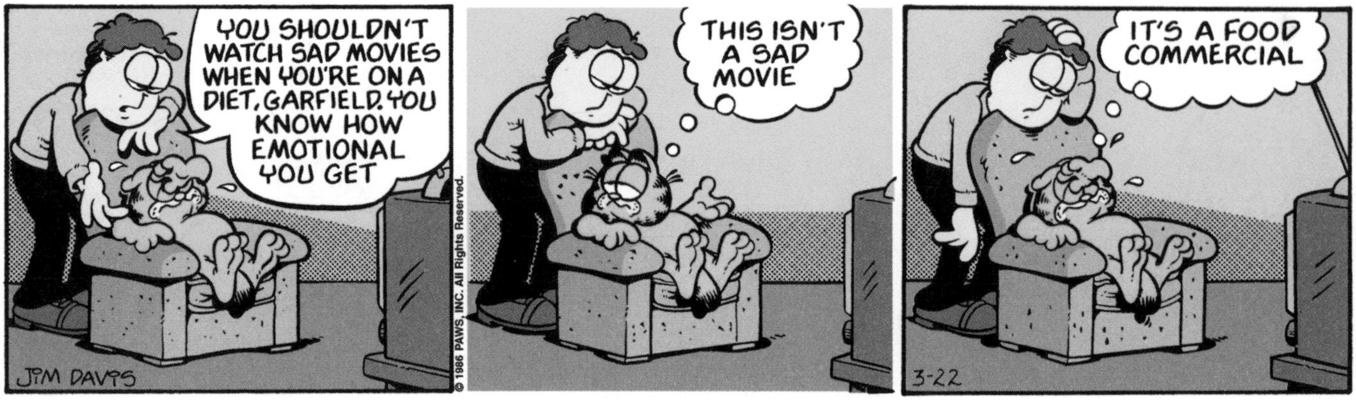
YOU SHOULDN'T WATCH SAD MOVIES WHEN YOU'RE ON A DIET, GARFIELD. YOU KNOW HOW EMOTIONAL YOU GET
JIM DAVIS
© 1986 PAWS, INC. All Rights Reserved.
THIS ISN'T A SAD MOVIE
IT'S A FOOD COMMERCIAL
3-22

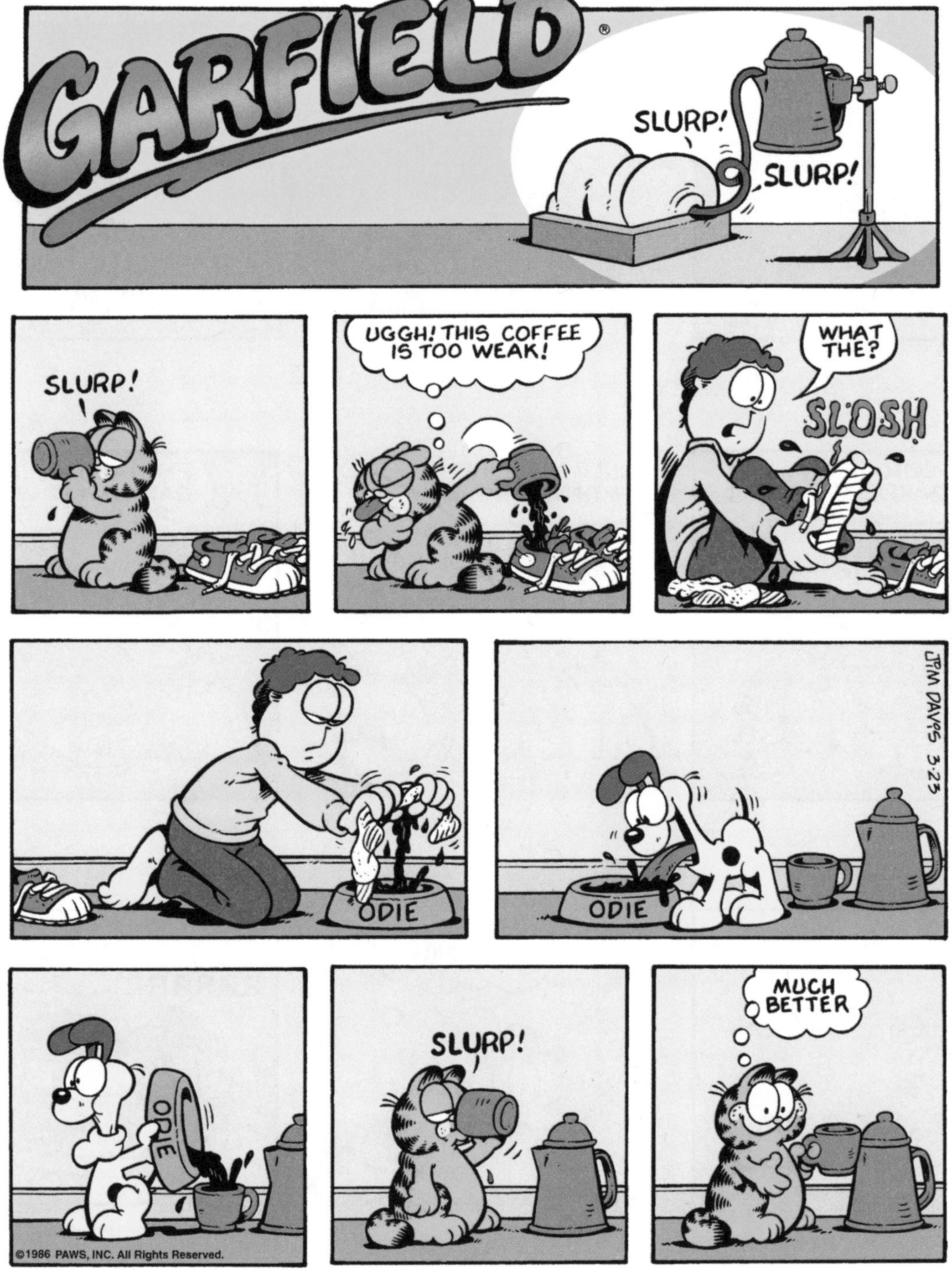
GARFIELD
SLURP!
SLURP!
SLURP!
UGGH! THIS COFFEE IS TOO WEAK!
WHAT THE?
SLOSH
JPM DAVPS 3-23
ODIE
ODIE
ODIE
SLURP!
MUCH BETTER
©1986 PAWS, INC. All Rights Reserved.

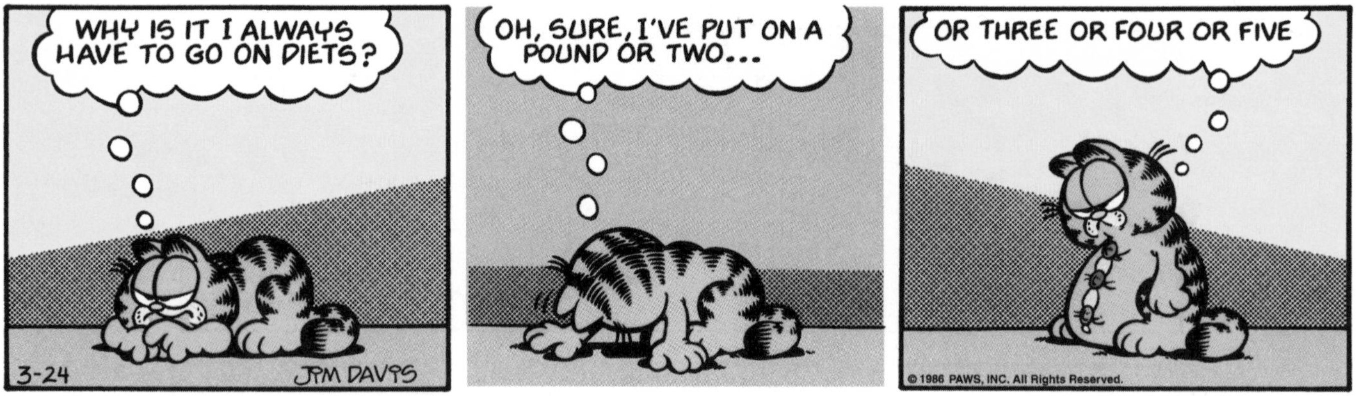
WHY IS IT I ALWAYS HAVE TO GO ON DIETS?
3-24
JIM DAVIS
OH, SURE, I'VE PUT ON A POUND OR TWO...
OR THREE OR FOUR OR FIVE
© 1986 PAWS, INC. All Rights Reserved.

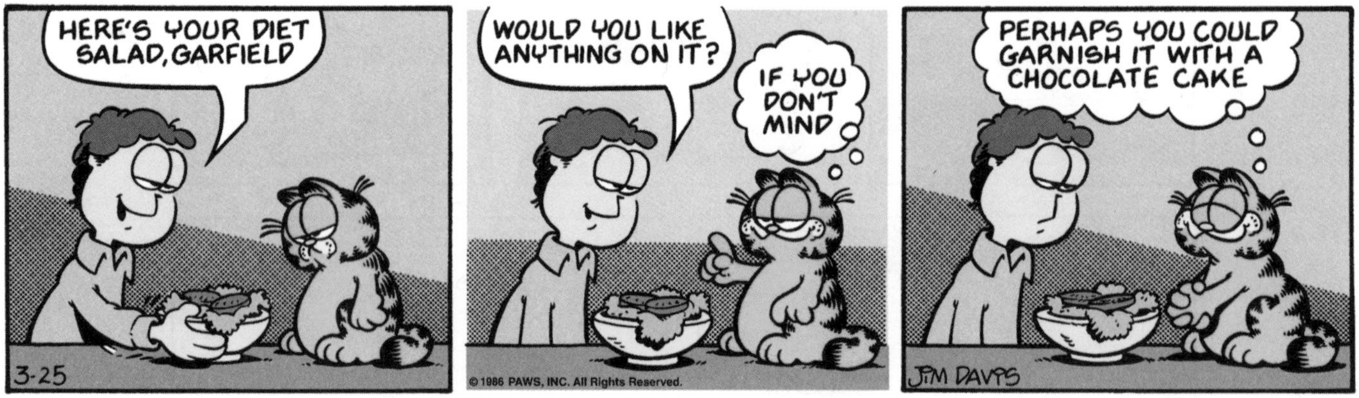
HERE'S YOUR DIET SALAD, GARFIELD
3-25
WOULD YOU LIKE ANYTHING ON IT?
IF YOU DON'T MIND
© 1986 PAWS, INC. All Rights Reserved.
PERHAPS YOU COULD GARNISH IT WITH A CHOCOLATE CAKE
JIM DAVIS

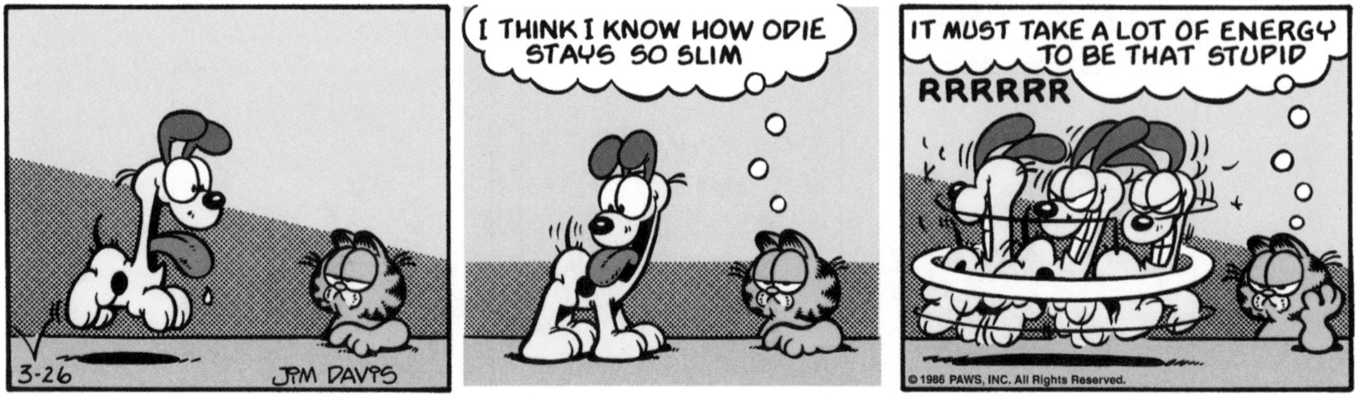
3-26
JIM DAVIS
I THINK I KNOW HOW ODIE STAYS SO SLIM
IT MUST TAKE A LOT OF ENERGY TO BE THAT STUPID
RRRRRR
© 1986 PAWS, INC. All Rights Reserved.

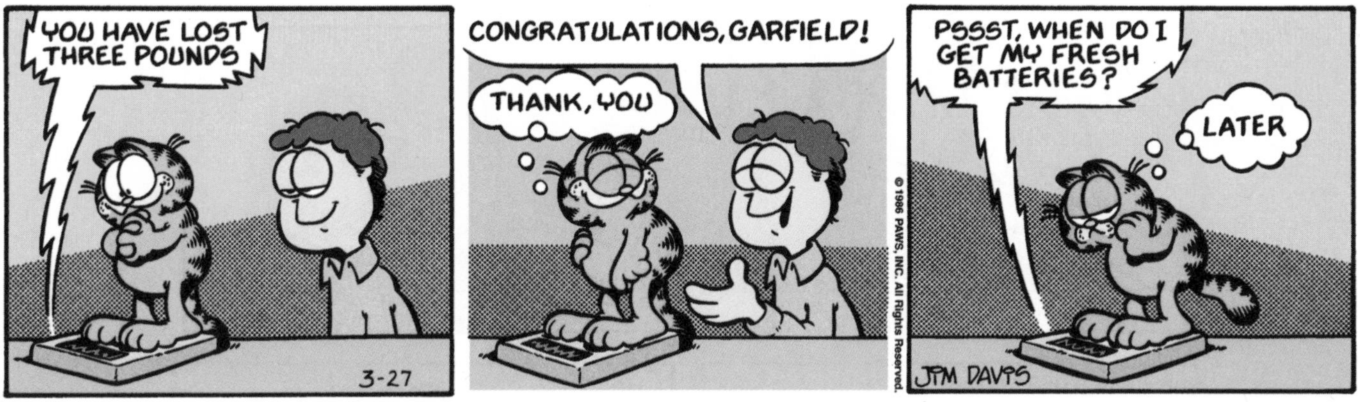
YOU HAVE LOST THREE POUNDS
3-27
CONGRATULATIONS, GARFIELD!
THANK, YOU
© 1986 PAWS, INC. All Rights Reserved.
PSSST, WHEN DO I GET MY FRESH BATTERIES?
LATER
JIM DAVIS

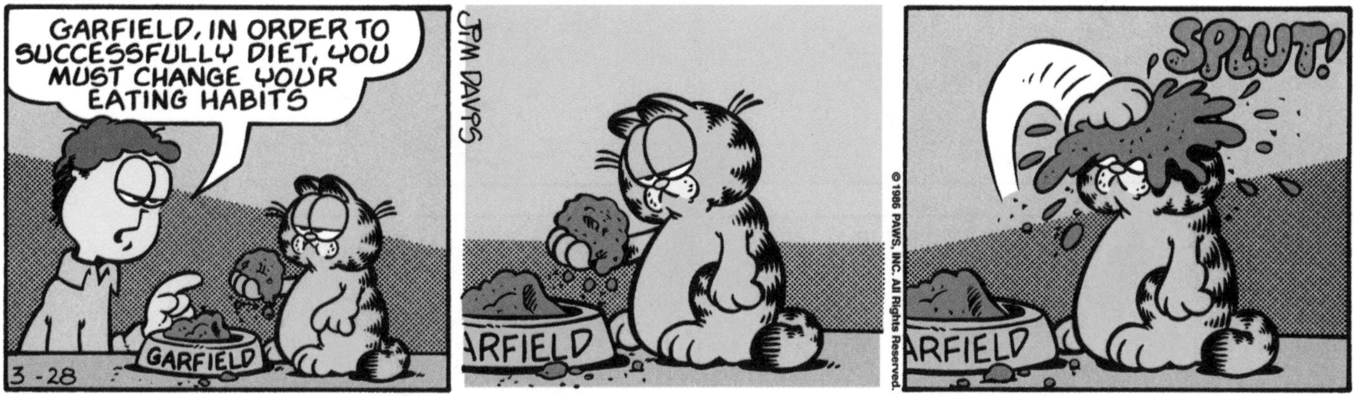
GARFIELD, IN ORDER TO SUCCESSFULLY DIET, YOU MUST CHANGE YOUR EATING HABITS
GARFIELD
3-28
JIM DAVIS
© 1986 PAWS, INC. All Rights Reserved.
SPLUT!

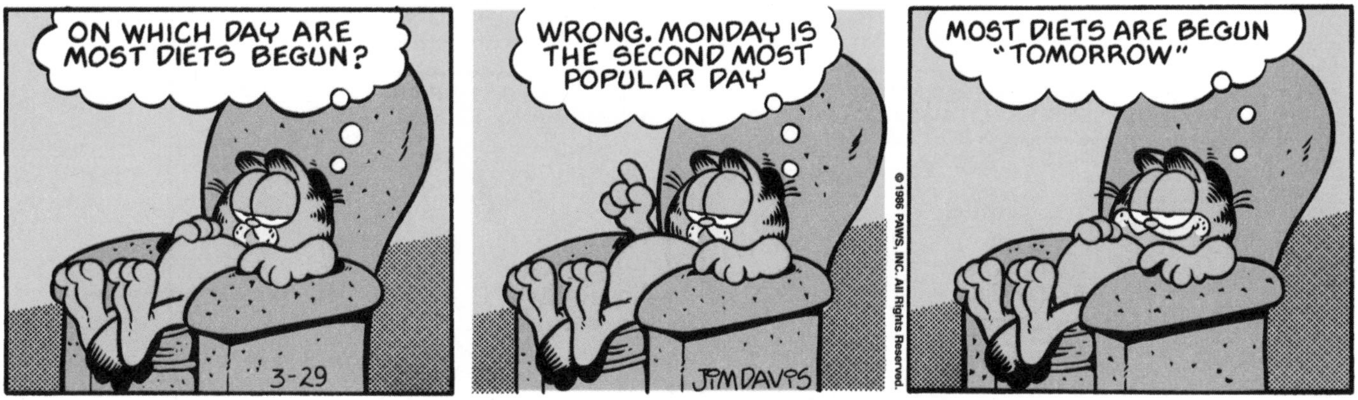
ON WHICH DAY ARE MOST DIETS BEGUN?
3-29
WRONG. MONDAY IS THE SECOND MOST POPULAR DAY
JIM DAVIS
© 1986 PAWS, INC. All Rights Reserved.
MOST DIETS ARE BEGUN "TOMORROW"

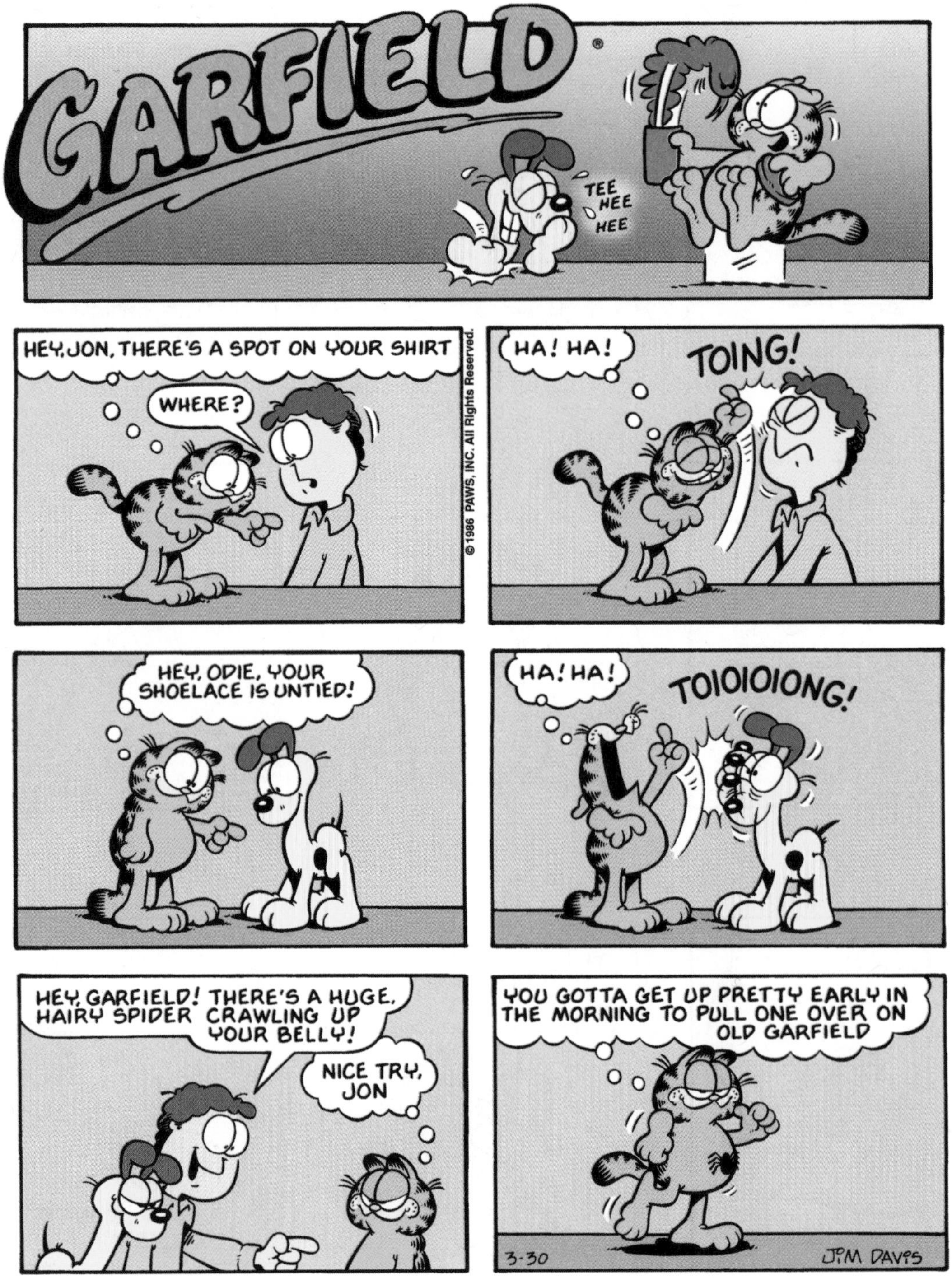

GARFIELD®
TEE HEE HEE
HEY, JON, THERE'S A SPOT ON YOUR SHIRT
WHERE?
© 1986 PAWS, INC. All Rights Reserved.
HA! HA!
TOING!
HEY, ODIE, YOUR SHOELACE IS UNTIED!
HA! HA!
TOIOIOIONG!
HEY, GARFIELD! THERE'S A HUGE, HAIRY SPIDER CRAWLING UP YOUR BELLY!
NICE TRY, JON
YOU GOTTA GET UP PRETTY EARLY IN THE MORNING TO PULL ONE OVER ON OLD GARFIELD
3-30
JIM DAVIS

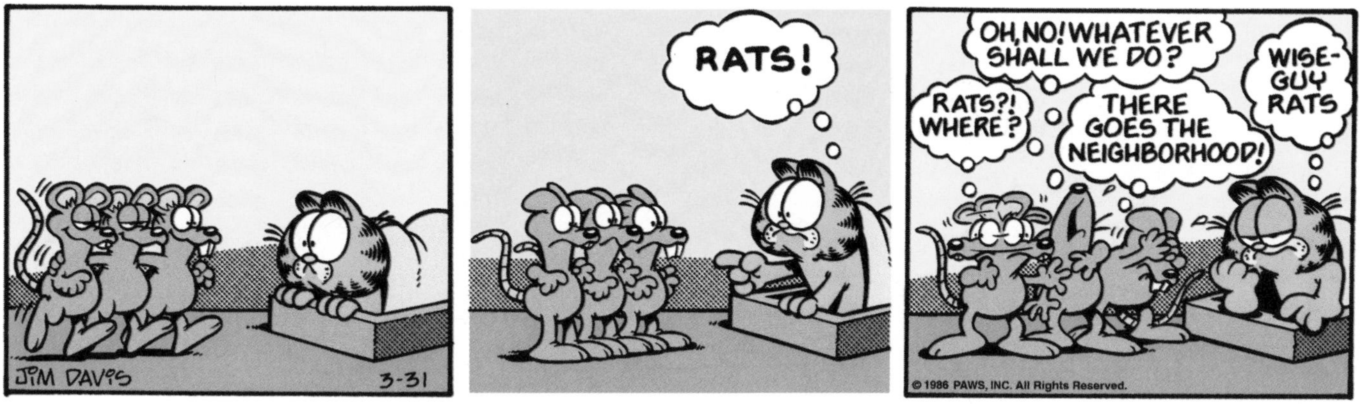
JIM DAVIS 3-31
RATS!
OH, NO! WHATEVER SHALL WE DO?
RATS?! WHERE?
THERE GOES THE NEIGHBORHOOD!
WISE-GUY RATS
© 1986 PAWS, INC. All Rights Reserved.

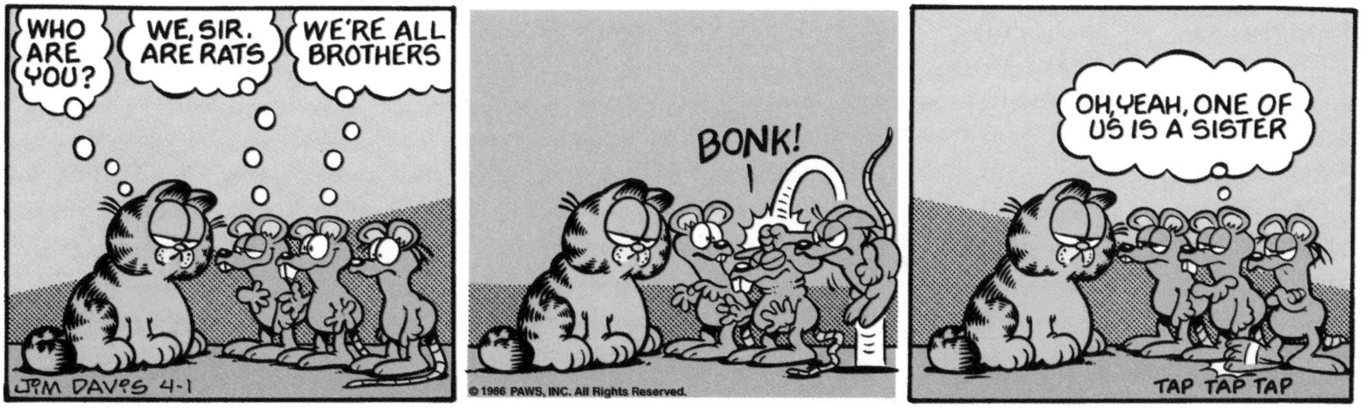
WHO ARE YOU?
WE, SIR, ARE RATS
WE'RE ALL BROTHERS
JIM DAVIS 4-1
BONK!
© 1986 PAWS, INC. All Rights Reserved.
OH, YEAH, ONE OF US IS A SISTER
TAP TAP TAP

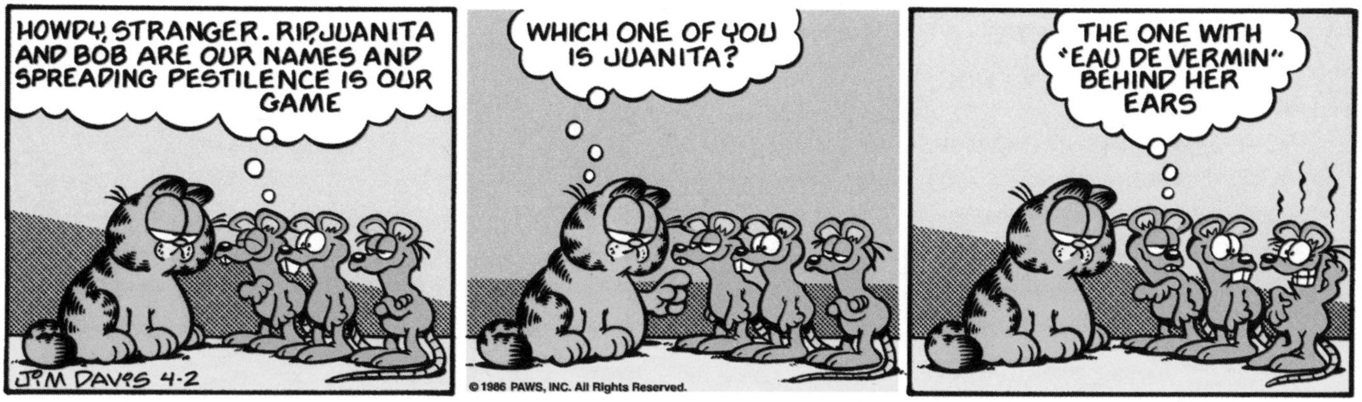
HOWDY, STRANGER. RIP, JUANITA AND BOB ARE OUR NAMES AND SPREADING PESTILENCE IS OUR GAME
JIM DAVIS 4-2
WHICH ONE OF YOU IS JUANITA?
© 1986 PAWS, INC. All Rights Reserved.
THE ONE WITH "EAU DE VERMIN" BEHIND HER EARS

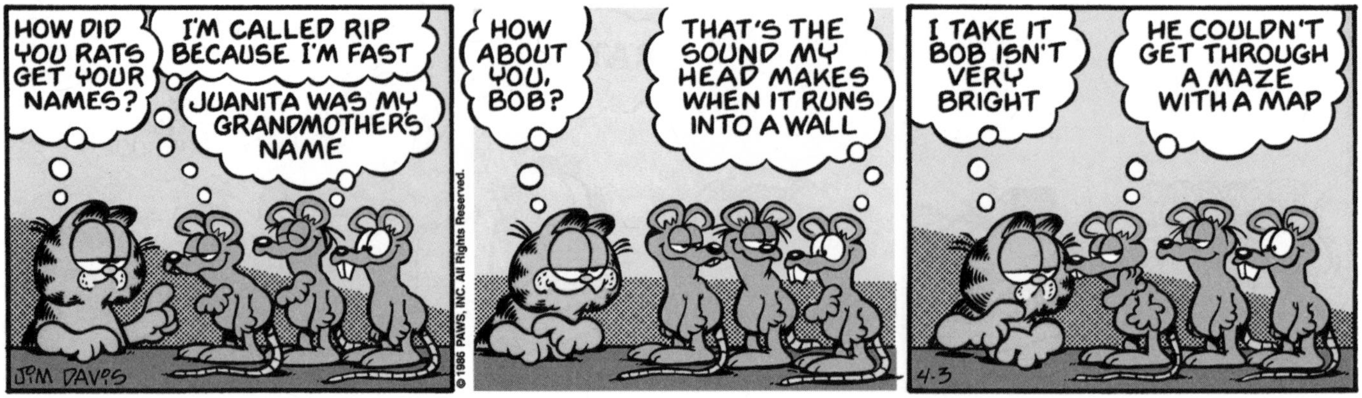
HOW DID YOU RATS GET YOUR NAMES?
I'M CALLED RIP BECAUSE I'M FAST
JUANITA WAS MY GRANDMOTHER'S NAME
JIM DAVIS
© 1986 PAWS, INC. All Rights Reserved.
HOW ABOUT YOU, BOB?
THAT'S THE SOUND MY HEAD MAKES WHEN IT RUNS INTO A WALL
I TAKE IT BOB ISN'T VERY BRIGHT
HE COULDN'T GET THROUGH A MAZE WITH A MAP
4-3

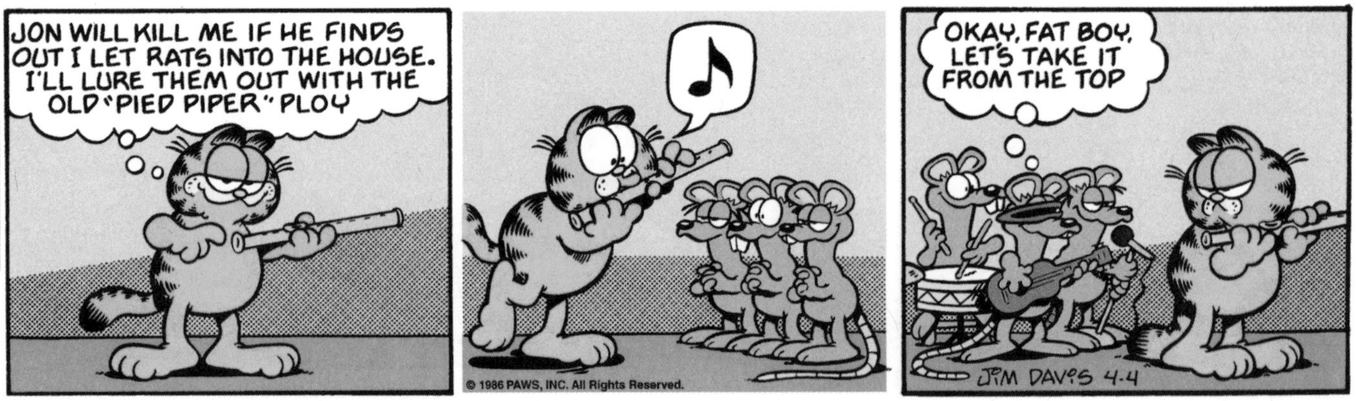
JON WILL KILL ME IF HE FINDS OUT I LET RATS INTO THE HOUSE. I'LL LURE THEM OUT WITH THE OLD "PIED PIPER" PLOY
♪
© 1986 PAWS, INC. All Rights Reserved.
OKAY, FAT BOY, LET'S TAKE IT FROM THE TOP
JIM DAVIS 4-4

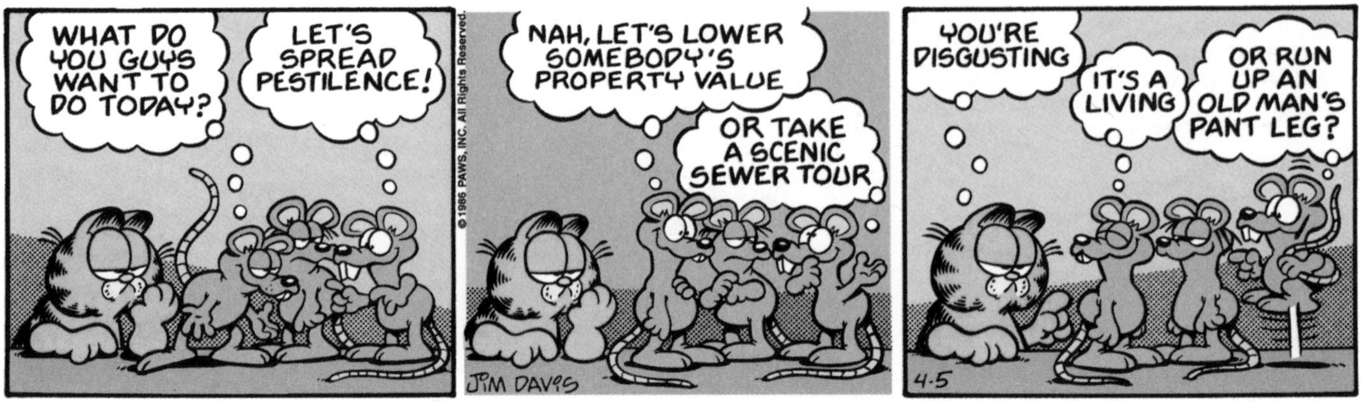
WHAT DO YOU GUYS WANT TO DO TODAY?
LET'S SPREAD PESTILENCE!
© 1986 PAWS, INC. All Rights Reserved.
NAH, LET'S LOWER SOMEBODY'S PROPERTY VALUE
OR TAKE A SCENIC SEWER TOUR
JIM DAVIS
YOU'RE DISGUSTING
IT'S A LIVING
OR RUN UP AN OLD MAN'S PANT LEG?
4-5

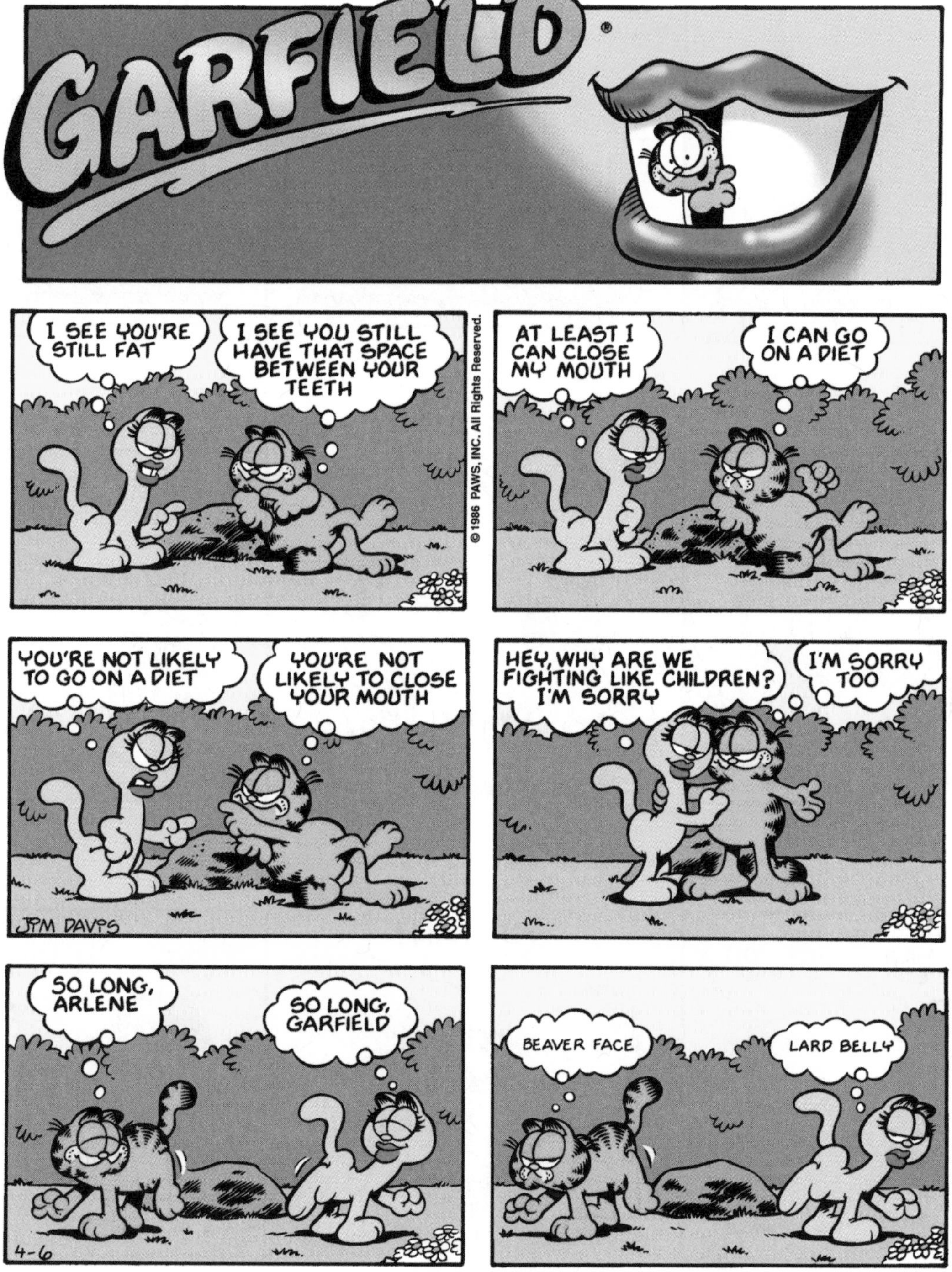
GARFIELD®
I SEE YOU'RE STILL FAT
I SEE YOU STILL HAVE THAT SPACE BETWEEN YOUR TEETH
AT LEAST I CAN CLOSE MY MOUTH
I CAN GO ON A DIET
YOU'RE NOT LIKELY TO GO ON A DIET
YOU'RE NOT LIKELY TO CLOSE YOUR MOUTH
HEY, WHY ARE WE FIGHTING LIKE CHILDREN? I'M SORRY
I'M SORRY TOO
SO LONG, ARLENE
SO LONG, GARFIELD
BEAVER FACE
LARD BELLY
JIM DAVIS
4-6

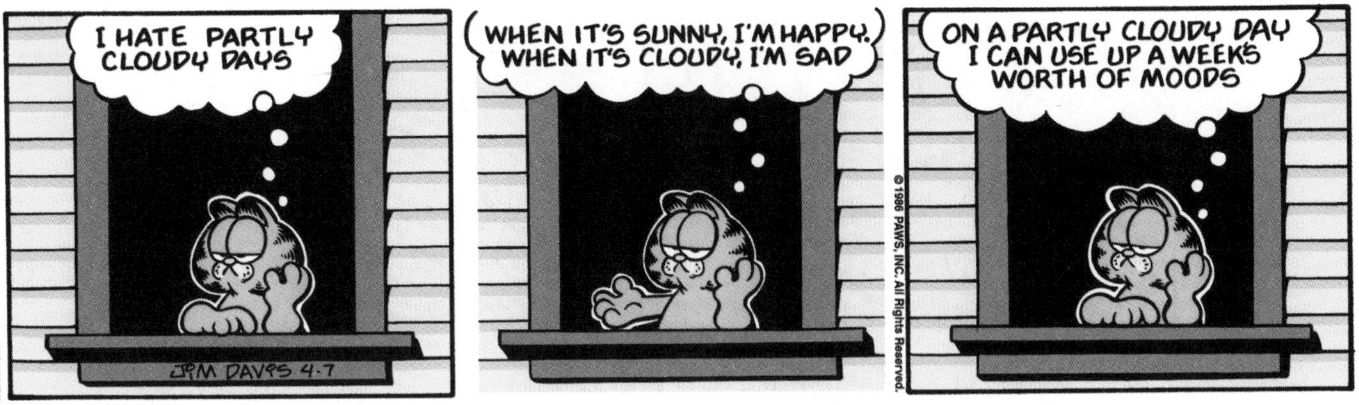
I HATE PARTLY CLOUDY DAYS
JIM DAVIS 4-7
WHEN IT'S SUNNY, I'M HAPPY. WHEN IT'S CLOUDY, I'M SAD
© 1986 PAWS, INC. All Rights Reserved.
ON A PARTLY CLOUDY DAY I CAN USE UP A WEEK'S WORTH OF MOODS

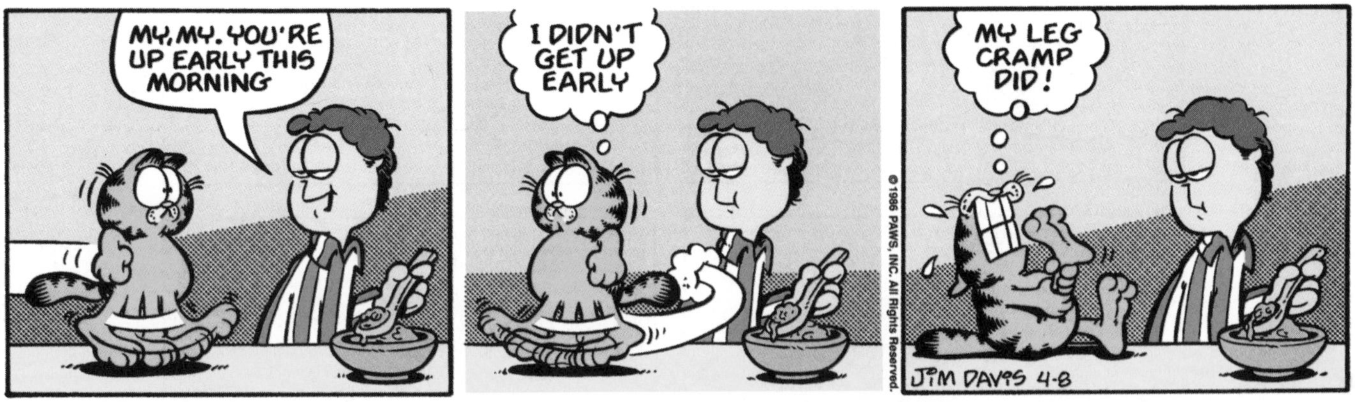
MY, MY. YOU'RE UP EARLY THIS MORNING
I DIDN'T GET UP EARLY
© 1986 PAWS, INC. All Rights Reserved.
MY LEG CRAMP DID!
JIM DAVIS 4-8

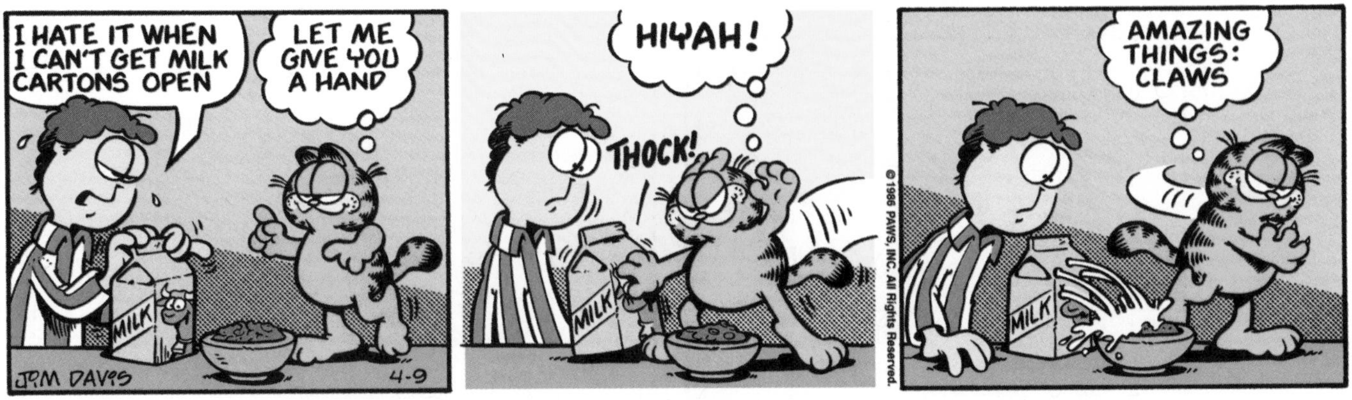
I HATE IT WHEN I CAN'T GET MILK CARTONS OPEN
LET ME GIVE YOU A HAND
MILK
JIM DAVIS
4-9
HIYAH!
THOCK!
MILK
© 1986 PAWS, INC. All Rights Reserved.
AMAZING THINGS: CLAWS
MILK

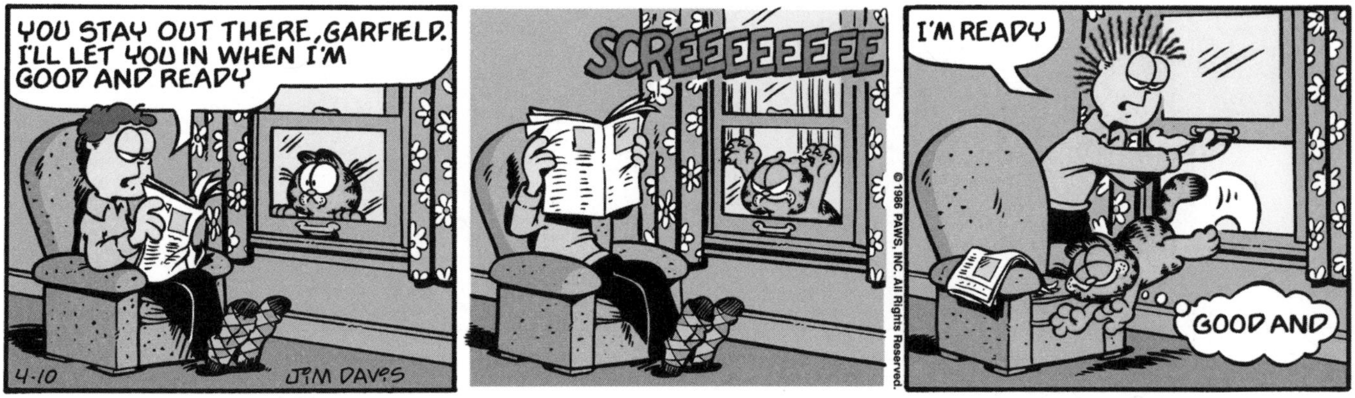
YOU STAY OUT THERE, GARFIELD. I'LL LET YOU IN WHEN I'M GOOD AND READY
4-10
JIM DAVIS
SCREEEEEEEEE
© 1986 PAWS, INC. All Rights Reserved.
I'M READY
GOOD AND

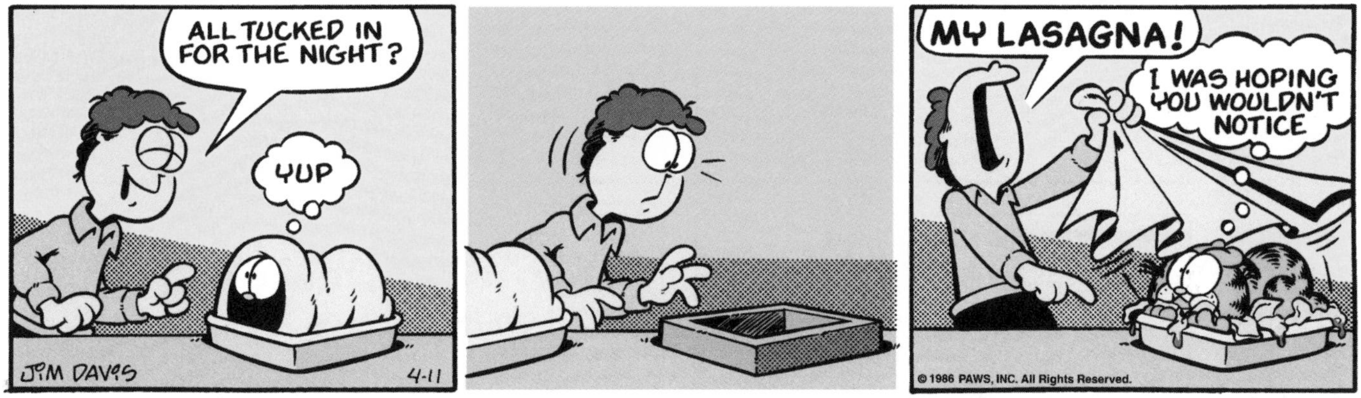
ALL TUCKED IN FOR THE NIGHT?
YUP
JIM DAVIS
4-11
MY LASAGNA!
I WAS HOPING YOU WOULDN'T NOTICE
© 1986 PAWS, INC. All Rights Reserved.

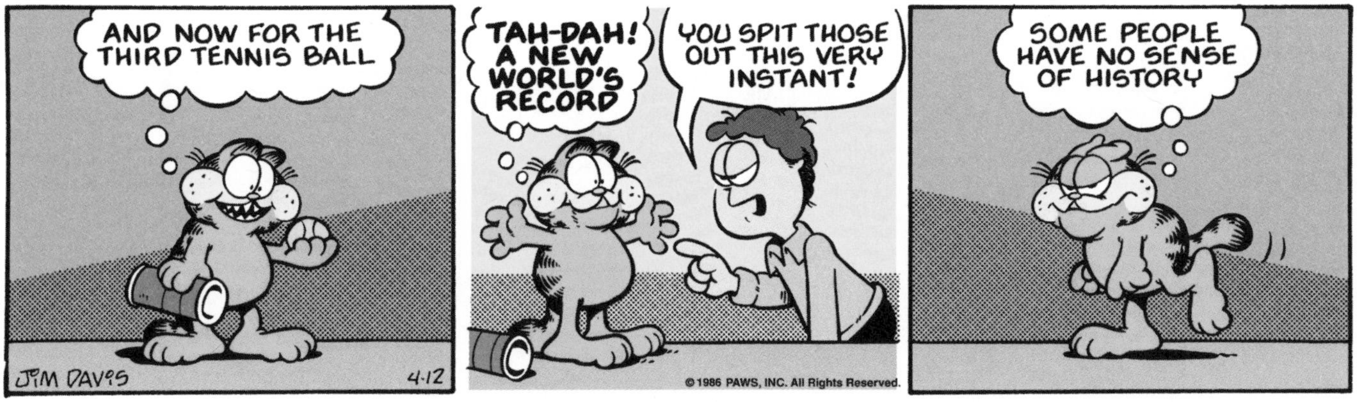
AND NOW FOR THE THIRD TENNIS BALL
JIM DAVIS
4-12
TAH-DAH! A NEW WORLD'S RECORD
YOU SPIT THOSE OUT THIS VERY INSTANT!
© 1986 PAWS, INC. All Rights Reserved.
SOME PEOPLE HAVE NO SENSE OF HISTORY

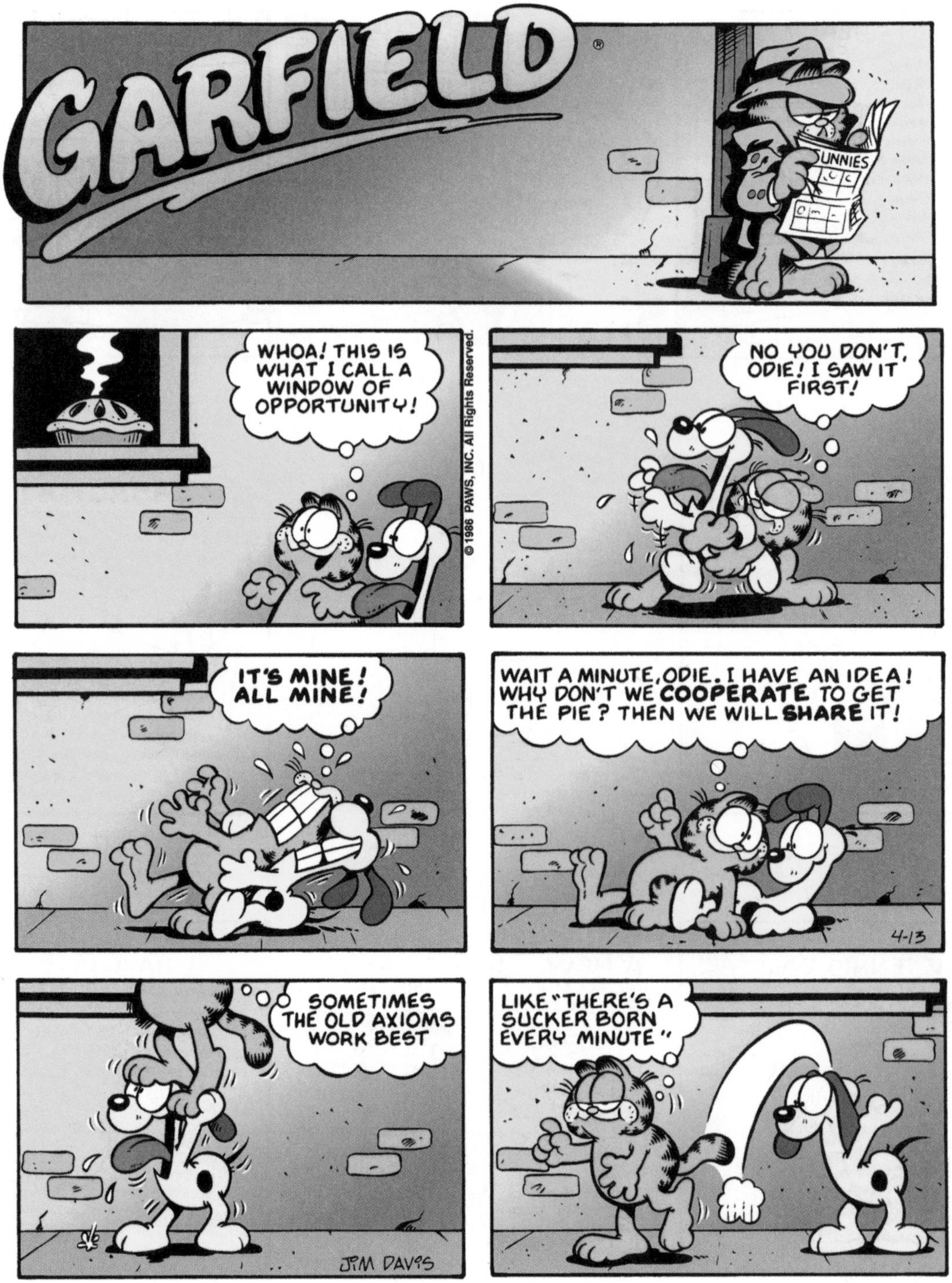
GARFIELD
SUNNIES
WHOA! THIS IS WHAT I CALL A WINDOW OF OPPORTUNITY!
© 1986 PAWS, INC. All Rights Reserved.
NO YOU DON'T, ODIE! I SAW IT FIRST!
IT'S MINE! ALL MINE!
WAIT A MINUTE, ODIE. I HAVE AN IDEA! WHY DON'T WE **COOPERATE** TO GET THE PIE? THEN WE WILL **SHARE** IT!
4-13
SOMETIMES THE OLD AXIOMS WORK BEST
JIM DAVIS
LIKE "THERE'S A SUCKER BORN EVERY MINUTE"

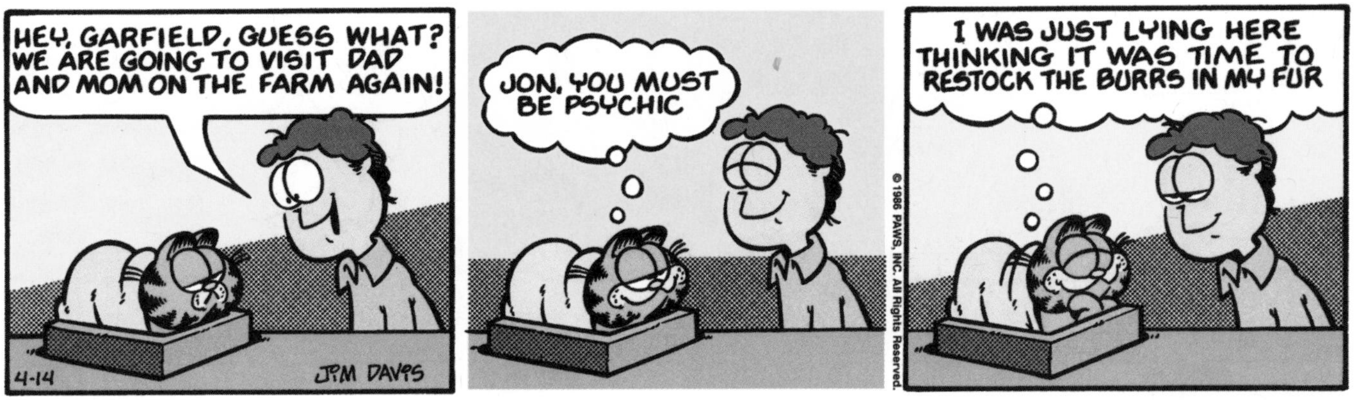
HEY, GARFIELD, GUESS WHAT? WE ARE GOING TO VISIT DAD AND MOM ON THE FARM AGAIN!
4-14
JIM DAVIS
JON, YOU MUST BE PSYCHIC
© 1986 PAWS, INC. All Rights Reserved.
I WAS JUST LYING HERE THINKING IT WAS TIME TO RESTOCK THE BURRS IN MY FUR

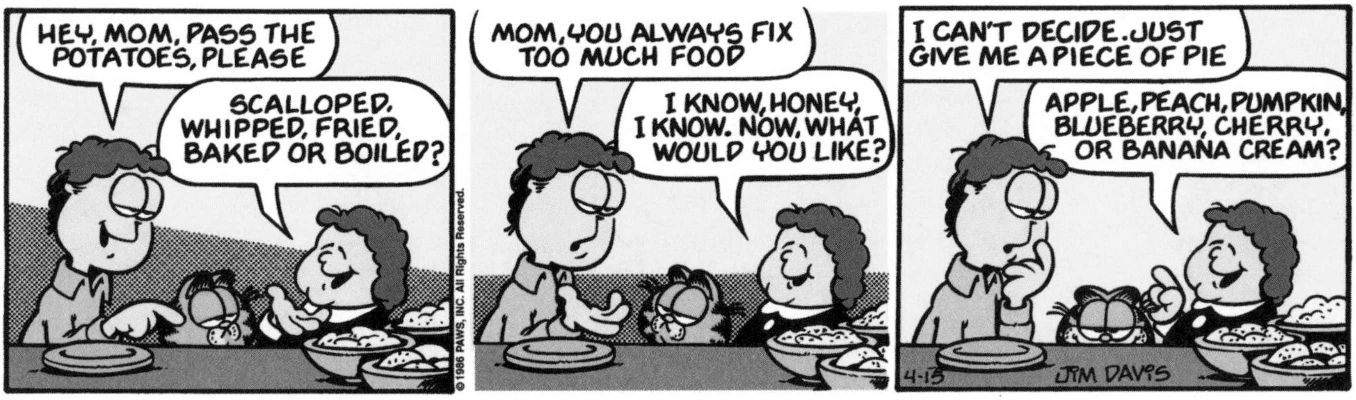
HEY, MOM, PASS THE POTATOES, PLEASE
SCALLOPED, WHIPPED, FRIED, BAKED OR BOILED?
© 1986 PAWS, INC. All Rights Reserved.
MOM, YOU ALWAYS FIX TOO MUCH FOOD
I KNOW, HONEY, I KNOW. NOW, WHAT WOULD YOU LIKE?
I CAN'T DECIDE. JUST GIVE ME A PIECE OF PIE
APPLE, PEACH, PUMPKIN, BLUEBERRY, CHERRY, OR BANANA CREAM?
4-15
JIM DAVIS

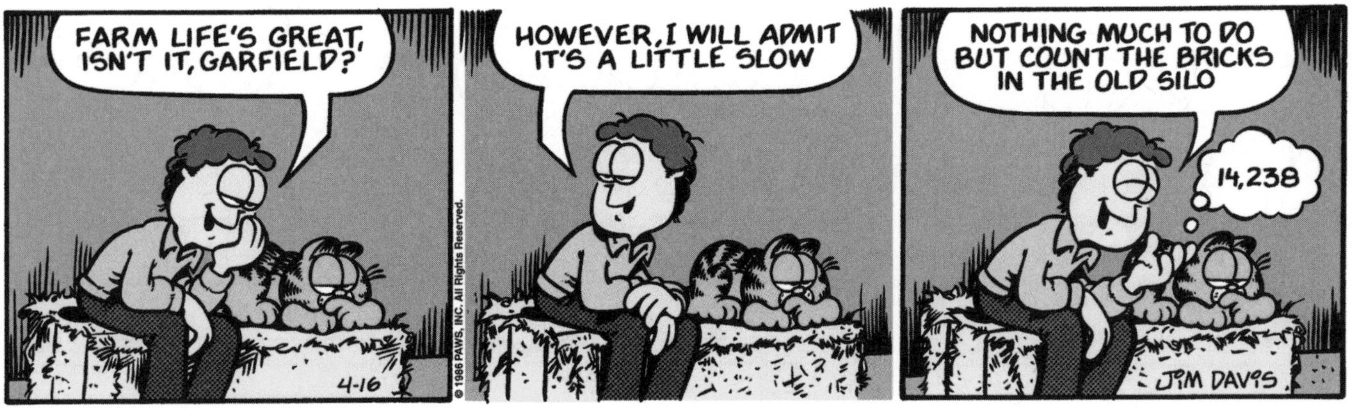
FARM LIFE'S GREAT, ISN'T IT, GARFIELD?
4-16
© 1986 PAWS, INC. All Rights Reserved.
HOWEVER, I WILL ADMIT IT'S A LITTLE SLOW
NOTHING MUCH TO DO BUT COUNT THE BRICKS IN THE OLD SILO
14,238
JIM DAVIS

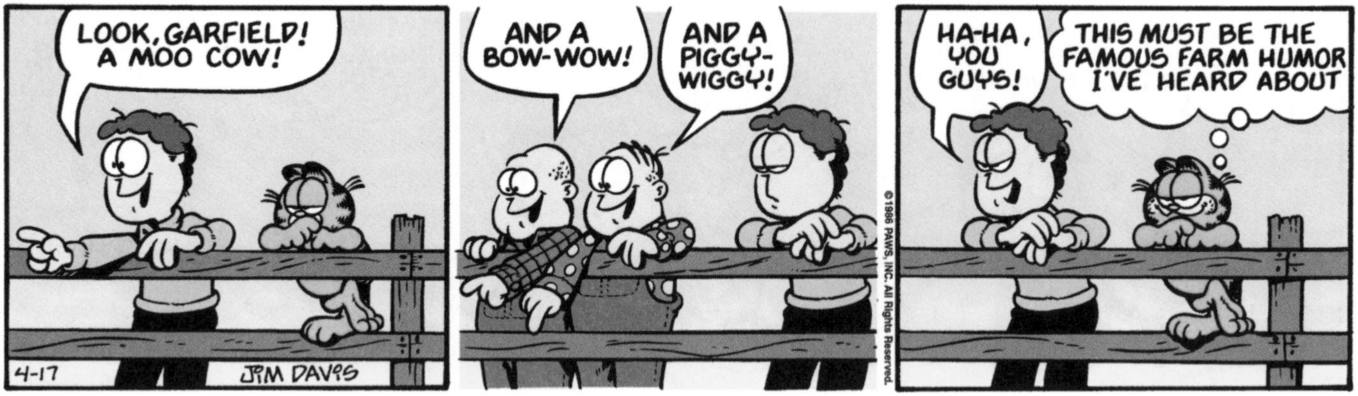
LOOK, GARFIELD! A MOO COW!
4-17
JIM DAVIS
AND A BOW-WOW!
AND A PIGGY-WIGGY!
© 1986 PAWS, INC. All Rights Reserved.
HA-HA, YOU GUYS!
THIS MUST BE THE FAMOUS FARM HUMOR I'VE HEARD ABOUT

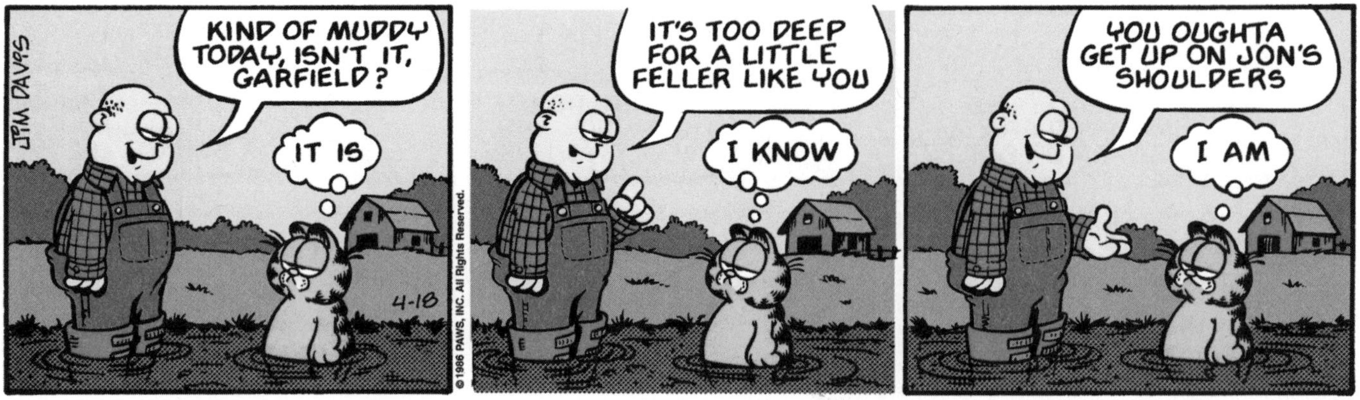
JIM DAVIS
KIND OF MUDDY TODAY, ISN'T IT, GARFIELD?
IT IS
4-18
© 1986 PAWS, INC. All Rights Reserved.
IT'S TOO DEEP FOR A LITTLE FELLER LIKE YOU
I KNOW
YOU OUGHTA GET UP ON JON'S SHOULDERS
I AM

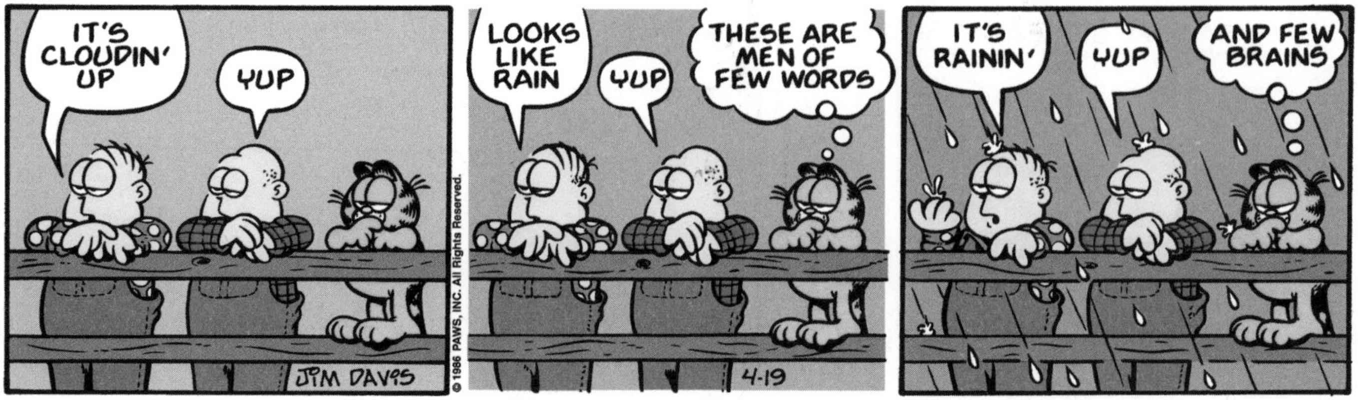
IT'S CLOUDIN' UP
YUP
JIM DAVIS
© 1986 PAWS, INC. All Rights Reserved.
LOOKS LIKE RAIN
YUP
THESE ARE MEN OF FEW WORDS
4-19
IT'S RAININ'
YUP
AND FEW BRAINS

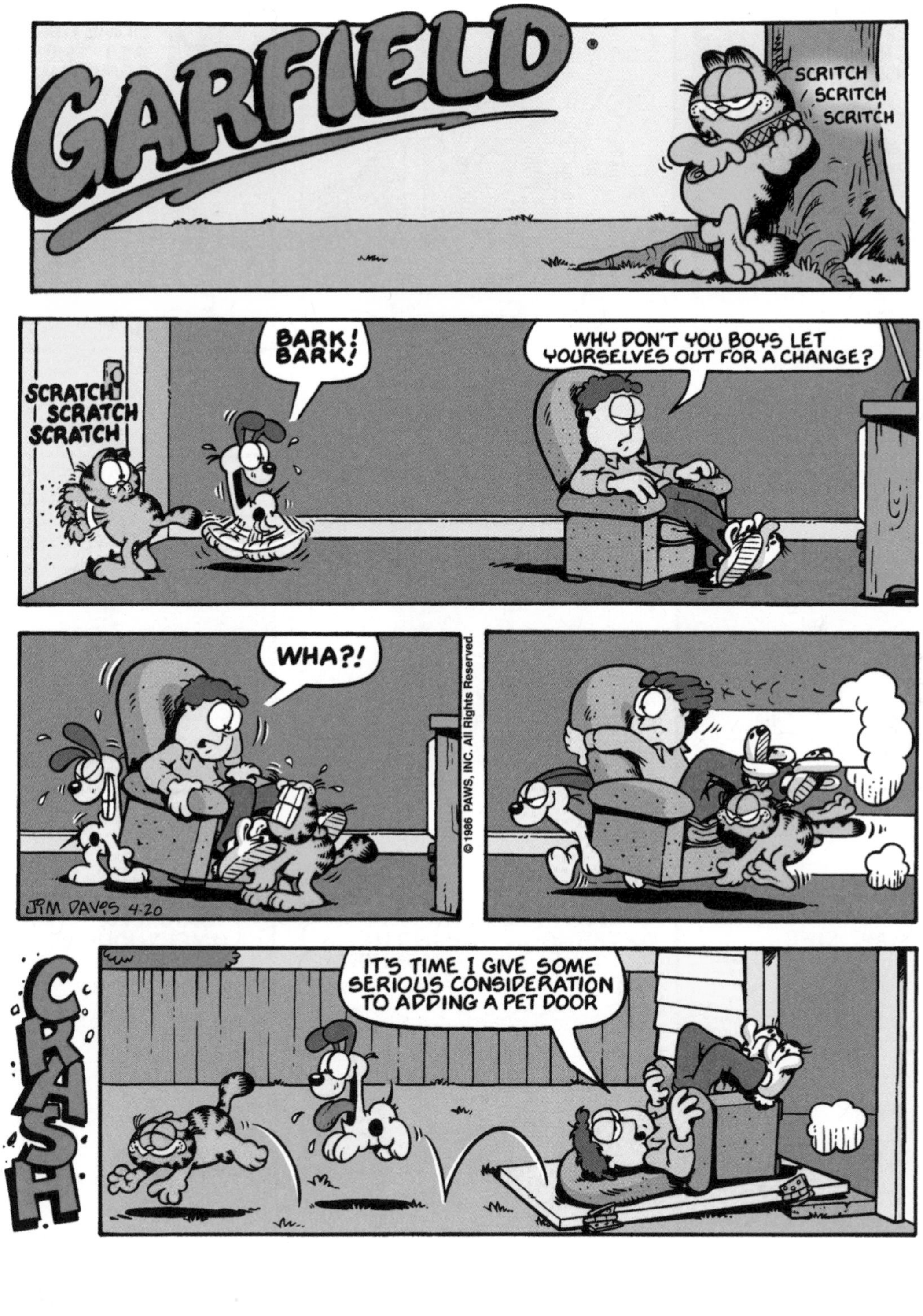
GARFIELD®
SCRITCH
SCRITCH
SCRITCH
SCRATCH
SCRATCH
SCRATCH
BARK! BARK!
WHY DON'T YOU BOYS LET YOURSELVES OUT FOR A CHANGE?
WHA?!
JIM DAVIS 4-20
© 1986 PAWS, INC. All Rights Reserved.
CRASH
IT'S TIME I GIVE SOME SERIOUS CONSIDERATION TO ADDING A PET DOOR

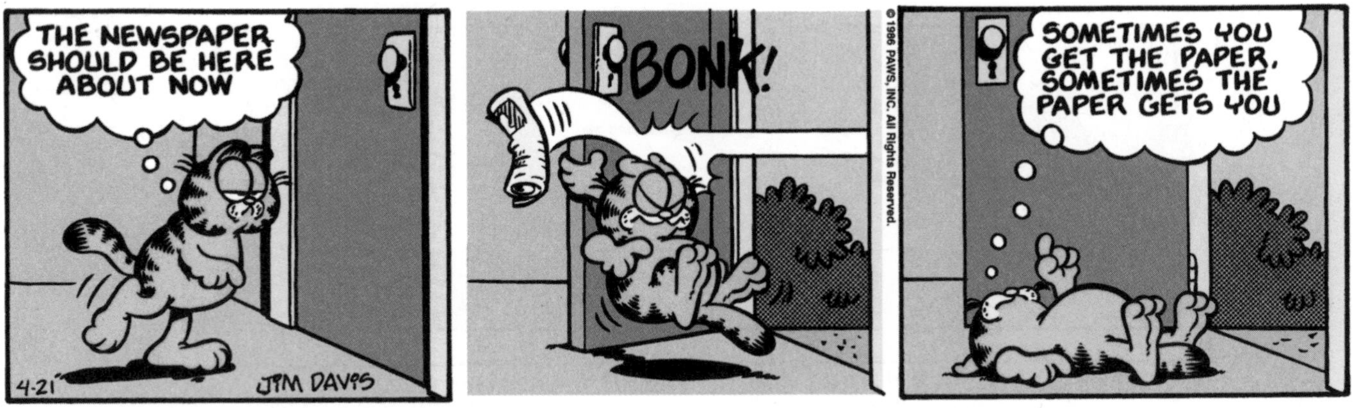
THE NEWSPAPER SHOULD BE HERE ABOUT NOW
4-21
JIM DAVIS
BONK!
© 1986 PAWS, INC. All Rights Reserved.
SOMETIMES YOU GET THE PAPER, SOMETIMES THE PAPER GETS YOU

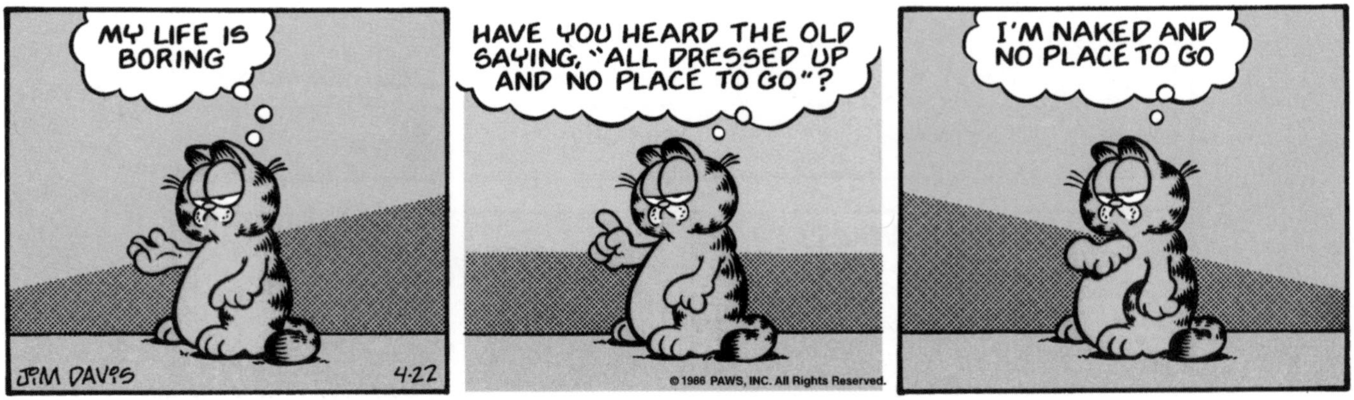
MY LIFE IS BORING
JIM DAVIS
4-22
HAVE YOU HEARD THE OLD SAYING, "ALL DRESSED UP AND NO PLACE TO GO"?
© 1986 PAWS, INC. All Rights Reserved.
I'M NAKED AND NO PLACE TO GO

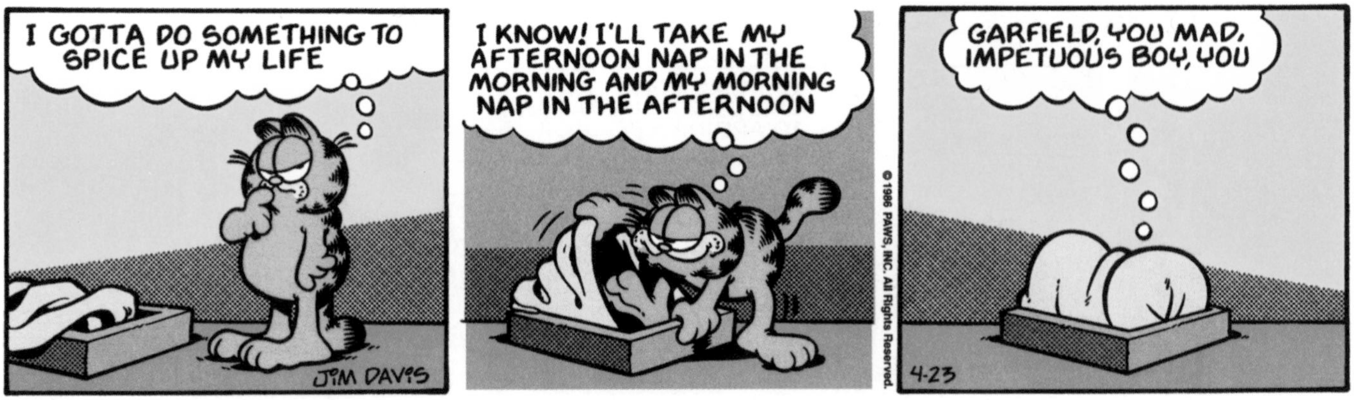
I GOTTA DO SOMETHING TO SPICE UP MY LIFE
JIM DAVIS
I KNOW! I'LL TAKE MY AFTERNOON NAP IN THE MORNING AND MY MORNING NAP IN THE AFTERNOON
© 1986 PAWS, INC. All Rights Reserved.
GARFIELD, YOU MAD, IMPETUOUS BOY, YOU
4-23

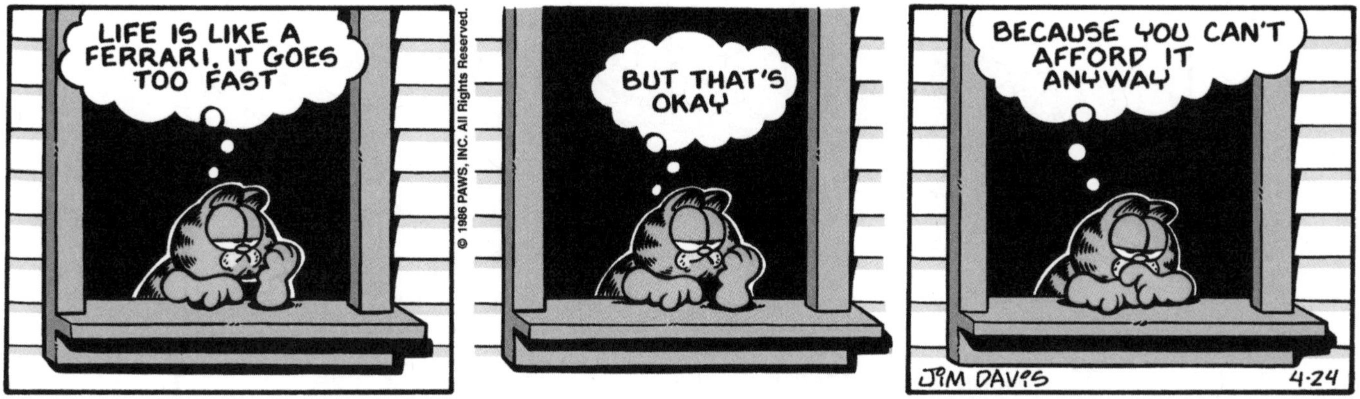
LIFE IS LIKE A FERRARI. IT GOES TOO FAST
© 1986 PAWS, INC. All Rights Reserved.
BUT THAT'S OKAY
BECAUSE YOU CAN'T AFFORD IT ANYWAY
JIM DAVIS
4-24

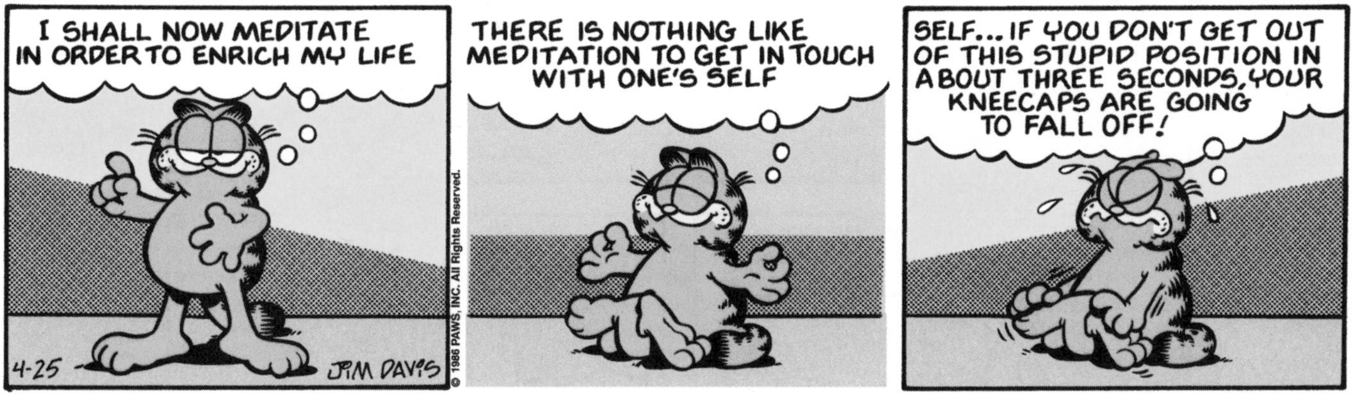
I SHALL NOW MEDITATE IN ORDER TO ENRICH MY LIFE
4-25
JIM DAVIS
© 1986 PAWS, INC. All Rights Reserved.
THERE IS NOTHING LIKE MEDITATION TO GET IN TOUCH WITH ONE'S SELF
SELF... IF YOU DON'T GET OUT OF THIS STUPID POSITION IN ABOUT THREE SECONDS, YOUR KNEECAPS ARE GOING TO FALL OFF!

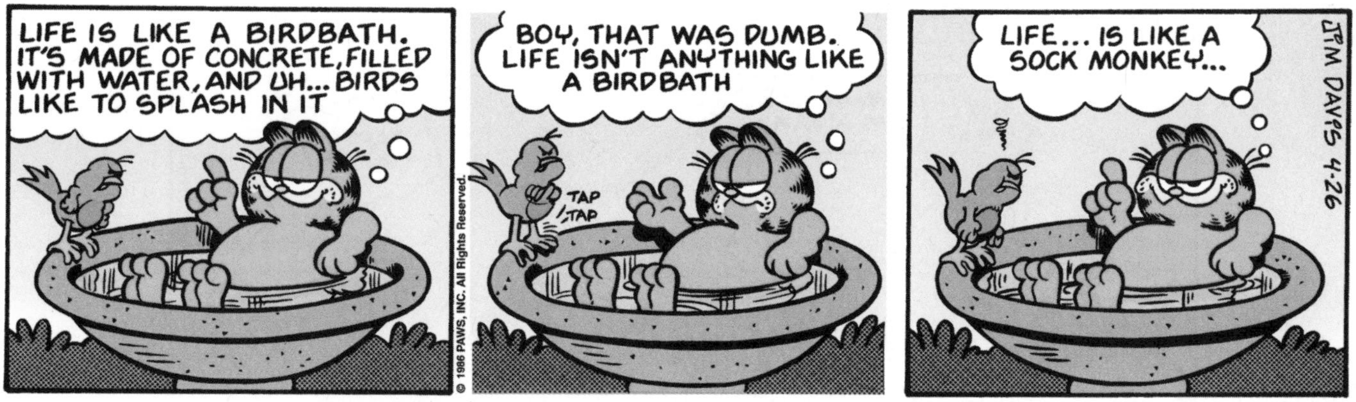
LIFE IS LIKE A BIRDBATH. IT'S MADE OF CONCRETE, FILLED WITH WATER, AND UH... BIRDS LIKE TO SPLASH IN IT
© 1986 PAWS, INC. All Rights Reserved.
BOY, THAT WAS DUMB. LIFE ISN'T ANYTHING LIKE A BIRDBATH
TAP TAP
LIFE... IS LIKE A SOCK MONKEY...
JIM DAVIS 4-26

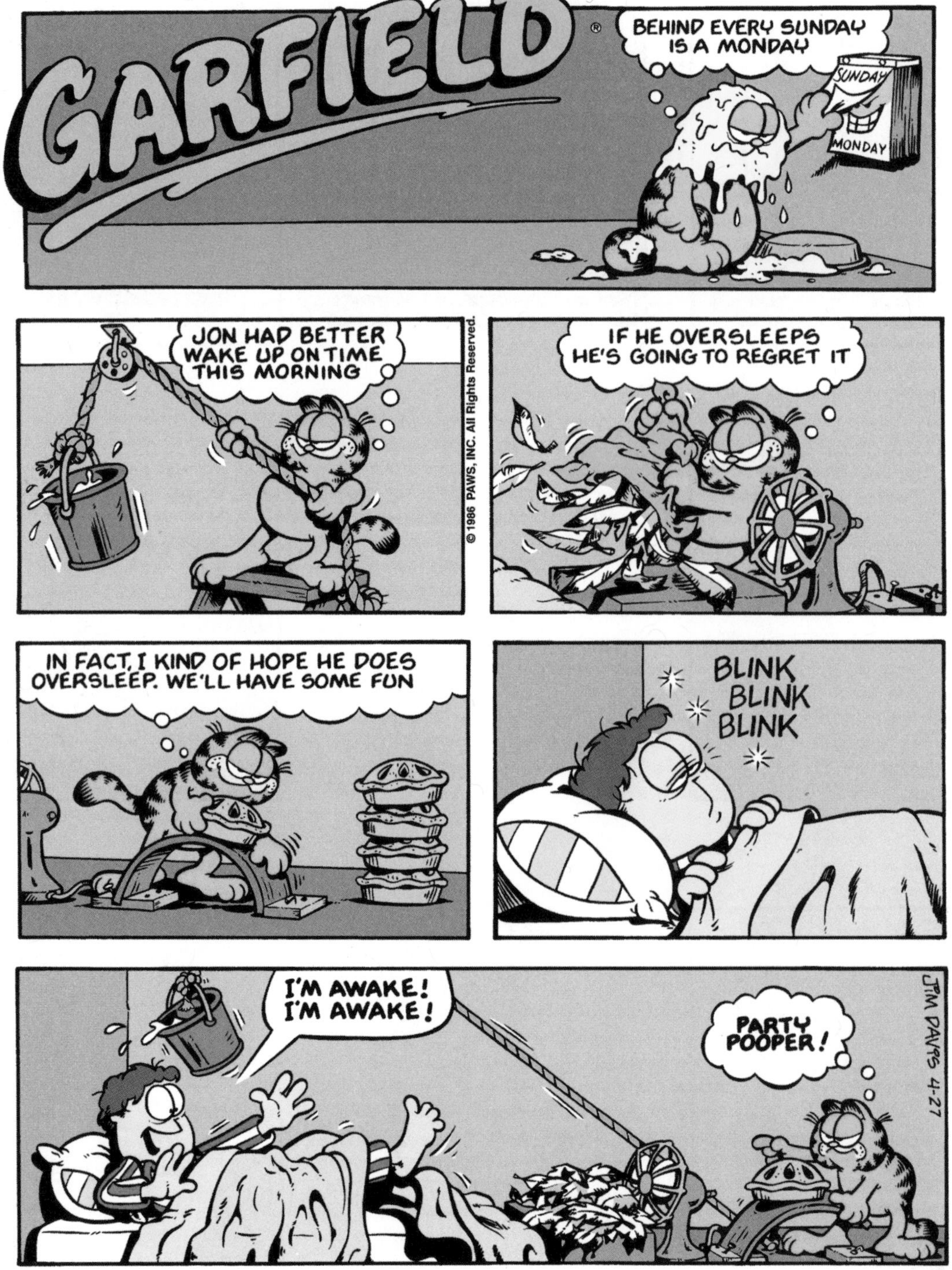
GARFIELD®
BEHIND EVERY SUNDAY IS A MONDAY
SUNDAY
MONDAY
JON HAD BETTER WAKE UP ON TIME THIS MORNING
© 1986 PAWS, INC. All Rights Reserved.
IF HE OVERSLEEPS HE'S GOING TO REGRET IT
IN FACT, I KIND OF HOPE HE DOES OVERSLEEP. WE'LL HAVE SOME FUN
BLINK BLINK BLINK
I'M AWAKE! I'M AWAKE!
PARTY POOPER!
JIM DAVIS 4-27

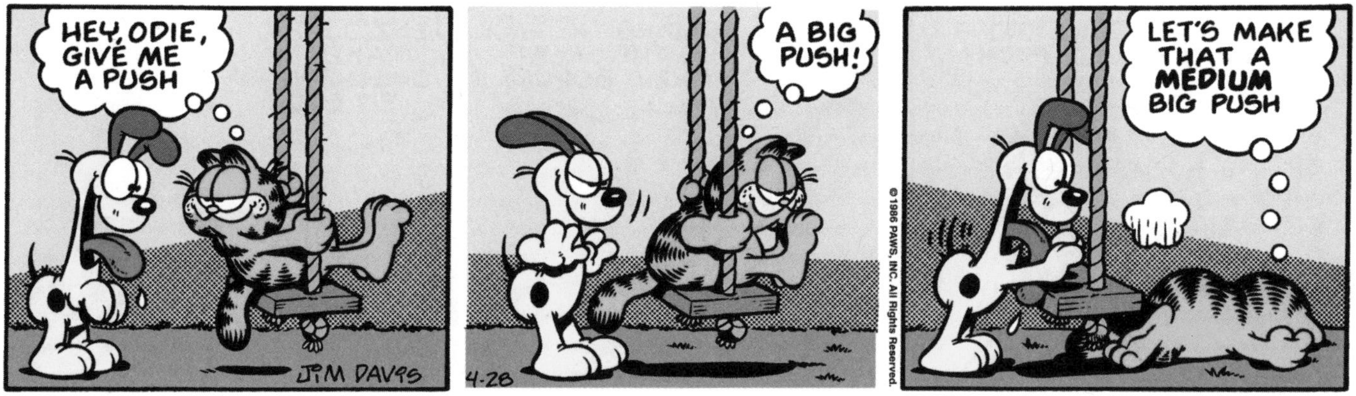
HEY, ODIE, GIVE ME A PUSH
JIM DAVIS
4-28
A BIG PUSH!
© 1986 PAWS, INC. All Rights Reserved.
LET'S MAKE THAT A **MEDIUM** BIG PUSH

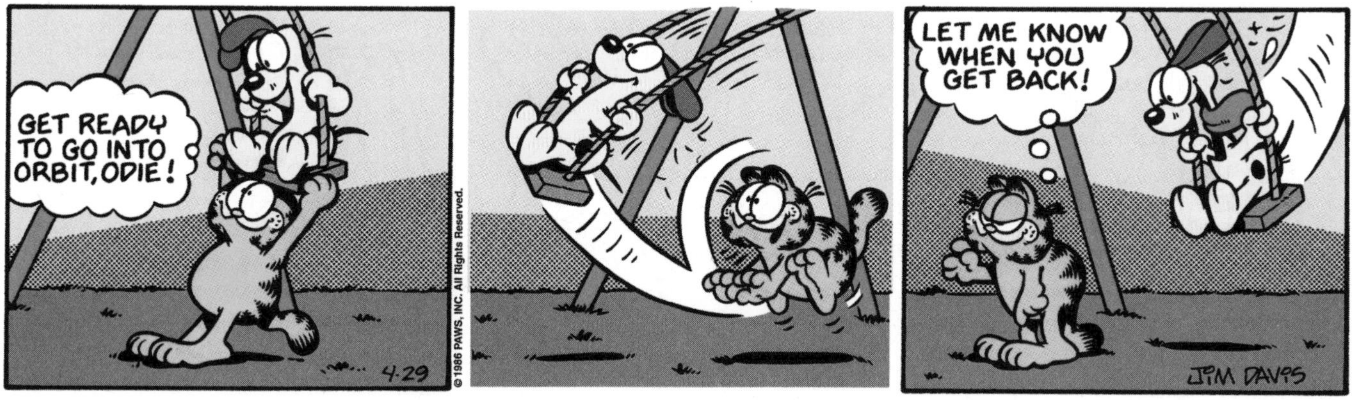
GET READY TO GO INTO ORBIT, ODIE!
4-29
© 1986 PAWS, INC. All Rights Reserved.
LET ME KNOW WHEN YOU GET BACK!
JIM DAVIS

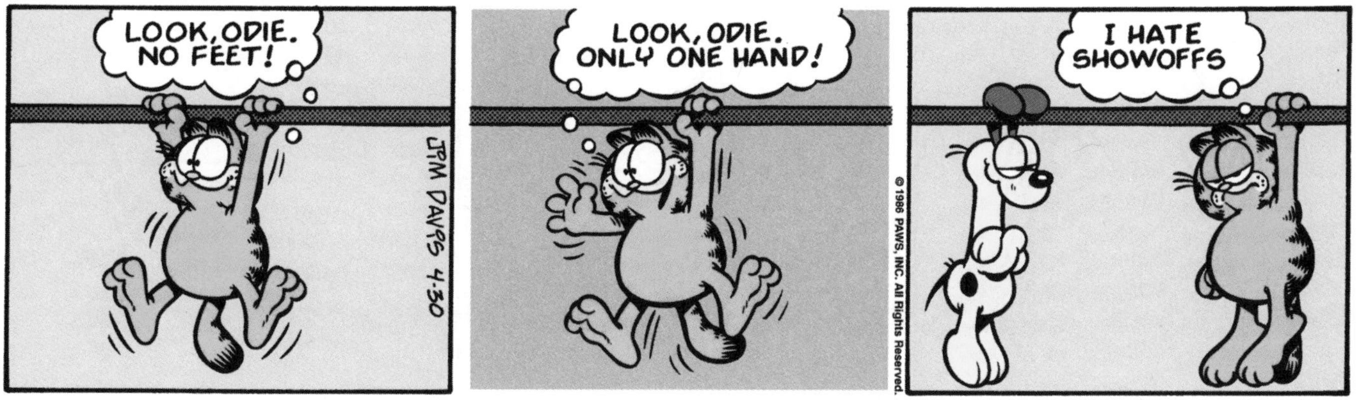
LOOK, ODIE. NO FEET!
JIM DAVIS 4-30
LOOK, ODIE. ONLY ONE HAND!
© 1986 PAWS, INC. All Rights Reserved.
I HATE SHOWOFFS

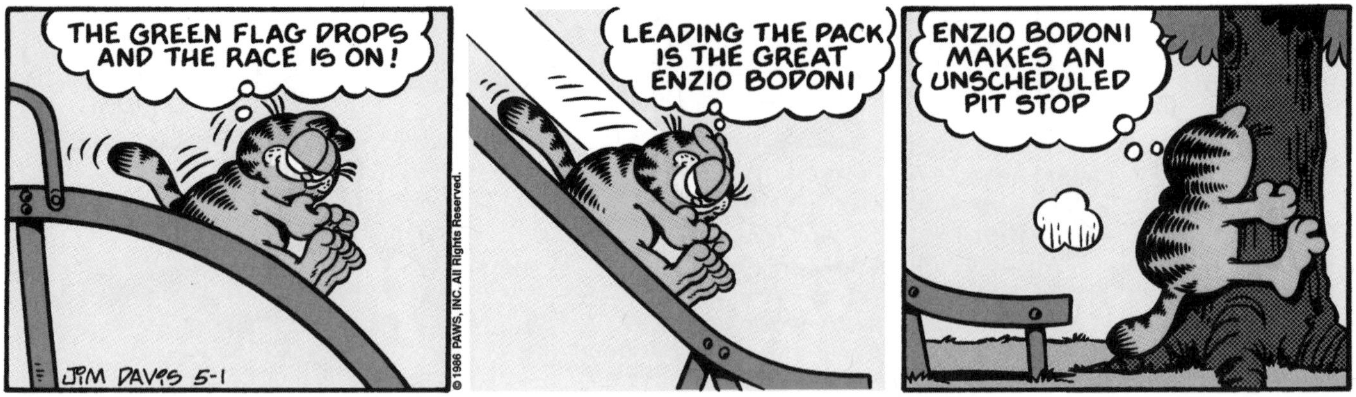
THE GREEN FLAG DROPS AND THE RACE IS ON!
JIM DAVIS 5-1
© 1986 PAWS, INC. All Rights Reserved.
LEADING THE PACK IS THE GREAT ENZIO BODONI
ENZIO BODONI MAKES AN UNSCHEDULED PIT STOP

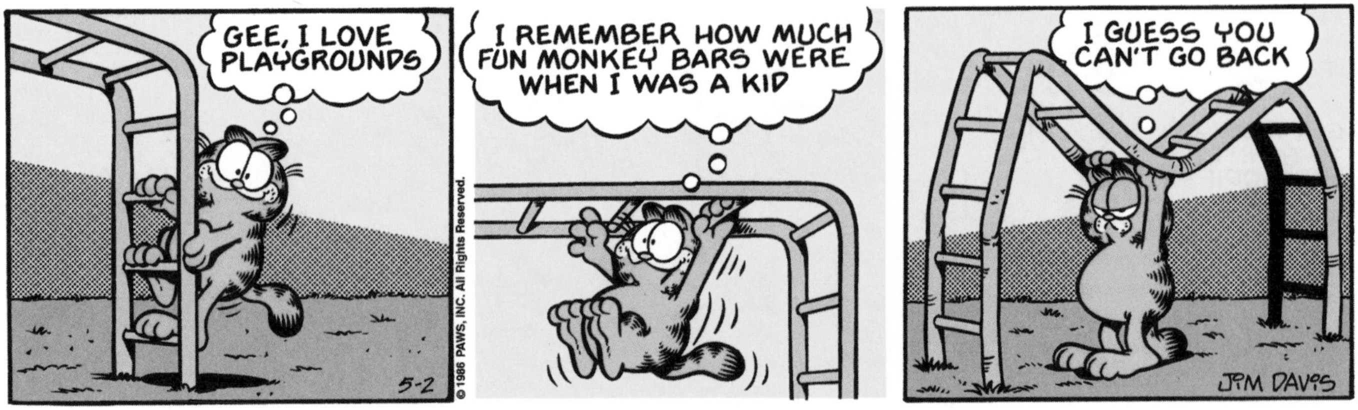
GEE, I LOVE PLAYGROUNDS
5-2
© 1986 PAWS, INC. All Rights Reserved.
I REMEMBER HOW MUCH FUN MONKEY BARS WERE WHEN I WAS A KID
I GUESS YOU CAN'T GO BACK
JIM DAVIS

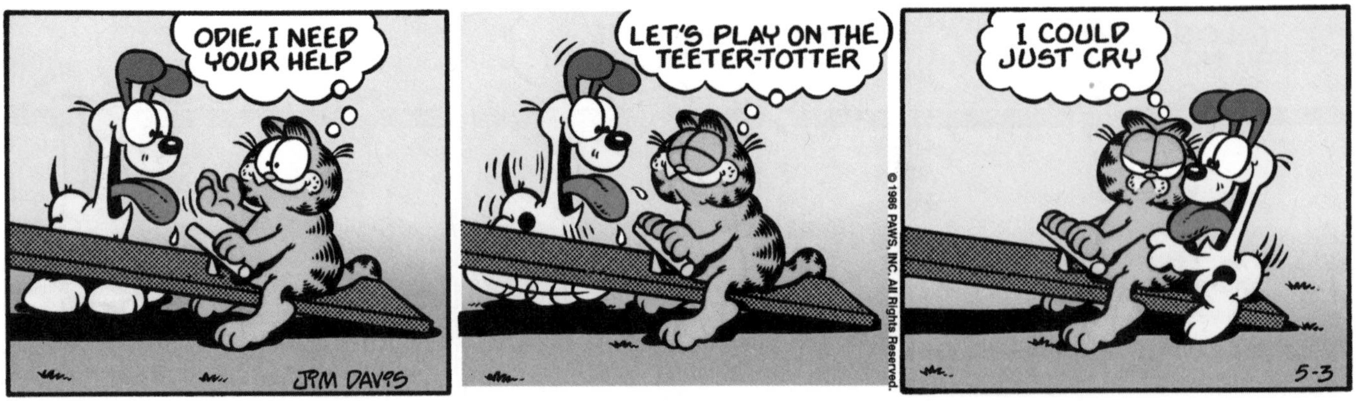
ODIE, I NEED YOUR HELP
JIM DAVIS
LET'S PLAY ON THE TEETER-TOTTER
© 1986 PAWS, INC. All Rights Reserved.
I COULD JUST CRY
5-3

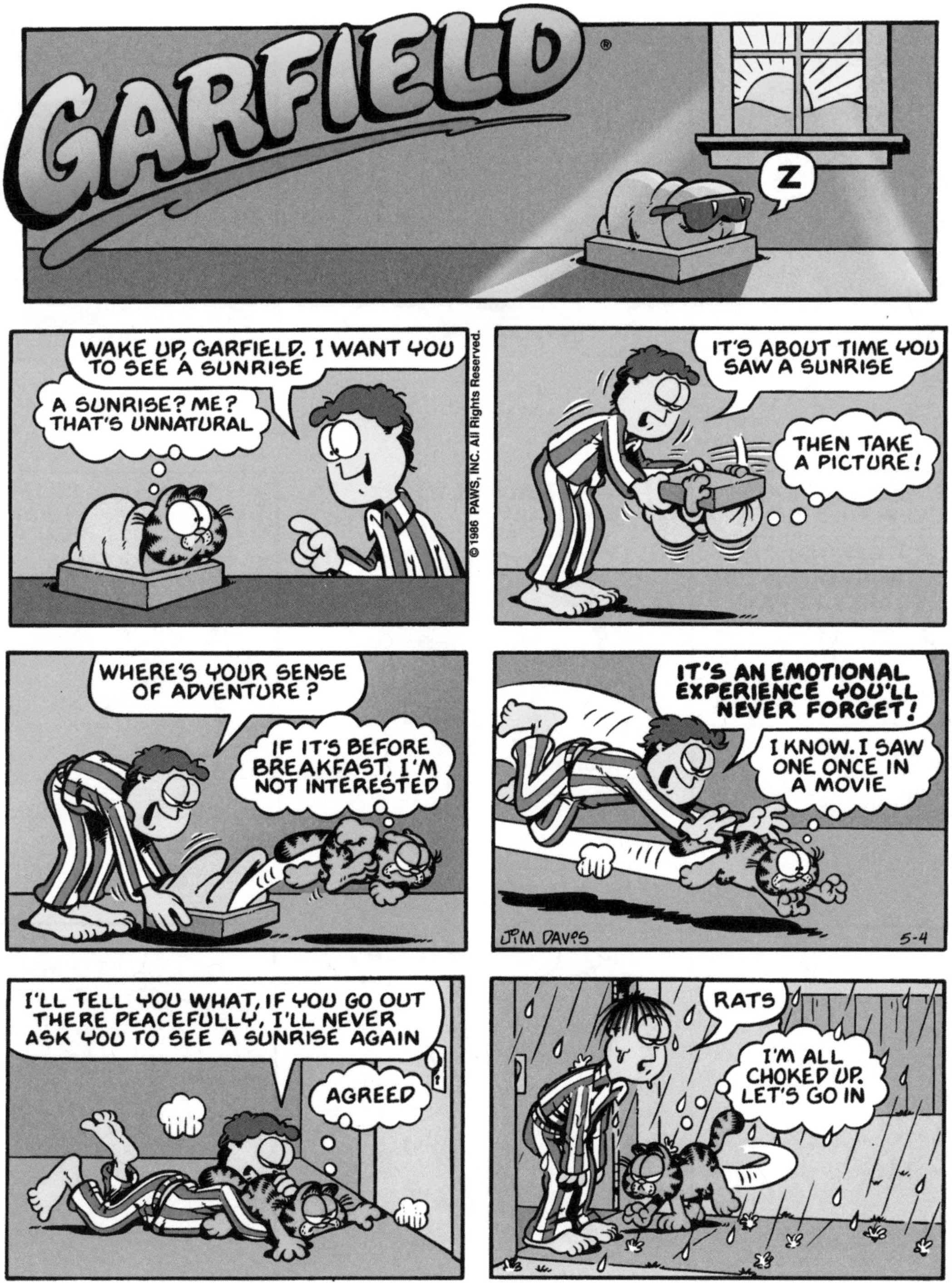
GARFIELD®
Z
WAKE UP, GARFIELD. I WANT YOU TO SEE A SUNRISE
A SUNRISE? ME? THAT'S UNNATURAL
© 1986 PAWS, INC. All Rights Reserved.
IT'S ABOUT TIME YOU SAW A SUNRISE
THEN TAKE A PICTURE!
WHERE'S YOUR SENSE OF ADVENTURE?
IF IT'S BEFORE BREAKFAST, I'M NOT INTERESTED
IT'S AN EMOTIONAL EXPERIENCE YOU'LL NEVER FORGET!
I KNOW. I SAW ONE ONCE IN A MOVIE
JIM DAVIS
5-4
I'LL TELL YOU WHAT, IF YOU GO OUT THERE PEACEFULLY, I'LL NEVER ASK YOU TO SEE A SUNRISE AGAIN
AGREED
RATS
I'M ALL CHOKED UP. LET'S GO IN

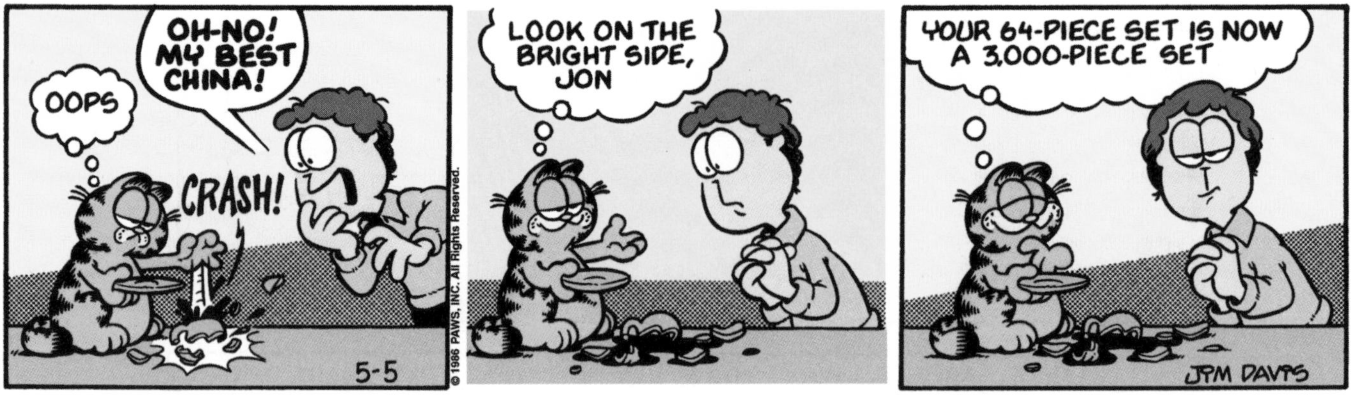
OH-NO! MY BEST CHINA!
OOPS
CRASH!
5-5
© 1986 PAWS, INC. All Rights Reserved.
LOOK ON THE BRIGHT SIDE, JON
YOUR 64-PIECE SET IS NOW A 3,000-PIECE SET
JIM DAVIS

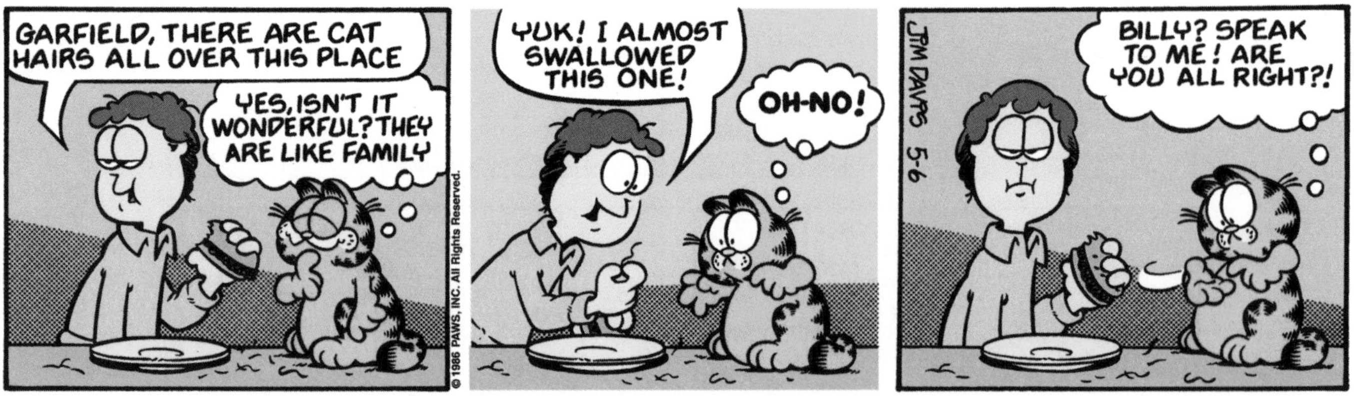
GARFIELD, THERE ARE CAT HAIRS ALL OVER THIS PLACE
YES, ISN'T IT WONDERFUL? THEY ARE LIKE FAMILY
© 1986 PAWS, INC. All Rights Reserved.
YUK! I ALMOST SWALLOWED THIS ONE!
OH-NO!
JIM DAVIS 5-6
BILLY? SPEAK TO ME! ARE YOU ALL RIGHT?!

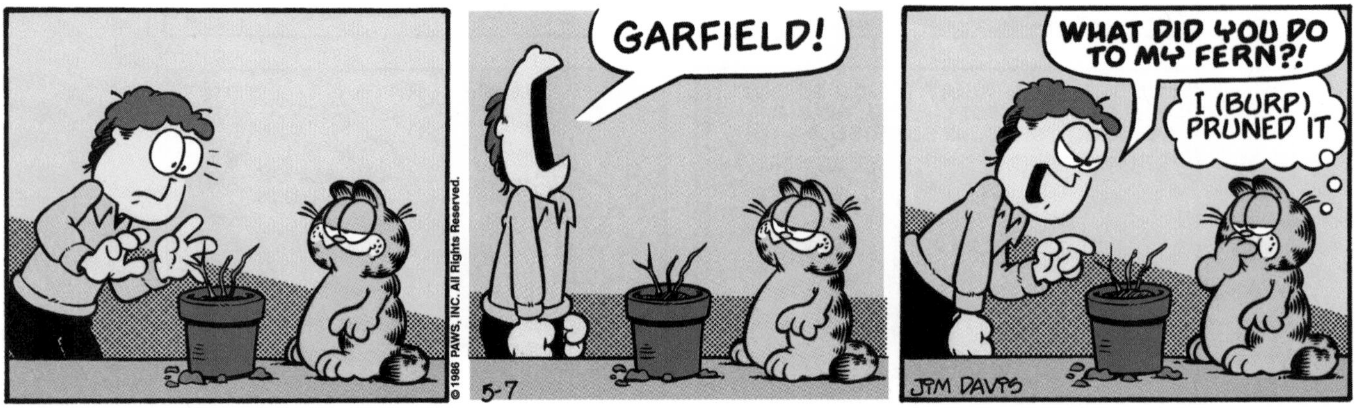
© 1986 PAWS, INC. All Rights Reserved.
GARFIELD!
5-7
WHAT DID YOU DO TO MY FERN?!
I (BURP) PRUNED IT
JIM DAVIS

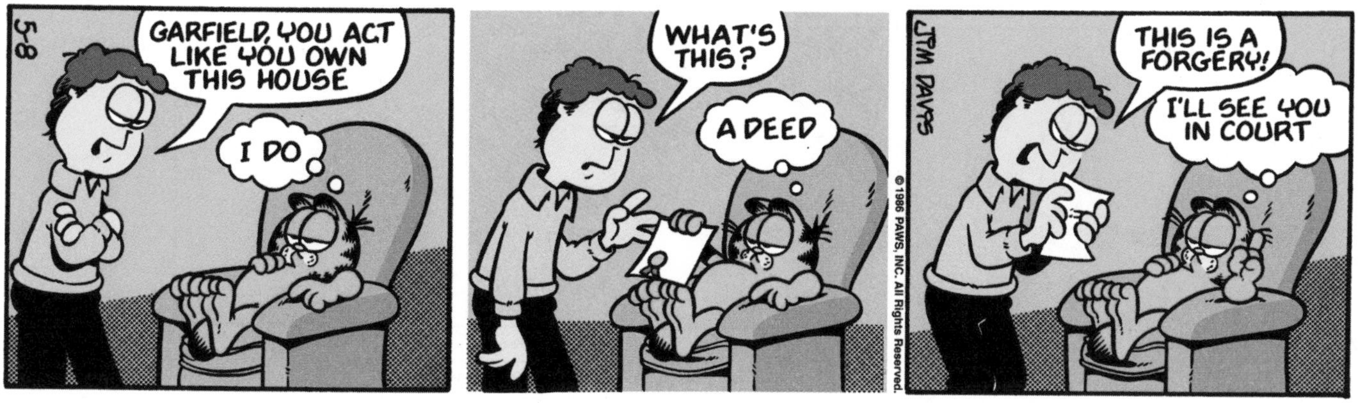
5-8
GARFIELD, YOU ACT LIKE YOU OWN THIS HOUSE
I DO
WHAT'S THIS?
A DEED
JIM DAVIS
© 1986 PAWS, INC. All Rights Reserved.
THIS IS A FORGERY!
I'LL SEE YOU IN COURT

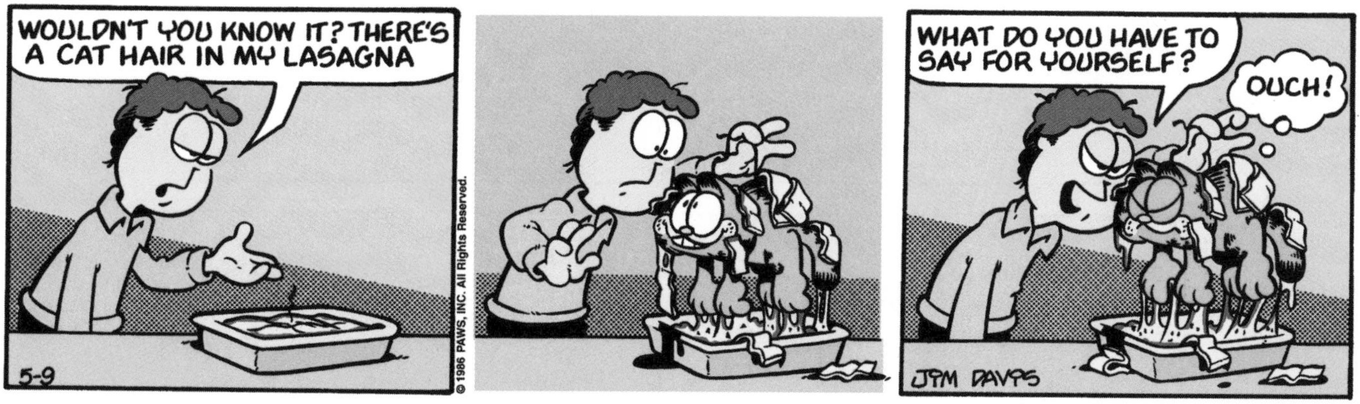
WOULDN'T YOU KNOW IT? THERE'S A CAT HAIR IN MY LASAGNA
5-9
© 1986 PAWS, INC. All Rights Reserved.
WHAT DO YOU HAVE TO SAY FOR YOURSELF?
OUCH!
JIM DAVIS

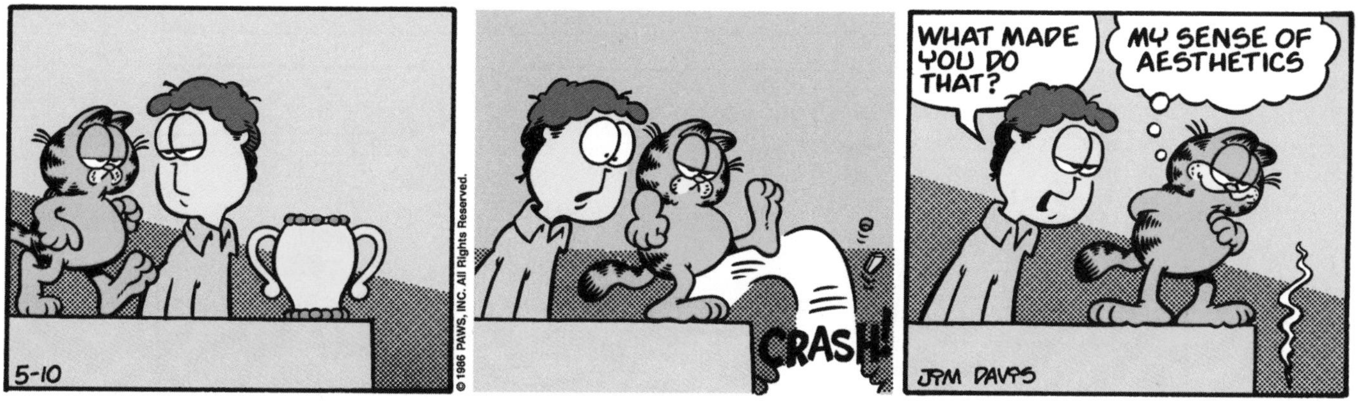
5-10
© 1986 PAWS, INC. All Rights Reserved.
CRASH!
WHAT MADE YOU DO THAT?
MY SENSE OF AESTHETICS
JIM DAVIS

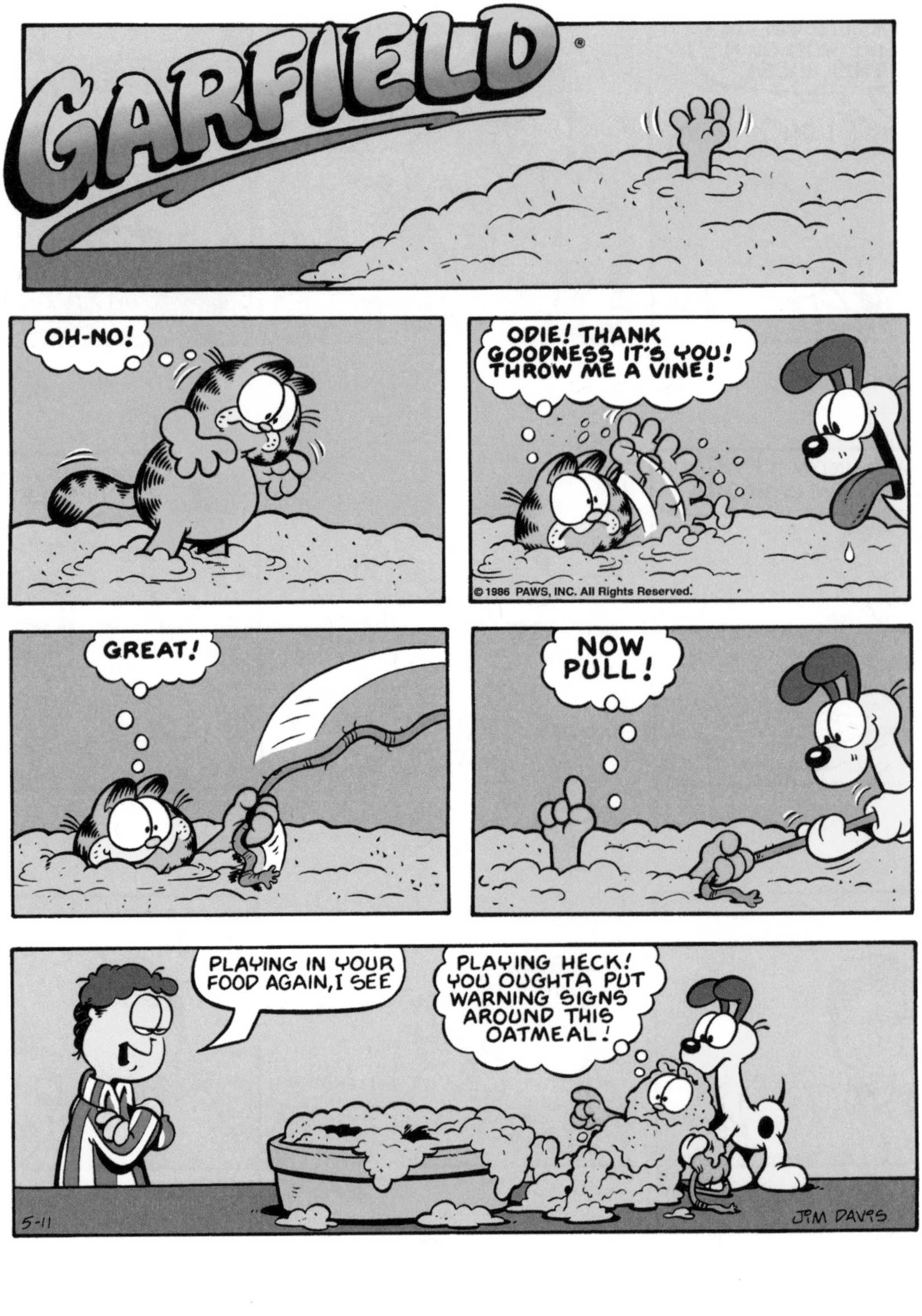
GARFIELD®
OH-NO!
ODIE! THANK GOODNESS IT'S YOU! THROW ME A VINE!
GREAT!
NOW PULL!
PLAYING IN YOUR FOOD AGAIN, I SEE
PLAYING HECK! YOU OUGHTA PUT WARNING SIGNS AROUND THIS OATMEAL!
5-11
JIM DAVIS

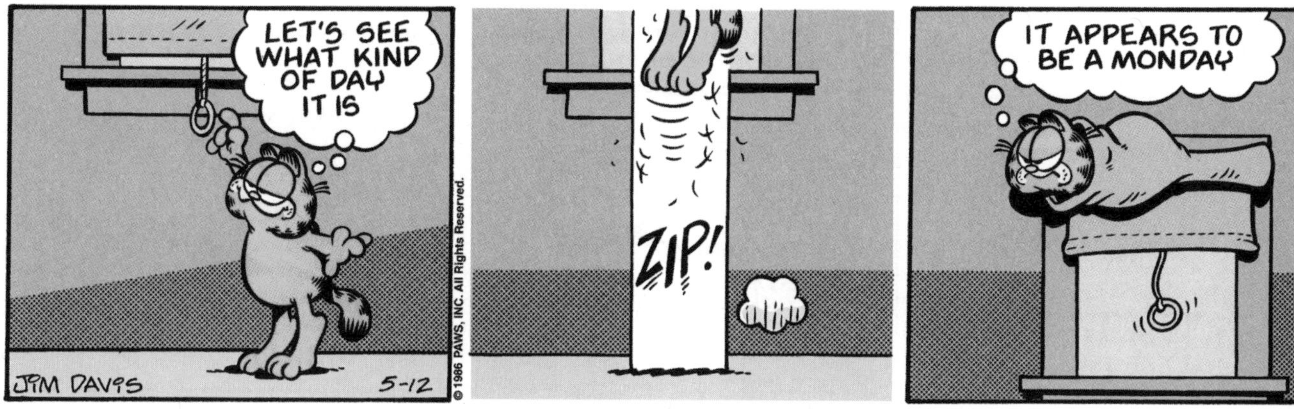
LET'S SEE WHAT KIND OF DAY IT IS
JIM DAVIS 5-12
© 1986 PAWS, INC. All Rights Reserved.
ZIP!
IT APPEARS TO BE A MONDAY

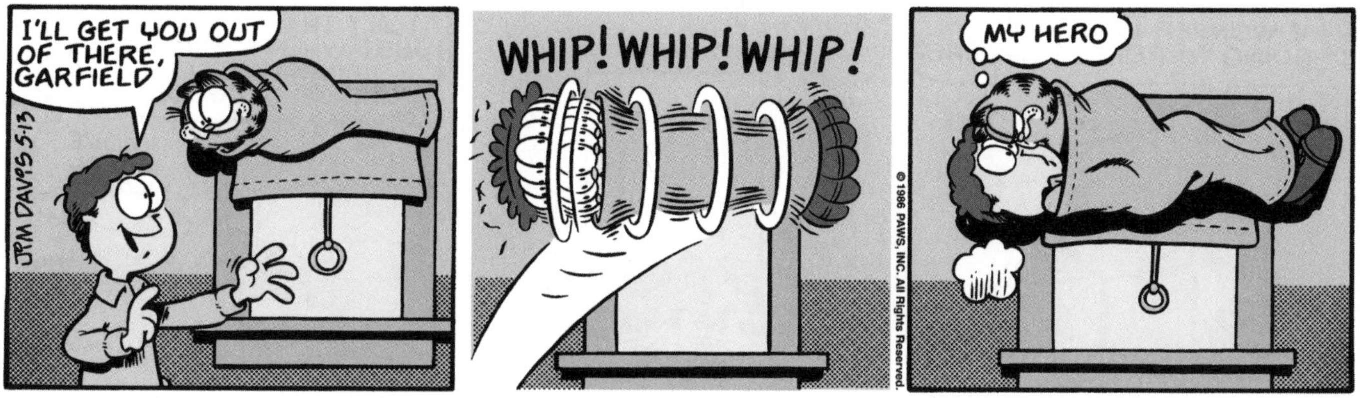
I'LL GET YOU OUT OF THERE, GARFIELD
JIM DAVIS 5-13
WHIP! WHIP! WHIP!
© 1986 PAWS, INC. All Rights Reserved.
MY HERO

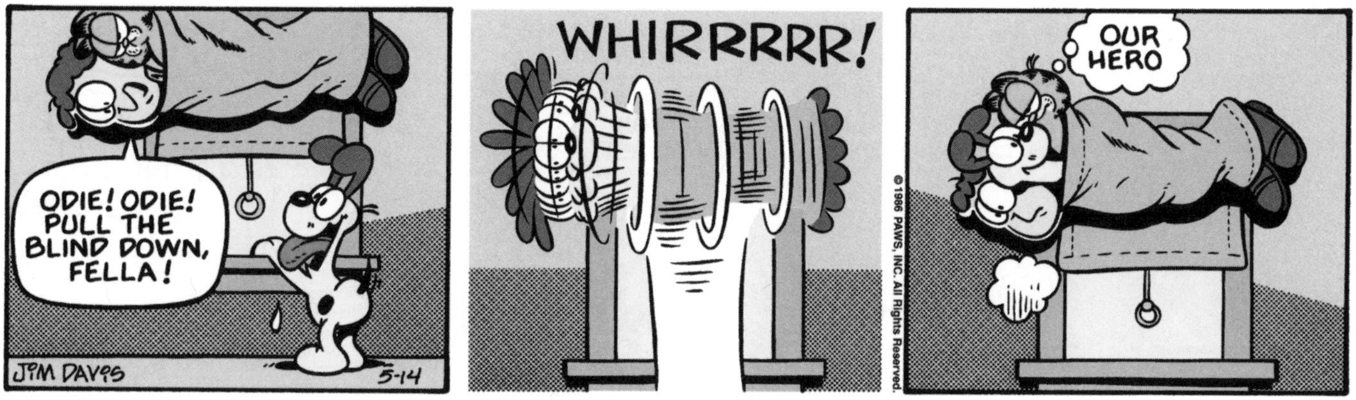
ODIE! ODIE! PULL THE BLIND DOWN, FELLA!
JIM DAVIS 5-14
WHIRRRRR!
© 1986 PAWS, INC. All Rights Reserved.
OUR HERO

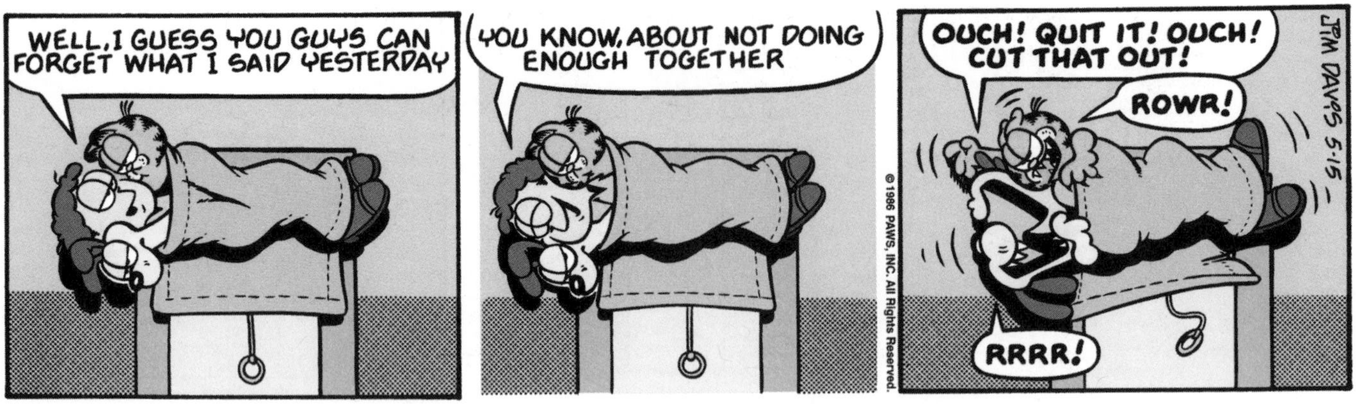
WELL, I GUESS YOU GUYS CAN FORGET WHAT I SAID YESTERDAY
YOU KNOW, ABOUT NOT DOING ENOUGH TOGETHER
OUCH! QUIT IT! OUCH! CUT THAT OUT!
ROWR!
RRRR!
JIM DAVIS 5-15
© 1986 PAWS, INC. All Rights Reserved.

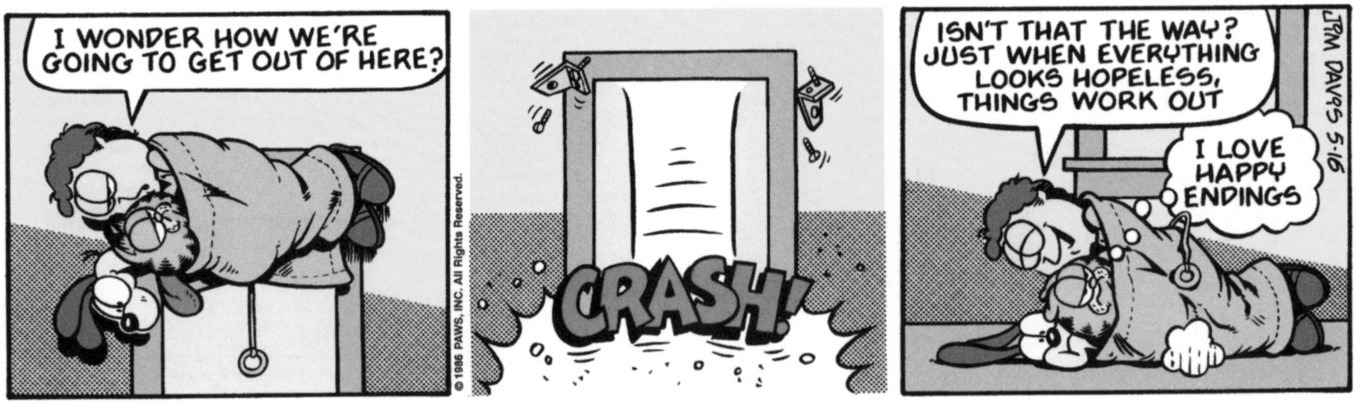
I WONDER HOW WE'RE GOING TO GET OUT OF HERE?
© 1986 PAWS, INC. All Rights Reserved.
CRASH!
ISN'T THAT THE WAY? JUST WHEN EVERYTHING LOOKS HOPELESS, THINGS WORK OUT
I LOVE HAPPY ENDINGS
JIM DAVIS 5-16

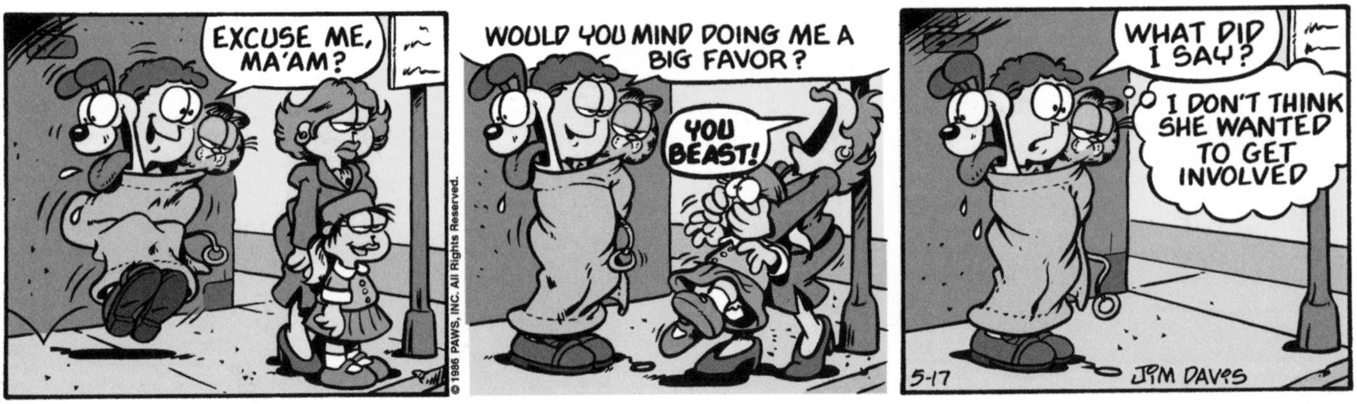
EXCUSE ME, MA'AM?
© 1986 PAWS, INC. All Rights Reserved.
WOULD YOU MIND DOING ME A BIG FAVOR?
YOU BEAST!
WHAT DID I SAY?
I DON'T THINK SHE WANTED TO GET INVOLVED
5-17
JIM DAVIS

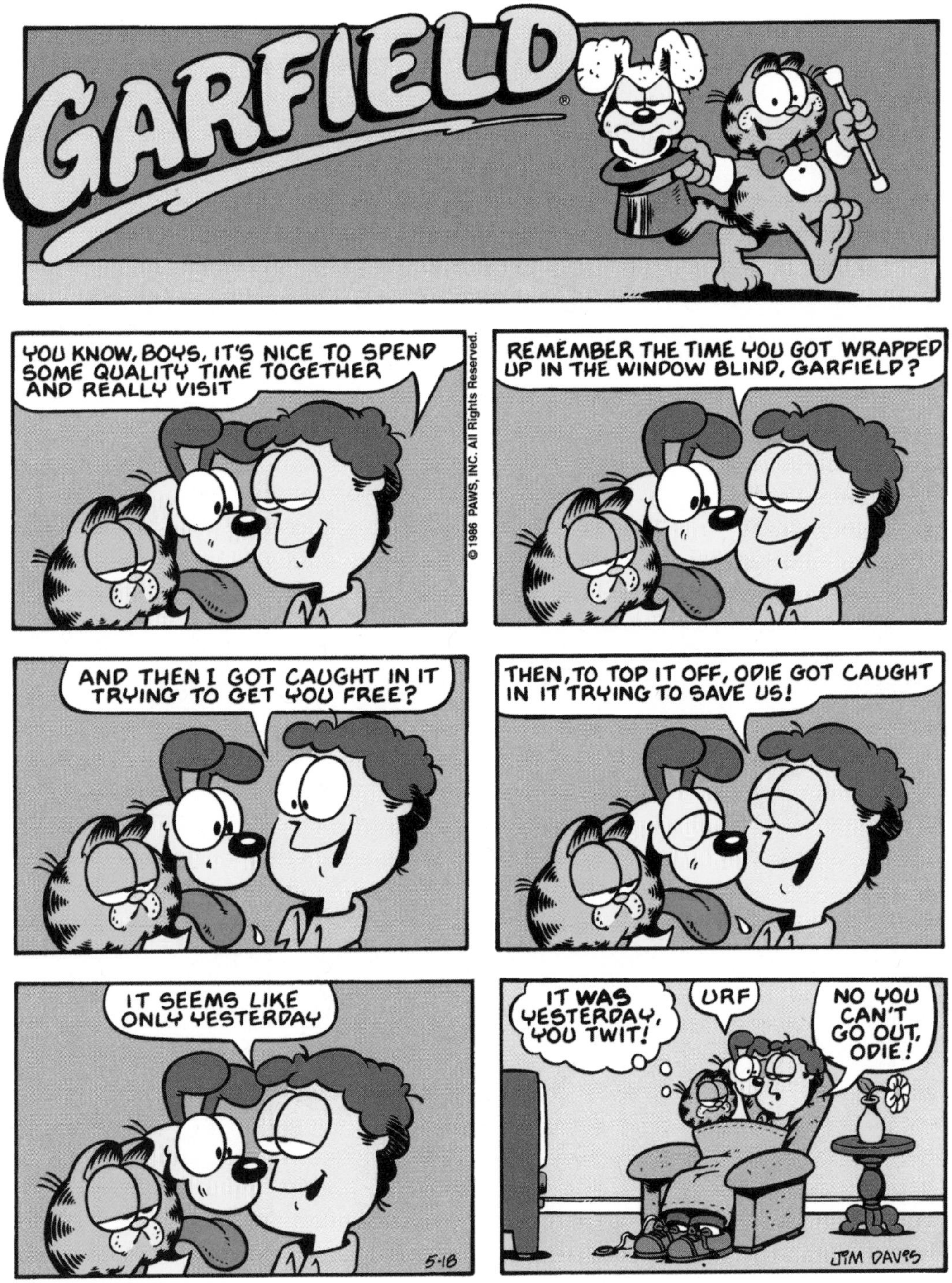
GARFIELD
YOU KNOW, BOYS, IT'S NICE TO SPEND SOME QUALITY TIME TOGETHER AND REALLY VISIT
REMEMBER THE TIME YOU GOT WRAPPED UP IN THE WINDOW BLIND, GARFIELD?
AND THEN I GOT CAUGHT IN IT TRYING TO GET YOU FREE?
THEN, TO TOP IT OFF, ODIE GOT CAUGHT IN IT TRYING TO SAVE US!
IT SEEMS LIKE ONLY YESTERDAY
5-18
IT WAS YESTERDAY, YOU TWIT!
URF
NO YOU CAN'T GO OUT, ODIE!
JIM DAVIS

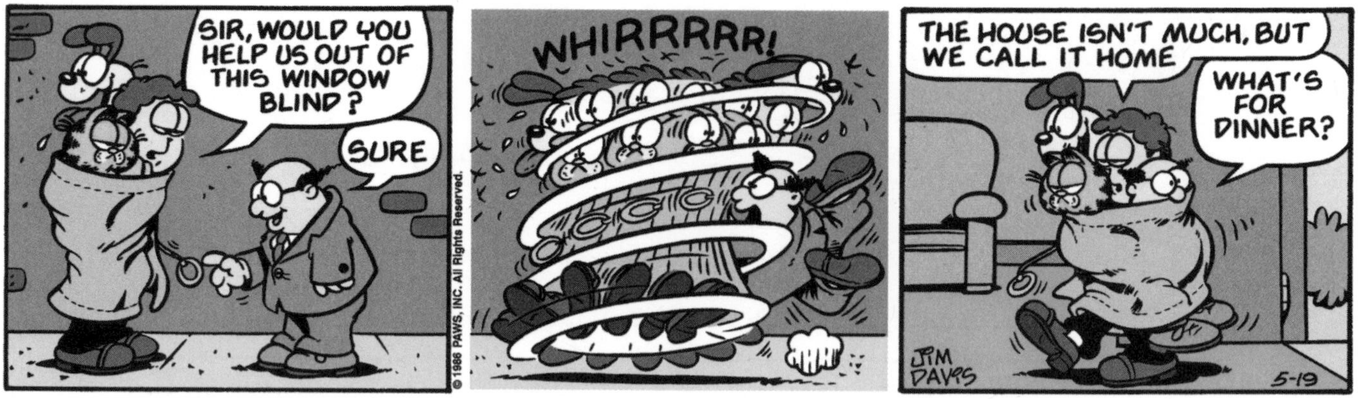
SIR, WOULD YOU HELP US OUT OF THIS WINDOW BLIND?
SURE
© 1986 PAWS, INC. All Rights Reserved.
WHIRRRRRR!
THE HOUSE ISN'T MUCH, BUT WE CALL IT HOME
WHAT'S FOR DINNER?
JIM DAVIS
5-19

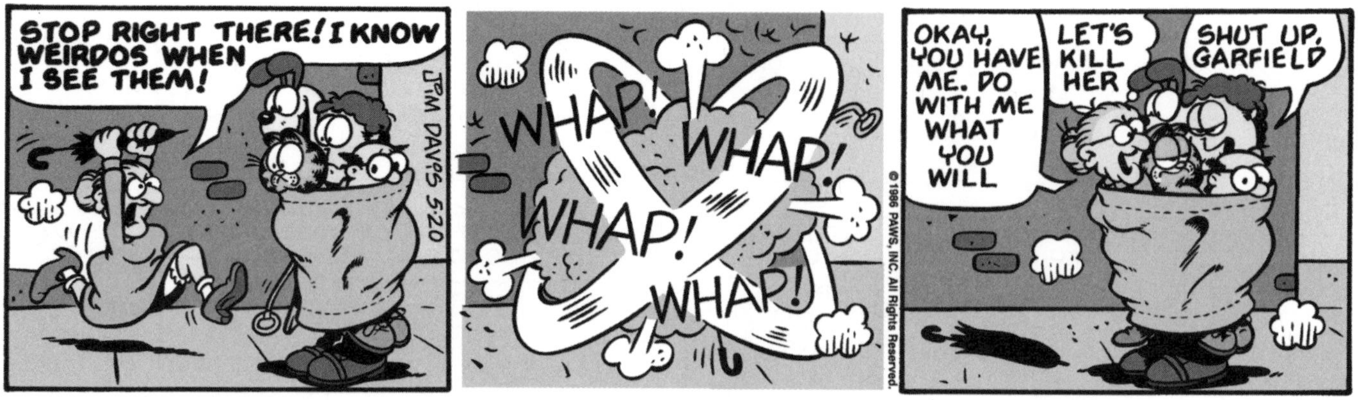
STOP RIGHT THERE! I KNOW WEIRDOS WHEN I SEE THEM!
JIM DAVIS 5-20
WHAP!
WHAP!
WHAP!
WHAP!
© 1986 PAWS, INC. All Rights Reserved.
OKAY, YOU HAVE ME. DO WITH ME WHAT YOU WILL
LET'S KILL HER
SHUT UP, GARFIELD

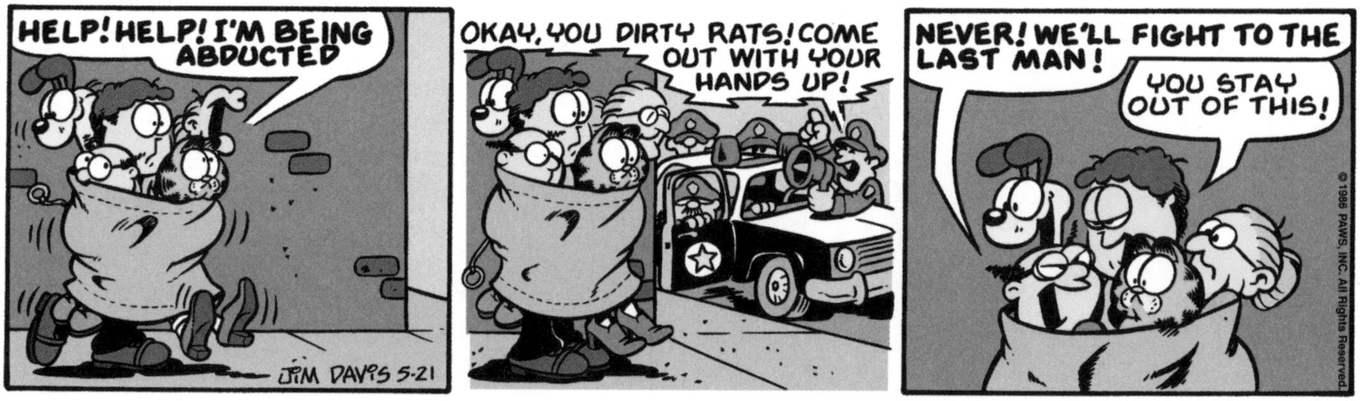
HELP! HELP! I'M BEING ABDUCTED
JIM DAVIS 5-21
OKAY, YOU DIRTY RATS! COME OUT WITH YOUR HANDS UP!
NEVER! WE'LL FIGHT TO THE LAST MAN!
YOU STAY OUT OF THIS!
© 1986 PAWS, INC. All Rights Reserved.

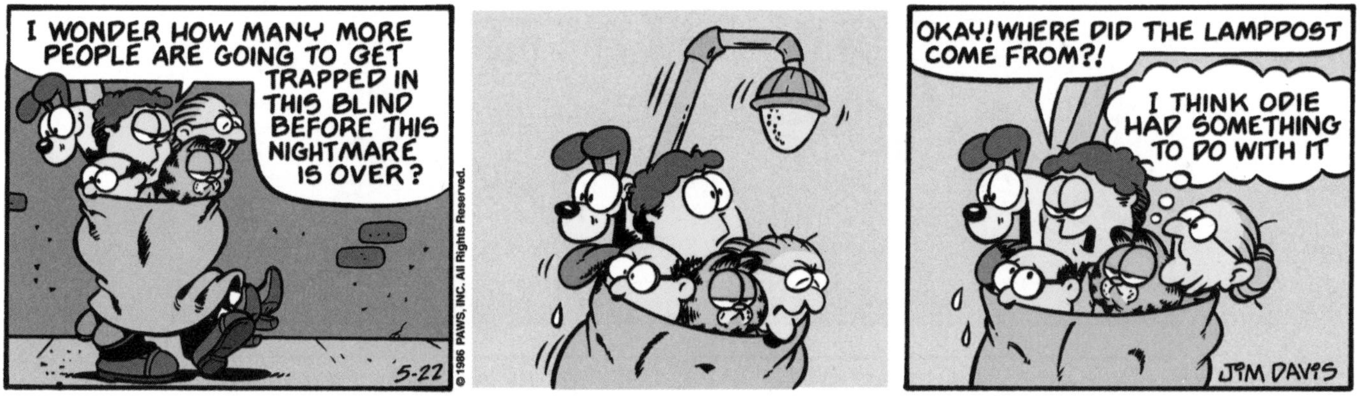
I WONDER HOW MANY MORE PEOPLE ARE GOING TO GET TRAPPED IN THIS BLIND BEFORE THIS NIGHTMARE IS OVER?
5-22
© 1986 PAWS, INC. All Rights Reserved.
OKAY! WHERE DID THE LAMPPOST COME FROM?!
I THINK ODIE HAD SOMETHING TO DO WITH IT
JIM DAVIS

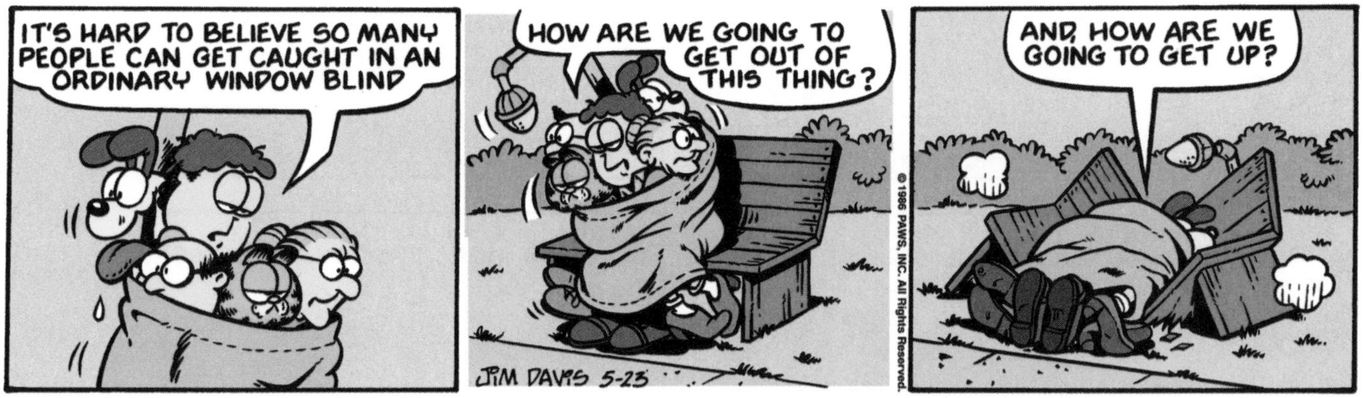
IT'S HARD TO BELIEVE SO MANY PEOPLE CAN GET CAUGHT IN AN ORDINARY WINDOW BLIND
HOW ARE WE GOING TO GET OUT OF THIS THING?
JIM DAVIS 5-23
© 1986 PAWS, INC. All Rights Reserved.
AND, HOW ARE WE GOING TO GET UP?

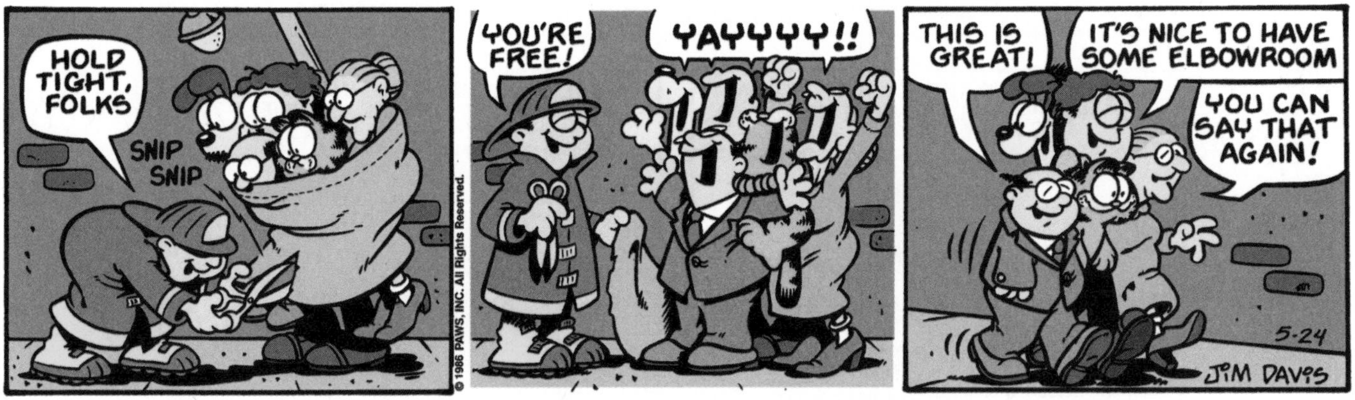
HOLD TIGHT, FOLKS
SNIP SNIP
© 1986 PAWS, INC. All Rights Reserved.
YOU'RE FREE!
YAYYYY!!
THIS IS GREAT!
IT'S NICE TO HAVE SOME ELBOWROOM
YOU CAN SAY THAT AGAIN!
5-24
JIM DAVIS

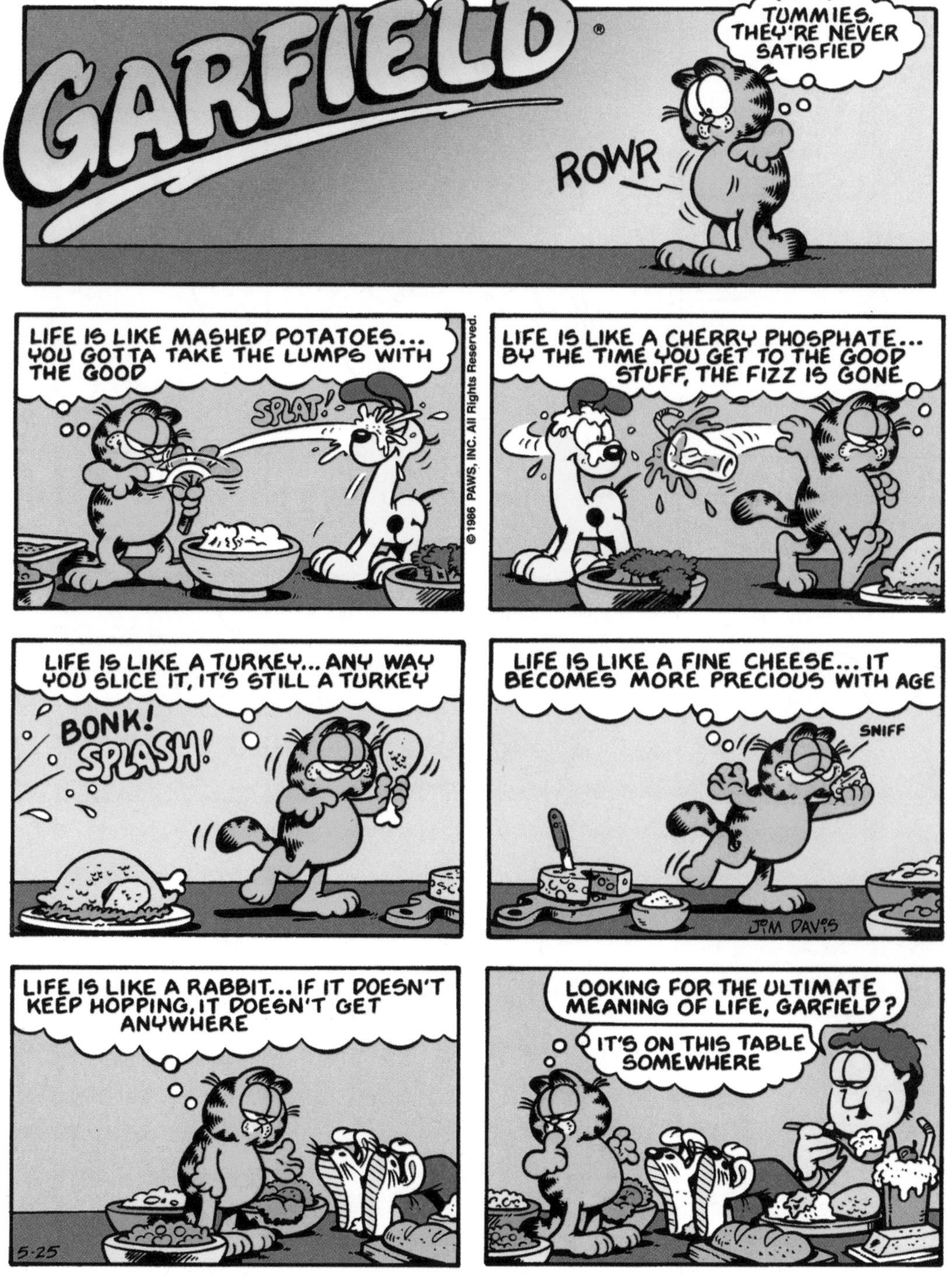
GARFIELD®
TUMMIES. THEY'RE NEVER SATISFIED
ROWR
LIFE IS LIKE MASHED POTATOES... YOU GOTTA TAKE THE LUMPS WITH THE GOOD
SPLAT!
© 1986 PAWS, INC. All Rights Reserved.
LIFE IS LIKE A CHERRY PHOSPHATE... BY THE TIME YOU GET TO THE GOOD STUFF, THE FIZZ IS GONE
LIFE IS LIKE A TURKEY... ANY WAY YOU SLICE IT, IT'S STILL A TURKEY
BONK!
SPLASH!
LIFE IS LIKE A FINE CHEESE... IT BECOMES MORE PRECIOUS WITH AGE
SNIFF
JIM DAVIS
LIFE IS LIKE A RABBIT... IF IT DOESN'T KEEP HOPPING, IT DOESN'T GET ANYWHERE
5-25
LOOKING FOR THE ULTIMATE MEANING OF LIFE, GARFIELD?
IT'S ON THIS TABLE SOMEWHERE

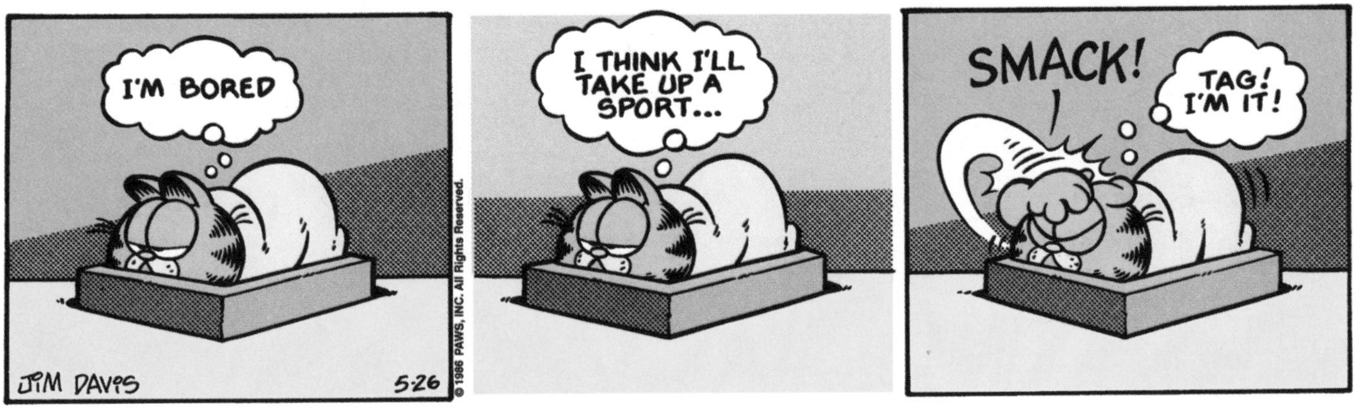
I'M BORED
JIM DAVIS
5-26
© 1986 PAWS, INC. All Rights Reserved.
I THINK I'LL TAKE UP A SPORT...
SMACK!
TAG! I'M IT!

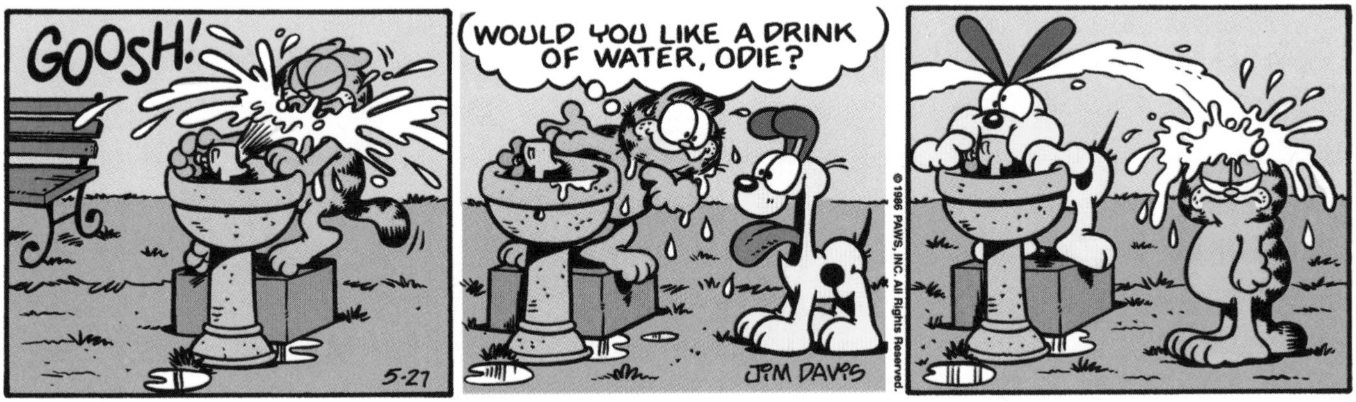
GOOSH!
5-27
WOULD YOU LIKE A DRINK OF WATER, ODIE?
JIM DAVIS
© 1986 PAWS, INC. All Rights Reserved.

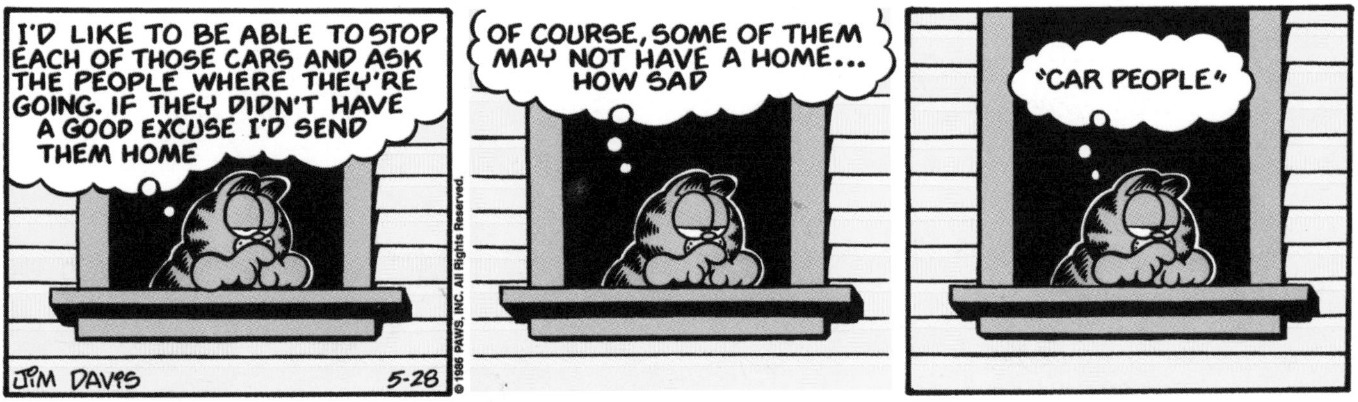
I'D LIKE TO BE ABLE TO STOP EACH OF THOSE CARS AND ASK THE PEOPLE WHERE THEY'RE GOING. IF THEY DIDN'T HAVE A GOOD EXCUSE I'D SEND THEM HOME
JIM DAVIS
5-28
© 1986 PAWS, INC. All Rights Reserved.
OF COURSE, SOME OF THEM MAY NOT HAVE A HOME... HOW SAD
"CAR PEOPLE"

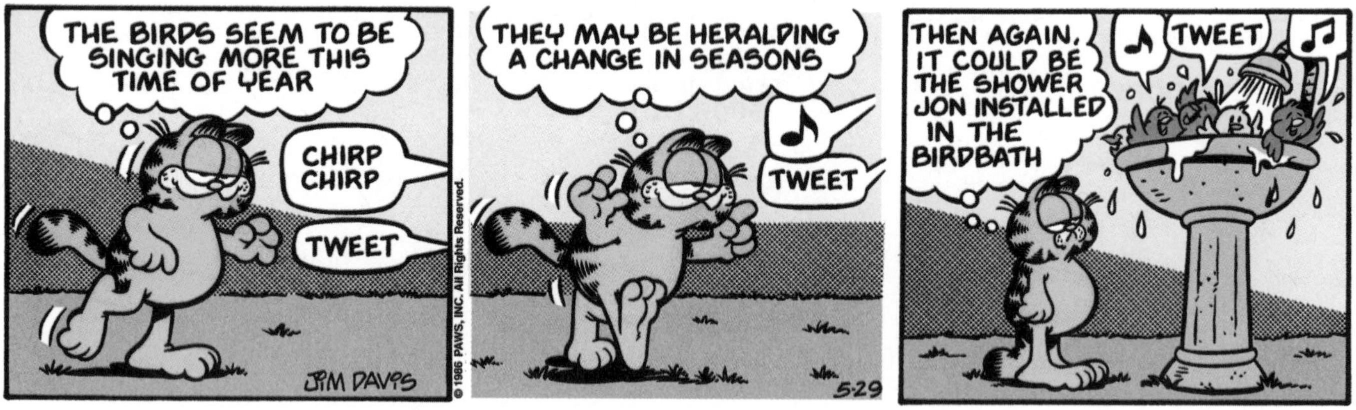
THE BIRDS SEEM TO BE SINGING MORE THIS TIME OF YEAR
CHIRP CHIRP
TWEET
JIM DAVIS
© 1986 PAWS, INC. All Rights Reserved.
THEY MAY BE HERALDING A CHANGE IN SEASONS
TWEET
5-29
THEN AGAIN, IT COULD BE THE SHOWER JON INSTALLED IN THE BIRDBATH
TWEET

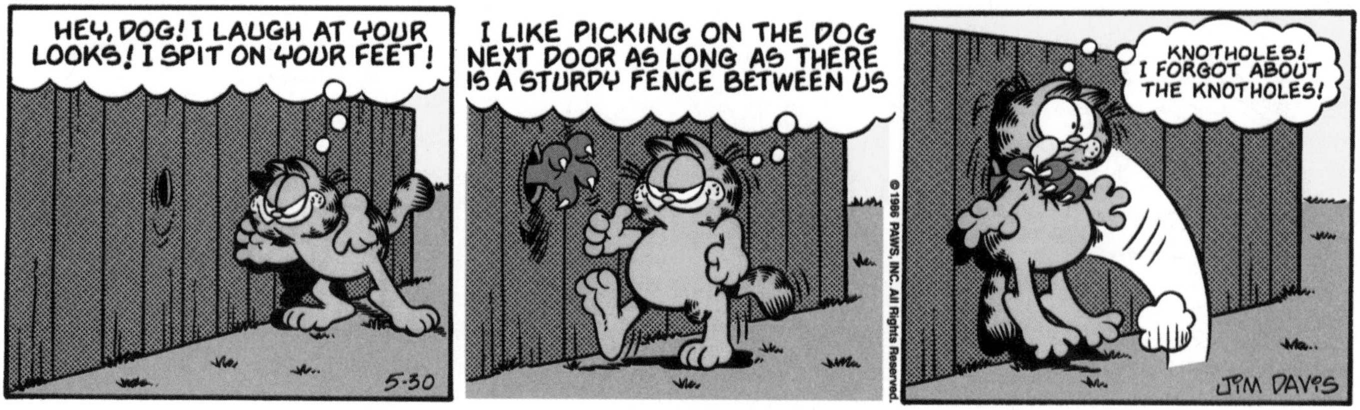
HEY, DOG! I LAUGH AT YOUR LOOKS! I SPIT ON YOUR FEET!
5-30
I LIKE PICKING ON THE DOG NEXT DOOR AS LONG AS THERE IS A STURDY FENCE BETWEEN US
© 1986 PAWS, INC. All Rights Reserved.
KNOTHOLES! I FORGOT ABOUT THE KNOTHOLES!
JIM DAVIS

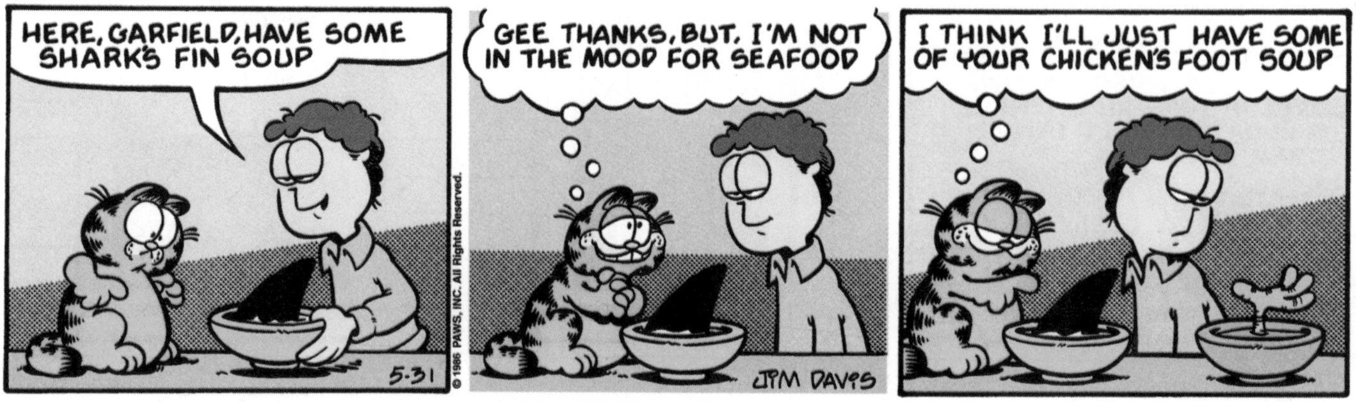
HERE, GARFIELD, HAVE SOME SHARK'S FIN SOUP
5-31
© 1986 PAWS, INC. All Rights Reserved.
GEE THANKS, BUT, I'M NOT IN THE MOOD FOR SEAFOOD
JIM DAVIS
I THINK I'LL JUST HAVE SOME OF YOUR CHICKEN'S FOOT SOUP

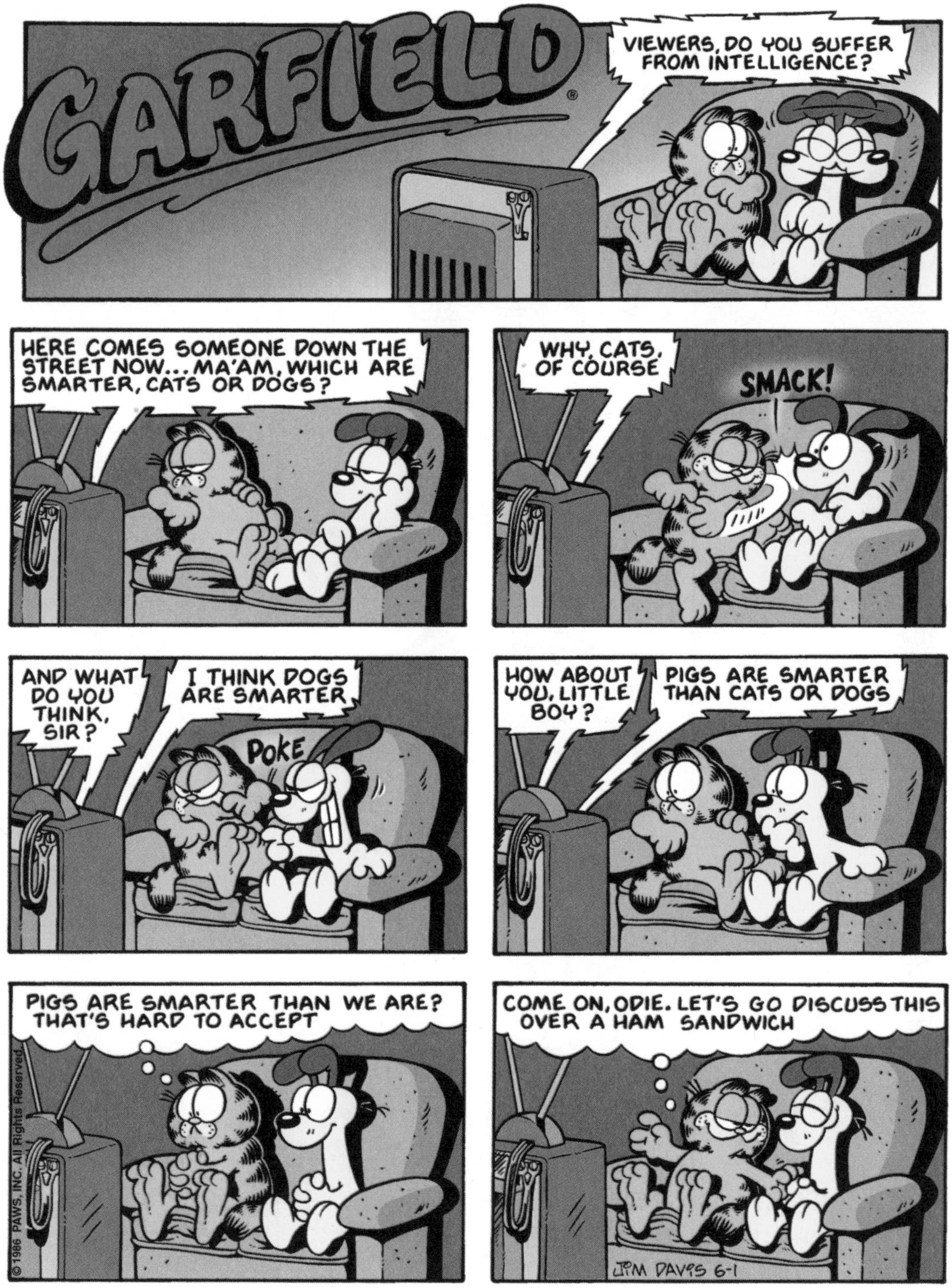
GARFIELD®
VIEWERS, DO YOU SUFFER FROM INTELLIGENCE?
HERE COMES SOMEONE DOWN THE STREET NOW... MA'AM, WHICH ARE SMARTER, CATS OR DOGS?
WHY, CATS, OF COURSE
SMACK!
AND WHAT DO YOU THINK, SIR?
I THINK DOGS ARE SMARTER
POKE
HOW ABOUT YOU, LITTLE BOY?
PIGS ARE SMARTER THAN CATS OR DOGS
PIGS ARE SMARTER THAN WE ARE? THAT'S HARD TO ACCEPT
COME ON, ODIE. LET'S GO DISCUSS THIS OVER A HAM SANDWICH
© 1986 PAWS, INC. All Rights Reserved.
JIM DAVIS 6-1

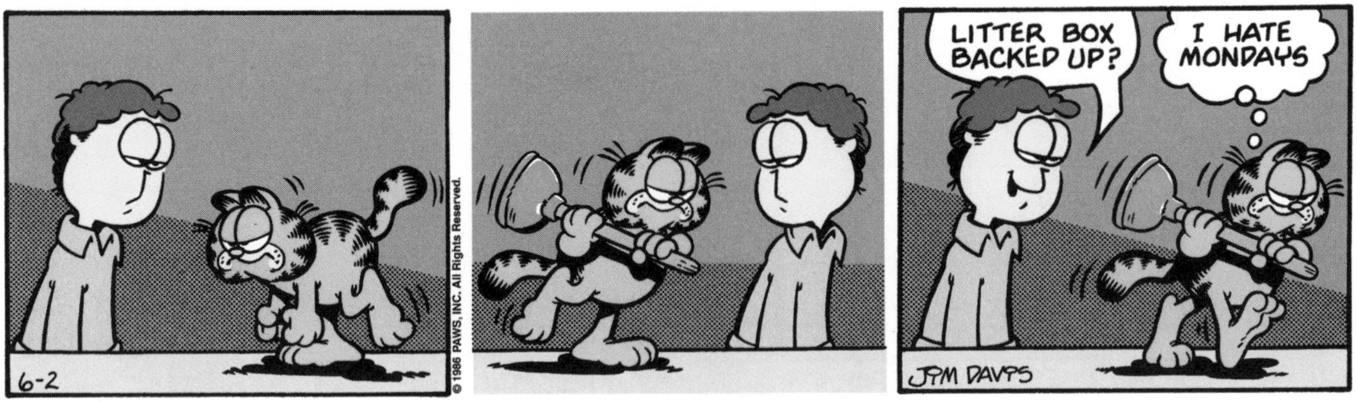
6-2
© 1986 PAWS, INC. All Rights Reserved.
LITTER BOX BACKED UP?
I HATE MONDAYS
JIM DAVIS

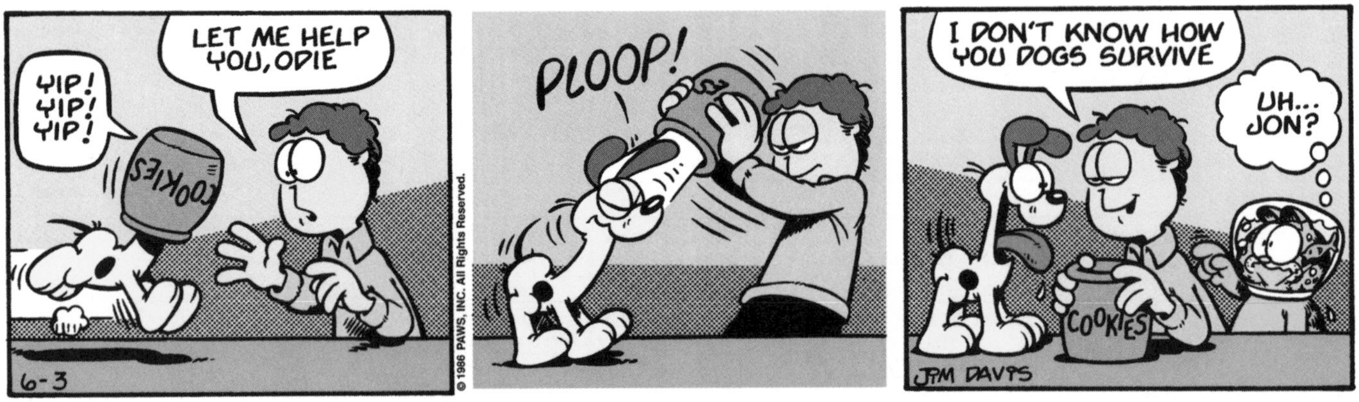
YIP! YIP! YIP!
LET ME HELP YOU, ODIE
COOKIES
6-3
© 1986 PAWS, INC. All Rights Reserved.
PLOOP!
I DON'T KNOW HOW YOU DOGS SURVIVE
UH... JON?
COOKIES
JIM DAVIS

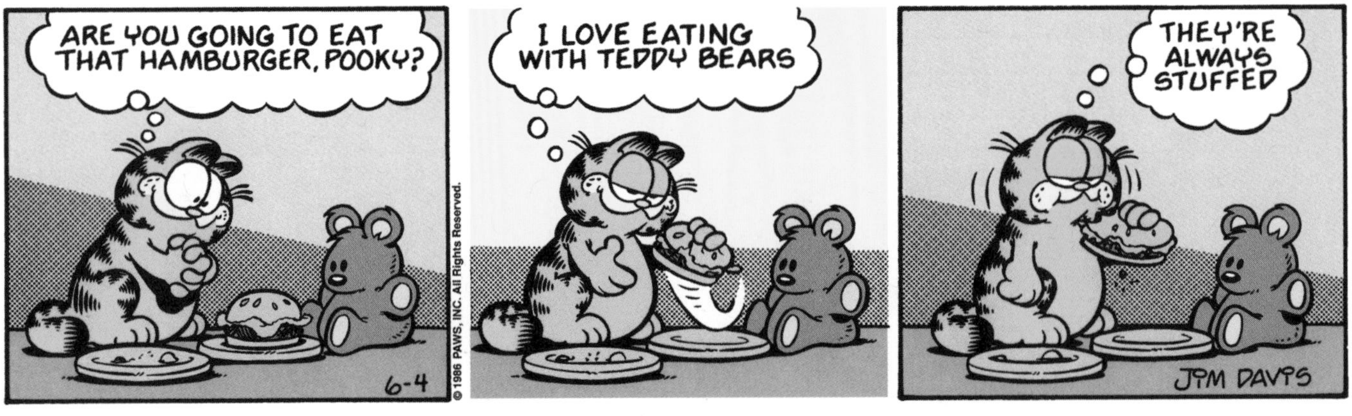
ARE YOU GOING TO EAT THAT HAMBURGER, POOKY?
6-4
© 1986 PAWS, INC. All Rights Reserved.
I LOVE EATING WITH TEDDY BEARS
THEY'RE ALWAYS STUFFED
JIM DAVIS

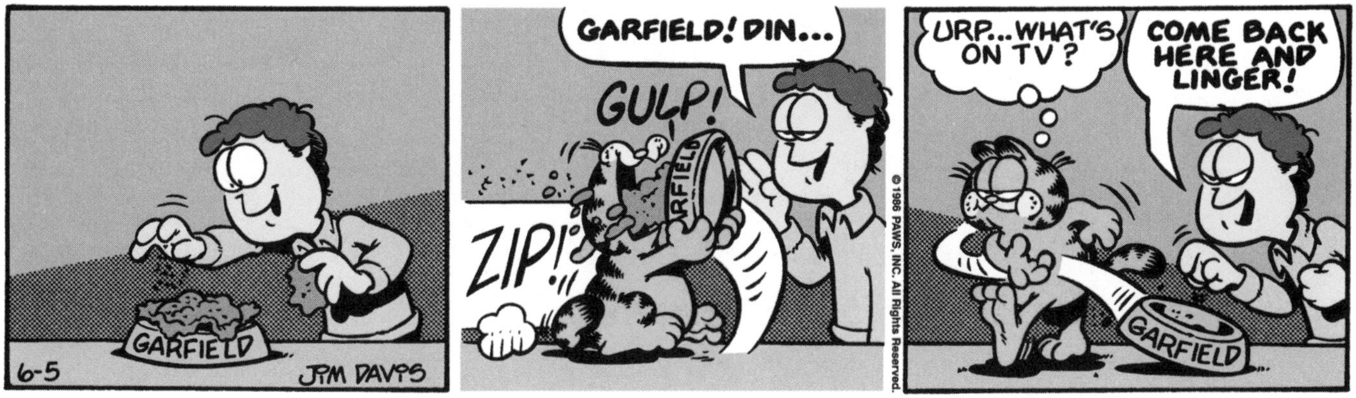
GARFIELD
6-5
JIM DAVIS
GARFIELD! DIN...
GULP!
GARFIELD
ZIP!
URP...WHAT'S ON TV?
COME BACK HERE AND LINGER!
GARFIELD
© 1986 PAWS, INC. All Rights Reserved.

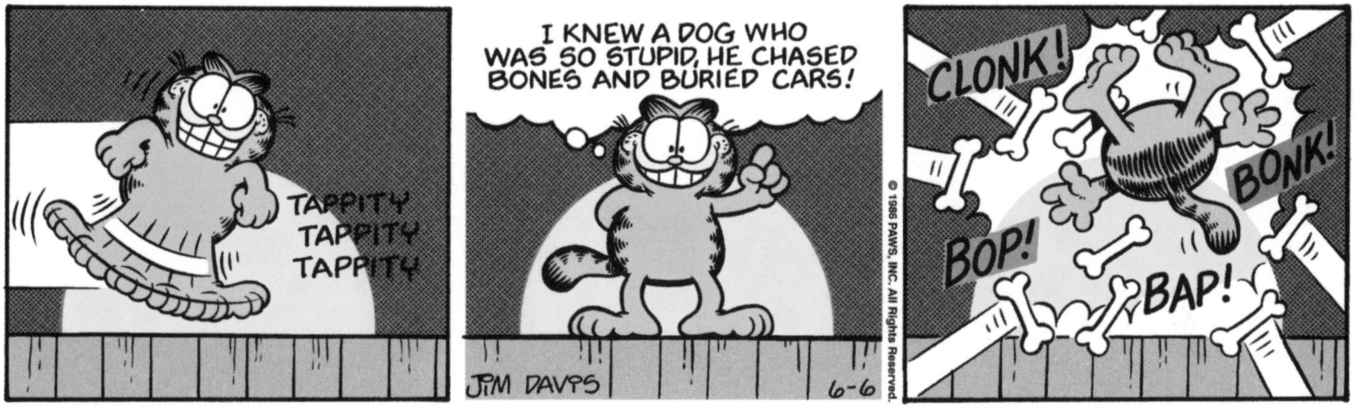
TAPPITY TAPPITY TAPPITY
I KNEW A DOG WHO WAS SO STUPID, HE CHASED BONES AND BURIED CARS!
JIM DAVIS
6-6
CLONK!
BONK!
BOP!
BAP!
© 1986 PAWS, INC. All Rights Reserved.

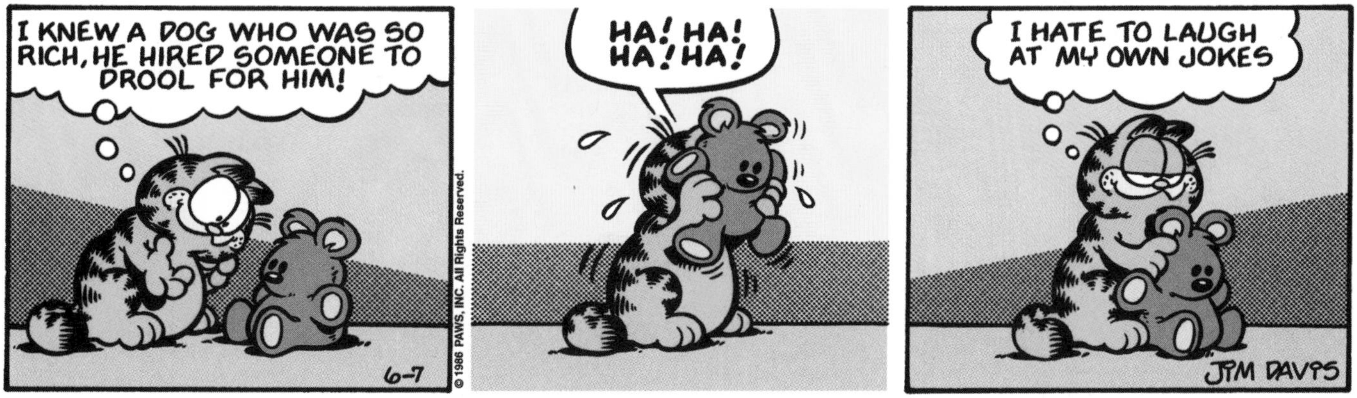
I KNEW A DOG WHO WAS SO RICH, HE HIRED SOMEONE TO DROOL FOR HIM!
6-7
© 1986 PAWS, INC. All Rights Reserved.
HA! HA! HA! HA!
I HATE TO LAUGH AT MY OWN JOKES
JIM DAVIS

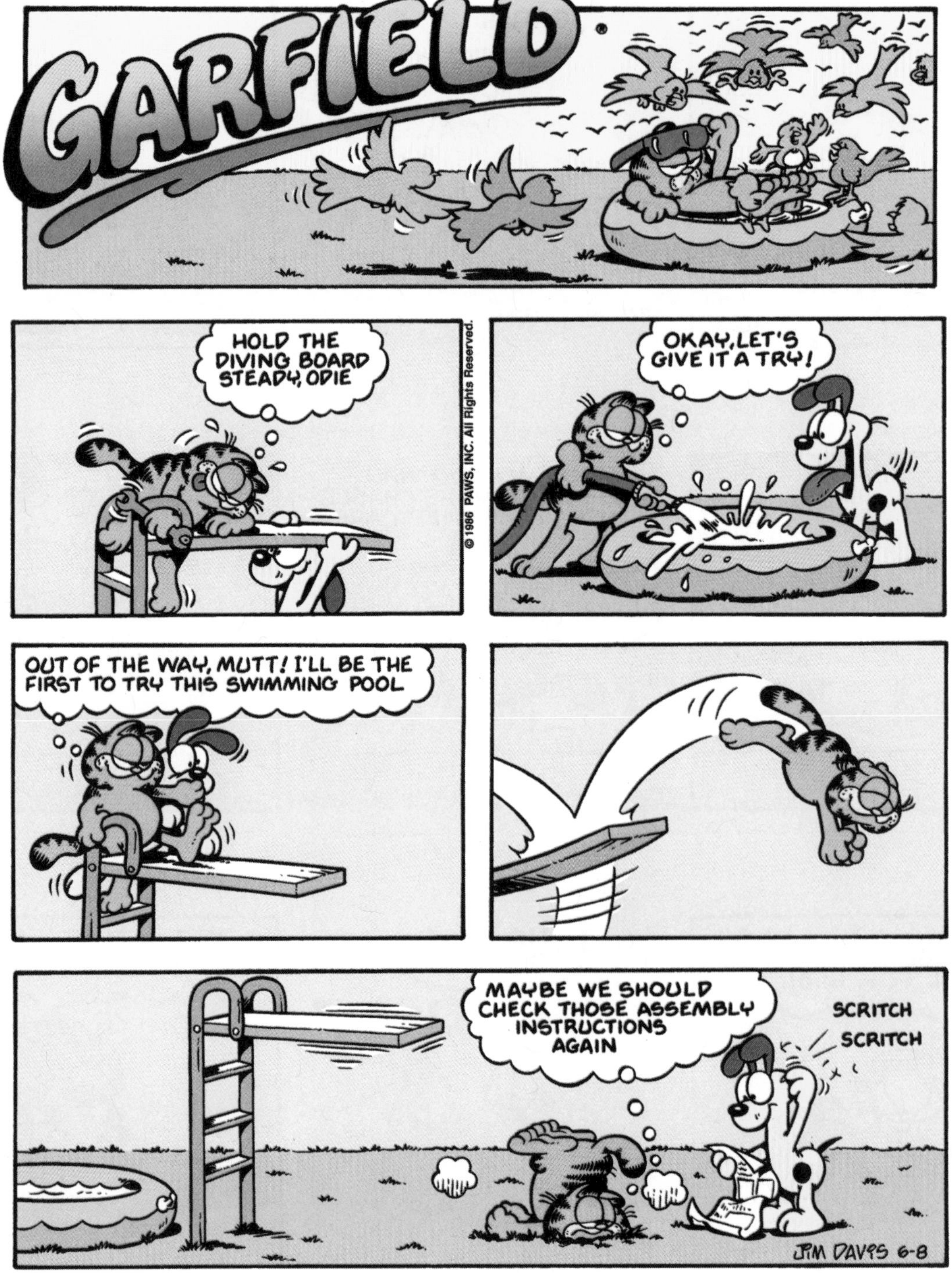
GARFIELD
HOLD THE DIVING BOARD STEADY, ODIE
© 1986 PAWS, INC. All Rights Reserved.
OKAY, LET'S GIVE IT A TRY!
OUT OF THE WAY, MUTT! I'LL BE THE FIRST TO TRY THIS SWIMMING POOL
MAYBE WE SHOULD CHECK THOSE ASSEMBLY INSTRUCTIONS AGAIN
SCRITCH
SCRITCH
JIM DAVIS 6-8

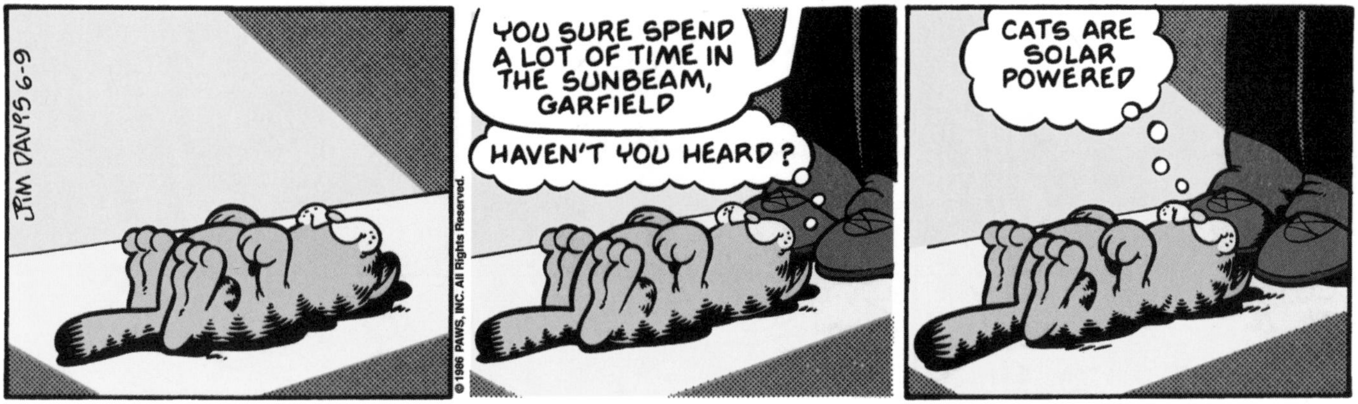
JIM DAVIS 6-9
YOU SURE SPEND A LOT OF TIME IN THE SUNBEAM, GARFIELD
HAVEN'T YOU HEARD?
© 1986 PAWS, INC. All Rights Reserved.
CATS ARE SOLAR POWERED

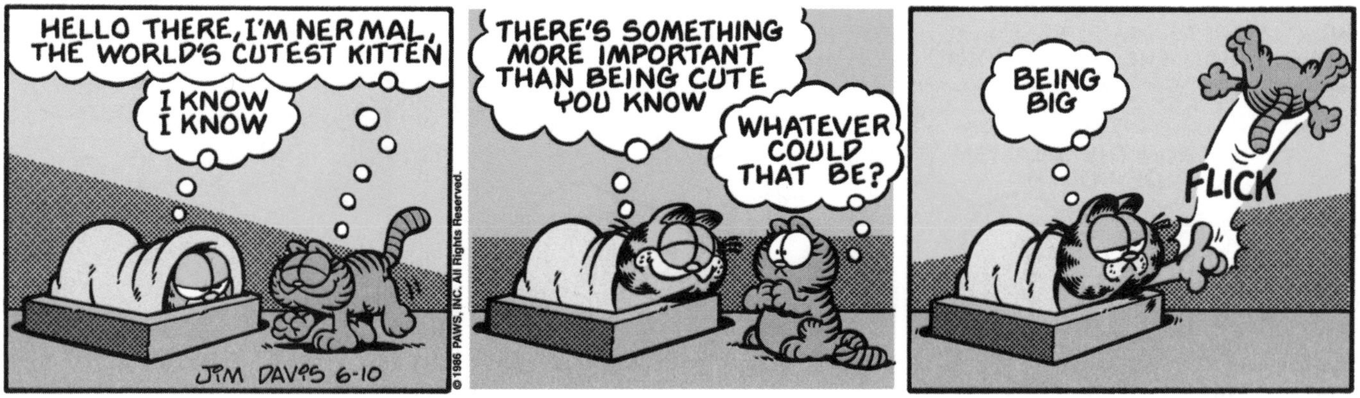
HELLO THERE, I'M NERMAL, THE WORLD'S CUTEST KITTEN
I KNOW I KNOW
JIM DAVIS 6-10
© 1986 PAWS, INC. All Rights Reserved.
THERE'S SOMETHING MORE IMPORTANT THAN BEING CUTE YOU KNOW
WHATEVER COULD THAT BE?
BEING BIG
FLICK

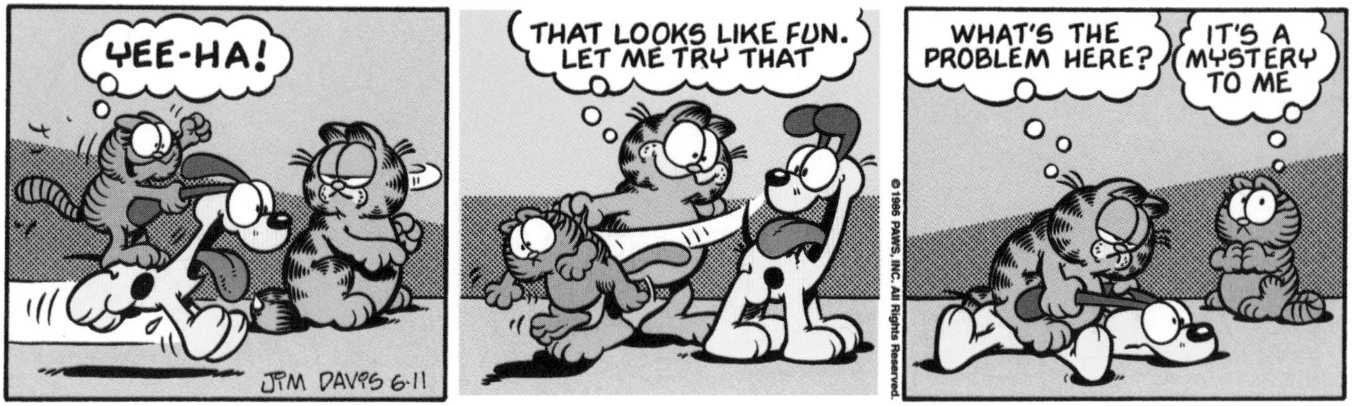
YEE-HA!
JIM DAVIS 6-11
THAT LOOKS LIKE FUN. LET ME TRY THAT
© 1986 PAWS, INC. All Rights Reserved.
WHAT'S THE PROBLEM HERE?
IT'S A MYSTERY TO ME

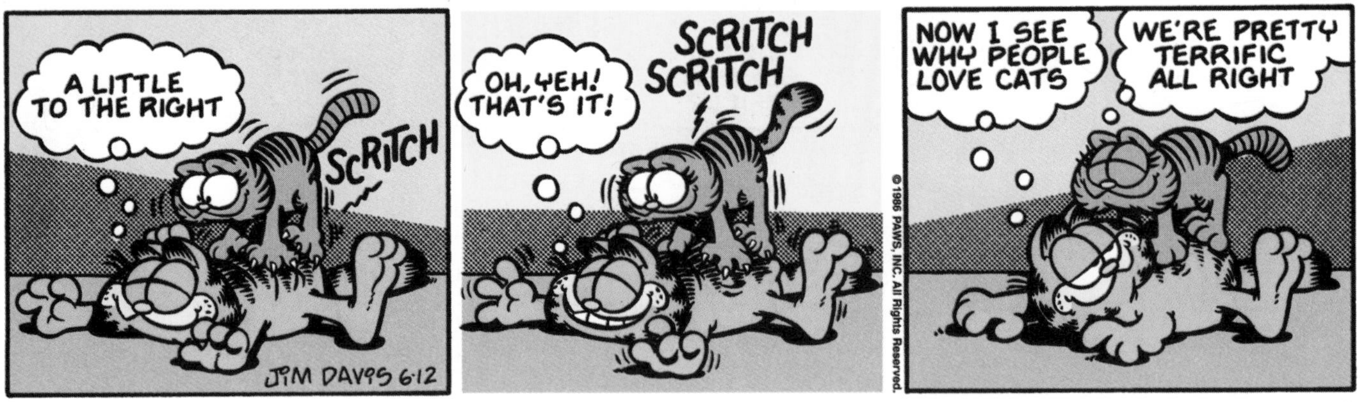
A LITTLE TO THE RIGHT
SCRITCH
JIM DAVIS 6-12
OH, YEH! THAT'S IT!
SCRITCH SCRITCH
© 1986 PAWS, INC. All Rights Reserved.
NOW I SEE WHY PEOPLE LOVE CATS
WE'RE PRETTY TERRIFIC ALL RIGHT

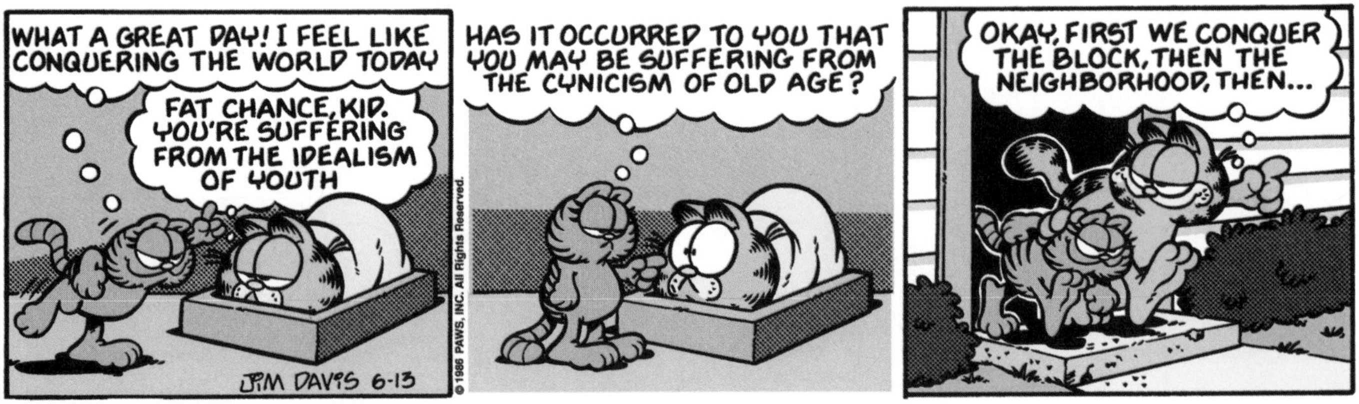
WHAT A GREAT DAY! I FEEL LIKE CONQUERING THE WORLD TODAY
FAT CHANCE, KID. YOU'RE SUFFERING FROM THE IDEALISM OF YOUTH
JIM DAVIS 6-13
© 1986 PAWS, INC. All Rights Reserved.
HAS IT OCCURRED TO YOU THAT YOU MAY BE SUFFERING FROM THE CYNICISM OF OLD AGE?
OKAY, FIRST WE CONQUER THE BLOCK, THEN THE NEIGHBORHOOD, THEN...

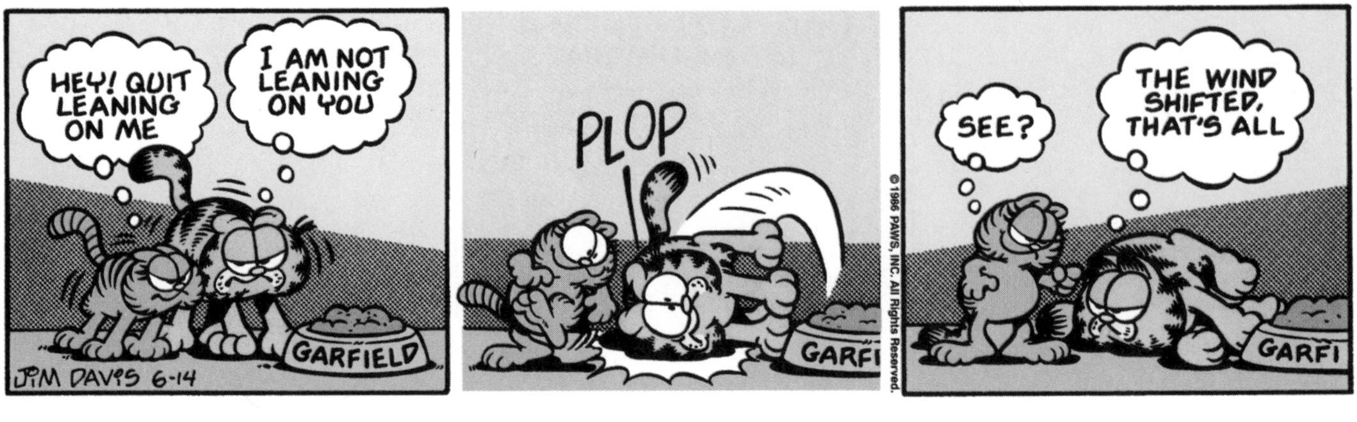
HEY! QUIT LEANING ON ME
I AM NOT LEANING ON YOU
GARFIELD
JIM DAVIS 6-14
PLOP
GARFI
© 1986 PAWS, INC. All Rights Reserved.
SEE?
THE WIND SHIFTED, THAT'S ALL
GARFI

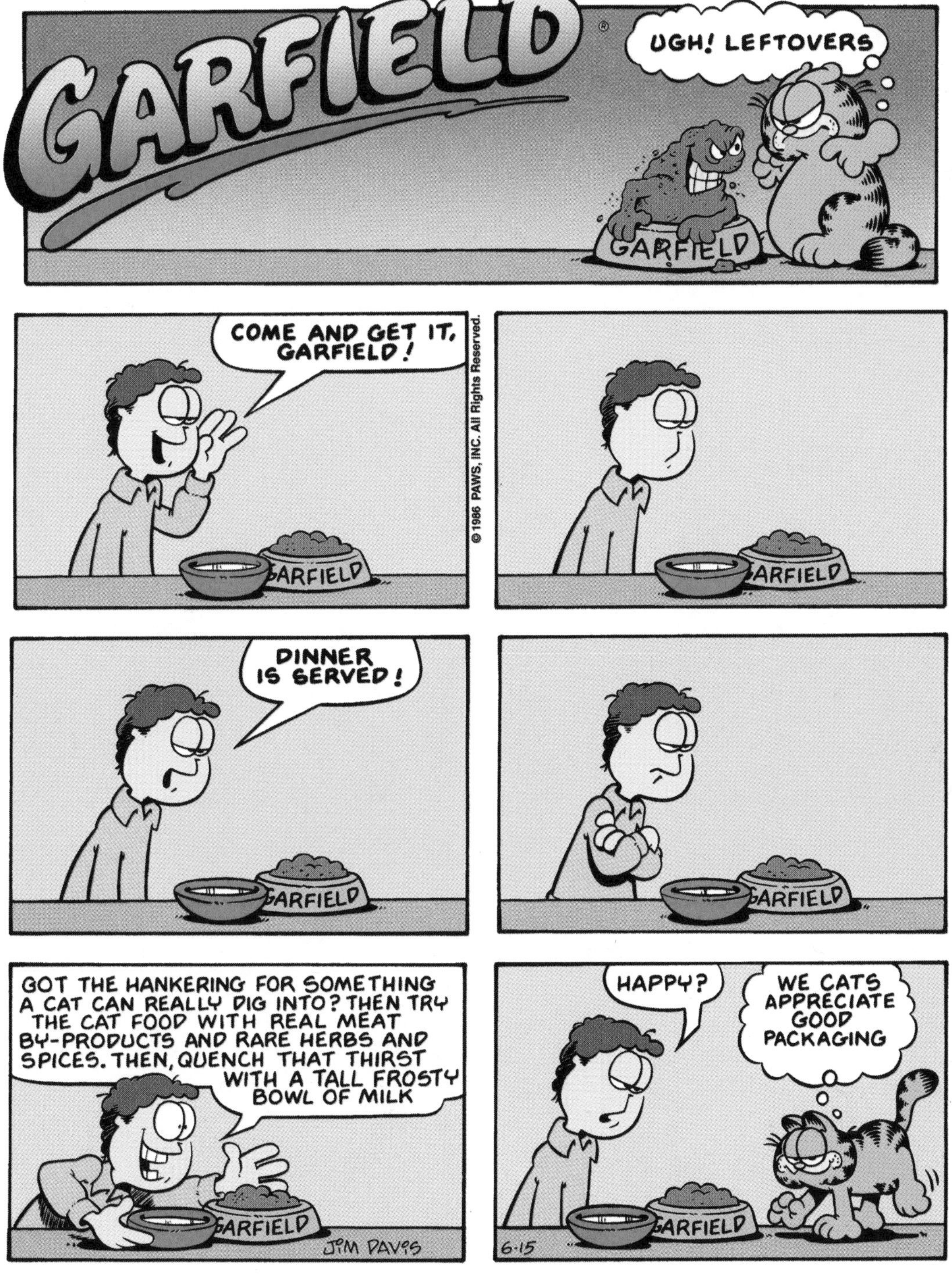
GARFIELD
UGH! LEFTOVERS
GARFIELD
COME AND GET IT, GARFIELD!
© 1986 PAWS, INC. All Rights Reserved.
GARFIELD
GARFIELD
DINNER IS SERVED!
GARFIELD
GARFIELD
GOT THE HANKERING FOR SOMETHING A CAT CAN REALLY DIG INTO? THEN TRY THE CAT FOOD WITH REAL MEAT BY-PRODUCTS AND RARE HERBS AND SPICES. THEN, QUENCH THAT THIRST WITH A TALL FROSTY BOWL OF MILK
GARFIELD
JIM DAVIS
HAPPY?
WE CATS APPRECIATE GOOD PACKAGING
GARFIELD
6-15

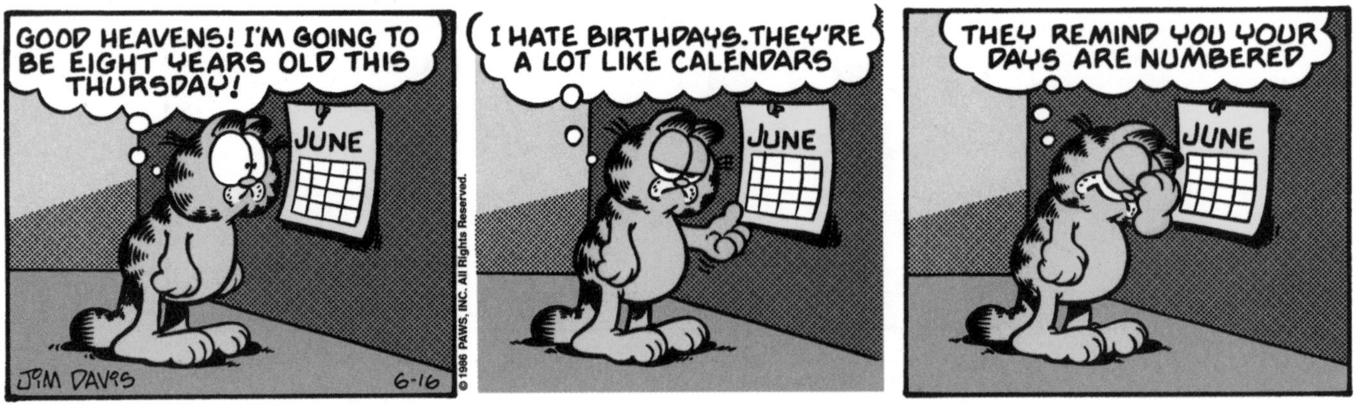
GOOD HEAVENS! I'M GOING TO BE EIGHT YEARS OLD THIS THURSDAY!
JUNE
JIM DAVIS
6-16
© 1986 PAWS, INC. All Rights Reserved.
I HATE BIRTHDAYS. THEY'RE A LOT LIKE CALENDARS
JUNE
THEY REMIND YOU YOUR DAYS ARE NUMBERED
JUNE

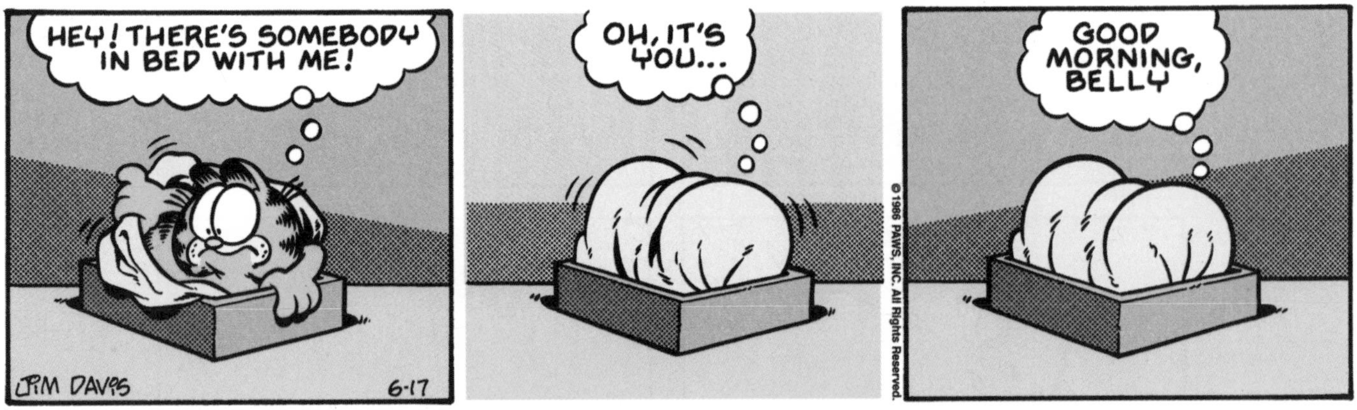
HEY! THERE'S SOMEBODY IN BED WITH ME!
JIM DAVIS
6-17
OH, IT'S YOU...
© 1986 PAWS, INC. All Rights Reserved.
GOOD MORNING, BELLY

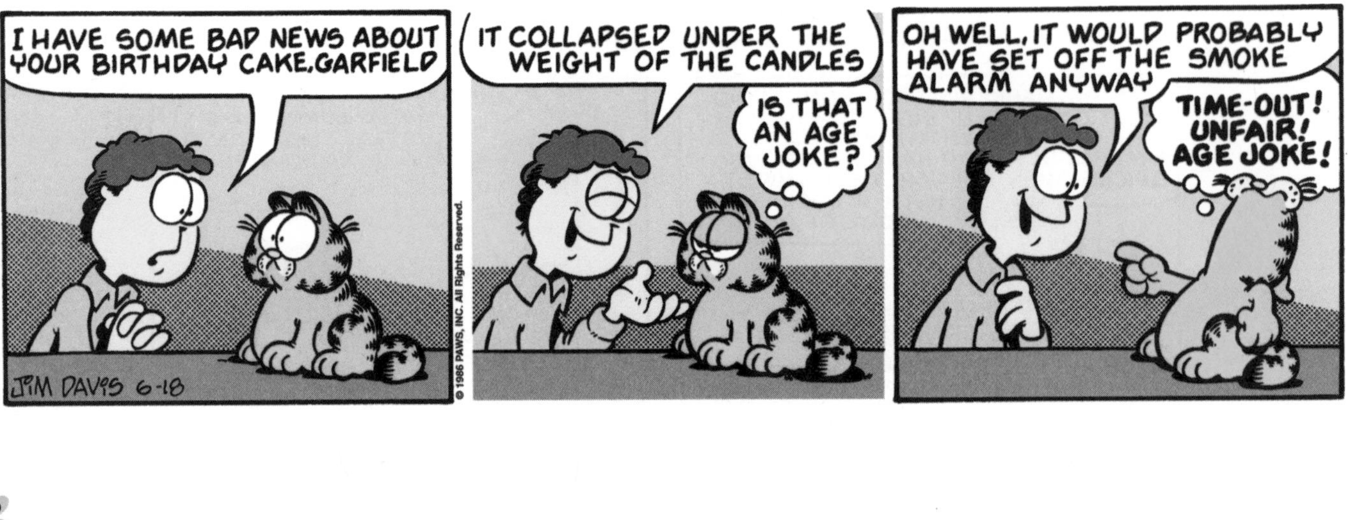
I HAVE SOME BAD NEWS ABOUT YOUR BIRTHDAY CAKE, GARFIELD
JIM DAVIS 6-18
© 1986 PAWS, INC. All Rights Reserved.
IT COLLAPSED UNDER THE WEIGHT OF THE CANDLES
IS THAT AN AGE JOKE?
OH WELL, IT WOULD PROBABLY HAVE SET OFF THE SMOKE ALARM ANYWAY
TIME-OUT! UNFAIR! AGE JOKE!

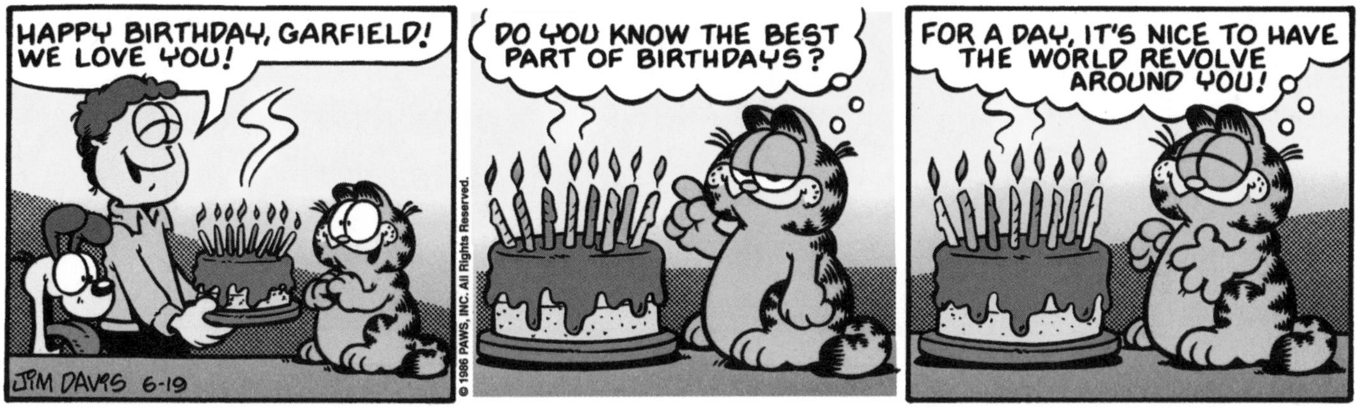
HAPPY BIRTHDAY, GARFIELD! WE LOVE YOU!
JIM DAVIS 6-19
© 1986 PAWS, INC. All Rights Reserved.
DO YOU KNOW THE BEST PART OF BIRTHDAYS?
FOR A DAY, IT'S NICE TO HAVE THE WORLD REVOLVE AROUND YOU!

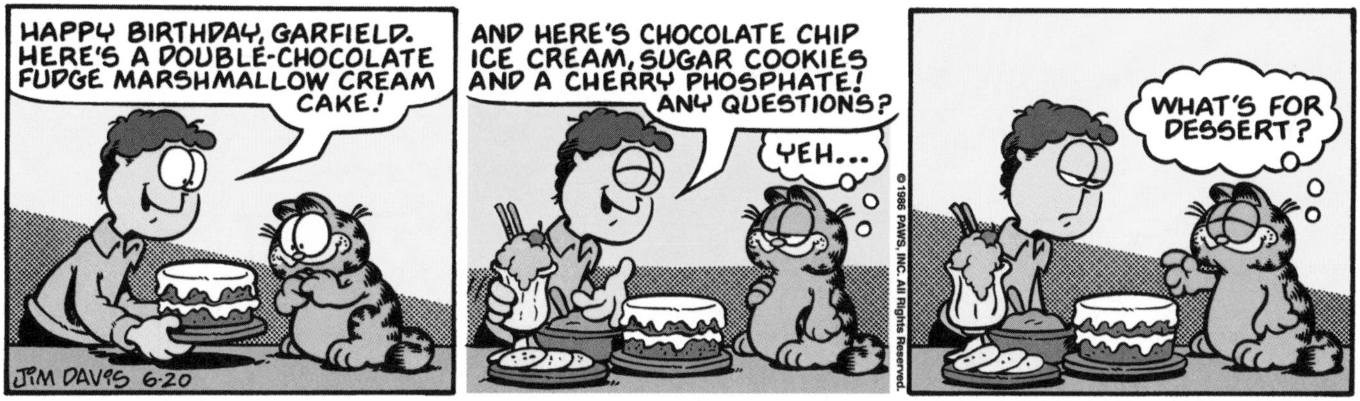
HAPPY BIRTHDAY, GARFIELD. HERE'S A DOUBLE-CHOCOLATE FUDGE MARSHMALLOW CREAM CAKE!
JIM DAVIS 6-20
AND HERE'S CHOCOLATE CHIP ICE CREAM, SUGAR COOKIES AND A CHERRY PHOSPHATE! ANY QUESTIONS?
YEH...
© 1986 PAWS, INC. All Rights Reserved.
WHAT'S FOR DESSERT?

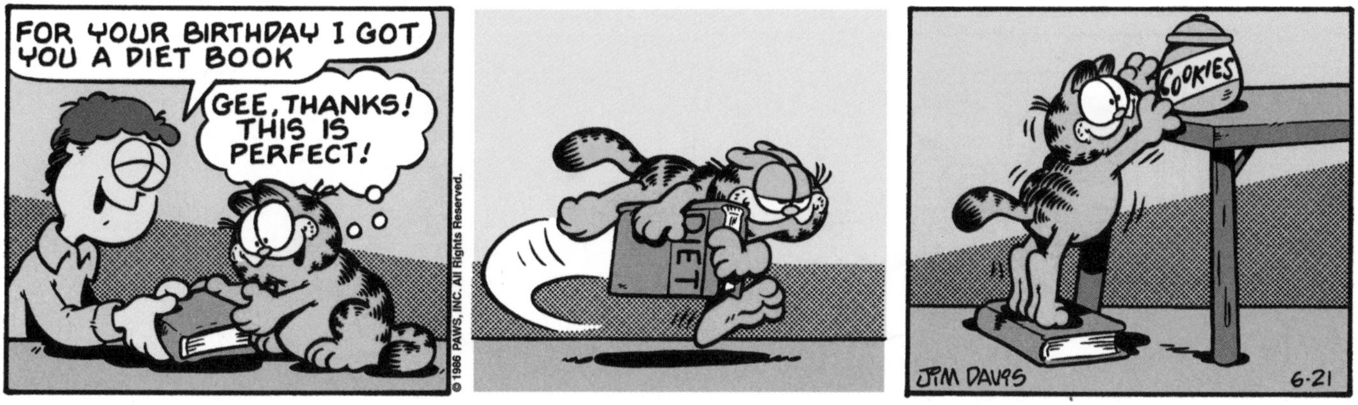
FOR YOUR BIRTHDAY I GOT YOU A DIET BOOK
GEE, THANKS! THIS IS PERFECT!
© 1986 PAWS, INC. All Rights Reserved.
DIET
COOKIES
JIM DAVIS
6-21

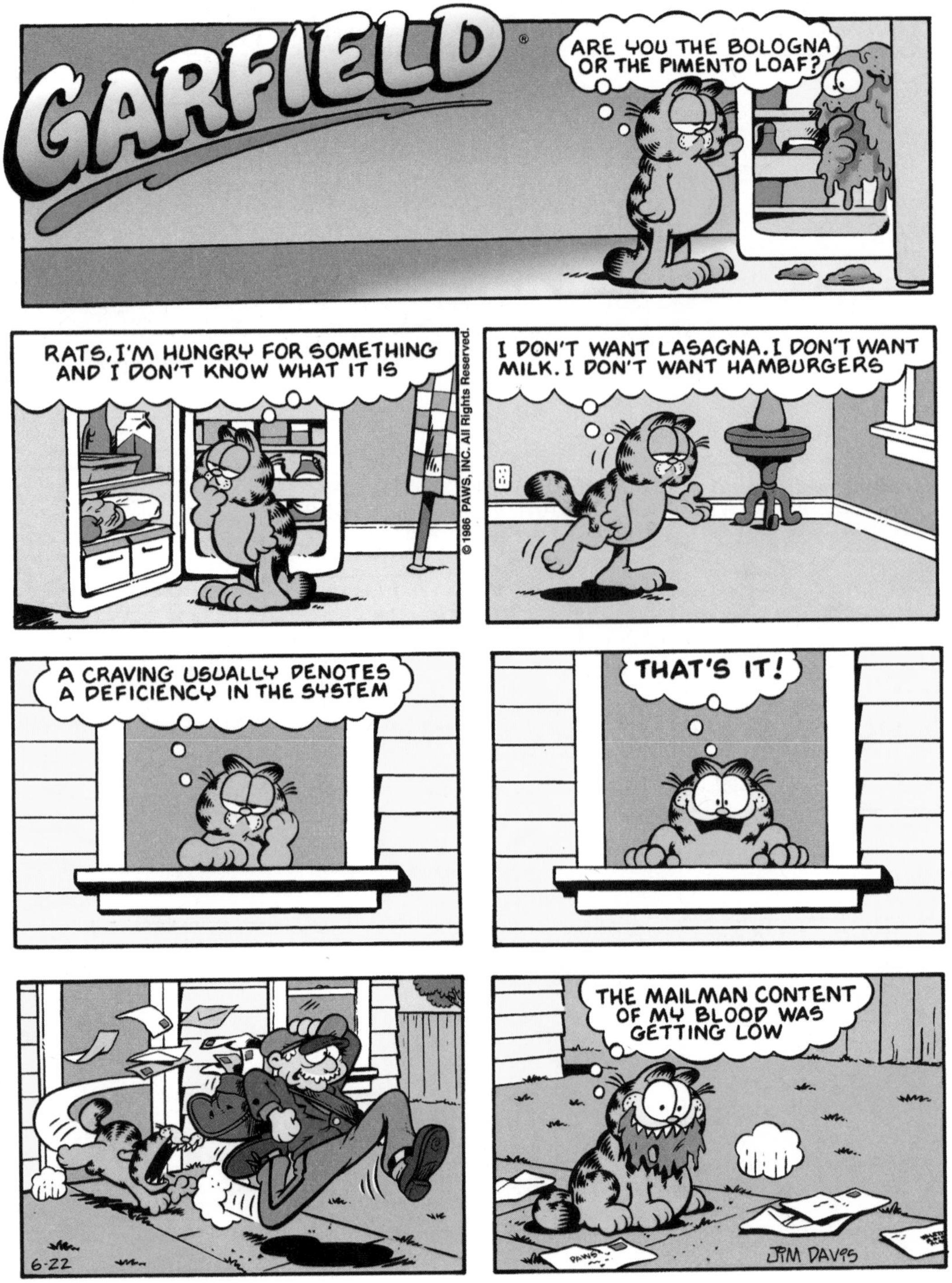
GARFIELD
ARE YOU THE BOLOGNA OR THE PIMENTO LOAF?
RATS, I'M HUNGRY FOR SOMETHING AND I DON'T KNOW WHAT IT IS
© 1986 PAWS, INC. All Rights Reserved.
I DON'T WANT LASAGNA. I DON'T WANT MILK. I DON'T WANT HAMBURGERS
A CRAVING USUALLY DENOTES A DEFICIENCY IN THE SYSTEM
THAT'S IT!
6-22
THE MAILMAN CONTENT OF MY BLOOD WAS GETTING LOW
JIM DAVIS

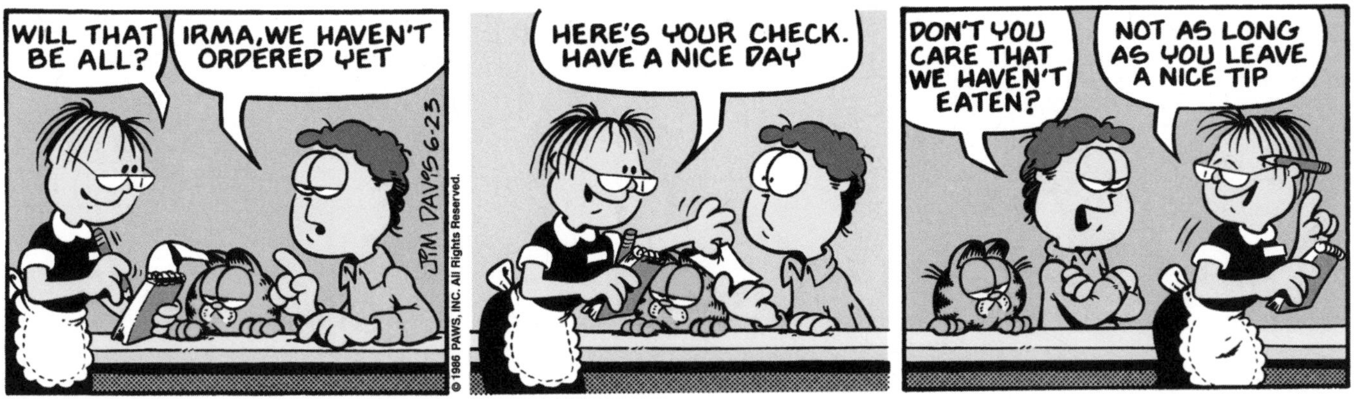
WILL THAT BE ALL?
IRMA, WE HAVEN'T ORDERED YET
JIM DAVIS 6-23
© 1986 PAWS, INC. All Rights Reserved.
HERE'S YOUR CHECK. HAVE A NICE DAY
DON'T YOU CARE THAT WE HAVEN'T EATEN?
NOT AS LONG AS YOU LEAVE A NICE TIP

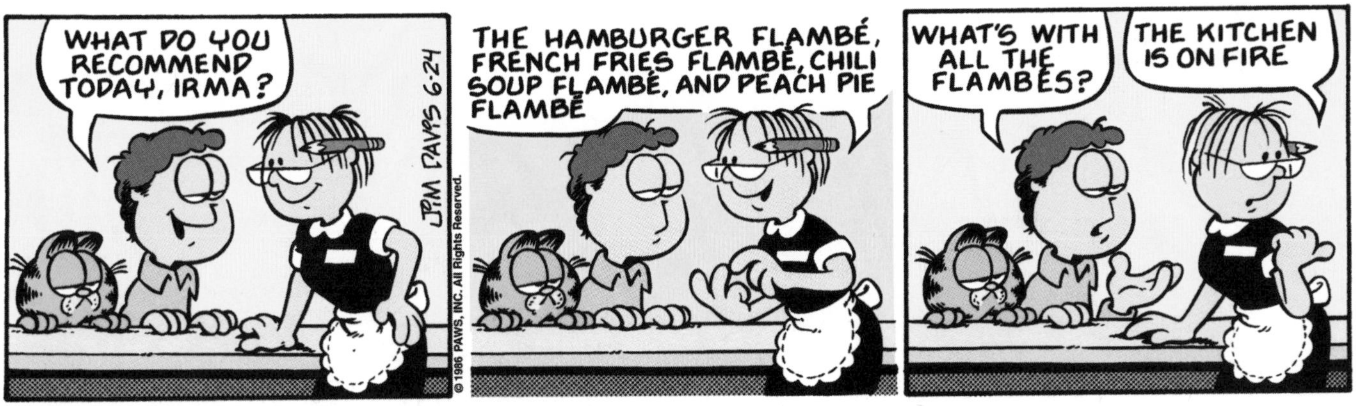
WHAT DO YOU RECOMMEND TODAY, IRMA?
JIM DAVIS 6-24
© 1986 PAWS, INC. All Rights Reserved.
THE HAMBURGER FLAMBÉ, FRENCH FRIES FLAMBÉ, CHILI SOUP FLAMBÉ, AND PEACH PIE FLAMBÉ
WHAT'S WITH ALL THE FLAMBÉS?
THE KITCHEN IS ON FIRE

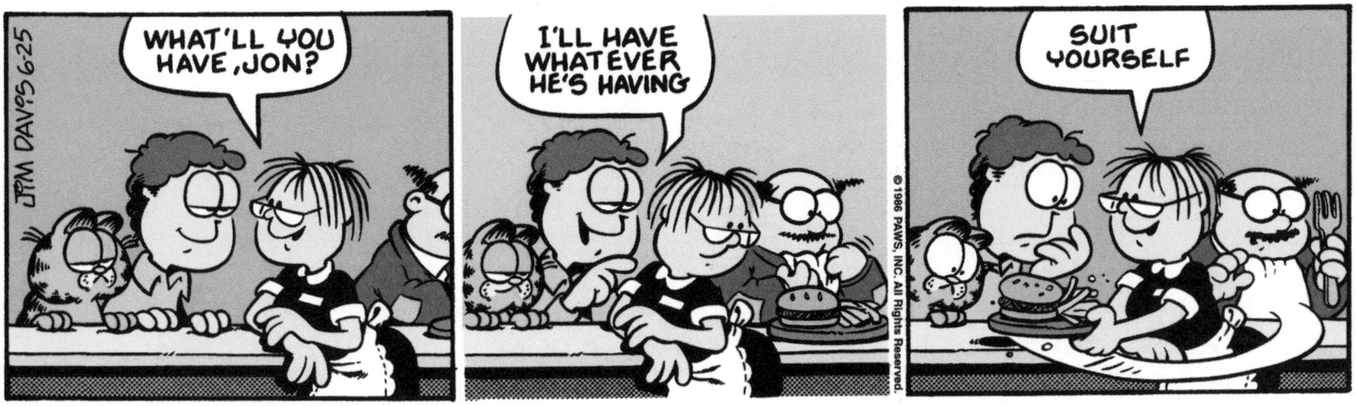
JIM DAVIS 6-25
WHAT'LL YOU HAVE, JON?
I'LL HAVE WHATEVER HE'S HAVING
© 1986 PAWS, INC. All Rights Reserved.
SUIT YOURSELF

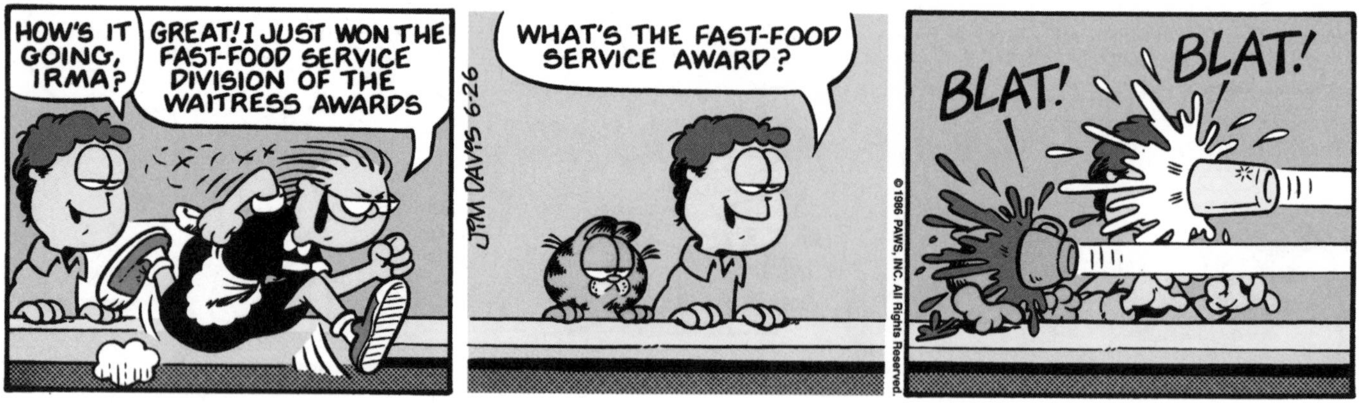
HOW'S IT GOING, IRMA?
GREAT! I JUST WON THE FAST-FOOD SERVICE DIVISION OF THE WAITRESS AWARDS
JIM DAVIS 6-26
WHAT'S THE FAST-FOOD SERVICE AWARD?
© 1986 PAWS, INC. All Rights Reserved.
BLAT!
BLAT!

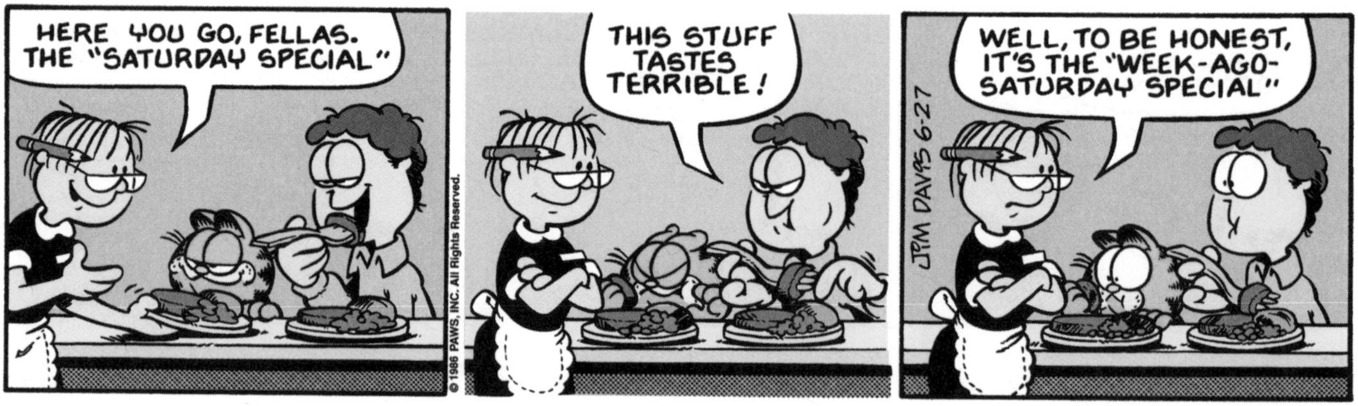
HERE YOU GO, FELLAS. THE "SATURDAY SPECIAL"
© 1986 PAWS, INC. All Rights Reserved.
THIS STUFF TASTES TERRIBLE!
JIM DAVIS 6-27
WELL, TO BE HONEST, IT'S THE "WEEK-AGO-SATURDAY SPECIAL"

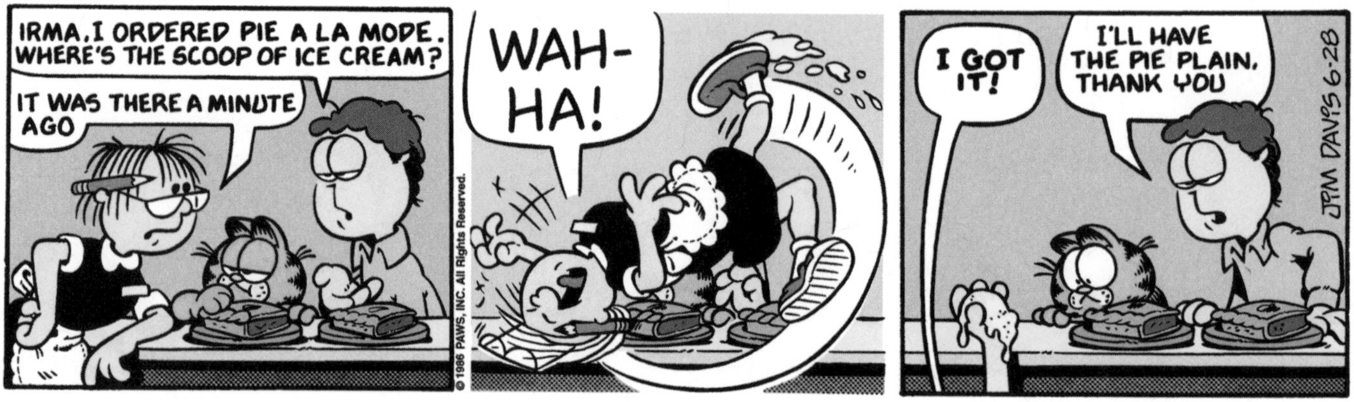
IRMA, I ORDERED PIE A LA MODE. WHERE'S THE SCOOP OF ICE CREAM?
IT WAS THERE A MINUTE AGO
© 1986 PAWS, INC. All Rights Reserved.
WAH-HA!
I GOT IT!
I'LL HAVE THE PIE PLAIN, THANK YOU
JIM DAVIS 6-28

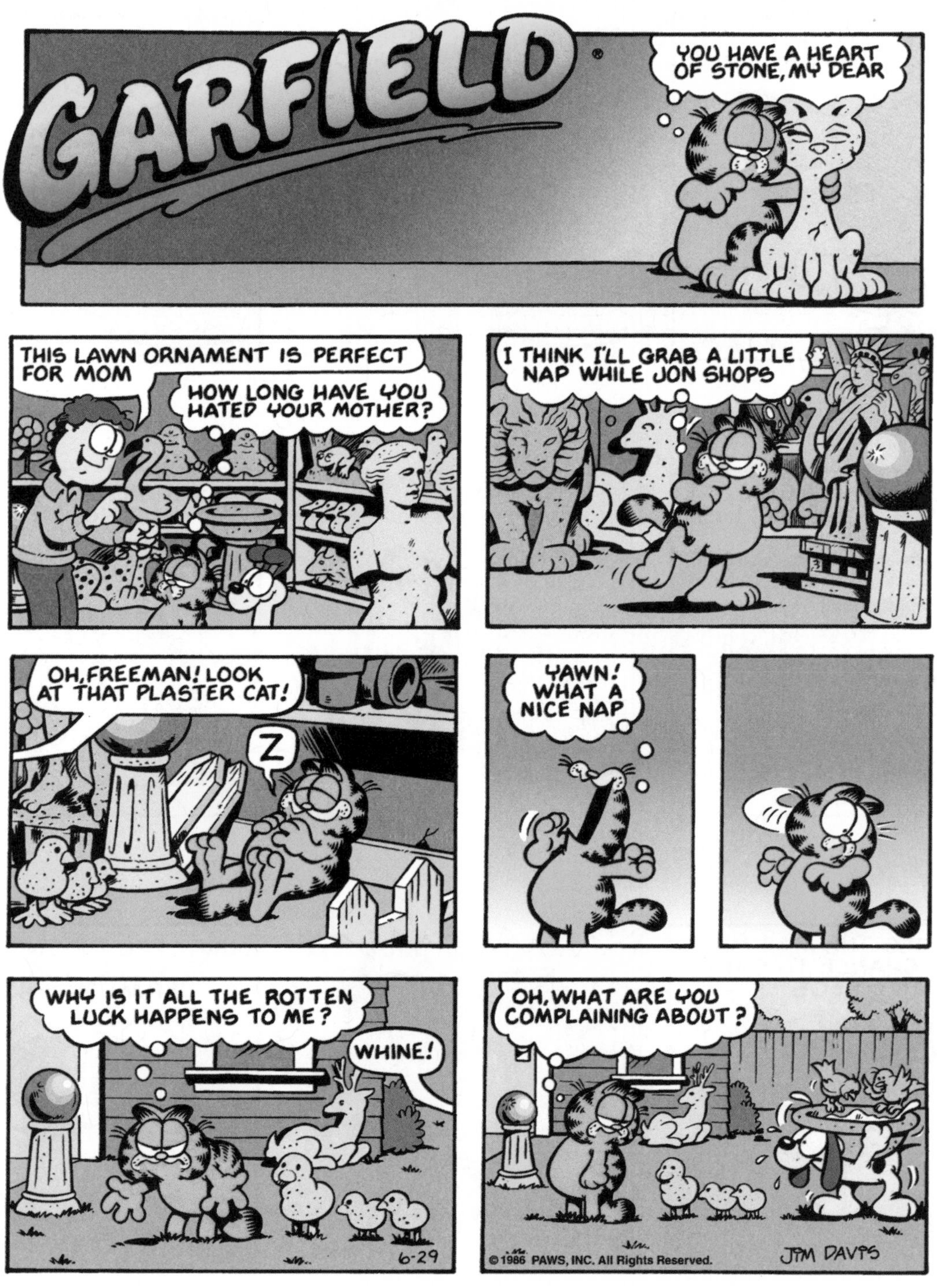
GARFIELD®
YOU HAVE A HEART OF STONE, MY DEAR
THIS LAWN ORNAMENT IS PERFECT FOR MOM
HOW LONG HAVE YOU HATED YOUR MOTHER?
I THINK I'LL GRAB A LITTLE NAP WHILE JON SHOPS
OH, FREEMAN! LOOK AT THAT PLASTER CAT!
Z
YAWN! WHAT A NICE NAP
WHY IS IT ALL THE ROTTEN LUCK HAPPENS TO ME?
WHINE!
OH, WHAT ARE YOU COMPLAINING ABOUT?
6-29
© 1986 PAWS, INC. All Rights Reserved.
JIM DAVIS

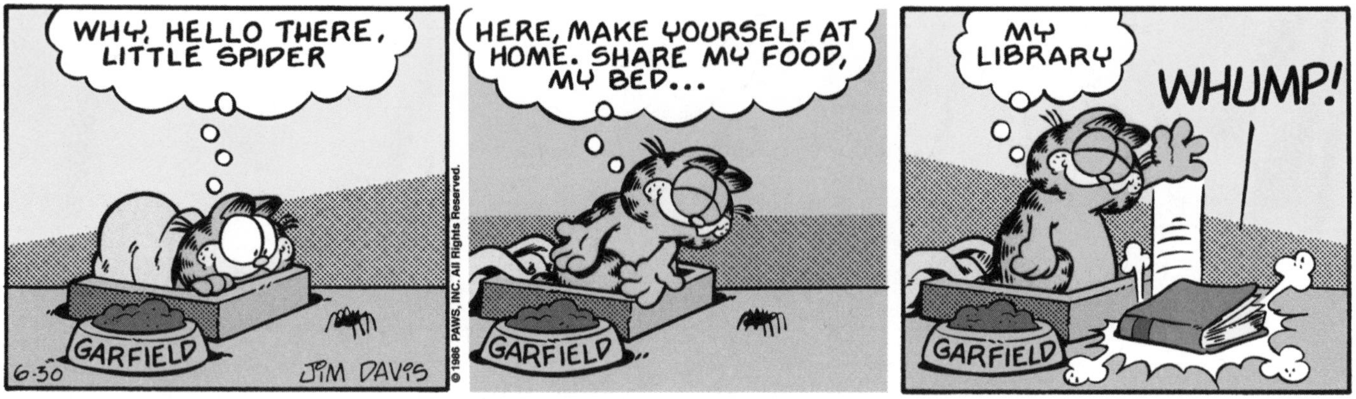
WHY, HELLO THERE, LITTLE SPIDER
6-30
JIM DAVIS
GARFIELD
© 1986 PAWS, INC. All Rights Reserved.
HERE, MAKE YOURSELF AT HOME. SHARE MY FOOD, MY BED...
GARFIELD
MY LIBRARY
WHUMP!
GARFIELD

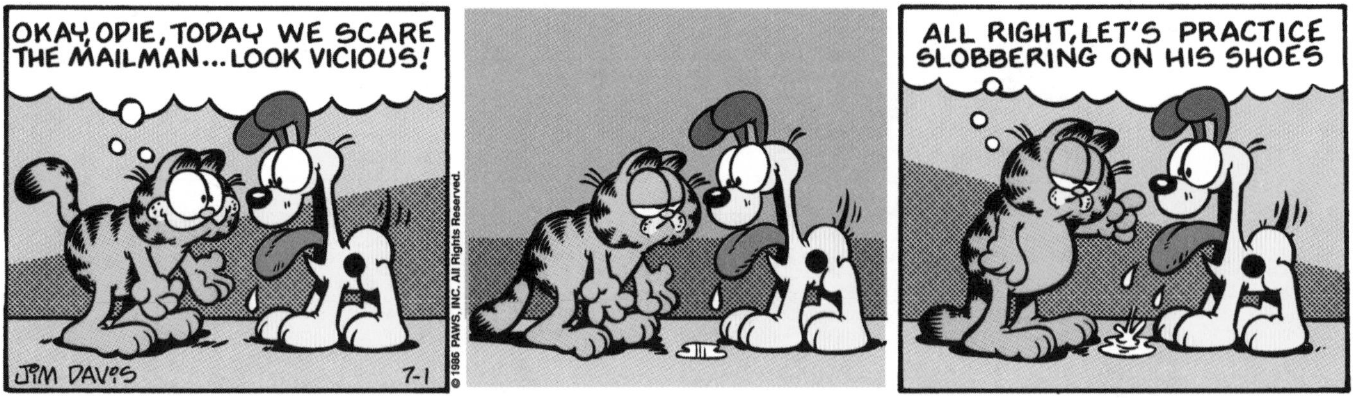
OKAY, ODIE, TODAY WE SCARE THE MAILMAN... LOOK VICIOUS!
JIM DAVIS
7-1
© 1986 PAWS, INC. All Rights Reserved.
ALL RIGHT, LET'S PRACTICE SLOBBERING ON HIS SHOES

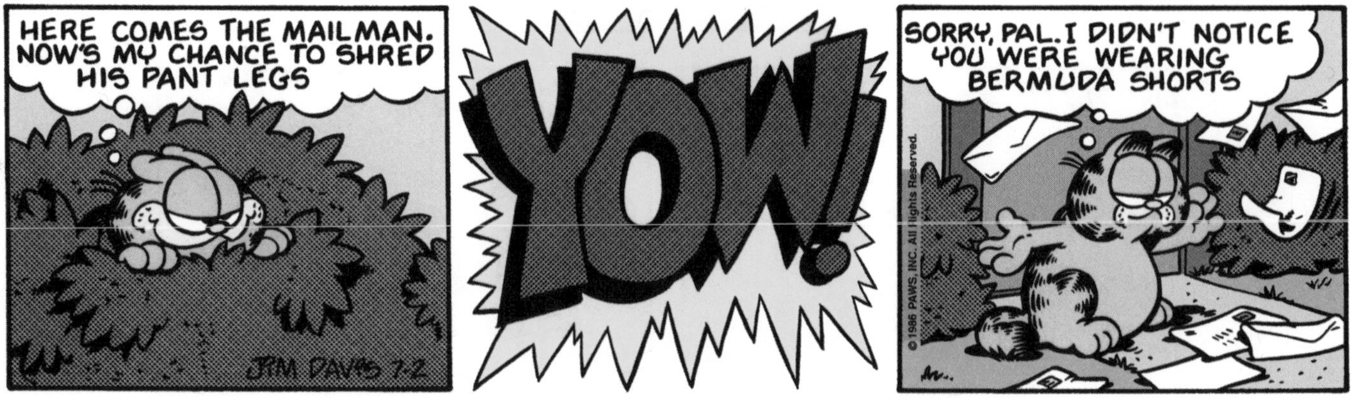
HERE COMES THE MAILMAN. NOW'S MY CHANCE TO SHRED HIS PANT LEGS
JIM DAVIS 7-2
YOW!
SORRY, PAL. I DIDN'T NOTICE YOU WERE WEARING BERMUDA SHORTS
© 1986 PAWS, INC. All Rights Reserved.

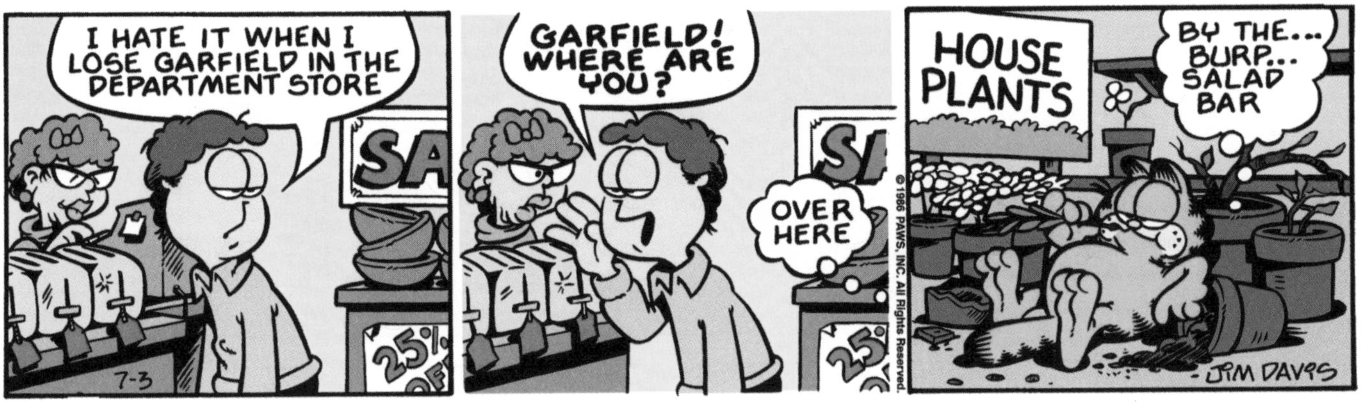
I HATE IT WHEN I LOSE GARFIELD IN THE DEPARTMENT STORE
7-3
GARFIELD! WHERE ARE YOU?
OVER HERE
© 1986 PAWS, INC. All Rights Reserved.
HOUSE PLANTS
BY THE... BURP... SALAD BAR
JIM DAVIS

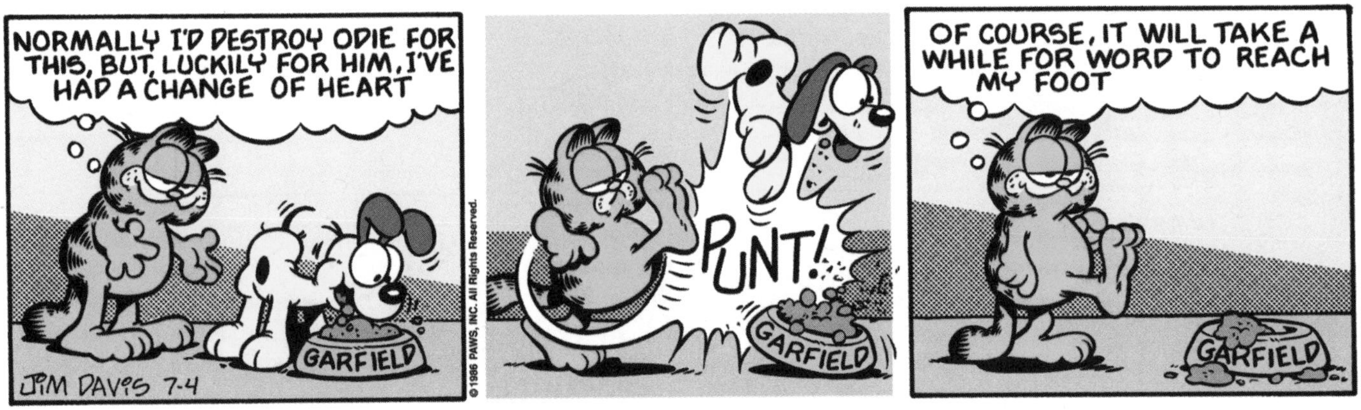
NORMALLY I'D DESTROY ODIE FOR THIS, BUT, LUCKILY FOR HIM, I'VE HAD A CHANGE OF HEART
GARFIELD
JIM DAVIS 7-4
© 1986 PAWS, INC. All Rights Reserved.
PUNT!
GARFIELD
OF COURSE, IT WILL TAKE A WHILE FOR WORD TO REACH MY FOOT
GARFIELD

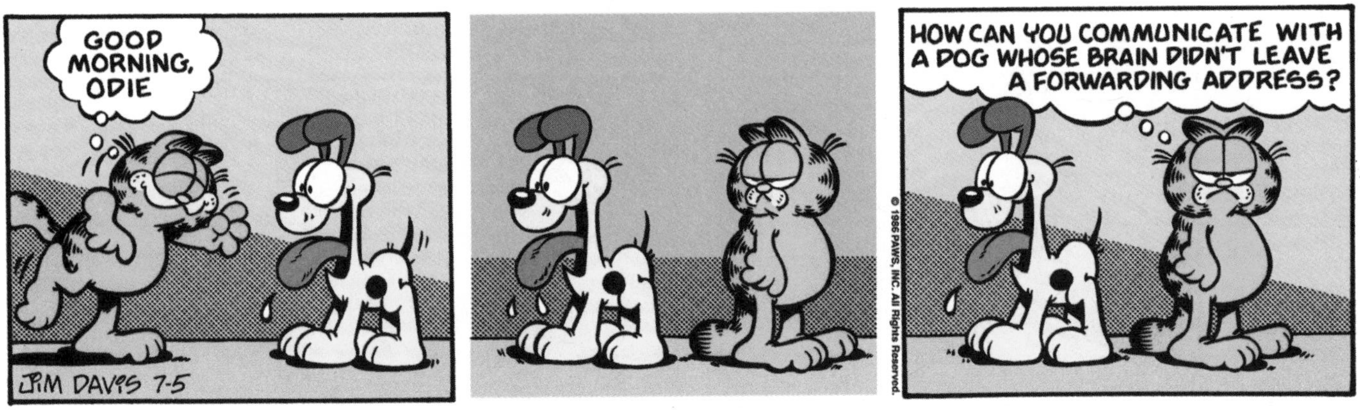
GOOD MORNING, ODIE
JIM DAVIS 7-5
© 1986 PAWS, INC. All Rights Reserved.
HOW CAN YOU COMMUNICATE WITH A DOG WHOSE BRAIN DIDN'T LEAVE A FORWARDING ADDRESS?

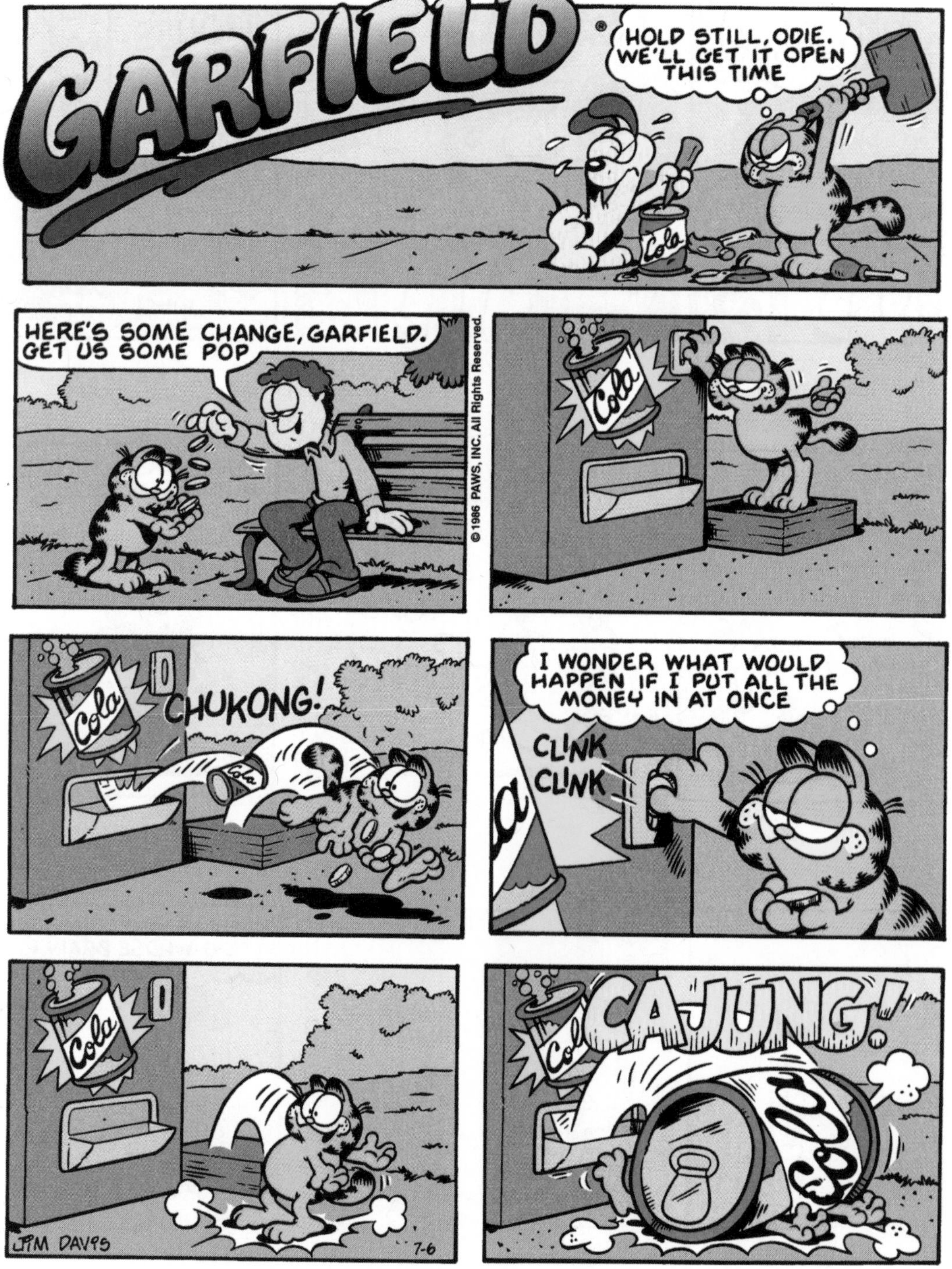
GARFIELD
HOLD STILL, ODIE. WE'LL GET IT OPEN THIS TIME
Cola
HERE'S SOME CHANGE, GARFIELD. GET US SOME POP
© 1986 PAWS, INC. All Rights Reserved.
Cola
CHUKONG!
I WONDER WHAT WOULD HAPPEN IF I PUT ALL THE MONEY IN AT ONCE
CLINK
CLINK
Cola
JIM DAVIS 7-6
CAJUNG!
Cola

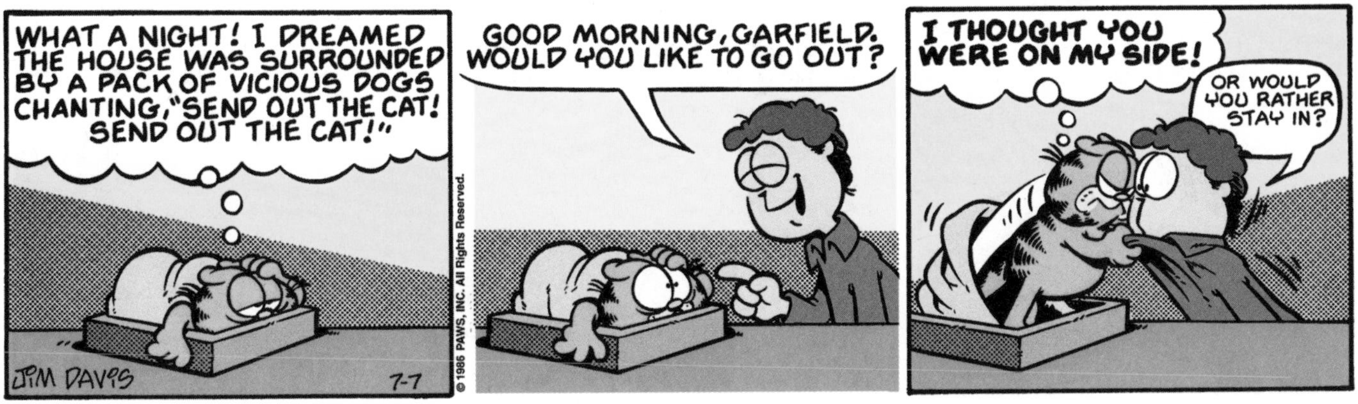
WHAT A NIGHT! I DREAMED THE HOUSE WAS SURROUNDED BY A PACK OF VICIOUS DOGS CHANTING, "SEND OUT THE CAT! SEND OUT THE CAT!"
JIM DAVIS 7-7
© 1986 PAWS, INC. All Rights Reserved.
GOOD MORNING, GARFIELD. WOULD YOU LIKE TO GO OUT?
I THOUGHT YOU WERE ON MY SIDE!
OR WOULD YOU RATHER STAY IN?

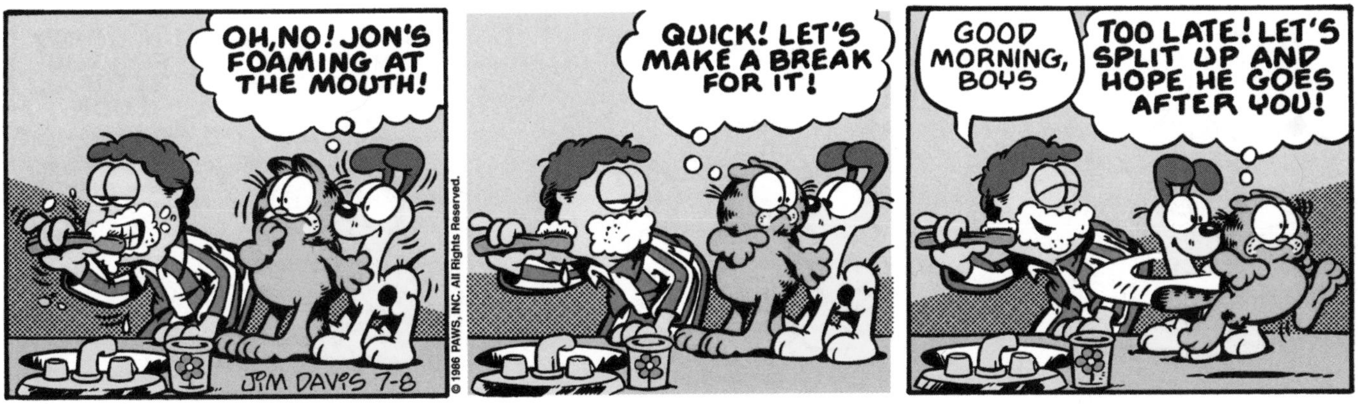
OH, NO! JON'S FOAMING AT THE MOUTH!
JIM DAVIS 7-8
© 1986 PAWS, INC. All Rights Reserved.
QUICK! LET'S MAKE A BREAK FOR IT!
GOOD MORNING, BOYS
TOO LATE! LET'S SPLIT UP AND HOPE HE GOES AFTER YOU!

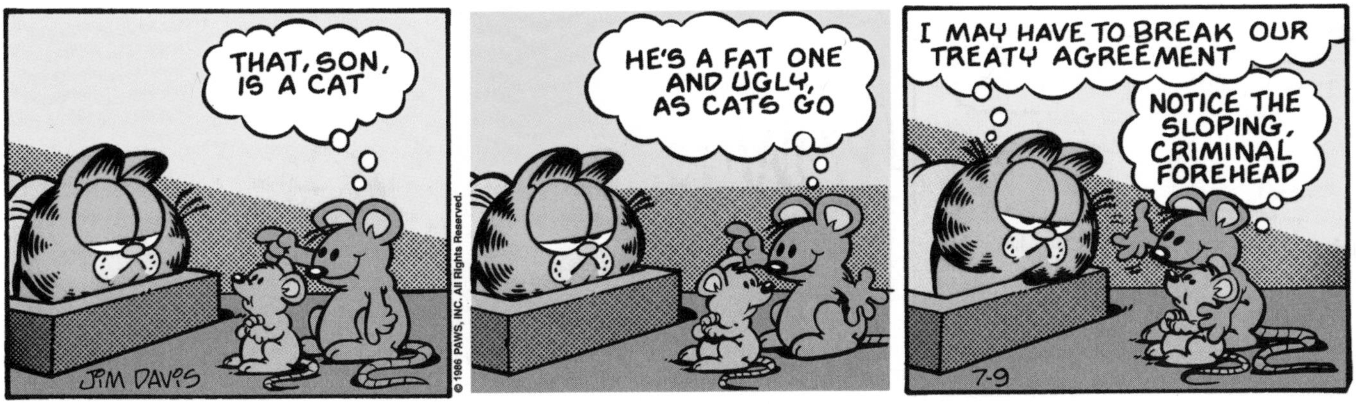
THAT, SON, IS A CAT
JIM DAVIS
© 1986 PAWS, INC. All Rights Reserved.
HE'S A FAT ONE AND UGLY, AS CATS GO
I MAY HAVE TO BREAK OUR TREATY AGREEMENT
NOTICE THE SLOPING, CRIMINAL FOREHEAD
7-9

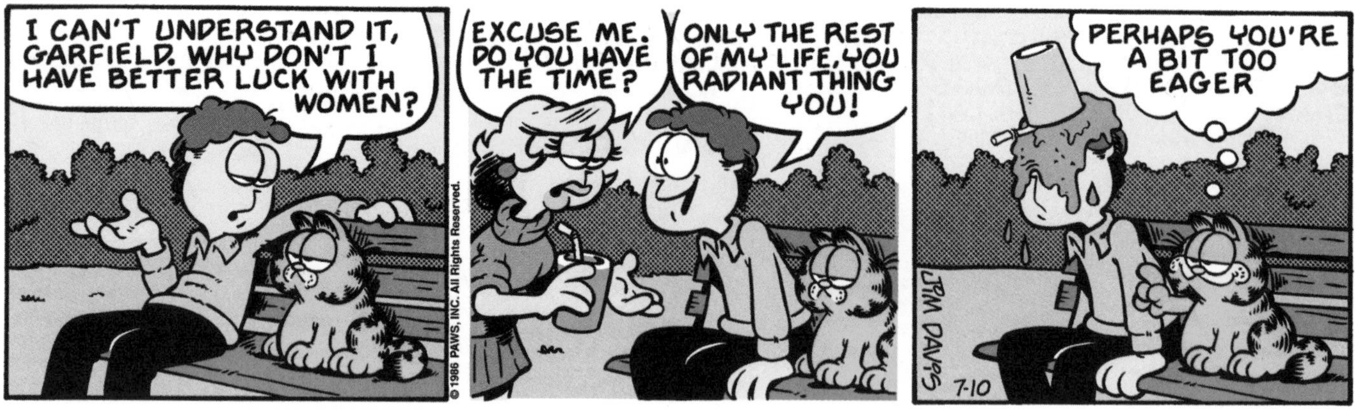
I CAN'T UNDERSTAND IT, GARFIELD. WHY DON'T I HAVE BETTER LUCK WITH WOMEN?
© 1986 PAWS, INC. All Rights Reserved.
EXCUSE ME. DO YOU HAVE THE TIME?
ONLY THE REST OF MY LIFE, YOU RADIANT THING YOU!
PERHAPS YOU'RE A BIT TOO EAGER
JIM DAVIS 7-10

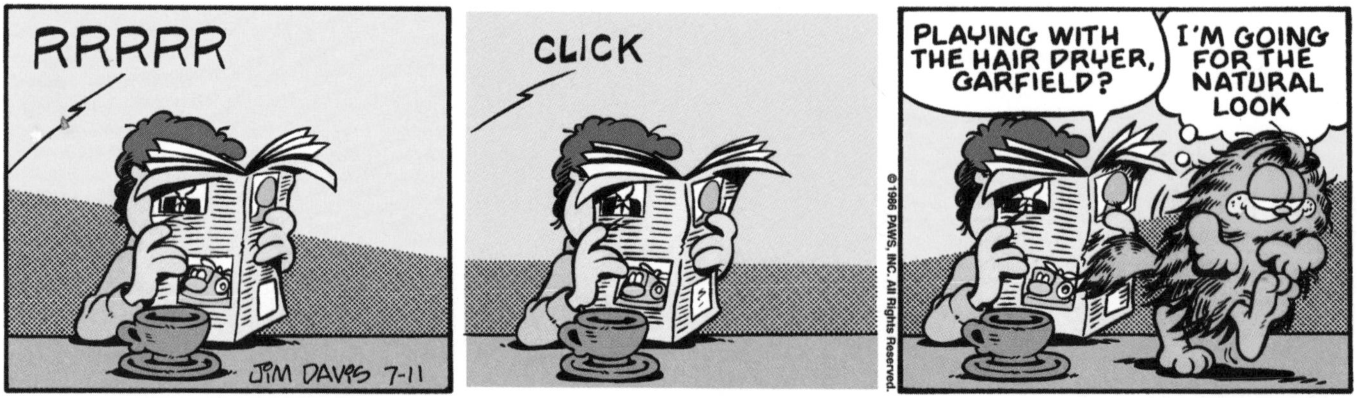
RRRRR
JIM DAVIS 7-11
CLICK
© 1986 PAWS, INC. All Rights Reserved.
PLAYING WITH THE HAIR DRYER, GARFIELD?
I'M GOING FOR THE NATURAL LOOK

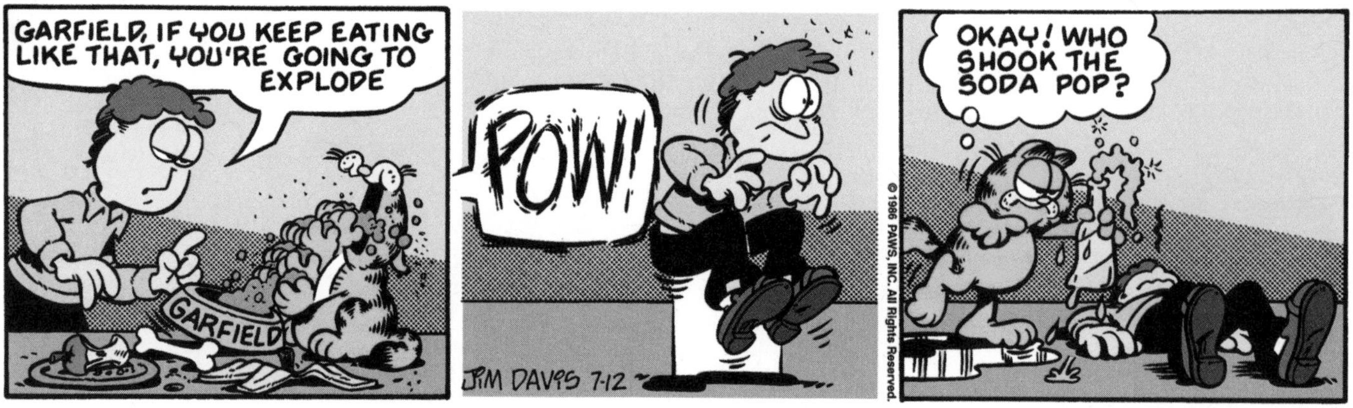
GARFIELD, IF YOU KEEP EATING LIKE THAT, YOU'RE GOING TO EXPLODE
GARFIELD
POW!
JIM DAVIS 7-12
© 1986 PAWS, INC. All Rights Reserved.
OKAY! WHO SHOOK THE SODA POP?

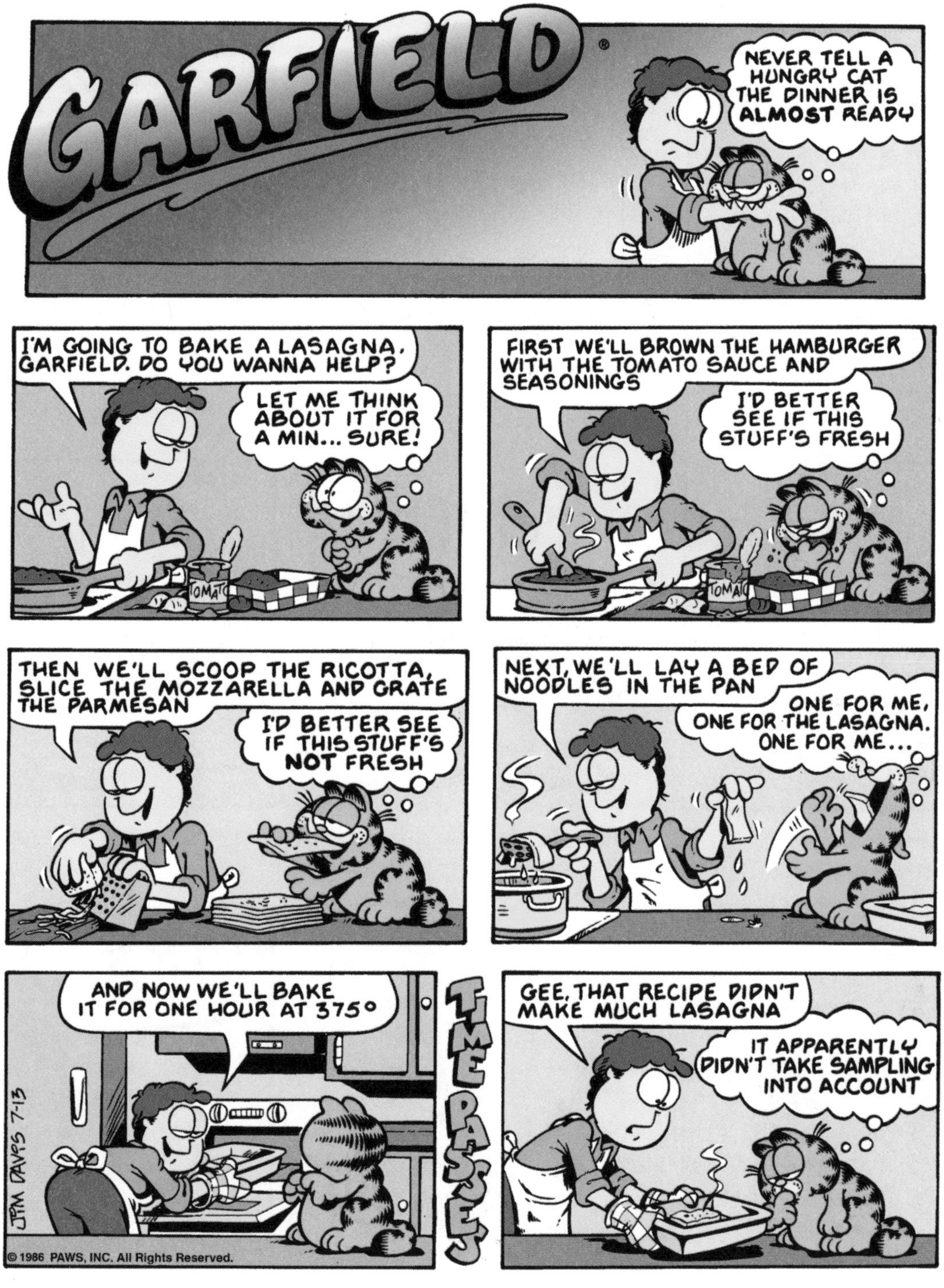
GARFIELD
NEVER TELL A HUNGRY CAT THE DINNER IS **ALMOST** READY
I'M GOING TO BAKE A LASAGNA, GARFIELD. DO YOU WANNA HELP?
LET ME THINK ABOUT IT FOR A MIN... SURE!
FIRST WE'LL BROWN THE HAMBURGER WITH THE TOMATO SAUCE AND SEASONINGS
I'D BETTER SEE IF THIS STUFF'S FRESH
THEN WE'LL SCOOP THE RICOTTA, SLICE THE MOZZARELLA AND GRATE THE PARMESAN
I'D BETTER SEE IF THIS STUFF'S **NOT** FRESH
NEXT, WE'LL LAY A BED OF NOODLES IN THE PAN
ONE FOR ME, ONE FOR THE LASAGNA. ONE FOR ME...
AND NOW WE'LL BAKE IT FOR ONE HOUR AT 375°
JPM DAVIS 7-13
© 1986 PAWS, INC. All Rights Reserved.
TIME PASSES
GEE, THAT RECIPE DIDN'T MAKE MUCH LASAGNA
IT APPARENTLY DIDN'T TAKE SAMPLING INTO ACCOUNT

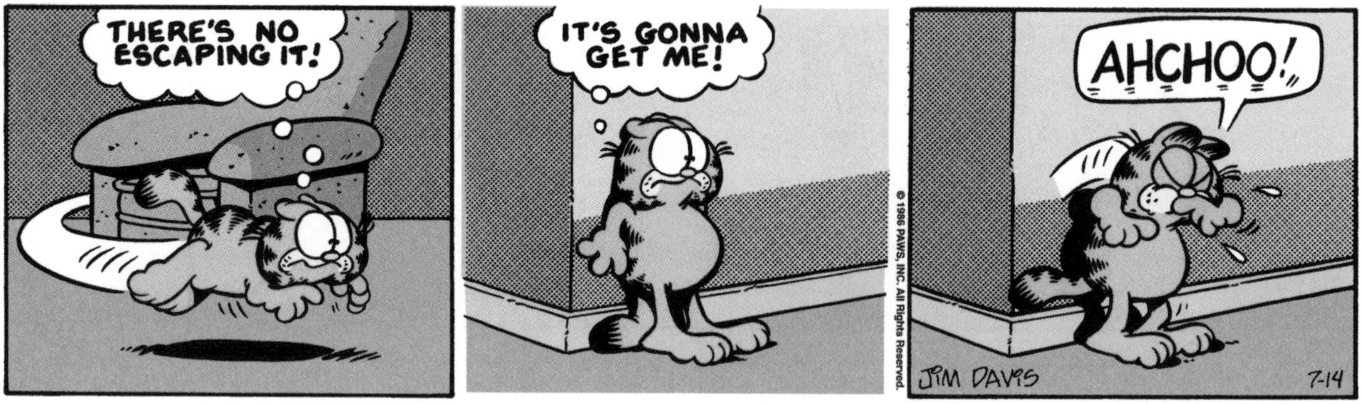
THERE'S NO ESCAPING IT!
IT'S GONNA GET ME!
AHCHOO!
JIM DAVIS
7-14

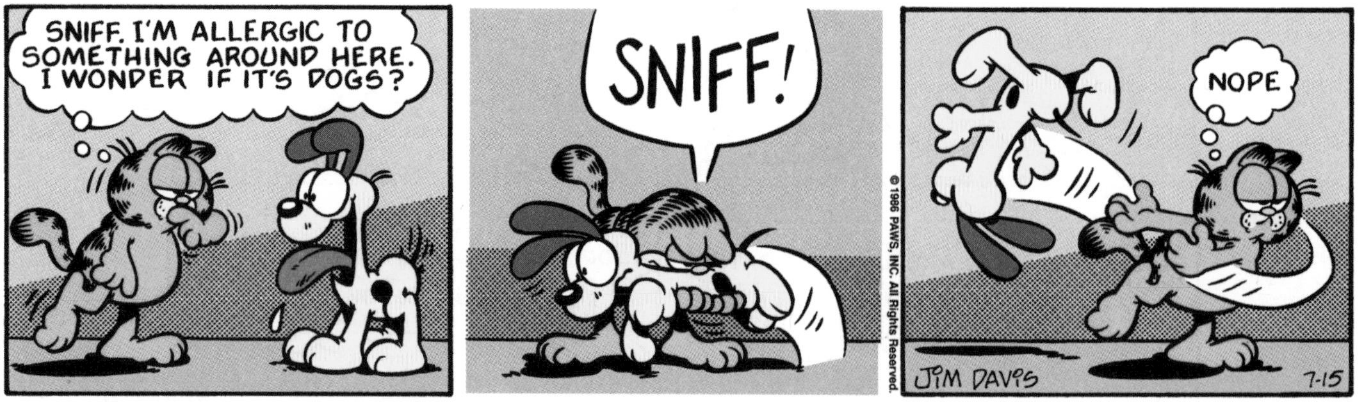
SNIFF. I'M ALLERGIC TO SOMETHING AROUND HERE. I WONDER IF IT'S DOGS?
SNIFF!
NOPE
JIM DAVIS
7-15

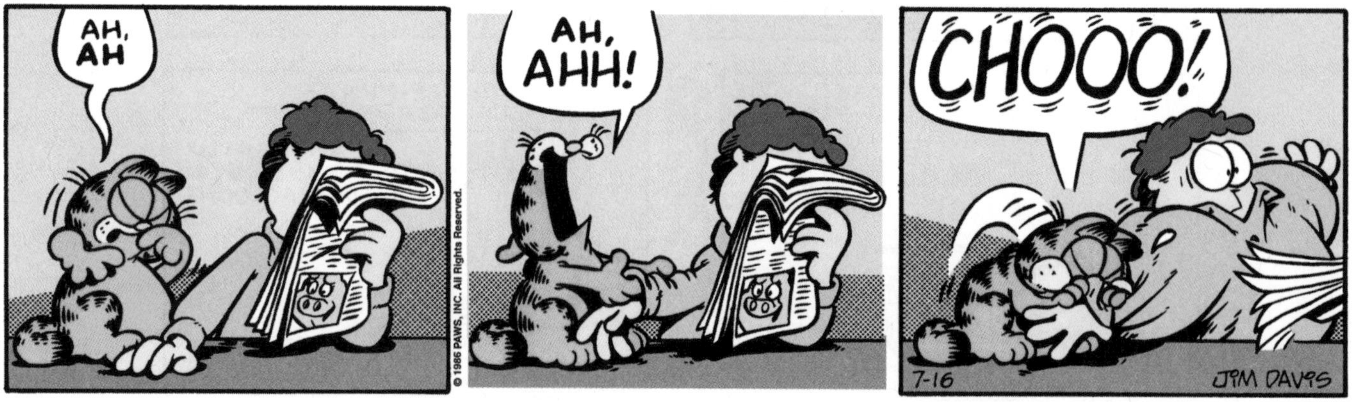
AH, AH
AH, AHH!
CHOOO!
7-16
JIM DAVIS

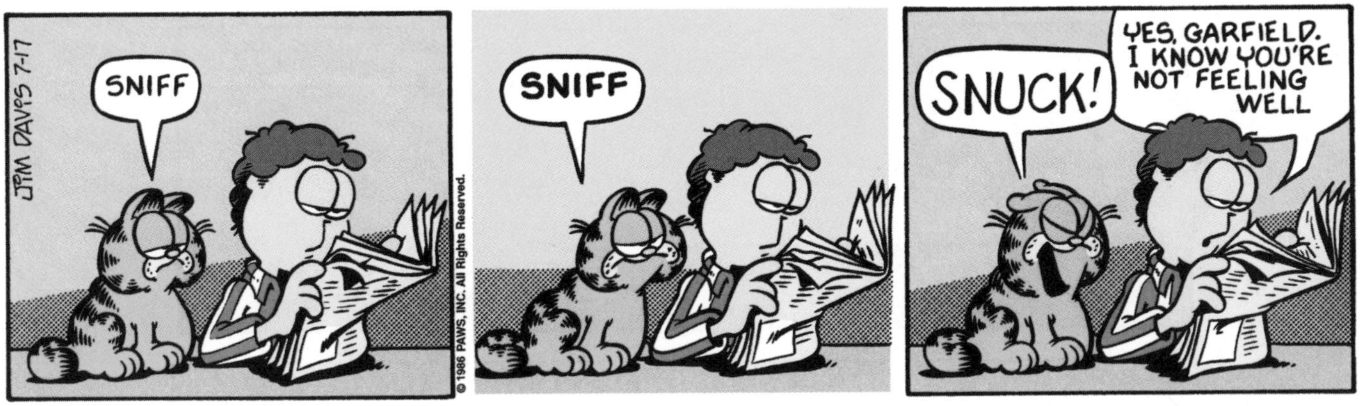
JIM DAVIS 7-17
SNIFF
SNIFF
© 1986 PAWS, INC. All Rights Reserved.
SNUCK!
YES, GARFIELD. I KNOW YOU'RE NOT FEELING WELL

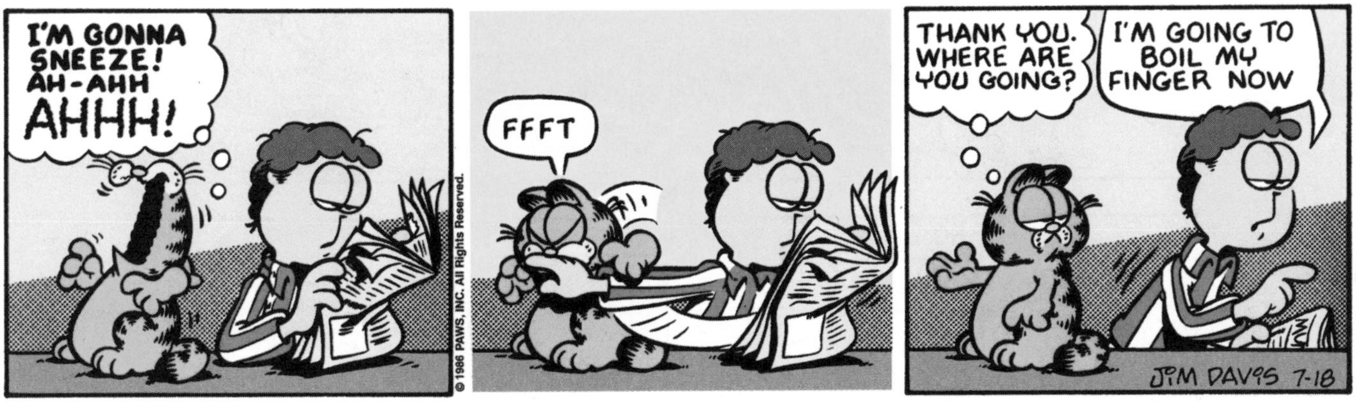
I'M GONNA SNEEZE! AH-AHH AHHH!
© 1986 PAWS, INC. All Rights Reserved.
FFFT
THANK YOU. WHERE ARE YOU GOING?
I'M GOING TO BOIL MY FINGER NOW
JIM DAVIS 7-18

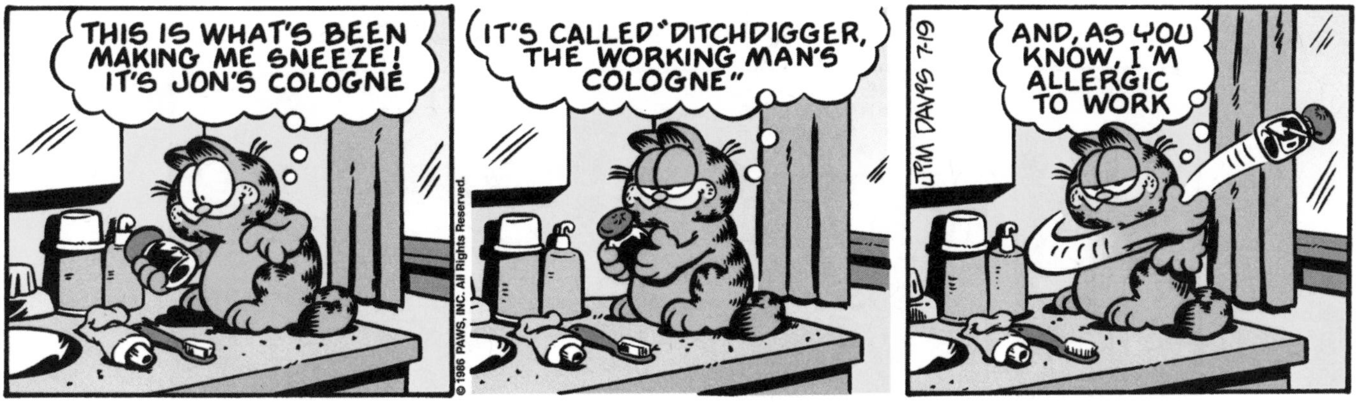
THIS IS WHAT'S BEEN MAKING ME SNEEZE! IT'S JON'S COLOGNE
© 1986 PAWS, INC. All Rights Reserved.
IT'S CALLED "DITCHDIGGER, THE WORKING MAN'S COLOGNE"
JIM DAVIS 7-19
AND, AS YOU KNOW, I'M ALLERGIC TO WORK

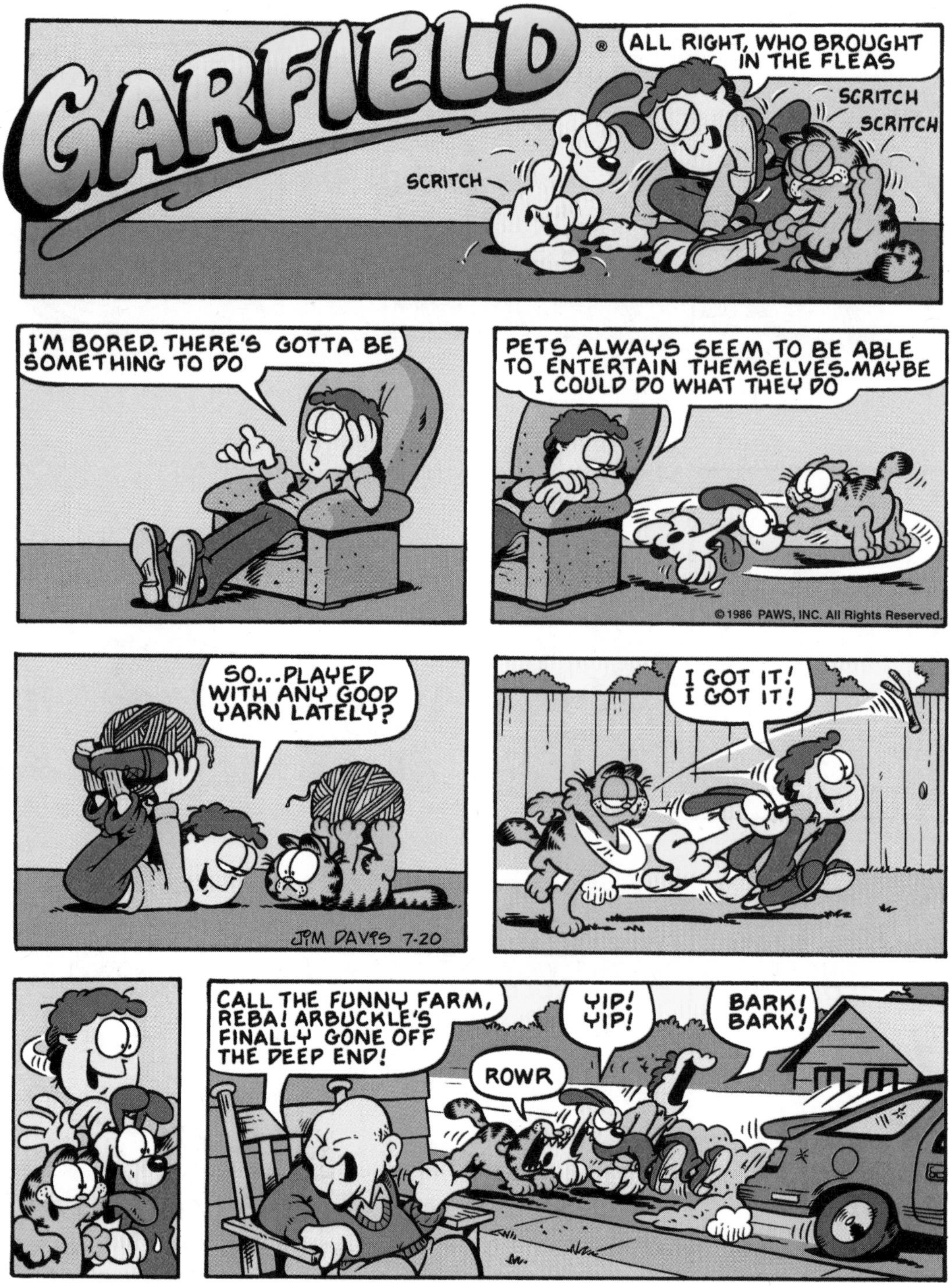
GARFIELD®
ALL RIGHT, WHO BROUGHT IN THE FLEAS
SCRITCH
SCRITCH
SCRITCH
I'M BORED. THERE'S GOTTA BE SOMETHING TO DO
PETS ALWAYS SEEM TO BE ABLE TO ENTERTAIN THEMSELVES. MAYBE I COULD DO WHAT THEY DO
© 1986 PAWS, INC. All Rights Reserved.
SO...PLAYED WITH ANY GOOD YARN LATELY?
JIM DAVIS 7-20
I GOT IT! I GOT IT!
CALL THE FUNNY FARM, REBA! ARBUCKLE'S FINALLY GONE OFF THE DEEP END!
ROWR
YIP! YIP!
BARK! BARK!

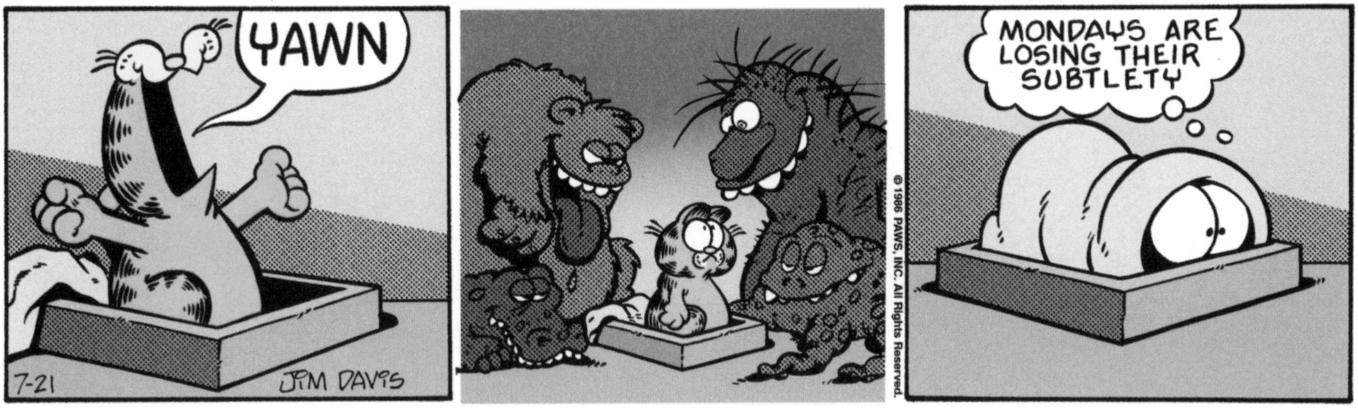
YAWN
7-21
JIM DAVIS
© 1986 PAWS, INC. All Rights Reserved.
MONDAYS ARE LOSING THEIR SUBTLETY

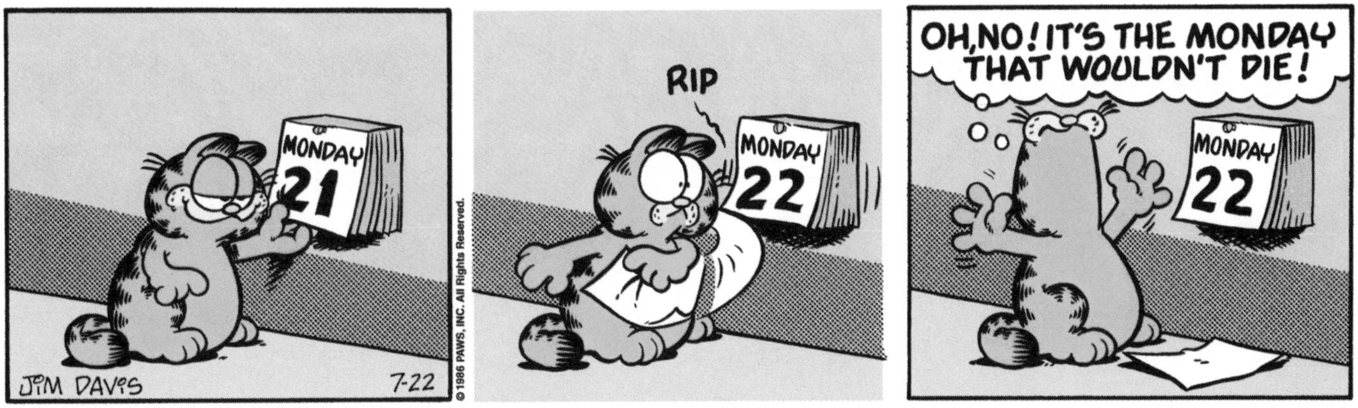
MONDAY
21
JIM DAVIS
7-22
© 1986 PAWS, INC. All Rights Reserved.
RIP
MONDAY
22
OH,NO! IT'S THE MONDAY THAT WOULDN'T DIE!
MONDAY
22

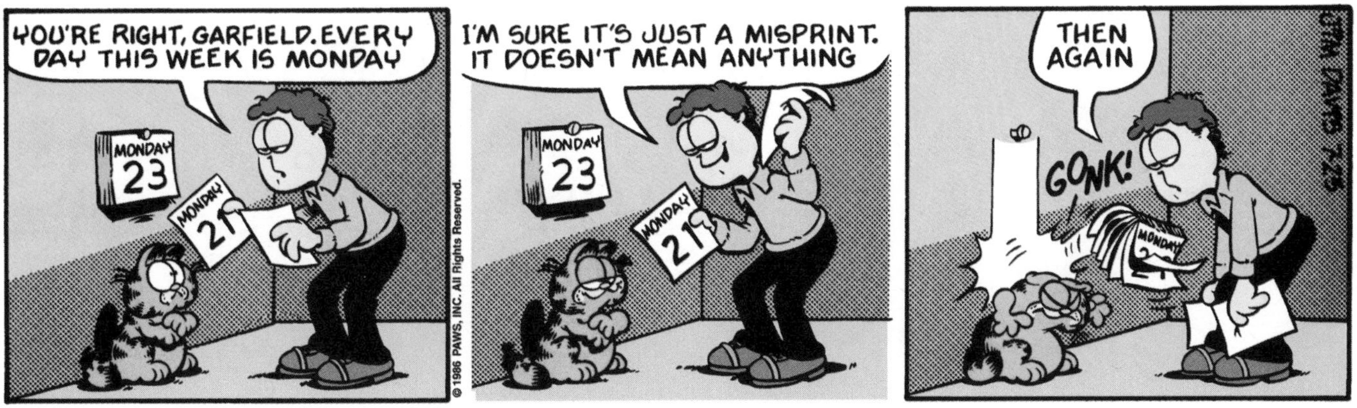
YOU'RE RIGHT, GARFIELD. EVERY DAY THIS WEEK IS MONDAY
MONDAY
23
MONDAY
21
© 1986 PAWS, INC. All Rights Reserved.
I'M SURE IT'S JUST A MISPRINT. IT DOESN'T MEAN ANYTHING
MONDAY
23
MONDAY
21
THEN AGAIN
GONK!
JIM DAVIS 7-23

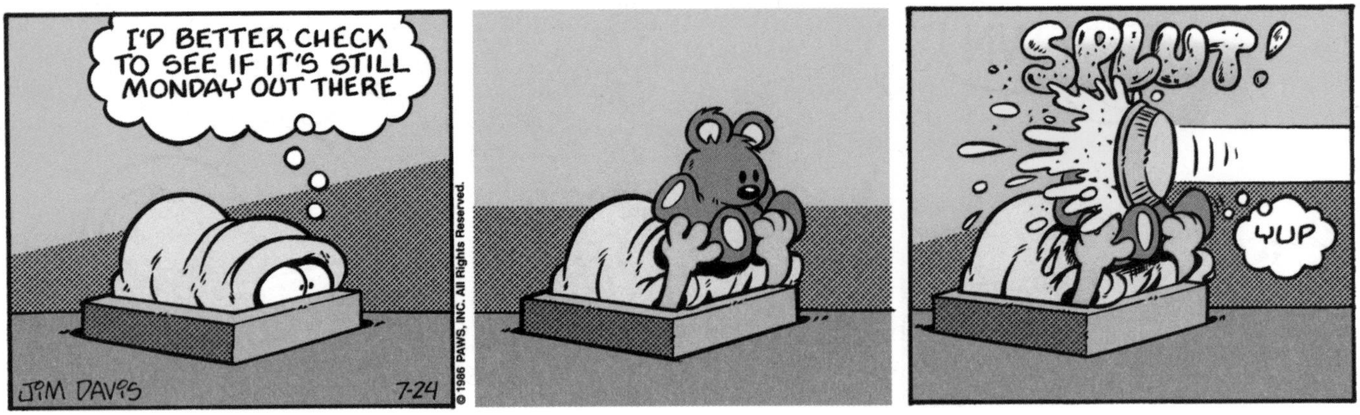
I'D BETTER CHECK TO SEE IF IT'S STILL MONDAY OUT THERE
JIM DAVIS
7-24
© 1986 PAWS, INC. All Rights Reserved.
SPLUT!
YUP

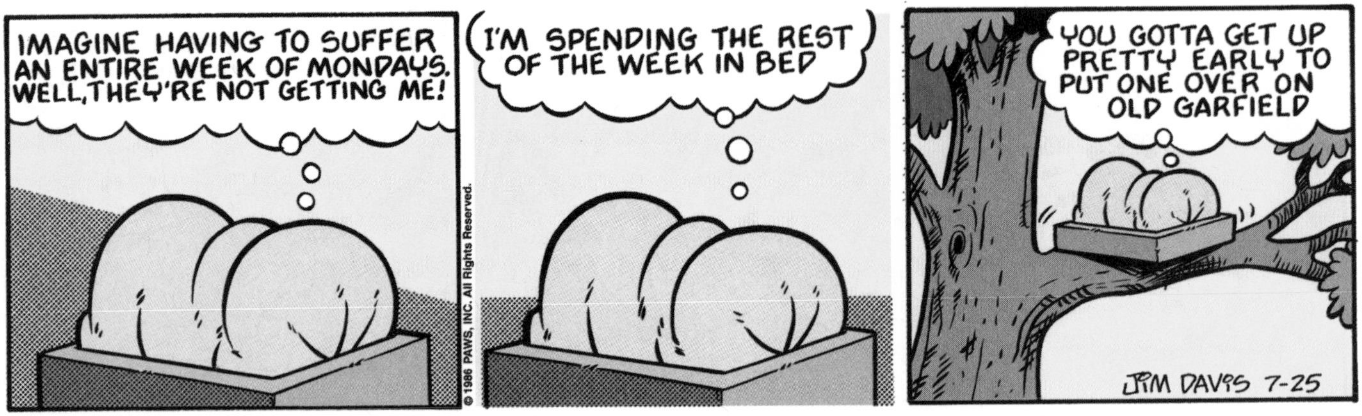
IMAGINE HAVING TO SUFFER AN ENTIRE WEEK OF MONDAYS. WELL, THEY'RE NOT GETTING ME!
© 1986 PAWS, INC. All Rights Reserved.
I'M SPENDING THE REST OF THE WEEK IN BED
YOU GOTTA GET UP PRETTY EARLY TO PUT ONE OVER ON OLD GARFIELD
JIM DAVIS 7-25

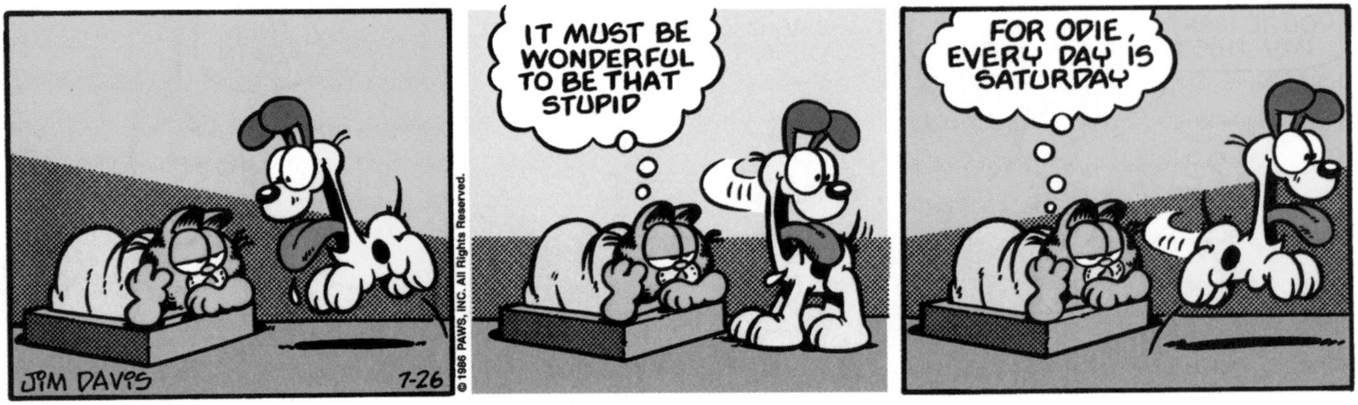
JIM DAVIS
7-26
© 1986 PAWS, INC. All Rights Reserved.
IT MUST BE WONDERFUL TO BE THAT STUPID
FOR ODIE, EVERY DAY IS SATURDAY

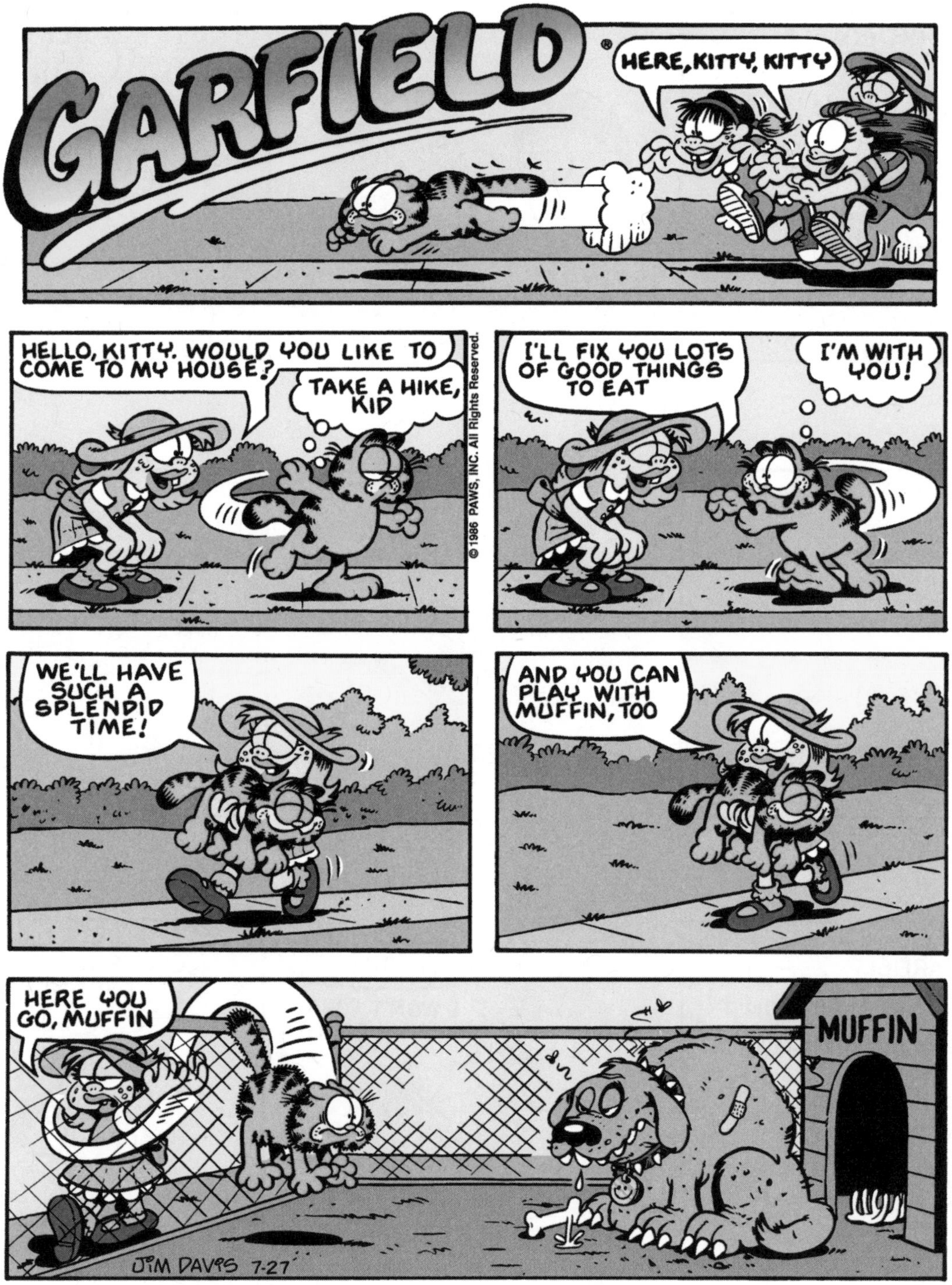
GARFIELD®
HERE, KITTY, KITTY
HELLO, KITTY. WOULD YOU LIKE TO COME TO MY HOUSE?
TAKE A HIKE, KID
© 1986 PAWS, INC. All Rights Reserved.
I'LL FIX YOU LOTS OF GOOD THINGS TO EAT
I'M WITH YOU!
WE'LL HAVE SUCH A SPLENDID TIME!
AND YOU CAN PLAY WITH MUFFIN, TOO
HERE YOU GO, MUFFIN
MUFFIN
JIM DAVIS 7-27

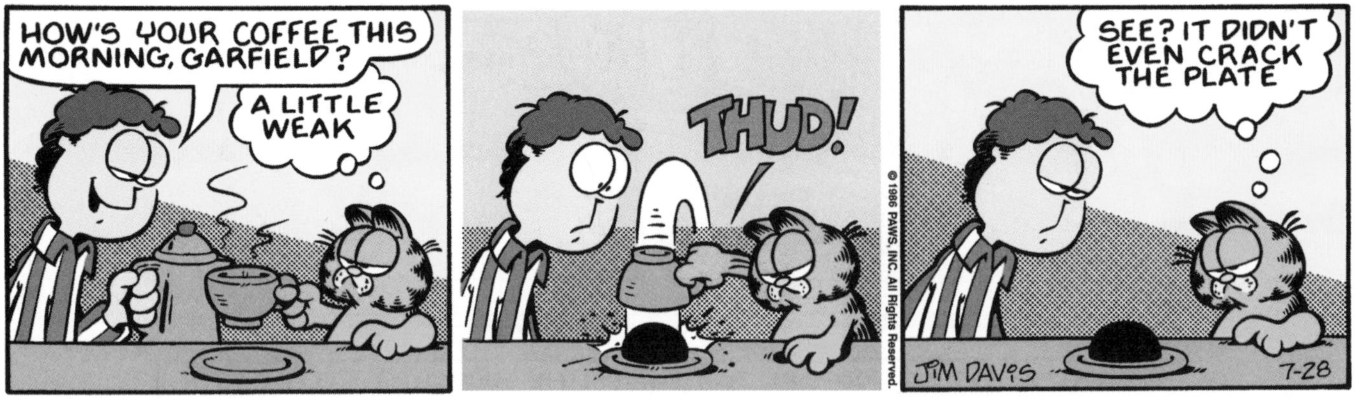
HOW'S YOUR COFFEE THIS MORNING, GARFIELD?
A LITTLE WEAK
THUD!
© 1986 PAWS, INC. All Rights Reserved.
SEE? IT DIDN'T EVEN CRACK THE PLATE
JIM DAVIS 7-28

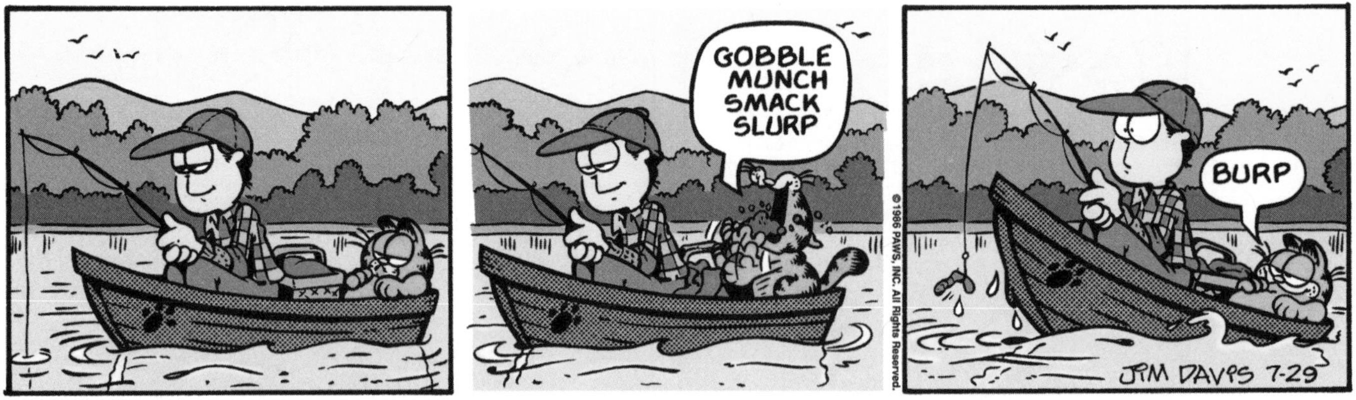
GOBBLE MUNCH SMACK SLURP
© 1986 PAWS, INC. All Rights Reserved.
BURP
JIM DAVIS 7-29

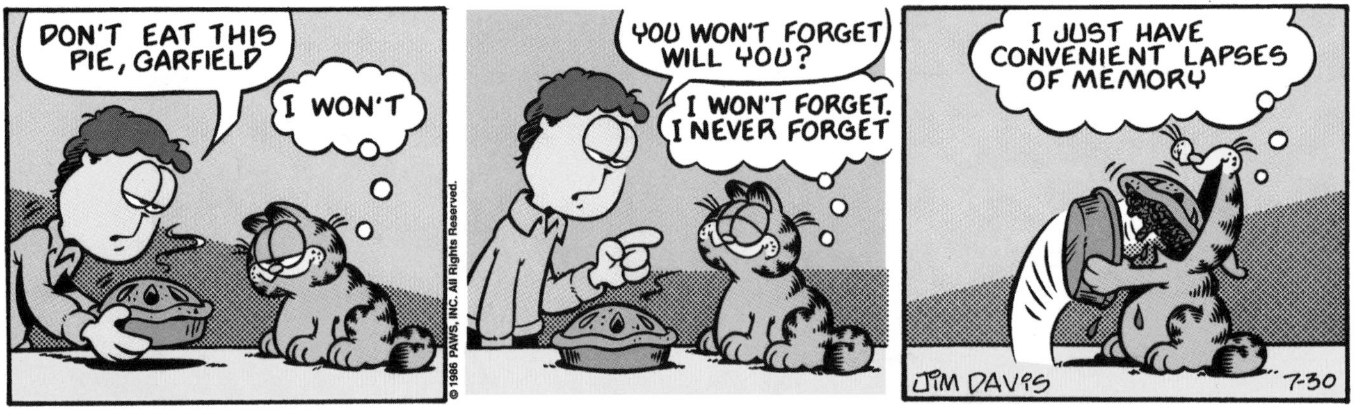
DON'T EAT THIS PIE, GARFIELD
I WON'T
© 1986 PAWS, INC. All Rights Reserved.
YOU WON'T FORGET WILL YOU?
I WON'T FORGET. I NEVER FORGET
I JUST HAVE CONVENIENT LAPSES OF MEMORY
JIM DAVIS 7-30

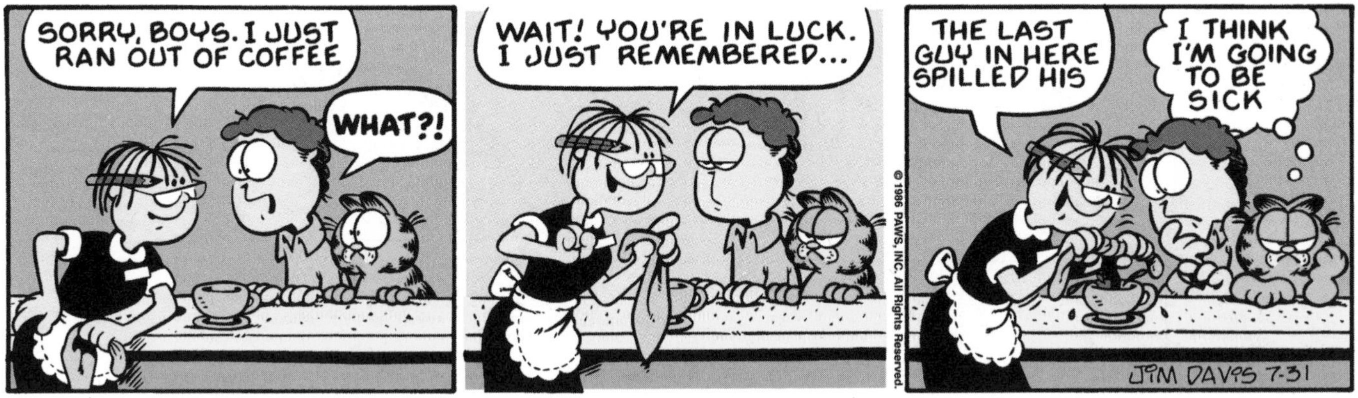
SORRY, BOYS. I JUST RAN OUT OF COFFEE
WHAT?!
WAIT! YOU'RE IN LUCK. I JUST REMEMBERED...
THE LAST GUY IN HERE SPILLED HIS
I THINK I'M GOING TO BE SICK
JIM DAVIS 7-31
© 1986 PAWS, INC. All Rights Reserved.

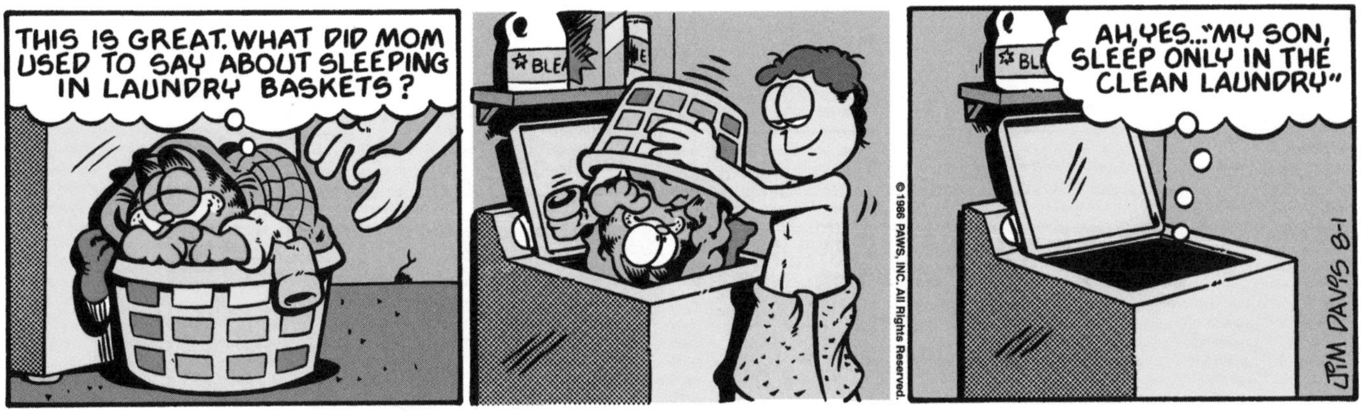
THIS IS GREAT. WHAT DID MOM USED TO SAY ABOUT SLEEPING IN LAUNDRY BASKETS?
AH, YES..."MY SON, SLEEP ONLY IN THE CLEAN LAUNDRY"
JIM DAVIS 8-1
© 1986 PAWS, INC. All Rights Reserved.

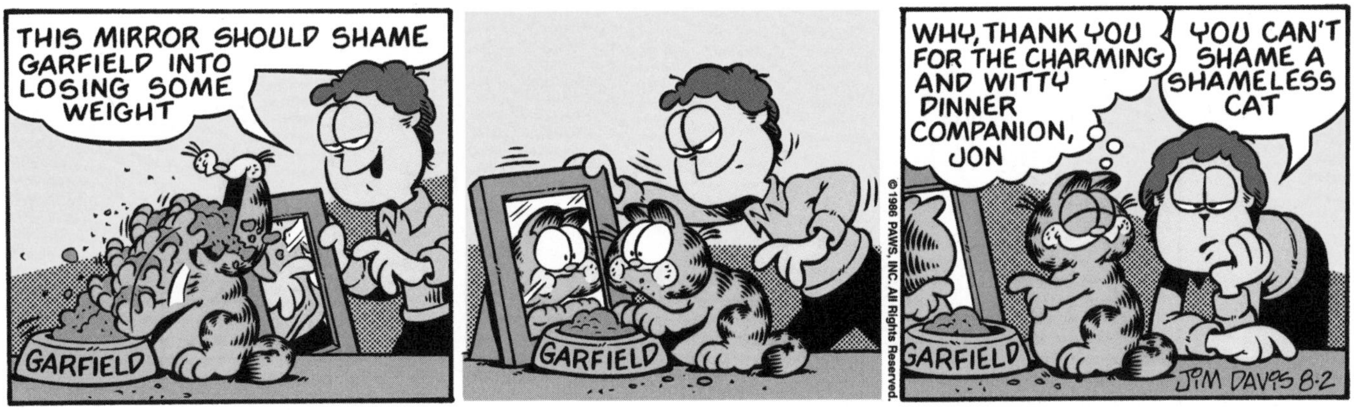
THIS MIRROR SHOULD SHAME GARFIELD INTO LOSING SOME WEIGHT
GARFIELD
GARFIELD
WHY, THANK YOU FOR THE CHARMING AND WITTY DINNER COMPANION, JON
YOU CAN'T SHAME A SHAMELESS CAT
GARFIELD
JIM DAVIS 8-2
© 1986 PAWS, INC. All Rights Reserved.

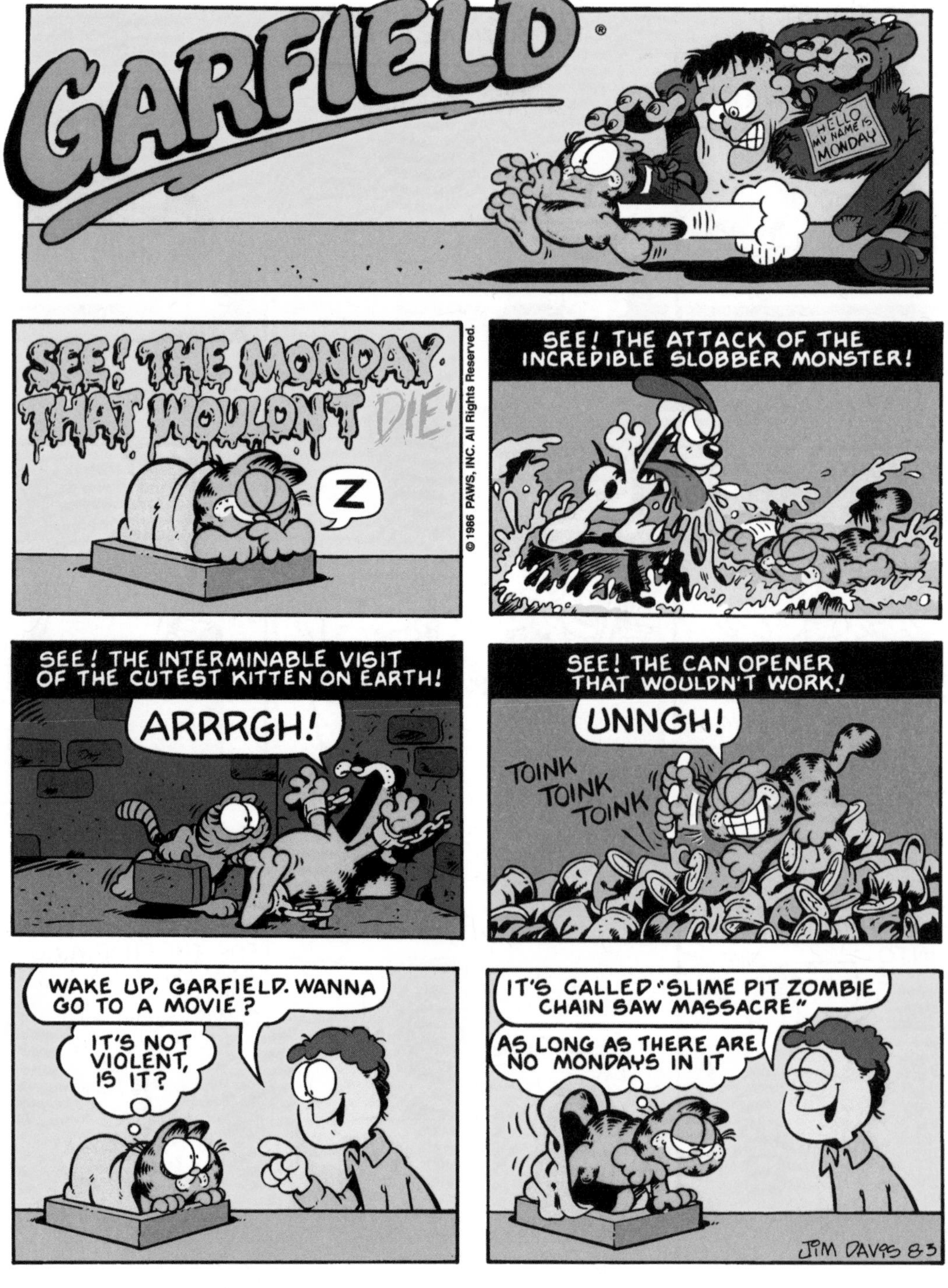
GARFIELD®
HELLO MY NAME IS MONDAY
SEE! THE MONDAY THAT WOULDN'T DIE!
Z
© 1986 PAWS, INC. All Rights Reserved.
SEE! THE ATTACK OF THE INCREDIBLE SLOBBER MONSTER!
SEE! THE INTERMINABLE VISIT OF THE CUTEST KITTEN ON EARTH!
ARRRGH!
SEE! THE CAN OPENER THAT WOULDN'T WORK!
UNNGH!
TOINK TOINK TOINK
WAKE UP, GARFIELD. WANNA GO TO A MOVIE?
IT'S NOT VIOLENT, IS IT?
IT'S CALLED "SLIME PIT ZOMBIE CHAIN SAW MASSACRE"
AS LONG AS THERE ARE NO MONDAYS IN IT
JIM DAVIS 8-3

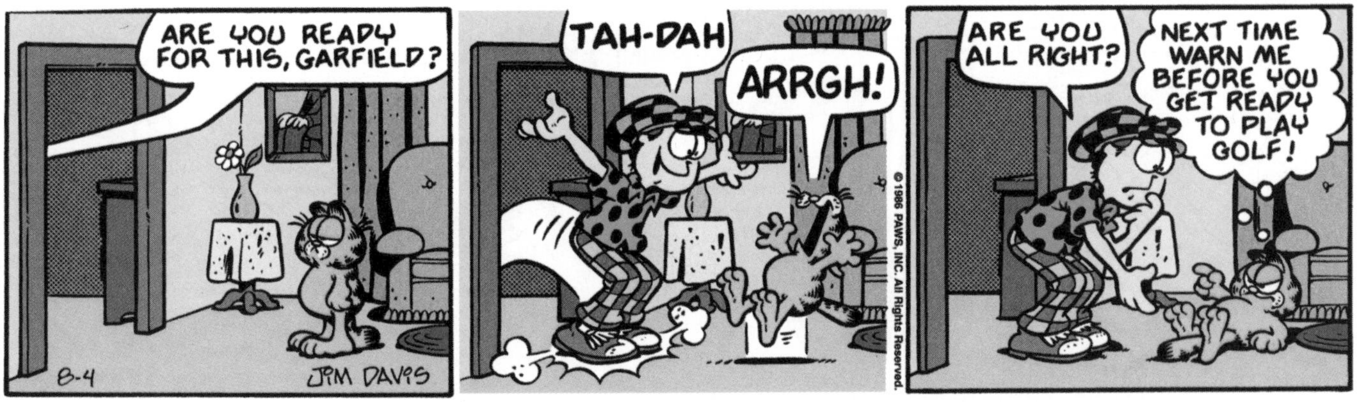
ARE YOU READY FOR THIS, GARFIELD?
8-4 JIM DAVIS
TAH-DAH
ARRGH!
© 1986 PAWS, INC. All Rights Reserved.
ARE YOU ALL RIGHT?
NEXT TIME WARN ME BEFORE YOU GET READY TO PLAY GOLF!

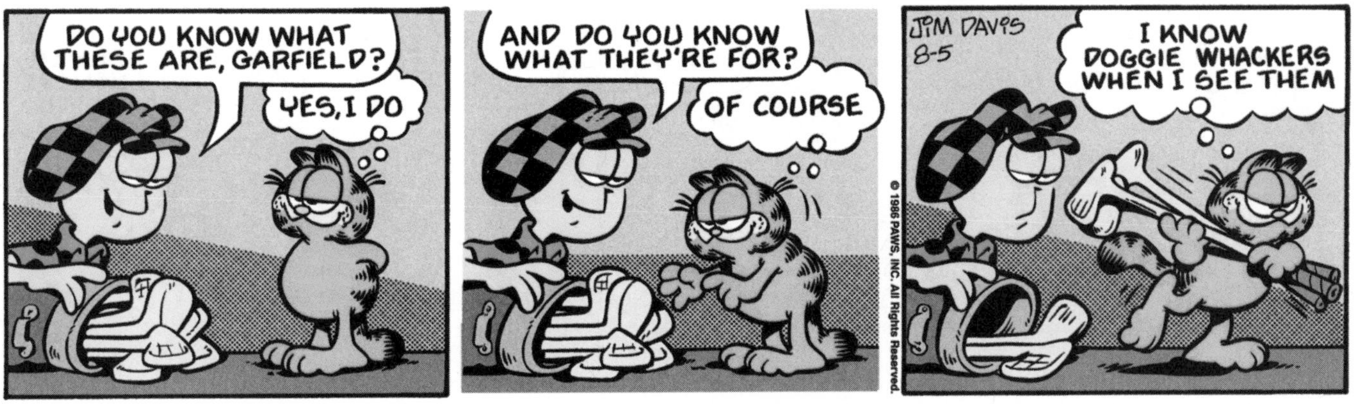
DO YOU KNOW WHAT THESE ARE, GARFIELD?
YES, I DO
AND DO YOU KNOW WHAT THEY'RE FOR?
OF COURSE
© 1986 PAWS, INC. All Rights Reserved.
JIM DAVIS 8-5
I KNOW DOGGIE WHACKERS WHEN I SEE THEM

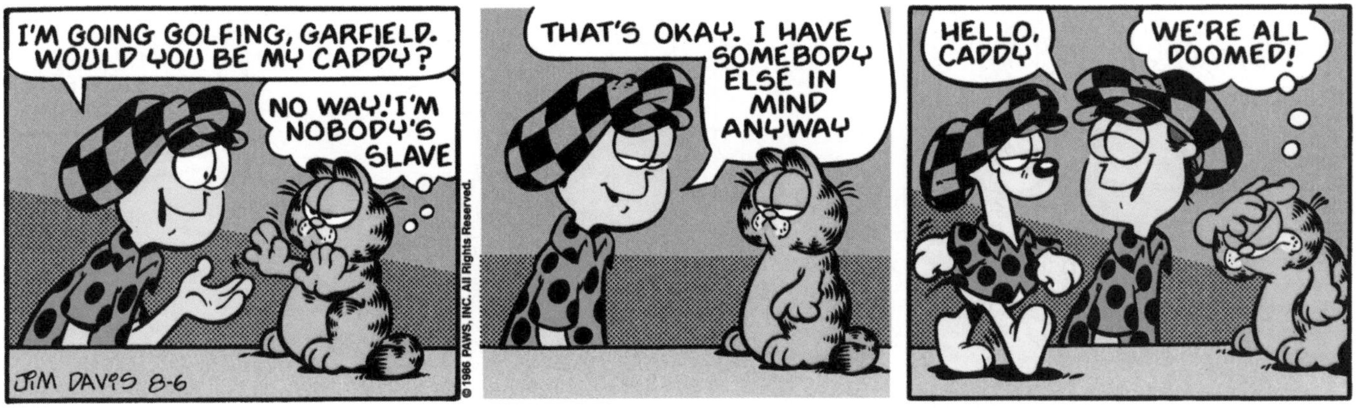
I'M GOING GOLFING, GARFIELD. WOULD YOU BE MY CADDY?
NO WAY! I'M NOBODY'S SLAVE
JIM DAVIS 8-6
© 1986 PAWS, INC. All Rights Reserved.
THAT'S OKAY. I HAVE SOMEBODY ELSE IN MIND ANYWAY
HELLO, CADDY
WE'RE ALL DOOMED!

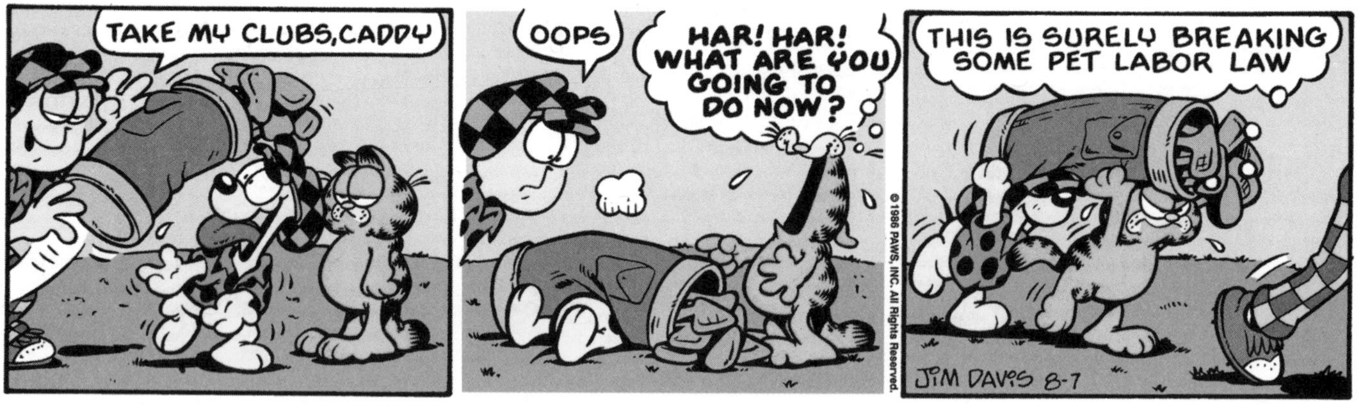
TAKE MY CLUBS, CADDY
OOPS
HAR! HAR! WHAT ARE YOU GOING TO DO NOW?
© 1986 PAWS, INC. All Rights Reserved.
THIS IS SURELY BREAKING SOME PET LABOR LAW
JIM DAVIS 8-7

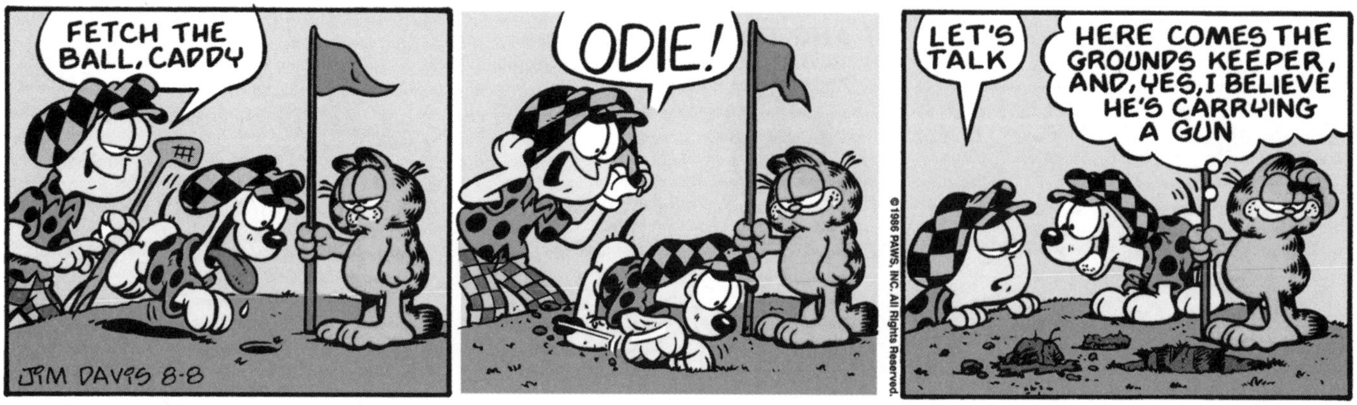
FETCH THE BALL, CADDY
JIM DAVIS 8-8
ODIE!
© 1986 PAWS, INC. All Rights Reserved.
LET'S TALK
HERE COMES THE GROUNDS KEEPER, AND, YES, I BELIEVE HE'S CARRYING A GUN

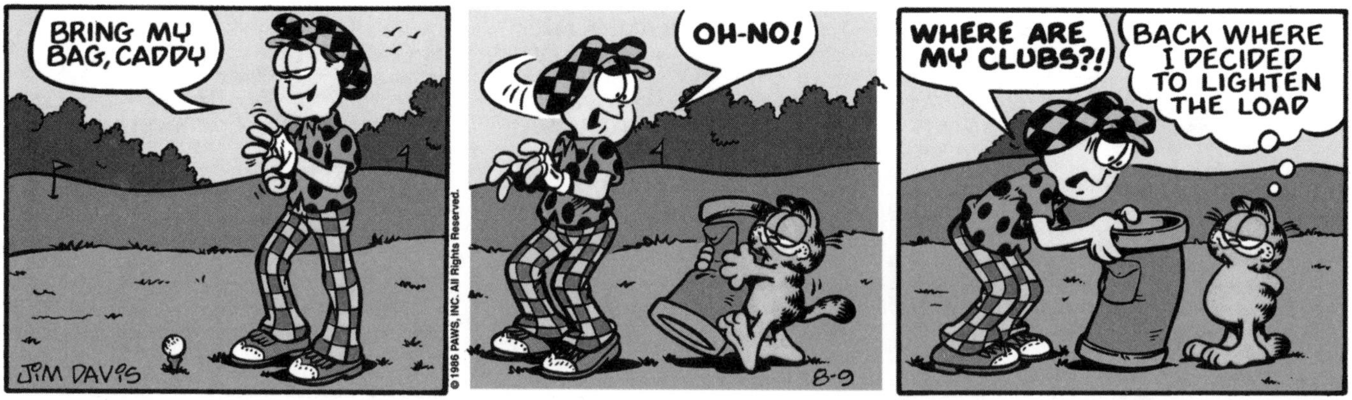
BRING MY BAG, CADDY
JIM DAVIS
© 1986 PAWS, INC. All Rights Reserved.
OH-NO!
8-9
WHERE ARE MY CLUBS?!
BACK WHERE I DECIDED TO LIGHTEN THE LOAD

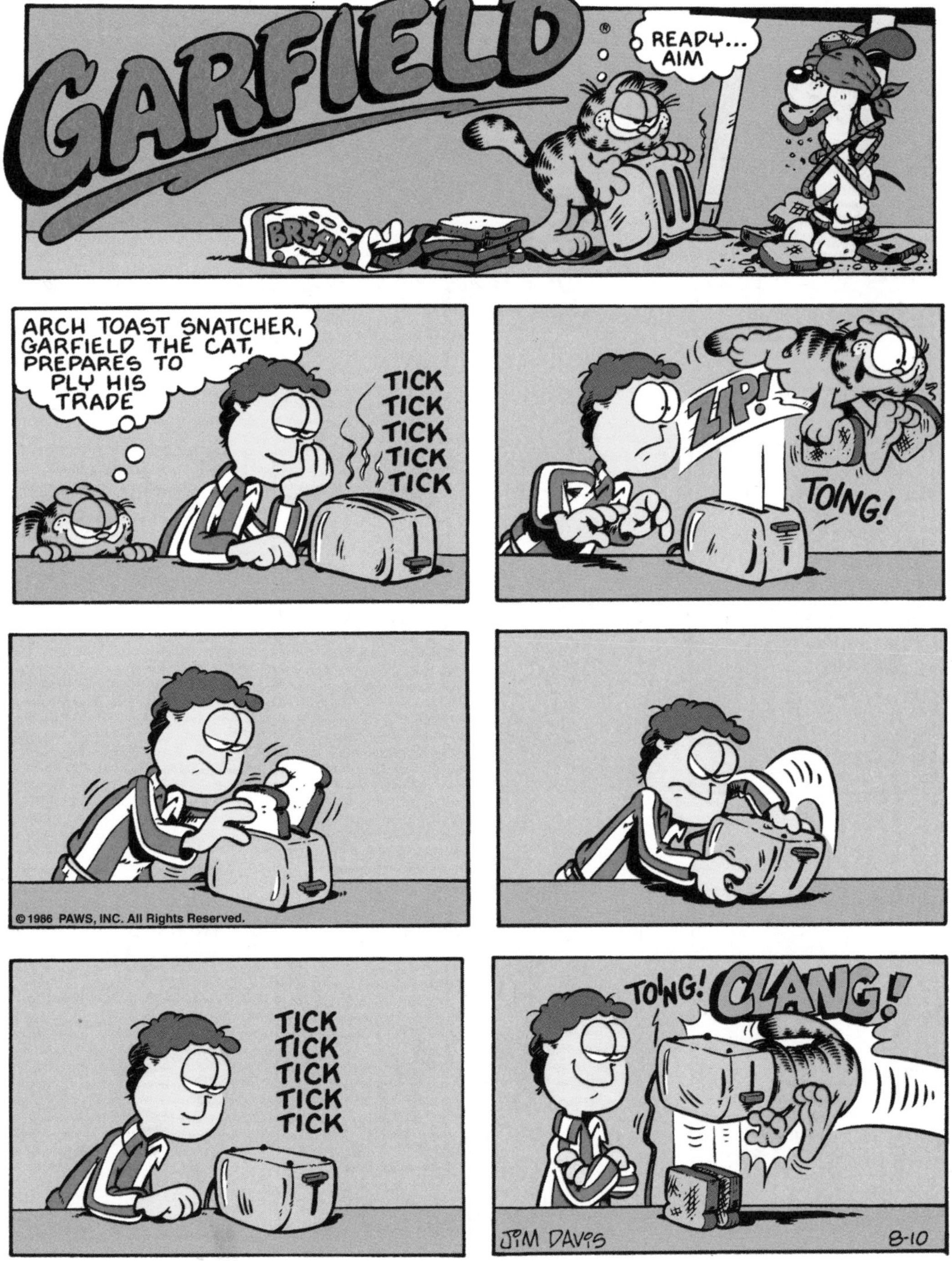
GARFIELD®
READY... AIM
BREAD
ARCH TOAST SNATCHER, GARFIELD THE CAT, PREPARES TO PLY HIS TRADE
TICK TICK TICK TICK TICK
ZIP!
TOING!
TICK TICK TICK TICK TICK
TOING!
CLANG!
JIM DAVIS
8-10

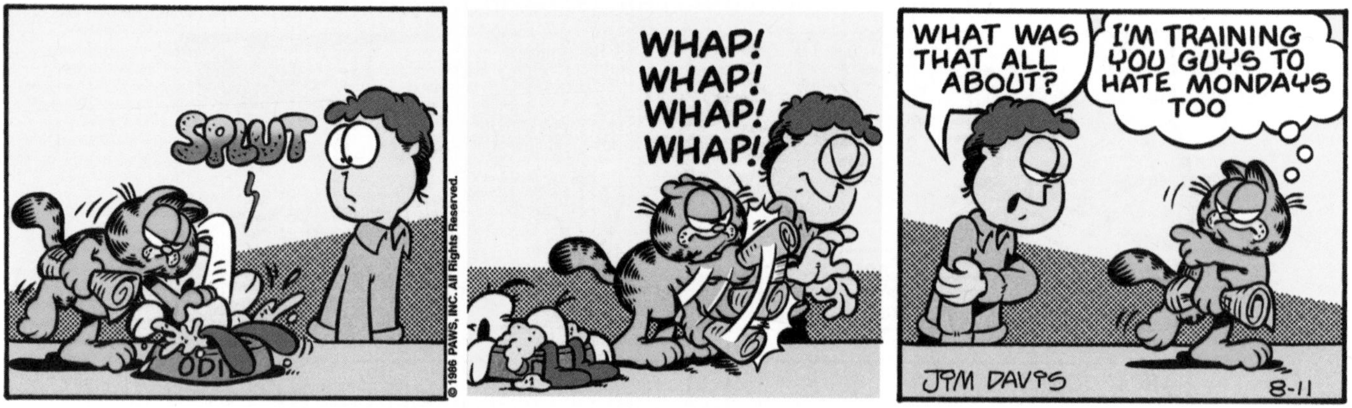
SPLUT
© 1986 PAWS, INC. All Rights Reserved.
WHAP! WHAP! WHAP! WHAP!
WHAT WAS THAT ALL ABOUT?
I'M TRAINING YOU GUYS TO HATE MONDAYS TOO
JIM DAVIS
8-11

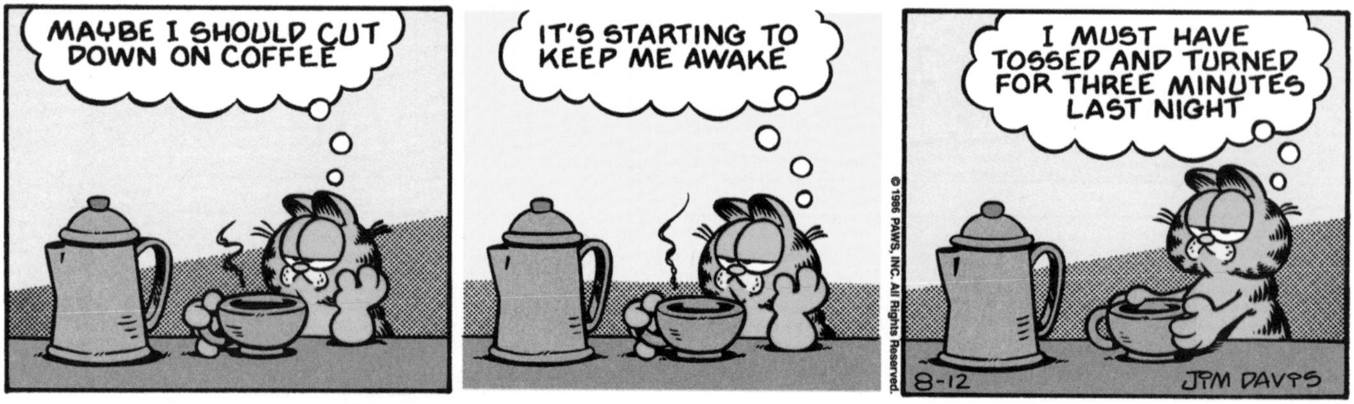
MAYBE I SHOULD CUT DOWN ON COFFEE
IT'S STARTING TO KEEP ME AWAKE
© 1986 PAWS, INC. All Rights Reserved.
I MUST HAVE TOSSED AND TURNED FOR THREE MINUTES LAST NIGHT
8-12
JIM DAVIS

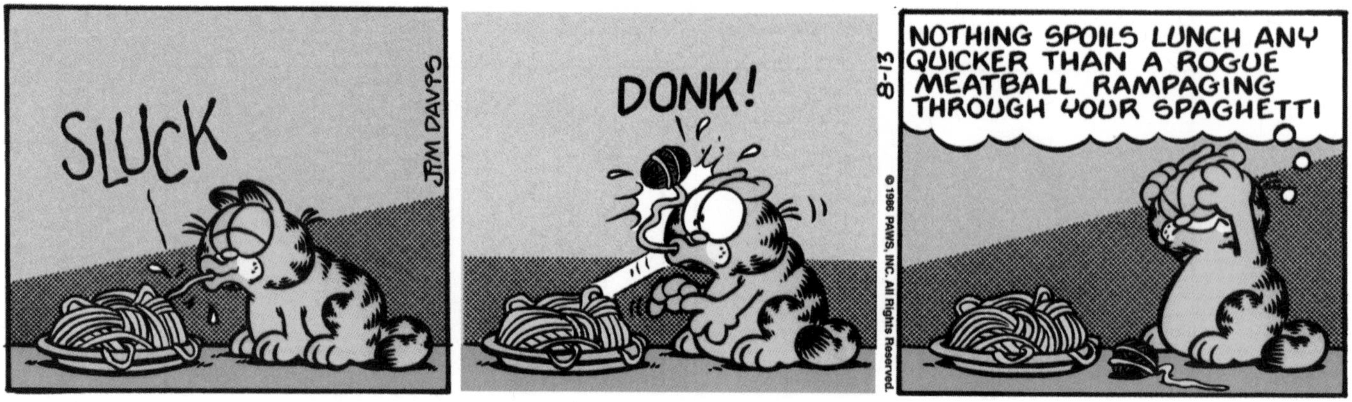
SLUCK
JIM DAVIS
DONK!
8-13
© 1986 PAWS, INC. All Rights Reserved.
NOTHING SPOILS LUNCH ANY QUICKER THAN A ROGUE MEATBALL RAMPAGING THROUGH YOUR SPAGHETTI

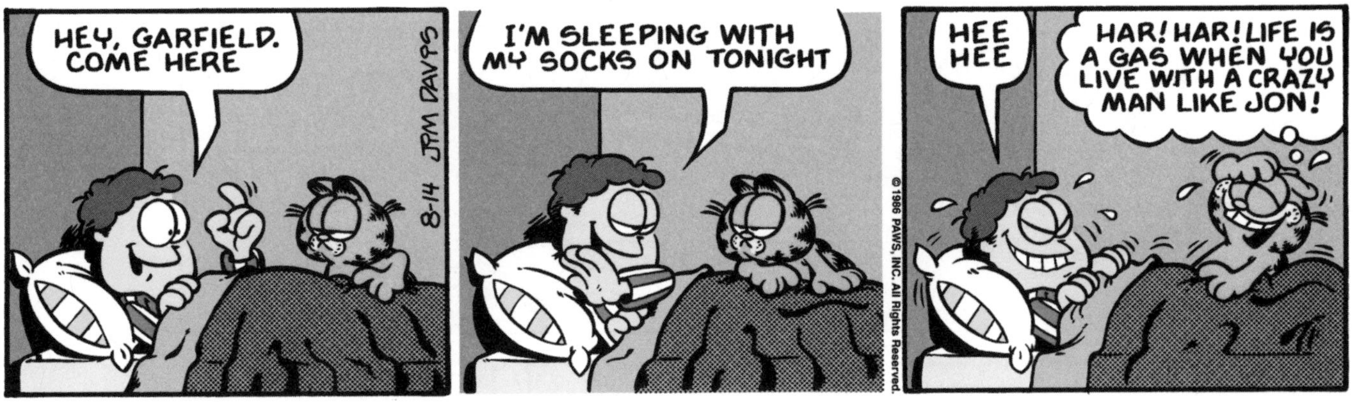
HEY, GARFIELD. COME HERE
JPM DAVPS 8-14
I'M SLEEPING WITH MY SOCKS ON TONIGHT
© 1986 PAWS, INC. All Rights Reserved.
HEE HEE
HAR! HAR! LIFE IS A GAS WHEN YOU LIVE WITH A CRAZY MAN LIKE JON!

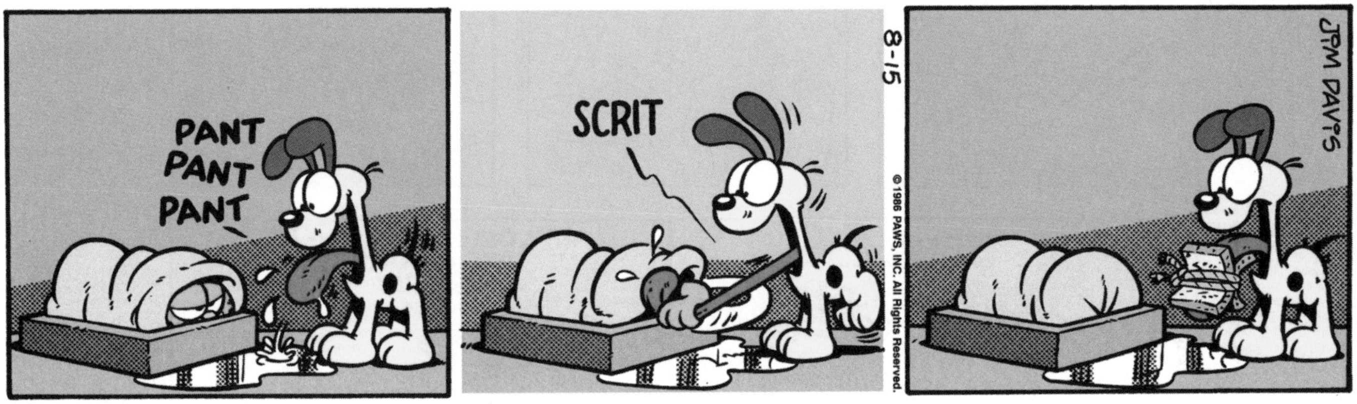
PANT PANT PANT
SCRIT
8-15
© 1986 PAWS, INC. All Rights Reserved.
JPM DAVPS

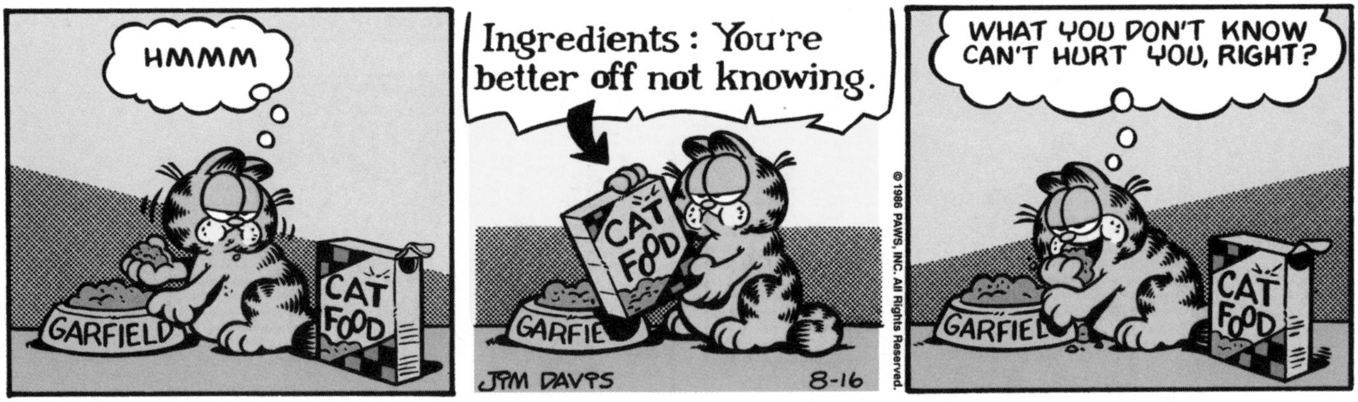
HMMM
GARFIELD
CAT FOOD
Ingredients : You're better off not knowing.
CAT FOOD
GARFIE
JPM DAVPS 8-16
© 1986 PAWS, INC. All Rights Reserved.
WHAT YOU DON'T KNOW CAN'T HURT YOU, RIGHT?
GARFIEL
CAT FOOD

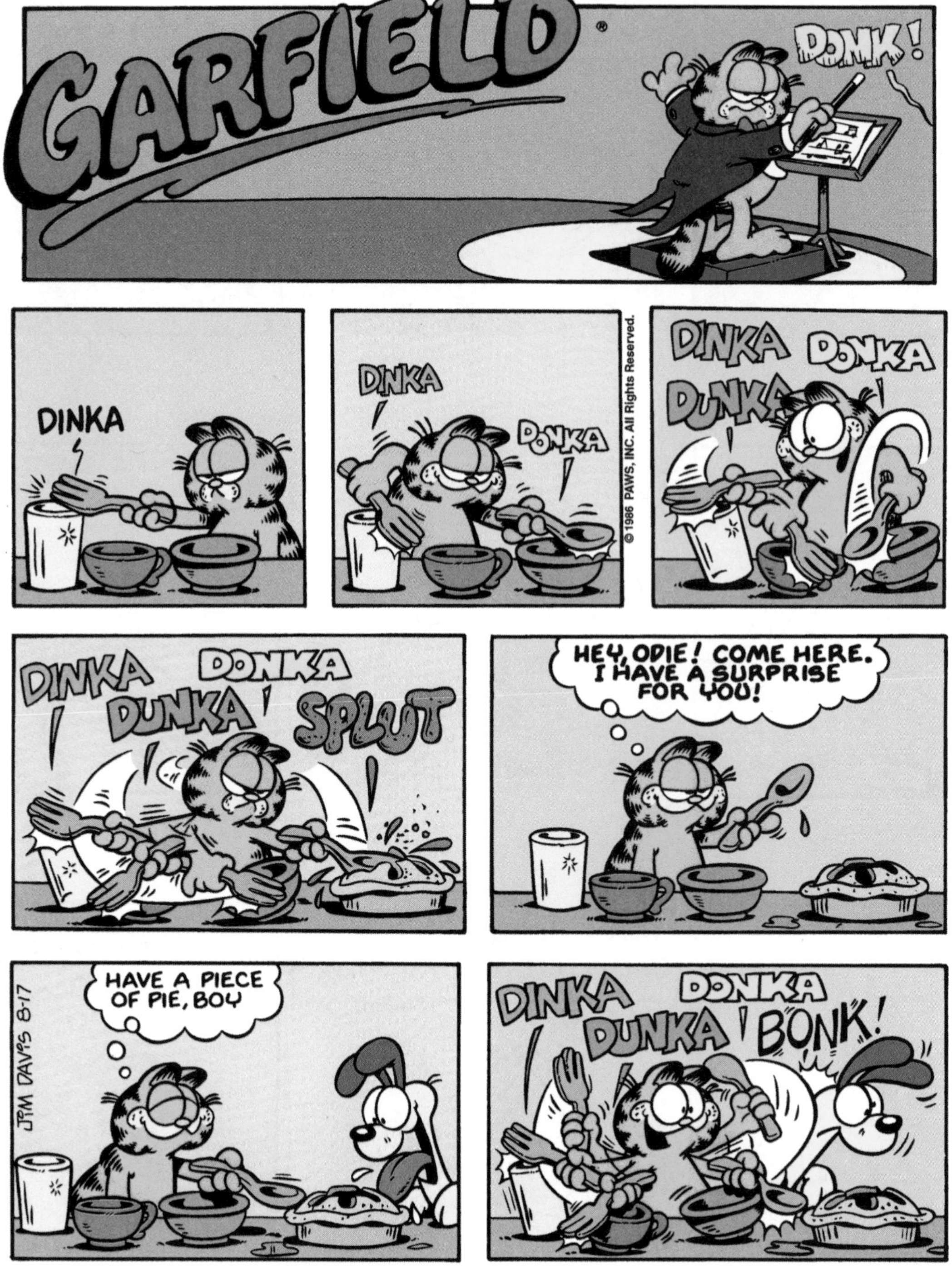
GARFIELD®
DONK!
DINKA
DINKA
DONKA
© 1986 PAWS, INC. All Rights Reserved.
DINKA DONKA
DUNKA
DINKA DONKA
DUNKA SPLUT
HEY, ODIE! COME HERE. I HAVE A SURPRISE FOR YOU!
JIM DAVIS 8-17
HAVE A PIECE OF PIE, BOY
DINKA DONKA
DUNKA BONK!

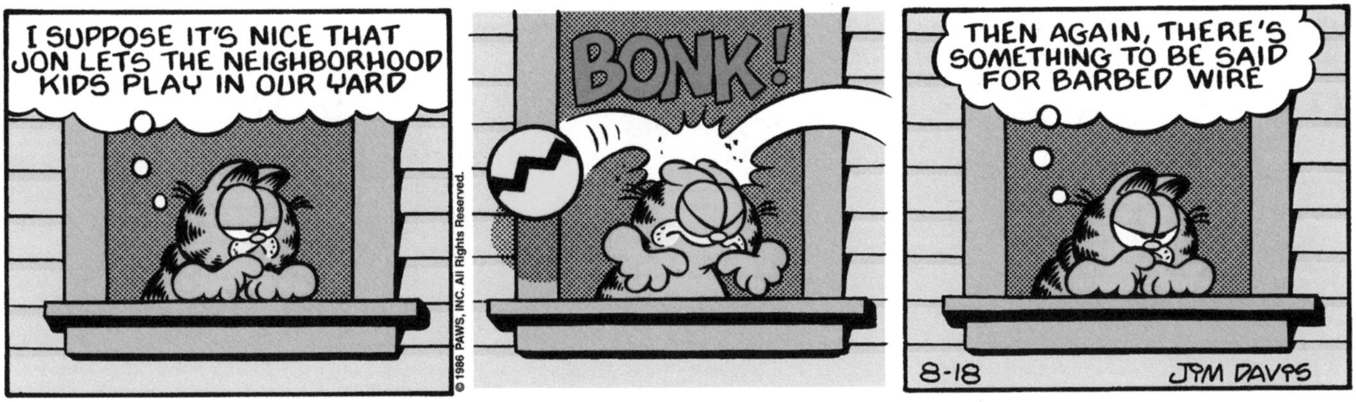
I SUPPOSE IT'S NICE THAT JON LETS THE NEIGHBORHOOD KIDS PLAY IN OUR YARD
BONK!
© 1986 PAWS, INC. All Rights Reserved.
THEN AGAIN, THERE'S SOMETHING TO BE SAID FOR BARBED WIRE
8-18
JIM DAVIS

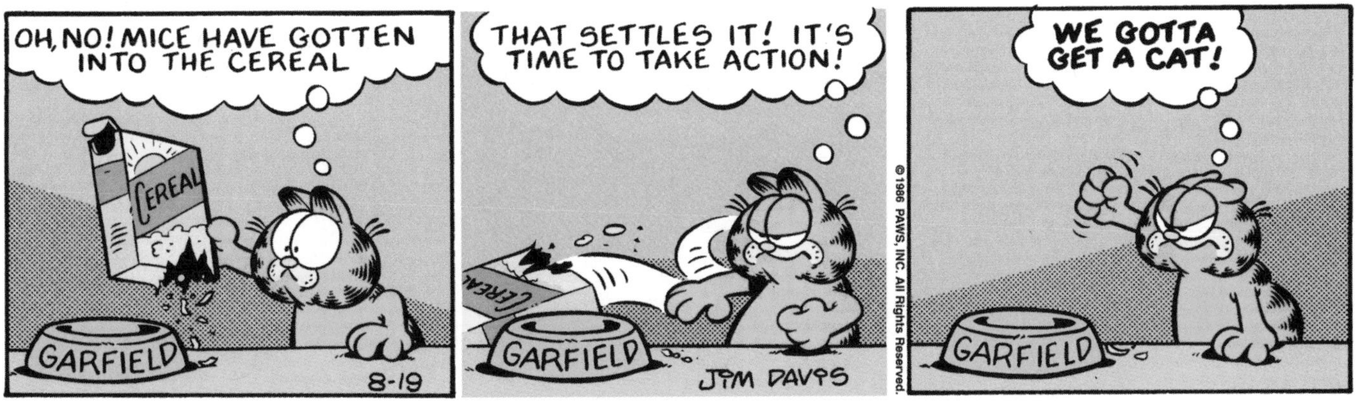
OH, NO! MICE HAVE GOTTEN INTO THE CEREAL
CEREAL
GARFIELD
8-19
THAT SETTLES IT! IT'S TIME TO TAKE ACTION!
CEREAL
GARFIELD
JIM DAVIS
© 1986 PAWS, INC. All Rights Reserved.
WE GOTTA GET A CAT!
GARFIELD

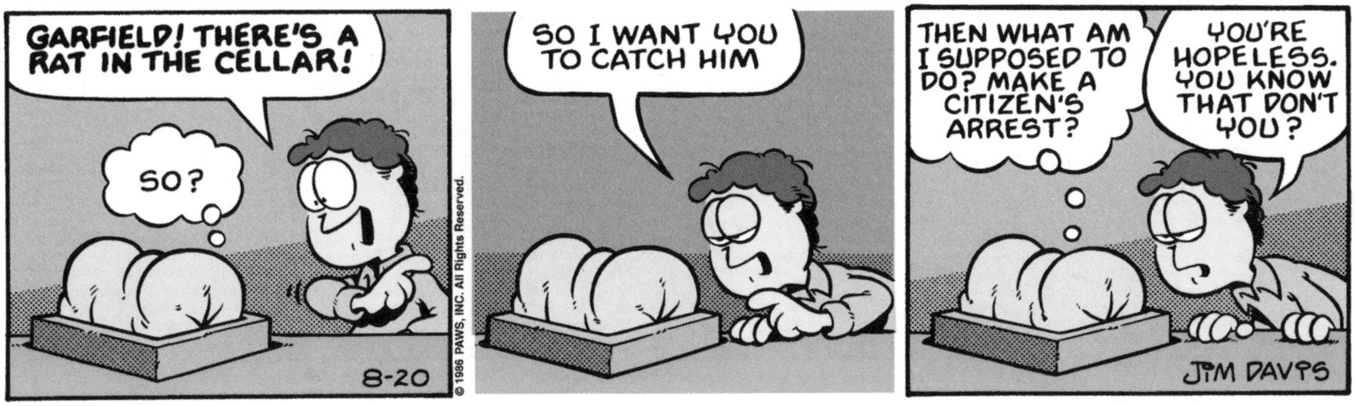
GARFIELD! THERE'S A RAT IN THE CELLAR!
SO?
8-20
© 1986 PAWS, INC. All Rights Reserved.
SO I WANT YOU TO CATCH HIM
THEN WHAT AM I SUPPOSED TO DO? MAKE A CITIZEN'S ARREST?
YOU'RE HOPELESS. YOU KNOW THAT DON'T YOU?
JIM DAVIS

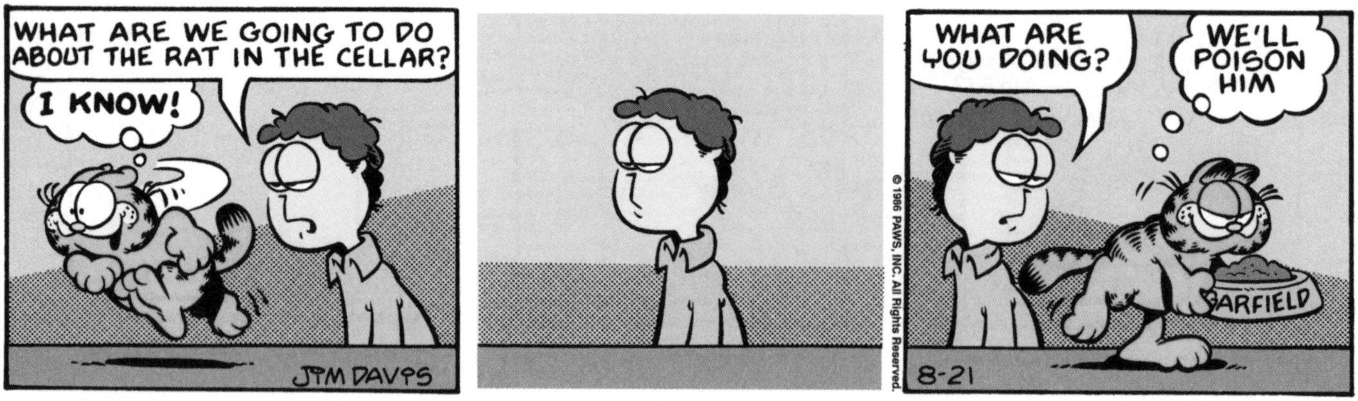
WHAT ARE WE GOING TO DO ABOUT THE RAT IN THE CELLAR?
I KNOW!
JIM DAVIS
© 1986 PAWS, INC. All Rights Reserved.
WHAT ARE YOU DOING?
WE'LL POISON HIM
GARFIELD
8-21

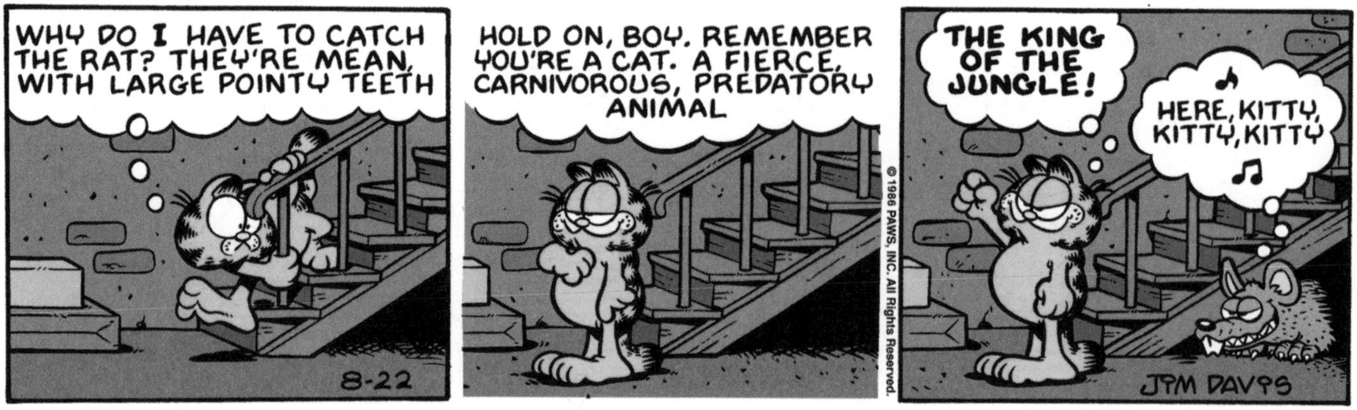
WHY DO I HAVE TO CATCH THE RAT? THEY'RE MEAN, WITH LARGE POINTY TEETH
8-22
HOLD ON, BOY. REMEMBER YOU'RE A CAT. A FIERCE, CARNIVOROUS, PREDATORY ANIMAL
© 1986 PAWS, INC. All Rights Reserved.
THE KING OF THE JUNGLE!
HERE, KITTY, KITTY, KITTY
JIM DAVIS

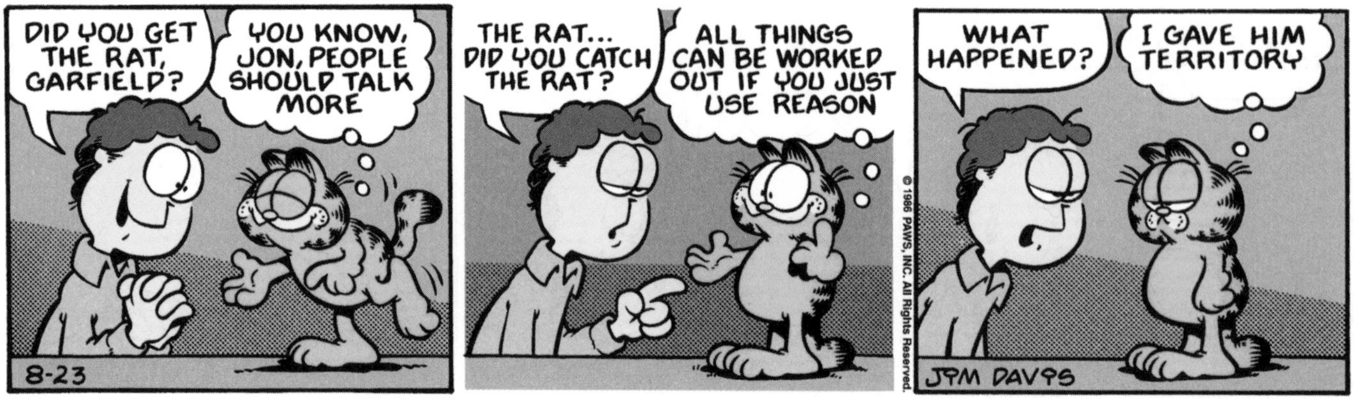
DID YOU GET THE RAT, GARFIELD?
YOU KNOW, JON, PEOPLE SHOULD TALK MORE
8-23
THE RAT... DID YOU CATCH THE RAT?
ALL THINGS CAN BE WORKED OUT IF YOU JUST USE REASON
© 1986 PAWS, INC. All Rights Reserved.
WHAT HAPPENED?
I GAVE HIM TERRITORY
JIM DAVIS

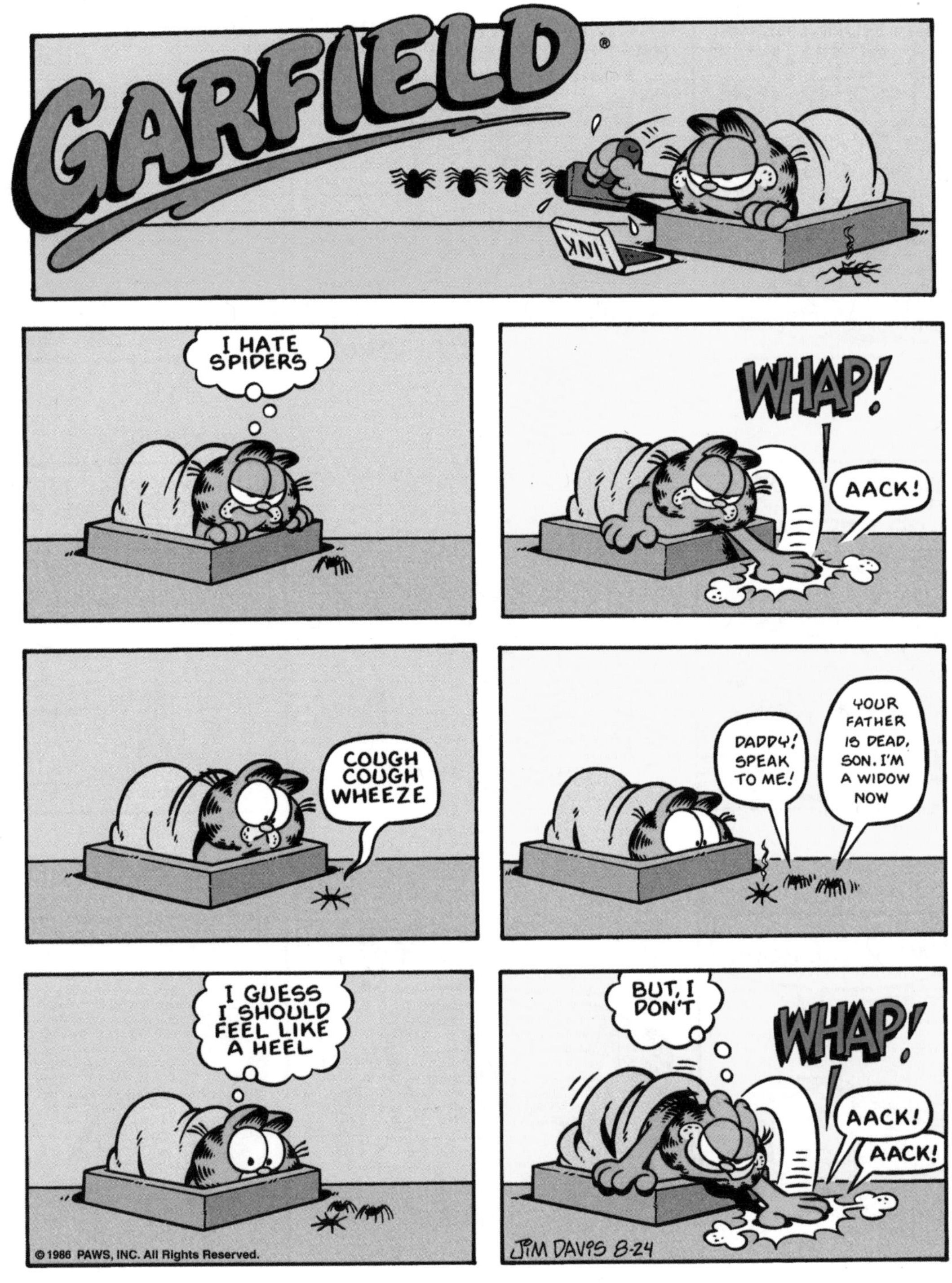
GARFIELD®
INK
I HATE SPIDERS
WHAP!
AACK!
COUGH COUGH WHEEZE
DADDY! SPEAK TO ME!
YOUR FATHER IS DEAD, SON. I'M A WIDOW NOW
I GUESS I SHOULD FEEL LIKE A HEEL
BUT, I DON'T
WHAP!
AACK!
AACK!
JIM DAVIS 8-24

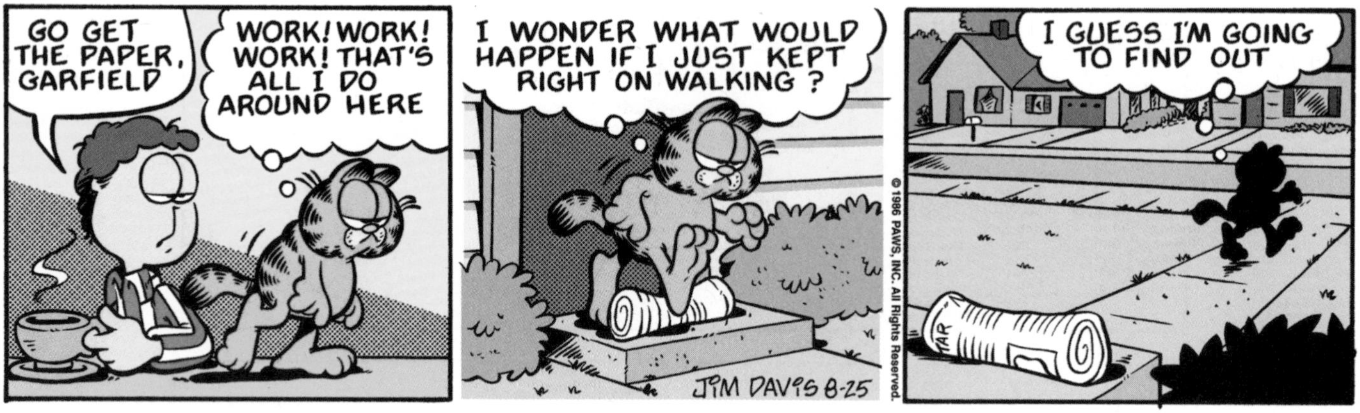
GO GET THE PAPER, GARFIELD
WORK! WORK! WORK! THAT'S ALL I DO AROUND HERE
I WONDER WHAT WOULD HAPPEN IF I JUST KEPT RIGHT ON WALKING ?
© 1986 PAWS, INC. All Rights Reserved.
JIM DAVIS 8-25
I GUESS I'M GOING TO FIND OUT

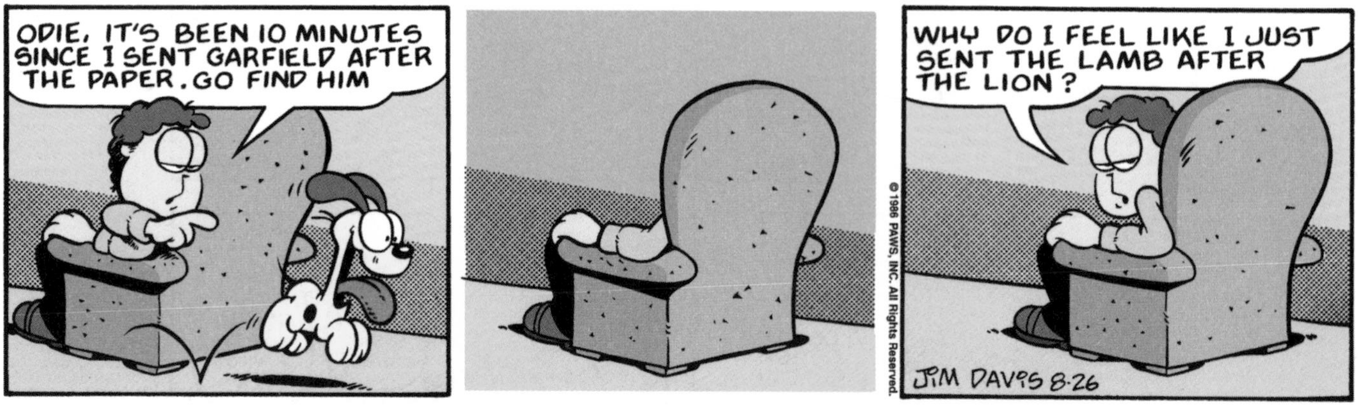
ODIE, IT'S BEEN 10 MINUTES SINCE I SENT GARFIELD AFTER THE PAPER. GO FIND HIM
© 1986 PAWS, INC. All Rights Reserved.
WHY DO I FEEL LIKE I JUST SENT THE LAMB AFTER THE LION ?
JIM DAVIS 8-26

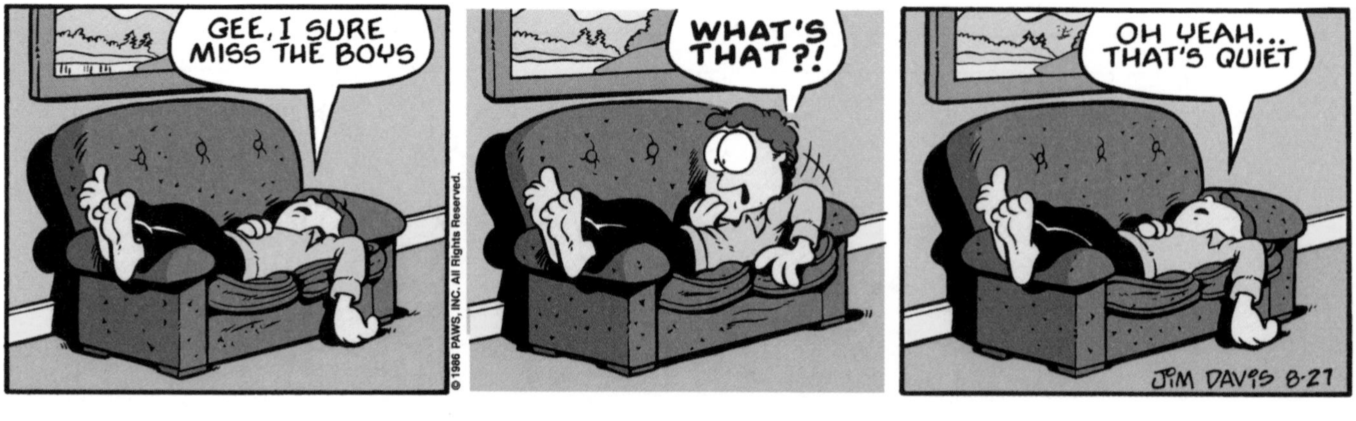
GEE, I SURE MISS THE BOYS
© 1986 PAWS, INC. All Rights Reserved.
WHAT'S THAT?!
OH YEAH... THAT'S QUIET
JIM DAVIS 8-27

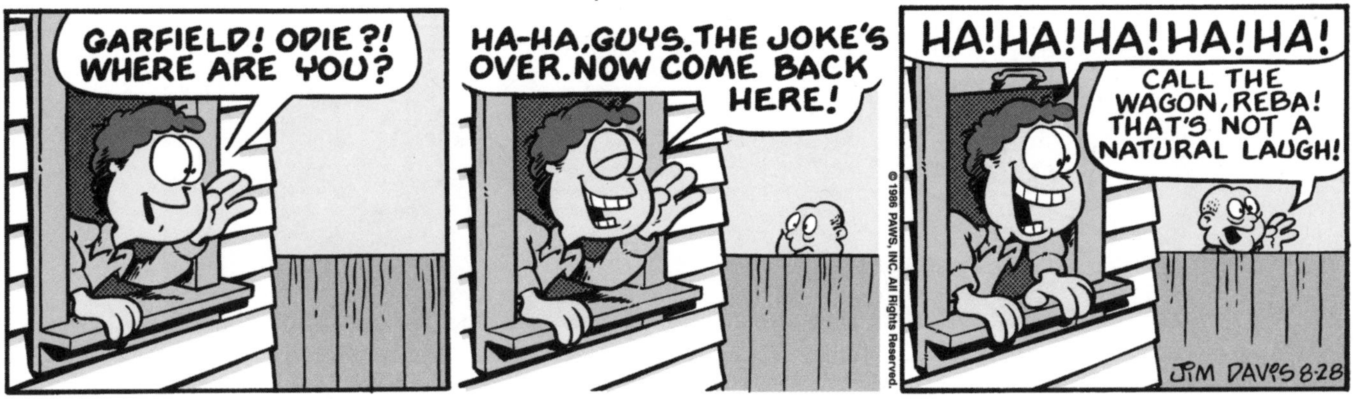
GARFIELD! ODIE?! WHERE ARE YOU?
HA-HA, GUYS. THE JOKE'S OVER. NOW COME BACK HERE!
HA! HA! HA! HA! HA!
CALL THE WAGON, REBA! THAT'S NOT A NATURAL LAUGH!
© 1986 PAWS, INC. All Rights Reserved.
JIM DAVIS 8-28

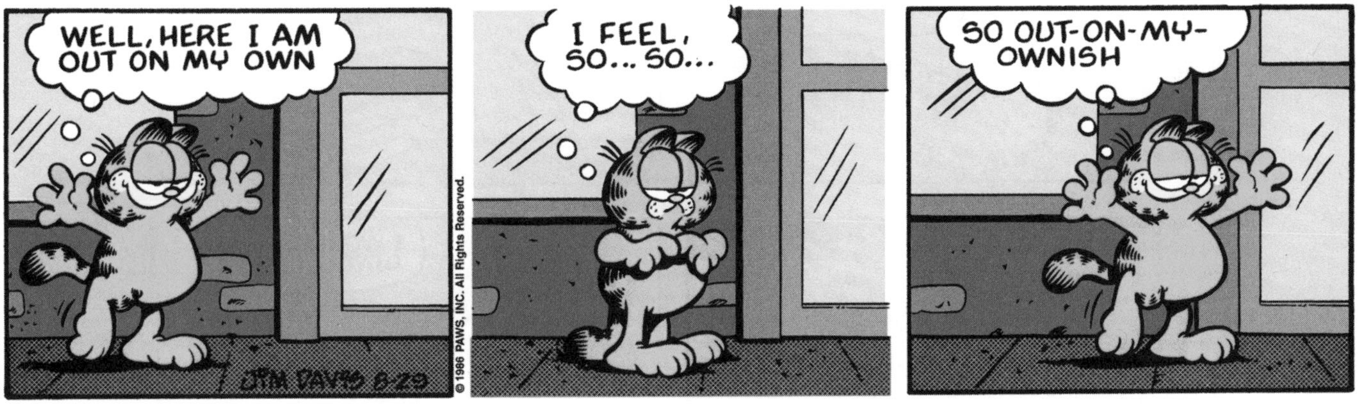
WELL, HERE I AM OUT ON MY OWN
JIM DAVIS 8-29
© 1986 PAWS, INC. All Rights Reserved.
I FEEL, SO... SO...
SO OUT-ON-MY-OWNISH

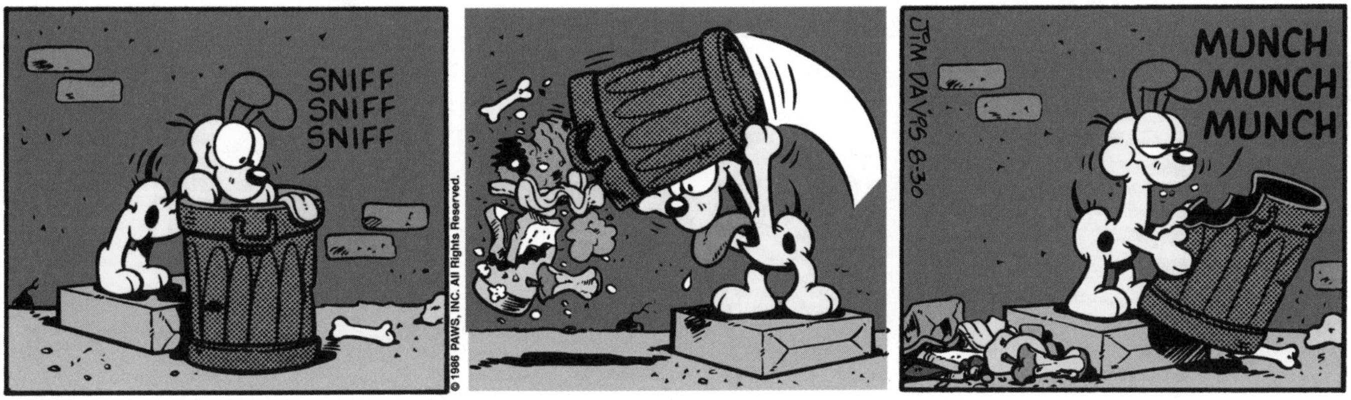
SNIFF SNIFF SNIFF
© 1986 PAWS, INC. All Rights Reserved.
JIM DAVIS 8-30
MUNCH MUNCH MUNCH

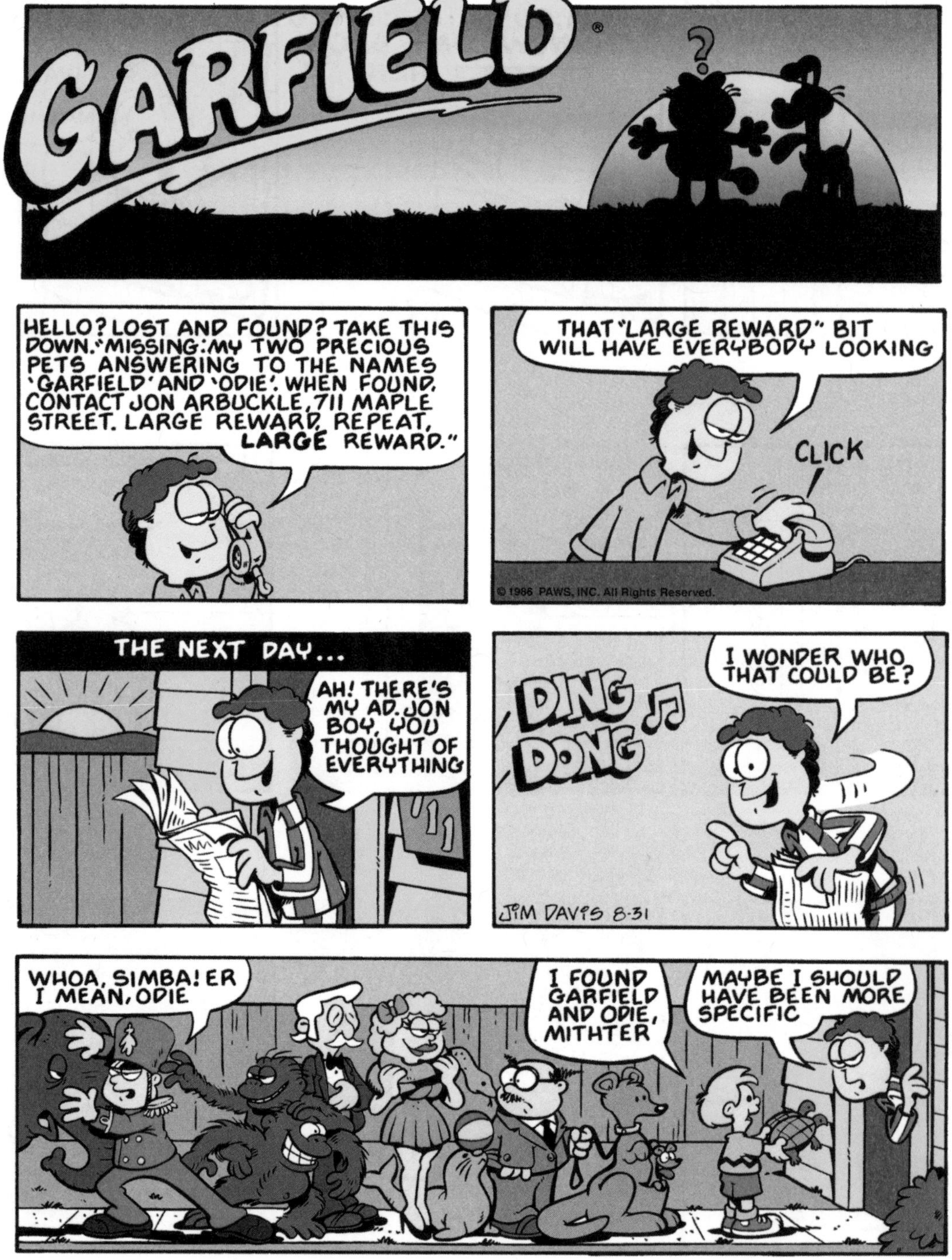
GARFIELD
HELLO? LOST AND FOUND? TAKE THIS DOWN. "MISSING: MY TWO PRECIOUS PETS ANSWERING TO THE NAMES 'GARFIELD' AND 'ODIE'. WHEN FOUND, CONTACT JON ARBUCKLE, 711 MAPLE STREET. LARGE REWARD, REPEAT, LARGE REWARD."
THAT "LARGE REWARD" BIT WILL HAVE EVERYBODY LOOKING
CLICK
© 1986 PAWS, INC. All Rights Reserved.
THE NEXT DAY...
AH! THERE'S MY AD. JON BOY, YOU THOUGHT OF EVERYTHING
DING DONG
I WONDER WHO THAT COULD BE?
JIM DAVIS 8-31
WHOA, SIMBA! ER I MEAN, ODIE
I FOUND GARFIELD AND ODIE, MITHTER
MAYBE I SHOULD HAVE BEEN MORE SPECIFIC

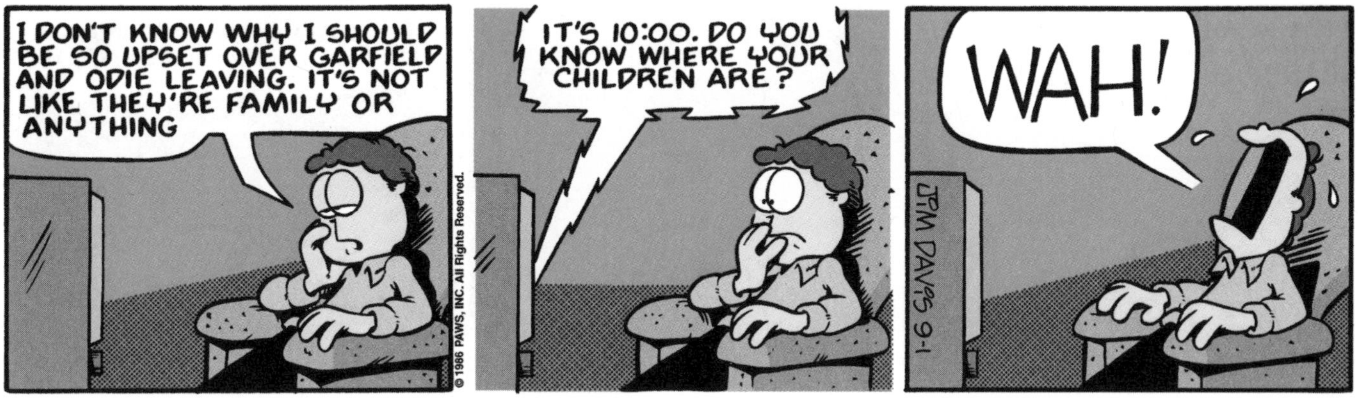
I DON'T KNOW WHY I SHOULD BE SO UPSET OVER GARFIELD AND ODIE LEAVING. IT'S NOT LIKE THEY'RE FAMILY OR ANYTHING
IT'S 10:00. DO YOU KNOW WHERE YOUR CHILDREN ARE?
WAH!
JIM DAVIS 9-1
© 1986 PAWS, INC. All Rights Reserved.

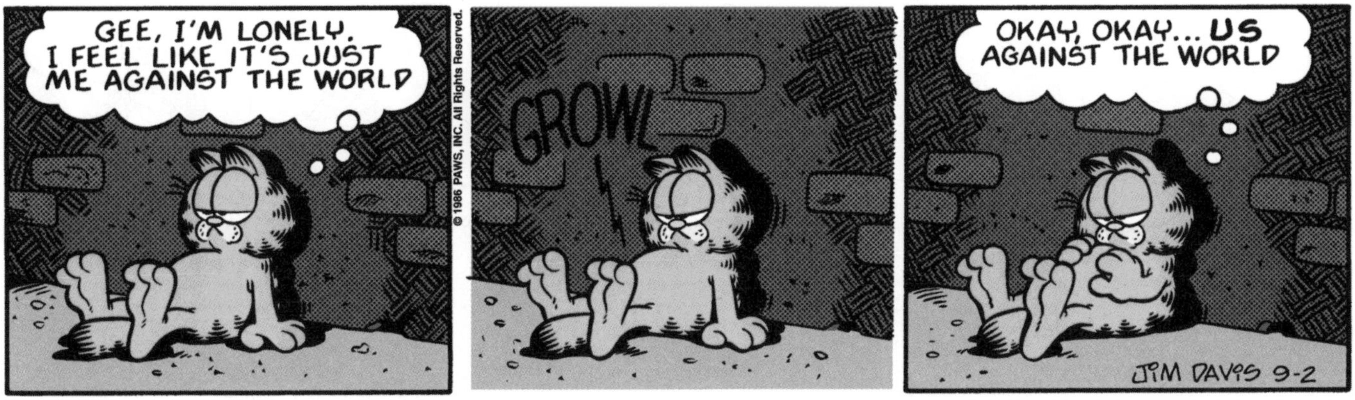
GEE, I'M LONELY. I FEEL LIKE IT'S JUST ME AGAINST THE WORLD
GROWL
OKAY, OKAY... US AGAINST THE WORLD
JIM DAVIS 9-2
© 1986 PAWS, INC. All Rights Reserved.

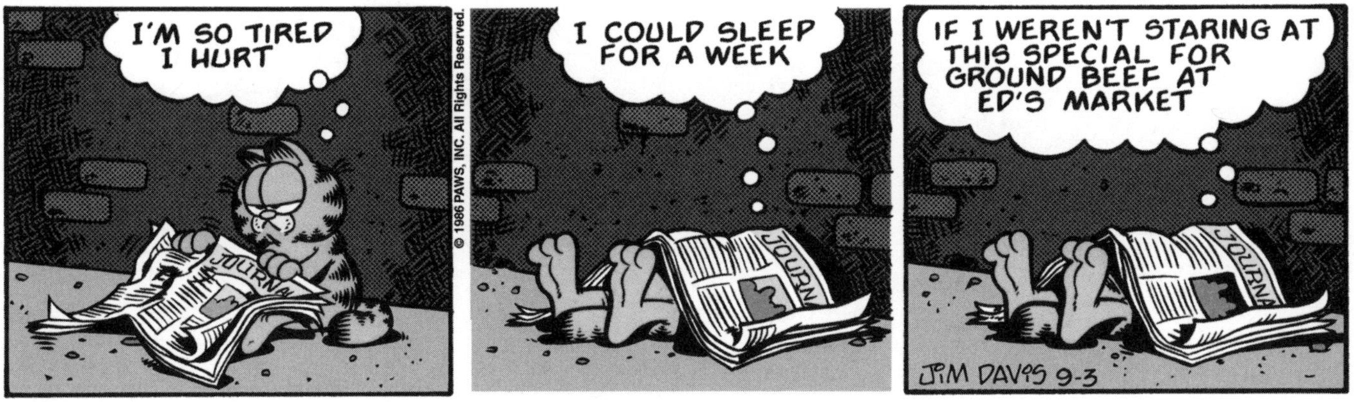
I'M SO TIRED I HURT
JOURNAL
I COULD SLEEP FOR A WEEK
IF I WEREN'T STARING AT THIS SPECIAL FOR GROUND BEEF AT ED'S MARKET
JIM DAVIS 9-3
© 1986 PAWS, INC. All Rights Reserved.

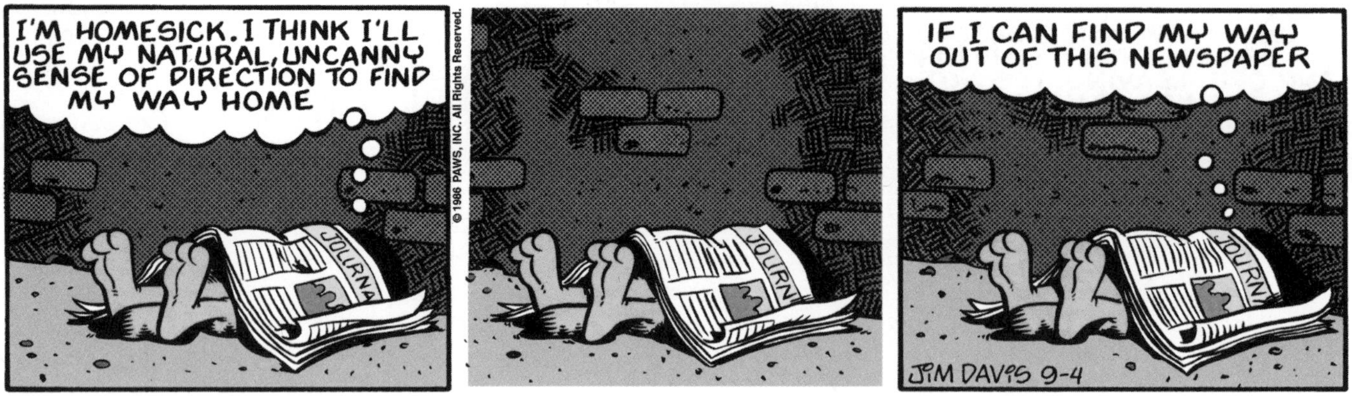
I'M HOMESICK. I THINK I'LL USE MY NATURAL, UNCANNY SENSE OF DIRECTION TO FIND MY WAY HOME
© 1986 PAWS, INC. All Rights Reserved.
IF I CAN FIND MY WAY OUT OF THIS NEWSPAPER
JIM DAVIS 9-4

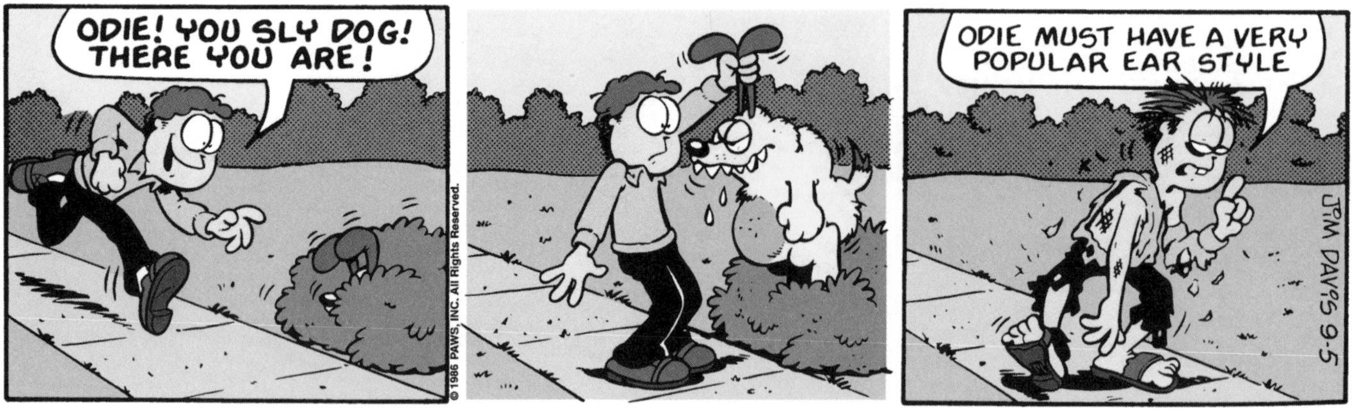
ODIE! YOU SLY DOG! THERE YOU ARE!
© 1986 PAWS, INC. All Rights Reserved.
ODIE MUST HAVE A VERY POPULAR EAR STYLE
JIM DAVIS 9-5

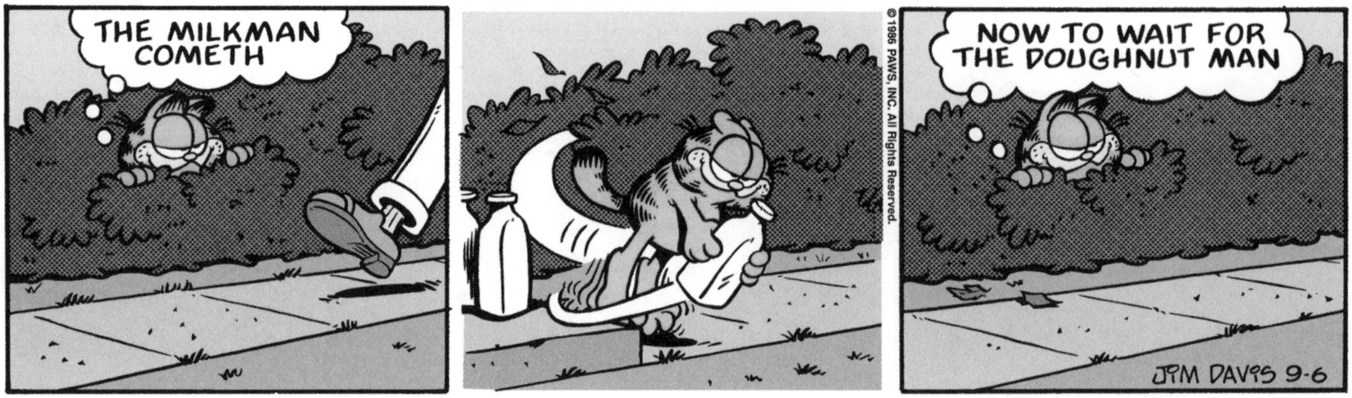
THE MILKMAN COMETH
© 1986 PAWS, INC. All Rights Reserved.
NOW TO WAIT FOR THE DOUGHNUT MAN
JIM DAVIS 9-6

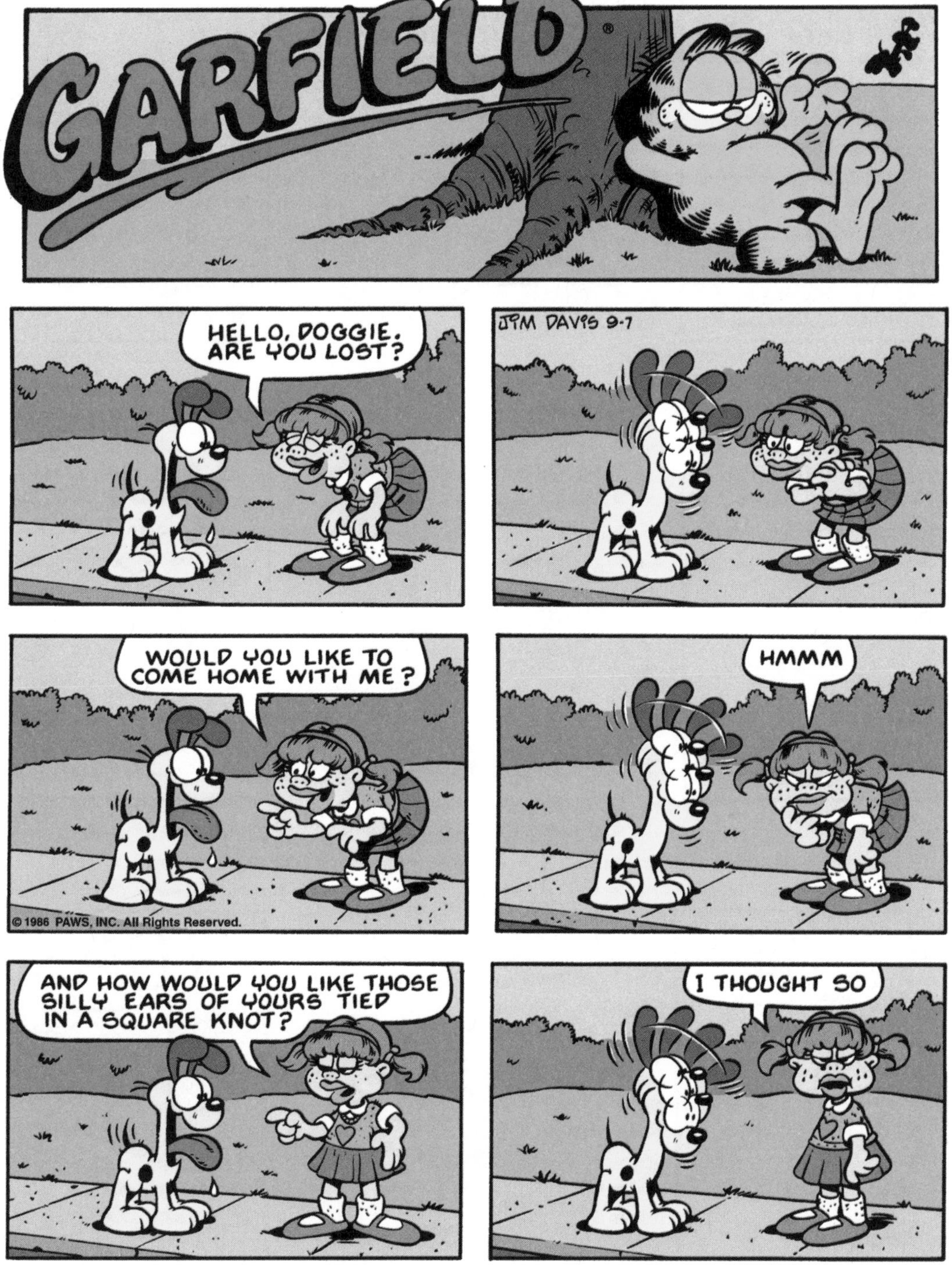
GARFIELD®
HELLO, DOGGIE. ARE YOU LOST?
JIM DAVIS 9-7
WOULD YOU LIKE TO COME HOME WITH ME?
HMMM
© 1986 PAWS, INC. All Rights Reserved.
AND HOW WOULD YOU LIKE THOSE SILLY EARS OF YOURS TIED IN A SQUARE KNOT?
I THOUGHT SO

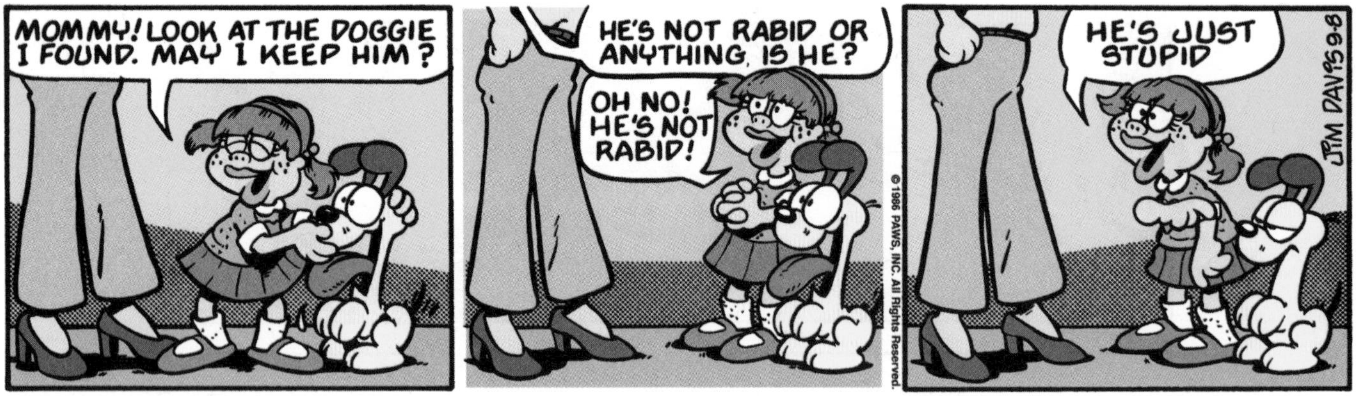
MOMMY! LOOK AT THE DOGGIE I FOUND. MAY I KEEP HIM?
HE'S NOT RABID OR ANYTHING, IS HE?
OH NO! HE'S NOT RABID!
HE'S JUST STUPID
JIM DAVIS 9-8
© 1986 PAWS, INC. All Rights Reserved.

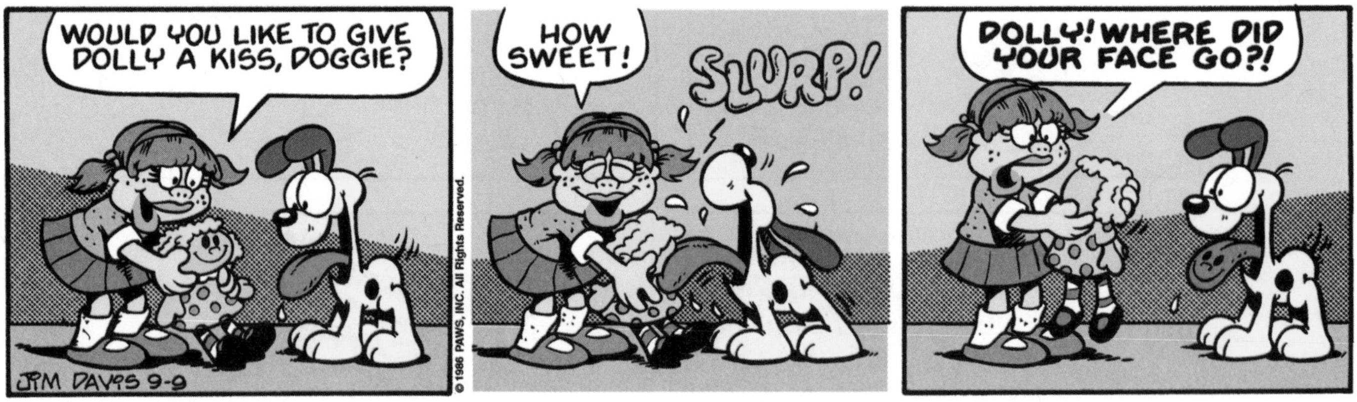
WOULD YOU LIKE TO GIVE DOLLY A KISS, DOGGIE?
JIM DAVIS 9-9
© 1986 PAWS, INC. All Rights Reserved.
HOW SWEET!
SLURP!
DOLLY! WHERE DID YOUR FACE GO?!

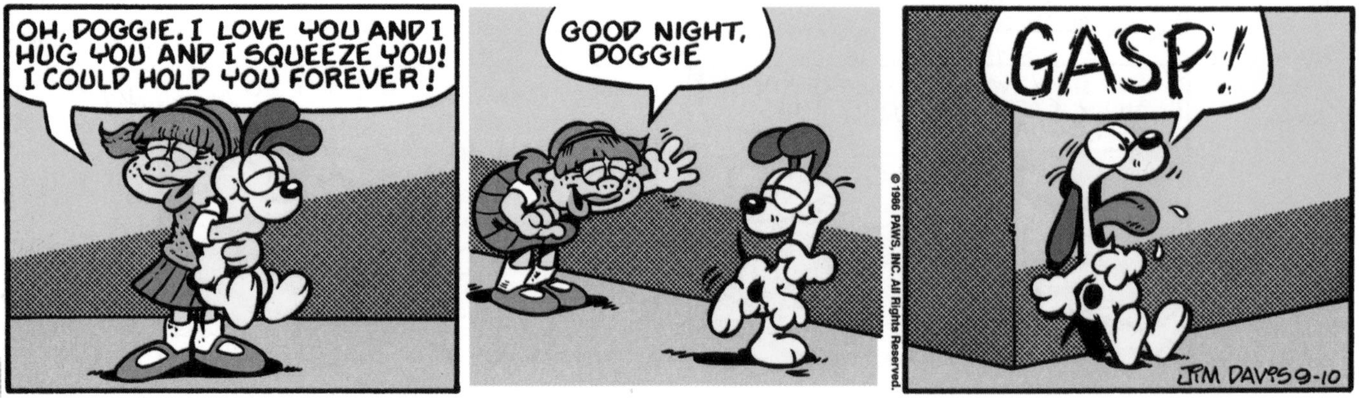
OH, DOGGIE. I LOVE YOU AND I HUG YOU AND I SQUEEZE YOU! I COULD HOLD YOU FOREVER!
GOOD NIGHT, DOGGIE
© 1986 PAWS, INC. All Rights Reserved.
GASP!
JIM DAVIS 9-10

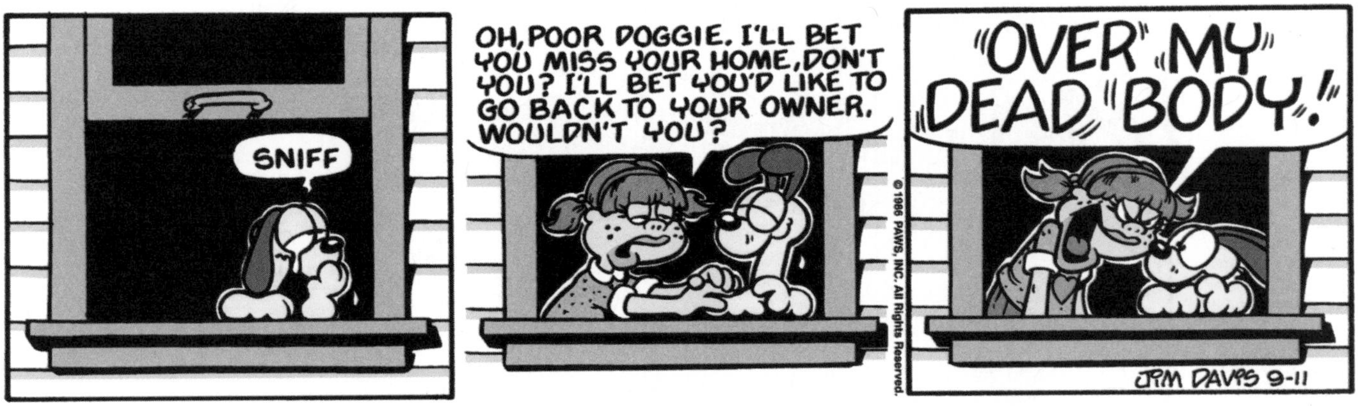
SNIFF
OH, POOR DOGGIE. I'LL BET YOU MISS YOUR HOME, DON'T YOU? I'LL BET YOU'D LIKE TO GO BACK TO YOUR OWNER, WOULDN'T YOU?
"OVER" "MY" "DEAD" "BODY"!
© 1986 PAWS, INC. All Rights Reserved.
JIM DAVIS 9-11

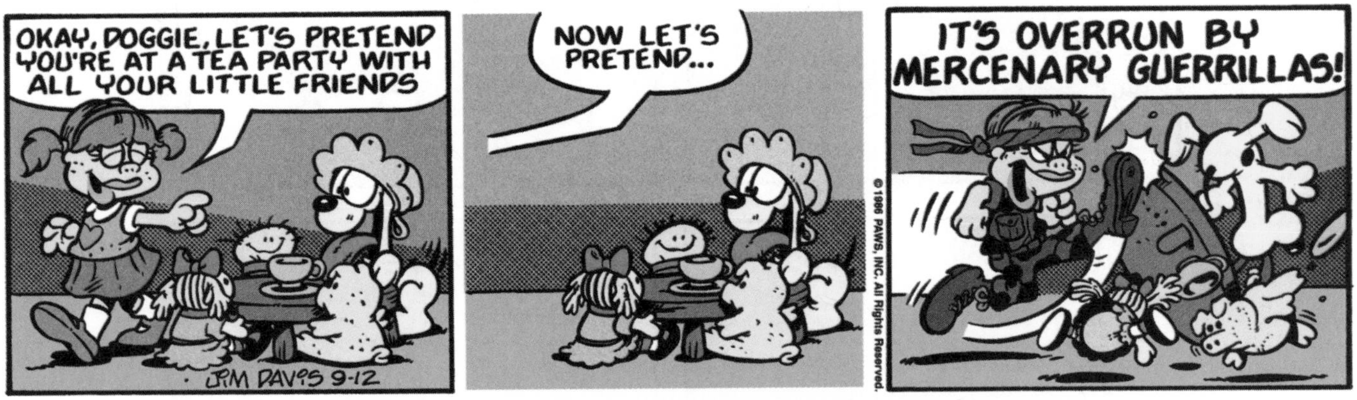
OKAY, DOGGIE, LET'S PRETEND YOU'RE AT A TEA PARTY WITH ALL YOUR LITTLE FRIENDS
JIM DAVIS 9-12
NOW LET'S PRETEND...
© 1986 PAWS, INC. All Rights Reserved.
IT'S OVERRUN BY MERCENARY GUERRILLAS!

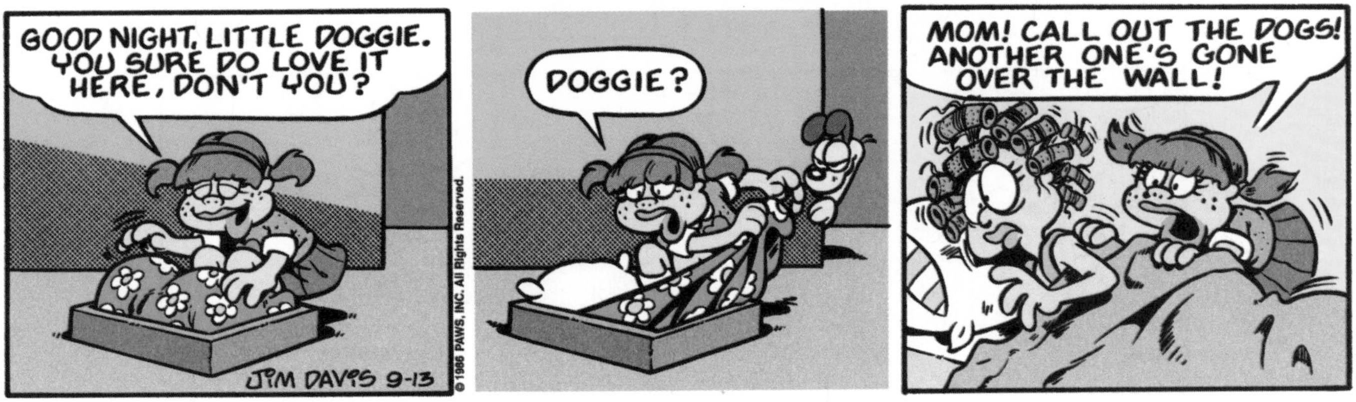
GOOD NIGHT, LITTLE DOGGIE. YOU SURE DO LOVE IT HERE, DON'T YOU?
JIM DAVIS 9-13
© 1986 PAWS, INC. All Rights Reserved.
DOGGIE?
MOM! CALL OUT THE DOGS! ANOTHER ONE'S GONE OVER THE WALL!

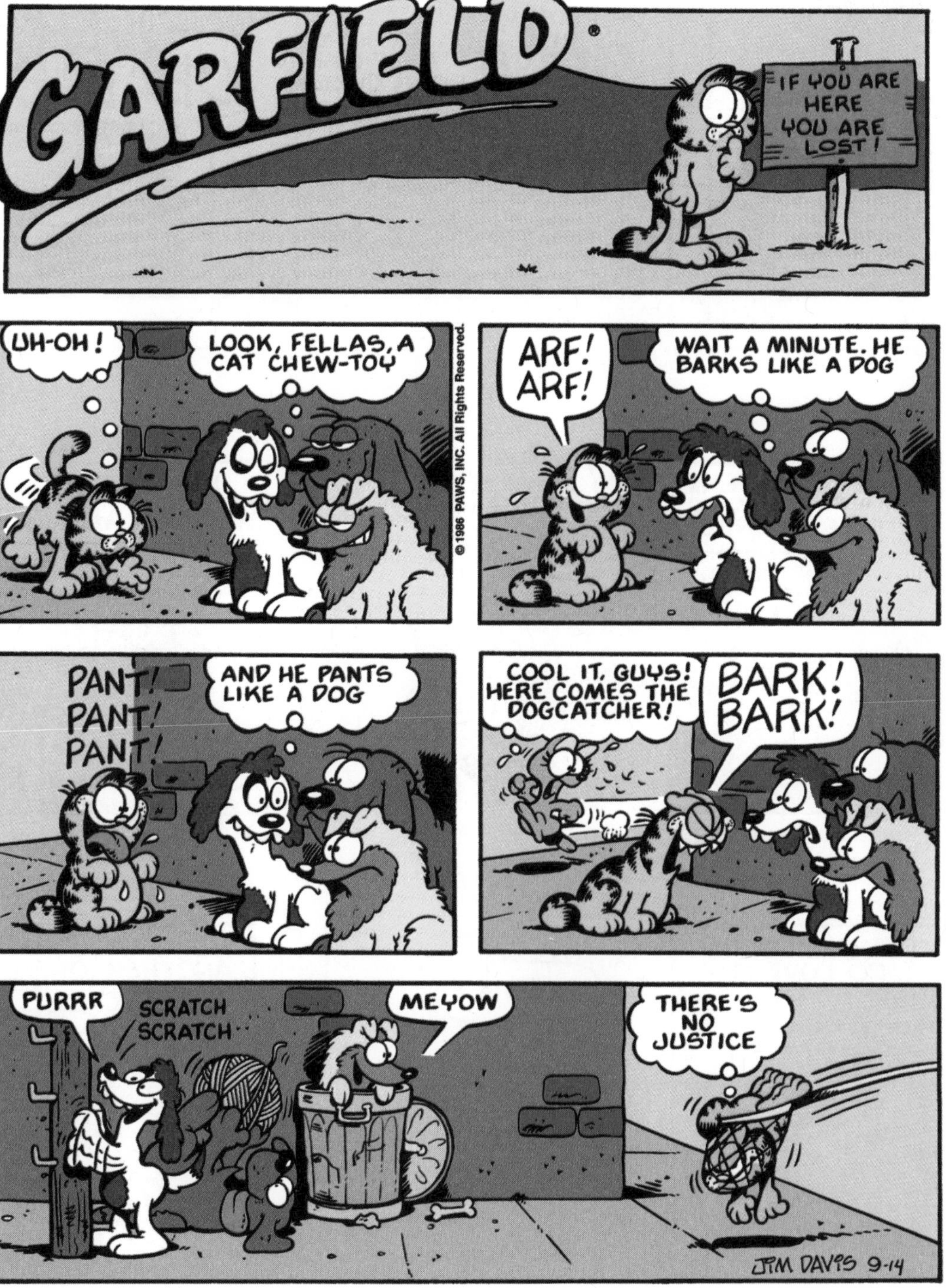
GARFIELD®
IF YOU ARE HERE YOU ARE LOST!
UH-OH!
LOOK, FELLAS, A CAT CHEW-TOY
© 1986 PAWS, INC. All Rights Reserved.
ARF! ARF!
WAIT A MINUTE. HE BARKS LIKE A DOG
PANT! PANT! PANT!
AND HE PANTS LIKE A DOG
COOL IT, GUYS! HERE COMES THE DOGCATCHER!
BARK! BARK!
PURRR
SCRATCH SCRATCH
MEYOW
THERE'S NO JUSTICE
JIM DAVIS 9-14

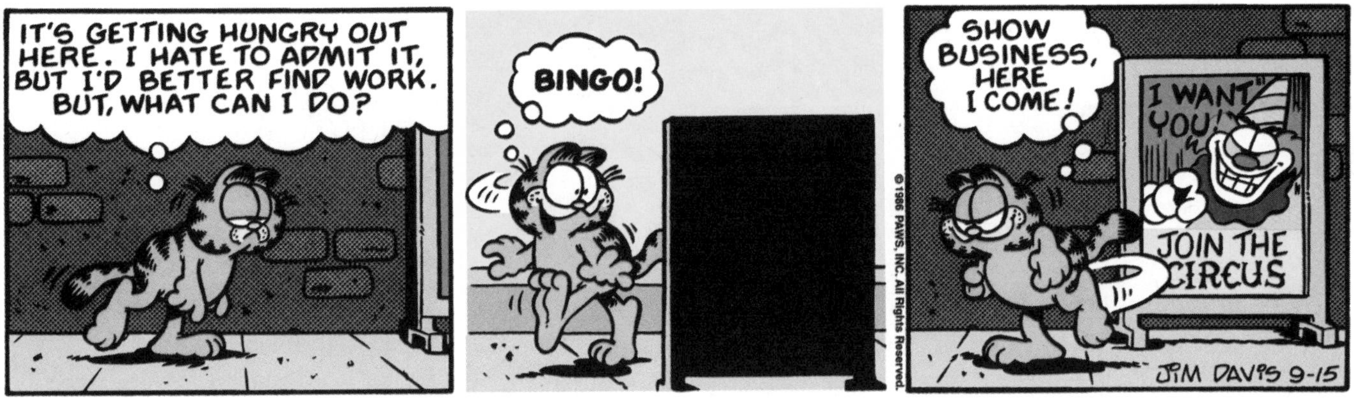
IT'S GETTING HUNGRY OUT HERE. I HATE TO ADMIT IT, BUT I'D BETTER FIND WORK. BUT, WHAT CAN I DO?
BINGO!
SHOW BUSINESS, HERE I COME!
I WANT YOU!
JOIN THE CIRCUS
JIM DAVIS 9-15
© 1986 PAWS, INC. All Rights Reserved.

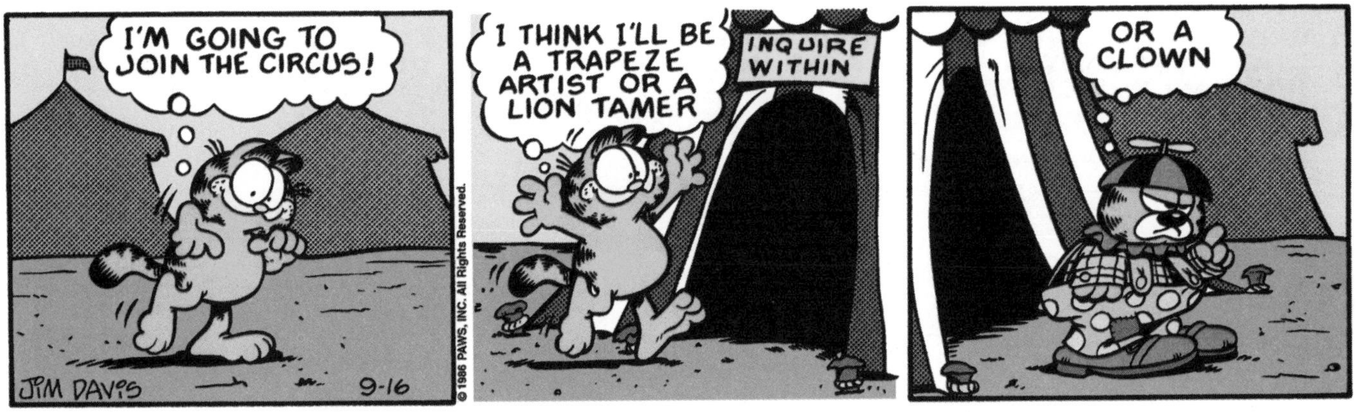
I'M GOING TO JOIN THE CIRCUS!
JIM DAVIS 9-16
© 1986 PAWS, INC. All Rights Reserved.
I THINK I'LL BE A TRAPEZE ARTIST OR A LION TAMER
INQUIRE WITHIN
OR A CLOWN

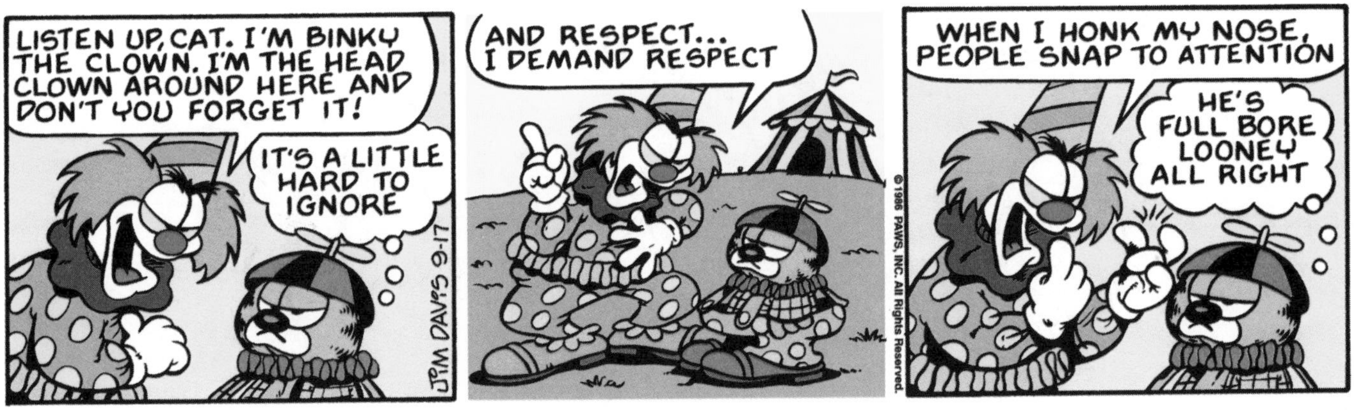
LISTEN UP, CAT. I'M BINKY THE CLOWN. I'M THE HEAD CLOWN AROUND HERE AND DON'T YOU FORGET IT!
IT'S A LITTLE HARD TO IGNORE
JIM DAVIS 9-17
AND RESPECT... I DEMAND RESPECT
© 1986 PAWS, INC. All Rights Reserved.
WHEN I HONK MY NOSE, PEOPLE SNAP TO ATTENTION
HE'S FULL BORE LOONEY ALL RIGHT

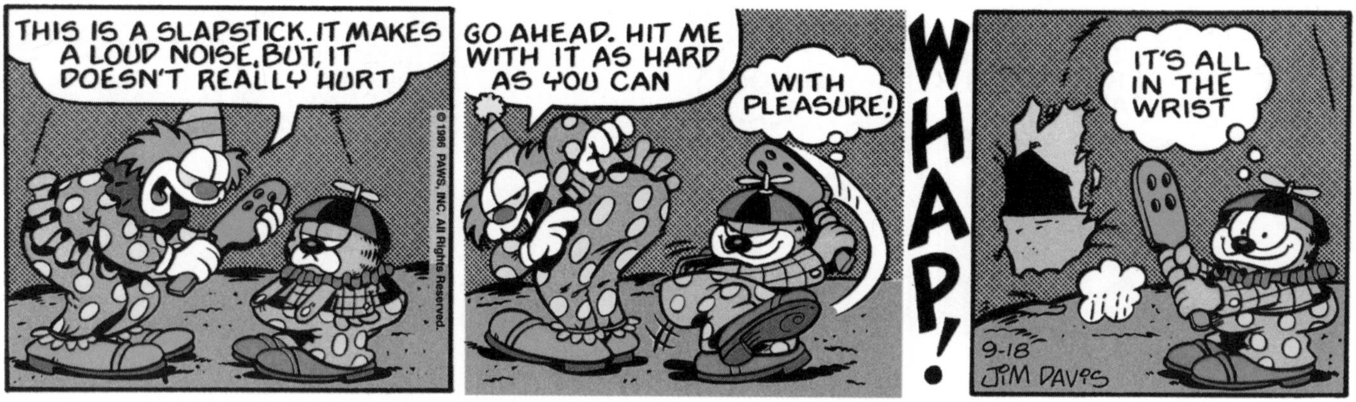
THIS IS A SLAPSTICK. IT MAKES A LOUD NOISE, BUT, IT DOESN'T REALLY HURT
© 1986 PAWS, INC. All Rights Reserved.
GO AHEAD. HIT ME WITH IT AS HARD AS YOU CAN
WITH PLEASURE!
WHAP!
IT'S ALL IN THE WRIST
9-18
JIM DAVIS

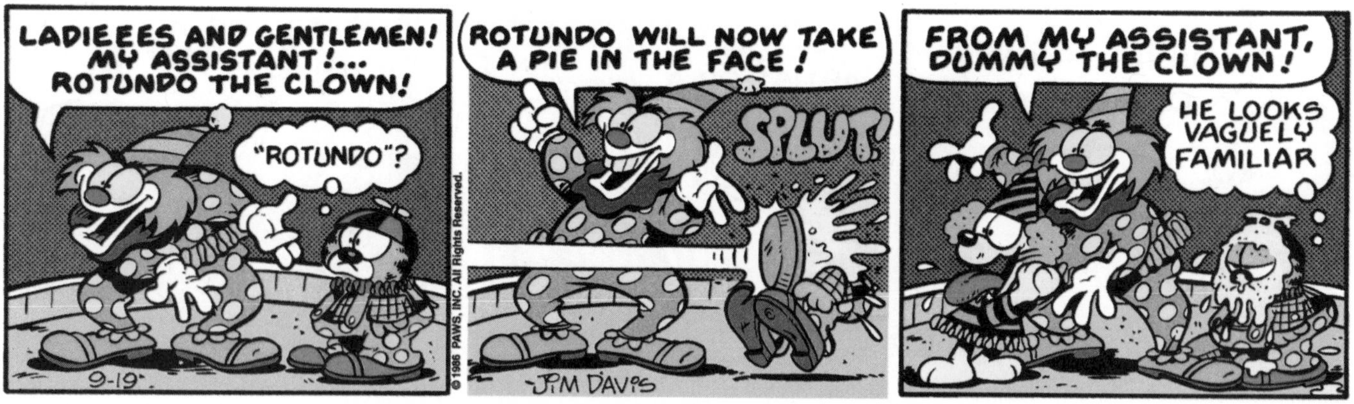
LADIEEES AND GENTLEMEN! MY ASSISTANT!... ROTUNDO THE CLOWN!
"ROTUNDO"?
9-19
© 1986 PAWS, INC. All Rights Reserved.
ROTUNDO WILL NOW TAKE A PIE IN THE FACE!
SPLUT!
JIM DAVIS
FROM MY ASSISTANT, DUMMY THE CLOWN!
HE LOOKS VAGUELY FAMILIAR

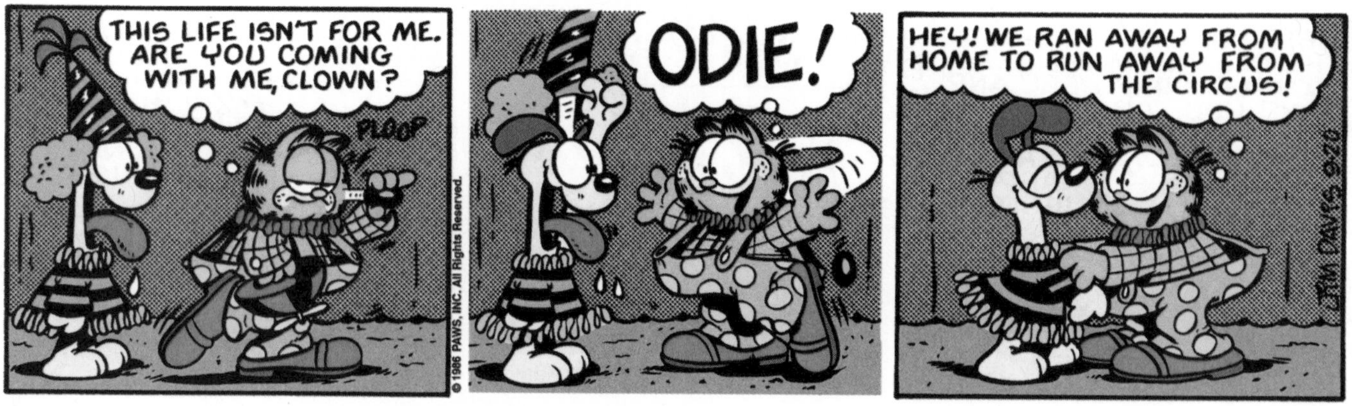
THIS LIFE ISN'T FOR ME. ARE YOU COMING WITH ME, CLOWN?
PLOOP
© 1986 PAWS, INC. All Rights Reserved.
ODIE!
HEY! WE RAN AWAY FROM HOME TO RUN AWAY FROM THE CIRCUS!
JIM DAVIS 9-20

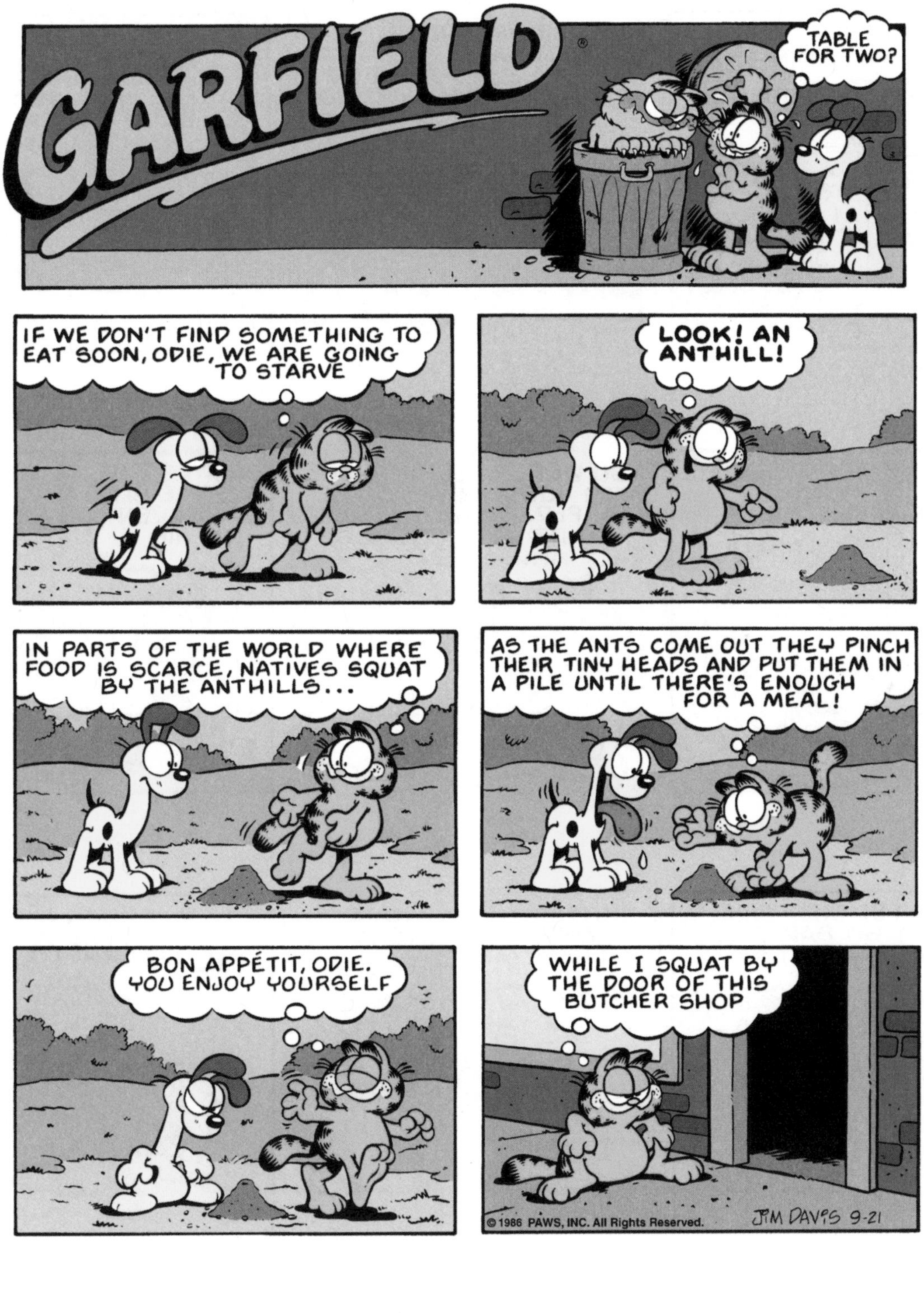
GARFIELD
TABLE FOR TWO?
IF WE DON'T FIND SOMETHING TO EAT SOON, ODIE, WE ARE GOING TO STARVE
LOOK! AN ANTHILL!
IN PARTS OF THE WORLD WHERE FOOD IS SCARCE, NATIVES SQUAT BY THE ANTHILLS...
AS THE ANTS COME OUT THEY PINCH THEIR TINY HEADS AND PUT THEM IN A PILE UNTIL THERE'S ENOUGH FOR A MEAL!
BON APPÉTIT, ODIE. YOU ENJOY YOURSELF
WHILE I SQUAT BY THE DOOR OF THIS BUTCHER SHOP
© 1986 PAWS, INC. All Rights Reserved.
JIM DAVIS 9-21

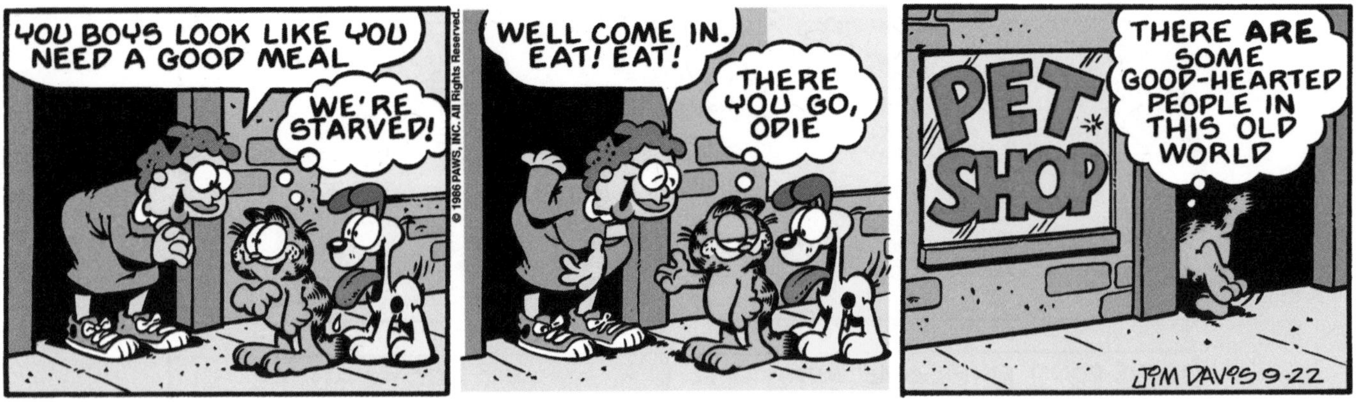
YOU BOYS LOOK LIKE YOU NEED A GOOD MEAL
WE'RE STARVED!
© 1986 PAWS, INC. All Rights Reserved.
WELL COME IN. EAT! EAT!
THERE YOU GO, ODIE
PET SHOP
THERE ARE SOME GOOD-HEARTED PEOPLE IN THIS OLD WORLD
JIM DAVIS 9-22

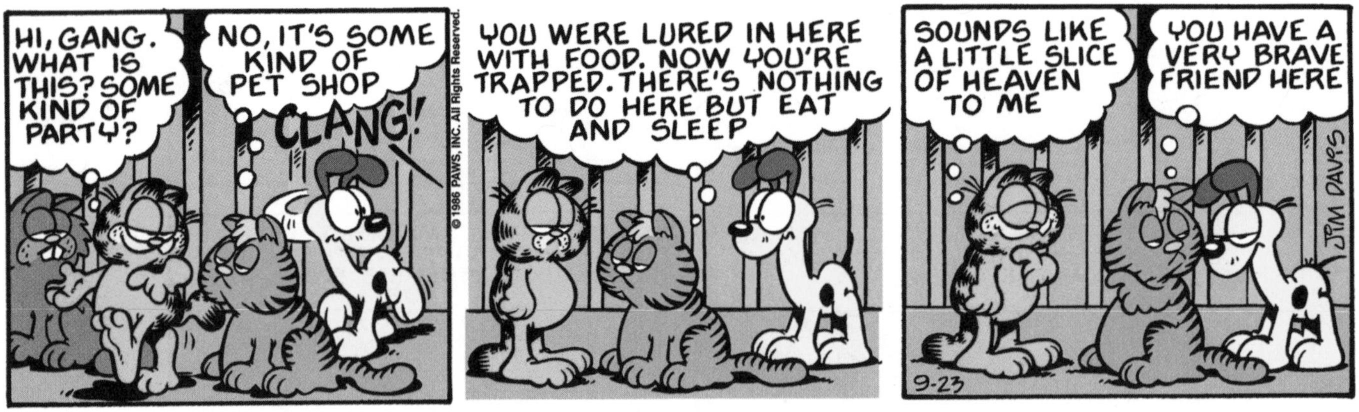
HI, GANG. WHAT IS THIS? SOME KIND OF PARTY?
NO, IT'S SOME KIND OF PET SHOP
CLANG!
© 1986 PAWS, INC. All Rights Reserved.
YOU WERE LURED IN HERE WITH FOOD. NOW YOU'RE TRAPPED. THERE'S NOTHING TO DO HERE BUT EAT AND SLEEP
SOUNDS LIKE A LITTLE SLICE OF HEAVEN TO ME
YOU HAVE A VERY BRAVE FRIEND HERE
JIM DAVIS
9-23

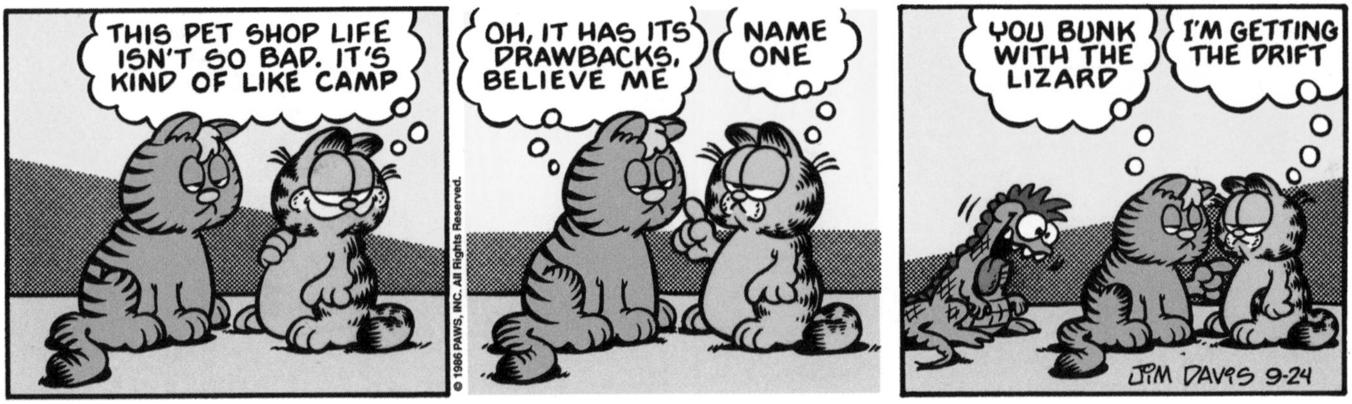
THIS PET SHOP LIFE ISN'T SO BAD. IT'S KIND OF LIKE CAMP
© 1986 PAWS, INC. All Rights Reserved.
OH, IT HAS ITS DRAWBACKS, BELIEVE ME
NAME ONE
YOU BUNK WITH THE LIZARD
I'M GETTING THE DRIFT
JIM DAVIS 9-24

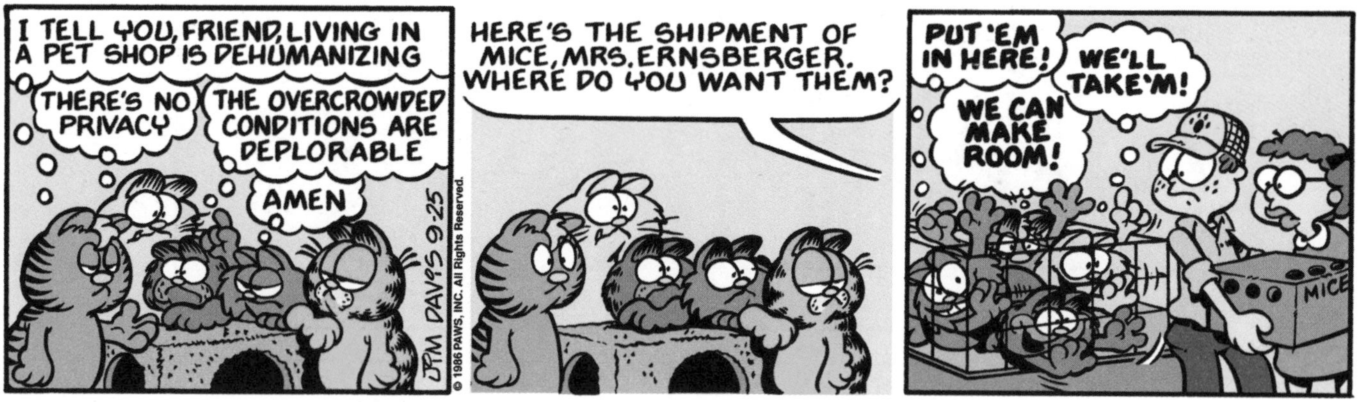
I TELL YOU, FRIEND, LIVING IN A PET SHOP IS DEHUMANIZING
THERE'S NO PRIVACY
THE OVERCROWDED CONDITIONS ARE DEPLORABLE
AMEN
JIM DAVIS 9-25
© 1986 PAWS, INC. All Rights Reserved.
HERE'S THE SHIPMENT OF MICE, MRS. ERNSBERGER. WHERE DO YOU WANT THEM?
PUT 'EM IN HERE!
WE'LL TAKE 'M!
WE CAN MAKE ROOM!
MICE

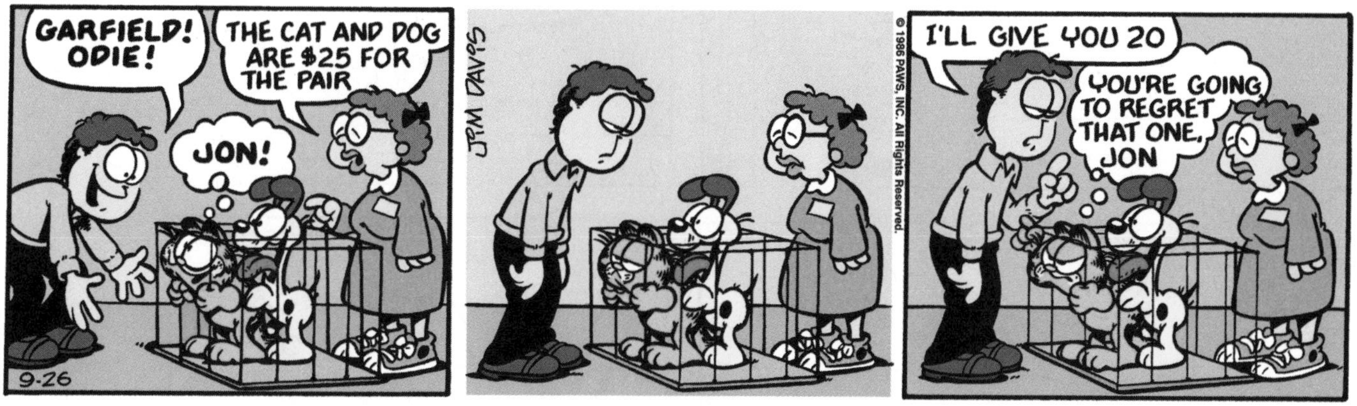
GARFIELD! ODIE!
THE CAT AND DOG ARE $25 FOR THE PAIR
JON!
9-26
JIM DAVIS
© 1986 PAWS, INC. All Rights Reserved.
I'LL GIVE YOU 20
YOU'RE GOING TO REGRET THAT ONE, JON

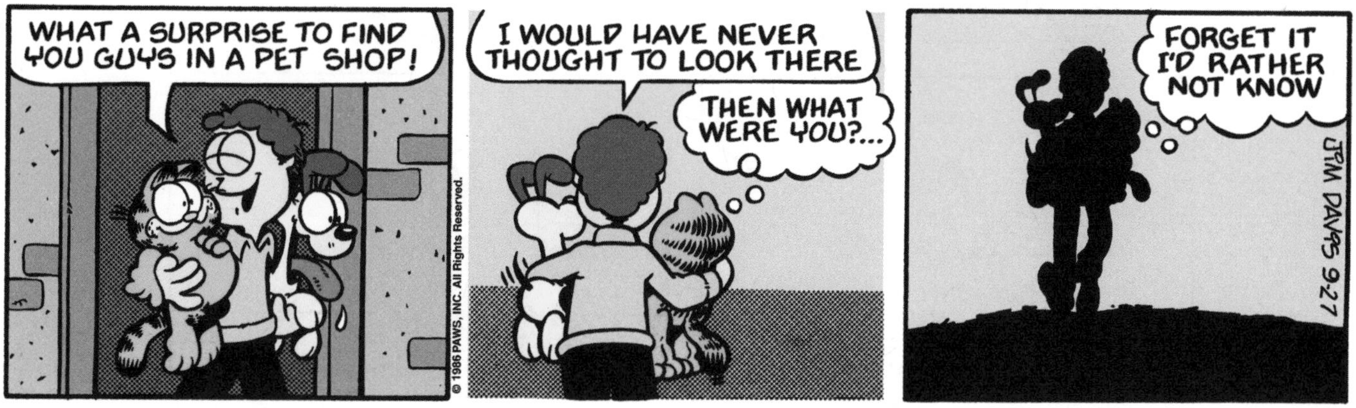
WHAT A SURPRISE TO FIND YOU GUYS IN A PET SHOP!
© 1986 PAWS, INC. All Rights Reserved.
I WOULD HAVE NEVER THOUGHT TO LOOK THERE
THEN WHAT WERE YOU?...
FORGET IT I'D RATHER NOT KNOW
JIM DAVIS 9-27

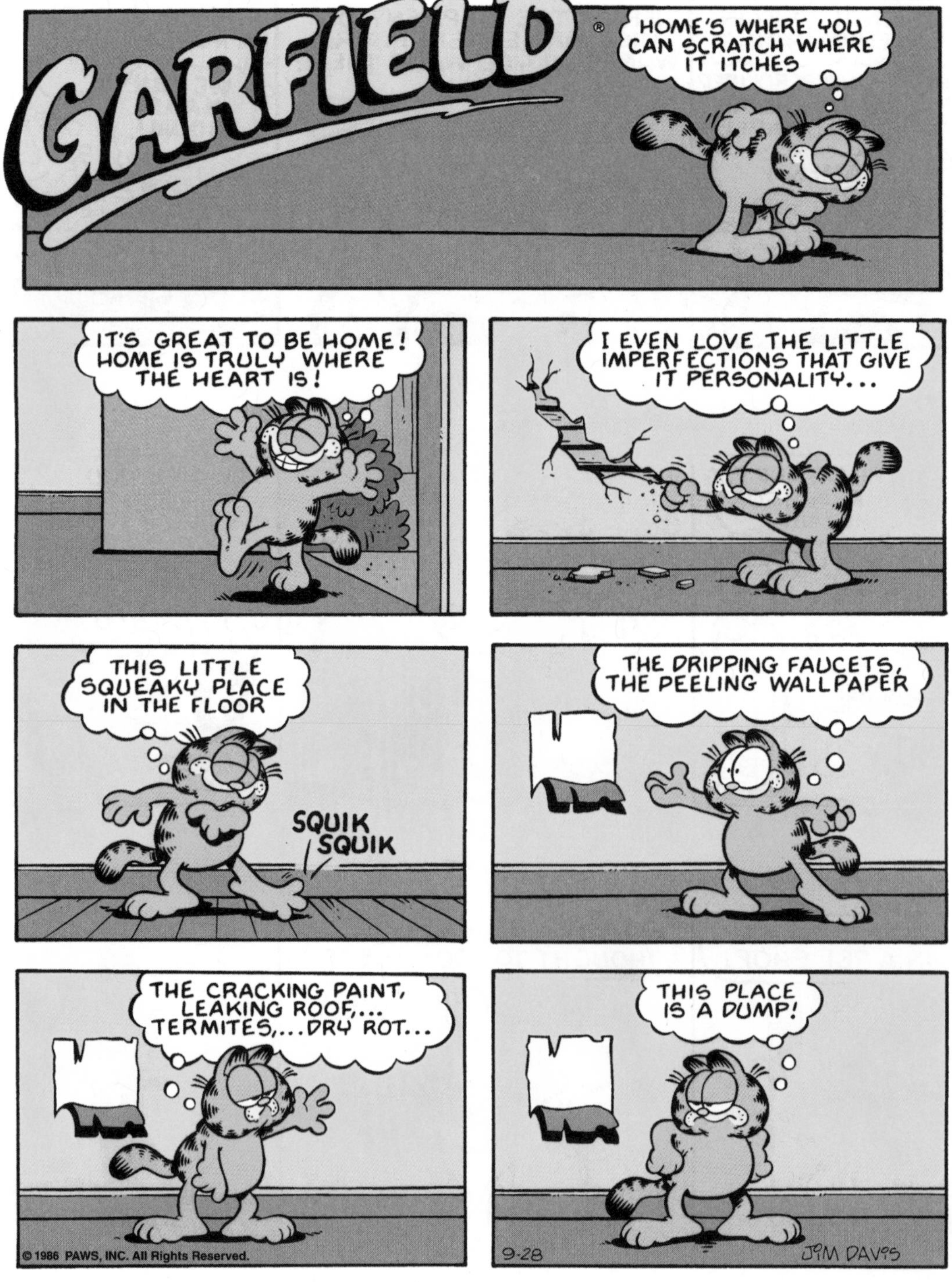
GARFIELD®
HOME'S WHERE YOU CAN SCRATCH WHERE IT ITCHES
IT'S GREAT TO BE HOME! HOME IS TRULY WHERE THE HEART IS!
I EVEN LOVE THE LITTLE IMPERFECTIONS THAT GIVE IT PERSONALITY...
THIS LITTLE SQUEAKY PLACE IN THE FLOOR
SQUIK SQUIK
THE DRIPPING FAUCETS, THE PEELING WALLPAPER
THE CRACKING PAINT, LEAKING ROOF,... TERMITES,... DRY ROT...
THIS PLACE IS A DUMP!
© 1986 PAWS, INC. All Rights Reserved.
9-28
JIM DAVIS

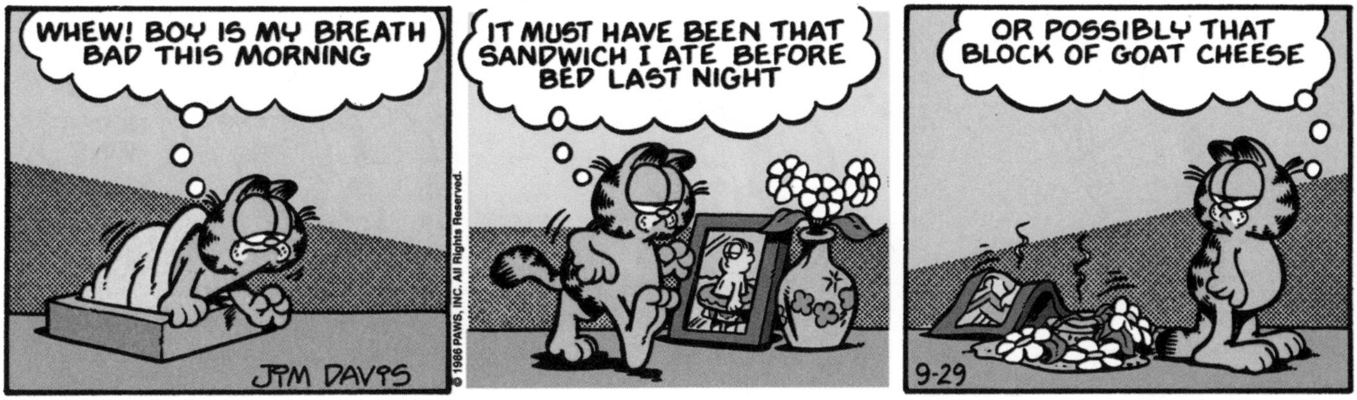
WHEW! BOY IS MY BREATH BAD THIS MORNING
JIM DAVIS
© 1986 PAWS, INC. All Rights Reserved.
IT MUST HAVE BEEN THAT SANDWICH I ATE BEFORE BED LAST NIGHT
OR POSSIBLY THAT BLOCK OF GOAT CHEESE
9-29

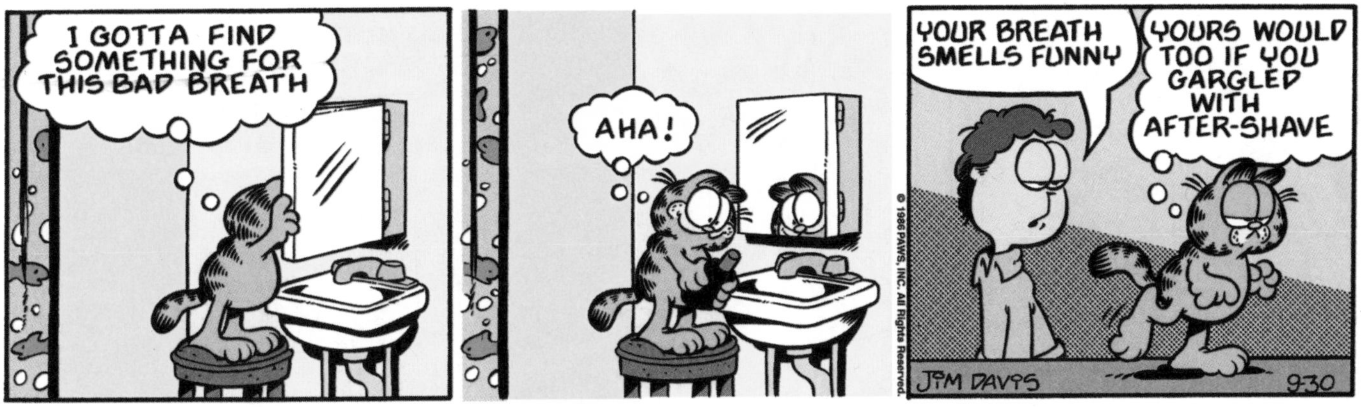
I GOTTA FIND SOMETHING FOR THIS BAD BREATH
AHA!
© 1986 PAWS, INC. All Rights Reserved.
YOUR BREATH SMELLS FUNNY
YOURS WOULD TOO IF YOU GARGLED WITH AFTER-SHAVE
JIM DAVIS
9-30

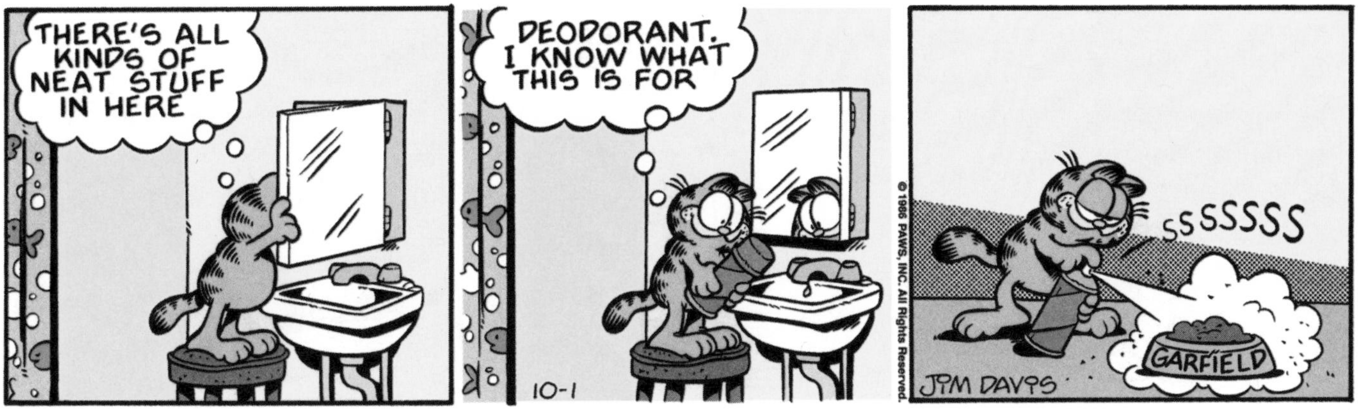
THERE'S ALL KINDS OF NEAT STUFF IN HERE
DEODORANT. I KNOW WHAT THIS IS FOR
10-1
© 1986 PAWS, INC. All Rights Reserved.
SSSSSSS
GARFIELD
JIM DAVIS

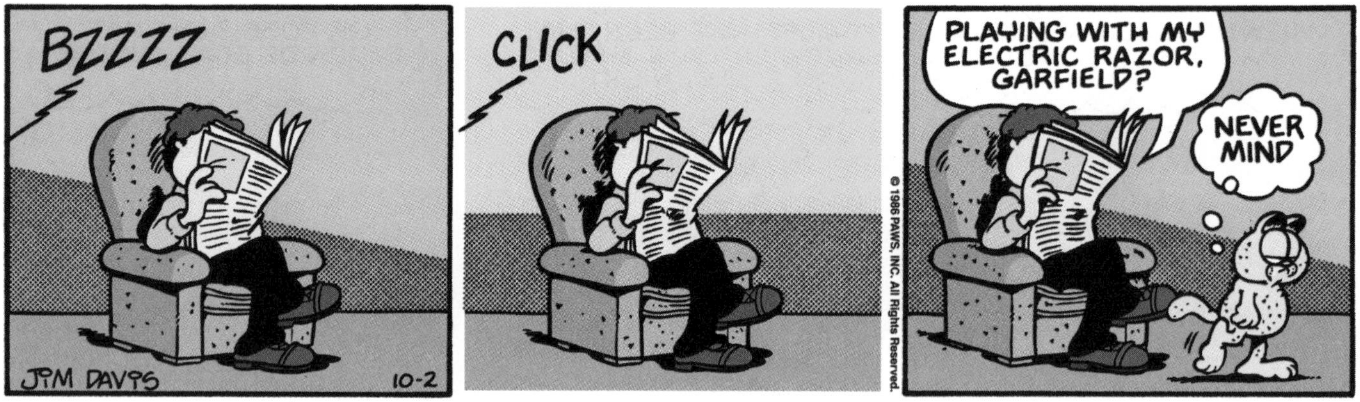
BZZZZ
JIM DAVIS
10-2
CLICK
PLAYING WITH MY ELECTRIC RAZOR, GARFIELD?
NEVER MIND
© 1986 PAWS, INC. All Rights Reserved.

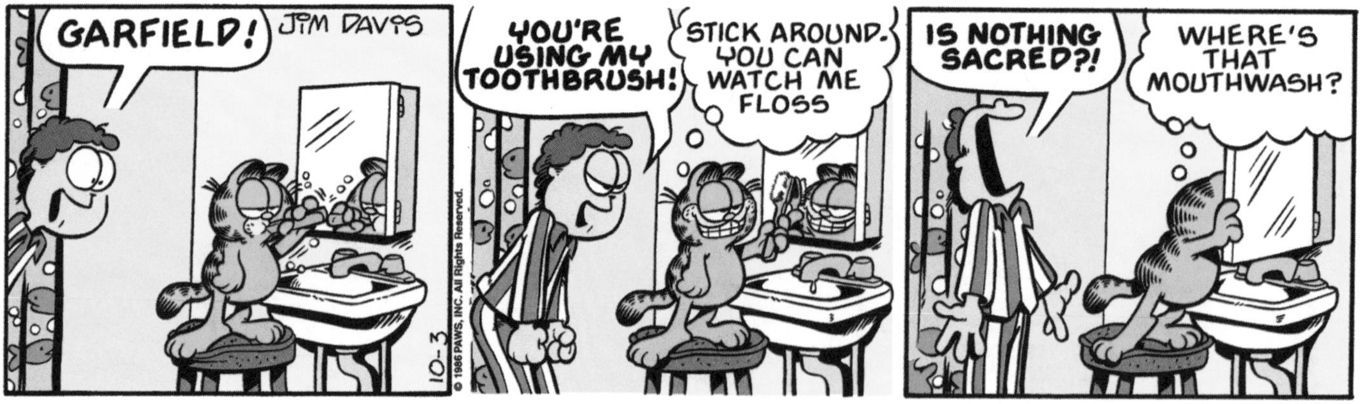
GARFIELD!
JIM DAVIS
10-3
© 1986 PAWS, INC. All Rights Reserved.
YOU'RE USING MY TOOTHBRUSH!
STICK AROUND. YOU CAN WATCH ME FLOSS
IS NOTHING SACRED?!
WHERE'S THAT MOUTHWASH?

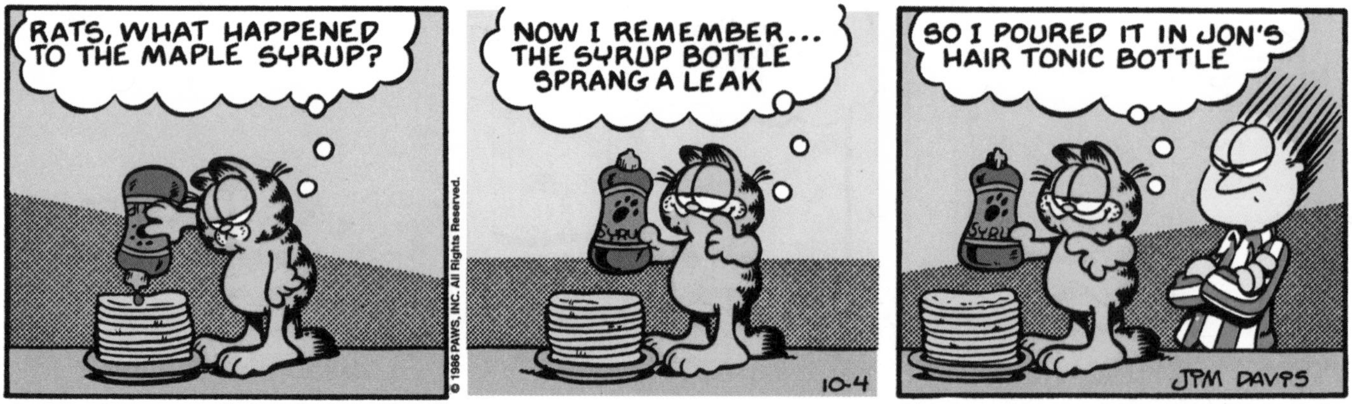
RATS, WHAT HAPPENED TO THE MAPLE SYRUP?
© 1986 PAWS, INC. All Rights Reserved.
NOW I REMEMBER... THE SYRUP BOTTLE SPRANG A LEAK
10-4
SO I POURED IT IN JON'S HAIR TONIC BOTTLE
JIM DAVIS

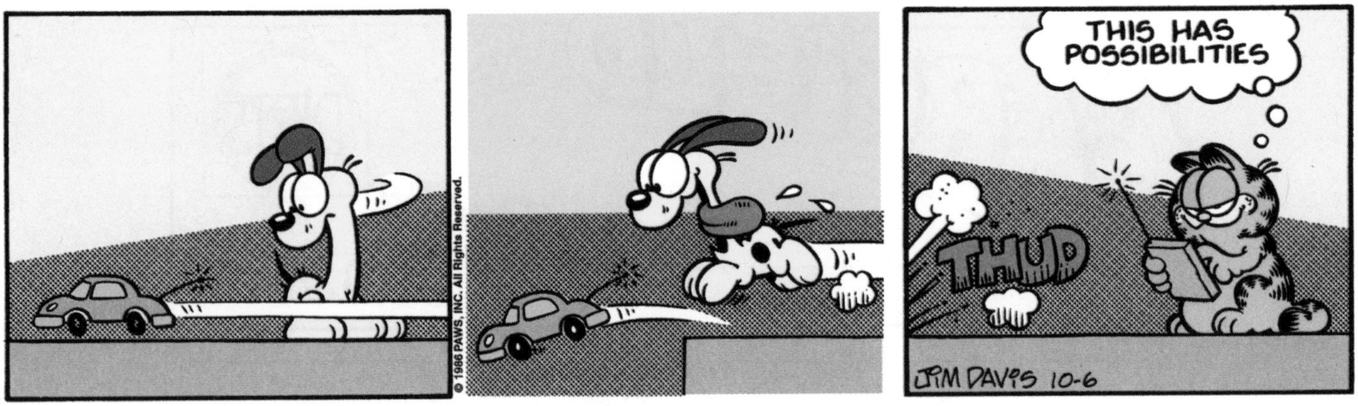
© 1986 PAWS, INC. All Rights Reserved.
THUD
THIS HAS POSSIBILITIES
JIM DAVIS 10-6

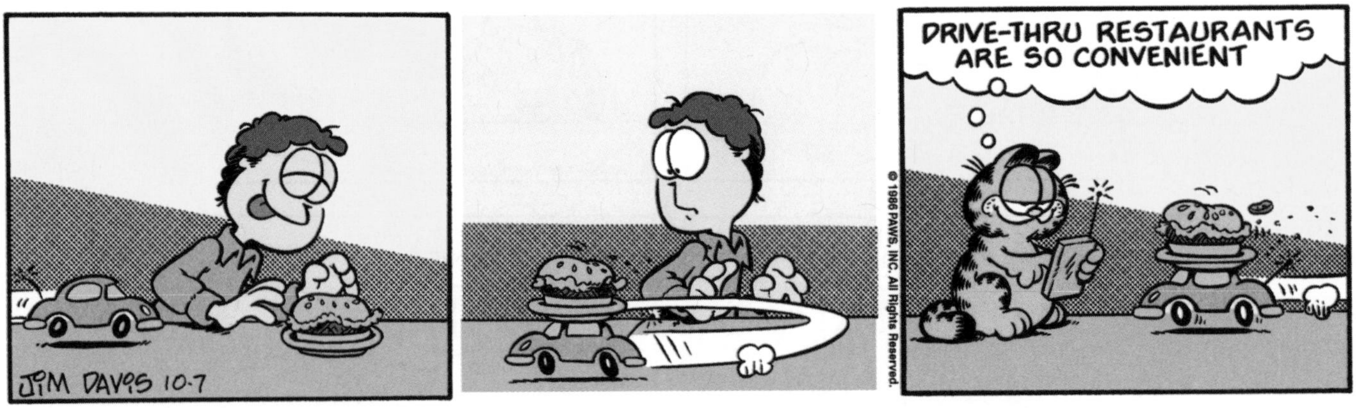
JIM DAVIS 10-7
© 1986 PAWS, INC. All Rights Reserved.
DRIVE-THRU RESTAURANTS ARE SO CONVENIENT

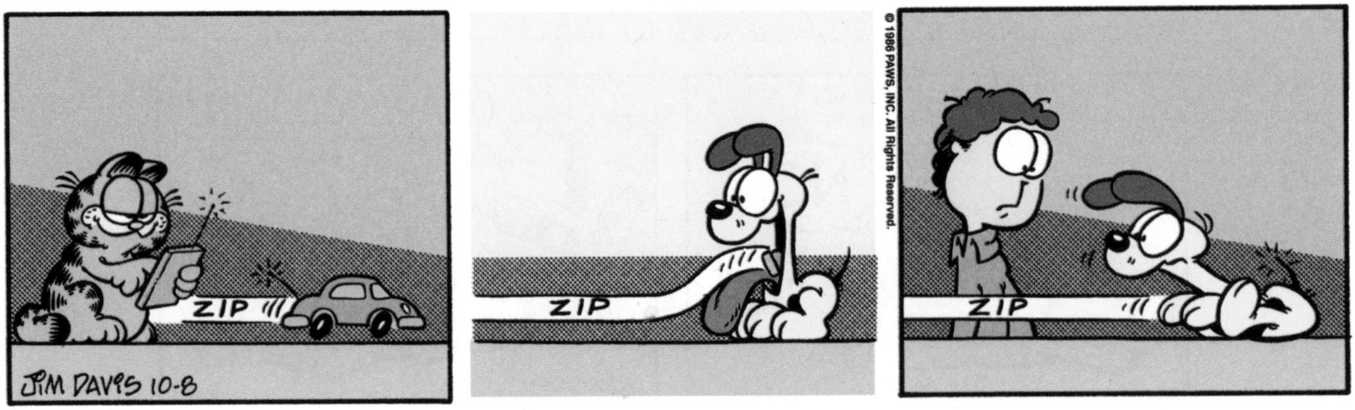
ZIP
JIM DAVIS 10-8
ZIP
© 1986 PAWS, INC. All Rights Reserved.
ZIP

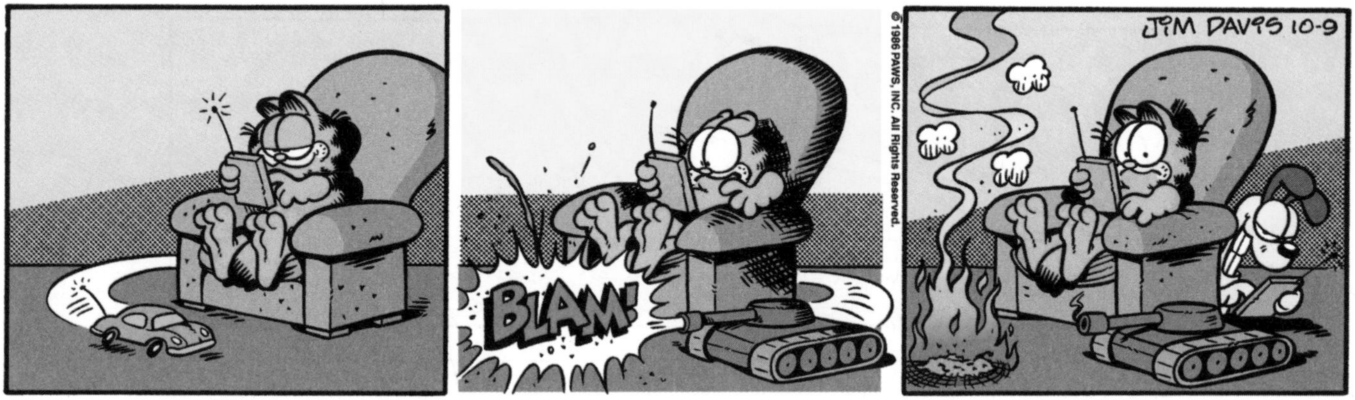
BLAM!
© 1986 PAWS, INC. All Rights Reserved.
JIM DAVIS 10-9

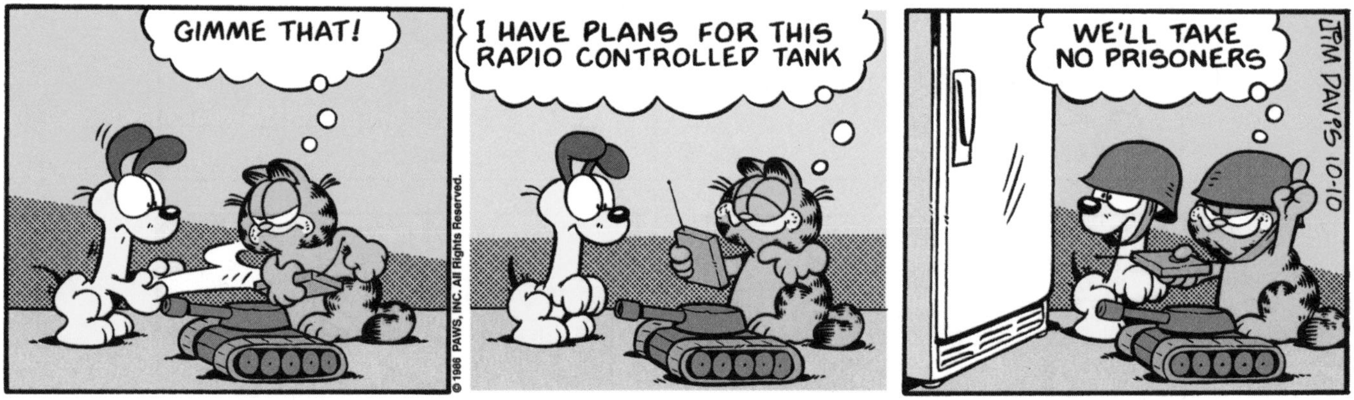
GIMME THAT!
© 1986 PAWS, INC. All Rights Reserved.
I HAVE PLANS FOR THIS RADIO CONTROLLED TANK
WE'LL TAKE NO PRISONERS
JIM DAVIS 10-10

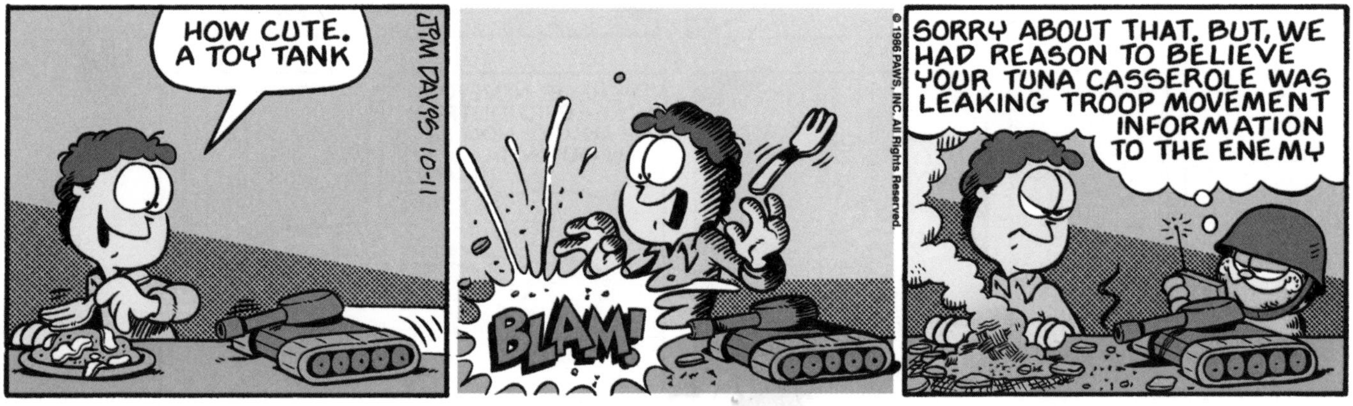
HOW CUTE. A TOY TANK
JIM DAVIS 10-11
BLAM!
© 1986 PAWS, INC. All Rights Reserved.
SORRY ABOUT THAT. BUT, WE HAD REASON TO BELIEVE YOUR TUNA CASSEROLE WAS LEAKING TROOP MOVEMENT INFORMATION TO THE ENEMY

Garfield
worldwide

BY JIM DAVIS

Ballantine Books • **New York**

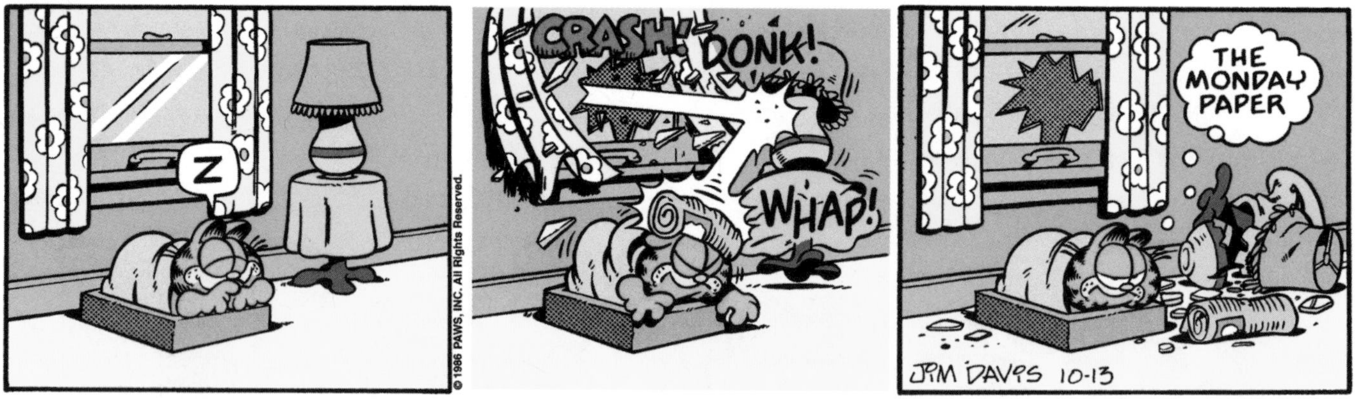
Z
© 1986 PAWS, INC. All Rights Reserved.
CRASH!
DONK!
WHAP!
THE MONDAY PAPER
JIM DAVIS 10-13

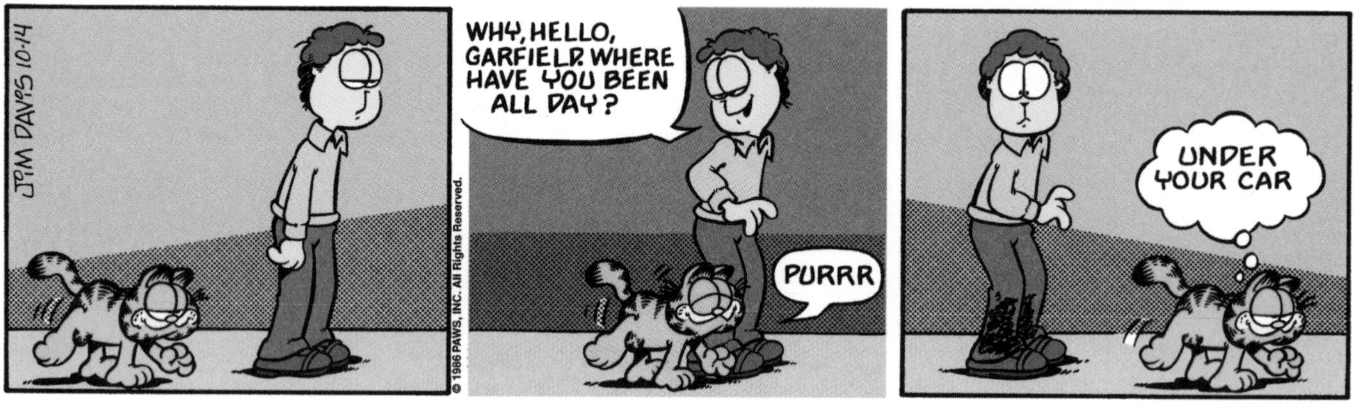
JIM DAVIS 10-14
© 1986 PAWS, INC. All Rights Reserved.
WHY, HELLO, GARFIELD. WHERE HAVE YOU BEEN ALL DAY?
PURRR
UNDER YOUR CAR

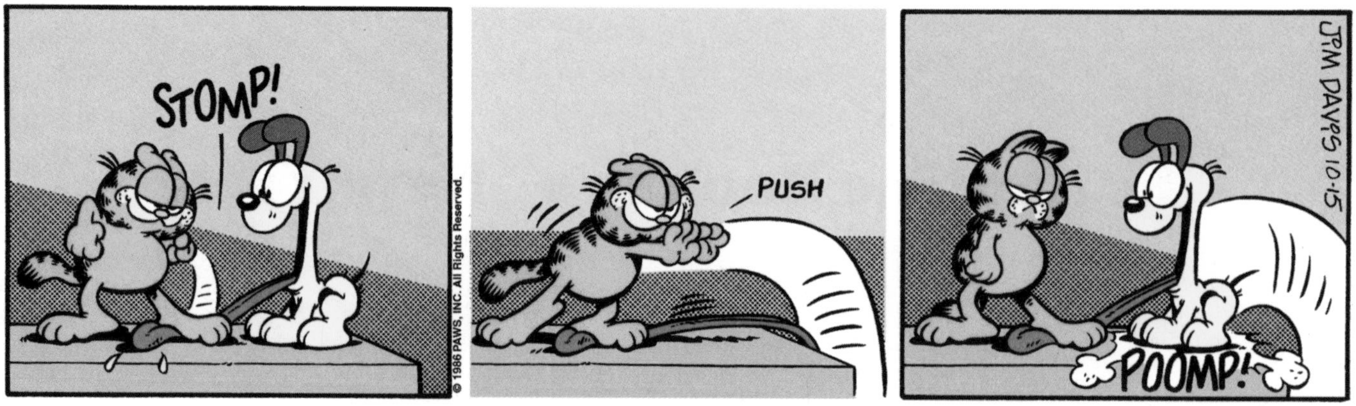
STOMP!
© 1986 PAWS, INC. All Rights Reserved.
PUSH
JIM DAVIS 10-15
POOMP!

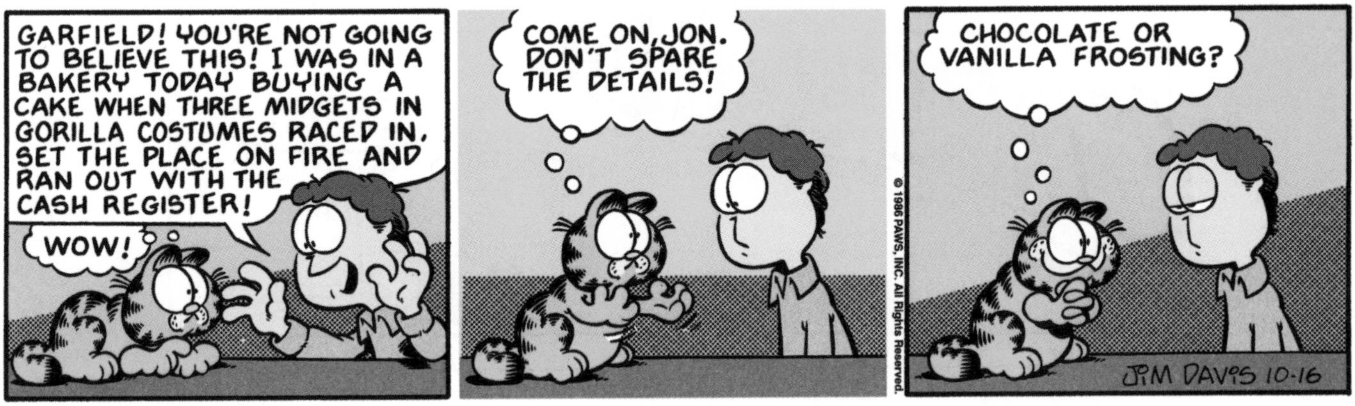
GARFIELD! YOU'RE NOT GOING TO BELIEVE THIS! I WAS IN A BAKERY TODAY BUYING A CAKE WHEN THREE MIDGETS IN GORILLA COSTUMES RACED IN, SET THE PLACE ON FIRE AND RAN OUT WITH THE CASH REGISTER!
WOW!
COME ON, JON. DON'T SPARE THE DETAILS!
© 1986 PAWS, INC. All Rights Reserved.
CHOCOLATE OR VANILLA FROSTING?
JIM DAVIS 10-16

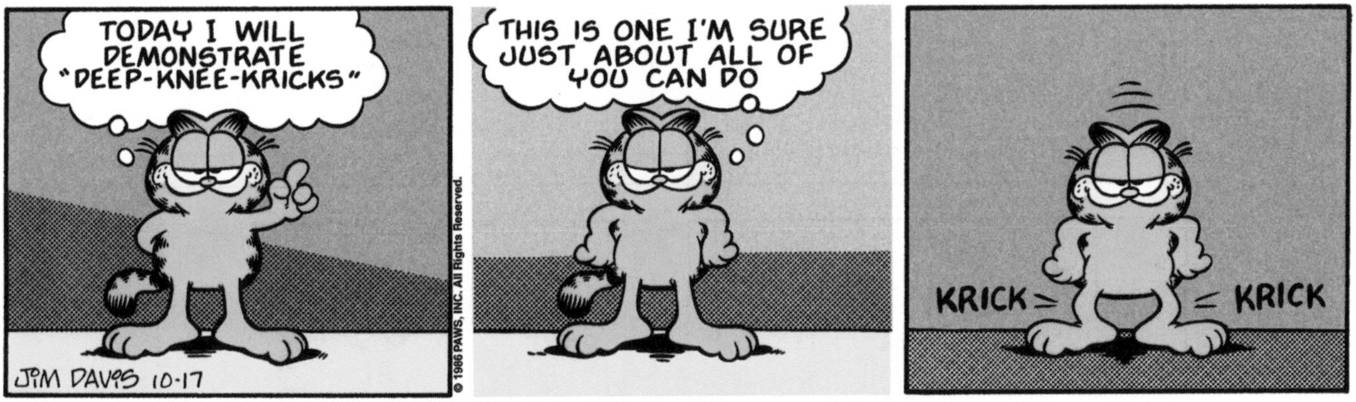
TODAY I WILL DEMONSTRATE "DEEP-KNEE-KRICKS"
JIM DAVIS 10-17
© 1986 PAWS, INC. All Rights Reserved.
THIS IS ONE I'M SURE JUST ABOUT ALL OF YOU CAN DO
KRICK
KRICK

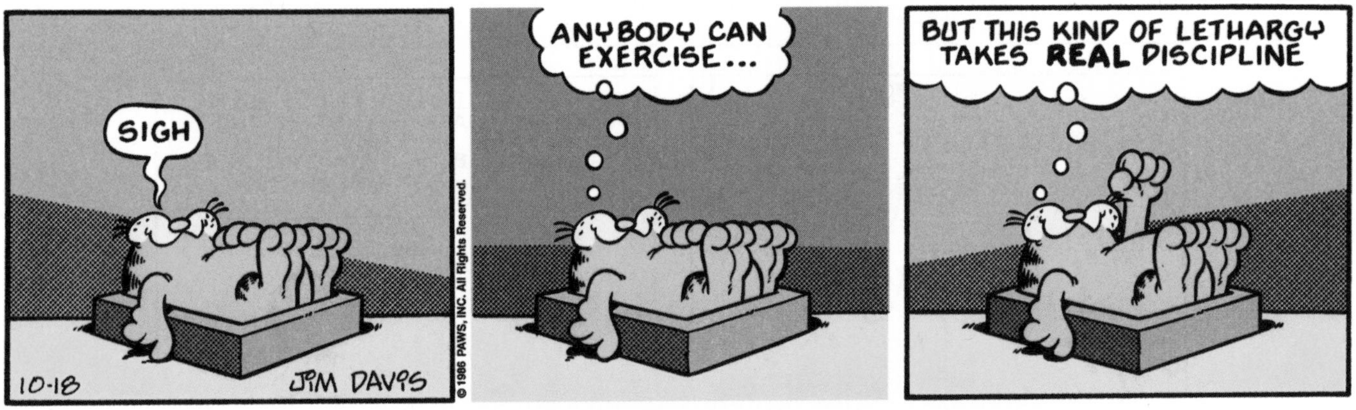
SIGH
10-18
JIM DAVIS
© 1986 PAWS, INC. All Rights Reserved.
ANYBODY CAN EXERCISE...
BUT THIS KIND OF LETHARGY TAKES REAL DISCIPLINE

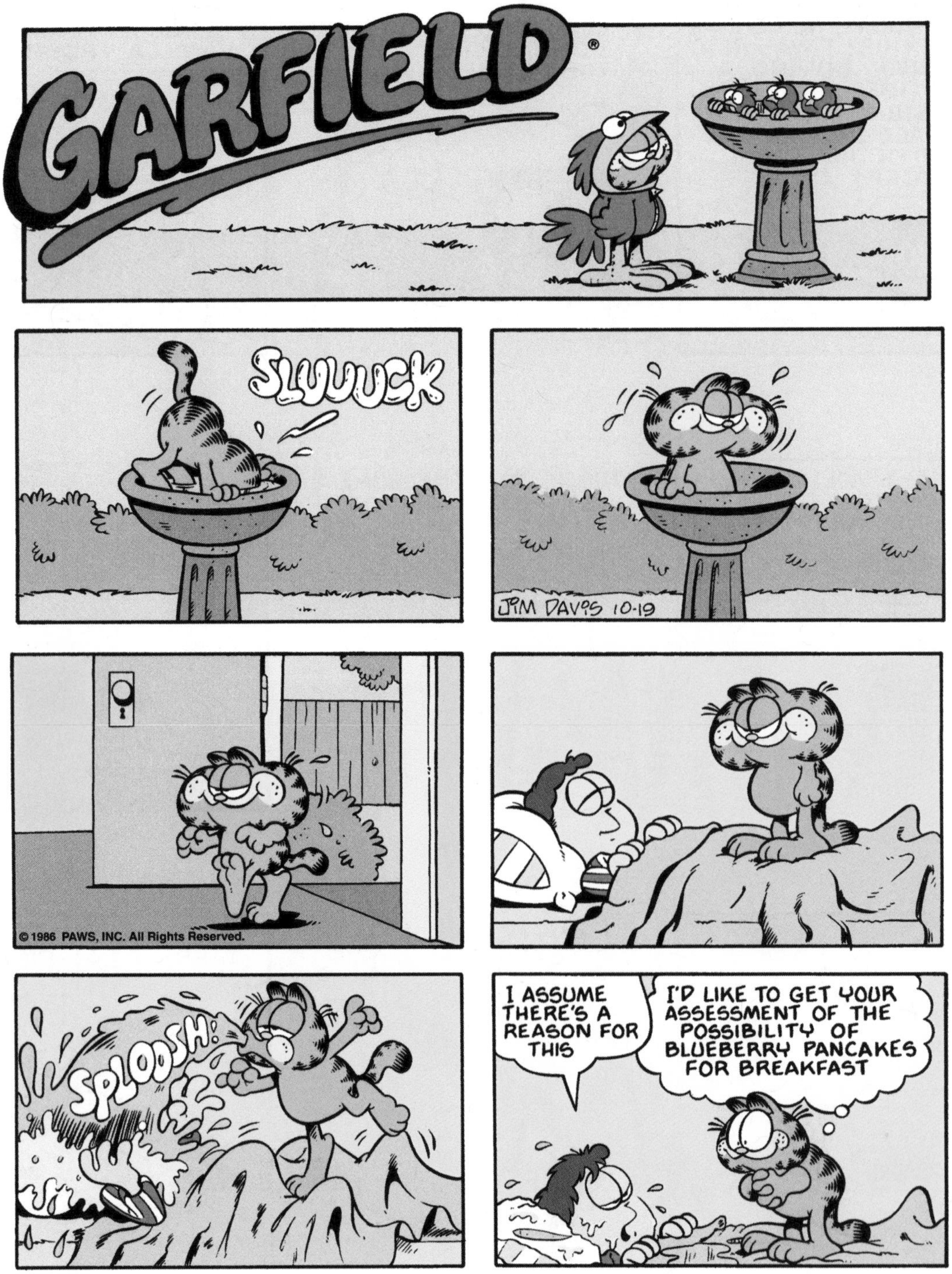
GARFIELD®
SLUUUCK
JIM DAVIS 10-19
© 1986 PAWS, INC. All Rights Reserved.
SPLOOSH!
I ASSUME THERE'S A REASON FOR THIS
I'D LIKE TO GET YOUR ASSESSMENT OF THE POSSIBILITY OF BLUEBERRY PANCAKES FOR BREAKFAST

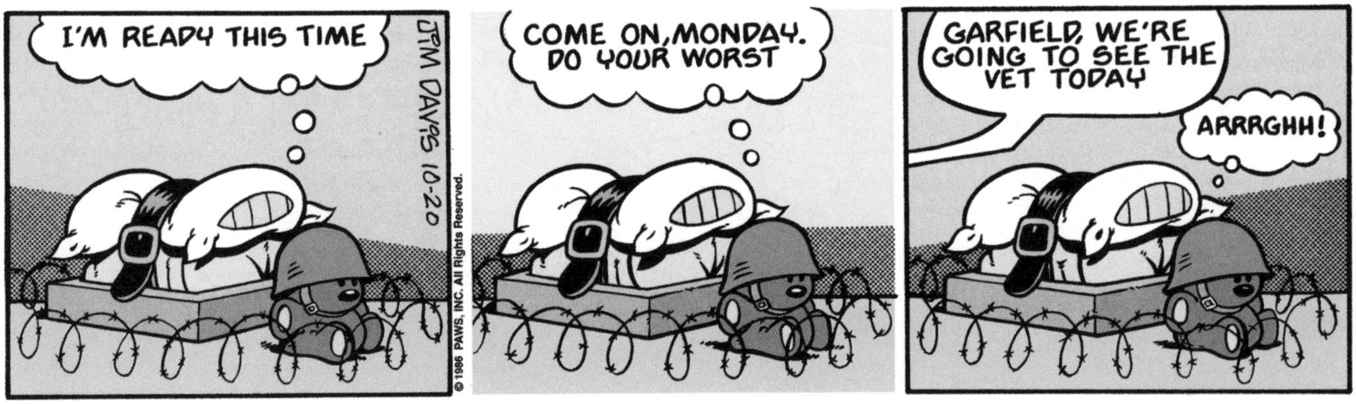
I'M READY THIS TIME
JIM DAVIS 10-20
© 1986 PAWS, INC. All Rights Reserved.
COME ON, MONDAY. DO YOUR WORST
GARFIELD, WE'RE GOING TO SEE THE VET TODAY
ARRRGHH!

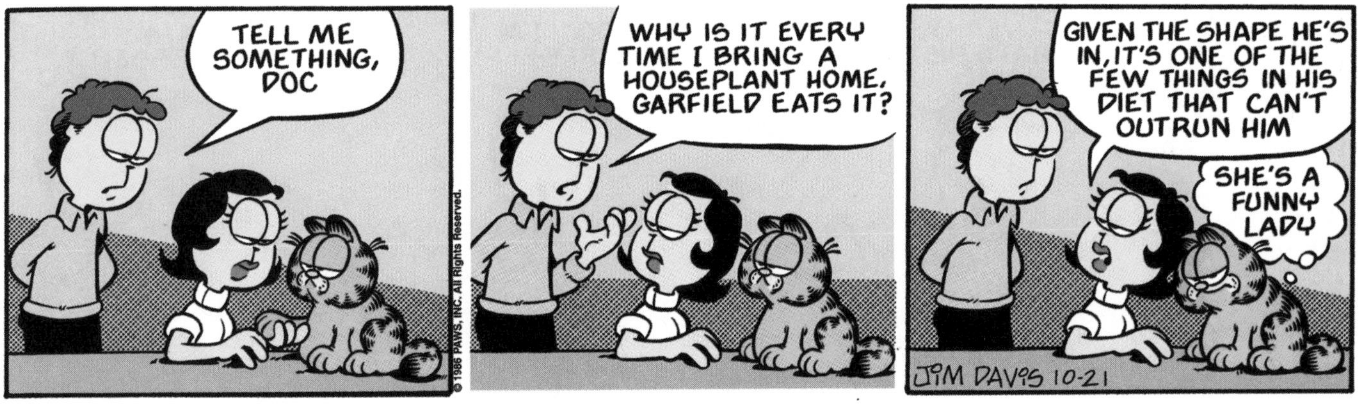
TELL ME SOMETHING, DOC
© 1986 PAWS, INC. All Rights Reserved.
WHY IS IT EVERY TIME I BRING A HOUSEPLANT HOME, GARFIELD EATS IT?
GIVEN THE SHAPE HE'S IN, IT'S ONE OF THE FEW THINGS IN HIS DIET THAT CAN'T OUTRUN HIM
SHE'S A FUNNY LADY
JIM DAVIS 10-21

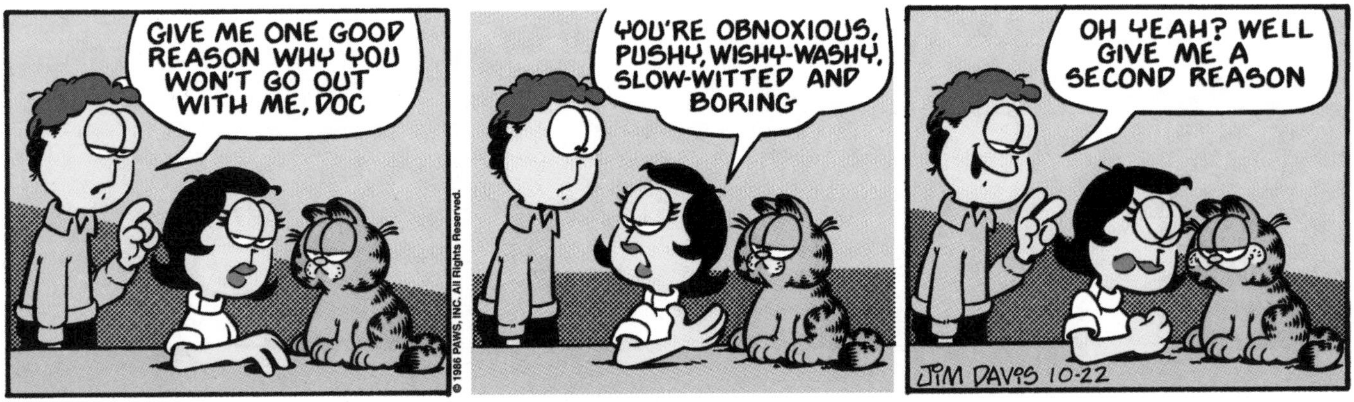
GIVE ME ONE GOOD REASON WHY YOU WON'T GO OUT WITH ME, DOC
© 1986 PAWS, INC. All Rights Reserved.
YOU'RE OBNOXIOUS, PUSHY, WISHY-WASHY, SLOW-WITTED AND BORING
OH YEAH? WELL GIVE ME A SECOND REASON
JIM DAVIS 10-22

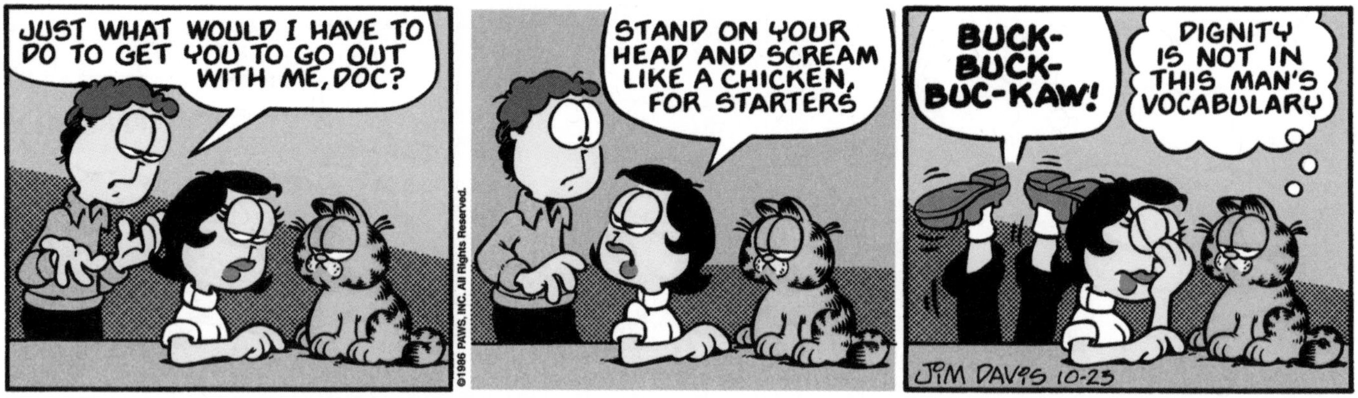
JUST WHAT WOULD I HAVE TO DO TO GET YOU TO GO OUT WITH ME, DOC?
STAND ON YOUR HEAD AND SCREAM LIKE A CHICKEN, FOR STARTERS
BUCK-BUCK-BUC-KAW!
DIGNITY IS NOT IN THIS MAN'S VOCABULARY
©1986 PAWS, INC. All Rights Reserved.
JIM DAVIS 10-23

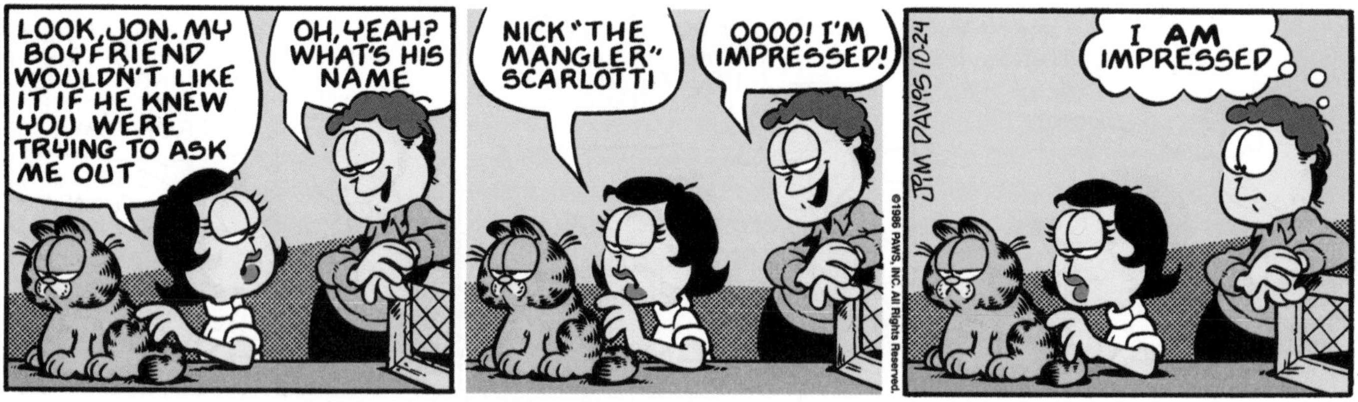
LOOK, JON. MY BOYFRIEND WOULDN'T LIKE IT IF HE KNEW YOU WERE TRYING TO ASK ME OUT
OH, YEAH? WHAT'S HIS NAME
NICK "THE MANGLER" SCARLOTTI
OOOO! I'M IMPRESSED!
JIM DAVIS 10-24
©1986 PAWS, INC. All Rights Reserved.
I AM IMPRESSED

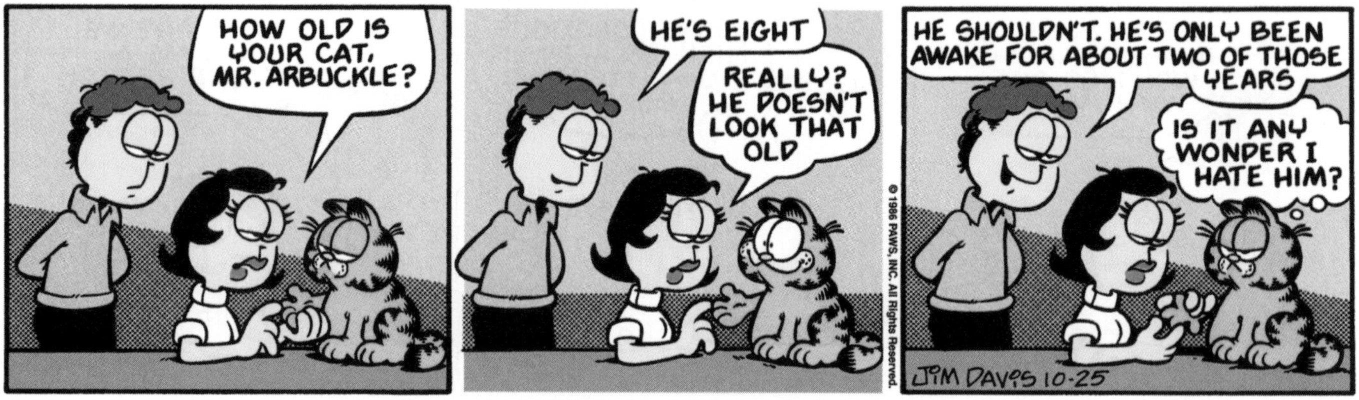
HOW OLD IS YOUR CAT, MR. ARBUCKLE?
HE'S EIGHT
REALLY? HE DOESN'T LOOK THAT OLD
© 1986 PAWS, INC. All Rights Reserved.
HE SHOULDN'T. HE'S ONLY BEEN AWAKE FOR ABOUT TWO OF THOSE YEARS
IS IT ANY WONDER I HATE HIM?
JIM DAVIS 10-25

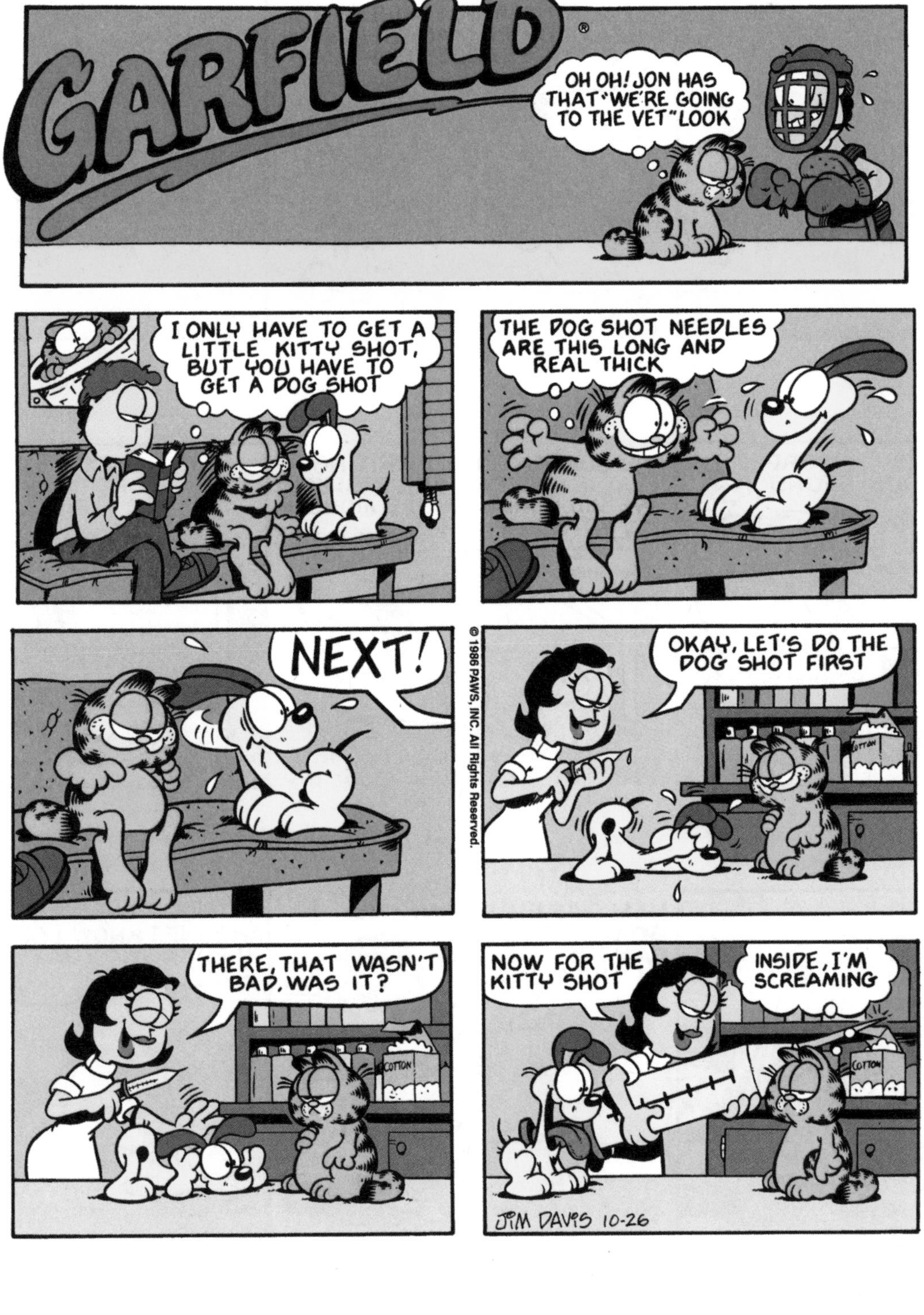
GARFIELD®
OH OH! JON HAS THAT "WE'RE GOING TO THE VET" LOOK
I ONLY HAVE TO GET A LITTLE KITTY SHOT, BUT YOU HAVE TO GET A DOG SHOT
THE DOG SHOT NEEDLES ARE THIS LONG AND REAL THICK
NEXT!
OKAY, LET'S DO THE DOG SHOT FIRST
COTTON
THERE, THAT WASN'T BAD, WAS IT?
COTTON
NOW FOR THE KITTY SHOT
INSIDE, I'M SCREAMING
COTTON
JIM DAVIS 10-26
© 1986 PAWS, INC. All Rights Reserved.

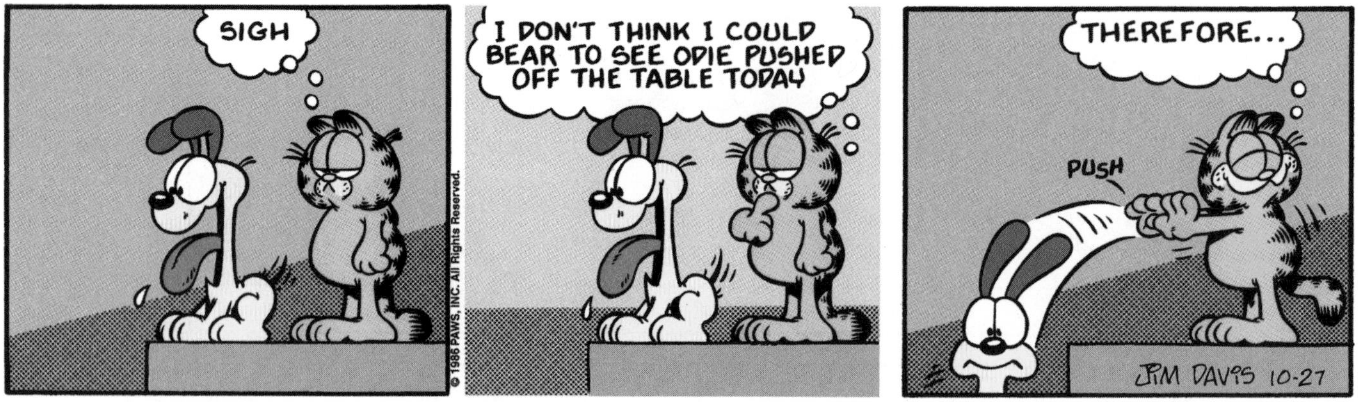
SIGH
I DON'T THINK I COULD BEAR TO SEE ODIE PUSHED OFF THE TABLE TODAY
THEREFORE...
PUSH
JIM DAVIS 10-27
© 1986 PAWS, INC. All Rights Reserved.

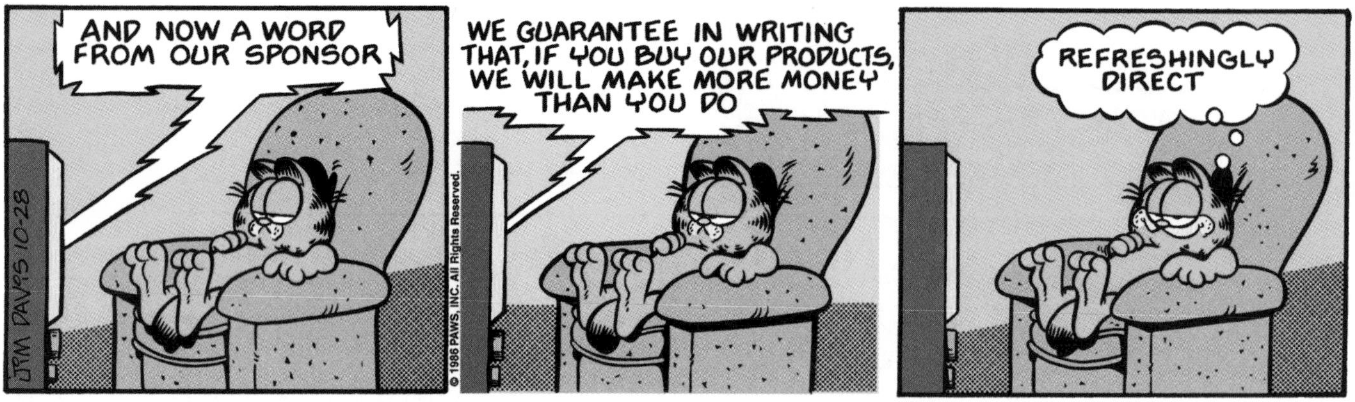
AND NOW A WORD FROM OUR SPONSOR
WE GUARANTEE IN WRITING THAT, IF YOU BUY OUR PRODUCTS, WE WILL MAKE MORE MONEY THAN YOU DO
REFRESHINGLY DIRECT
JIM DAVIS 10-28
© 1986 PAWS, INC. All Rights Reserved.

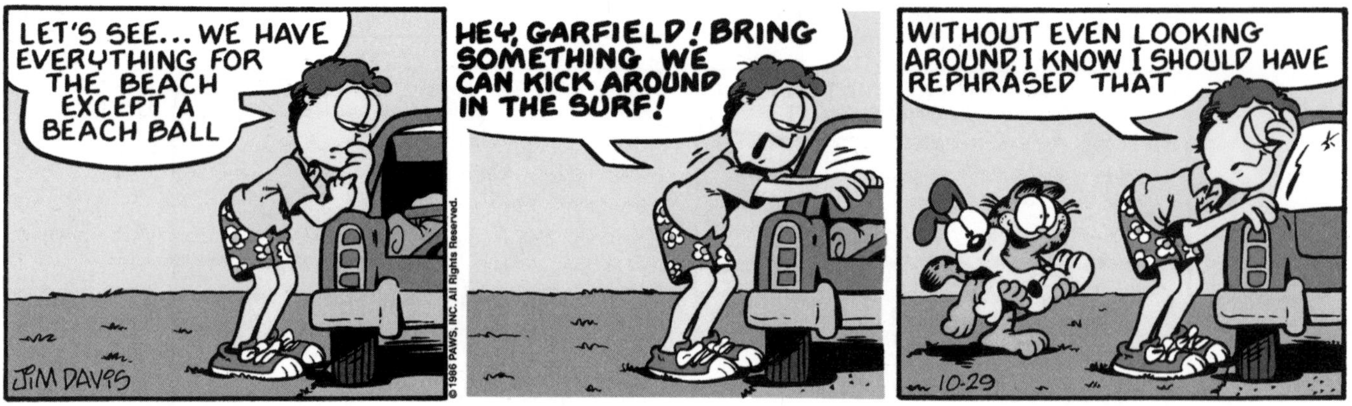
LET'S SEE... WE HAVE EVERYTHING FOR THE BEACH EXCEPT A BEACH BALL
HEY, GARFIELD! BRING SOMETHING WE CAN KICK AROUND IN THE SURF!
WITHOUT EVEN LOOKING AROUND, I KNOW I SHOULD HAVE REPHRASED THAT
JIM DAVIS
10-29
© 1986 PAWS, INC. All Rights Reserved.

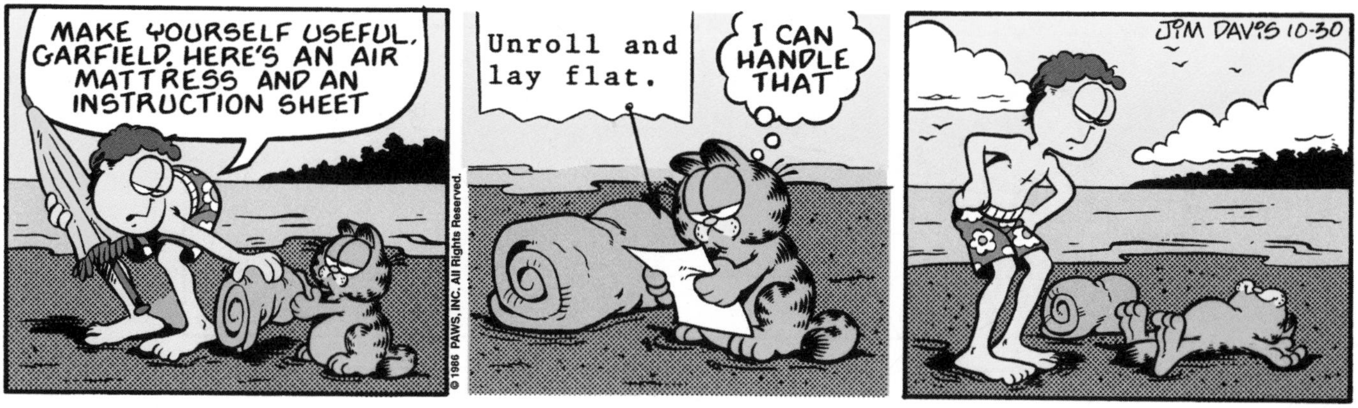
MAKE YOURSELF USEFUL, GARFIELD. HERE'S AN AIR MATTRESS AND AN INSTRUCTION SHEET
© 1986 PAWS, INC. All Rights Reserved.
Unroll and lay flat.
I CAN HANDLE THAT
JIM DAVIS 10-30

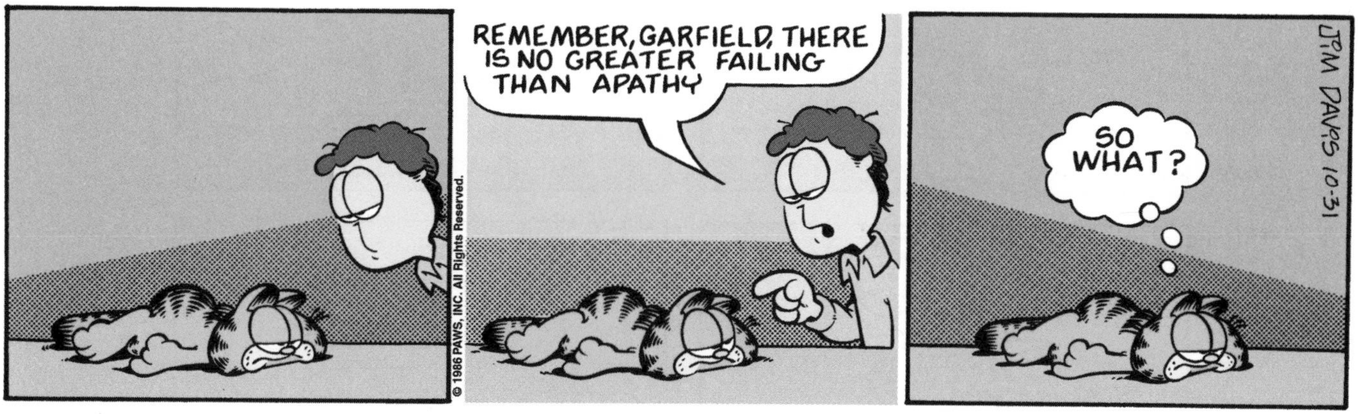
© 1986 PAWS, INC. All Rights Reserved.
REMEMBER, GARFIELD, THERE IS NO GREATER FAILING THAN APATHY
SO WHAT?
JIM DAVIS 10-31

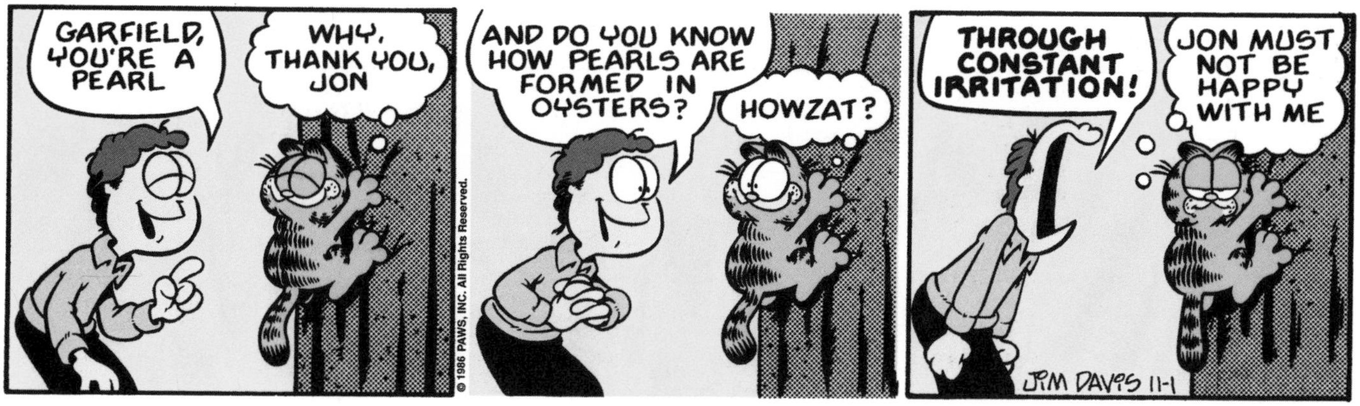
GARFIELD, YOU'RE A PEARL
WHY, THANK YOU, JON
© 1986 PAWS, INC. All Rights Reserved.
AND DO YOU KNOW HOW PEARLS ARE FORMED IN OYSTERS?
HOWZAT?
THROUGH CONSTANT IRRITATION!
JON MUST NOT BE HAPPY WITH ME
JIM DAVIS 11-1

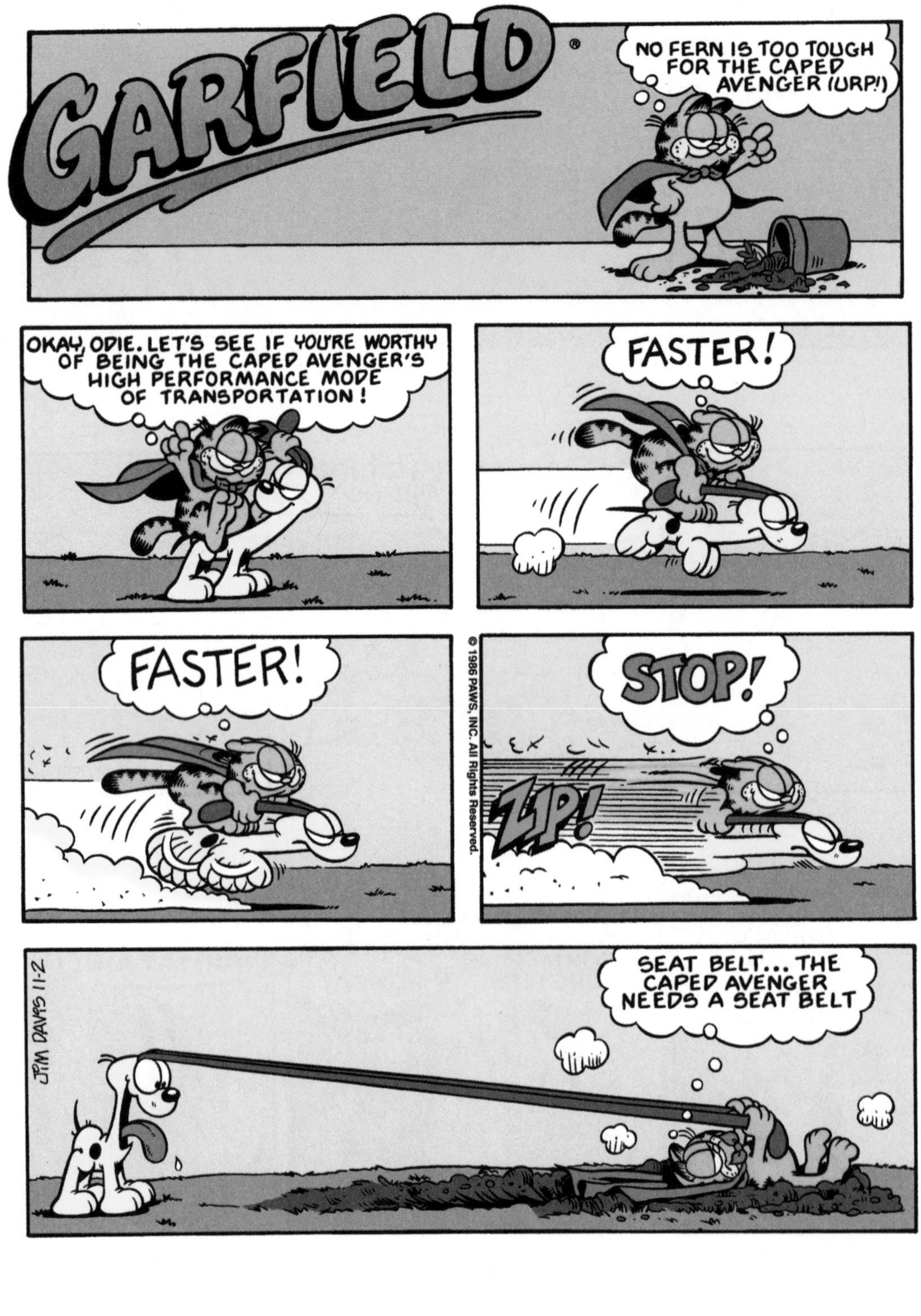
GARFIELD®
NO FERN IS TOO TOUGH FOR THE CAPED AVENGER (URP!)
OKAY, ODIE. LET'S SEE IF YOU'RE WORTHY OF BEING THE CAPED AVENGER'S HIGH PERFORMANCE MODE OF TRANSPORTATION!
FASTER!
FASTER!
STOP!
ZIP!
© 1986 PAWS, INC. All Rights Reserved.
SEAT BELT... THE CAPED AVENGER NEEDS A SEAT BELT
JPM DAVPS 11-2

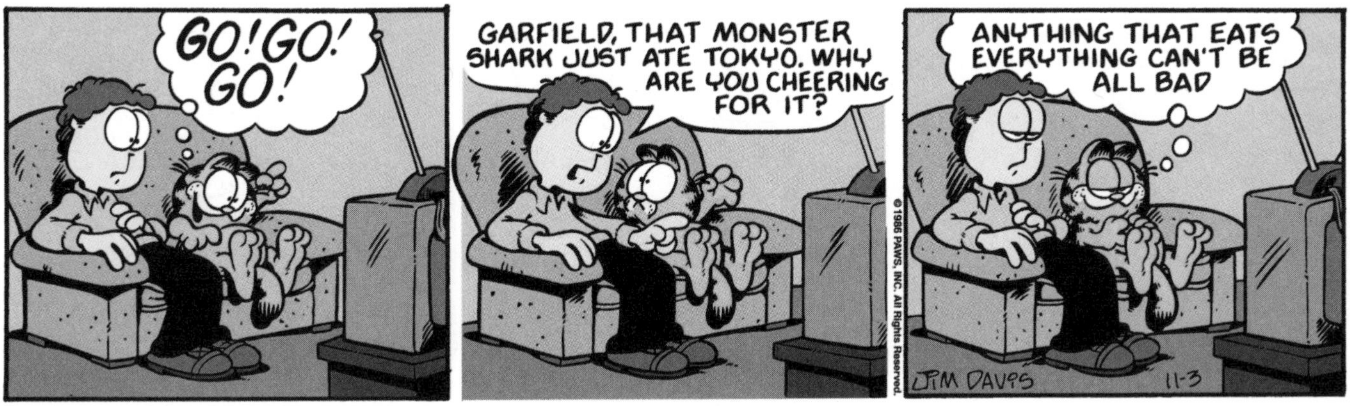
GO! GO! GO!
GARFIELD, THAT MONSTER SHARK JUST ATE TOKYO. WHY ARE YOU CHEERING FOR IT?
© 1986 PAWS, INC. All Rights Reserved.
ANYTHING THAT EATS EVERYTHING CAN'T BE ALL BAD
JIM DAVIS 11-3

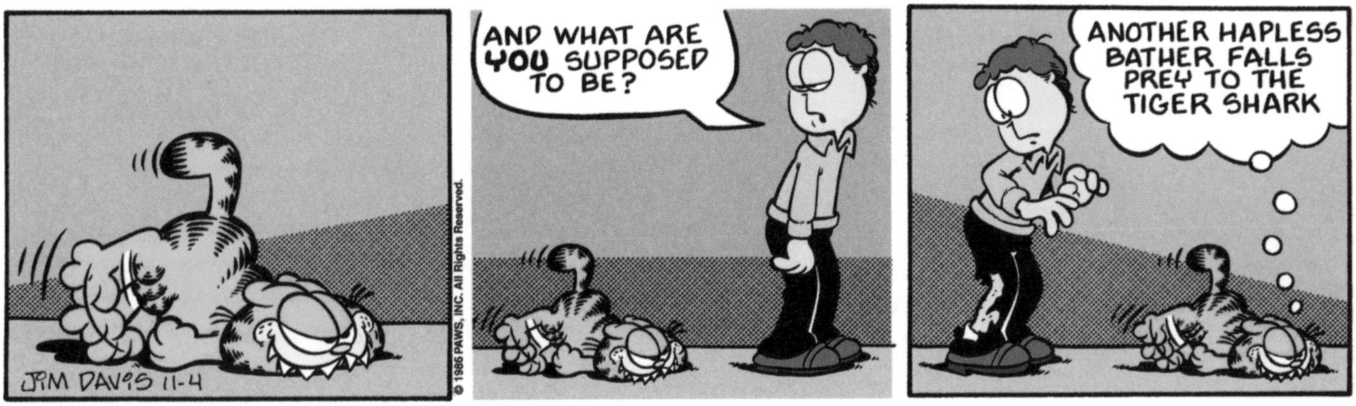
JIM DAVIS 11-4
© 1986 PAWS, INC. All Rights Reserved.
AND WHAT ARE YOU SUPPOSED TO BE?
ANOTHER HAPLESS BATHER FALLS PREY TO THE TIGER SHARK

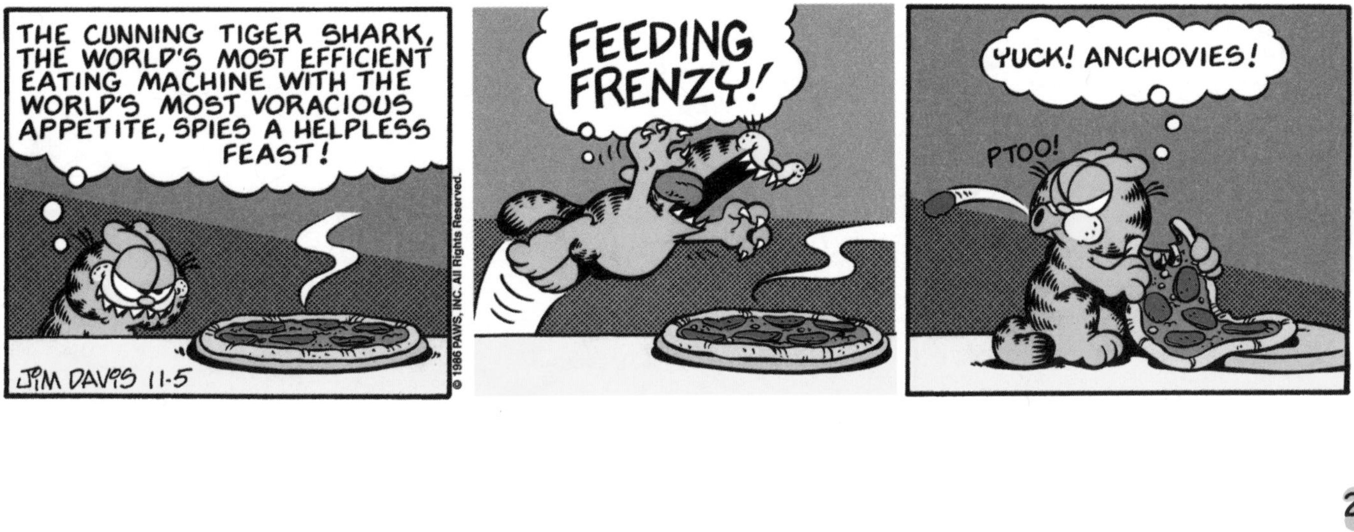
THE CUNNING TIGER SHARK, THE WORLD'S MOST EFFICIENT EATING MACHINE WITH THE WORLD'S MOST VORACIOUS APPETITE, SPIES A HELPLESS FEAST!
JIM DAVIS 11-5
© 1986 PAWS, INC. All Rights Reserved.
FEEDING FRENZY!
YUCK! ANCHOVIES!
PTOO!

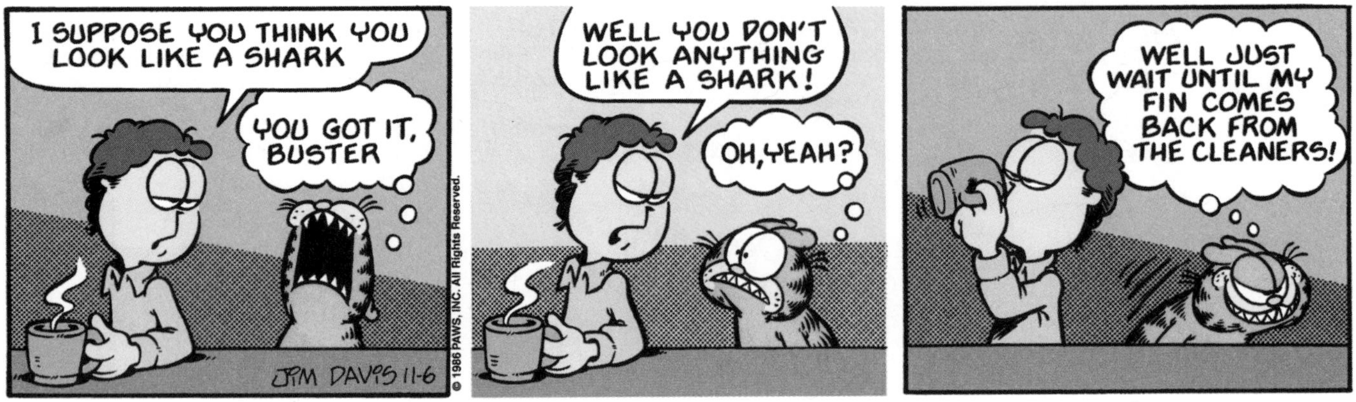
I SUPPOSE YOU THINK YOU LOOK LIKE A SHARK
YOU GOT IT, BUSTER
JIM DAVIS 11-6
© 1986 PAWS, INC. All Rights Reserved.
WELL YOU DON'T LOOK ANYTHING LIKE A SHARK!
OH, YEAH?
WELL JUST WAIT UNTIL MY FIN COMES BACK FROM THE CLEANERS!

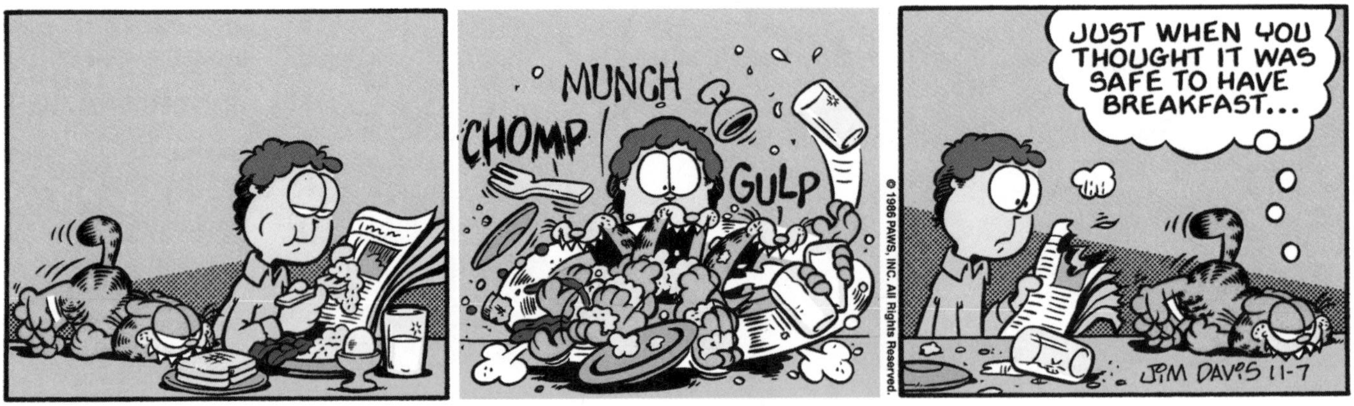
MUNCH
CHOMP
GULP
© 1986 PAWS, INC. All Rights Reserved.
JUST WHEN YOU THOUGHT IT WAS SAFE TO HAVE BREAKFAST...
JIM DAVIS 11-7

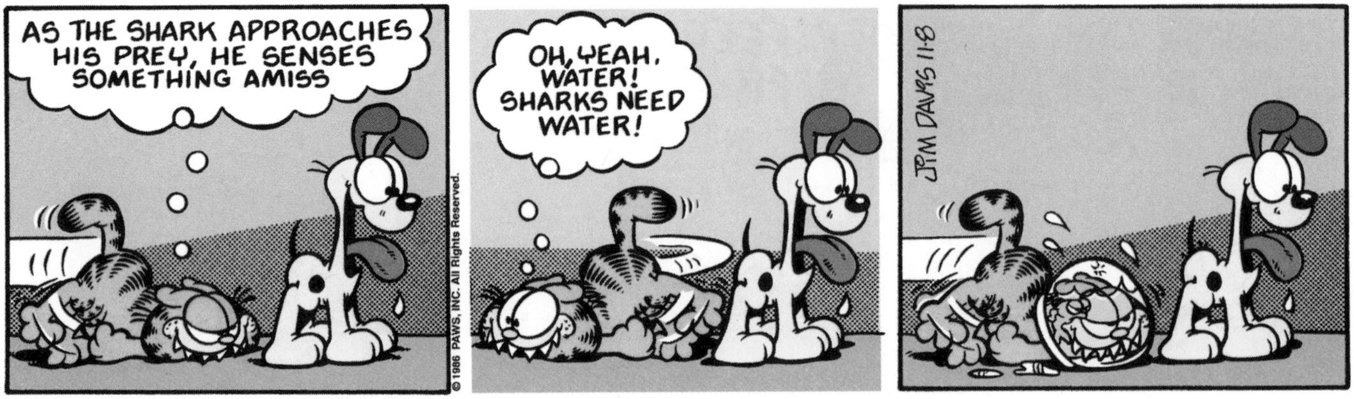
AS THE SHARK APPROACHES HIS PREY, HE SENSES SOMETHING AMISS
© 1986 PAWS, INC. All Rights Reserved.
OH, YEAH. WATER! SHARKS NEED WATER!
JIM DAVIS 11-8

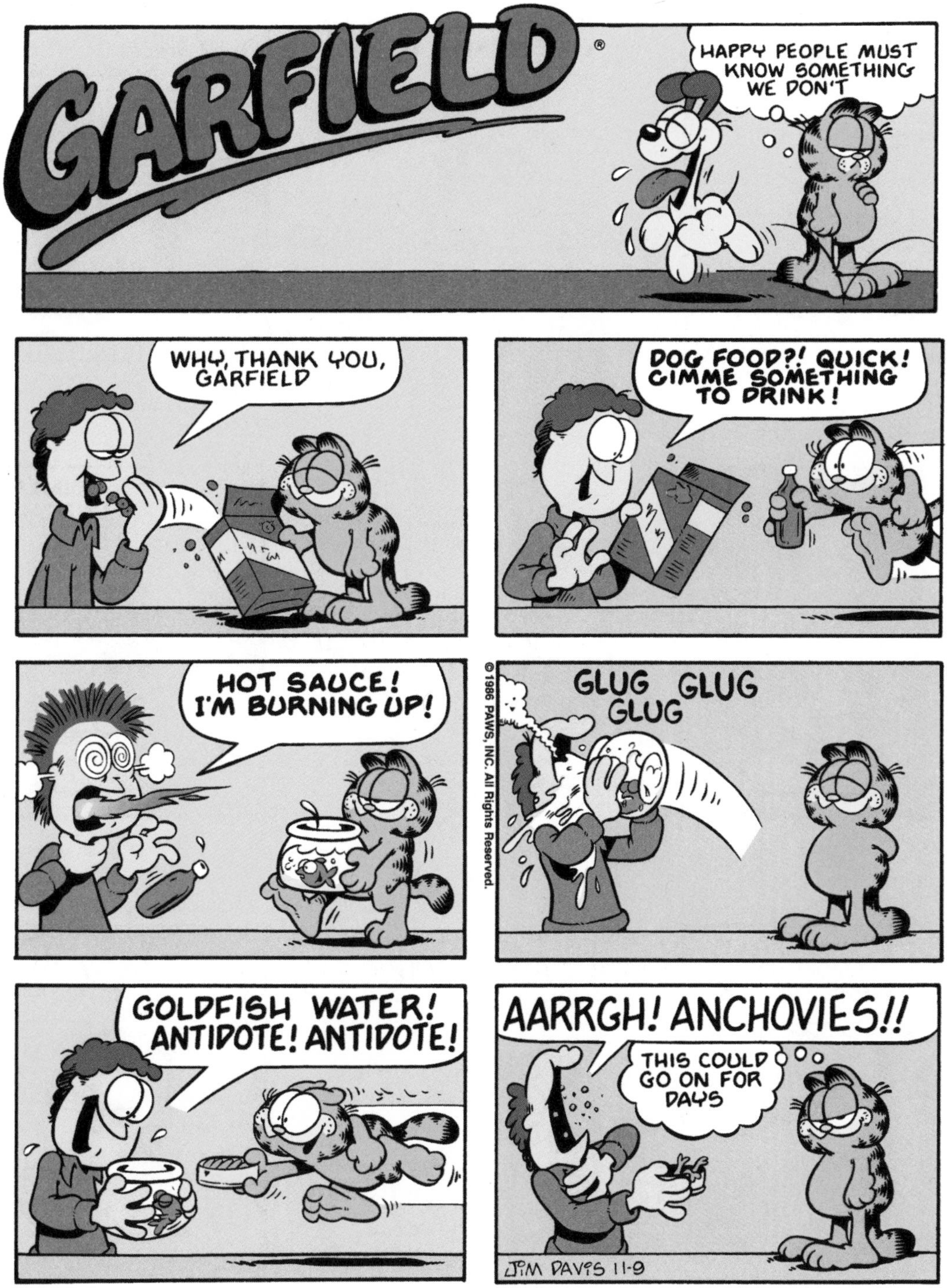
GARFIELD®
HAPPY PEOPLE MUST KNOW SOMETHING WE DON'T
WHY, THANK YOU, GARFIELD
DOG FOOD?! QUICK! GIMME SOMETHING TO DRINK!
HOT SAUCE! I'M BURNING UP!
© 1986 PAWS, INC. All Rights Reserved.
GLUG GLUG GLUG
GOLDFISH WATER! ANTIDOTE! ANTIDOTE!
AARRGH! ANCHOVIES!!
THIS COULD GO ON FOR DAYS
JIM DAVIS 11-9

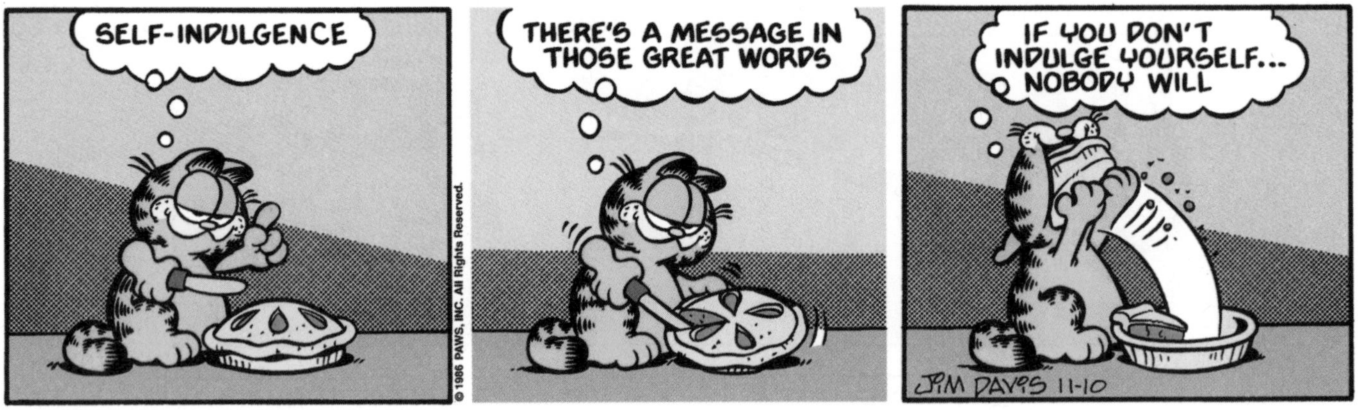
SELF-INDULGENCE
© 1986 PAWS, INC. All Rights Reserved.
THERE'S A MESSAGE IN THOSE GREAT WORDS
IF YOU DON'T INDULGE YOURSELF... NOBODY WILL
JIM DAVIS 11-10

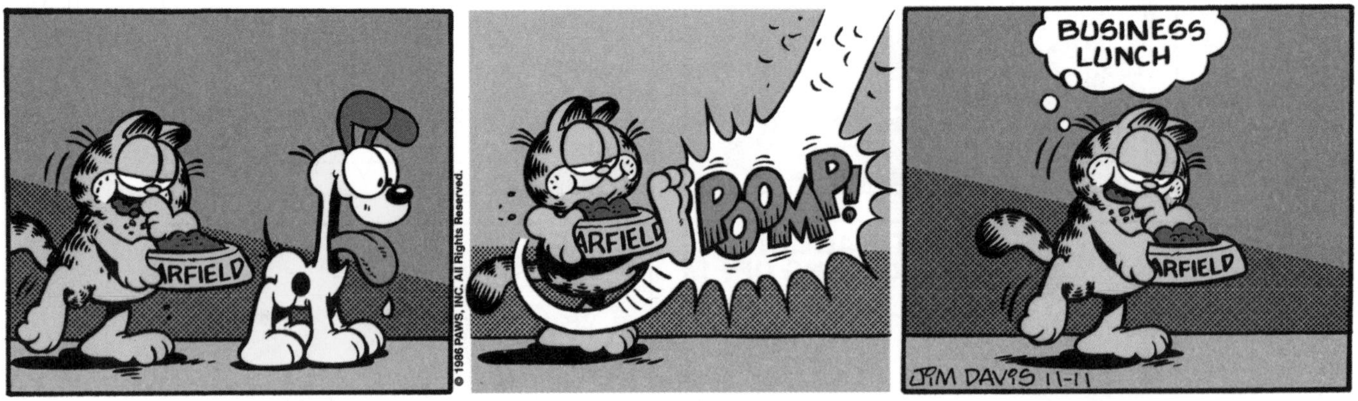
ARFIELD
© 1986 PAWS, INC. All Rights Reserved.
ARFIELD
POMP!
BUSINESS LUNCH
ARFIELD
JIM DAVIS 11-11

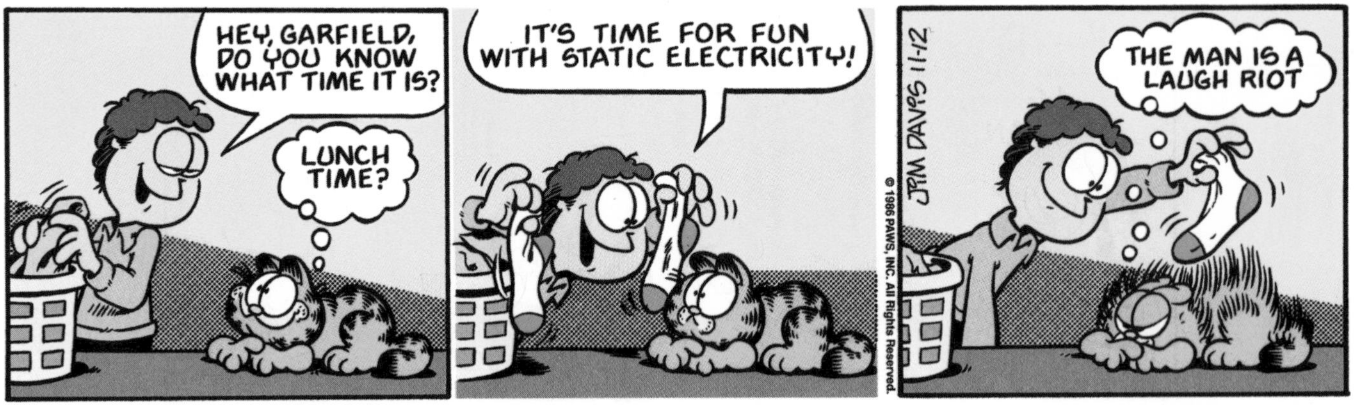
HEY, GARFIELD, DO YOU KNOW WHAT TIME IT IS?
LUNCH TIME?
IT'S TIME FOR FUN WITH STATIC ELECTRICITY!
JIM DAVIS 11-12
© 1986 PAWS, INC. All Rights Reserved.
THE MAN IS A LAUGH RIOT

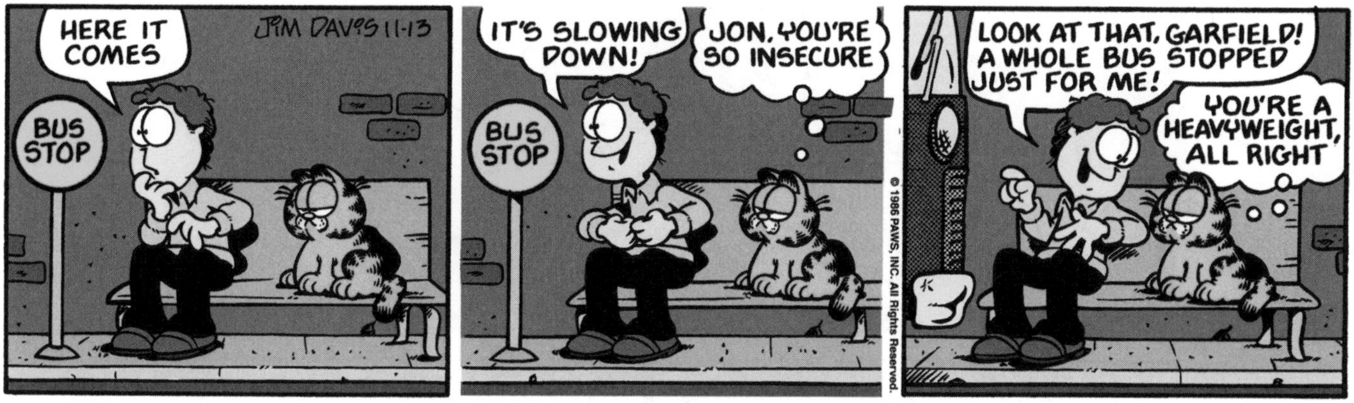
JIM DAVIS 11-13
HERE IT COMES
BUS STOP
IT'S SLOWING DOWN!
JON, YOU'RE SO INSECURE
© 1986 PAWS, INC. All Rights Reserved.
LOOK AT THAT, GARFIELD! A WHOLE BUS STOPPED JUST FOR ME!
YOU'RE A HEAVYWEIGHT, ALL RIGHT

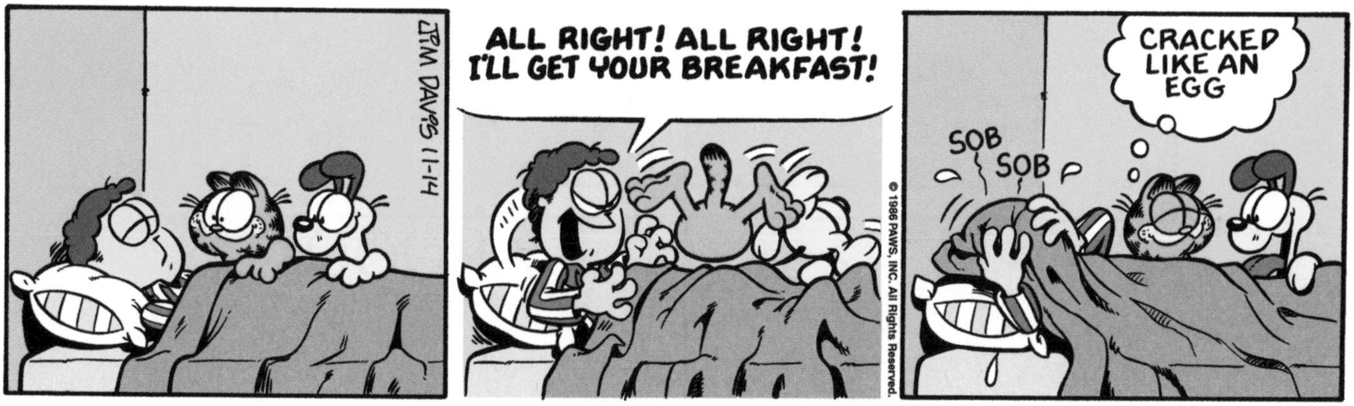
JIM DAVIS 11-14
ALL RIGHT! ALL RIGHT! I'LL GET YOUR BREAKFAST!
© 1986 PAWS, INC. All Rights Reserved.
SOB SOB
CRACKED LIKE AN EGG

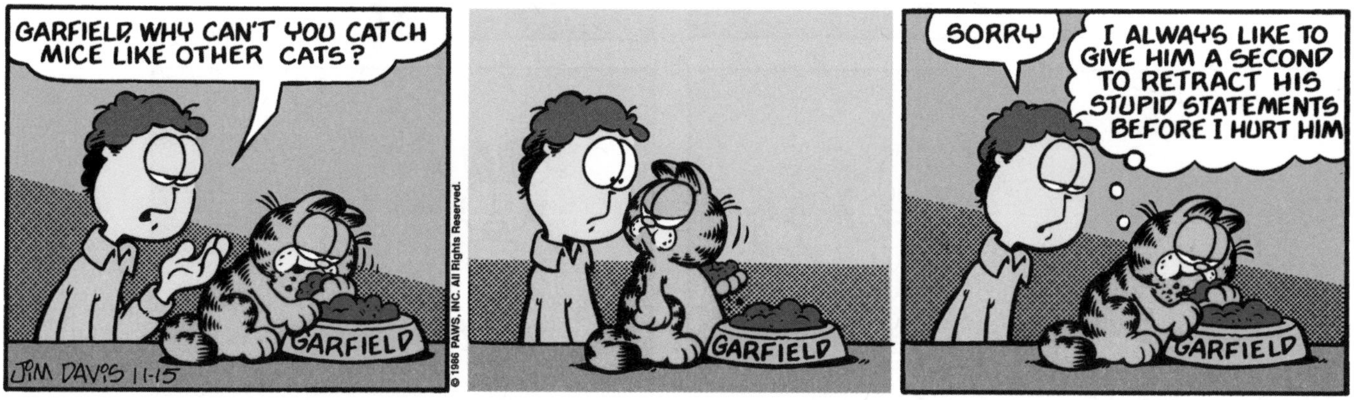
GARFIELD, WHY CAN'T YOU CATCH MICE LIKE OTHER CATS?
GARFIELD
JIM DAVIS 11-15
© 1986 PAWS, INC. All Rights Reserved.
GARFIELD
SORRY
I ALWAYS LIKE TO GIVE HIM A SECOND TO RETRACT HIS STUPID STATEMENTS BEFORE I HURT HIM
GARFIELD

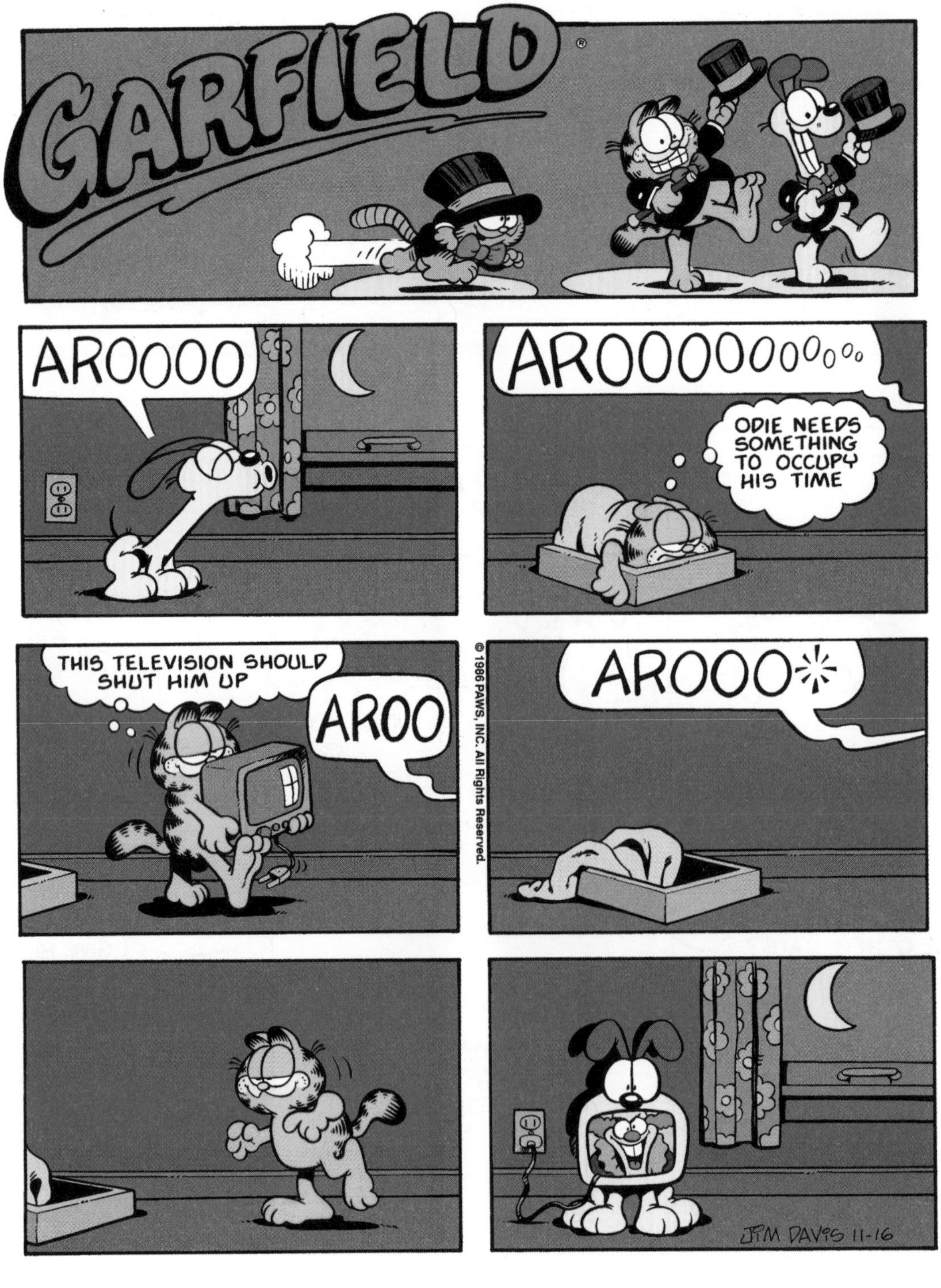
GARFIELD®
AROOOO
AROOOOOOOOOo
ODIE NEEDS SOMETHING TO OCCUPY HIS TIME
THIS TELEVISION SHOULD SHUT HIM UP
AROO
AROOO
JIM DAVIS 11-16

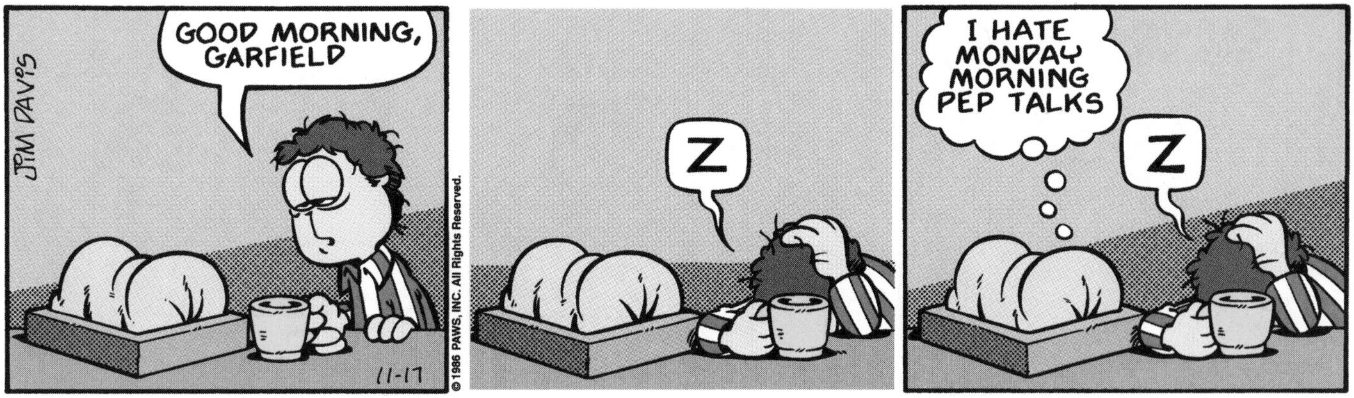
JIM DAVIS
GOOD MORNING, GARFIELD
11-17
© 1986 PAWS, INC. All Rights Reserved.
Z
I HATE MONDAY MORNING PEP TALKS
Z

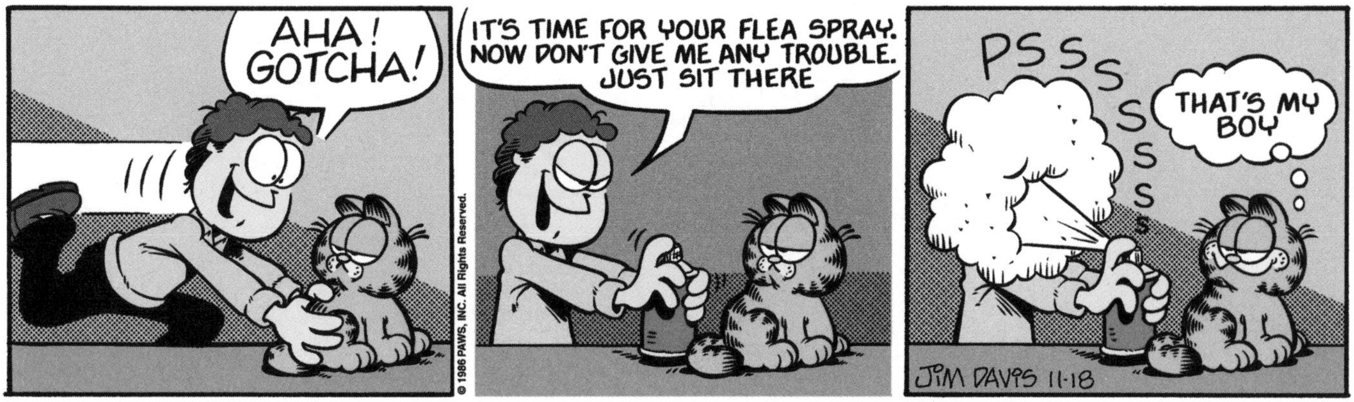
AHA! GOTCHA!
© 1986 PAWS, INC. All Rights Reserved.
IT'S TIME FOR YOUR FLEA SPRAY. NOW DON'T GIVE ME ANY TROUBLE. JUST SIT THERE
PSSSSSSSS
THAT'S MY BOY
JIM DAVIS 11-18

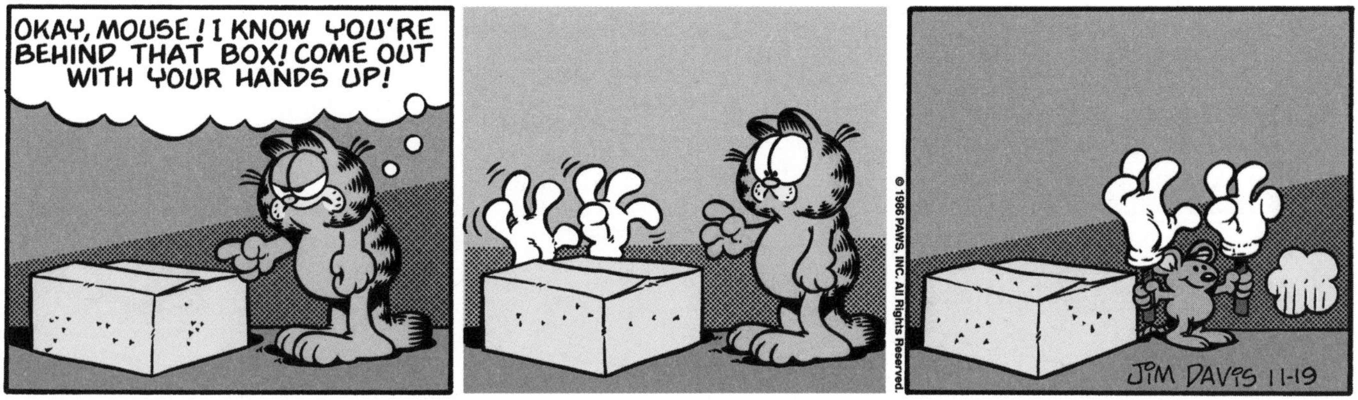
OKAY, MOUSE! I KNOW YOU'RE BEHIND THAT BOX! COME OUT WITH YOUR HANDS UP!
© 1986 PAWS, INC. All Rights Reserved.
JIM DAVIS 11-19

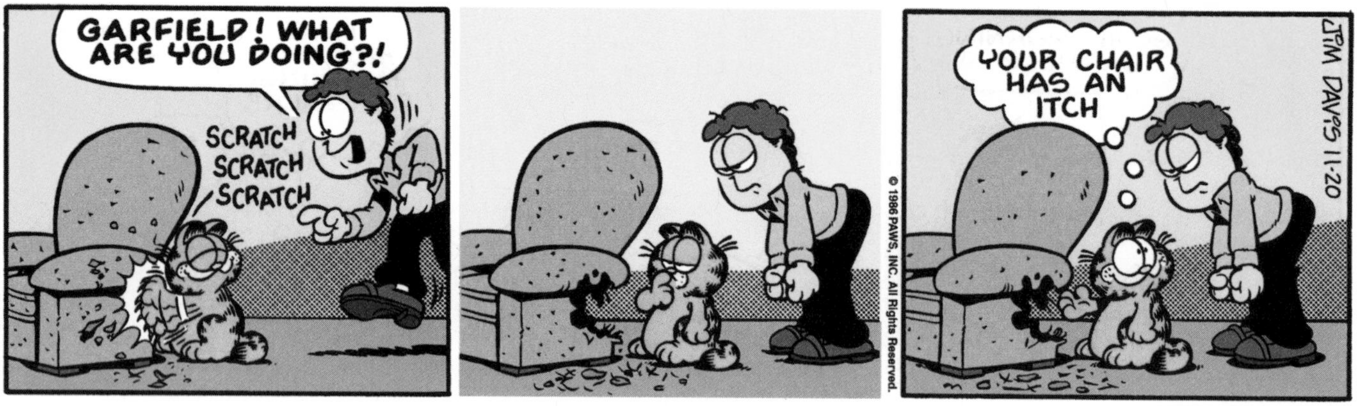
GARFIELD! WHAT ARE YOU DOING?!
SCRATCH SCRATCH SCRATCH
© 1986 PAWS, INC. All Rights Reserved.
YOUR CHAIR HAS AN ITCH
JIM DAVIS 11-20

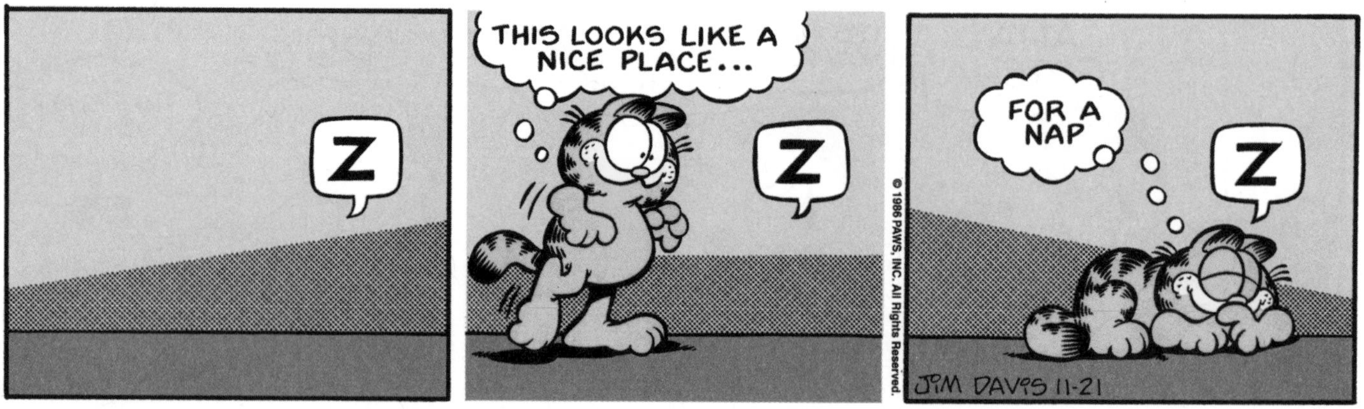
Z
THIS LOOKS LIKE A NICE PLACE...
Z
© 1986 PAWS, INC. All Rights Reserved.
FOR A NAP
Z
JIM DAVIS 11-21

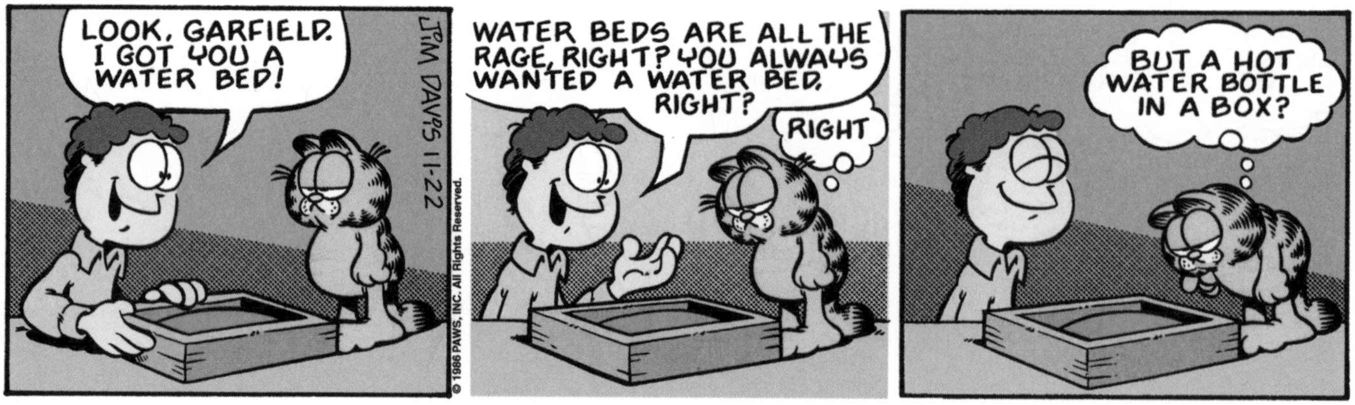
LOOK, GARFIELD. I GOT YOU A WATER BED!
JIM DAVIS 11-22
© 1986 PAWS, INC. All Rights Reserved.
WATER BEDS ARE ALL THE RAGE, RIGHT? YOU ALWAYS WANTED A WATER BED, RIGHT?
RIGHT
BUT A HOT WATER BOTTLE IN A BOX?

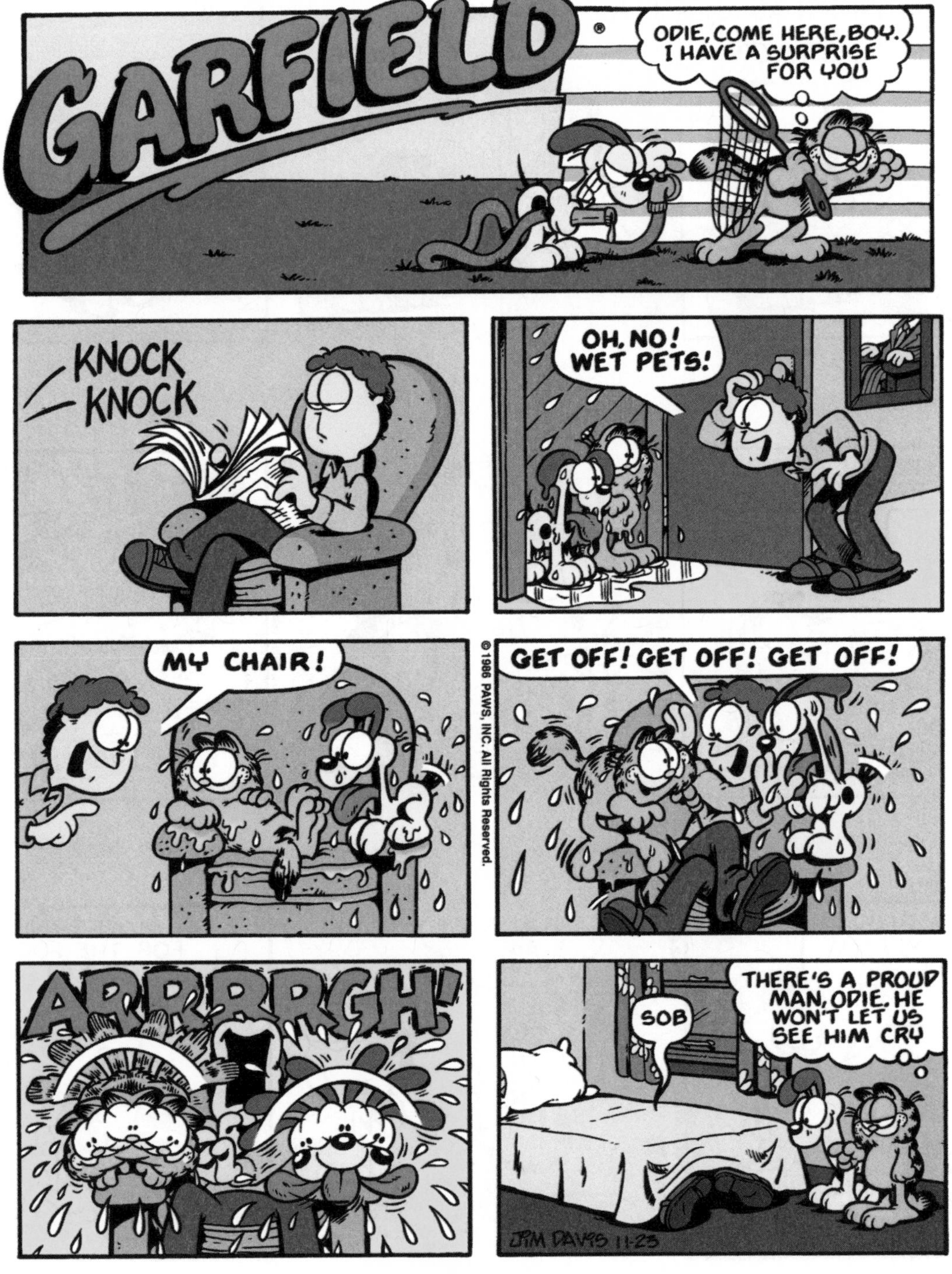

GARFIELD®
ODIE, COME HERE, BOY. I HAVE A SURPRISE FOR YOU
KNOCK KNOCK
OH, NO! WET PETS!
MY CHAIR!
GET OFF! GET OFF! GET OFF!
ARRRRGH!
SOB
THERE'S A PROUD MAN, ODIE. HE WON'T LET US SEE HIM CRY
JIM DAVIS 11-23

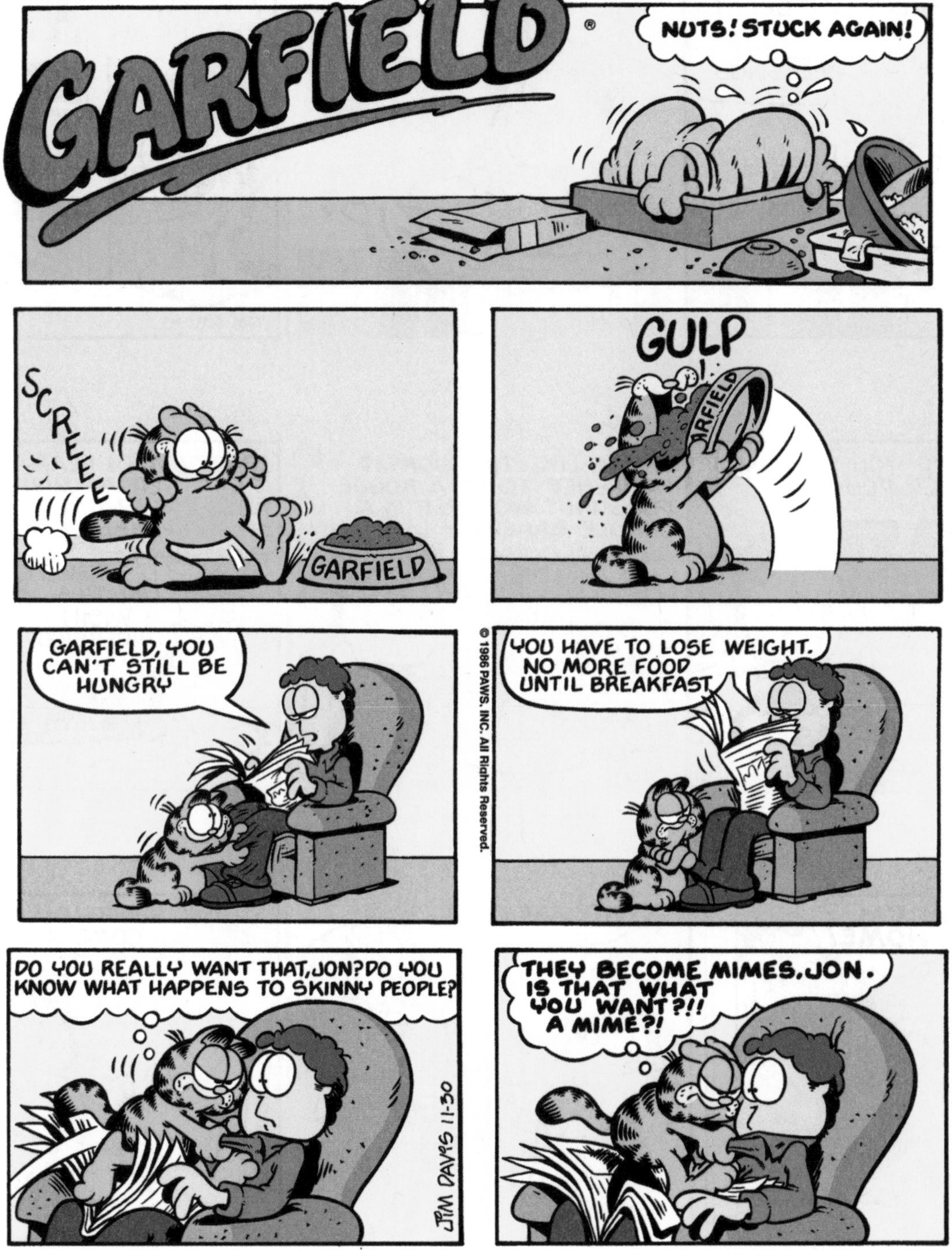
GARFIELD
NUTS! STUCK AGAIN!
SCREEEE
GARFIELD
GULP
GARFIELD
GARFIELD, YOU CAN'T STILL BE HUNGRY
YOU HAVE TO LOSE WEIGHT. NO MORE FOOD UNTIL BREAKFAST
© 1986 PAWS, INC. All Rights Reserved.
DO YOU REALLY WANT THAT, JON? DO YOU KNOW WHAT HAPPENS TO SKINNY PEOPLE?
JIM DAVIS 11-30
THEY BECOME MIMES, JON. IS THAT WHAT YOU WANT?!! A MIME?!

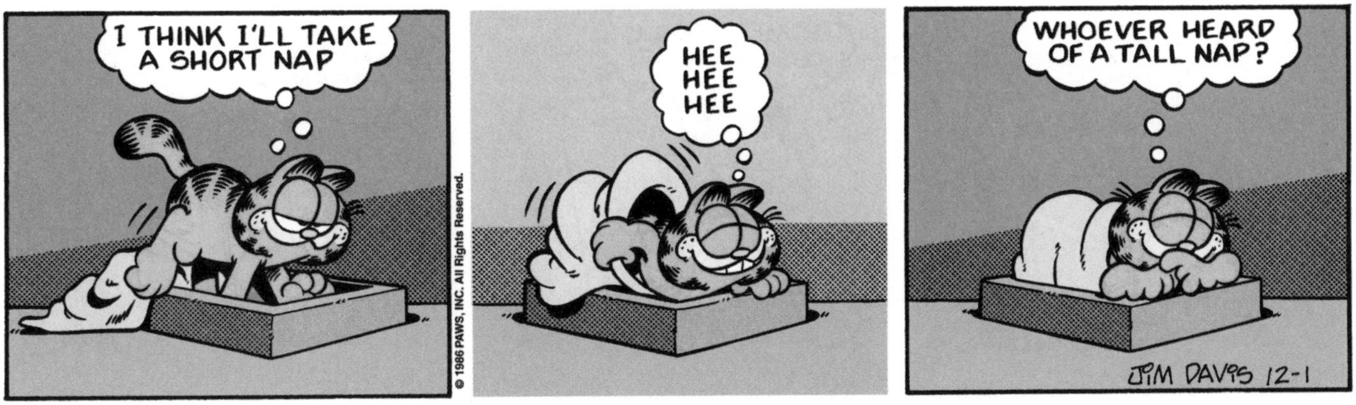
I THINK I'LL TAKE A SHORT NAP
© 1986 PAWS, INC. All Rights Reserved.
HEE HEE HEE
WHOEVER HEARD OF A TALL NAP?
JIM DAVIS 12-1

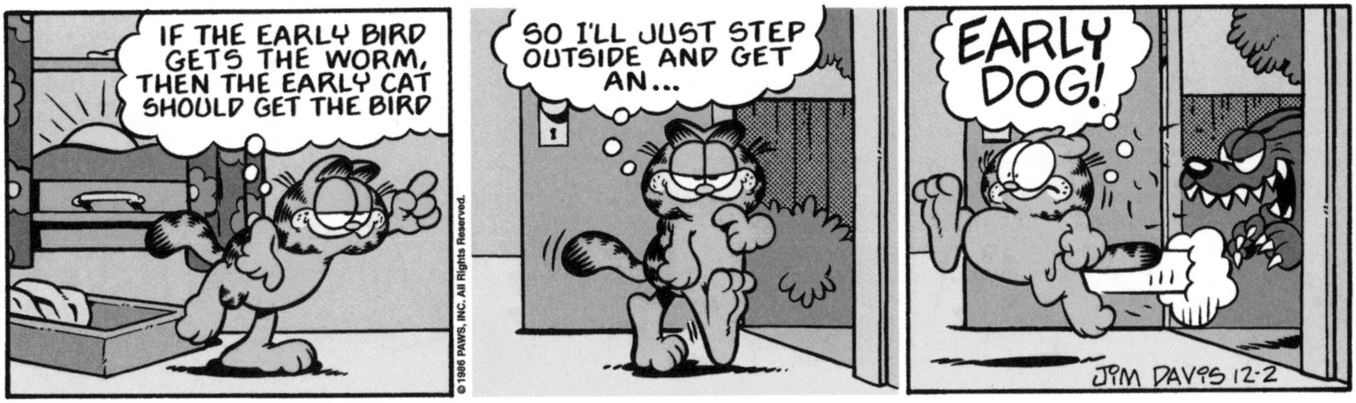
IF THE EARLY BIRD GETS THE WORM, THEN THE EARLY CAT SHOULD GET THE BIRD
© 1986 PAWS, INC. All Rights Reserved.
SO I'LL JUST STEP OUTSIDE AND GET AN...
EARLY DOG!
JIM DAVIS 12-2

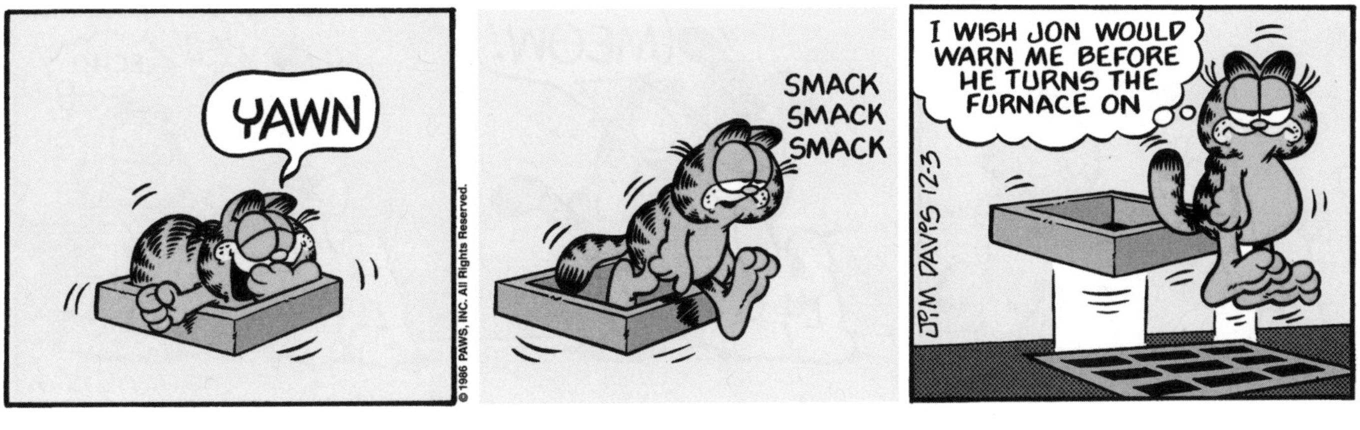
YAWN
© 1986 PAWS, INC. All Rights Reserved.
SMACK SMACK SMACK
JIM DAVIS 12-3
I WISH JON WOULD WARN ME BEFORE HE TURNS THE FURNACE ON

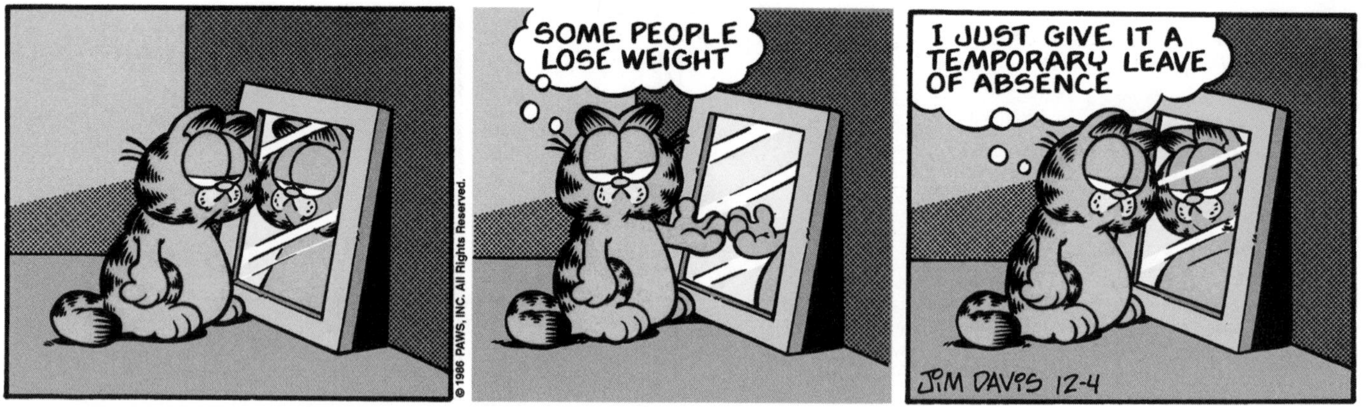
© 1986 PAWS, INC. All Rights Reserved.
SOME PEOPLE LOSE WEIGHT
I JUST GIVE IT A TEMPORARY LEAVE OF ABSENCE
JIM DAVIS 12-4

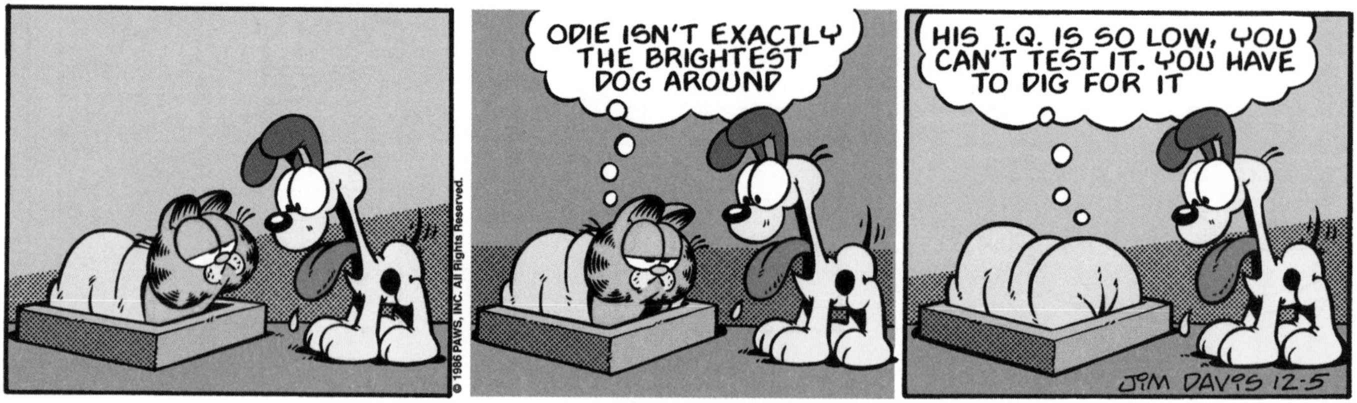
© 1986 PAWS, INC. All Rights Reserved.
ODIE ISN'T EXACTLY THE BRIGHTEST DOG AROUND
HIS I.Q. IS SO LOW, YOU CAN'T TEST IT. YOU HAVE TO DIG FOR IT
JIM DAVIS 12-5

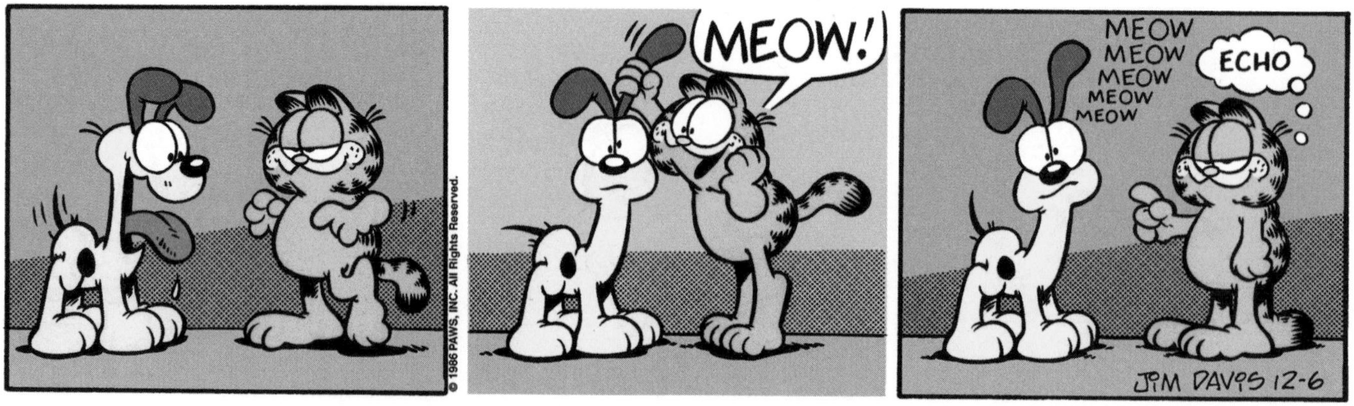
© 1986 PAWS, INC. All Rights Reserved.
MEOW!
MEOW MEOW MEOW MEOW MEOW
ECHO
JIM DAVIS 12-6

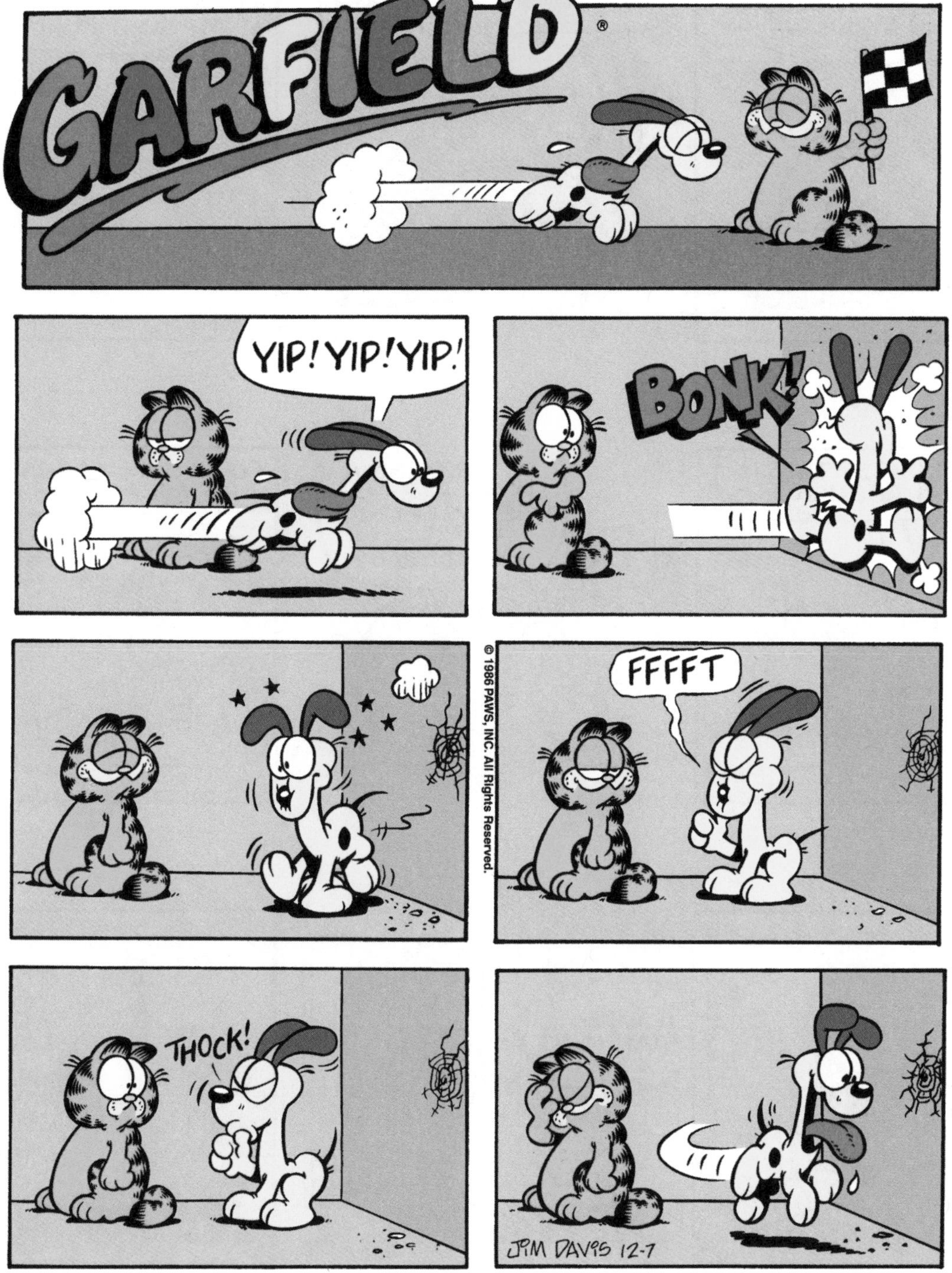
GARFIELD
YIP! YIP! YIP!
BONK!
FFFFT
THOCK!
JIM DAVIS 12-7

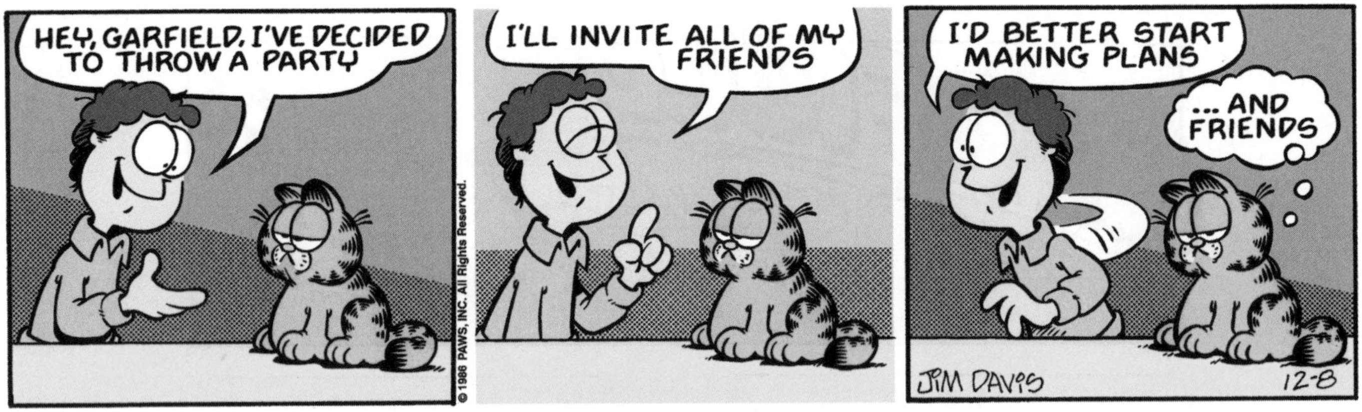
HEY, GARFIELD, I'VE DECIDED TO THROW A PARTY
I'LL INVITE ALL OF MY FRIENDS
I'D BETTER START MAKING PLANS
... AND FRIENDS
JIM DAVIS 12-8
© 1986 PAWS, INC. All Rights Reserved.

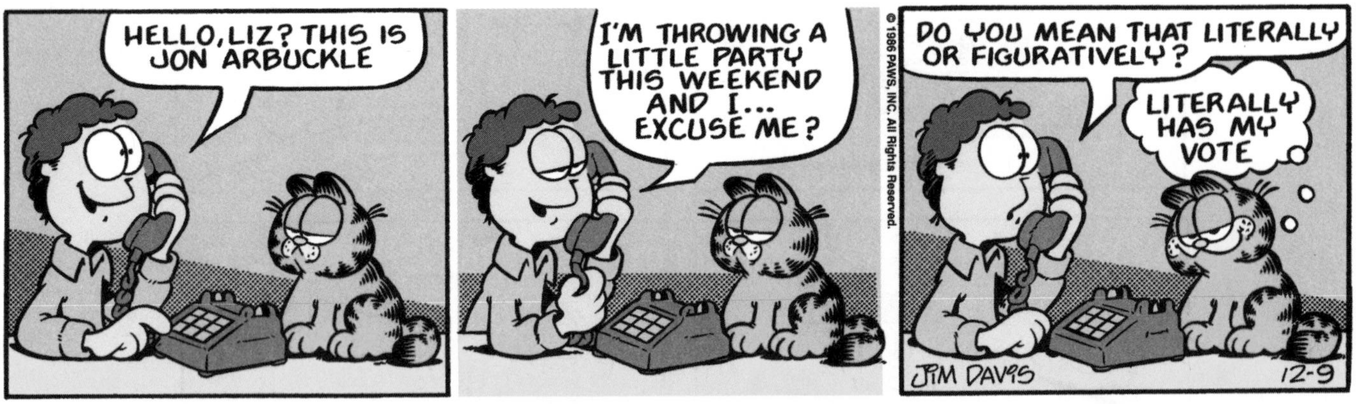
HELLO, LIZ? THIS IS JON ARBUCKLE
I'M THROWING A LITTLE PARTY THIS WEEKEND AND I... EXCUSE ME?
DO YOU MEAN THAT LITERALLY OR FIGURATIVELY?
LITERALLY HAS MY VOTE
JIM DAVIS 12-9
© 1986 PAWS, INC. All Rights Reserved.

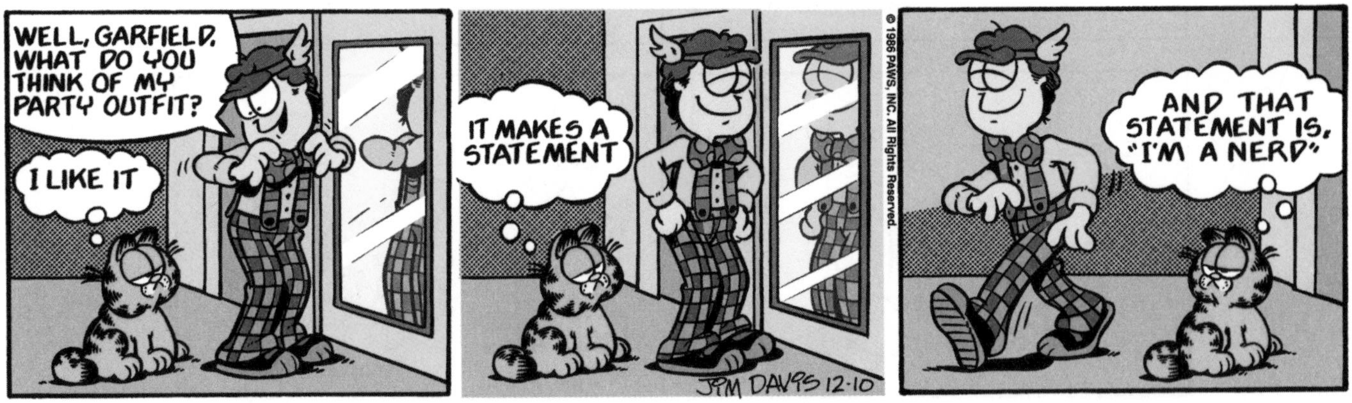
WELL, GARFIELD, WHAT DO YOU THINK OF MY PARTY OUTFIT?
I LIKE IT
IT MAKES A STATEMENT
AND THAT STATEMENT IS, "I'M A NERD"
JIM DAVIS 12-10
© 1986 PAWS, INC. All Rights Reserved.

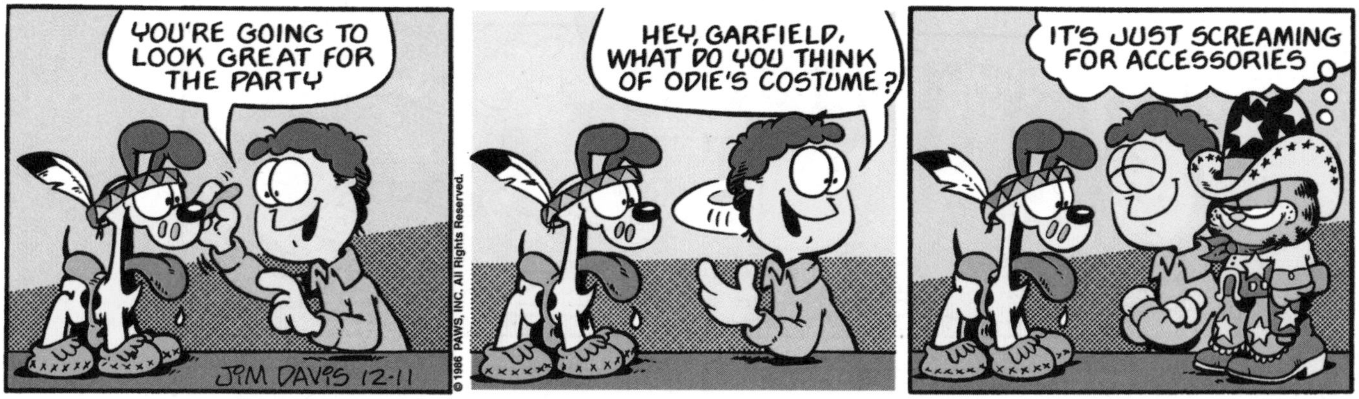
YOU'RE GOING TO LOOK GREAT FOR THE PARTY
JIM DAVIS 12-11
© 1986 PAWS, INC. All Rights Reserved.
HEY, GARFIELD, WHAT DO YOU THINK OF ODIE'S COSTUME?
IT'S JUST SCREAMING FOR ACCESSORIES

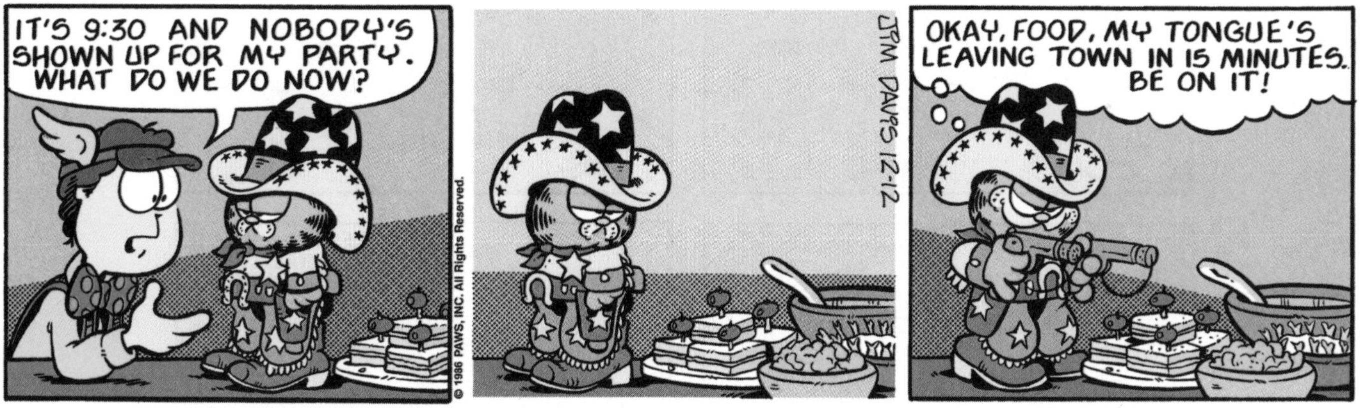
IT'S 9:30 AND NOBODY'S SHOWN UP FOR MY PARTY. WHAT DO WE DO NOW?
© 1986 PAWS, INC. All Rights Reserved.
JIM DAVIS 12-12
OKAY, FOOD, MY TONGUE'S LEAVING TOWN IN 15 MINUTES. BE ON IT!

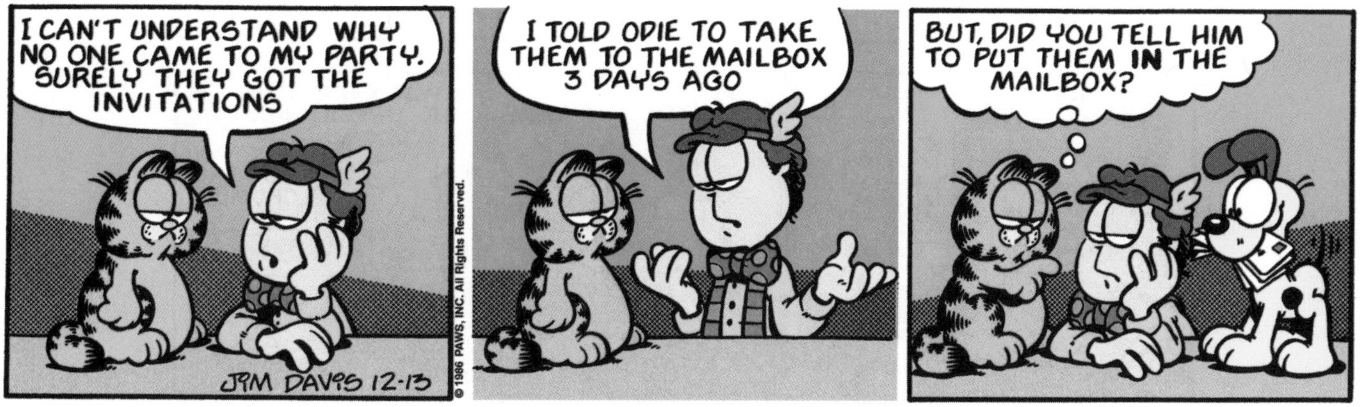
I CAN'T UNDERSTAND WHY NO ONE CAME TO MY PARTY. SURELY THEY GOT THE INVITATIONS
JIM DAVIS 12-13
© 1986 PAWS, INC. All Rights Reserved.
I TOLD ODIE TO TAKE THEM TO THE MAILBOX 3 DAYS AGO
BUT, DID YOU TELL HIM TO PUT THEM IN THE MAILBOX?

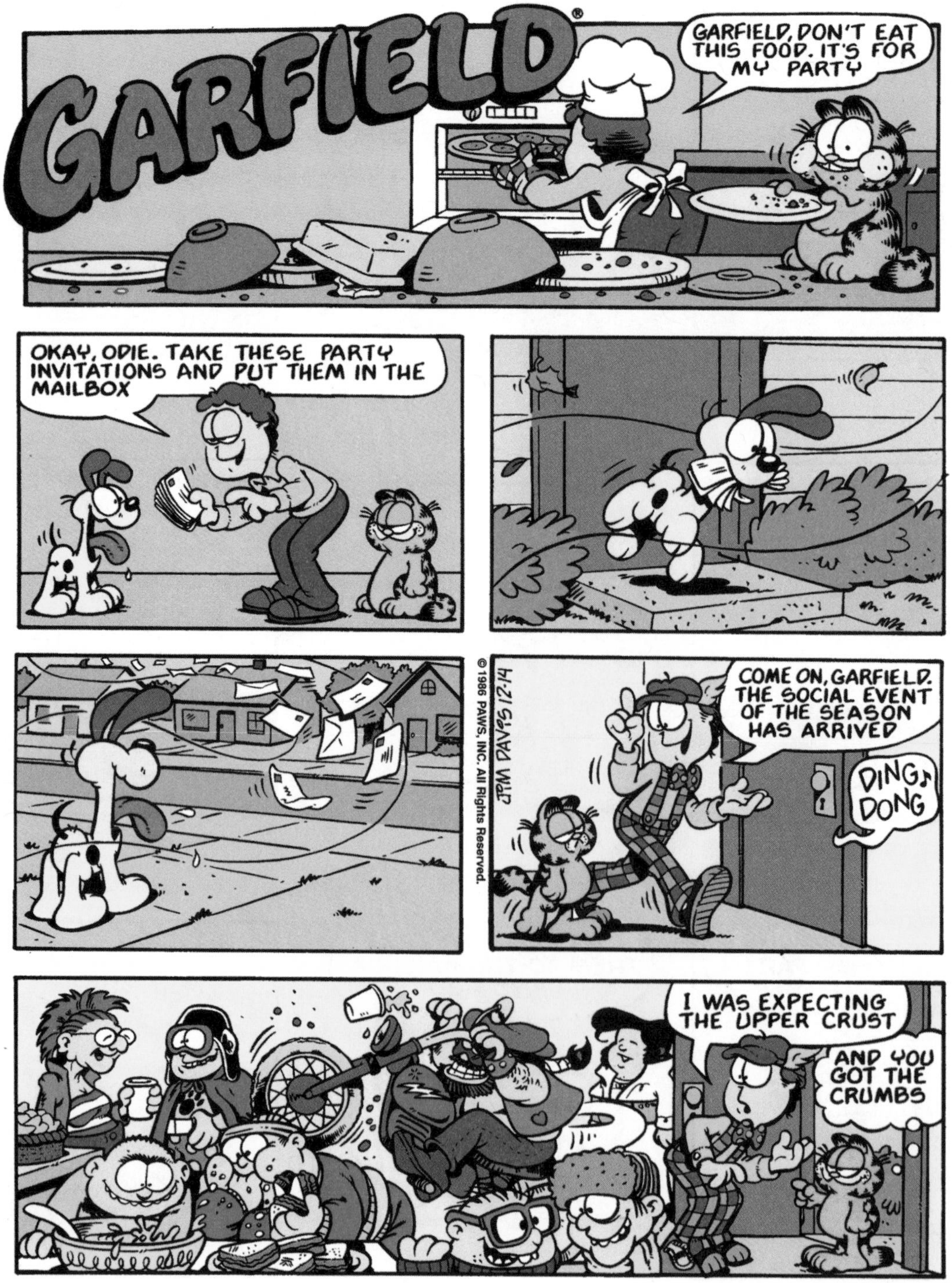
GARFIELD®
GARFIELD, DON'T EAT THIS FOOD. IT'S FOR MY PARTY
OKAY, ODIE. TAKE THESE PARTY INVITATIONS AND PUT THEM IN THE MAILBOX
© 1986 PAWS, INC. All Rights Reserved.
JIM DAVIS 12-14
COME ON, GARFIELD. THE SOCIAL EVENT OF THE SEASON HAS ARRIVED
DING DONG
I WAS EXPECTING THE UPPER CRUST
AND YOU GOT THE CRUMBS

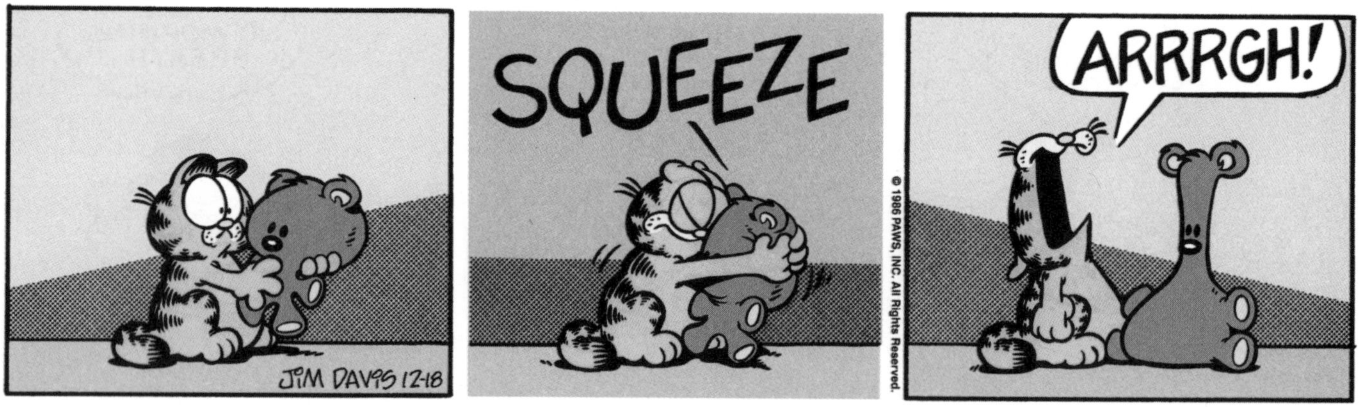
JIM DAVIS 12-18
SQUEEEZE
© 1986 PAWS, INC. All Rights Reserved.
ARRRGH!

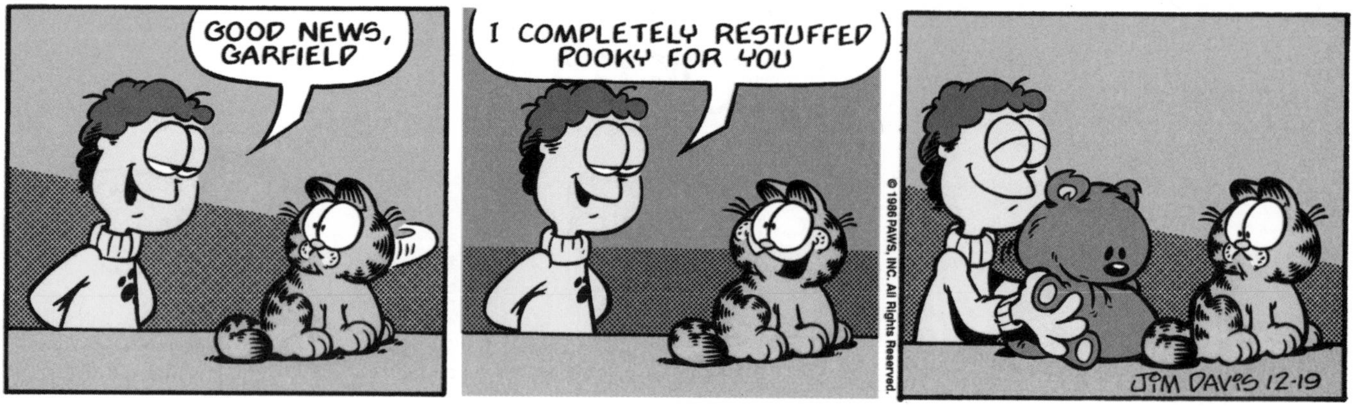
GOOD NEWS, GARFIELD
I COMPLETELY RESTUFFED POOKY FOR YOU
© 1986 PAWS, INC. All Rights Reserved.
JIM DAVIS 12-19

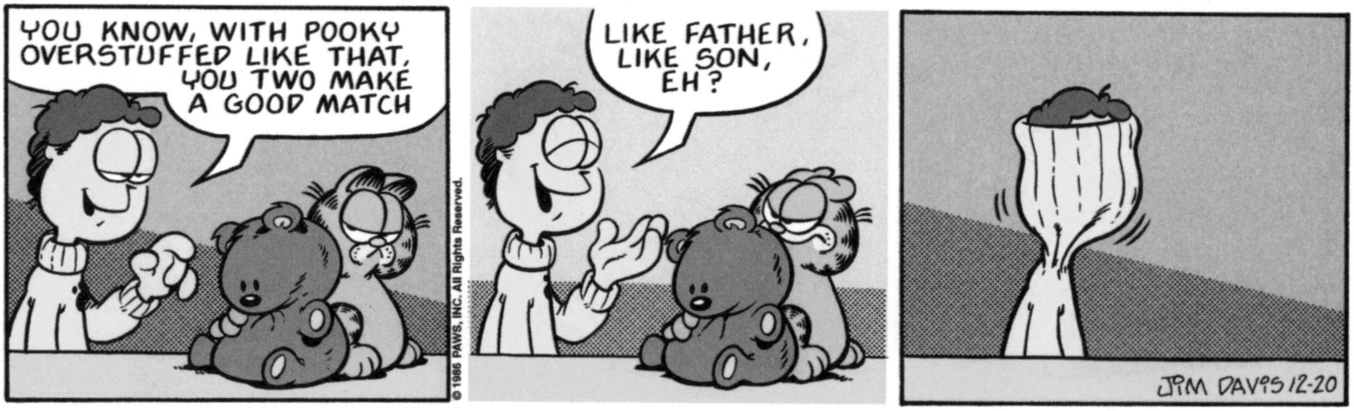
YOU KNOW, WITH POOKY OVERSTUFFED LIKE THAT, YOU TWO MAKE A GOOD MATCH
© 1986 PAWS, INC. All Rights Reserved.
LIKE FATHER, LIKE SON, EH?
JIM DAVIS 12-20

230

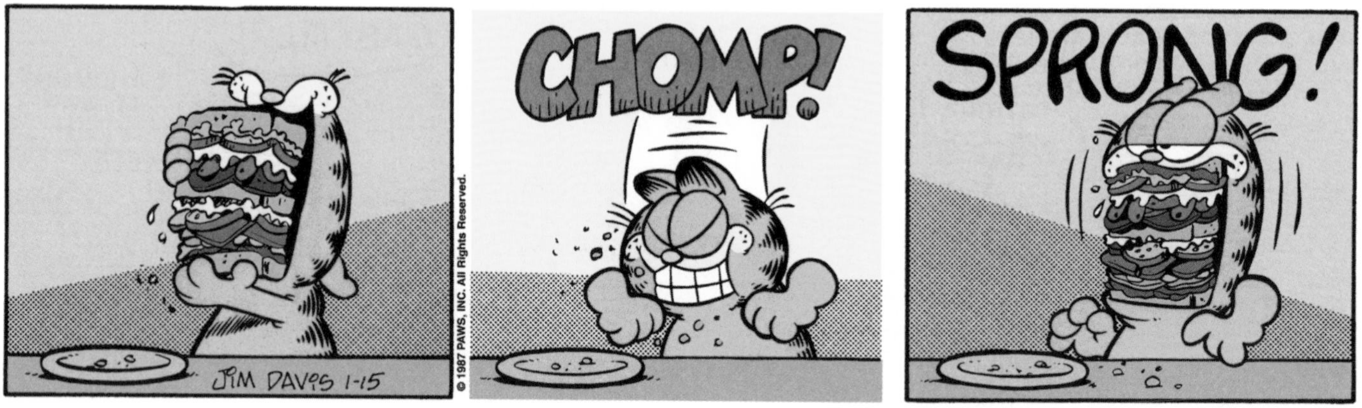
JIM DAVIS 1-15
CHOMP!
© 1987 PAWS, INC. All Rights Reserved.
SPRONG!

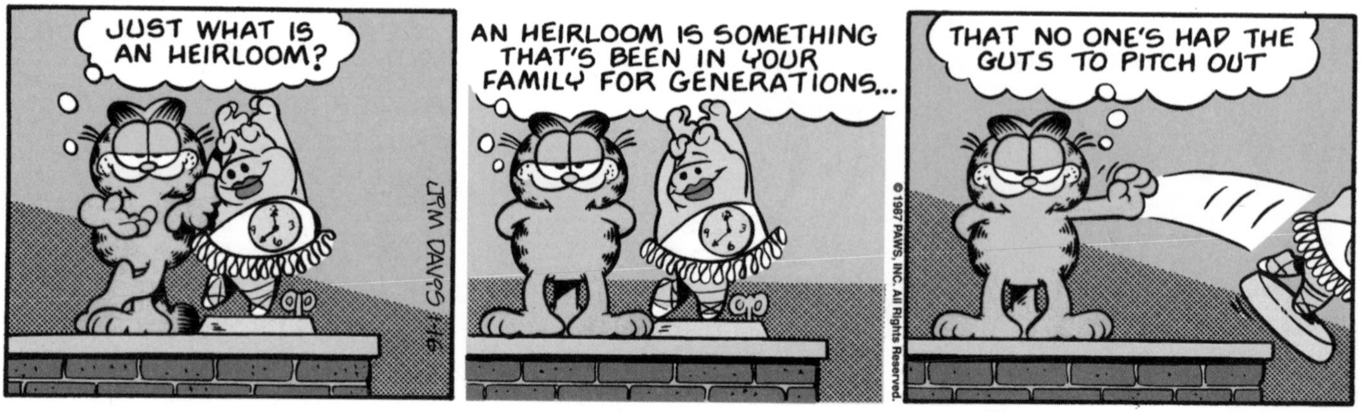
JUST WHAT IS AN HEIRLOOM?
JIM DAVIS 1-16
AN HEIRLOOM IS SOMETHING THAT'S BEEN IN YOUR FAMILY FOR GENERATIONS...
© 1987 PAWS, INC. All Rights Reserved.
THAT NO ONE'S HAD THE GUTS TO PITCH OUT

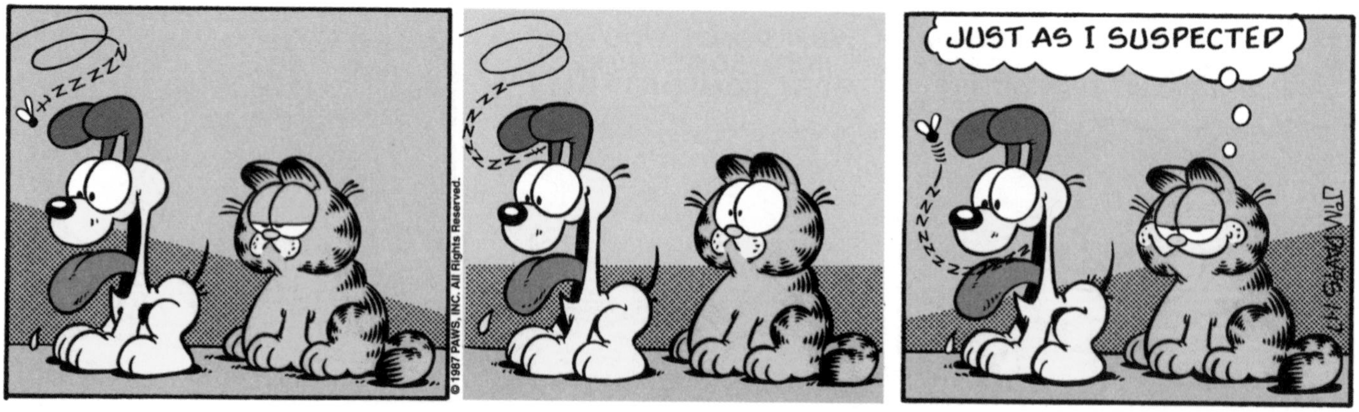
ZZZZZ
© 1987 PAWS, INC. All Rights Reserved.
JUST AS I SUSPECTED
JIM DAVIS 1-17

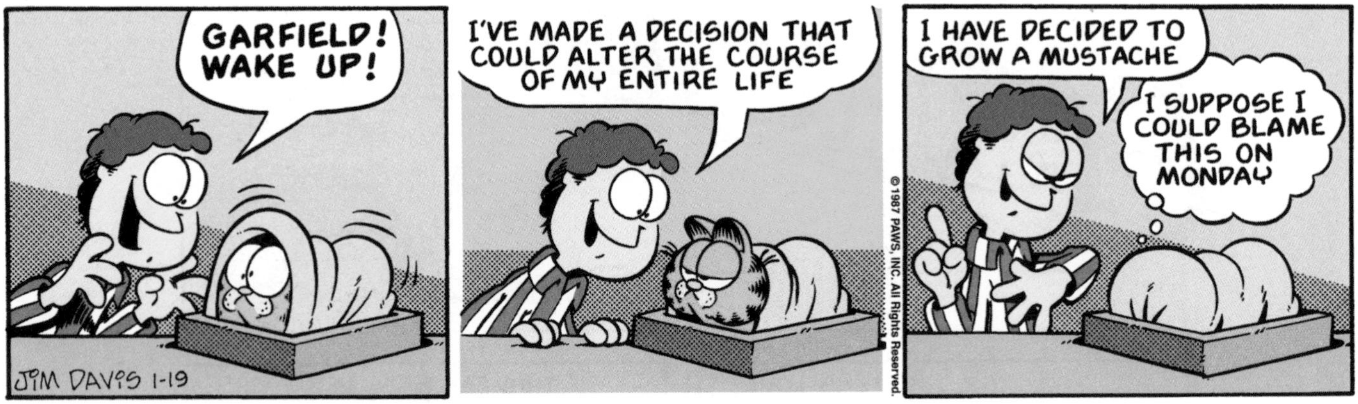
GARFIELD! WAKE UP!
JIM DAVIS 1-19
I'VE MADE A DECISION THAT COULD ALTER THE COURSE OF MY ENTIRE LIFE
© 1987 PAWS, INC. All Rights Reserved.
I HAVE DECIDED TO GROW A MUSTACHE
I SUPPOSE I COULD BLAME THIS ON MONDAY

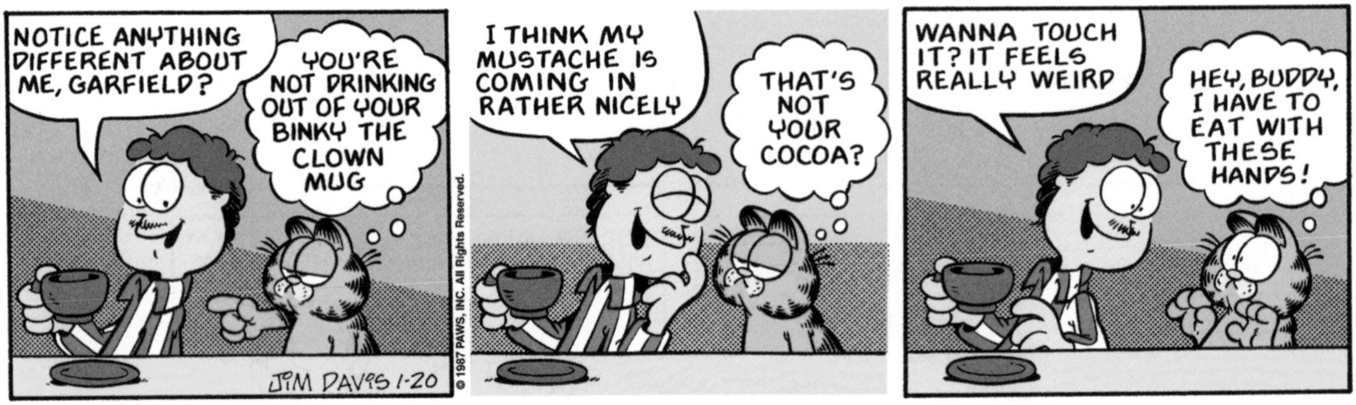
NOTICE ANYTHING DIFFERENT ABOUT ME, GARFIELD?
YOU'RE NOT DRINKING OUT OF YOUR BINKY THE CLOWN MUG
JIM DAVIS 1-20
© 1987 PAWS, INC. All Rights Reserved.
I THINK MY MUSTACHE IS COMING IN RATHER NICELY
THAT'S NOT YOUR COCOA?
WANNA TOUCH IT? IT FEELS REALLY WEIRD
HEY, BUDDY, I HAVE TO EAT WITH THESE HANDS!

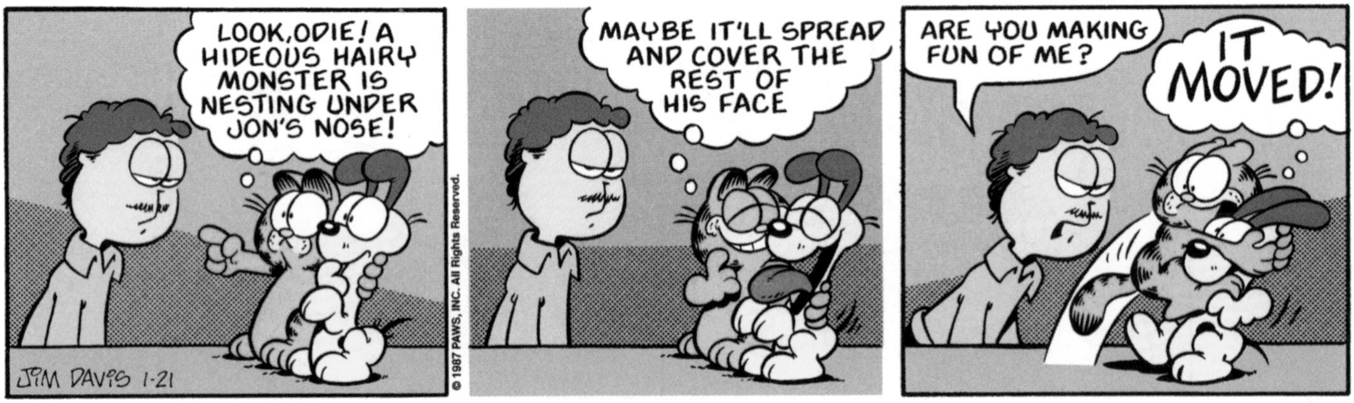
LOOK, ODIE! A HIDEOUS HAIRY MONSTER IS NESTING UNDER JON'S NOSE!
JIM DAVIS 1-21
© 1987 PAWS, INC. All Rights Reserved.
MAYBE IT'LL SPREAD AND COVER THE REST OF HIS FACE
ARE YOU MAKING FUN OF ME?
IT MOVED!

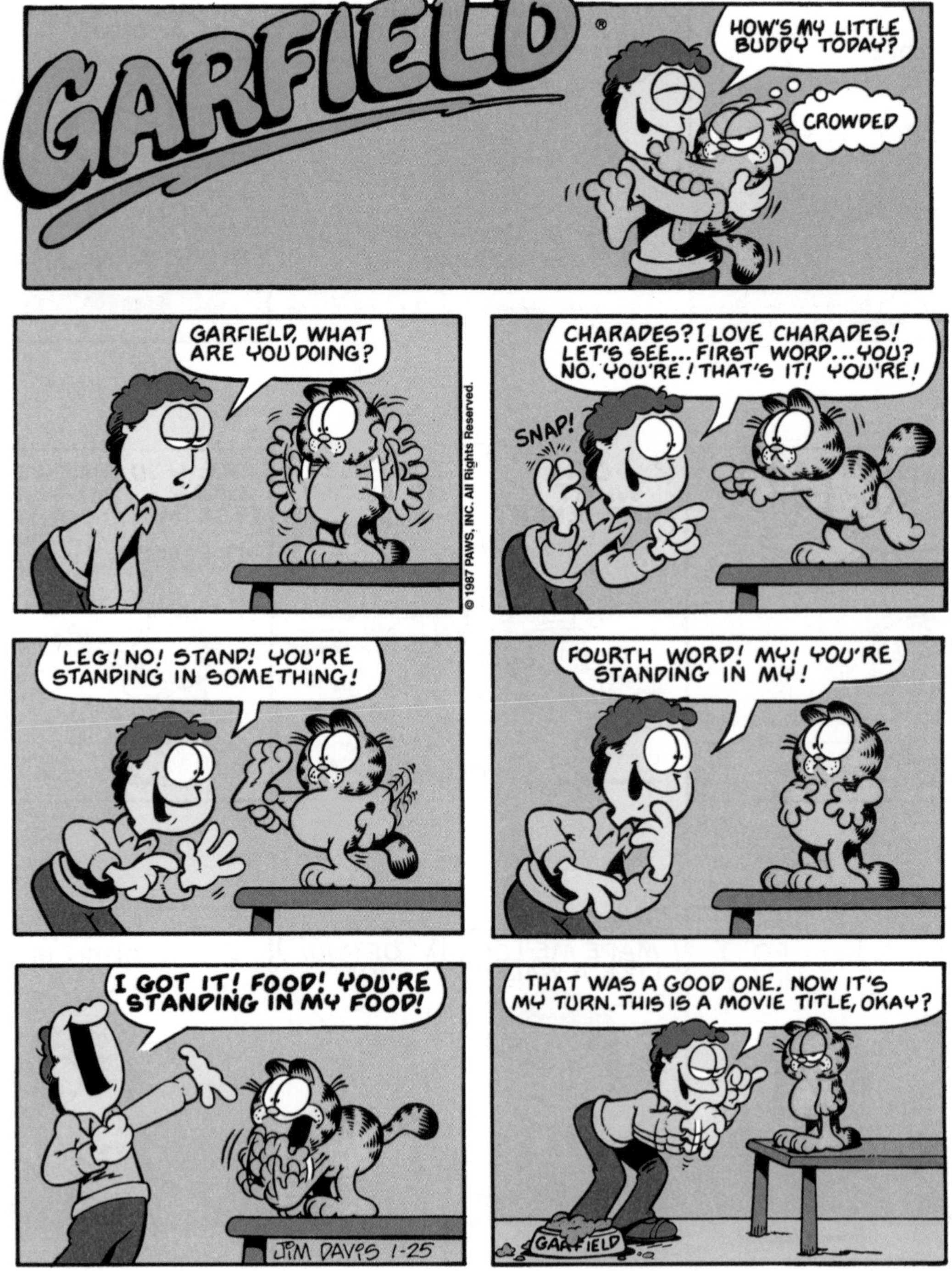
GARFIELD®
HOW'S MY LITTLE BUDDY TODAY?
CROWDED
GARFIELD, WHAT ARE YOU DOING?
CHARADES? I LOVE CHARADES! LET'S SEE... FIRST WORD...YOU? NO, YOU'RE! THAT'S IT! YOU'RE!
SNAP!
LEG! NO! STAND! YOU'RE STANDING IN SOMETHING!
FOURTH WORD! MY! YOU'RE STANDING IN MY!
I GOT IT! FOOD! YOU'RE STANDING IN MY FOOD!
THAT WAS A GOOD ONE. NOW IT'S MY TURN. THIS IS A MOVIE TITLE, OKAY?
GARFIELD
JIM DAVIS 1-25

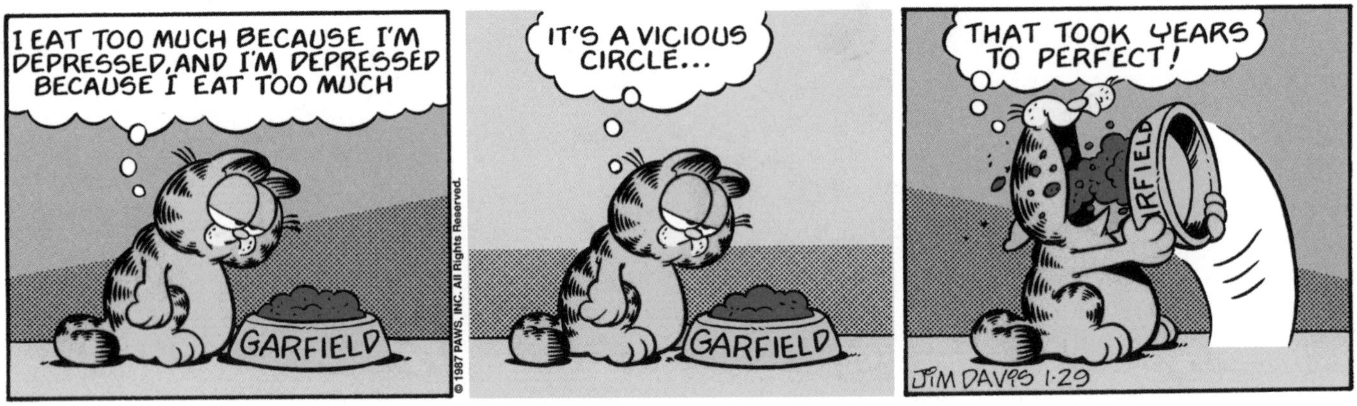
I EAT TOO MUCH BECAUSE I'M DEPRESSED, AND I'M DEPRESSED BECAUSE I EAT TOO MUCH
GARFIELD
IT'S A VICIOUS CIRCLE...
GARFIELD
© 1987 PAWS, INC. All Rights Reserved.
THAT TOOK YEARS TO PERFECT!
RFIELD
JIM DAVIS 1·29

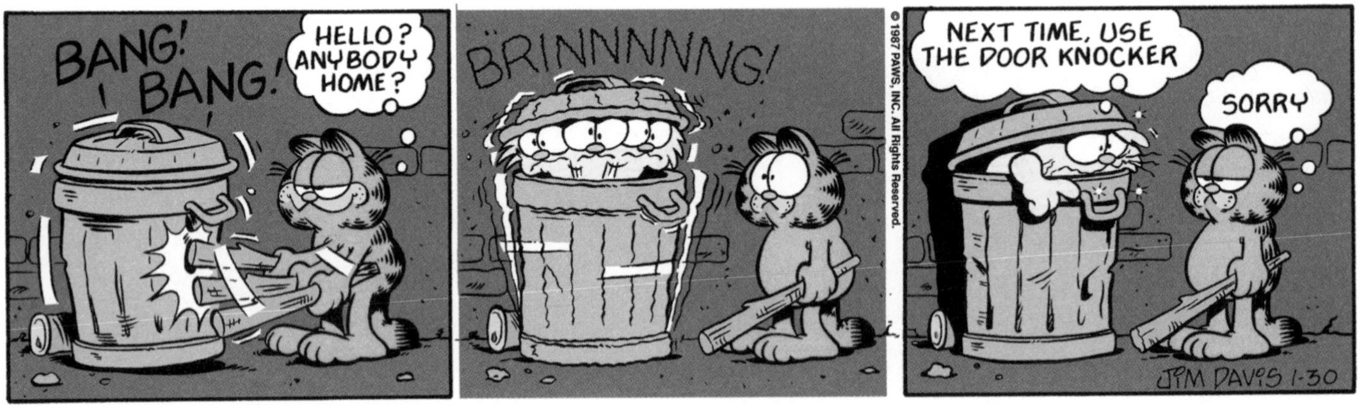
BANG! BANG!
HELLO? ANYBODY HOME?
BRINNNNNG!
© 1987 PAWS, INC. All Rights Reserved.
NEXT TIME, USE THE DOOR KNOCKER
SORRY
JIM DAVIS 1·30

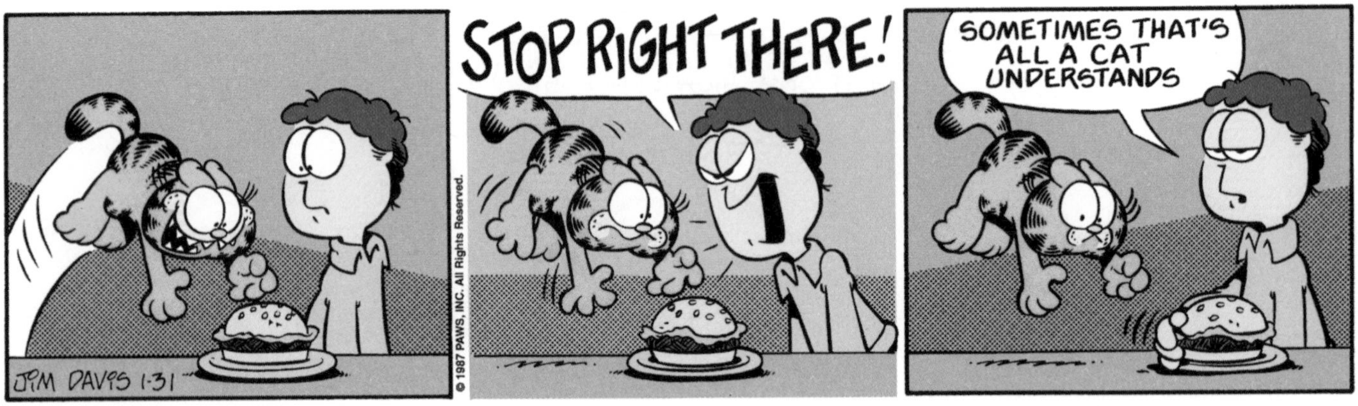
JIM DAVIS 1·31
© 1987 PAWS, INC. All Rights Reserved.
STOP RIGHT THERE!
SOMETIMES THAT'S ALL A CAT UNDERSTANDS

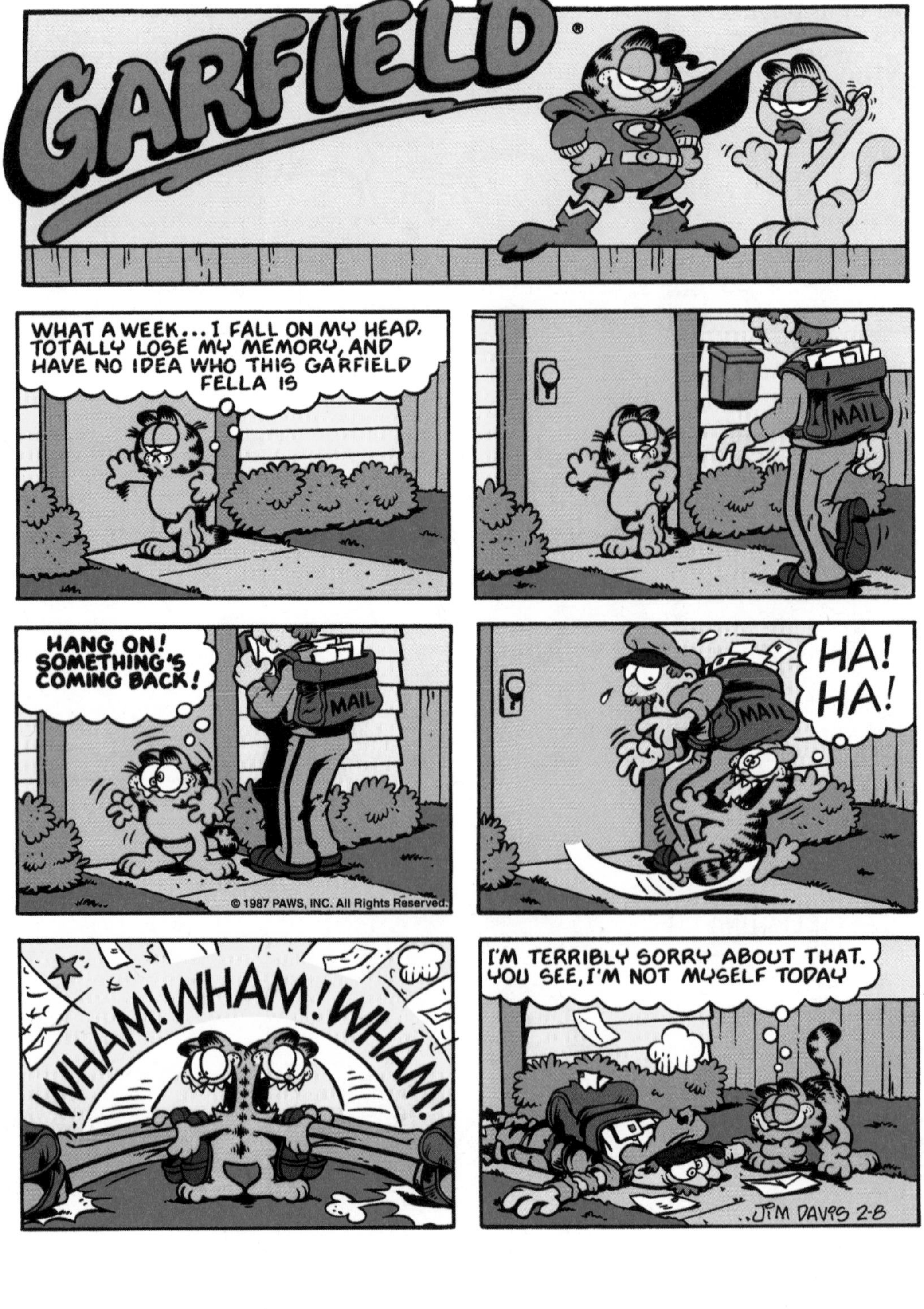
GARFIELD
WHAT A WEEK... I FALL ON MY HEAD, TOTALLY LOSE MY MEMORY, AND HAVE NO IDEA WHO THIS GARFIELD FELLA IS
MAIL
HANG ON! SOMETHING'S COMING BACK!
MAIL
HA! HA!
MAIL
WHAM! WHAM! WHAM!
I'M TERRIBLY SORRY ABOUT THAT. YOU SEE, I'M NOT MYSELF TODAY
JIM DAVIS 2-8

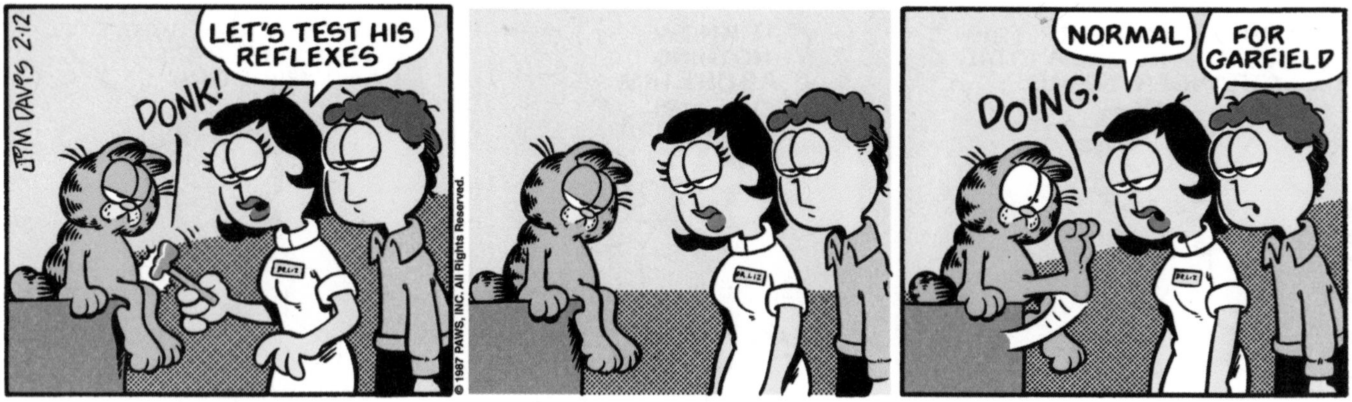
JIM DAVIS 2-12
LET'S TEST HIS REFLEXES
DONK!
© 1987 PAWS, INC. All Rights Reserved.
DOING!
NORMAL
FOR GARFIELD

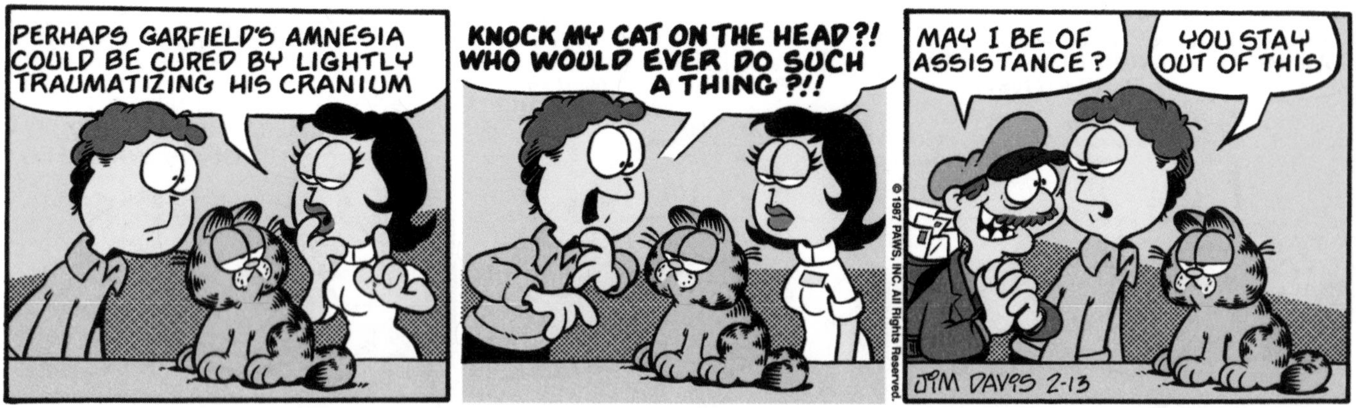
PERHAPS GARFIELD'S AMNESIA COULD BE CURED BY LIGHTLY TRAUMATIZING HIS CRANIUM
KNOCK MY CAT ON THE HEAD?! WHO WOULD EVER DO SUCH A THING?!!
© 1987 PAWS, INC. All Rights Reserved.
MAY I BE OF ASSISTANCE?
YOU STAY OUT OF THIS
JIM DAVIS 2-13

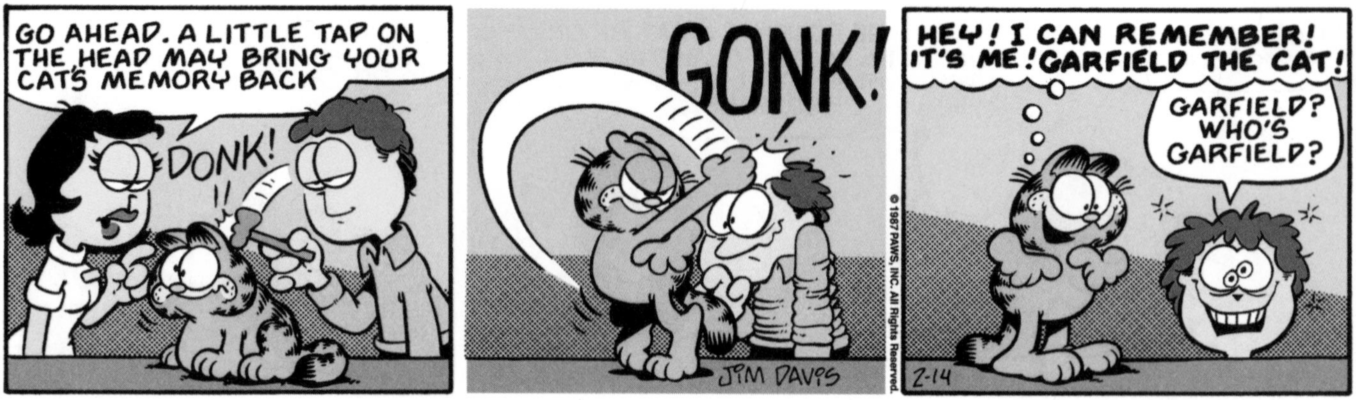
GO AHEAD. A LITTLE TAP ON THE HEAD MAY BRING YOUR CAT'S MEMORY BACK
DONK!
GONK!
JIM DAVIS
© 1987 PAWS, INC. All Rights Reserved.
HEY! I CAN REMEMBER! IT'S ME! GARFIELD THE CAT!
GARFIELD? WHO'S GARFIELD?
2-14

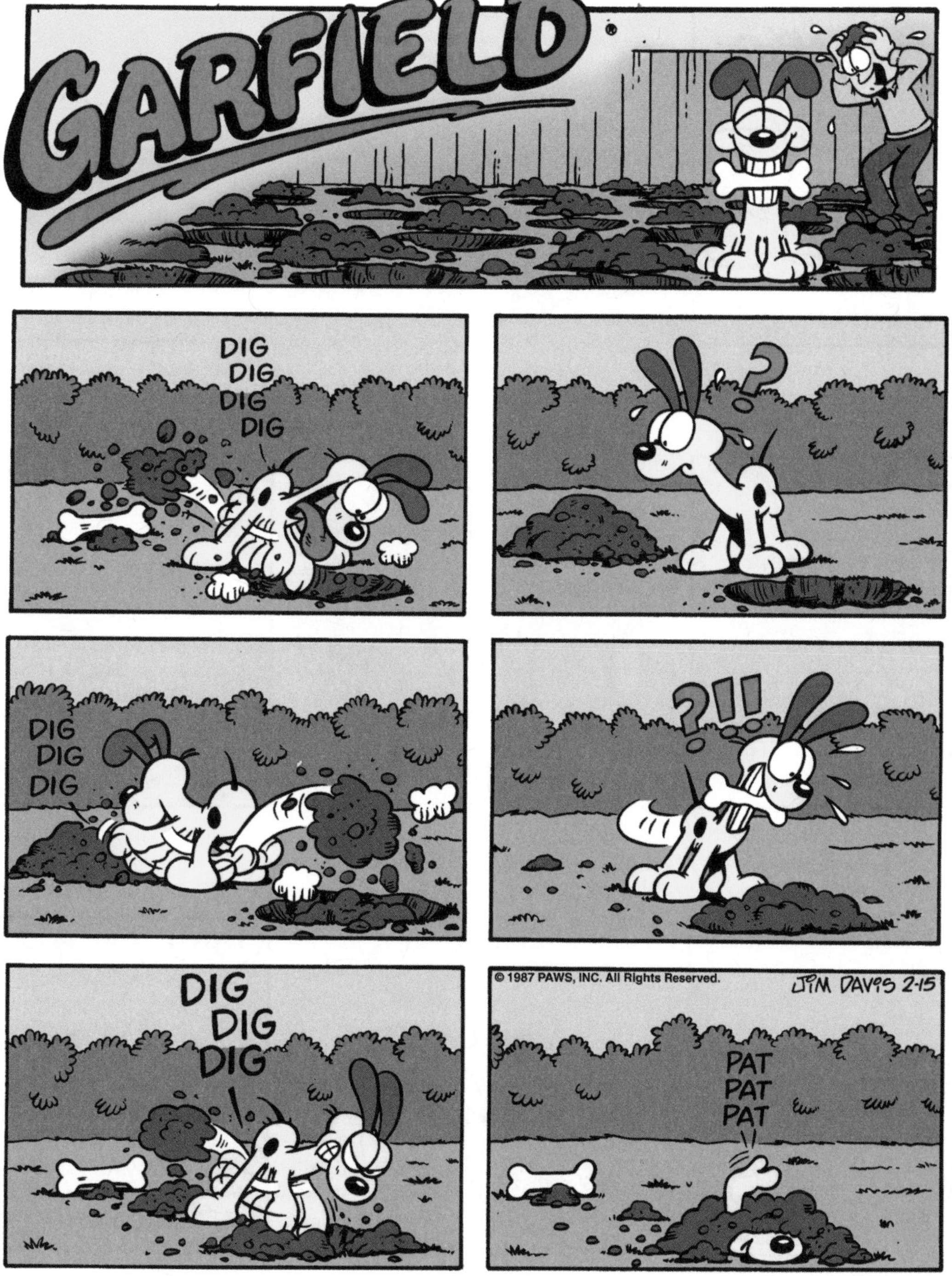
GARFIELD
DIG DIG DIG DIG
?
DIG DIG DIG
?!!
DIG DIG DIG
PAT PAT PAT
JIM DAVIS 2-15

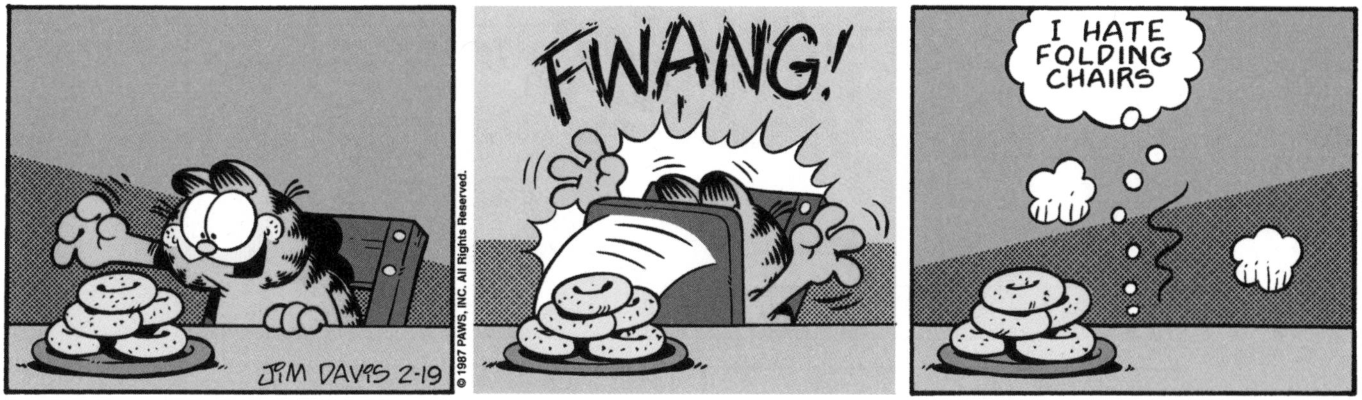
JIM DAVIS 2-19
© 1987 PAWS, INC. All Rights Reserved.
FWANG!
I HATE FOLDING CHAIRS

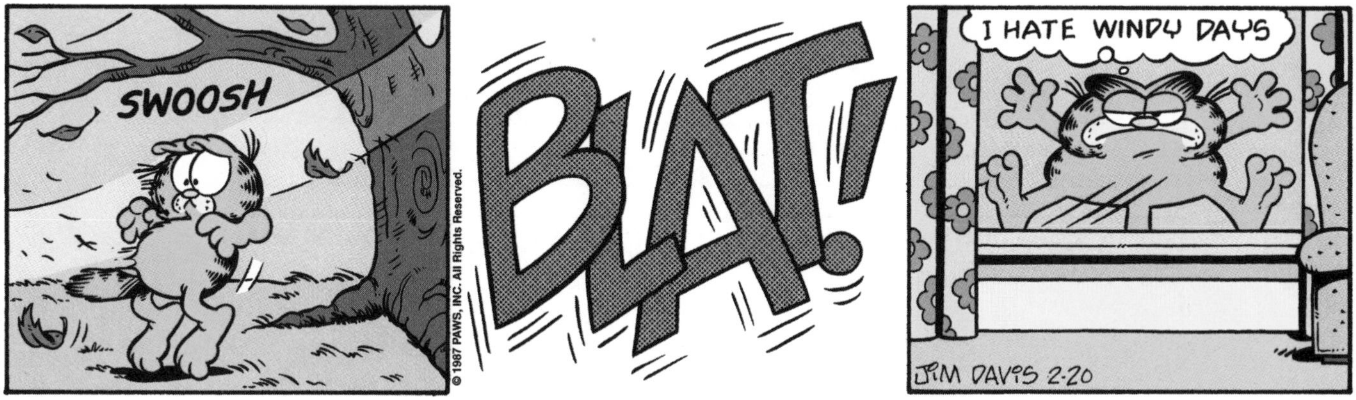
SWOOSH
© 1987 PAWS, INC. All Rights Reserved.
BLAT!
I HATE WINDY DAYS
JIM DAVIS 2-20

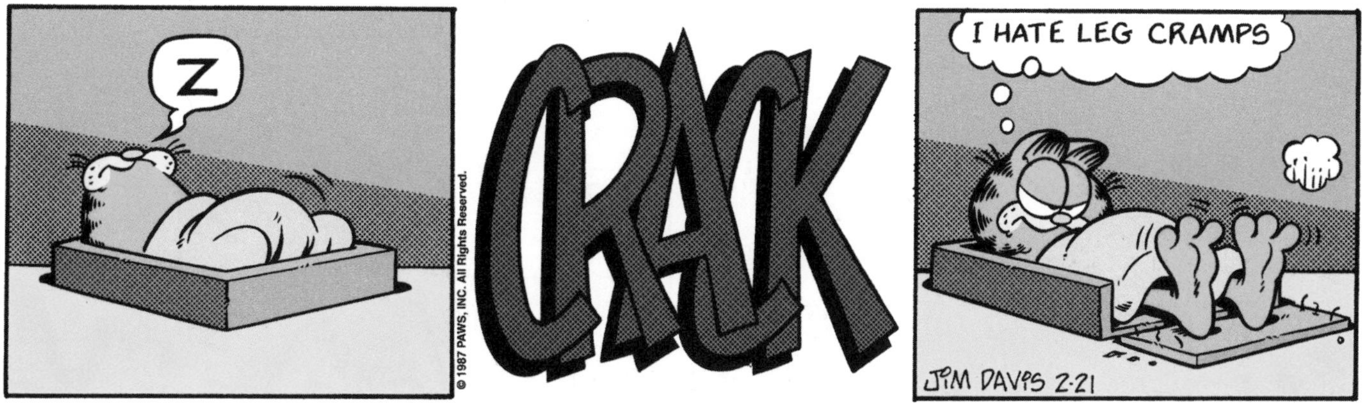
Z
© 1987 PAWS, INC. All Rights Reserved.
CRACK
I HATE LEG CRAMPS
JIM DAVIS 2-21

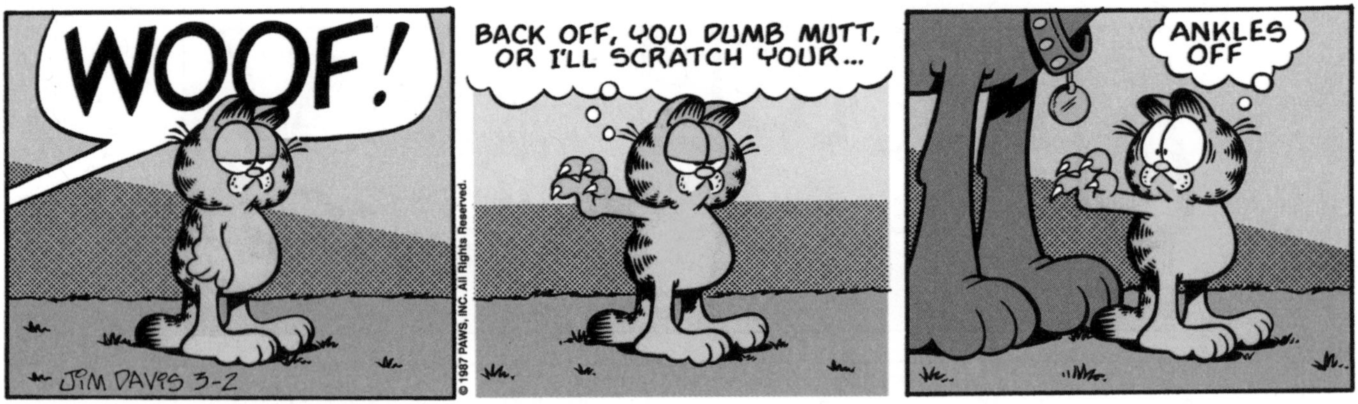
WOOF!
JIM DAVIS 3-2
© 1987 PAWS, INC. All Rights Reserved.
BACK OFF, YOU DUMB MUTT, OR I'LL SCRATCH YOUR...
ANKLES OFF

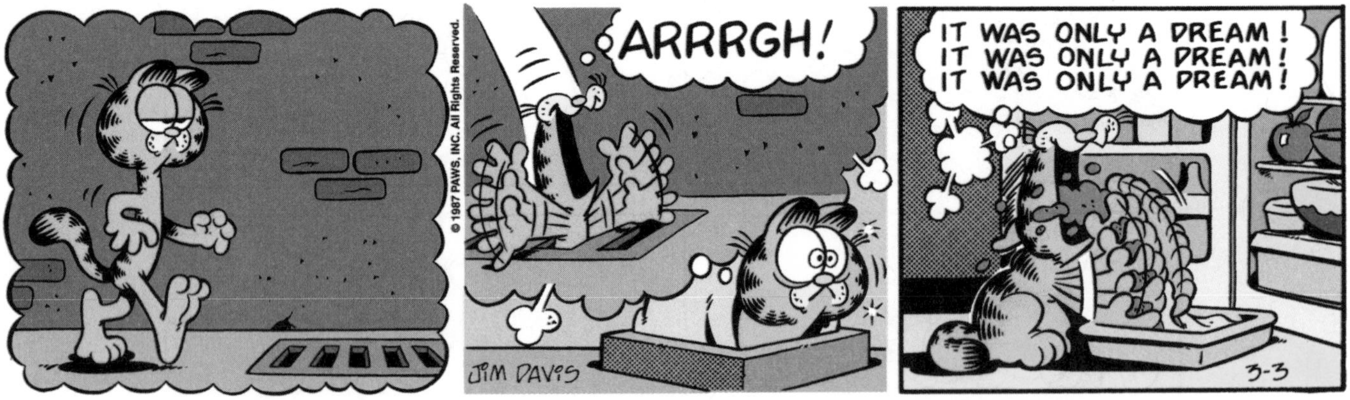
© 1987 PAWS, INC. All Rights Reserved.
ARRRGH!
JIM DAVIS
IT WAS ONLY A DREAM! IT WAS ONLY A DREAM! IT WAS ONLY A DREAM!
3-3

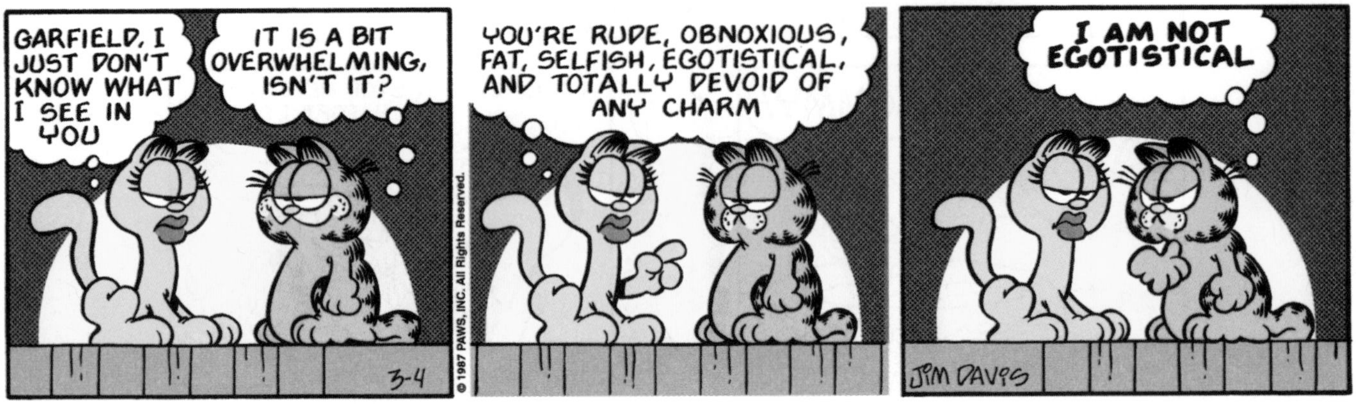
GARFIELD, I JUST DON'T KNOW WHAT I SEE IN YOU
IT IS A BIT OVERWHELMING, ISN'T IT?
3-4
© 1987 PAWS, INC. All Rights Reserved.
YOU'RE RUDE, OBNOXIOUS, FAT, SELFISH, EGOTISTICAL, AND TOTALLY DEVOID OF ANY CHARM
I AM NOT EGOTISTICAL
JIM DAVIS

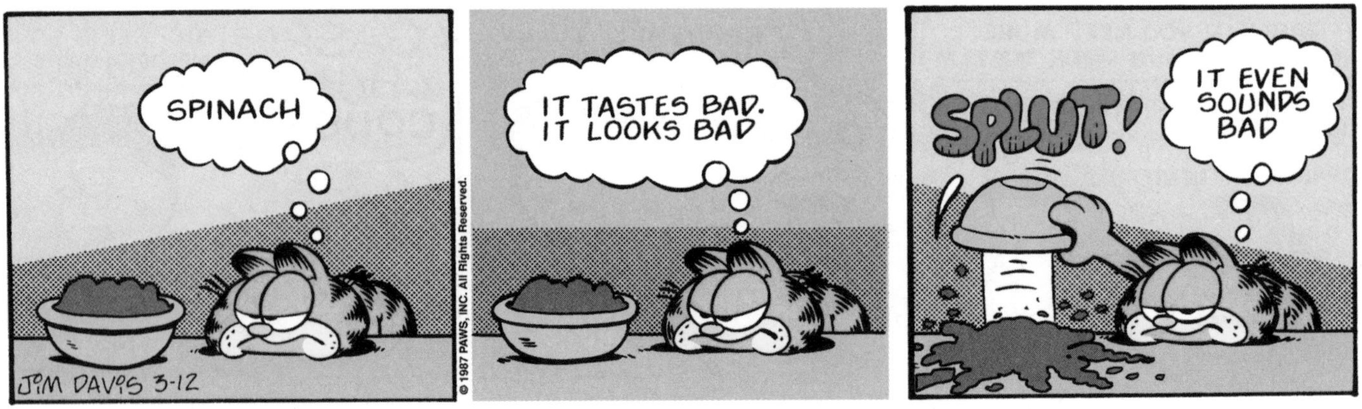
SPINACH
JIM DAVIS 3-12
IT TASTES BAD.
IT LOOKS BAD
SPLUT!
IT EVEN SOUNDS BAD

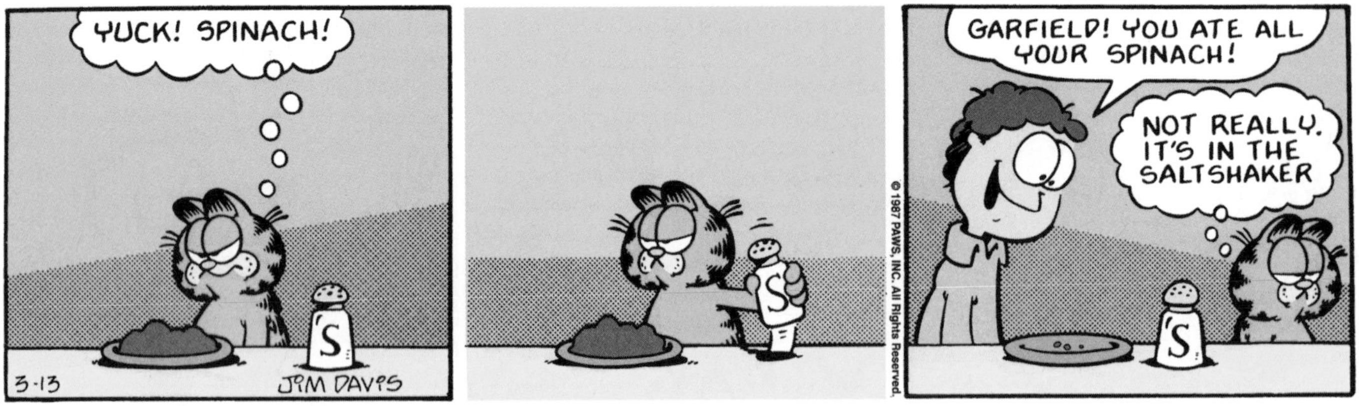
YUCK! SPINACH!
3-13
JIM DAVIS
S
GARFIELD! YOU ATE ALL YOUR SPINACH!
NOT REALLY. IT'S IN THE SALTSHAKER

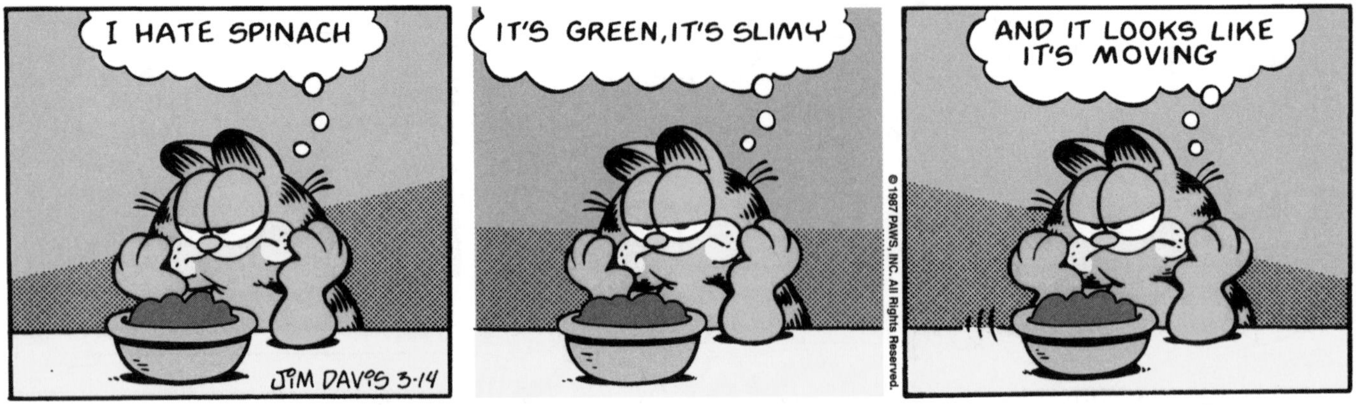
I HATE SPINACH
JIM DAVIS 3-14
IT'S GREEN, IT'S SLIMY
AND IT LOOKS LIKE IT'S MOVING

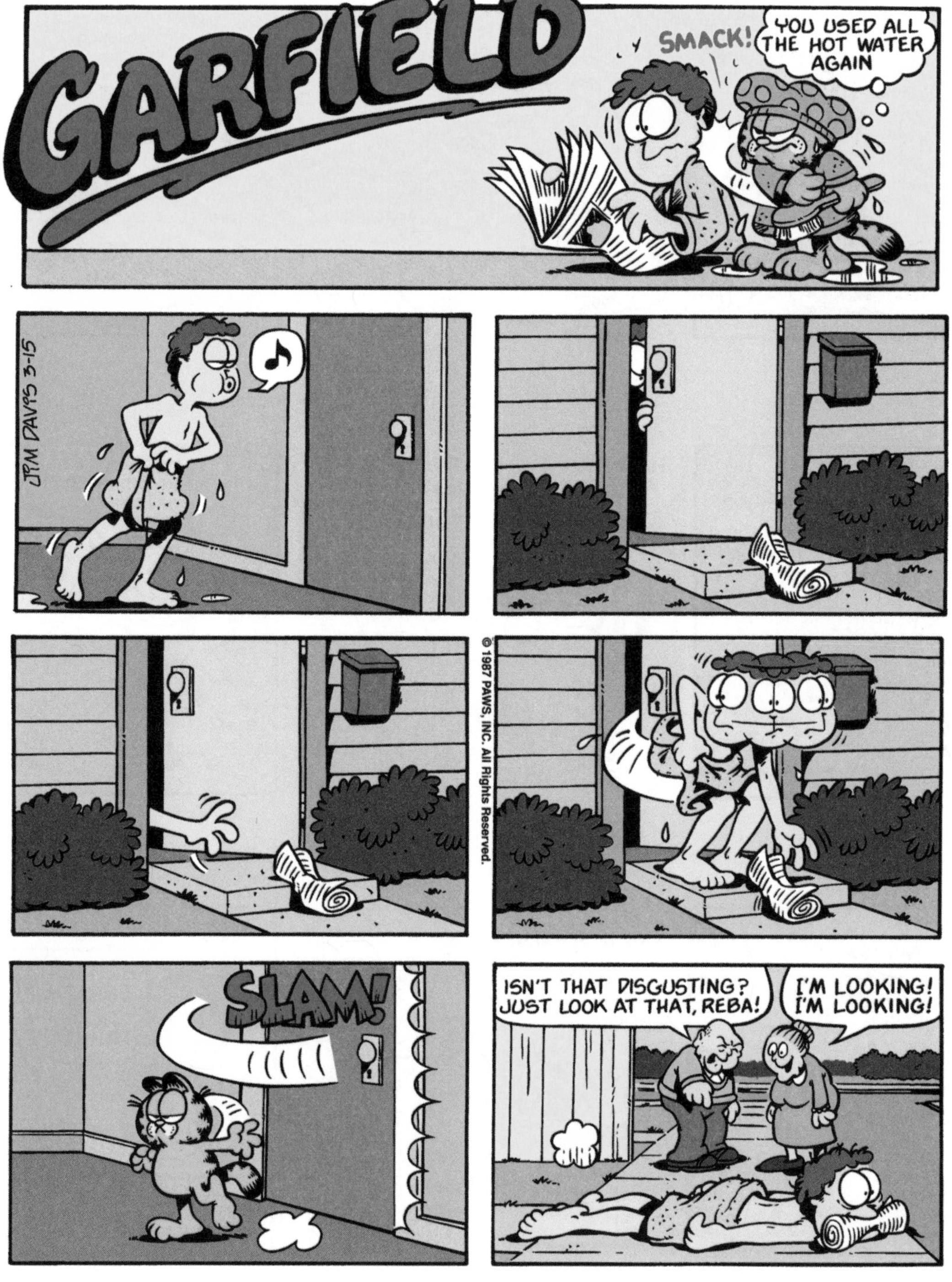
GARFIELD®
SMACK!
YOU USED ALL THE HOT WATER AGAIN
JIM DAVIS 3-15
© 1987 PAWS, INC. All Rights Reserved.
SLAM!
ISN'T THAT DISGUSTING? JUST LOOK AT THAT, REBA!
I'M LOOKING! I'M LOOKING!

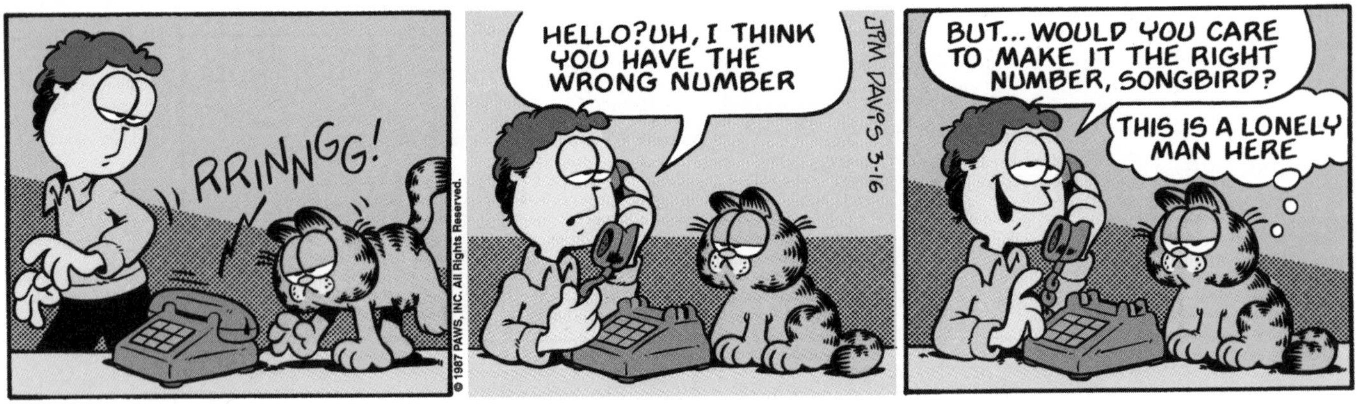
RRINNGG!
© 1987 PAWS, INC. All Rights Reserved.
HELLO? UH, I THINK YOU HAVE THE WRONG NUMBER
JIM DAVIS 3-16
BUT... WOULD YOU CARE TO MAKE IT THE RIGHT NUMBER, SONGBIRD?
THIS IS A LONELY MAN HERE

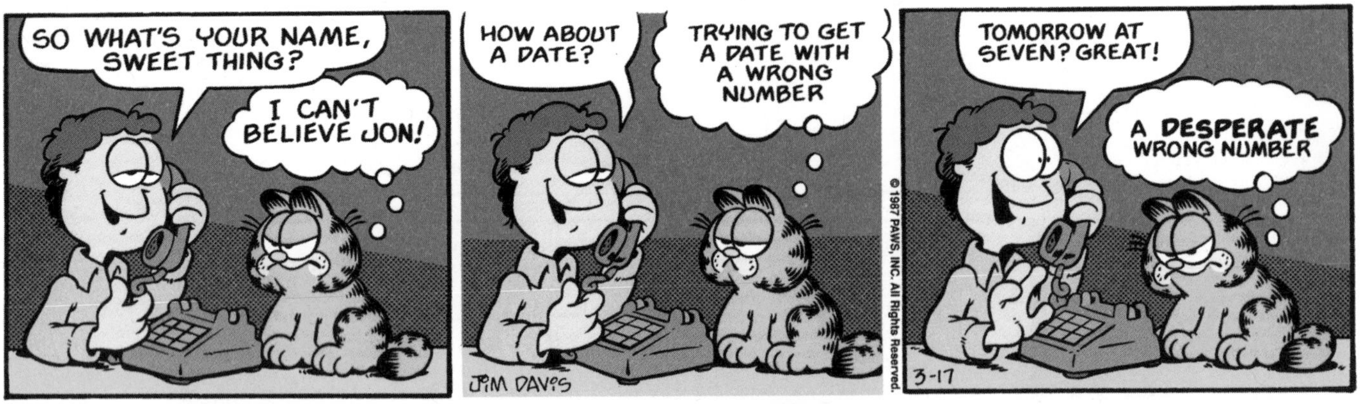
SO WHAT'S YOUR NAME, SWEET THING?
I CAN'T BELIEVE JON!
HOW ABOUT A DATE?
TRYING TO GET A DATE WITH A WRONG NUMBER
JIM DAVIS
© 1987 PAWS, INC. All Rights Reserved.
TOMORROW AT SEVEN? GREAT!
A DESPERATE WRONG NUMBER
3-17

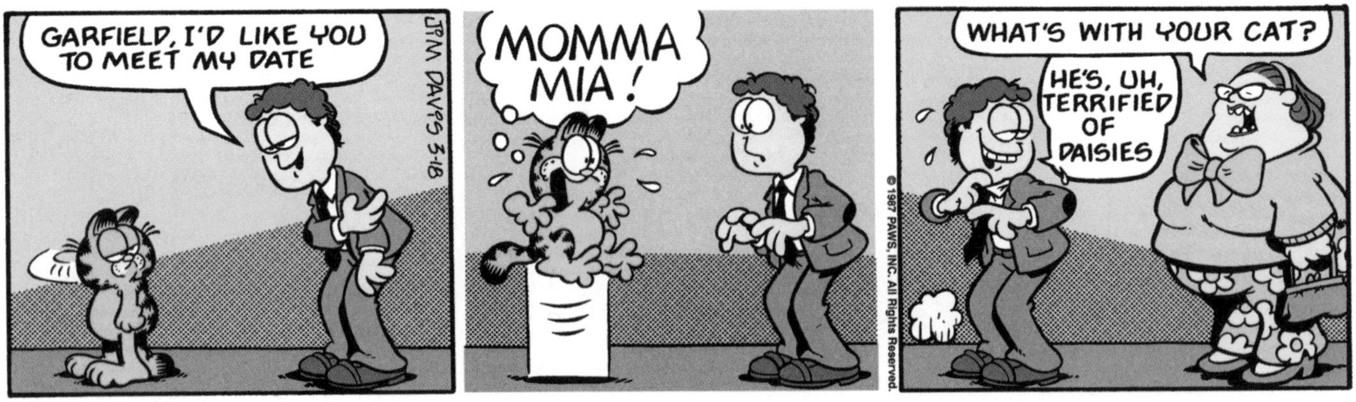
GARFIELD, I'D LIKE YOU TO MEET MY DATE
JIM DAVIS 3-18
MOMMA MIA!
© 1987 PAWS, INC. All Rights Reserved.
WHAT'S WITH YOUR CAT?
HE'S, UH, TERRIFIED OF DAISIES

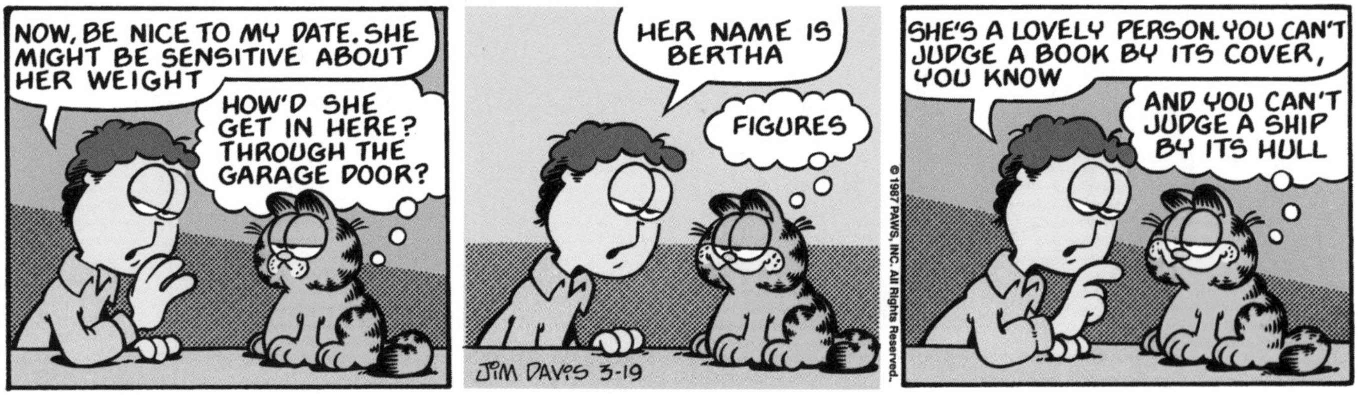
NOW, BE NICE TO MY DATE. SHE MIGHT BE SENSITIVE ABOUT HER WEIGHT
HOW'D SHE GET IN HERE? THROUGH THE GARAGE DOOR?
HER NAME IS BERTHA
FIGURES
JIM DAVIS 3-19
© 1987 PAWS, INC. All Rights Reserved.
SHE'S A LOVELY PERSON. YOU CAN'T JUDGE A BOOK BY ITS COVER, YOU KNOW
AND YOU CAN'T JUDGE A SHIP BY ITS HULL

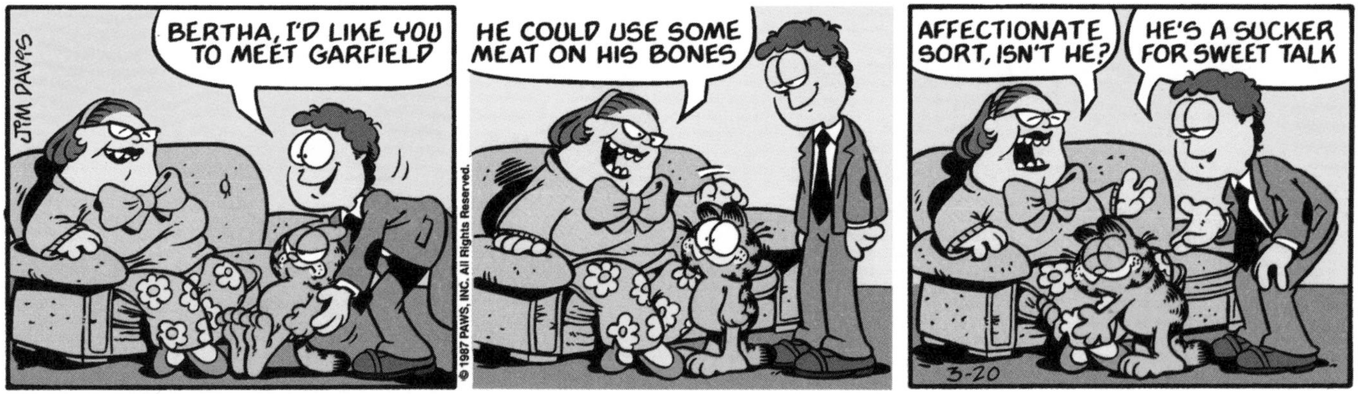
JIM DAVIS
BERTHA, I'D LIKE YOU TO MEET GARFIELD
© 1987 PAWS, INC. All Rights Reserved.
HE COULD USE SOME MEAT ON HIS BONES
AFFECTIONATE SORT, ISN'T HE?
HE'S A SUCKER FOR SWEET TALK
3-20

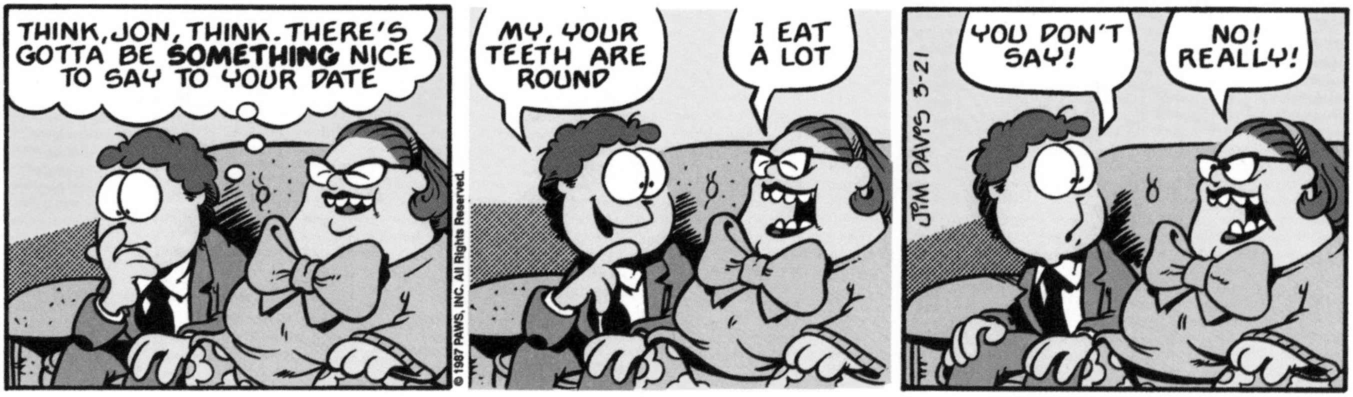
THINK, JON, THINK. THERE'S GOTTA BE SOMETHING NICE TO SAY TO YOUR DATE
© 1987 PAWS, INC. All Rights Reserved.
MY, YOUR TEETH ARE ROUND
I EAT A LOT
JIM DAVIS 3-21
YOU DON'T SAY!
NO! REALLY!

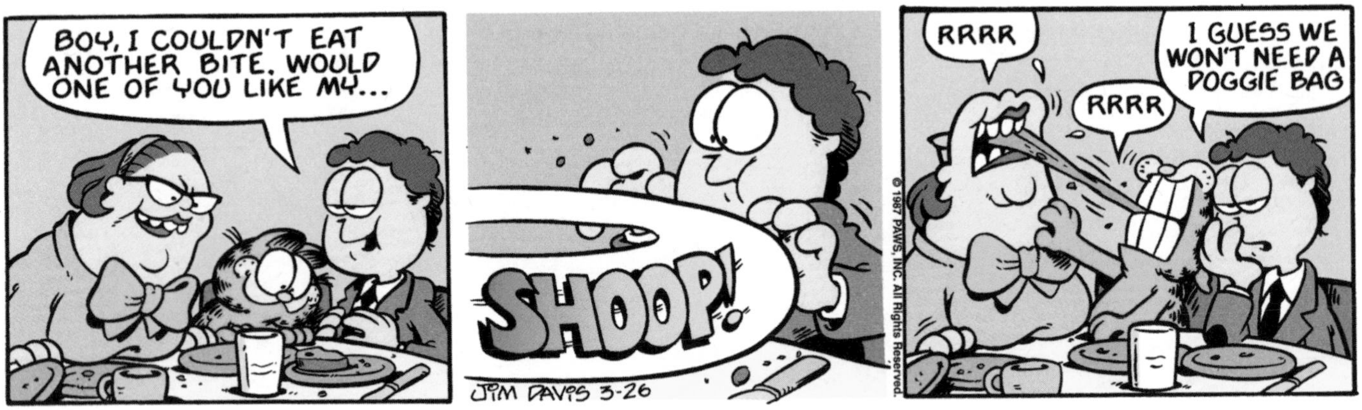
BOY, I COULDN'T EAT ANOTHER BITE. WOULD ONE OF YOU LIKE MY...
SHOOP!
JIM DAVIS 3-26
© 1987 PAWS, INC. All Rights Reserved.
RRRR
RRRR
I GUESS WE WON'T NEED A DOGGIE BAG

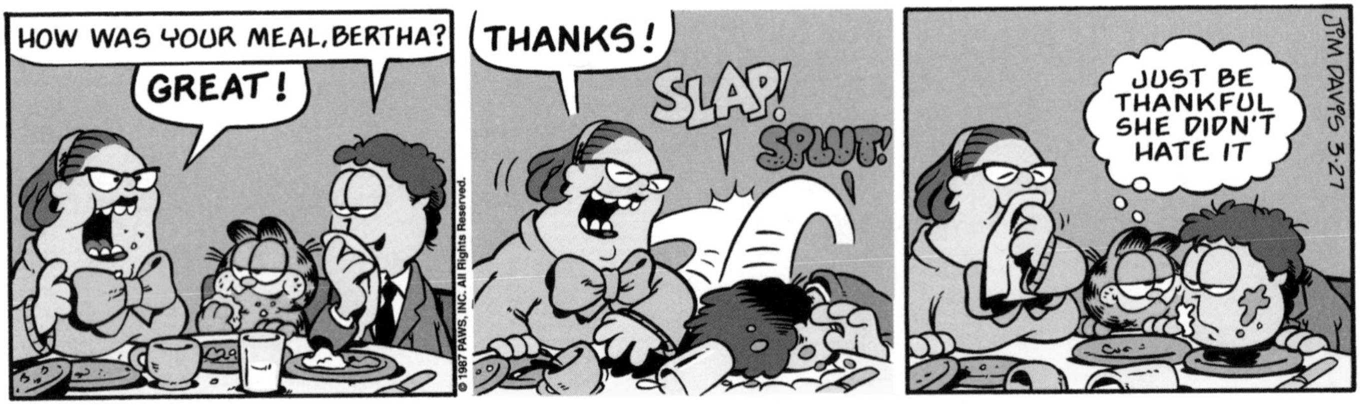
HOW WAS YOUR MEAL, BERTHA?
GREAT!
© 1987 PAWS, INC. All Rights Reserved.
THANKS!
SLAP!
SPLUT!
JIM DAVIS 3-27
JUST BE THANKFUL SHE DIDN'T HATE IT

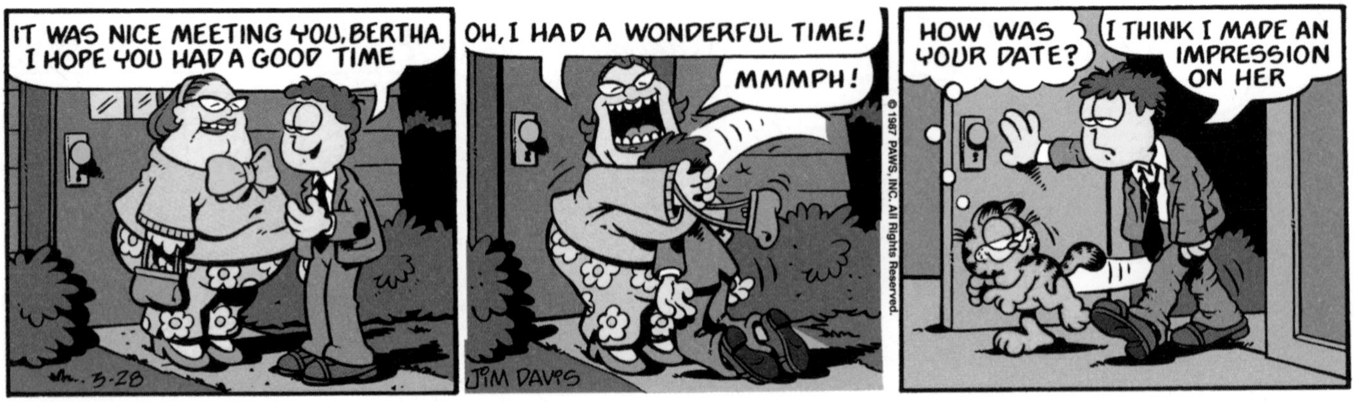
IT WAS NICE MEETING YOU, BERTHA. I HOPE YOU HAD A GOOD TIME
OH, I HAD A WONDERFUL TIME!
MMMPH!
JIM DAVIS
© 1987 PAWS, INC. All Rights Reserved.
HOW WAS YOUR DATE?
I THINK I MADE AN IMPRESSION ON HER

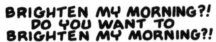

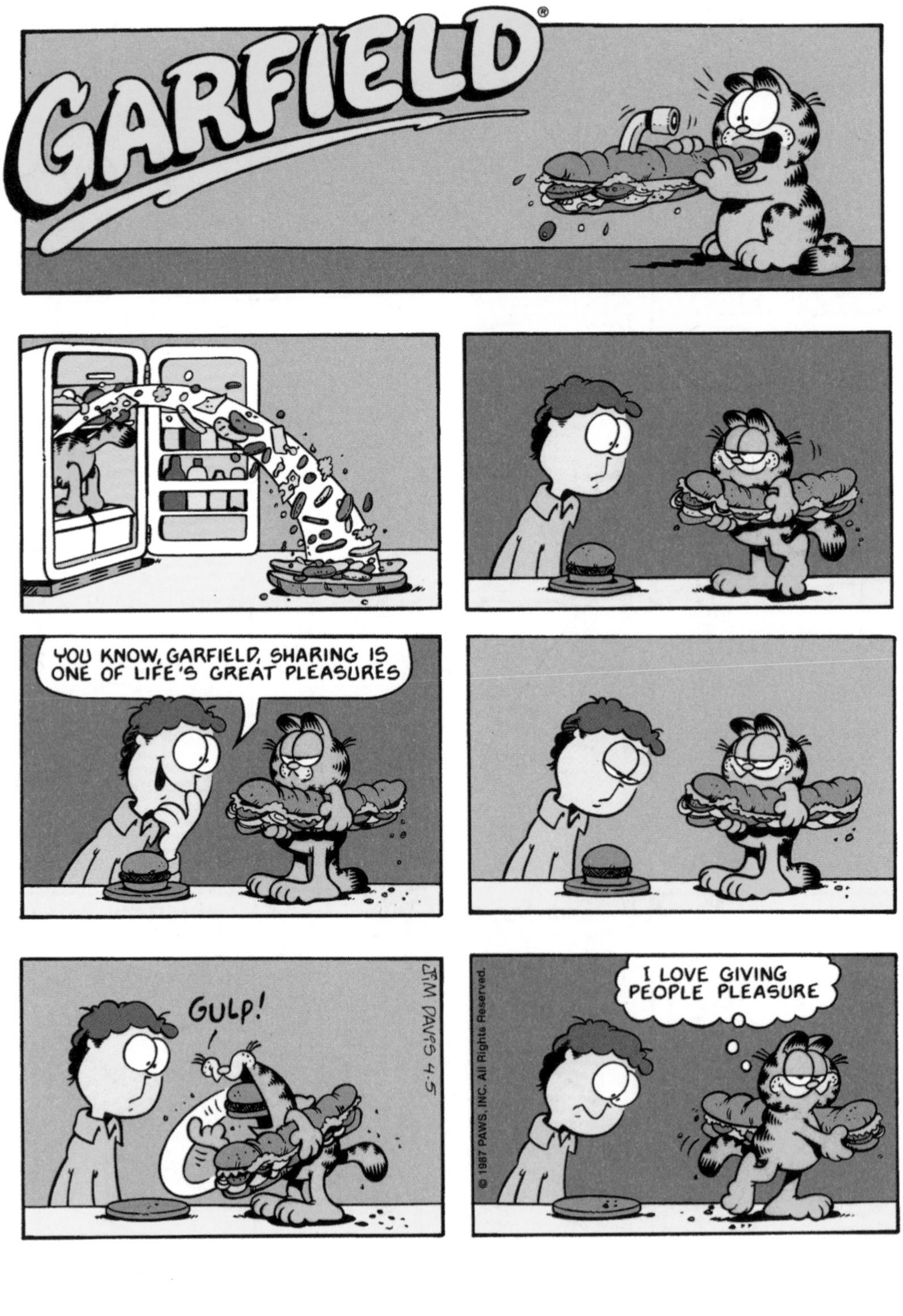
GARFIELD®
YOU KNOW, GARFIELD, SHARING IS ONE OF LIFE'S GREAT PLEASURES
GULP!
JIM DAVIS 4-5
© 1987 PAWS, INC. All Rights Reserved.
I LOVE GIVING PEOPLE PLEASURE

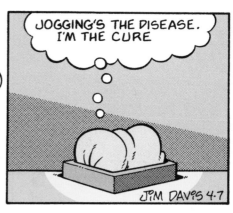

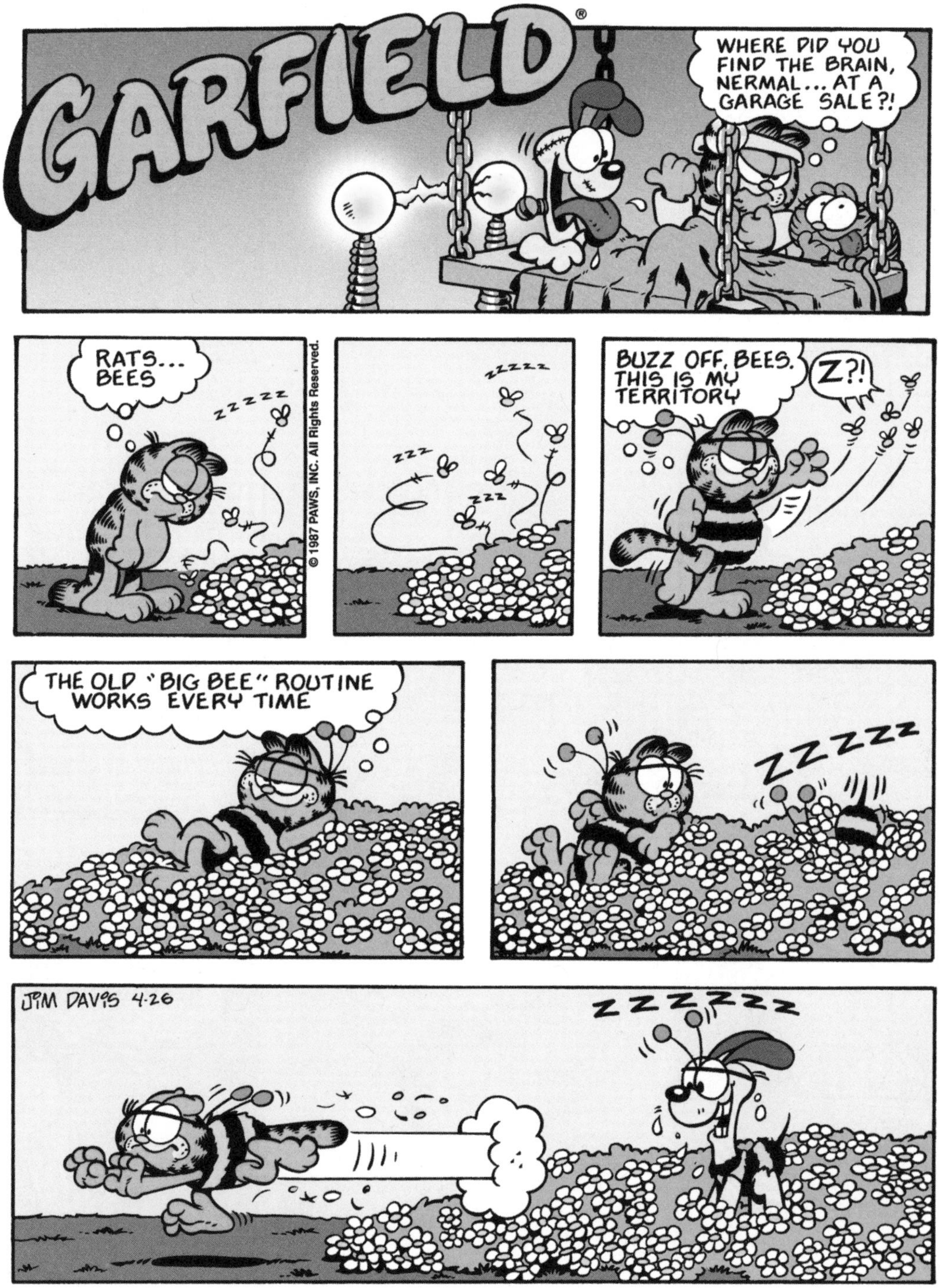
GARFIELD®
WHERE DID YOU FIND THE BRAIN, NERMAL... AT A GARAGE SALE?!
RATS... BEES
© 1987 PAWS, INC. All Rights Reserved.
ZZZZZ
ZZZZZ
ZZZ
ZZZ
BUZZ OFF, BEES. THIS IS MY TERRITORY
Z?!
THE OLD "BIG BEE" ROUTINE WORKS EVERY TIME
ZZZZZ
JIM DAVIS 4-26
ZZZZZZZ

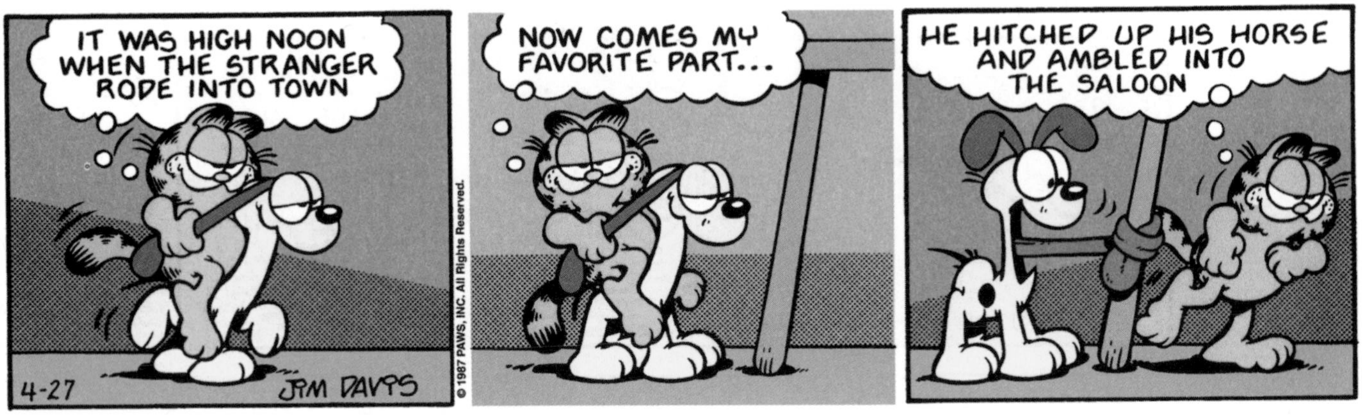
IT WAS HIGH NOON WHEN THE STRANGER RODE INTO TOWN
4-27
JIM DAVIS
© 1987 PAWS, INC. All Rights Reserved.
NOW COMES MY FAVORITE PART...
HE HITCHED UP HIS HORSE AND AMBLED INTO THE SALOON

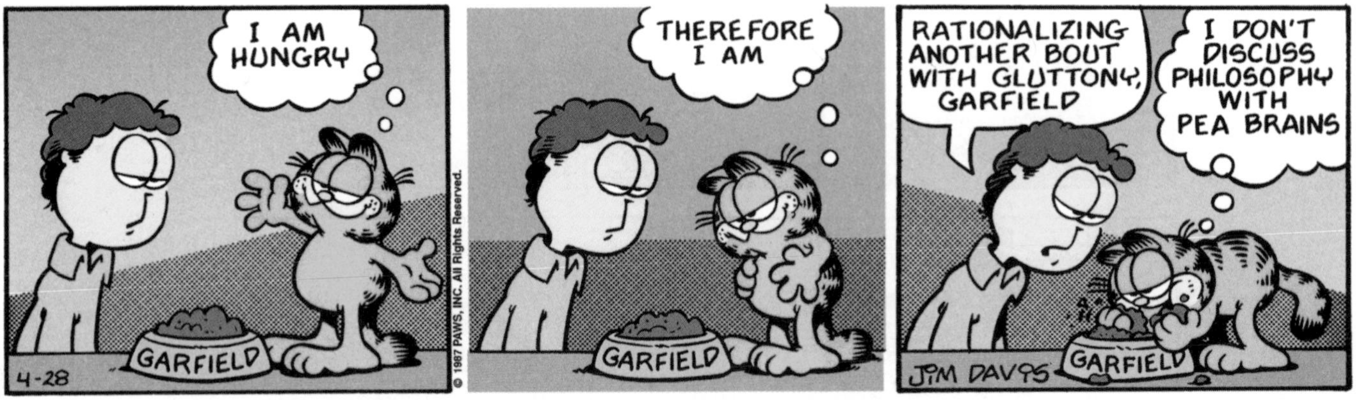
I AM HUNGRY
GARFIELD
4-28
© 1987 PAWS, INC. All Rights Reserved.
THEREFORE I AM
GARFIELD
RATIONALIZING ANOTHER BOUT WITH GLUTTONY, GARFIELD
I DON'T DISCUSS PHILOSOPHY WITH PEA BRAINS
JIM DAVIS
GARFIELD

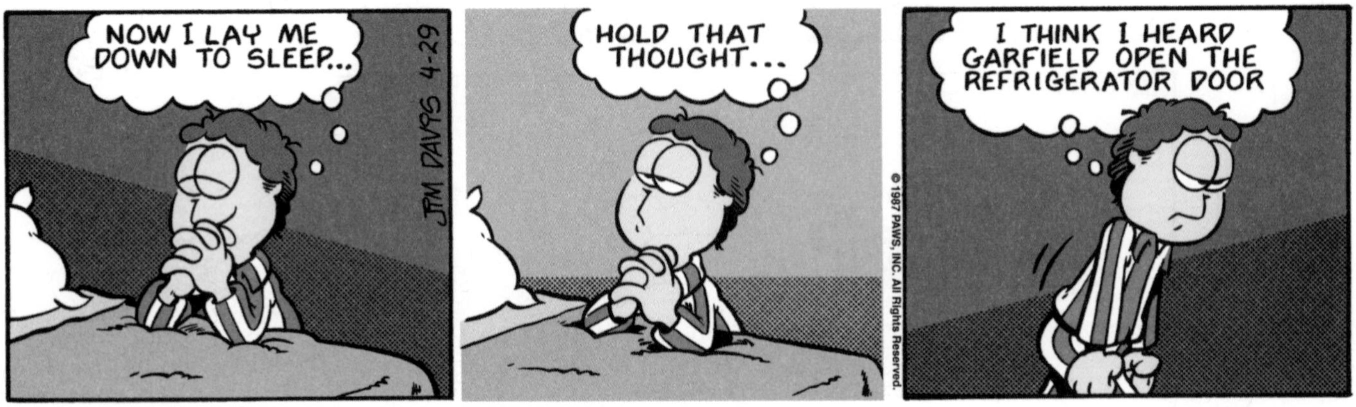
NOW I LAY ME DOWN TO SLEEP...
JIM DAVIS 4-29
HOLD THAT THOUGHT...
© 1987 PAWS, INC. All Rights Reserved.
I THINK I HEARD GARFIELD OPEN THE REFRIGERATOR DOOR

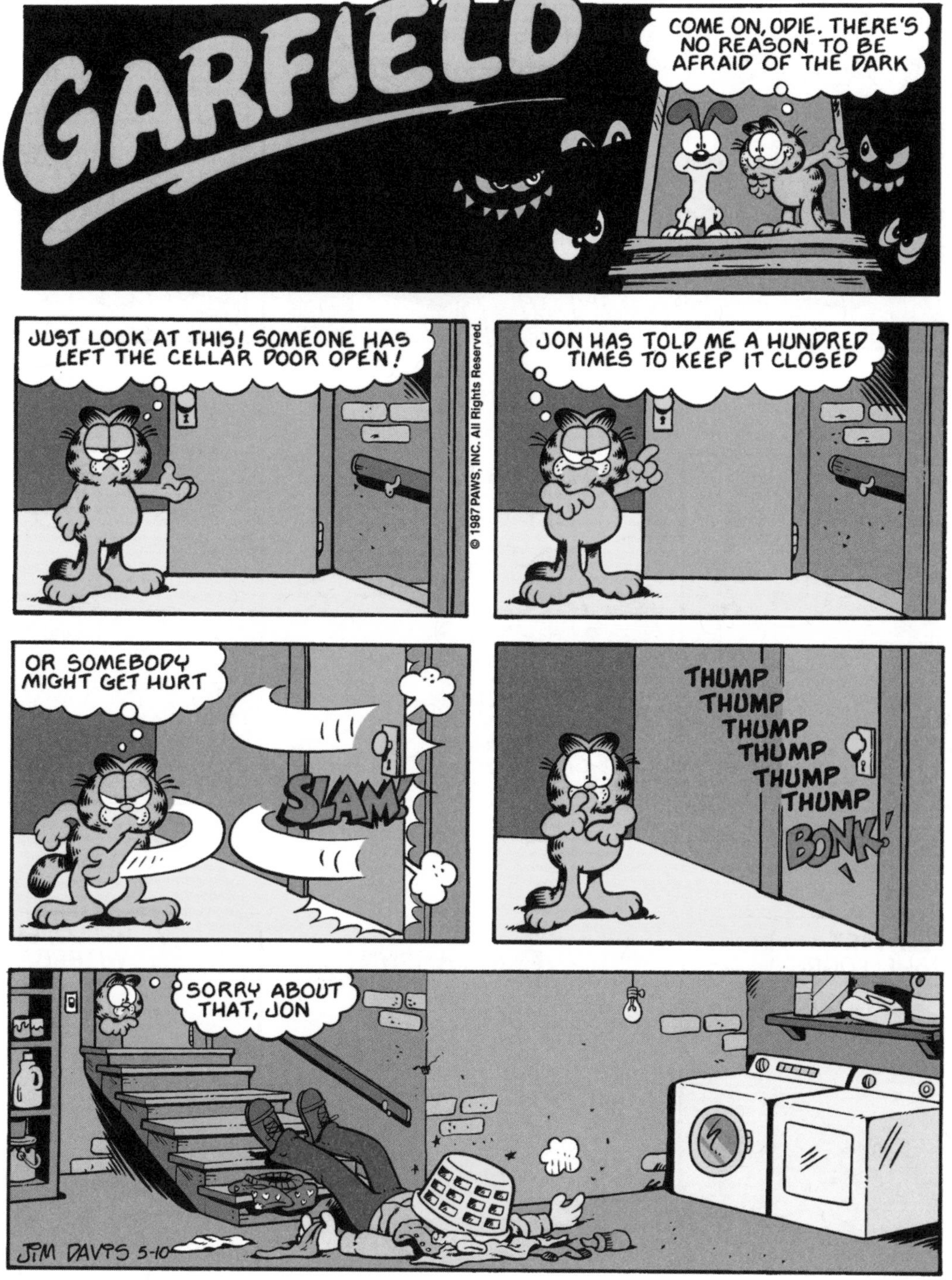
GARFIELD®
COME ON, ODIE. THERE'S NO REASON TO BE AFRAID OF THE DARK
JUST LOOK AT THIS! SOMEONE HAS LEFT THE CELLAR DOOR OPEN!
JON HAS TOLD ME A HUNDRED TIMES TO KEEP IT CLOSED
OR SOMEBODY MIGHT GET HURT
SLAM!
THUMP THUMP THUMP THUMP THUMP THUMP
BONK!
SORRY ABOUT THAT, JON
JIM DAVIS 5-10

HOW TO DRAW GARFIELD

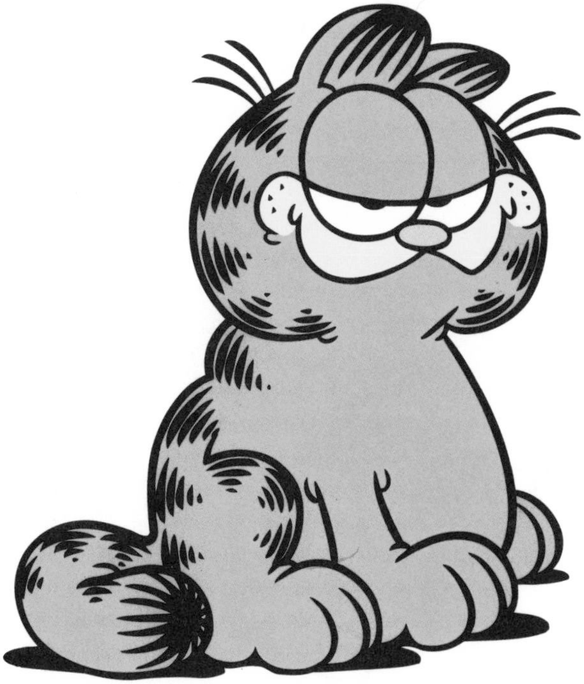

RIGHT

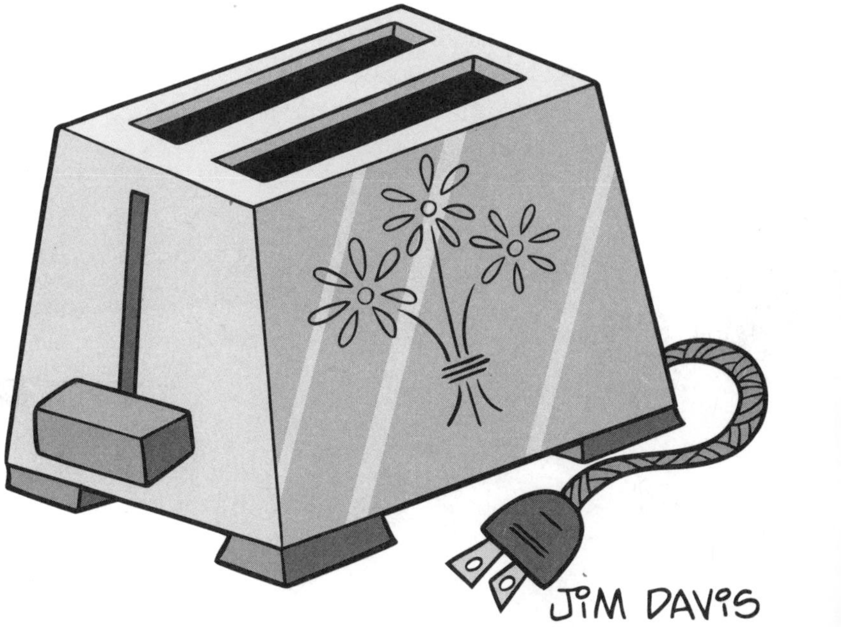
JIM DAVIS

WRONG

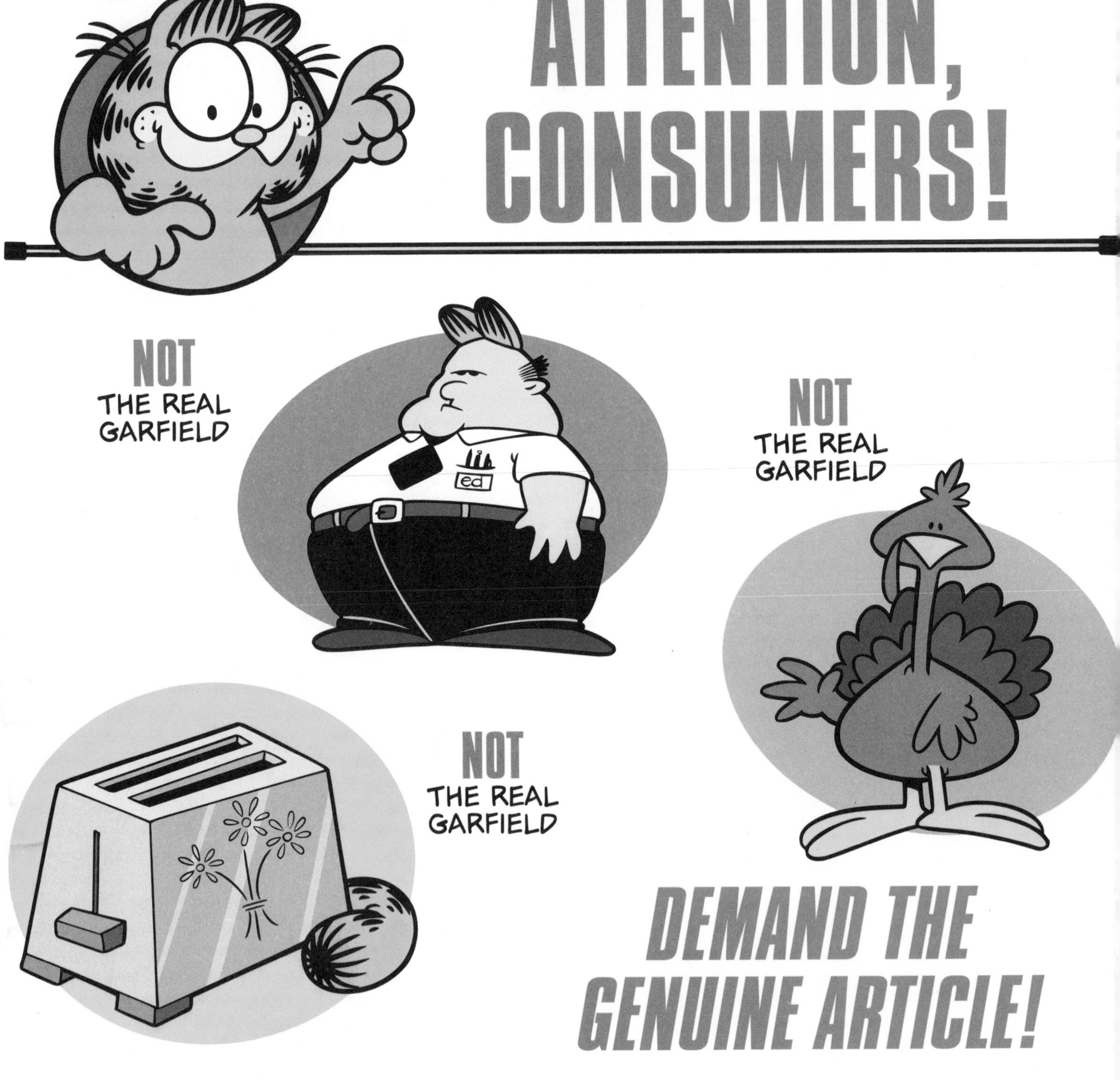
ATTENTION, CONSUMERS!
NOT THE REAL GARFIELD
ed
NOT THE REAL GARFIELD
NOT THE REAL GARFIELD
DEMAND THE GENUINE ARTICLE!